# THE
# PSYCHOLOGY
# OF
# SYMBOLIC
# ACTIVITY

**HOWARD R. POLLIO** *The University of Tennessee*

**ADDISON-WESLEY
PUBLISHING COMPANY**
READING, MASSACHUSETTS · MENLO PARK, CALIFORNIA
LONDON · DON MILLS, ONTARIO

Cover design: *Head*, a sculpture by Henry Moore, executed in 1937, and reproduced here by courtesy of Henry Moore. Other photographs throughout the book are also reproduced by courtesy of Henry Moore.

# PREFACE

Along with sweet, moist, warm air, Spring always brings something else to Tennessee: bookmen from the North. It was three or four years ago—I'm not sure which—that one of these bookmen, having found his way to my office, proceeded to ask me his annual question:

"Are there any books that you might like to see us publish? That is, are there any areas that you think need a new book?"

"How about one on symbolic activity," I replied. "You know, things like language and thinking and problem-solving and stuff like that."

"You suggested that one last year, and our editor feels that such a book won't sell or make any money for him or the publisher. If you want to see such a book on the market, I'm afraid, you're going to have to write it yourself and find your own publisher."

Little did I realize then that this conversation and others like it would lead me to write a book that no one thought would make any money, but one that I felt nonetheless was needed.

The area covered in the present book—human symbolic activity—has been a long time in emerging as a separate speciality in psychology. In the recent past, Roger Brown's book, *Words and Things* (1957) and the fourth section of Osgood's classic *Method and Theory in Experimental Psychology* (1953) gave some hints as to the broader regions of this field, but their coverage was a bit too specialized to define the more general area I had in mind. Indeed, the major purpose of the present book is to give some guidelines as to the nature of this broader field, and to provide a textbook for courses dealing with an area too often treated only indirectly by hard-nosed experimental psychologists.

My first real exposure to the more general area of symbolic activity came in 1966 when I was a participant in the Kentucky symposium on *Verbal Behavior and General Behavior Theory* (1968). What with all the milling and mulling around, I became quite confused, and then quite convinced that there were a number of different and perfectly valid approaches to a psychology of human symbolic activity, but that in order to appreciate any one of them it was first necessary to develop a "feel" for what that particular approach was trying to do. Since I had been trained by Melton and Peak in the associationistic tradition at Michigan and nurtured in operationism by Verplanck at Tennessee, I felt reasonably secure in my ability to empathize with this group.  At the Kentucky conference, it became painfully clear to me—and anyone who has ever crossed verbal swords with a transformational linguist will tell you how painful it can be—that I had to learn about different approaches to symbolic activity if I were to be able to write a relatively unbiased account of the area.

The next two years were spent in doing my homework at the University of Tennessee.  In 1968 I was awarded a USPHS Special Research Fellowship, which allowed me to spend a year (1968–1969) in the very stimulating environment of the Psycholinguistics Research Unit of the University of London, headed by Frieda Goldman-Eisler.  It was there, in discussion with Dr. Eisler and Dr. Peter Wason and their students—Michele Cohen, Brian Butterworth, and Rae Kennedy—that I began work on the present manuscript, completing an early draft in the fall of 1969.

Much of the next six months were spent in enabling a publisher to find me, and thanks to the help of Charlotte and Jim Doyle, Addison-Wesley parted the bushes and there I were.  But a first draft and nice comments, pleasant as they are, do not mean a completed book; and so beginning in the spring of 1971 until the present, I have reworked (and reworked and *re*worked, it seems) this manuscript until I have produced the only book to have a fourth edition in advance of its first printing.  Well, the fifth edition should be easier anyway.

Despite these revisions I am sure many readers will find the coverage somewhat selective and idiosyncratic.  I have tried in this book to cover what I consider significant theoretical points of view and to show how the experimental literature growing out of these approaches makes a consistent whole if one is willing to "get into" a theoretical tradition other than his own.  One often has to pass over a lot of clever things that have been done because they do not fit with one's own preconceptions.

In this book I have picked two general approaches to symbolic activity—hopefully the most significant ones—and tried to develop their argument in a way that I hope is consistent with their orienting attitudes and prejudices. For this reason, the same topic—say memory—will occur in two different chapters of the book with almost no cross-referencing between the two. Probably for some teaching purposes it might be helpful to assign such chapters in sequence and thereby give complete coverage to a single area rather than to a single theoretical position as I have done.  It is also conceivable (but I for one would be distressed by it) to teach only one of the two orientations all the way through and never get to the opposing points of view.  If that's your intention, well . . . .

It is always a pleasure to acknowledge individuals who have had a hand in helping you in some way in doing something you consider important.  (To be completely fair, I should probably also list those who hindered me, but be that as it may.) Two colleagues were particularly helpful in this regard: Merrill Garrett of M.I.T., who suffered through the whole of this book, and David Hakes of the University of Texas, who suffered through Parts I and III. Both of these gentlemen provided me, through their reviews, with an excellent learning experience. Reading through their wise and extensive comments improved my perspective on human symbolic activities and served to correct many errors and misapprehensions I had. Although I am sure that not all these errors are now gone, there is only so much two wise reviewers can do, and both Garrett and Hakes have done their job very well indeed.

Although I have taken account of about 80% of their comments, all of which materially improved my presentation, there is one point on which I have consistently refused their counsel: Both wanted me to be a bit more critical in a number of places than I have actually been. While almost all their critical analyses were valid and correct, I have tried to write each chapter as an "insider" might. So, for example, if I were writing an associative chapter, I have tried to write as an associative psychologist might, and if I were writing an information-processing chapter, I have tried to write as an information psychologist might. There seems to me to be little point in continually littering up each area with conceptual caveats, even if such caveats can be clearly seen from a different point of view. Then, too, I've always been a kind of a Pollyanna, preferring to give most people (theorists included) the benefit of the doubt that they, too, see the caveats as well as I do.

Many different secretaries—Hyacynth Mason and Justine Brener in London—worked on this book, although only Lillian Bussell, my secretary in Knoxville, had to type it three times. One more time and—had the manuscript been lost—she could probably have produced it by rote. Ann H. Bailey helped in securing permissions and in seeing the present book through to press.

Finally, there is the continuing debt I owe to Marilyn Pollio. Both in London and Knoxville and elsewhere, her ability to put up with noisy kids, a crazy husband and a peripatetic existence have provided a thread of sanity and continuity to an otherwise freely associated life style. It is to her that this book is sincerely dedicated.

In addition, I would like to thank Sir Henry Moore for his generous permission to use photographs of his sculptures in the present book. They have always been a source of inspiration for me, and I am delighted now to be able to present them to a new generation of students.

*Knoxville, Tennessee*                                                        H.R.P.
*June 1973*

# CONTENTS

# PART I
## SYMBOLS AND SYMBOLIC ACTIVITY

# CHAPTER 1

# SIGNS, SYMBOLS, AND SUCH

Human beings have always considered their symbols and their symbolic activities quite important, even should these activities and symbols get in the way of what it is that needs doing. For example, when Neil Armstrong stepped from his lunar module onto the surface of the moon, he went through a number of extraordinary, nontechnical, rituals. First of all, he had carefully prepared what his opening lines were to be: "A single step for man, a great leap for mankind," and shortly thereafter he, and fellow astronaut Edwin Aldrin, planted the American flag on the moon. If this weren't enough, they next set up a plaque telling the world that the Mission of Apollo had been undertaken in peace toward all men. Throughout their entire $2\frac{1}{2}$-hour stay on the moon, such symbolic acts regularly interrupted the orderly progress of their scientific exploration.

From one point of view, these behaviors are, or should be, quite surprising. In Armstrong and Aldrin we have two of the finest products of technological education, and yet neither they nor we found these nonuseful and nontechnical interruptions unnecessary or even superfluous. The fact of the matter is that modern man—even if he is a technical realist such as Armstrong —lives not only, or even primarily, in a world of things and objects as in a world of symbols. A coin is a symbol for a certain amount of work done, a word or a concept is a symbol of a thing or a relationship, and a book is a fantastic pile of accumulated symbols. Many of the most important aspects of our world are, in fact, symbols for something else.

Placing a high premium on symbols and symbolic activity is not peculiar to our own country or to our modern world alone. In ancient history it was not uncommon for kings or pharoahs to seek the advice of oracles or soothsayers before undertaking a new military or political venture. In the Bible Joseph rose to high office not only because he appealed to Potiphar's wife, but because he was able to interpret the Pharoah's dream as well.

Planting flags and plaques, interpreting dreams, and consulting soothsayers, however, do not exhaust the many ways in which symbols determine the day-to-day activities of people. Science, poetry, painting, mathematics, drama, dance, literature, etc., all describe modes of symbolic activity that are extremely important to us, whether the "us" lived 2000 years ago or now.

1

The artist or scientist is appropriately considered a person of special worth, primarily because his vision extends and often changes the direction of our everyday life.

Unfortunately, symbolic activity does not always enrich or ennoble; sometimes it misdirects and oppresses. No popular group has fought the irrational use of symbols more than the intellectual movement known as General Semantics. In his book *Language and Thought in Action* (1949), S. I. Hayakawa shows how the same object or situation may be depicted in two entirely different lights. The parallel columns below* illustrate how the same objective reality may lead to entirely different reactions, depending on the words used:

| | |
|---|---|
| "Finest quality filet mignon." | First-class piece of dead cow. |
| Cubs trounce Giants 5–3. | Score: Cubs 5, Giants 3. |
| McCormick bill steam-rollered through Senate. | Senate passes McCormick bill over strong opposition. |
| She has her husband under her thumb. | She is deeply interested in her husband's affairs. |
| French armies in rapid retreat! | The retirement of the French forces to previously prepared positions in the rear was accomplished briskly and efficiently. |
| The governor appeared to be gravely concerned and said that a statement would be issued in a few days after careful examination of the facts. | The governor was on the spot. |

These illustrations are intended to show how profoundly words can be used to confuse or to bias an issue if the listener (or speaker) does not ask "To what do these words really refer?"

In the present book we will concentrate primarily on the nature of man's symbolic activities; more accurately, on how a relatively small group of investigators known as psychologists and psycholinguists study these activities. A great many other disciplines—philosophy and mathematics to mention only two—also have had a good deal to say about these topics. In order to set the psychologists' task in this larger context, we will need to consider some of the issues raised by other disciplines. Such issues do not involve questions of the type that the psychologist usually considers. They deal instead with questions of personal attitudes and philosophy—mute questions that always set the stage for any scientific investigation.

---

* From *Language in Thought and Action*, by S. I. Hayakawa, New York: Harcourt, Brace and Jovanovich, 1949, page 85.

But why concern ourselves with mute questions and unspoken assumptions? Largely because how we answer any one of these questions, even implicitly, determines how we answer our experimental questions explicitly. For example, if we take the position that there is no qualitative difference in how a subhuman animal and a human animal "thinks," we can then study animal thinking to understand human thinking. If we assume in the business of language that man is a creature apart, then we can study language only by observing what human beings do, with any and all other data gathered on a subhuman species irrelevant to this task. Although the distinctions philosophers draw are not the distinctions psychologists draw, they nonetheless provide an uninvited, but necessary, backdrop against which all psychological research must be evaluated. Much of this first chapter is concerned precisely with these issues; a *potpourri* of unresolved background questions about symbols and symbol users.

## SOME TECHNICAL DISTINCTIONS

In order to understand the ways in which symbolic events influence human behavior, it is first necessary to examine the nature and characteristics of symbolic events in general. Although a number of different criteria have been proposed to define the essential characteristics of a symbol, Ludwig Von Bertalanffy (1965) has suggested the following three criteria, all of which must be applied at the same time to qualify an event as a symbol:

1. It must be representative.
2. It must be freely created.
3. It must be transmitted by culture.

These three criteria obviously represent a minimal set in defining symbols. As a starting point it seems necessary to define each of these terms briefly and let further discussion clarify their meaning. By *representative* we simply mean that some event stands for or represents some other event; by *free creation* we simply mean to stress the fact that there is no logical or necessary reason why any particular symbol need stand for any particular object or event; and by *cultural transmission* we hope to emphasize the taught and learned aspects of most symbols.

## 1. Representation

The first of these criteria specifies one essential aspect of any symbol: It must stand for something else. Given this as a basic property it is quite clear, as philosophers often remind us, that any symbolic event has various components: the term, a concept lying behind the term that may be likened to some object or event, and the person using the term. Given these components, meaning may enter in one of two ways: The symbol "means" the object to the person, or the person "means" the object by the symbol. In the first case we are talking philosophically; in the second, psychologically. The important difference between a philosophical and a psychological analysis of symbols is that for a philosophical analysis we are interested mainly in symbols and symbol systems, while for a psychological analysis we are interested primarily in people and only secondarily in symbols and symbol systems. In this introductory chapter we will be interested in analyzing symbols and symbol systems; in subsequent chapters our interest will be in symbol users.

**Varieties of representation.**    Since we want to understand the ways in which terms relate to their objects, it is necessary at the outset to realize that a number of different relations are possible between terms and objects. Sometimes, however, this relationship turns out to be pretty complicated. Consider the following example:

In the sentence "John shot a lion," we can reasonably say that *lion* refers to some specific object. Essentially what this means is that in order for me to say this *truthfully*, there must be a lion that some individual, "John," engaged in some action, "shooting," the object of which is our very palpable lion. Now consider a closely related statement, "John hunted a lion." Is "lion" here referring to a specific object? The answer is: It may be. On one reading, there exists a lion and John hunted it (his name was Leo and he escaped from the circus this morning). On another reading, however, "lion" doesn't stand for any particular lion as in the expression "John hunted a lion but gave up after several hours because he didn't find one." Note that for the first interpretation one would have to say that he didn't find *it* rather than *one*.

But what about meaning in all this? The intuitively correct conclusion would seem to be that "lion" *means* the same in all three sentences. The difference is in whether or not we expect to find a specific object. But if the term means the same in cases that differ in whether or not they refer to objects, then we have to talk about a meaning not only in terms of symbols and objects, but also in terms of concepts that may or may not be linked to some object or event.

One term–[concept]–object relationship that occurs quite frequently is called a *sign*. This term is used to describe those conditions under which the existence—past, present, or future—of an event, thing, or condition is indicated. Birds are a sign of spring, cold is a sign of winter, watery catprints on the windshield are a sign that it has begun to rain, while a salty fragrance indicates the nearness of an ocean. All these are examples of *natural signs*; that is, where one component of a total situation gives an indication of a larger natural unit.

Just as there are natural signs, so too we must recognize *artificial signs*. Here the same sort of correlational relationship between two events applies; the only difference in this case is that the correlation has been arbitrarily established with the specific purpose of providing an easily available event to serve as a sign for a more significant or elaborate one, i.e., to establish a correlation where none exists in nature. The behavior of Pavlov's dogs in the conditioning experiment is a good example. A bell, a buzzer, a light (or any other easily controlled physical event) is repeatedly paired with the presentation of food or shock (the more significant environmental event). After a sufficient number of pairings the bell comes to be a sign that food or shock is imminent. The presentation of the sign elicits behavior appropriate to the event anticipated: The dog salivates or withdraws. Pavlov himself realized the sign-function of the bell when he termed the conditioned response a "psychic secretion."

Since there is no necessary (natural) relationship between artificial signs and their correlated events, the possibility of multiple connection is usual. As Susanne Langer has noted with specific reference to a commonly used artificial sign:

> As for bells, the world is mad with their messages. Somebody at the front door, the back door, the side door, the telephone—toast is ready—typewriter line is ended—school begins, work begins, church begins, church is over—street car starts—cashbox registers—knife grinder passes— time for dinner, time to get up—fire in town!*

Although symbols also share with signs the property of using an arbitrary term to represent some other entity, event, or condition, their mode of representation is entirely different from that of signs.

> A term which is used symbolically and not signally does *not* evoke action appropriate to the presence of its object. If I say: "Napoleon," you do not bow to the conqueror of Europe as though I had introduced him, but merely think of him. If I mention a Mr. Smith of our common acquaintance, you may be led to tell me something about him "behind his back," which is just what you would *not* do in his presence. Thus the symbol for Mr. Smith—his name—may very well initiate an act appropriate peculiarly to his absence. Raised eyebrows and a look at the door, interpreted as a *sign* that he is coming, would stop you in the midst of your narrative; *that* action would be directed toward Mr. Smith in person.
>
> Symbols are not proxy for their objects, but are *vehicles for the conception of objects*. To conceive a thing or a situation is not the same thing as to "react toward it" overtly, or to be aware of its presence. In talking

---

* From *Philosophy in a New Key*, by Susanne K. Langer, Cambridge, Mass.: Harvard University Press; third edition, 1957, page 60.

*about* things we have conceptions of them, not the things themselves: and *it is the conceptions, not the things, that symbols directly "mean."**

Although these are perfectly valid philosophical distinctions, they are not completely helpful for a psychological analysis. For the psychologist, both signs and symbols must be conceptualized as the reaction(s) of an organism to some event, be this reaction as overt as Pavlov's dogs perking up their ears or salivating or as covert as the feeling and subsequent rating of pleasantness or unpleasantness evoked by a particular word or event. While the psychologist does agree with the philosopher that symbols do not evoke "overt actions appropriate to the presence of its object," he is forced to recognize that the phrase "vehicles for the conception of objects" must itself somehow or other be thought of as a reaction of an organism to an event. For the psychologist, symbols relate to internal reactions or events, not overtly observable, while signs refer to actual or potentially observable reaction patterns. Signs are correlative; symbols, substitutive.

To what types of internal events do symbols refer? It is quite clear that for a logical analysis, symbols can refer only to conceptions or to other symbols. The relation of one symbol to another or to many other symbol(s)—say the one we are interested in—is called its *connotation*, while the relation of a symbol to its object is called its *denotation*. Hayakawa describes the difference between the connotative and denotative modes of meaning as follows:

> From this point on, it will be necessary to employ some special terms in talking about meaning: *extensional meaning*, which will also be referred to as *denotation*, and *intensional meaning*—note the *s*—which will also be referred to as connotation. Briefly explained, the extensional meaning of an utterance is that which it *points to* or denotes in the extensional world. That is to say, the extensional meaning is something that *cannot be expressed in words*, because it is that which words stand for. An easy way to remember this is to put your hand over your mouth and point whenever you are asked to give an extensional meaning . . .
>
> The *intensional meaning* of a word or expression, on the other hand, is that which is *suggested* (connoted) inside one's head. Roughly speaking, whenever we express the meaning of words by uttering more words, we are giving intensional meaning, or connotations. To remember this, put your hand over your eyes and let the words spin around in your head.†

While there is only one mode of denotation, connotation has at least two different subvarieties. *Informative connotation* is often a substitute for

---

*Langer, *op. cit.*, page 61.
† Hayakawa, *op. cit.*, pages 58–59.

denotation. Suppose, for example, we are describing New York City to a child who lives in Knoxville, Tennessee. In this case it is obviously impossible to give the phrase "New York City" denotational meaning. What we do is to give the phrase its informative connotation: "That's where Grandma lives . . . where there are subways . . . the Mets and the Yankees . . . Coney Island and the rides . . . (and for a particularly cultured or perhaps pretentious parent) the Museum of Modern Art . . . the Metropolitan Museum of Art . . . the Lincoln Center . . . the Cloisters . . ."

Some symbols are capable only of informative connotation, as in the case of logical or mathematical symbols: $y^2 = a^2 + b^2$. While this definition may have denotative application, the formal or connotative definition specifies the meaning completely.

*Affective connotation*, the second major subvariety, does not attempt to provide any denotational referent at all; rather the use of particular symbols is meant to arouse emotional reactions, without regard to its informative connotation or denotation. "Communism is anti-democratic and un-American." Not one of the words in this sentence can be checked out for denotational accuracy. Similarly, words are often used in advertising for the particular emotional effect they produce rather than for any extensional information they might carry.

## 2. Free Creation

The second criterion proposed by Von Bertalanffy to characterize an event as a symbol implies that there is no necessary connection between a symbol and the object or condition symbolized. Words that sound like the reality they represent are an exception rather than the rule. This is a point about which General Semanticists have been particularly adamant: There is nothing magical or sacred about the relationships of a symbol (a word, a coin, a flag, etc.) to the object it represents. Indeed Korzybski, the patriarch of General Semantics, felt that many social and personal problems were brought about by the modern counterparts of word magic and incantation.

In order to correct for difficulties caused by careless language, it is necessary to break down our ordinary ways of evaluating what we say by using *dating, etcetering, quotation-marking,* and *hyphenating.* These techniques all involve the extension of a number of already available rules. $Republican_1$, $Republican_2$, $Republican_3$; . . . etc.; $Republican_{1870}$, $Republican_{1880}$, $Republican_{1890}$ . . . all present examples of the first three of these techniques. Indexing or dating a particular individual who happens to have membership in a particular group is meant to show that despite the fact that there is some degree of similarity between $Republican_1$ and $Republican_2$, or among members of the Republican Party in 1880 and 1890, the differences among these individuals are likely to be as significant as their similarities.

If we substitute Barry Goldwater for Republican$_1$ and Henry Kissinger for Republican$_2$, the example takes on more contemporary significance. Dating also serves to remind us that the context of a belief, or of an opinion or of an attitude, profoundly affects the extensional or denotational referent of the symbol.

*Etc.* and *quotation marks* can also be useful to clarify careless language. The term *etc.* is used to remind speakers and listeners that no symbol is a perfect representation of its referent idea, object, or event. Quotation marks are used to remind us that words such as *race, mind, truth*, etc., are not to be trusted even though they are the only terms available in the language.

In general, semanticists compare the relationship of language to reality with the relationship of *maps* to *territories*. That is, symbols are maps of events, conditions, states, or objects that stand for (represent) denotatively valid territories. Obviously maps are nowhere near as complicated or as complete as the territories they represent, and it is the mistaken notion that maps are identical with their territories that causes so much semantic and conceptual trouble.

One obvious, yet powerful, way in which to describe the relationship of maps to territories is through the use of what the semanticists call the *structural differential*, or more simply, the *Ladder of Abstraction*. To take Hayakawa's example (1949): Consider a particular cow immediately before us as an object of immediate perception—unnamed, uncategorized; just simply there. This is the lowest rung of the ladder, an object of direct perception. At the next level, let us name this particular object *Bessie* and recognize that the name is not the object, for the object is constantly changing over time. If we next consider Bessie as a *cow*, we have moved up another rung on the abstraction ladder, for the word *cow* stands for characteristics we have abstracted as common to Bessie, and Cow$_2$, Cow$_3$, ..., etc. When Bessie is referred to as *livestock*, we have moved up again, and when she is referred to as a *farm asset*, we have taken another step, and so on as we climb Bessie's Ladder. At each step we lose more and more of the particular reality immediately before us, and at each step we run the risk of increased semantic confusion if we mistake the map for its territory.

What are the criteria of a good map? The most important criterion would seem to be the degree to which it agrees with the territory it describes. It is never exact and it never has as many details as its territory: What it does provide is a set of abstracted properties that ultimately are open to extensional observation. So too with words. We should always ask how accurately does a thought, word, or symbol represent its extensional referent. In order to do this, we must realize that a useful definition points down the abstraction ladder, or if absolutely necessary remains at the same level. Definitions that go up the ladder often end up by confusing an issue rather than clarifying it.

With all this concern about symbols, it would certainly seem that of all the animal kingdom man should use his symbols best. Stuart Chase, deploring the confusion created by symbolization—in particular language—wistfully observes his cat, Hobie Baker, who never mistakes a symbol for its referent. He is free "from the hallucination evoked by bad language." The poet Walt Whitman similarly caught some of this dilemma when he wrote:

> I think I could turn, and live with animals, they are so placid and self-contain'd.
>
> They do not sweat and whine about their condition,
>
> They do not lie awake in the dark and weep for their sins,
>
> They do not make me sick discussing their duty to God,
>
> Not one is dissatisfied, not one is demented with the mania of owning things,
>
> Not one kneels to another, nor to his own kind that lived thousands of years ago.
>
> Not one is respectable, or unhappy the whole world over.*

Although the General Semantics movement has stressed the dangers of nonextensional symbolization, the significance of such symbolization should be obvious. Much of our knowledge—of geography, of history, of philosophy, of mathematics, of theology, etc.—comes from nonextensional or connotational sources. These are profoundly important to the nature of Man as a symbol-using organism, even if they result in occasional difficulty if uncritically used.

Susanne Langer has been sufficiently impressed by the fact that many symbolic activities seem to hinder man's quest for biological survival so as to suggest that a different motivation must underlie symbolic activity. Her admittedly speculative hypothesis is that symbolization—defined as the continual transformation of input (sensory or otherwise) into conception or ideation—is a basic human need termed *the need of symbolization.*

> I propose, therefore, to try a new general principle: to conceive the mind, still as an organ in the service of primary needs, but of characteristically human needs; instead of assuming that the human mind tried to do the same thing as a cat's mind, but by the use of a special talent which miscarries four times out of five, I shall assume that the human mind is trying to do something else; and that the cat does not act humanly because he does not need to. This difference in fundamental needs, I

---

* From "Song of Myself," Section 32 of *Leaves of Grass*, by Walt Whitman, New York: The New American Library.

believe, determines the difference of function which sets man so far apart from all his zoological brethren; and the recognition of it is the key to those paradoxes in the philosophy of mind which our too consistently zoological model of human intelligence has engendered.*

The upshot of this discussion is not that we need accept Langer's need nor Hayakawa's anxiety, but that symbols can be treated either with reverence or fear. The person who is overawed or even only slightly awed by symbols is likely to have his or her life fall into a constant semantic muddle, while the person who fears symbols is likely to have his or her life fall into a nightmare of continual definition. Although neither attitude by itself is a particularly reasonable one, both do contain an element of truth. Misused symbols can cause emotional and conceptual havoc, but fear of symbols can deprive human beings of such significant experiences as poetry, music, and mathematics. Under the sign of either Aquarius or Apollo—and whether they like it or not—human beings are thoroughly symbolic creatures.

**Symbols and symbol systems.**   Up to this point, we have concentrated on the individual symbol, yet it is clear that many individual symbols—be these words, musical notes, or mathematical $x$'s, $y$'s and $z$'s—are parts of larger units called *symbol systems*. The major way in which such systems have been talked about involves a distinction between *discursive* and *presentational* symbol systems.

Let us begin with a rather commonplace example:

An average high school baseball player stranded on first base after his teammate had made the third out had a problem: "In order to get to my position at third base," he pondered, "would it be better to cut a diagonal across the infield or to get there by going around the bases? Which is shortest? If it's 90 feet to second base and 90 feet from second to third, running around the bases is 180 feet. If I cut across the infield it's $90^2 + 90^2$ or $8100 + 8100$ or $16,200$. If I take a rough square root of $16,200 \ldots$ it's about $160. \ldots$ Let's see, 160 squared $\ldots$ Oh the hell with it! I'll run across the infield and figure it out later. $\ldots$"

What this student accomplished (or almost did) was to use one of the most significant characteristics of symbols: their ability to be applied to a variety of different situations. Consider the properties of the Pythagorean formula: $a^2 + b^2 = c^2$. First of all, use of this formula requires the user to know what a right triangle is, as well as the rules of squaring, and of addition. Once these operations are performed, the formula may be applied to any set of numbers describing any right triangle. The proof of $a^2 + b^2 = c^2$ was not made in terms of showing that this equation exactly fits every possible set of

---

*Langer, *op. cit.*, pages 43–44.

three different lengths found in right triangles. Rather it was proved by showing it to be logically consistent with other statements, all of which also had been proved in the same way, except for a few "undefined" terms such as *line* and *point*. Although it turns out to be true that $a^2 + b^2 = c^2$ applies to an infinity of right triangles, this is not the way in which it was proved initially.

Mathematics represents one of the highest and most important symbolic achievements of Man. The power of mathematics lies in the fact that mathematical symbols do not stand alone but are organized into systems governed by explicit rules. These rules provide this particular symbol system with the ability to generate increasingly more general and more powerful statements. Such rules also define any and all statements that are permissible within a given system. Because of this property an expression such as $4 + 2 = (7 + 3) + 6$ is meaningless within the rules of our number system. Mathematics, as well as its less rigorously defined and more natural counterpart, language, obviously contains rules of combination that appropriately may be termed the grammar or logical syntax of the system. Both mathematics and language (in addition to many other disciplines containing a vocabulary and combinatorial rules to operate on vocabulary elements—science, philosophy, logic, etc.) constitute the class of symbolic forms known as *discursive* or *propositional* symbolism.

In addition to a vocabulary and a syntax, discursive symbolism also has the property of multiple expression: That is, alternative statements are possible, for example, $2 + 2 = 3 + 1 = 4$; "A pig is a quadruped mammal"; etc. This property makes it possible in the case of language to construct a dictionary, and in all cases to translate from one form to another as well as to translate from one system to another if the rules of the translation are known; i.e., from English to German; from algebra to geometry. To be sure, "translation" is more precise for constructed systems such as mathematics than for natural systems such as language. The key to discursive symbolism is that all its statements, to a greater or lesser degree, are subject to verification or falsification by other statements, and that such statements are perfectly general, i.e., not bound to a specific place or time.

But is there not another mode of symbolization? On the day-to-day level it seems clear that banners, anthems, slogans, insignias, etc., cannot be referred to other statements and are appropriate only to a particular culture at a particular time. At a more significant level of nondiscursive symbolism, we have the production of painting, both abstract and representative, of poetry and music, and of ritual and myth. To be sure, some or all of these activities involve discursive elements; e.g., poetry is made up of words and music of notes, but for these activities such usage is not intended to yield contradictable or general statements. Rather it is intended to re-evoke in the listener the experience of its creator. When Goethe talks about "the movement of his heart," he is certainly not giving us a lecture on human physiology.

It is quite hard to characterize all the attributes that define *nondiscursive* symbolism, except perhaps to note in a general way that it deals both with unique experience and values. The entire realm of nondiscursive or *presentational* symbolism has been said to deal with the "unspeakable," the "logical beyond," and similar terms.

> There is, however, a kind of symbolism peculiarly adapted to the explication of "unspeakable" things, though it lacks the cardinal virtue of language, which is denotation. The most highly developed type of such purely connotational semantic is music. We are not talking non-sense when we say that a certain musical progression is significant, or that a given phrase lacks meaning, or a player's rendering fails to convey the import of a passage. Yet such statements make sense only to people with a natural understanding of the medium, whom we describe, therefore, as "musical." . . . Speech and music have essentially different functions, despite their oft-remarked union in song. Their original relationship lies much deeper than any such union . . . and can be seen only when their respective natures are understood.*

Before we can close the present section, or for that matter before we can open the next, we need take a close look at some of the specific properties serving to define the discursive symbol system we call language. For this rather special system, the linguist Charles Hockett has three times (in 1959, 1960, and 1963) tried to develop a set of design properties that would serve once and for all to characterize the essential properties of human language. In order to do this, Hockett uses a test battery approach: A particular communication system is considered the equivalent of human language only if it passes each test successfully. Although Hockett has provided as many as 13 significant tests, the three that seem most critical are semanticity, arbitrariness, and productivity or openness.

By semanticity, Hockett means what we have termed *representativeness*, or the ability of a word to stand for something else, while by *arbitrariness* he means to stress the fact that there need be no necessary relationship between a word and its meaning: *Whale* is a small word for a large object, *microorganism* is a large word for a small object, and the word *salt* is neither salty nor granular. *Productivity* or *openness* means the ability of a speaker or listener to say or understand things that have never been said or heard before. Language is *open* largely because it possesses a grammar, or a set of implicit rules that serves to coin new sentences by putting together words so as to produce new meanings. So, for example, when a newspaper announces: "The moon and President Nixon's trip . . . dominate the headlines" we have

---

* Langer, *op. cit.*, page 93.

no trouble in understanding this sentence, although it is unlikely that we have ever seen or heard it before. It is precisely this last criterion that will turn out to be of crucial importance in the next section.

## 3. Transmission by Culture

Von Bertalanffy's third criterion is meant to stress the taught and learned aspects of most symbols for no child is ever born with a knowledge of his society's particular symbols. These are learned and altered by each successive generation in much the same way that preceding and succeeding generations were, or will be, required to do so. Originally meaningless articulations slowly develop into language, meaningless rhythms evolve into dance and music, and meaningless scribbles into art. All these symbolic activities are profoundly affected by specific education and individual learning. The languages, the dances, and the artifacts of different societies are manifestly different, yet all reveal the operation of specific acculturation and learning.

Although it is absolutely certain that subhuman organisms do learn rudimentary symbolic activities, such as signs and signaling, it is not at all clear that they are able to transmit this "information" or "knowledge" to their offspring or peers. Unlike the human animal, no subhuman mother has ever been able to build abstraction upon abstraction without concomitant experience with any or all of the events symbolized. In comparison to lower-order organisms, this capacity in man allows for a continuity of human experiences and serves to bind the present with the past and both with the future.

Why should we be concerned with whether or not subhuman organisms can use the same order of symbolization as man? Roger Brown (1958) has parodied the spirit of this dilemma when he noted:

> I grant a mind to every human being, to each a full stock of feelings, thoughts, motives, and meanings. I hope they grant as much to me. How much of this mentality that we allow one another ought we allow to the monkey, the sparrow, the goldfish, the ant? Hadn't we better reserve something for ourselves alone, perhaps consciousness or self-consciousness, possibly linguistic reference?
>
> Most people are determined to hold the line against animals. Grant them the ability to make linguistic reference and they will be putting in a claim for minds and souls. The whole phyletic scale will come trooping into Heaven demanding immortality for every tadpole and hippopotamus. Better to be firm now and make it clear that man alone can use language to make reference. There is a qualitative difference of mentality separating us from the animals.*

* From *Words and Things,* by Roger Brown, New York: The Free Press, 1958, page 155.

A more serious reason for this concern has to do with the number of different classes of laws needed to deal with symbolic behavior. If we accept human and subhuman symbolization as essentially the same kinds of phenomena, with the human variety simply being the more elaborate of the two, then a single set of principles will do. If, however, we make a qualitative rather than a quantitative distinction, then different sets of principles need be employed to describe human and subhuman symbolization.

**Of bees and monkeys and their language:** But aren't there subhuman organisms who do communicate with one another in a truly representative way? The best-documented example of this would seem to be provided by the "language of the bees." These remarkable creatures are able to communicate the distance, direction, and quality of a nectar source to bees still in the hive and all by means of the so-called "bee dance." This "dance" actually consists of two different patterns, with the first of these called the *round* dance and the second, the *wagging* or *circle* dance. Basically the round dance is used to communicate food sources close to the hive (from 150–300 feet), while the circle dance is used to communicate food sources far from the hive (i.e., at distances greater than 300 feet).

The great zoologist, Karl von Frisch (1954) and his associates have studied the characteristics of the circle dance in great detail and find that the frequency of turns performed by the forager bee gives a reasonable estimate of these longer distances. When, for example, the feeding place was about 300 feet away, the bee made 10 turns in 15 seconds. When the nectar source was about a mile and a half away, the returning bee made only 3 turns in 13 seconds. Thus the number of turns made by the forager provides a relatively precise estimate of distance when the circle dance is performed. It should be noted that a "lead dancer" is always followed in her dance by her hive mates (food foraging, like all other hive work, is carried out by the female).

But what about direction? Certainly no bee would ever find a honey source if it had to fly a circle having a mile and a half radius. The bee dance also provides information as to direction, and this information is usually communicated by the direction of the middle section of the circle dance with respect to the sun. Since von Frisch and his coworkers have found that different species of bees tend to use slightly different means to communicate direction, these differences have been termed "dialects in the language of the bees."

Do all these results indicate that the language of the bees is in fact a true symbol system—that is, a language? Karl von Frisch himself has noted:

> I should like to emphasize the limitations of the language metaphor. The true comparative linguist is concerned with one of the subtlest products of man's powerfully developed thought processes. The brain of a

bee is the size of a grass seed and is not made for thinking. The actions of bees are mainly governed by instinct. Therefore the student of even so complicated and purposeful an activity as the communication dance must remember that he is dealing with innate patterns, impressed on the nervous system of the insects over the immense reaches of time of their phylogenetic development.*

A second major distinction between the language of the bees and human language is that for the bee appropriate stimuli always elicit the response appropriate to the stimulus, whereas in human language it is extremely rare for an adult speaker to name all the objects he comes in contact with. In essence the language of the bees involves relatively invariant sign usage, whereas human language is capable of both sign and symbol usage. As Brown (1958) put it:

> The follower bee reacts to the dance of the finder as if the follower had experienced the stimulus causing the dance. Because the follower reacts to the dance as a sign the dance is like a linguistic name but again it is unlike it, because the follower's reaction is *too* reliable. A human being who hears the name of some food does not usually go in search of the referent. What he does is contingent on other things in the situation and in himself. If he is hungry, likes the food in question, and takes the name for an invitation to eat, he may act as if he had seen the food itself. The contingencies governing the reaction of the follower bee are fewer and quite different.†

Now these considerations all deal with Hockett's criterion of semanticity; what about openness or productivity? Although bees do seem able to communicate many diverse facts about their food-gathering activities, they do not seem to be able to go beyond this topic. Their total vocabulary is quite small —how far and in what direction—and although their "language" works quite well for locating specific nectar sources, it has no symbols for meanings other than those related to foraging activities.

The result of this discussion is that although the observations made by von Frisch and others do indicate that subhuman organisms are capable of representative activity, these activities are not the same as human language. They show no evidence of being transmitted by culture, they are not freely created, and they do not involve either a semantic or syntactical system capable of expressing infinitely many distinct messages. Although the language of the bees does provide for representative symbolization, it is far too

* From Karl von Frisch, *Dialects in the Language of Bees*, Sci. Amer., August 1962, page 79.

† From *Words and Things*, by Roger Brown, New York: The Free Press, 1958, pages 171–172.

limited in scope to interpret as equivalent to human language in any meaningful sense of the term.

In terms of evolution, however, it isn't too surprising to find that the language of the bees fails to meet most, or even many, of the criteria usually used to classify a communication system as language. In order to give the notion of subhuman language a fair run for its money, we ought to try a species somewhat closer to man. This strategy has been tried three times with chimpanzees in the past 70 years. The first attempt at teaching a chimp to speak was made by Winthrop and Luella Kellogg about 40 years ago. They raised a female chimp by the name of Gua under conditions identical to those for their son, Donald. Although Gua originally exceeded Donald in a number of developmental indices, she never did learn to speak. She did, however, come to understand a number of English phrases such as "come here," "shake hands," and "kiss-kiss."

The second attempt at teaching a chimp to speak was undertaken by Keith and Cathy Hayes, who raised a female chimp by the name of Viki. Although the Kelloggs had only incidentally tried to teach Gua to speak, the Hayeses spared no effort in trying to teach Viki to talk. As a result of their efforts, Viki came to understand a number of English sentences and phrases. But despite this intensive training, she was able to produce only a very small number of clearly recognizable words, such as *mama, cup,* etc. Films of Viki show that for her to articulate a word like *cup* was no easy task and one that required great effort on her part.

Twice in recent history psychologists have failed to teach man's closest relative to speak. Under ordinary circumstances this would be enough to discourage anyone from trying to teach a chimpanzee to speak, particularly since the Hayeses used quite sophisticated teaching methods. Recently, however, Allan and Beatrice Gardner (1969a; 1969b) have attempted this problem again, but with a new twist. Although both the Kelloggs and Hayeses attempted to teach chimps to speak, the Gardners began their study under a different assumption: namely, that the ability to use language does not necessarily require an ability to make sounds. Largely because the essential aspects of language can and have been mastered by people who are unable to speak, the Gardners reasoned that since the vocal apparatus of the chimpanzee is quite different from that of man, it seemed unlikely that a chimp could be trained to make refined use of vocalization. Instead, they argued, why not teach a chimp to use sign language? Since such communication does not require vocalization, Viki and Gua may have failed to use language not because of an essential linguistic incapacity but because of a motor failing unrelated to language.

There are, however, further advantages to using sign language. For one, chimpanzees are very skillful in using their hands for manipulating objects; for another, laboratory chimpanzees often develop begging and playful gestures which they use to good effect in the laboratory.

What is the American Sign Language (ASL) like? Basically there are two systems used by the deaf, one involving finger spelling and the other involving idea coding. The finger-spelling approach assumes knowledge of spoken language, since specific manual patterns represent specific letters. Idea coding, however, uses symbols that are independent of ordinary speech. So, for example, the symbol for *flower* is made by holding the fingers of one hand extended with all five fingertips touching and then touching the fingertips first to one nostril and then to the other as in sniffing a flower, while the symbol for *more* is usually made by repeatedly bringing together the tips of the fingers on both hands. Some of the symbols in this language are therefore quite iconic or realistically representative (e.g., *flower*), while some are perfectly arbitrary (e.g., *more*). Although many of these arbitrary signs may have had an iconic meaning a few years ago, such imagery seems to have been lost through years of stylized use.

But enough of the formal structure of the American Sign Languages; what about the Gardners' chimpanzee? Washoe, the chimp chosen for this experiment, was between 8 and 14 months of age when she first arrived in the Gardners' laboratory at the University of Nevada (Washoe, by the way, was named for Washoe County, home of the University of Nevada). Chimps at this age are quite similar to human infants: Eye–hand coordination is moderately poor, crawling has just begun, and both baby chimp and human spend the vast majority of their time sleeping.

Since the Gardners wanted to develop conversational behavior in Washoe, it was decided to give Washoe an unstructured environment much like that of a growing child. Confinement was minimal, and she was usually surrounded by friendly adults and interesting activities and toys. Only one requirement was made of all Washoe's human companions—that they use only ASL symbols when in Washoe's presence. In addition, they were encouraged to use intense sounds—hand clapping, whistling, laughing, etc.— with the provision that all sounds used must be sounds that a chimpanzee could imitate.

Since there were no handbooks for teaching a chimp (or a human for that matter) to speak, a number of rough-and-ready methods were used. Among the more prevalent of these were direct shaping and imitation. Many signs were introduced to Washoe by shaping Washoe's hands into an appropriate configuration and then putting them through the movements of the sign. Some of Washoe's signs seem to have been acquired by delayed imitation. A good example is provided by the sign for toothbrush. As the Gardners tell it:

A part of the daily routine has been to brush her teeth after every meal. When this routine was first introduced Washoe generally resisted it.

She gradually came to submit with less and less fuss, and after many months she would even help or sometimes brush her teeth herself. Usually, having finished her meal, Washoe would try to leave her high-chair; we would restrain her, signing "First, toothbrushing, then you can go." One day, in the 10th month of the project, Washoe was visiting the Gardner home and found her way into the bathroom. She climbed up on the counter, looked at our mug full of toothbrushes, and signed "toothbrush." At the time, we believed that Washoe understood this sign but we had not seen her use it. She had no reason to ask for the toothbrushes, because they were well within her reach, and it is most unlikely that she was asking to have her teeth brushed. This was our first observation, and one of the clearest examples, of behavior in which Washoe seemed to name an object or an event for no obvious motive other than communication.

Following this observation, the toothbrushing routine at mealtime was altered. First, imitative prompting was introduced. Then as the sign became more reliable, her rinsing-mug and toothbrush were displayed prominently until she made the sign. By the 14th month she was making the "toothbrush" sign at the end of meals with little or no prompting; in fact she has called for her toothbrush in a peremptory fashion when its appearance at the end of a meal was delayed. The "toothbrush" sign is not merely a response cued by the end of a meal; Washoe retained her ability to name toothbrushes when they were shown to her at other times.*

Although this description indicates that Washoe was able to use the sign *toothbrush* in a truly representative way, it seems reasonable to ask how many and what kind of words Washoe did learn. Table 1.1 (see pages 20–23) presents some of the 30 signs reliably used by Washoe at age 36 months, as well as the contexts within which these were used.

An examination of the entry "More" indicates that Washoe is quite able to detach her use of a sign from a specific context and generalize it to other acceptable contexts. The sign for *more*, which started out as a request for more tickling, ended up as a request for more food or for a continuation or repetition of some performance. In other words, this sign shows profound and correct generalization.

These results pretty soundly seem to satisfy two of Hockett's criteria: semanticity and arbitrariness. Washoe seems to be able to make genuinely representative use of arbitrary signs. This leaves only one criterion—productivity or syntax—and here again Washoe seems to be doing quite well. As soon as Washoe had 8 or 10 signs, she began to combine them spon-

---

* From R. A. and B. T. Gardner, "Teaching Sign Language to a Chimpanzee," *Science*, August 15, 1969, page 667.

taneously. These combinations—such as "more tickle" or "gimme tickle"—often appeared before they had been produced first by the Gardners. The major types of signs used in combination seem to fall in one of three classes: emphasizers ("please," "hurry," "more," "come–gimme"), verblike specifiers ("go" "out," "in" "open," "hear–listen") and pronouns ("I–me" and "you"). Some of the characteristic constructions produced, involving each of the three classes are: "please open hurry" for emphasizers; "hear–listen dog" for specifiers; and "You out go" for pronouns.

This, then, is Washoe's verbal world. Is it equal to human language? In so far as representativeness and/or ability to name is concerned, the data seem overwhelmingly in favor of conceding that Washoe can do these things about as well as a child of comparable age. But what about her ability to make new sentences, i.e., her syntactic ability? Roger Brown (1970) has attempted an answer to this question by comparing Washoe's "combination sentences" with those produced by children between the ages of 18 months and 4 years. The first problem to be decided is whether or not Washoe's combinations are simply signs distributed over time, or if they represent grammatical constructions. One way in which to decide this is to see if sentences are "marked off" in any way, as for example what we do in normal speech when we lower our voice at the end of a declarative sentence, or end questions with a rising pitch. In sign language declarative sentences are usually indicated by returning the hands to a position of repose, while questions are indicated by holding the hands in the position of the last sign or by moving the hands out toward the other person. In both cases Washoe makes use of these signaling devices indicating that she does, in fact, have these techniques to define the ends of sentences.

There is, however, one aspect of Washoe's language behavior that is not yet resolvable from the available data. In English, word order is very important in understanding what it is a sentence means. For example, *Jim bit Charlotte* is quite different from *Charlotte bit Jim*, and this difference is given by word order. In all the combinations used by Washoe, there is not a single case that could not be understood by reference to immediate context. In Washoe's world there has been no need to develop the syntactic relationship of actor-to-person or object acted upon (i.e., Jim bit Charlotte versus Charlotte bit Jim). If, however, Washoe is able to develop this type of syntactic relationship, then it will be possible to feel somewhat more confident that she does indeed have the ability to use language.

This evaluation, based largely on Brown's analysis, is quite supportive of the contention that Washoe may eventually attain the estate of human language. A different analysis by Bronowski and Bellugi (1970) is much less sanguine in this regard. Their approach begins by providing a characterization of human language in terms of two primary factors: the ability of humans to disengage from their immediate environment and their ability to under-

**Table 1.1** Signs used reliably by chimpanzee Washoe within 22 months of the beginning of training, listed in order of their original appearance*

| Signs | Description | Context |
|---|---|---|
| Come–gimme | Beckoning motion, with wrist or knuckles as pivot. | Sign made to persons or animals, also for objects out of reach. Often combined: "come tickle," "gimme sweet," etc. |
| More | Fingertips are brought together, usually overhead. (Correct ASL form: tips of the tapered hand touch repeatedly.) | When asking for continuation or repetition of activities such as swinging or tickling, for second helpings of food, etc. Also used to ask for repetition of some performance, such as a somersault. |
| Up | Arm extends upward, and index finger may also point up. | Wants a lift to reach objects such as grapes on vine, or leaves; or wants to be placed on someone's shoulders; or wants to leave potty-chair. |
| Sweet | Index or index and second fingers touch tip of wagging tongue. (Correct ASL form: index and second fingers extended side by side.) | For dessert; used spontaneously at end of meal. Also, when asking for candy. |
| Open | Flat hands are placed side by side, palms down, then drawn apart while rotated to palms up. | At door of house, room, car, refrigerator, or cupboard; on containers such as jars; and on faucets. |
| Tickle | The index finger of one hand is drawn across the back of the other hand. (Related to ASL "touch.") | For tickling or for chasing games. |
| Go | Opposite of "come–gimme." | While walking hand-in-hand or riding on someone's shoulders. Washoe usually indicates the direction desired. |
| Out | Curved hand grasps tapered hand; then tapered hand is withdrawn upward. | When passing through doorways; until recently, used for both "in" and "out." Also, when asking to be taken outdoors. |

| | | |
|---|---|---|
| Hurry | Open hand is shaken at the wrist. (Correct ASL form: index and second fingers extended side by side.) | Often follows signs such as "come-gimme," "out," "open," and "go," particularly if there is a delay before Washoe is obeyed. Also, used while watching her meal being prepared. |
| Hear–listen | Index finger touches ear. | For loud or strange sounds: bells, car horns, sonic booms, etc. Also, for asking someone to hold a watch to her ear. |
| Toothbrush | Index finger is used as brush, to rub front teeth. | When Washoe has finished her meal, or at other times when shown a toothbrush. |
| Drink | Thumb is extended from fisted hand and touches mouth. | For water, formula, soda pop, etc. For soda pop, often combined with "sweet." |
| Hurt | Extended index fingers are jabbed toward each other. Can be used to indicate location of pain. | To indicate cuts and bruises on herself or on others. Can be elicited by red stains on a person's skin or by tears in clothing. |
| Sorry | Fisted hand clasps and unclasps at shoulder. (Correct ASL form: fisted hand is rubbed over heart with circular motion.) | After biting someone, or when someone has been hurt in another way (not necessarily by Washoe). When told to apologize for mischief. |
| Funny | Tip of index finger presses nose, and Washoe snorts. (Correct ASL form: index and second fingers used; no snort.) | When soliciting interaction play, and during games. Occasionally, when being pursued after mischief. |
| Please | Open hand is drawn across chest. (Correct ASL form: fingertips used, and circular motion.) | When asking for objects and activities. Frequently combined: "Please go," "Out, please," "Please drink." |
| Food-eat | Several fingers of one hand are placed in mouth. (Correct ASL form: fingertips of tapered hand touch mouth repeatedly.) | During meals and preparation of meals. |

---

* From Gardner and Gardner, *op. cit.*

**Table 1.1** (*continued*)

| Signs | Description | Context |
|---|---|---|
| Flower | Tip of index finger touches one or both nostrils. (Correct ASL form: tips of tapered hand touch first one nostril, then the other.) | For flowers. |
| Cover-blanket | Draws one hand toward self over the back of the other. | At bedtime or naptime, and, on cold days, when Washoe wants to be taken out. |
| Dog | Repeated slapping on thigh. | For dogs and for barking. |
| You | Index finger points at a person's chest. | Indicates successive turns in games. Also used in response to questions such as "Who tickled?" "Who brush?" |
| Napkin-bib | Fingertips wipe the mouth region. | For bib, for washcloth, and for Kleenex. |
| In | Opposite of "out." | Wants to go indoors, or wants someone to join her indoors. |
| Brush | The fisted hand rubs the back of the open hand several times. (Adapted from ASL "polish.") | For hairbrush, and when asking for brushing. |
| Hat | Palm pats top of head. | For hats and caps. |
| I-me | Index finger points at, or touches, chest. | Indicates Washoe's turn, when she and a companion share food, drink, etc. Also used in phrases, such as "I drink," and in reply to questions such as "Who tickle?" (Washoe: "you"); "Who I tickle?" (Washoe: "Me.") |
| Shoes | The fisted hands are held side by side and strike down on shoes or floor. (Correct ASL form: the sides of the fisted hands strike against each other.) | For shoes and boots. |

| Smell | Palm is held before nose and moved slightly upward several times. | For scented objects: tobacco, perfume, sage, etc. |
| Pants | Palms of the flat hands are drawn up against the body toward waist. | For diapers, rubber pants, trousers. |
| Clothes | Fingertips brush down the chest. | For Washoe's jacket, nightgown, and shirts; also for our clothing. |
| Cat | Thumb and index finger grasp cheek hair near side of mouth and are drawn outward (representing cat's whiskers). | For cats. |
| Key | Palm of one hand is repeatedly touched with the index finger of the other. (Correct ASL form: crooked index finger is rotated against palm.) | Used for keys and locks and to ask us to unlock a door. |
| Baby | One forearm is placed in the crook of the other, as if cradling a baby. | For dolls, including animal dolls such as a toy horse and duck. |
| Clean | The open palm of one hand is passed over the open palm of the other. | Used when Washoe is washing, or being washed, or when a companion is washing hands or some other object. Also used for "soap." |

stand their environment by "analyzing it into parts and then making new combinations from the parts." (Bronowski and Bellugi, 1970, page 168.) Obviously, these criteria are meant to tie language to a more general evaluation of human symbolic activities, as indeed Bronowski had done in a previous paper. (1968)

When Bronowski and Bellugi compared Washoe's linguistic development with that of normal children, they found Washoe consistently deficient in her ability to disengage her signing behavior from the immediate situation, as well as her lack of ability to show any consistent marking for the actor-verb-object construction noted by Brown. Similarly, she is relatively deficient in making statements that refer either to the past or present, and there are "only a few indicators that gesture language is used as an instrument of reflection by Washoe." Stating the matter more philosophically, Bronowski and Bellugi put it as follows:

> When we watch the way a child learns to speak from his point of view, we become aware of his mental activity in finding for himself inductive rules of usage which constitute both a grammar of language and a philosophy of the structure of reality. What the example of Washoe shows in a profound way is that it is the process of total reconstitution which is the evolutionary hallmark of the human mind, and for which so far we have no evidence in the mind of the nonhuman primate, even when he is given the vocabulary ready-made.

Ultimately, then, it becomes a matter of philosophy or world view as to whether Washoe has human language ability. Those who are willing to see a simple continuity between man and ape see Washoe as having "true" language; while those who see the human mind as qualitatively different from that of a chimp deny Washoe the estate of human language. There is an old story by Frank R. Stockton called *Lady or the Tiger?* in which the hero is asked to choose one of two doors leading from an arena. Behind one of these doors is a ferocious lion; behind the other, a waiting lady. The hero makes his choice and the story ends by asking: "Did he pick the lady or the tiger?" After listening to arguments about Washoe—both pro and con—it seems appropriate to ask: "The lady, or the chimpanzee?"

## LANGUAGE AND OUR VIEW OF THE WORLD

In Washoe's world the issue is clear: language or no language? In our human world the issue is also clear: which language? For the past few years or so the Avis car renting agency has been running an advertisement, in which the same phrase—WE TRY HARDER—is presented in 20 different languages.

As they point out in their advertising copy: "The closest the Germans can get to 'We Try Harder' is 'We give of ourselves more effort'." Now although it is a commonplace experience for those of us who were required to learn a second language to feel that the way in which certain ideas were expressed in two different languages was different, we nonetheless believed that ideas expressed in one language could also be expressed in a second language. Never did we question the assumption that what was "thinkable" in Language *A* was also "thinkable" in Language *B*.

The linguist Benjamin Whorf, on the basis of his analysis of languages belonging to widely disparate language families (e.g., English and Hopi) came to the conclusion that the way a person perceives and understands reality (that is, constructs his world view) depends on the lexical (variety of available words) and grammatical possibilities of the language he speaks. Such a view is contrary to the usual assumption that speech (language) is merely an incidental tool used to communicate, but not to formulate, the content of discourse. "Thought is primary; speech simply expressive" runs the dictum. Under this assumption, different languages are really trying to "say the same thing" with varying degrees of success in any particular instance ("We Try Harder" versus "We Give of Ourselves More Effort").

The poet W. H. Auden has described his feelings about the relationship of language to thought in the following terms: "Language is the mother, not the handmaiden of thought; words will tell you things you never thought or felt before." (*Life Magazine*, June 1970.) Such a view is clearly contrary to the naive assertion that language is indeed "the handmaiden of thought." For Auden, words are not incidental to communication, but serve to formulate what is finally thought or said. In the beginning there is the word.

What types of things did Whorf have in mind when he specified grammatical factors as of importance in affecting our construction of reality? One of his analyses concerned the difference between nouns and verbs. As schoolchildren we were taught to distinguish between nouns and verbs in the following ways: A noun names a person, place, or thing, and persons, places, or things tend to be relatively enduring, whereas verbs name actions or processes which are of relatively short duration. Although there are many exceptions to this classificatory scheme, Whorf (1961) put it well when he noted:

> If it be said that "strike, turn, run," are verbs because they denote temporary or short-lasting events, i.e., actions, why then is "fist" a noun? It also is a temporary event. Why are "lightning, spark, wave, eddy, pulsation, flame, storm, phase, cycle, spasm, noise, emotion" nouns? they are temporary events. If "man" and "house" are nouns because they are longlasting and stable events, i.e., things, what then are "keep, adhere, extend, project, continue, persist, grow, dwell," and so on doing among the verbs? If it be objected that "possess, adhere" are verbs because they

are stable relationships rather than stable percepts, why then should "equilibrium, pressure, current, peace, group, nation, society, tribe, sister," or any kinship term be among the nouns? It will be found that an "event" to us means "what our language classes as a verb" or something analogized therefrom. And it will be found that it is not possible to define "event, thing, object, relationship," and so on, from nature, but that to define them always involves a circuitous return to the grammatical categories of the definer's language.

Indeed it is possible to argue that the idea of cause and effect so common in Western scientific thinking may at base simply reflect the subject–predicate form of the Indo-European language common to these countries. In Hopi, for example, there is no way in which to mark time, i.e., there are no markings such as *will* for future, *ing* for present, and *ed* for past. Among the properties of Hopi time "are that it varies with each observer, does not persist simultaneously, . . . and cannot be given a number greater than one." Because of this it is possible for a Hopi Indian to describe the universe without recourse to time. Thus, according to Whorf, any science developed by a Hopi-speaking community would certainly produce a physics different from that developed in communities speaking an Indo-European language, for such a physics would have to be constructed without the time dimension in its equations.

A second major point to Whorf's hypothesis is that the vocabulary of different languages also affects the speaker's perception and conception of reality.

We have the same word for falling snow, snow on the ground, snow packed hard like ice, slushy snow, wind-driven flying snow—whatever the situation may be. To an Eskimo, this all-inclusive word would be almost unthinkable; he would say that falling snow, slushy snow, and so on, are sensuously and operationally different, different things to contend with; he uses different words for them and for other kinds of snow. The Aztecs go even farther than we in the opposite direction, with "cold," "ice," and "snow" all represented by the same basic word with different terminations: "ice" is the noun form; "cold," the adjectival form; and for "snow," "ice mist."

In an attempt to see whether colors that can be named with a single word, e.g., *red*, are recognized and responded to more readily than words requiring a phrase, e.g., a *purplish-brown-red*, Brown and Lenneberg (1954) first had a group of college students name 24 color chips. From these data they computed the degree to which subjects agreed in naming a particular color. Agreement among subjects in naming a color was called *color codability*. In an attempt to see whether colors that are more codable (i.e., appear as separate words in the language) are also more easily recognized and remembered, Brown and Lenneberg presented a different group of subjects with a number of sets of four different colors which the subjects then had to point out on a chart after the initial set had been removed. Results showed that color codability correlated with the degree to which subjects were able to recognize and recall colors.

In a cross-language test of this hypothesis, Brown and Lenneberg report the results of a similar experiment involving Zuni Indian subjects. These results showed that colors which were highly codable for English-speaking subjects were not the same as those that were highly codable for Zuni-speaking subjects. Further, Zuni speakers had great trouble in recognizing and remembering colors that were easily coded in English but not in Zuni and had little trouble recognizing and remembering colors that were easily coded in Zuni but not in English. This experiment would seem to provide some support for the view that where a language provides clear distinctions, speakers tend to organize their perception of reality on the basis of these distinctions.

Further work on this topic by Lantz (1963) indicates that the linguistic codability of a particular color is more important the harder the task a subject is required to perform. In the first part of Lantz's study, 20 subjects had to invent a name for each of 20 chips varying in hue. Phrases such as "dirty gold," "canary yellow," etc., were used in some cases to identify specific chips. In the second part of the experiment, a new group of subjects was asked to pick out of a set of 100 colors the specific chips named in the first part of the experiment. Each of the 20 names varied in their ability to specify the correct chip, and on this basis it was possible to get a *communication efficiency* or *codability score* for each color name. For the third part of the experiment a new group of subjects saw four different poker chips for a brief time period. Following this a five-second interval passed, after which time subjects were asked to select the four colors from a set of colors presented to them. Although there were a number of interesting results, the most important one for purposes of the present discussion was that the correlation between color codability and color recall was 0.71. What this means is that colors having high codability scores are the ones that are best recalled; or items that are given a clear and consistent name are easier to recognize than items having less distinct tags.

These experiments and analysis in no way really make an iron-clad case for Whorf's hypothesis. What they do suggest is that there are specific instances—i.e., in a memory task—in which the vocabulary of different languages may be correlated with what a person is likely to do in that par-ticular situation. In no way do these data conclusively prove that the same person could not have done something else; i.e., code and recall colors for which there are no specific words. To say this somewhat differently, widely diverse languages may share many of the same concepts, even if these concepts are more easily expressible in one or the other of these languages. In this regard, it is interesting to note that Whorf was able to make his theoretical point understood by individuals who speak none of the Indian languages from which he derived his hypotheses. Obviously his key references are translatable, however crudely, from one language to another.

The linguistic relativity hypothesis originally described by Whorf has recently been revived by Marshall McLuhan under the catchwords *The Medium is the Message* (McLuhan, 1964). This phrase is meant to emphasize McLuhan's contention that media analysts pay far too much attention to the content of a medium and not enough attention to the properties of the medium itself. McLuhan's definition of media is considerably broader than any we have been considering, and consequently, he is perfectly willing to discuss such topics as clocks, bicycles, roads, and light bulbs—to mention an assorted few—in the context of media.

What McLuhan wants to emphasize is that the specific properties of a medium significantly affect the mental habits a person brings to bear in solving problems and making choices essentially unrelated to the medium. In the case of books, for example, McLuhan is adamant in stressing the role of printing in bringing about our modern technological world. The significant thing about printing is its uniformity, its repeatability, and its separateness. McLuhan feels that many of the significant ideas of modern Western man came from this experience with the printed word:

> Socially, the typographic extension of man brought in nationalism, industrialism, mass markets, and universal literacy and education. For print presented an image of repeatable precision that inspired totally new forms of extending social energies.... Perhaps the most significant of the gifts of typography to man is that of detachment and noninvolvement—the power to act without reacting. Science since the Renaissance has exalted this gift which has become an embarrassment in the electric age, in which all people are involved in all others at all times.... The fragmenting and analytic power of the printed word in our psychic lives gave us that "dissociation of sensibility" which in the arts and literature since Cézanne and since Baudelaire has been a top priority for elimination in every program of reform in taste and knowledge. In the "implosion" of the electric age the separation of thought and feeling has come to seem as strange as the departmentalization of knowledge in schools and universities. Yet it was precisely the power to separate thought and feeling, to be able to act without reacting, that split literate man out of the tribal world of close family bonds in private and social life.*

---

* From *Understanding Media*, by Marshall McLuhan, New York: McGraw-Hill, 1964, pages 172–173.

But the Gutenberg dream is now fading in the glare of a television set: a medium vastly different in form from that of typography. In contrast to print, television projects an image of low definition; one that requires the viewer to connect the electronic dots in order to produce a meaningful picture. In contrast to print, which is primarily a superficial visual medium, TV requires participation at all levels if one is to get the message.

What social and cognitive changes should we expect to accompany this change in medium? For one, the habits of thought brought by TV should produce an intense and immediate involvement in people and things that should ultimately reduce sectionalism and nationalism, and, in McLuhan's word, result in a "tribalization" of man. Intellectually, habits of thinking derived from TV should bring about a Now Generation more interested in total experiencing than in piecemeal technological thinking. Television, the mosaic mesh, is serving to bring about a turned-on, arational, existential child who doesn't read very well and who isn't really very concerned by this turn of events. Johnny can't read simply because TV has made a bookish point of view obsolete.

The distinction between TV and typography gives rise to one of McLuhan's more important concepts: the principle of "hot" and "cool" media. A hot medium is one of high definition that fails to invite participation, whereas a cool medium is of low definition that invites completion or participation by the user. Do these differences bring about different psychological effects? McLuhan describes a study (McLuhan, 1964, page 332) in which three groups of students were asked to answer a quiz concerning material that had been presented over three different media: two hot—radio and print—and one cool—TV. For both the TV and radio groups the information was presented in a straightforward, verbal flow by a lecturer without any discussion. Results showed that students did better with TV and radio than with print; and that the TV group did better than the radio group. A second experiment was then done in which each of the three media was "hotted-up"; for radio and TV the material was dramatized with many new auditory and visual features, while for the printed form, novel typographic settings were used to emphasize each salient point.

The results of this new experiment again showed TV and radio to produce better test scores than print, but the surprising thing about these results was that radio was now better than TV. McLuhan feels an explanation should be made in the following terms:

It was a long time before the obvious reason declared itself, namely that TV is a cool, participant medium. When hotted up by dramatization and stingers, it performs less well because there is less opportunity for participation. Radio is a hot medium. When given additional intensity, it performs better. It doesn't invite the same degree of participation in its users. Radio will serve as background-sound or as noise-level control, as when the ingenious teenager employs it as a means of privacy. TV will not work as background. It engages you. You have to be with it.*

McLuhan has certainly made it possible for us to "get with" Whorf's hypothesis in its modern form. As with Whorf, McLuhan is interested in showing that all media, not only language, have strong and pervasive effects on human thinking and symbolizing. Unfortunately, or perhaps fortunately, McLuhan has not couched his arguments in anything other than terms that lead either to blanket acceptance or blanket rejection. For this reason he has angered a number of more bookish critics who have dismissed him as a con-man and charlatan. Although it is true that his writings contain a good deal of confetti, this hypothesis is sufficiently challenging in its general form to require further experimentation and elaboration. As it now stands, McLuhan has produced a series of glib, yet provocative, hypotheses about the effects of different media on human thinking.

## SUMMARY

In the present chapter we have gone a long way. We began by showing that man does not regard his symbolic activity as unimportant; quite the contrary, even biologically nonadaptive symbolization such as ritual is, and always has been, considered extremely significant. In order to embark on a psychological analysis of symbolic behavior we needed first to understand a few of the complexities involved in symbols and symbol users. These complexities set the stage for a psychological analysis of symbolic activity which, of necessity, can deal only indirectly with such questions.

For this reason we began by defining the essential properties of symbols in terms of: (1) *representation*, (2) *free creation*, and (3) *cultural transmission*. By representation we meant simply that a symbol stands for something else. There are a number of different ways in which a term can serve to stand for something else; the two major divisions involve signs and symbols. Although it is possible to distinguish between signs and symbols on the basis of a number of different criteria, the essential difference is that signs "announce" their objects, while symbols lead us to conceive of their objects.

The terms *connotation* and *denotation* were also discussed as modes of representation. Denotative meaning was described as the relation of a symbol to its object, with an ever present possibility of actually "pointing it out" to another individual. Connotation was considered as the relationships of one symbol to one, or many other, symbols. Under this mode of meaning, "point-outableness" is not required or even possible.

---

* McLuhan, *op. cit.*, pages 311–312.

The criterion of *free creation* was used to emphasize the fact that in almost all cases there is no logical or basic reason why a particular symbol is used to stand for a particular object or concept. The relationship is arbitrary and man-made. Although word magic (i.e., the belief that a word and its object are inseparable) is no longer common, its modern counterparts, as the General Semanticists have noted, still exist. In order to combat such strong magic, Semanticists such as Korzybski and Hayakawa suggest a number of techniques, all involving a clear recognition of the fact that words and things are not identical, and that the further you move away from the denotation of concepts the more careful you need be in language usage.

The third criterion, *transmission by culture,* is obviously related to the criterion of free creation in stressing the taught and learned aspects of symbols and symbol usage. This criterion in its elaborated sense has also been used to distinguish human from animal languages. For example, the language of the bees studied by von Frisch certainly is "representative." However, this language does not meet the criterion of productivity or openness and the criterion of transmission by learning. We can teach a dog all sorts of tricks, but we have never heard that a particularly clever dog has taught her puppies to do them.

When, however, we come to the linguistic ability of chimpanzees, more particularly one special chimp named Washoe, the issue of animal languages is not so easily decided. From the detailed records collected by her mentors, it is clear that Washoe has been able to acquire a reasonably extensive vocabulary, and that many of her signs have the arbitrary property required by a definition of human language. In addition to possessing a rather large vocabulary, Washoe had also begun, by the age of 36 months, to produce multiple sign combinations. The question as to whether these signs are simply sequences of words or whether they imply the use of productive syntactical rules is at present an undecided and undecidable point. In any event, the decision as to whether to grant Washoe human linguistic estate seems to be one of definition. If you define language in terms of productive communication—as the Gardners do—then Washoe has language; if you define language not as a specific linguistic faculty but as a constellation of general mental faculties—as Bronowski and Bellugi do— then Washoe clearly does not have language. In any case the final decision is still open.

Symbolic activities also have other characteristics to a greater or lesser degree. One of these, *productivity* (or the ability to utilize a general rule in an infinity of particular cases), is limited to *discursive* symbol systems. The essential characteristic of such systems is that they possess a basic set of elements as well as rules for manipulating and/or recombining these elements. The two most obvious examples are language and mathematics.

*Nondiscursive* (or *presentational*) symbolism is a second mode of symbolic activity. Such symbolism is considered to deal with the "unspeakable," the "logical beyond," or similar terms, and reflects time-bound experiences and values. Since language is itself discursive, it is really an unfit vehicle for dealing with this realm of symbolic activity. Music, poetry, painting, etc., all provide instances of nondiscursive symbolic forms.

Within a given discursive realm such as language, it is obvious that there are many different and distinct subgroupings possible. English, French, German, etc., constitute one group; Hebrew, Arabic, etc., another; Hopi, Zuni, and Shawnee, still another. The linguist Whorf has hypothesized that language is more than a mirror of thought; rather it shapes and directs the world view of its speaker. Although he and others have provided some anecdotal and experimental evidence showing that both the lexical and grammatical possibilities of a language do affect thinking in theoretically meaningful ways, such scattered data in no way prove his point conclusively. Perhaps the major argument against such a view is that widely diverse languages and language families share many of the same concepts even if these concepts are more easily expressible in one language than in another. Whatever differences there are among concepts arising from different languages seem to be of minor importance when compared with their similarities. Even where such differences exist, man's symbolic capabilities are usually sufficient to allow for some sort of cross translation of both language and concept. A more modern version of this theme—that is, of relating medium to message—stresses the contribution of media rather than content to general modes of thinking. Although McLuhan's hypothesis is an intriguing one, the evidence on which it rests is too fragmentary at present to justify it with any degree of certainty.

# CHAPTER 2

# THE DAYDREAMER AND THE FISHERMAN: SOME PRELIMINARY THOUGHTS ON THINKING

The operations of human mentality are varied and complex; convincing descriptions, few and far between. Psychology has been particularly unsuccessful in providing an effective description of these operations that is both intuitively meaningful and scientifically respectable. Sometimes the operations of mind have been described as a gigantic switchboard, complete with complicated switching machinery; sometimes they have been localized and described as movements in the peripheral muscles, complete with implicit responses; sometimes they have been described as elementary sensations, complete with variegated and multicolored images; and sometimes they have not even been described, for thinking has been considered by some an unfit topic for scientific study. Regardless of the description, all fall far short of providing a useful and convincing account of what seems to be happening when the phrase "I think" is used.

Fortunately, novelists are not as constrained as psychologists in describing the nature of human thinking. Consequently, their descriptions more convincingly approximate the complexities of thoughtful activities so that laymen and scientist alike agree: "Now that's more like it!" To be sure, such descriptions still do have their own special constraints; namely, that the description be expressible in words. Yet despite this, novelists seem to present a more intuitively satisfying account than any psychologist has so far ever been able to do.

For this reason it seems wise to begin an analysis of thought by examining in detail two different fictional accounts of these processes; one by Marcel Proust and the other by Ernest Hemingway. These particular descriptions present with extraordinary clarity a number of the most significant facets of human thought. Both also reveal something of their authors. The selection from Proust deals with the recollections of a sensitive and introspective adult about his life in the pampered days of his youth; while the selection from Hemingway deals with the attempt of an old fisherman to wrest one last catch from the sea.

Since historically Proust represents an earlier view, it is appropriate to begin with an excerpt from *Swann's Way*:

And so it is with our own past.  It is a labour in vain to attempt to recapture it: all the efforts of our intellect must prove futile.  The past is hidden somewhere outside the realm, beyond the reach of intellect, in some material object (in the sensation which that material object will give us) which we do not suspect.  And as for that object, it depends on change whether we come upon it or not before we ourselves must die.

Many years had elapsed during which nothing of Combray, ... had any existence for me, when one day in winter, as I came home, my mother, seeing that I was cold, offered me some tea, a thing I did not ordinarily take.  I declined at first, and then, for no particular reason, changed my mind.  She sent out for one of those short, plump little cakes called "petites madeleines," which look as though they had been moulded in the fluted scallop of a pilgrim's shell.  And soon, mechanically, weary after a dull day with the prospect of a depressing morrow, I raised to my lips a spoonful of the tea in which I had soaked a morsel of the cake.  No sooner had the warm liquid, and the crumbs with it, touched my palate than a shudder ran through my whole body, and I stopped, intent upon the extraordinary changes that were taking place.  An exquisite pleasure had invaded my senses, but individual, detached, with no suggestion of its origin.  And at once the vicissitudes of life had become indifferent to me, its disasters innocuous, its brevity illusory— this new sensation having had on me the effect which love has of filling me with a precious essence; or rather this essence was not in me, it was myself.  I had ceased now to feel mediocre, accidental, mortal.  Whence could it have come to me, this all-powerful joy?  I was conscious that it was connected with the taste of tea and cake, but that it infinitely transcended those savours, could not, indeed, be of the same nature as theirs.  Whence did it come?  What did it signify?  How could I seize upon and define it?

I drink a second mouthful, in which I find nothing more than in the first, a third, which gives me rather less than the second.  It is time to stop, the potion is losing its magic.  It is plain that the object of my quest, the truth, lies not in the cup but in myself.  The tea has called up in me, but does not itself understand, and can only repeat indefinitely, with a gradual loss of strength, the same testimony; which I, too, cannot interpret, though I hope at least to be able to call upon the tea for it again and to find it there presently, intact and at my disposal, for my final enlightenment. ...

Undoubtedly what is thus palpitating in the depths of my being must be the image, the visual memory which, *being linked to that taste*, has tried to follow if into my conscious mind.  But its struggles are too far off, too much confused; scarcely can I perceive the colourless re- flection in which are blended the uncaptureable whirling medley of radiant hues, and I cannot distinguish its form, cannot invite it, as the one possible interpreter, to translate to me the evidence of its contemporary, its inseparable paramour, the taste of cake soaked in tea; cannot ask it to inform me what special circumstance is in question, of what period in my past life. . . .

And suddenly the memory returns. The taste was that of the little crumb of madeleine which on Sunday mornings at Combray (because on those mornings I did not go out before church-time), when I went to say good day to her in her bedroom my aunt Leonie used to give me, dipping it first in her own cup of real or of lime-flower tea. The sight of the little madeleine had recalled nothing to my mind before I tasted it; perhaps because I had so often seen such things in the interval, without tasting them, on the trays in pastry-cooks' windows, that their image had dissociated itself from those Combray days to take its place among others more recent; perhaps because of those memories, so long abandoned and put out of mind, nothing now survived, everything was scattered; . . .

And once I had recognized the taste of the crumb of madeleine soaked in her decoction of lime-flowers which my aunt used to give me (although memory made me so happy) immediately the old grey house upon the street, where her room was, rose up like the scenery of a theatre to attach itself to the little pavilion, opening on to the garden, which had been built out behind it for my parents (the isolated panel which until that moment had been all that I could see) and with the house the town, from morning to night and in all weathers, the Square where I was sent before luncheon, the streets along which I used to run errands, the country roads we took when it was fine. And just as the Japanese amuse themselves by filling a porcelain bowl with water and steeping in it little crumbs of paper which until then are without character or form, but, the moment they become wet, stretch themselves and bend, take on colour and distinctive shape, become flowers or houses or people, permanent and recognisable, so in that moment all the flowers in our garden and in Swann's park, and the water-lillies on the Vivonne and the good folk of the village and their little dwellings and the parish church and the whole of Combray and of its surroundings, taking their proper shapes and growing solid, sprang into being, town and gardens alike, from my cup of tea.*

How can this remarkable quote be handled in psychological terms? First it is clear that the environmental event producing (the narrator) Marcel's initial reaction is a piece of madeleine cake soaked in tea. This

---

* From *Remembrance of Things Past*, by Marcel Proust, New York: Random House, 1934.

event, tea plus madeleine, must be considered the stimulus in psycholgical parlance. The first response evoked by the tea–madeleine stimulus is a diffuse emotional one: "an all-powerful joy." In some psychological notation this state of affairs would be written:

$$S_{t+m} \xrightarrow{\hspace{2cm}} r_{internal("joy")}.$$

Such notation uses upper-case letters, $S$, $R$, etc., for directly observable events or stimuli in the environment, and lower-case letters, $s$, $r$, to indicate internal, nonobservable or hypothetical stimuli and responses.

Marcel, in an attempt to strengthen the pleasant feeling evoked by the tea and madeleine compound, drinks a second, and then a third draught. As he soon discovers, the potion loses its power to evoke the pleasant sensation ($r_{int}$). This is the same type of observation that can be made about overt, observable responses ($R$) on the basis of either haphazard or laboratory experience. With repetition, responses habituate or fatigue. In life, after the same movement has been repeated over and over again, we say we are "tired"; in the laboratory we note a sharp decrease in the efficiency with which an animal performs the required response even if external conditions remain the same.

From this experience, Marcel makes an important discovery: The essence of his experience is not within the object (stimulus) itself but rather within him. This is an important point, for it implies that what a person "knows" about an object or event (and let's use the Semanticist's quotes at this moment) does not reside in the object itself, but rather in the person. Objects not previously encountered do not mean anything to a person unless they can be assimilated to objects previously experienced. It is only through experience that reactions, attitudes, meanings, etc., develop. Although there are stimuli that do evoke an unfailing reaction from the very first, these responses are usually considerably simpler than those involved in human symbolic activity. With these exceptions, Proust's point seems well taken: "The truth lies not in the cup but in myself."

After the initial, vague, emotional response by the tea-soaked madeleine, Marcel experiences a very confusing period in which something seems to be going on within him, yet he is unable to capture it. It is as if the initial response had set up a ring of ripples that spread out in his consciousness looking for some place to land. Marcel is in the midst of a tip-of-the-tongue state.

"And suddenly the memory returns."

The internal response, $r_{int}$, seems to have evoked some sort of internal stimulus, $s_{int}$, that now evokes other internal responses, which in turn lead to an overt description of this memory. This extended sequence may be diagrammed:

$$S_{t+m} \rightarrow r_{int_1} - s_{int_1} \rightarrow r_{int_2} - s_{int_2} \rightarrow R_{description}.$$

The $r_{\text{int}_2}$ represents the recollection of Aunt Leonie. The connection here is largely one of similarity in reaction: Both the present cups of tea and the cups of tea tasted at Aunt Leonie's house evoke similar internal reactions ($r_{\text{int}_1}$ and $r_{\text{int}_2}$). This memory is evoked on the basis of one of the most venerable laws of mental operation, the *Law of Similarity*. Two events are likely to occur together in thought to the degree that they are similar in some way (in this case, similar in emotional reaction).

The operation of this same principle is also in evidence in the next set of memories evoked: the "old greyhouse on the street"; then to "the little pavilion" to "the garden" and from "the house, the town" and finally the "town" and the environs of Combray. In addition to similarity of emotional reaction, these memories are also related by another important property: The sequence of memories evoked by the madeleine cake mirrors the sequence of events Marcel had experienced in walking from his room to the garden and then to the town. In the case of these memories, the overt order of recall depends on each of the constituent parts having been experienced previously in a certain temporal order; with items close together in experience also close together in recall. This stream of memories illustrates the operation of still another classic law of association, the *Law of Contiguity*: Two items occur in close temporal contiguity in thought to the degree that they occurred in contiguity in experience. Once this law is assumed, it follows that the manifest flow of behavior is produced by an underlying mental process that is similar in all important respects to the manifest flow. According to this law, if behaviour is sequential, so too is its underlying mechanism.

Once all this is understood, a psychological diagram of Marcel's remembrance of things past might well look like Fig. 2.1 on page 38.

What this diagram attempts to capture is the multiply connected and highly sequential lattice that makes up the type of consciousness understood and described by Proust. An initial stimulus evokes an emotional reaction; this reaction serves to evoke a series of memories, all dependent on preceding memories and based on the same emotional response. These memories, however, are themselves fine grained; that is, each successive memory cluster may be broken down into a number of components, and the flow of these components is determined by the order of events in the environment. These components serve to connect the present cluster with the memory already experienced and to enable further memories to make their appearance. The elements of each cluster have a great many more connections with other items in their own cluster than with specific items in succeeding clusters.

Proust also describes the essential nature of a theory of forgetting when he notes: "The sight of the little madeleine had recalled nothing to my mind before I tasted it; perhaps because I had so often seen such things in the interval, without tasting them ... (so) that their image has dissociated itself

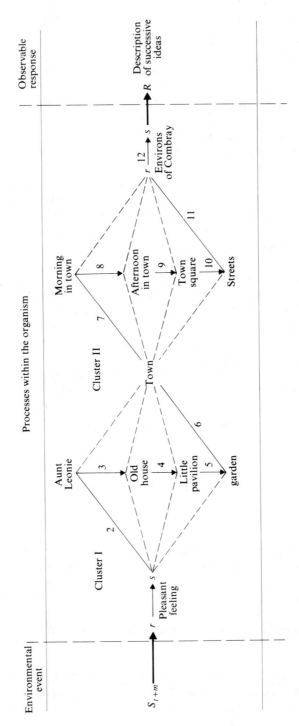

**Fig. 2.1**  Diagram of conceptual processes described in Proust's *Swann's Way*.

from those Combray days . . . ." Psychologically, this implies that a stimulus event fails to evoke an associated response if a second incompatible response has somehow or other gotten connected to the original stimulus. This process, which forms the cornerstone of an associative analysis of memory and forgetting, is called the *principle of unlearning*; that is, the original response is unlearned (forgotten) to the degree that a new response is connected to the same stimulus event. If the second response is not incompatible with the first, as is true in Marcel's case, it will still be "on call" when the stimulus is presented, but the probability that it will be recalled is reduced.

\* \* \* \*

Consider now the inner machinations of Hemingway's Old Man as he exhibits an entirely different mode of thinking:

Now, he thought, I must think about the drag. It has its perils and its merits. I may lose so much line that I will lose him, if he makes his effort and the drag made by the oars is in place and the boat loses all her lightness. Her lightness prolongs both our suffering but it is my safety since he has great speed that he has never yet employed. No matter what passes I must gut the dolphin so he does not spoil and eat some of him to be strong.

Now I will rest an hour more and feel that he is solid and steady before I move back to the stern to do the work and make the decisions. In the meantime I can see how he acts and if he shows any changes. . . .

He rested for what he believed to be two hours. The moon did not rise now until late and he had no way of judging the time. Nor was he really resting except comparatively. He was still bearing the pull of the fish across his shoulders but he placed his left hand on the gunwale of the bow and confided more and more of the resistance to the fish to the skiff itself.

How simple it would be if I could make the line fast, he thought. But with one small lurch he could break it. I must cushion the pull of the line with my body and at all times be ready to give line with both hands.

"But you have not slept yet, old man," he said aloud. "It is half a day and a night and now another day and you have not slept. You must devise a way so that you sleep a little if he is quiet and steady. If you do not sleep you might become unclear in the head."

He started to work his way back to the stern on his hands and knees, being careful not to jerk against the fish. He may be half asleep himself, he thought. But I do not want him to rest. He must pull until he dies . . . .

The old man dropped the line and put his foot on it and lifted the harpoon as high as he could and drove it down with all his strength, and more strength he had just summoned, into the fish's side just behind the great chest fin that rose high in the air to the altitude of the man's chest. He felt the iron go in and he leaned on it and drove it further and then pushed all his weight after it.

Then the fish came alive, with his death in him, and rose high out of the water showing all his great length and width and all his power and his beauty. He seemed to hang in the air above the old man in the skiff. Then he fell into the water and over all of the skiff . . . .

"Keep my head clear," he said against the wood of the bow. "I am a tired old man. But I have killed this fish which is my brother and now I must do the slave work."

Now I must prepare the nooses and the rope to lash him alongside, he thought. Even if we were two and swamped her to load him and bailed her out, this skiff would never hold him. I must prepare everything, then bring him and lash him well and step the mast and set sail for home.

He started to pull the fish in to have him alongside so that he could pass a line through his gills and out of his mouth and make his head fast alongside the bow. I want to see him, he thought, and to touch and to feel him. I think I felt his heart, he thought. When I pushed on the harpoon shaft the second time. Bring him in now and make him fast and get the noose around his tail and another around his middle to bind him to the skiff . . . .

When he was even with him and had the fish's head against the bow he could not believe his size. But he untied the harpoon rope from the bit, passed it through the fish's gills and out his jaws, made a turn around his sword then passed the rope through the other gill, made another turn around the bill and knotted the double rope and made it fast to the bit in the bow. He cut the rope then and went astern to noose the tail. The fish had turned silver from his original purple and silver, and the stripes showed the same pale violet colour as his tail. They were wider than a man's hand with his fingers spread and the fish's eye looked as detached as the mirrors in a periscope or as a saint in a procession.

"It was the only way to kill him," the old man said. He was feeling better since the water and he knew he would not go away and his head was clear. He's over fifteen hundred pounds the way he is, he thought. Maybe much more. If he dresses out two-thirds of that at thirty cents a pound?

"I need a pencil for that," he said, "my head is not that clear. But I think the great DiMaggio would be proud of me today. I had no bone spurs. But the hands and the back hurt truly." I wonder what a bone spur is, he thought. Maybe we have them without knowing of it.

He made the fish fast to bow and stern and to the middle thwart. He was so big it was like lashing a much bigger skiff alongside. He cut a piece of line and tied the fish's lower jaw against his bill so his mouth would not open and they would sail as cleanly as possible. Then he stepped the mast and, with the stick that was his gaff and with his boom rigged, the patched sail drew, the boat began to move, and half lying in the stern he sailed south-west.*

In this extended quote from Hemingway, as well as in the previous quote from Proust, thinking has been depicted as a sequential activity. In Proust's example the sequence of thought is determined by the structure of mind: One thought follows another either because the objects and events they represent have been experienced together in that order in the past (i.e., follow the Law of Contiguity), or because they are similar in some way (i.e., follow the Law of Similarity). In the case of the sequence of behavior exhibited by the fishermen, it is clear that the flow of both thought and action is more synchronized, and clearly under the control of some overall design, perhaps described as "Catch the Fish." Although specific thoughts and actions follow each other in time, the overall progression of both is determined by a very general understanding of what it is that has to be done.

In the execution of each step of this overall plan, the fisherman constantly checks the usefulness of his actions against some imagined outcome: "How simple it would be if I could make the line fast ... but with one lurch he could break it." Here he is forced to determine whether making the line fast fits in with being able to hold on and bring his catch to shore. What the Old Man does is to compare a contemplated course of action against the overall aim or standard of his total program of action. If the plan meets the standard, the action is performed; if it does not, it is discarded.

This type of continual try and check has much in common with the properties of a thermostat in a heater or air conditioner. In this case the manufacturer or the user first establishes a standard: Room temperature should be at 72°. If the temperature drops below 72°, the criterion is not met and the heater kicks on. As warmth spreads over the room, the thermostat reacts; when this reaction indicates the room is at 72°, the heater shuts off. All during the time that the heater is on, the thermostat continuously compares the incoming information about temperature with its predesignated standard value. As long as the standard is not reached, the heat continues. This continuous testing of present temperature against desired temperature goes on at the same time that heat is being produced.

The continuous trial and check that characterizes the operation of both the thermostat and Hemingway's Old Man is called a *feedback loop*. Perhaps

---

* From *The Old Man and the Sea*, by Ernest Hemingway, New York: Charles Scribner's Sons, 1952.

the most important aspect of such a feedback loop is that a course of future action is strongly determined by how well the results of the present action serve to make the standard a reality. This is true for the operation of both man and machine.

Such a situation is quite different from one, let us say, in which incoming temperature evokes a "one-shot" reaction. Suppose, for example, that the heater were set to be turned on in accordance with the severity of cold in the room, so that if the room were at 50° the heater would kick on for a 6-hour period, whereas if it were at 65° the heater would kick on for only 2 hours. At 72° the heater would never make a response. In this case the level of incoming cold stimulation is correlated with the "strength" of the evoked reaction. A temperature of 75° is below the evocation threshold (72°) and consequently does not evoke any response on the part of the heater.

This latter model, in which the strength of the heater's reaction is fixed and determined by input temperature level, is comparable to one type of $S$–$R$ model employed in psychological theory. For this approach, an organism responds only when there is some above-threshold stimulus (even if the stimulus must be assumed) with the characteristics of the response determined by certain intensive or qualitative properties of the stimulus. Give a shock, the organism withdraws; present food, the organism salivates. In both cases the magnitude of the response is determined by the quality and magnitude of the input.

Although it is quite easy to find numerous examples of the "fixed response heater" in psychological theory, there are fewer realizations of the "feedback heater" model. What would such an analysis look like? Consider for a moment Hemingway's Fisherman, and endow him with the following standard: The normal drag on a fishing line is, let us say, 10lb. When the fisherman feels 10lb drag, the fish is let alone until either the pull is more than 10lb (in which case, the Fisherman gives line) or less than 10lb (in which case, he reels in line). At any given moment, the amount of tug on the line is continuously evaluated by its pressure on the Fisherman's finger. If there is "just" 10lb of pressure, nothing is done. Such a situation could be diagrammed:

$$\text{INPUT}_{(\text{tautness})} \rightarrow \text{TEST}_{(\text{if equal to 10lb})} \rightarrow \text{EXIT}_{(\text{do nothing})}$$

If the input tautness is either more or less than 10lb, a more extended diagram is required. Consider the following situation, in which input tautness is less than 10lb. [Note that this model contains a provision for action: i.e., doing something in order to get tautness back to 10lb (see illustration).]

In this case, input information is tested for tautness [step (1)]. If this tautness is less than 10 lb, as it is in this case, the input doesn't match the standard [step (2)] and the fisherman must do something to make it congruent. In this case he would reel in [step (3)]. After reeling in, he does a

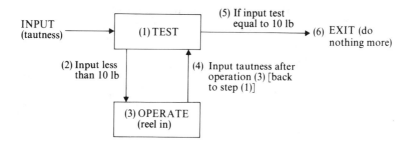

subsequent test [step (4)]: if this test now shows that after "reeling-in" the input tests equal to the standard (1), the fisherman need do nothing more and therefore stops or exits [step (6)]. The important part of this analysis comes when the test performed at step (4) still produces a tautness of less than (or perhaps, more than) 10 lb. Because the test does not meet the standard, the loop is still open and the chain is still at step (2), which then produces another cycle. Such continual Test-Operate-Test behavior proceeds until the standard is reached and for the moment an Exit is possible.

Throughout this discussion the use of the word *exit* obviously represents an odd word choice. The reason for using this word has to do with the fact that taking the first letters of the sequence, Test-Operate-Test-Exit, forms the easily remembered word *TOTE*, a word coined by Miller, Galanter, and Pribram (1961) to describe what they consider an appropriate unit for the psychological analysis of behavior sequences. The advantage of using a TOTE unit in place of the more familiar stimulus-response (S–R) unit is that it provides a systematic place for the concept of feedback. If behavior is considered only in the light of S–R (or s–r) units, no real test phase is possible: A temperature of 50° will cause the heater to respond for a 6-hour period even if the temperature rises to 75° after the first hour. For a TOTE unit, present and immediately preceding actions are constantly being tested against the standard. If temperature rises to 75° in one hour, the heater stops; if temperature fails to get to 72° after 6 hours, the heater still continues to operate. In a real sense the heater is behaving more appropriately in this latter case. The operation of TOTE units are irrelevant to the experience of Proust's daydreamer, although they are strongly implied by Hemingway's Fisherman.

Hemingway's Fisherman also displays other interesting aspects to his behavior. Perhaps one of the more significant of these is that almost everything he does throughout the course of his day and night on the ocean is guided by a single consideration. Every action, regardless of how simple or complex, regardless of how much or how little time it takes, is geared to catching a fish. Once we come to this realization, it is possible to see that planful activity is not only, or even necessarily, the result of thought or action sequences that are similar or that in the past have occurred close together in time. Rather such sequences may be considered controlled or generated by a single overriding plan or rule.

When, however, we try to identify subparts of the overall plan, such as: "Once the fish is hooked, reel him in," we note that such subparts can also be broken down into subparts. "Give him line when he pulls, reel him in when he rests." Each of these subcomponents can also be specified more precisely: "Let the line run out from a coil"; "Set it across your shoulders and over your right hand while your left hand is placed on the gunwale of the bow . . ." As a matter of fact, it seems possible to carry this description to many further levels of more precise description, with each level expanding the description of the next-higher level.

This analysis suggests that it is impossible to consider planful activity as simply the running off of a set of habits at one and the same level. Rather, such activity may be considered in terms of a hierarchical organization, with each lower (more specific) level completely preprogrammed by decisions, rules, or criteria, imposed at the next, or higher, levels. The Fisherman would never have gone into the boat (with all the skilled movements required so as not to upset it) or set sail if he did not have some goal in mind: catching a fish. What needs special emphasis is that when we talk about hierarchies and TOTE's and so on, *we are not talking about directly observable behaviors, but about theoretical descriptions of these behaviors.* In the hierarchical case, we must also emphasize that descriptions at different levels of the hierarchy are all different descriptions of the same behaviors.

A small portion of the hierarchical organization that might be involved in the sequence of actions performed by the Fisherman is presented in Fig. 2.2.

The first thing to note about this diagram is that reading the description across sequential points at the same level specifies a series of behaviors. At Level 2, for example, such a description would read: "Sail, set lines, hook fish, kill fish, reel in, etc . . . ." Hemingway himself seems to describe the Fisherman's behavior at about the third level of the diagram:

> He made the fish fast to bow and stern and to the middle thwart. He was so big it was like lashing a much bigger skiff alongside. He cut a piece of line and tied the fish's lower jaw against his bill so his mouth would not open and they would sail as cleanly as possible. Then he stepped the mast and, with the stick that was his gaff and with his boom rigged, the patched sail drew, the boat began to move, and half lying in the stern he sailed south-west.

A second thing to note about this diagram is that TOTE units have been omitted, although their inclusion is clearly compatible with, and even implied

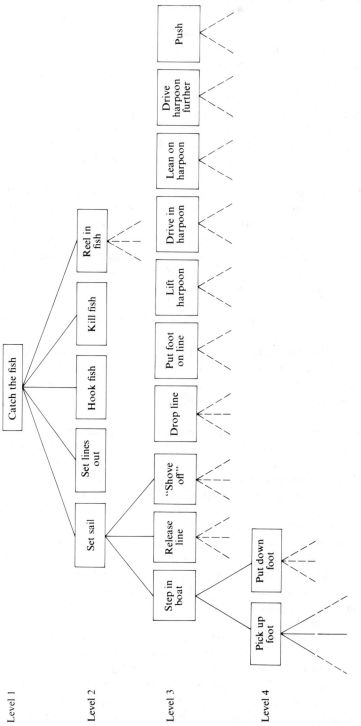

**Fig. 2.2**  Fragment of the Fisherman's organizational hierarchy.

by, this type of hierarchical analysis. For example, the last four behaviors described at Level 3 clearly constitute such a unit. Assume the Fisherman's internal standard is "drive the harpoon in until the fish stops moving." As the last two behaviors in this sequence indicate, the Fisherman obviously makes this test, finds the fish still alive (moving), and therefore operates (drives the harpoon in again) so as to achieve the standard. When the fisherman no longer feels movement, the standard is met and the plan is ready to move on to the next series of behaviors specified by the description "reel in fish" appearing at Level 2.

The differences between the type of thinking so well described by Proust and Hemingway are real and give rise to a number of theoretically interesting considerations. Both descriptions recognize the fact that thinking, like all behavior, is sequential; one idea or action follows another in time. The S–R or associative orientation stresses that the sequence produced is largely determined by the thinker's past experiences with the objects represented in his thoughts. In the madeleine cake incident, the particular series of memories rolls along a track arranged in accordance with Marcel's experience and populated by events which in the past had followed each other in experience. The sequence—from Aunt Leonie's room, to the house, to the garden, to the street, etc.—must certainly depict the way in which the physical environment presented itself to young Marcel as he walked from his aunt's room to the town. These bits of memory are cemented together not by an overall plan, but rather by an emotional reaction: All Marcel's memories on that particular day were pleasant.

Although it is quite clear that experience is quite important in determining the Fisherman's thoughts and action, it is also clear that the overall course of thought and action is not entirely organized on the basis of past sequential experiences that occurred in the now-occurring order. For one, the Fisherman had never before hooked a fish of this size and his behavior must in some sense be novel in response to this fact. Although thinking and acting are still sequential in execution, this sequentiality is seen not to reflect an underlying process that is itself sequential. Rather the sequential aspects of the Fisherman's behavior arise from a hierarchical organization of a number of subplans, each acquired from past experience, each of a lesser degree of scope, and each under the control of the aims of a plan at the next-higher level. Often a previously successful subplan has to be modified or discarded to meet the overall demands of the next-highest-level plan (i.e., "How simple it would be if I could make the line fast," he thought. "But with one small lurch he could break it. I must cushion the pull of the line with my body and at all times be ready to give line with both hands"). Thinking involves a continuous process of trial and check to see how well any given subroutine meets the overall plan. The description of planful behavior at any given level is subject both to further expansion (i.e., moving to a "lower" level) or to further foreshortening (i.e., moving to a "higher" level), with the implication that decisions made at higher levels automatically control the sequence at lower levels. If the thermostat says "It's hot enough now," the heater automatically shuts off.

These two ways of looking at human thinking raise a rather interesting issue: Is mind to be considered a passive mechanism acting simply on the basis of the similarity or contiguity between two events, or should this mechanism be considered in terms of processes that actively transform information as it is received, stored or utilized? In the first—or associative—case, stimulus inputs "trigger off" responses, these responses produce other further responses . . . and a sequence of responses is thereby produced. Given this assumption, responses are organized on the basis of past experience and creative thought is simply a fortuitous or serendipitous activity of certain minds particularly suited for recombining originally disparate responses. Experience serves to build vast $S-R$ networks that are capable in principle of leading from anything to almost anything else. These vast associative networks can also serve to direct the flow of thought in ways that often are prosaic or stereotyped.

From an information-processing or generative view, simple linkages between events may exist, but the major operation of mind is to transform information rather than respond to it directly. In the case of memory, for example, George Miller described what seemed to be an extraordinary feat of memory (1956) when he observed that communications engineers could remember exactly the on and off patterns of a series of as many as 21 lights. Miller soon discovered that no one attempted to deal with the series in its entirety; rather each series was broken down by a code into smaller sets ("chunks") of 3 items each. For example, a series of 15 lights required the memorizer to retain only 5 different "chunks" of information rather than all 15. In this case these engineers used something like the following code: If all 3 lights were off, they labeled it 0, if the first 2 lights to the left were off and the third one was on, they labeled it 1, and so on, until the case in which all three lights were on, which was labeled 7.

Thus, if the first 15 lights had the form on, on, off, off, on, off, off, on, on, off, on, on, off, on, off, they would first be grouped into 5 groups of three each, and then each group would be given its appropriate code number:

```
on  on  off = 6
off on  off = 2
off on  on  = 3
off on  on  = 3
off on  off = 2
```

The sequence of numbers 6, 2, 3, 3, 2 would specify the sequence completely. There would be no need to remember which lights were on; knowing the code would take care of that. Recalling the sequence of lights could then be accomplished by transforming the numbers back into lights. The total process involved in this task consists of three operations: (1) observe display, (2) code according to rule, (3) recode back to lights. This is representable as follows (figure adapted from Miller, 1956c).

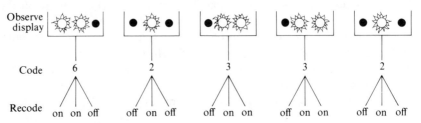

The initial transformation involves a reduction of input information to a manageable form, while the final transformation involves re-expanding the code back to lights on the basis of an already existing rule. The final sequence as it appears in recall is generated not on the basis of a serial process but on the basis of a hierarchical coding rule. In this case the sequential flow of behavior is controlled by a nonsequential process.

*A final remark.* The daydreamer and the Fisherman present two different types of thinking, and the differences between the two are real and important. As we have tried to show, reverie and directed thinking provide the fertile soil from which two different *theoretical* orientations of thinking have developed. This does not mean that each of these theories is accepted as appropriate for one type of thinking but not for the other. Rather it means that *S–R* or associationistic theories begin with certain assumptions growing out of an analysis of relatively unconstrained sequences of thought, while information-processing or generative theories grow out of an analysis of goal-directed thinking. What we will try to show in subsequent sections is how both these theoretical orientations have attempted to extend their hypotheses to include topics not dealt with in their original formulations. What these topics are is itself the topic of the next section.

## WHAT IS STUDIED WHEN THOUGHT IS STUDIED?

The quotes from both Hemingway and Proust serve to define at least two different areas considered under the general topic of thought: memory and problem solving. Even if both memory and problem solving are defined as broadly as possible, they do not exhaust the areas generally considered when the psychologist or the layman thinks of thinking. The major omission, at least as far as a broad topic heading is concerned, is concept formation. By concept formation we mean to imply such questions as: How do people form concepts? What materials and procedures should be used to study concept formations? How should we consider concepts theoretically? And so on.

These three areas—memory, problem solving and concept formation—are probably the major topical headings considered in the rather nebulous area called human symbolic activity. Now while precise-sounding (although not really exact) definitions could be offered for all three areas, it is perhaps better to let the various procedures involved in the study of these phenomena specify the differences more exactly. Instead let us use the words with their more or less everyday connotations.

*Memory* for example is taken to deal with the ability of a subject to retain or revive previously experienced thoughts, movements, images, ideas, etc.

*Problem solving* deals with what an organism says and does when presented with problems that can vary in complexity from disentangling two mechanical puzzles to proving a mathematical theorem.

*Concept formation* involves an examination of what goes on when a subject attempts to put into a single class a collection of items differing in a number of "nonessential" ways, e.g., labeling a set of objects as "round" or "tall" or "triangular" or "whatnot."

To be sure, all these areas overlap and any one of the three is often involved in the other two. So, for example, recalling specific aspects of the materials presented may be a prerequisite for either (or both) problem solving and concept formation (Bourne, 1966), while a memory task can be considered as a novel problem in need of some new conceptualization in order to produce the greatest degree of recall. The major reason for dividing symbolic activity into these topics is that such divisions seem intuitively reasonable and serve to describe areas currently under intensive investigation. These divisions are meant to be provisional, not absolute.

The processes involved in memory, problem solving, and concept formation, like almost all activities of mind, are not fully articulated in the infant. They develop and change as a result of increases in both developmental and learned sophistication. Although the study of the growth of mind has an extensive history in philosophy, psychoanalysis, and early structural psychology (see Locke's *Tabula Rasa*, Freud and Abraham's *Psychosexual Stages*, and Asch's *Determining Tendencies*), few psychologists until recently have attempted to trace the course of cognitive growth except in a completely normative way: Developmental data were gathered, but for use only as indicators of what a 4-, 5-, 6-, or 10-year-old child could be expected to do. The requirements and dictates of mental measurement were of primary importance.

The obvious exception to this trend has been the work of Piaget and his collaborators, who have studied the growth of many different facets of intelligence. One of the basic assumptions behind Piaget's work is that the development of thought and conception in the child parallels the historical development of epistomological conceptions in philosophy culminating in scientific thought. In its most obvious outlines, Piaget's work falls within, or is at least consonant with, a rule-governed approach to thinking. The child as he develops is not the passive recipient of experience, but rather the active shaper of information on the basis of his present construction of reality.

As in more experimental realms, two trends can be distinguished in talking about the growth of mind: Human mentality may be viewed either as the accumulation of environmental inputs and of their subsequent combinations and recombinations; or alternatively, as the accumulation of different "schemata" for conceptualizing and organizing the nature of these experiences. The development of thought, along with the establishment of memory, the ability to solve problems, and the potential for concept formation seem obvious divisions for examining experimental work. In Part II we will examine experimental work done on the topic of thinking that has its origins in an associationistic or ($S-R$) tradition, while in Part III we will examine data derived from a generative or informational viewpoint. In both cases research work will be organized around the topics of *Memory, Concept Formation, Problem Solving* and *Cognitive Development.*

## ON UNDERSTANDING THOUGHT; OR WHEN ARE WE SATISFIED WE KNOW WHAT WE KNOW ABOUT KNOWING?

As an object of study, thinking is a particularly tough customer. For one thing, it is extremely difficult to get thinking out in the open for all to see. Traditionally, thinking implies covert activity, something private and unobservable. Behaviorally, thinking has a tendency to stop or at least to interfere with ongoing responses; "Stop and think" is an oft-quoted adage. Like so many interesting problems, the initiation and progression of thought must remain an inference from observable behavior—but what kind of behavior? A number of different approaches have been followed in attempting to decide on what is the appropriate way to study thought experimentally. In the sections that follow, three different orientations are considered. Each in its own way offers a different and useful entering wedge.

### 1. The Controlled Response

In 1954 W. S. Verplanck took 17 members of a class in experimental psychology and set them loose on their friends, dates, parents, or anyone else who would talk to them, with the instructions: "Every time the person you're talking to begins a phrase with the words 'I think...' 'I believe...' 'It seems to me . . .,' etc., I want you to record it.  Do this for 10 min.  At the end of this period, I want you to agree with the next statement he (she) makes containing these or similar phrases.  Indicate your agreement by saying things such as 'You're right,' 'I agree,' 'That's so'; or if they're in the middle of a sentence just nod your head.  Do this for 10 min.  During the next, and final, 10 minute period neither agree nor disagree with any statement your respondent makes. Simply record the number and type of statements made.

The students heard and they obeyed.  The data they gathered are presented in Fig. 2.3.

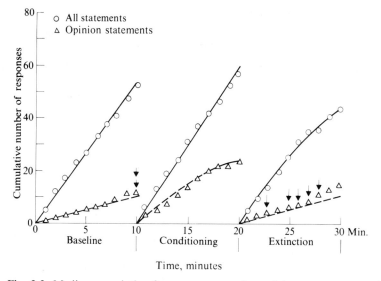

**Fig. 2.3** Median cumulative frequency curves for opinion statements, and all statements, for the three periods: baseline, conditioning, and extinction.  (From Verplanck, 1955)

The first 10-minute period is called the *base-line period* during which time the number of freely emitted statements of opinion are plotted (lower curve) along with the total number of statements recorded (upper curve). The next block of time, called the *conditioning period*, presents the rate at which opinion statements were produced when each statement was followed by some statement of agreement.  During the final 10 minutes, the number of opinion statements, as well as the total number of statements produced, were recorded but not agreed with.  The arrows over the curves presented for *extinction* indicate those points at which subjects said they "had to leave, could they be excused, etc. . . ."

The striking aspect of this experiment is that although the total number of responses made did not differ during the three periods, the number of opinion statements did differ significantly, with the greatest number occurring during conditioning and the smallest number during extinction. This was true regardless of the topic of conversation, the particular setting in which the responses were monitored, or the relationship of Experimenter to Subject. Agreement affects the rate of producing opinion statements.

This experiment provides a good example of one approach to the problem of deciding whether or not an investigator has an "understanding" of thinking. By the rules of this orientation, if an experimenter can bring the "mental" behavior he is interested in under his control, and demonstrate that indeed it is under his control, he may be said to "understand" the phenomenon. Control is equal to understanding.

For this approach there is no problem in specifying thinking or conceptual behavior—they are simply responses, similar in character to all other responses, and as such capable of being brought under the control of reinforcement. Since "thinking," by investigator preference, can be only an overt or observable response, the problems involved in attempting to describe or control what goes on "inside" the thinker are sidestepped. The only valid subject matter is the behavior itself; all internal and nonobservable processes are studiously not studied.

## 2. Proof by Prediction

There are a great many pairs of words in the English language that sound alike, but have two completely different meanings. This is particularly true for a class of *homophones* that has both a hostile and nonhostile interpretation; e.g., *lick, pound, trip*, etc. This fact raises the problem of why speakers and listeners seldom mistake a hostile for a nonhostile usage.

In an attempt to test the hypothesis that linguistic context serves to determine which usage is implied, Pollio, Wilcox, and Sundland (1966) secured a large collection of hostilely ambiguous words and then gathered word associations to them. Figure 2.4 shows one possible pattern for the word *pound* as derived from these norms.

As these results indicate, *pound* has word associates belonging to two different categories of words; one hostile and the other nonhostile. After similar preliminary data had been gathered for a number of different ambiguous–stimulus words, these stimuli were divided into three groups: those words that had a strong tendency to produce a hostile associate (e.g., *slug*), those that had a medium tendency to produce hostile associates (e.g., *pound*); and those that had a weak tendency to produce hostile associates (e.g., *sock*). After these groupings were established, all words were preceded by either 1, 2, or 3 context words. For three different groups of subjects, all stimulus words were preceded by context words that were neutral with respect to hostility, e.g., *gum, job*, etc. For another three groups of subjects,

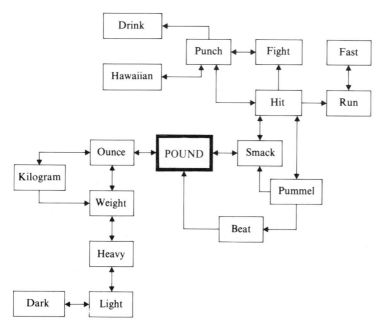

**Fig. 2.4**  Pattern of associative interconnections involving stimulus word *pound*.

all stimulus words were preceded by context words that were chosen so as to be specifically hostile, e.g., *bullet, rape, . . .* , etc.

The basic hypothesis proposed in this experiment was that each context word served to arouse the tendency to say that word as a response.  For example, if a subject saw the word *hit*, his first response would be to repeat the word to himself.  In so doing, it was felt that this implicit evocation would serve to arouse many of the other words in the associative network fathered by the word *hit*.  If we keep this in mind, then seeing the word *hit* and the word *pound* should serve to evoke a response common to the associative networks aroused by both (e.g., *smack*) more readily than one connected to *pound* alone (e.g., *ounce*).  By this logic, longer prior contexts (*hit, smack, fist, pound*) should evoke a hostile response (e.g. *beat*) more often than shorter contexts.  Similarly, if *pound* were preceded by a context of nonhostile words, the likelihood of a hostile response should be decreased.

Figure 2.5 presents the results of this experiment for stimulus words initially high in producing hostile responses.  As can be seen, the number of hostile word associates is significantly greater for stimuli preceded by hostile contexts than for words preceded by neutral contexts.  Furthermore, this effect is stronger over more extensive prior contexts.  Context serves to resolve the ambiguity of hostilely ambiguous homophones.

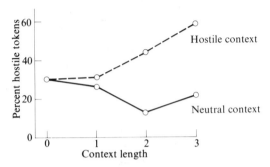

**Fig. 2.5**  Proportion of hostile response tokens as a function of context length. (From Pollio, Wilcox, and Sundland, 1966)

What philosophy of "understanding" is implied by this and similar experiments? Usually, an event is said to be understood when an investigator can specify the principles he expects to operate in a particular situation and then can use these principles to predict how an organism will behave in that situation. In order to do this, he usually begins by asking specific questions about the nature of the experimental task and about the nature of the behaving subject. Since the experimenter usually controls the experimental situation, he spends most of his time in describing the pattern of relationships that exists among the relevant units of behavior. This immediately raises the question of what units need be considered. Here the usual procedure is to choose some unit that can be specified reliably by a number of different observers, and that is, or can be, intuitively related to the area under consideration. In the case of symbolic activities, the word is one unit that obviously fulfils these requirements even though words do have substructures such as prefixes, tenses, possessives, etc. In addition, the word has the added advantage of providing readily available tables of frequency of occurrence, of word associates, of rated meaning, and so on. In short, we know a good deal about words.

Once the units problem has been decided, it is then necessary to describe the nature of the relevant organization of units involved in the present task. This organization is usually called *psychological structure*. Structure, however, is useful only to the degree that knowing about that structure leads the investigator to predictions about potentially observable behavior. In the case of verbal structure, diagrammed in Fig. 2.4, one theoretical basis on which to predict what will happen is to use a principle of multiple inputs. One version of such a principle might run: "When stimulus words provide multiple input to the same word, both the speed and probability of occurrence of that word are facilitated. In the case of two context stimuli (*A* and *B*) having an associative connection with a third or target stimulus (*C*), the occurrence of (*C*) depends jointly on the *A–C* and *B–C* probabilities. . . ."

The logic of the proof-by-prediction approach runs roughly as follows: If you can predict how a subject will behave in a novel experimental setting, then you can feel somewhat more confident about your theoretical analysis of the situation. This is not to say that you can feel completely certain that your understanding is correct, but only that the probability of its being correct is somewhat greater after your prediction was verified than before. If, however, a particular prediction is not verified, there are a number of directions in which an investigator can go, depending in large measure on his analysis of what went wrong. Such analyses usually involve a reconsideration of the theoretical principle thought to operate in that situation, or a reconsideration of the experimental task in terms of its appropriateness for the principle under consideration, or any of a number of other possibilities. The ways in which experiments can go wrong (i.e., not come out as predicted) are as numerous as the types of experiments done. The important point, however, is that for this approach, understanding consists of a continual try and check of observation to theory, and theory to observation. Where observation is inconsistent with theory, some change in either theory or experiment is required. In this way, new evidence continuously shapes the nature of useful theory and experimental procedure.

## 3. Turing's Test: Simulation and Understanding

In 1950, the eminent English mathematician A. M. Turing asked a rather pertinent impertinent question: "Can a machine think?" As he correctly noted, the answer to this question hinges on the definition of two key words: "machine" and "think." The first, "machine," was quickly disposed of when Turing specified the digital computer as "his machine." The definition of "think" was not handled immediately, but sidestepped in favor of the following line of argument: "Suppose I were to let you ask two different people, one male and one female, any question or set of questions you choose in an attempt to determine which one was female. In order to keep the game on the up and up, however, I never let you see Person *A* or Person *B*, and I never let you know when *A* or *B* was lying or telling the truth. Would it be possible for you to tell me which one was female?"

Once Turing specified his game in this way, the issue of whether or not a computer can "think" becomes sort of a red herring. Turing's game won't really help us decide this question simply because we can make the answer come out any way we want. The decision really rests on whether or not we demand that the word "think" include "animalness" or possibly even "humanness": Those who do not see the necessity of a humanness criterion will be ready to extend the courtesy of thinking to a machine; those who do will never accept the machine's behavior as thinking, no matter how expert the imitation.

To return to Turing's question: If we had to decide whether *A* or *B* were the lady, we would need to take account of whether or not Person *A* (the male) was trying to fool you into believing he was *A* or whether he was trying to help you. If the answer is the former—that he was trying to fool you—then *B* would be said to be *imitating A*.

The object of the game for *A* is to help the questioner. She can say, "Don't believe a word of what he says—I'm the woman." This would of course do nothing for us if *B* responded in the same way. If the questioner were unable to make the correct decision, then it would be proper to say that *B* is imitating or *simulating A*'s response to such a degree that an impartial judge could not tell them apart.

This type of experimental logic depends strongly on the characteristics and perceptions of the judge. Whether or not we have simulated or imitated an answer precisely—or simulated or imitated a segment of behavior—depends on the same sort of judgment required to determine whether or not "we can distinguish between oleomargarine and the high-price spread." This is precisely what is implied by Turing's test: Can an expert distinguish between the protocol of a flesh and blood subject and the protocol of an electrically enervated machine.

As should be clear from this discussion, simulation is a general procedure and not specifically tied to electronic computers. The important aspect of simulation is the logical program directing it, not the physical similarity of the machine's output to the human's behavior. "(Computers) ... need not scurry around the room like a rat in a maze or resemble the three pints of brain matter they were supposed to imitate" in order for simulation to be intelligible or significant. (Miller, Galanter, and Pribram, 1960, page 48.)

Before, however, a simulation can be accepted, there are a number of problems that need be handled. Consider, for example, the use of a phonograph to simulate human speech, i.e., where it would be impossible to determine whether a phonograph were playing in the next room or whether a person were speaking in the next room (Fodor, 1968). Although this is a trial case, our analysis of what's wrong does exhibit at least two problems: (1) "Phonographs do what speakers do, not what they can do" and (2) "Phonographs do what they do differently from the way in which speakers do what they do."

The first of these considerations shows that it is necessary to distinguish between performance (any specific behavior) and competence (what an organism could do). Although probably no speaker would ever produce a sentence such as "My automobile has turned into a pumpkin again," it is clear that any speaker could understand it. With regard to the second point, Fodor has offered the following situation:

Suppose we had a theorem-proving machine that proved theorems of the propositional calculus by using the method of truth-tables. Then the potential output of this machine (viz., the infinite set of theorems of the propositional calculus) would be, in one relevant respect, identical to the potential output of anyone who knows how to do proofs in propositional calculus. Yet the machine would be inadequate as an explanation of theorem-proving insofar as it does not do proofs in the same way as a human mathematician does them. In particular, since it is incapable of employing the sorts of heuristics that mathematicians can employ, the operation of the machine provides very little (possibly no) insight into the mental operations that constitute this kind of mathematical reasoning.*

It is the latter case that provides a solution for evaluating the usefulness of a simulation. Although the output of the machine and the mathematician would be identical in terms of the specific theorems produced, it would still be possible to find cases that the machine finds easy to solve and that provide great difficulty for the mathematician, and vice versa. What this means is that it is necessary to compare a great many different aspects of how men and machines go about doing a number of different tasks in order to evaluate the adequacy of any given simulation. Not only must we look at a wide variety of tasks, but we must also look at tasks which, on independent grounds, relate to the area we are observing. It isn't just the number or variety of tasks successfully simulated; rather it's their intrinsic relationship to the area under consideration.

If simulations can be evaluated by comparing different aspects of their performance with the performance of men, it is also obvious that simulations can be evaluated in terms of their ability to mimic human behavior in novel situations. It is precisely in this way that our phonograph fails to simulate human speech. If we ask it a question—"Where's the Right Guard?"—it cannot answer, whereas a human speaker could, even if only to say "I don't know."

In contrast to other evaluation procedures, Turing's test does not seem at first to require as many controls as either the controlled-response or proof-by-prediction strategies. On closer examination, however, it is clear that successful simulation is possible only when we specify in advance what would constitute acceptable and significant ground rules. As is true in both other cases, the nature of an acceptable output changes as the investigator acquires more experience in using his program. In simulation, postdiction is a perfectly acceptable way of revising a program used to simulate particular behaviors.

---

* From J. Fodor, *Psychological Explanation*, New York: Random House, 1968, page 136.

## Some Differences Between Associative and Generative Theories of Mind

The daydreamer and the Fisherman represent two different types of thinking, and each of these serves as a point of reference for a different approach to the psychology of symbolic activity. Perhaps the best way to summarize the differences between associative and generative (or informational) analyses is to compare them in terms of their respective positions on a series of questions. This is done in outline form in Table 2.1.

**Table 2.1** Some significant differences between associative and generative analyses of symbolic activities

| Topics | Associative | Generative |
|---|---|---|
| 1. Role of subject in mental activity | Passive, reproductive | Active, constructive |
| 2. Major principles of mental operation | Laws of association: contiguity, similarity; $S$–$R$ (or $S \rightarrow (r - s) \rightarrow R$); habits | Plans, rules, heuristics, TOTEs |
| 3. Characteristic organization of ongoing activity | Linear—left to right | Hierarchical—top to bottom |
| 4. Number of simultaneously active processes | Many | One |
| 5. Reference cognitive activity | Associative thinking: word association, reverie, dreaming | Planful activity: Problem solving, rule learning and rule using |
| 6. Role of biological endowment | *Tabula*—more or less *rasa* | *Tabula*—more or less well writ-on |
| 7. Experimental technique to demonstrate "understanding" | Prediction; control | Simulation; demonstration |
| 8. Research strategy | Understand simple phenomena first; then study complex ones | Complex to simple |

Many of these topics have been discussed to a greater or lesser extent in the present chapter, and will be discussed in more detail in future chapters. The first two of these topics are straightforward enough, and concern the role of the subject in thinking and the major principles by which such thinking progresses. The third topic concerns the distinction between a left-to-right approach to thinking and a top-to-bottom approach. This distinction revolves around the question of whether or not the underlying principles that govern the flow of thought need be identical to the behavior observed. If thinking is sequential, need its underlying process develop in a left-to-right or sequential order?

The fourth topic grows out of some considerations raised by Neisser in an article entitled "The multiplicity of thought" (1963). Perhaps the simplest way to ask this question is to phrase it in terms of how a computer might go about recognizing a printed letter. In the case of a one-at-a-time process the job would get done as follows:

> We begin by asking whether there is a vertical straight line? If so, the letter is *B* or *D* or *E* or ...; if not, the letter is *A* or *C* or *V*, etc. This question divides the universe of possibilities into two categories. The next question depends on the answer to the first. If there is a vertical line, one might ask if there is also a right angle. This divides *E*, *F*, *T*, etc., from *N*, *M*, *U*, etc. A series of such questions is called a "logic" or a "decision tree," and can easily be devised to make an unequivocal decision about every input. Many programs for letter recognition have been written on this basis. They work rather well, *provided the input is restricted to printed characters in particular founts.*
>
> (Neisser in Wason and Johnson-Laird, page 313, 1968)

The multiple-process approach works by asking all these questions at once, instead of:

> ... letting each answer determine the next question. Suppose the program examines the input for many different properties simultaneously. Letters are ultimately identified by weighted averages of the results. Such features as vertical line and right angle are given weights which increase the probability that the program will decide *T* and decrease its chances of saying 0. Even a great deal of variability need not lead the program astray, because letters are effectively defined by the totality of their features.
>
> (Neisser in Wason and Johnson-Laird, page 314, 1968)

The fifth category requires no explanation, primarily because the present chapter has been devoted largely to examining this issue. The sixth deals with the relative emphasis of both positions on heredity and environment, and here the associative group stands largely in favor of a strong environmental influence, while information-processing approaches—particularly with regard to language—stress the role of biological endowment. The last two topics deal with questions of research strategy, and, since these have been discussed previously, there is no need to review them again.

Although Table 2.1 draws the distinctions between associative and information-processing approaches quite sharply, these distinctions are often not nearly as distinct as Table 2.1 and the accompanying text would suggest. They are meant, instead, to describe *some* topics on which one or another specific representatives of these theoretical approaches differ. Perhaps it is best to consider these questions as general mnemonics rather than as absolute and unfailing distinctions. Then, too, there is no reason why any specific associative (or generative) theory need have the same position on all eight topics as we have presented them. The total pattern, however, represents a set of assumptions that, historically, has tended to be made together, although any specific theory need not touch base on all eight in exactly the same way as we characterized them in Table 2.1.

## SUMMARY

Beginning with extended quotes from Proust and Hemingway, the present chapter set out to illuminate the snares involved in dealing with thinking. The excerpt selected from *Swann's Way* provided a view of human mentality in which external and internal events serve to instigate chains of thought. In the language of an associative analysis, thought is a series of chained responses evoked either by some observable environmental event (a stimulus such as the *petit madeleine*) or by the sensory consequences of an internal response (such as the little $s$'s arising from the initial feeling response of pleasantness, $r_{joy}$). For an $S-R$ analysis involving only upper-case letters, the internal $s$'s and $r$'s are dispensed with and only overt responses, such as movements or words, are admissible for the scientific study of thought.

Given the operation of internal, hypothetical $s$'s and $r$'s, the flow of thought is given direction largely by the classical laws of association; The Law of Contiguity, The Law of Similarity, and so on. In the case of Proust's Marcel, the flow of thought reflects the previously experienced flow of the environment as determined by The Law of Contiguity. The Law of Similarity comes into play when it is noted that all the resting places of Marcel's imagination are emotionally similar. Similarity of emotion cements these resting places together. The cornerstone of this approach to mentality is well put by Proust: "The truth lies not in the cup, but in myself."

Hemingway's Fisherman is remarkable for the planful (albeit occasionally reminiscent and distorted) mental activity exhibited. In all his thinking and doing, the Fisherman is guided by a single overriding consideration— what has come to be called a Plan—and all his actions are tested against the requirements of this plan. Such testing consists of a "looping" sequence of actions beginning and ending with a Test Phase designed to determine whether the requirements of the plan have been met. Miller, Galanter, and Pribram have termed such a unit a TOTE unit, where the four letters stand for Test, Operate, Test, and Exit. Perhaps the most significant aspect of the Fisherman's behavior—and planful behavior in general—is that the behavior and thought sequence produced is generated not by a sequential process, but rather by a hierarchical one. At any one level the action is sequential; the sequence, however, is not determined at that level, but at one higher "upstream."

The general topic of thinking consists of a number of subtopics. The major ones that have been considered experimentally concern memory, concept formation, and problem solving. As is the case with almost all human processes, thought has an extensive developmental history which must also be considered. The growth of mind, similar to memory, concept formation and problem solving, has been conceptualized both in terms of an S–R and a hierarchical model. In the chapters that follow, both orientations will be considered.

As an object of study, thinking poses difficult experiment problems, as by definition it is covert activity—something unseen. Three different approaches to the study of thought have been offered: the controlled-response technique, the proof-by-prediction technique, and Turing's test. In the first of these the investigator convinces himself that he is studying thinking if he can control overt responses presumably having an intuitively meaningful relationship to cognitive activity. The controlled-response strategy successfully avoids the problem of whether the response ($R$) observed is an appropriate index of thought, since, by definition, the overt response is thinking.

The proof-by-prediction strategy always builds on prior knowledge about a particular situation, problem, or organism. For word-association studies, such prior knowledge involves the pattern of relationships revealed through the use of word-association tests. Understanding is demonstrated by predicting what an organism will do in a constrained or experimental setting, and prediction is the proof of understanding.

Turing's test assumes that a process such as thinking is understood when a machine can be built that will produce a similar (or exact) replica of selected aspects of the performance of an organism involved in thinking. This is called *simulation*. One important aspect of behavior simulated by an automaton is that the automaton's performance need not be similar to the subject's performance except in the way originally agreed on when trying out Turing's test. The fact that some engineers have devised mechanical rats, mice, or what have you, to simulate how certain behavior is learned, is irrelevant. Such demonstrations add nothing that is not given in the output record of the computer and should be taken for what they are: cute demonstrations. The basic features of simulation depend neither on physical resemblance nor on electronic computers. What is important is that what a man and a machine do in a particular situation must be functionally interchangeable and significant in that situation.

# PART II
# ASSOCIATIVE APPROACHES
# TO THINKING

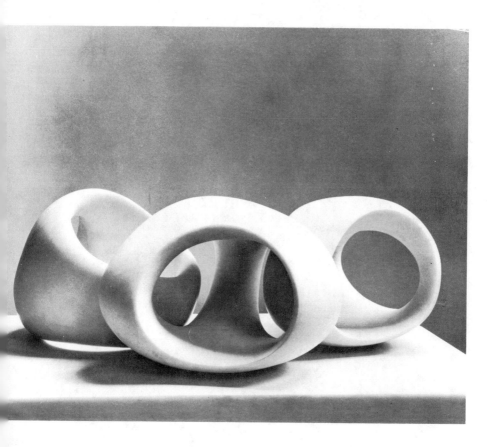

# CHAPTER 3

# FROM *S* TO *R*:
# THE ROLE OF ASSOCIATIONS
# IN THOUGHT

The *S–R* or associative approach to thinking can be considered as a herculean effort to get thought out into the open so that its development, operation, and growth become accessible to unequivocal observation and experimentation. This is certainly the motivating force behind many of the demonstrations and experiments carried out in this tradition; a tradition that considers thought, in some way or other, as equivalent to covert responding.

Consider, for a moment, the following informal demonstration: Take a fragile container such as a martini glass and fill it with an appropriate liquid. Next balance the circular base of the glass on the tips of the fingers of the preferred hand or even on the fingertips of both hands. When the glass is sufficiently well balanced, have someone read you a set of complicated arithmetic problems. If the problems involve a great deal of "carrying," so much the better. What happens in this situation, at least on the basis of casual observation, is that the speed and reliability with which mental arithmetic operations are performed are significantly depressed by balancing the glass. This is obviously not true for all people at all times, and the demonstration actually works better if the contents of the glass are emptied a few times before beginning the experiment.

Why should anyone expect this demonstration to work? The reasoning seems to be that little children originally learn to count on their fingers and to some extent this tendency continues into adulthood, although in much reduced form. Holding a glass while trying to do arithmetic problems effectively interferes with addition simply because the much-reduced overt response of counting on one's fingers still persists. Such a demonstration is quite within the mainstream of *S–R* psychology, for it attempts to show that the covert operations of mind can be assessed by noting the very observable properties of the peripheral response system. In this way numerical calculation can be brought out into the open and thereby made publicly observable.

For just this reason it has been useful to consider thought as implicit speech, for such a view implies that peripheral speech muscles (such as control the lips and tongue) can be used to tell an experimenter when a subject is thinking. Unfortunately, the first time this experiment was tried a number of years ago (Thorson, 1925), the results were anything but impressive: There was little or no correlation between the movements of the tongue when the subject spoke and thought the same word. By this crude test, at least, no similarity was found.

But should we expect the exact duplication of an overt response when the subject merely thinks a word? Perhaps a more justifiable expectation is that the rhythm of such activities would be the same. In line with this analysis, Jacobson (1932), using a much more refined recording system than Thorson, found that the temporal characteristics of responses produced by the tongue and lips during "thinking a word" were similar to those produced by subjects softly speaking the same word. In addition, if subjects were asked to count aloud softly, the temporal pattern of tongue and lip movements were similar to those produced by asking subjects to count silently in their head.

Recording tongue and lip movements can be a rather cumbersome procedure, particularly for the subject, and it is always possible that using such apparatus may suggest to the subject that somehow or other he is expected to move his lips and tongue. If this interpretation is correct, Jacobson's results tend to be equivocal and prove little. In an attempt to overcome such objections, Max (1935, 1937) used deaf mutes as subjects and recorded minute movements of their arms and fingers during the course of doing problems such as the following,

1.  Which of these words would look exactly the same if the card was reversed and seen in a mirror?

    OHIO    SAW    MOTOR    NOON    OTTO

2.  Add together all the numbers from 1 to 9.

3.  Read this carefully, so as to remember it:

    *Anna Wyczoikowska wrote an article called "Theoretical and Experimental Studies in the Mechanism of Speech."*

Max used deaf mutes as subjects for two very good reasons: (1) It allowed him to record the activity of those arm muscles which control finger movements involved in sign language, and (2) it enabled him to avoid any suggestion that subjects were "expected" to move their fingers during thought problems, since he was recording arm and not finger movements.

Max's results, contrary to earlier work, were uniformly impressive. When the records of 18 deaf and 16 normal subjects were compared, the deaf mutes showed noticeable action currents in 84% of the cases as compared to only 31% for hearing subjects. In simultaneous recordings deaf subjects showed positive responses in 73% of the records taken from their arms (the locus of speech) and only 19% in control records taken from electrodes attached to their legs. When both normal and deaf subjects were presented with tasks involving motor components such as "Imagine holding a wriggling snake behind your head," hearing subjects produced muscle potentials in 44 of 60 such situations, whereas deaf subjects produced measurable potentials in 36 of 41 situations. For motor imagery tasks, there were no appreciable differences between groups. Finally, over all 18 deaf subjects, correlations between the size of the muscle potentials produced and the intelligence of these subjects ranged between $-0.22$ and $-0.92$. In other words, more intelligent deaf subjects tended to have less-noticeable muscle response during thought than less-intelligent deaf subjects. The more intelligent the person, the less overt his symbolic activity.

Another, and perhaps better, way in which thought can be measured in terms of motor responses involves demonstrating that "thinking responses" follow the same principles as overt responses such as those involved in verbal behavior. This type of strategy is perhaps best exemplified in an early study by N. E. Miller (1935). In this experiment Miller conditioned a galvanic skin response (*GSR*) to the letter *T*. Every time the letter *T* was presented, the subject was required to read it aloud and this verbalization was then followed by shock. During the training series, subjects were also asked to pronounce the number 4 aloud. Reading this number aloud, however, was never followed by shock. After a discrimination had been established, the subject was presented with a series of dots and asked "to think (but not say aloud)" the letter *T* to the first dot and the number 4 to the second dot, and so on alternately. Miller's results were clear: A large *GSR* deflection was correlated with every other dot; in other words with every time the subject thought "*T*," but not when he thought "4."

Perhaps the most important result of Miller's experiment was that it was now possible to describe thinking in terms of responses, even if these responses were themselves not subject to direct observation. In principle, covert thinking responses are no different from overt ones, and consequently, whatever facts are known about observable responses are transferable to covert thinking responses. Given this demonstration, all the vast classical and instrumental conditioning literature becomes directly relevant to the problems of symbolic behavior in general, and to thought in particular.

This is the major reason why *S–R* psychologists use upper-case letters, such as *S* and *R*, to represent overt stimuli and response, and lower-case letters, such as *s* and *r*, to represent internal events. If overt and covert stimuli and responses follow the same laws, it is then possible to predict covert response sequences on the basis of principles discovered in experiments involving overt responses. If overt *R*'s fatigue, so too do covert *r*'s; if overt *S*'s generalize, so too do covert *s*'s, and so on. By this strategy, the covert is made overt and thereby subject to direct observation and test.

## MEDIATION EFFECTS

Armed with this analytic approach, we can study more complex forms of covert activity. One of the more significant of these covert processes is met whenever we observe that two items that have never been experienced together somehow come to mind either at the same time, or at least in reasonably close temporal succession. It is not unlikely, for example, for someone to think of the words *sparrow* and *penguin* at the same time if he is asked to think of different kinds of birds. This will occur despite the fact that these words probably have never occurred together in experience.

One way in which to get these responses to occur together is to think in terms of *mediating associations*; that is, to assume that a single word (such as *bird*) has been separately associated with each response word (e.g., *sparrow–bird*; *penguin–bird*) and that this common element mediates the contiguity of these items in thinking.

The principle of mediated association can be described formally in the following terms: Initially separate elements (words, ideas, and so on) can be brought together in thought to the degree that a common element (a word or idea) is, or has been, associated with both. The British associationistic philosophers called these bridging elements *mediate associates*, because they mediated between two originally unrelated ideas. Such associative connections were carefully distinguished from direct associates which arose through contiguity of items in time or space. In this latter case the stream of mental associates was thought to mirror the actual order of occurrence of events and ideas in the experience of the thinker.

Now although mediation is a plausible theory, it is also necessary that such mediating events be demonstrated experimentally, and if such events can be made directly observable, so much the better. Fortunately, in 1933 Shipley was able to demonstrate the existence of *overt* mediators, and six years later Lumsdaine repeated these observations, employing more precise measures of the mediating event. Together these procedures have come to be called the *Shipley–Lumsdaine paradigms*.

In the first stage of one of the Shipley–Lumsdaine experiments, a faint light was paired with a tap on the subject's cheek. This tap was of sufficient force so as to evoke a wink. After repeated pairings of the light and the tap, presenting the light alone led to the occurrence of the wink. So far so good—simple classical conditioning. In the next part of the experiment the tap was presented first and then paired with a small shock to the finger, eliciting finger withdrawal. Thus a second connection was established between the tap (and its reflexive wink) and finger withdrawal. Given the existence of the conditioned pairs, light–wink and tap–finger withdrawal, what would happen if a light were now presented by itself? Letting $L$ stand for light, $W$ for wink, and $R$ for finger withdrawal, we can present the stages of the experiment in the following terms:

| Training I | Training II | Test |
|---|---|---|
| $L \rightarrow W$ | Tap $(W) \rightarrow R$ | $L \rightarrow (W) \rightarrow R$; therefore $L \rightarrow R$ |

In this case the wink could serve as a mediating element if the light were to produce finger withdrawal. Results showed that despite the fact that the light had never before been paired directly with shock, it nonetheless came to evoke finger withdrawal. This would seem to be explained best on the basis of the pre-established mediating connection between the light and the wink (i.e., the $L-W$ connection established during the first training session).

If the wink actually mediated the occurrence of finger withdrawal, it should be possible to observe the occurrence of a wink after the presentation of the light but before the occurrence of finger withdrawal. This is precisely what Lumsdaine did: He recorded the temporal order of occurrence of wink and finger-withdrawal responses and found that in most cases, for most subjects, the wink did in fact occur before finger withdrawal. On this basis, Lumsdaine argued that the wink served to mediate the occurrence of finger withdrawal.

Although not all subjects produced exactly this sequence, most $S-R$ psychologists were sufficiently encouraged by successful instances to extend the notion of mediating elements to covert "thought" responses. The major line of research dealing with these covert responses involves the use of words, with connections between words assessed by asking a group of students to tell an experimenter what other word they thought of first when they saw a particular word. The responses produced by such groups were taken as direct associates evoked by the stimulus word. These associates were then used by Jenkins (1963) and his co-workers in studies of mediated learning. Such studies were run as follows: Subjects were first required to learn a set of paired associates of the form, $ZUG-Table$, $BOP-King$ and so on. After this learning was complete they were next asked to learn a second list consisting of pairs such as $ZUG-Chair$, $BOP-Queen$, etc. Although it took subjects a number of trials to learn the first set of pairs (say 10), the second list was learned almost immediately.

In terms of mediating associates, the total set of relationships in this situation can be diagrammed as a chain.

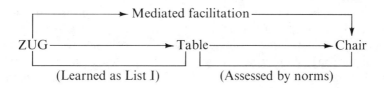

In this study, and in others like it, subjects often told the experimenter that they were very much aware of the fact that Table–Chair and King–Queen were obviously related and that once they had learned the first list, ZUG–Table, BOP–King, learning the second list was "obvious."

Russell and Storms (1955), working in Jenkins' laboratory at the University of Minnesota, were able to demonstrate the effects of mediated transfer over a chain having more than a single link. They used pairs of words of the type ZUG–Soldier and then asked subjects to learn the pair ZUG–Navy. The total sequence involved in this particular case can be represented as follows:

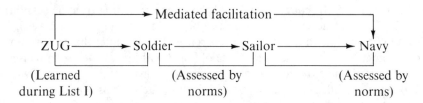

In all cases Russell and Storms found that facilitation occurred over two mediational links.

In all these experiments, mediation effects were tested on the response side (*R*) of *S–R* word pairs. Further experiments done by the Minnesota group were also able to demonstrate mediation effects due to pre-existing connections between first and second list stimuli (Ryan, 1960). In these experiments the first set of pairs might be something like Man–ZUG, with the corresponding List II pair Woman–ZUG, and so on for a number of pairs. In general, mediation effects were found for both stimulus and response terms.

Analyzing mediation effects through word-association norms also provides other interesting experimental possibilities. For one, normative sets of word associates always show that some words produce the same response from a large group of respondents, e.g., out of a group of 1008 students at the University of Minnesota, 768 gave *girl* as a response to *boy*. At the other extreme are idiosyncratic responses which are given by only one student in 1008 (for example, *Winslow* to the stimulus *boy*). Since it is possible to sample the total range of such associative response probabilities, Jenkins and his students expected that the size of this probability would predict the ease and strength of mediation.

Unfortunately, this has not always turned out to be the case; instead, almost any associate, of almost any strength (down to 0.002) is capable of producing facilitative mediation (Jenkins, 1963). When, however, a number of complicating factors peculiar to paired-associates learning (i.e., the task usually used to measure mediation effects), are eliminated, small differences between response probabilities do occur. Shapiro (1970), for example, found differences in mediation between high pairs (mean probability equal to 0.55) and low (mean equal to 0.11). Earlier work by Palermo and Jenkins and others (Palermo and Jenkins, 1964; Wicklund, Palermo, and Jenkins, 1964) had also found small effects of association strength on mediated learning in child subjects, although similar results had not previously been found for college-age subjects (Haun, 1960).

Another way in which to find out how mediation works is to build in mediators in the laboratory rather than use natural language mediators such as one measured by word-association tasks. In 1961 Horton and Kjelder-gaard did precisely this in an attempt to check the effects of eight different mediation procedures or paradigms. These paradigms are presented in Table 3.1.

**Table 3.1**  Three-stage mediation paradigms

|       | I     | II    |                            |
|-------|-------|-------|----------------------------|
| Learn | A–B   | B–C   | Simple chains              |
| Learn | B–C   | A–B   | $(A \rightarrow B \rightarrow C)$ |
| Test  | A–C   | A–C   |                            |

|       | III   | IV    |                            |
|-------|-------|-------|----------------------------|
| Learn | B–A   | C–B   | Reverse chains             |
| Learn | C–B   | B–A   | $(A \leftarrow B \leftarrow C)$ |
| Test  | A–C   | A–C   |                            |

|       | V     | VI    |                            |
|-------|-------|-------|----------------------------|
| Learn | A–B   | C–B   | Stimulus equivalence       |
| Learn | C–B   | A–B   | $(A \rightarrow B \leftarrow C)$ |
| Test  | A–C   | A–C   |                            |

|       | VII   | VIII  |                            |
|-------|-------|-------|----------------------------|
| Learn | B–A   | B–C   | Response equivalence       |
| Learn | B–C   | B–A   | $(A \leftarrow B \rightarrow C)$ |
| Test  | A–C   | A–C   |                            |

Any subject in a given paradigm went through the sort of learning experiences described in the table. So, for example, subjects tested under Paradigm I, first learned the pair *A–B*, then learned the *B–C*, and were tested to see how fast pair *A–C* was learned. If this pair was learned more rapidly than a new pair *A–D*, such an outcome would demonstrate the facilitative effects of mediation. Horton and Kjeldergaard found that all paradigms showed mediation effects, with the exception of Number III, which failed to show any significant transfer effects.

These results are all extremely consistent in demonstrating mediational effects. Such effects have been found over assumed linkages of one and even two steps. Although early work by Jenkins (1963) paralleling that of Horton and Kjeldergaard failed to find mediation over more than two steps when the mediating event was learned in the laboratory, later results (James and Hakes, 1965; Grover, Horton, and Cunningham, 1967) have shown that four-stage mediation is possible even with laboratory materials.

Although such procedures can get a bit complicated, it is clear that mediate associations are capable of leading the mind from any one word to another word. As Hobbes (1839) put it well over a century ago:

> "From St. Andrew the mind runneth to St. Peter, because their names are read together; from St. Peter to a *stone*, for the same cause; from *stone* to *foundation* because we see them together; ... from *foundation* to *church*, and from *church* to *people*, and from *people* to *tumult*; and according to this example, the mind may run almost from anything to anything." To which a proper or even an improper associationist would add, "Amen!"

## SYNESTHESIA AND METAPHOR

If mediated associations give the mind a certain agility in bringing together initially disparate ideas, then the processes involved in synesthesia and metaphor augment this agility in a number of new directions. Synesthesia refers to a cross-modality matching—that is, matching the sensations provided by one sensory modality with sensations provided by a second modality, e.g., cold sensations are felt as a pressure around the teeth (Dallenback, 1926) while certain pains are specified as "pinkish" or "bluish" (Helson, 1964). Sometimes musical notes are paired with specific colors (Langfeld, 1914), and so on.

Osgood (1953) has summarized much of this earlier work on synesthesia and his conclusions seem well justified by the data: Far from being a rare phenomenon, many individuals (about 13% of the college students tested), habitually engage in this kind of cross-modality thinking (Karwoski and Odbert, 1938). This is particularly true in the case of music, in which matches are often reported between geometric figures and musical selections or between colors and musical selections. Subjects who do not usually engage in synesthetic thinking can, however, also be made to show many cross-modality effects if instructed to do so.

Although synesthetic thinking, even when evoked by directed approaches such as described by Osgood, is still a rather esoteric phenomena, metaphor— another type of substitution process—is much more readily encountered. Somehow human beings can't control themselves when it comes to metaphor (or to its more direct and obvious relative, simile); they invent them, good and bad, by the hundreds. For example, in terms of parts of the body we have standard or frozen metaphors such as: the *head* (*foot*) of a bed, the *mouth* of a river, the *finger* of fate, being *nosy*, having *eyes* for someone or thing, *male* plugs and *female* sockets, *hairy* problems, and a list as long as your *arm*. Sensory experiences provide another good source of nonliteral phrases: mood *indigo*, true *blue*, a *cool* manner, a *red*-letter day, *frigid*, *purple*-passion prose, *green* with envy, *bright*-eyed, and many other variations on these themes.

Anthropomorphizing animals is another fertile source of metaphor: *goose*, *hawks*, and *doves*, to *wolf* food or girls, a *whale* of a time, a *snake* in the grass, as well as a *flock* of others. The list is enough to make the stout-hearted blanch, or at least turn green.

Authors of fiction often christen their characters with names describing their importance. Thus the main character in each volume of Durrell's *Alexandria Quartet* provides some hint as to how reality will be presented in that particular book: *Justine* (the sexual heroine), *Balthazar* (the mystical), *Mountolive* (the political), and *Clea* (the artistic). Even less esoteric fiction features characters such as Terry Southern's *Candy*, or Ian Fleming's *Pussy Galore*.

Psychologists, such as Solomon Asch, who have studied how people form impressions of others, note a tendency for impressions to depend strongly on the metaphorical use of words such as *warm* or *cold*, where *warm* and *cold* are used to describe personality traits. In one study, for example, Asch (1946) presented two groups of subjects with the following set of terms presumably describing two different people:

Person A.　　Intelligent—skillful—industrious—*warm*—determined—
　　　　　　　practical—cautious.

Person B.　　Intelligent—skillful—industrious—*cold*—determined—
　　　　　　　practical—cautious.

The introduction of the term *warm* was sufficient to cause subjects to describe Person A as wise, generous, and popular, while the simple use of the term *cold* led to a description of Person B as restrained, unhappy, and unsociable.

Metaphorically tinged adjectives have often been used to describe operatic voices. It is not uncommon for music critics to use phrases such as a "cold, or flat" or "gravelly voiced rendition," and so on. In an attempt to determine whether these usages convey any meaning to the listening public, Brown, Leiter, and Hildum (1957) asked students to judge a series of operatic selections on ten antonym pairs, and to pick which of a set of 20 critic-derived adjectives (*pinched, chromium,* etc.) best described the voice. The first result of interest was that the pattern of adjectives chosen to describe tenors was different from that chosen to describe baritones or sopranos. In general, baritones were "duller," "coarser," "heavier," and "thicker" than the "brighter," "softer," "lighter," and "thinner" sopranos and tenors.

Of even more interest was the result that when the pattern of adjectives clustering together was examined by factor analysis, Brown *et al.* found natural adjective groupings. Their first and strongest grouping contained adjectives such as *cold–warm, like–dislike, lustrous–dull,* and *pinched–expansive.* Although further groupings were also uncovered, these were nowhere as clearly defined as this initial cluster. Taken in combination with Asch's results on impression formation, such results suggest that adjectives travel in groups, and that these groups can include both literal (*strong*) and nonliteral (*warm*) usages.

Further support for the view that adjectives travel in well-structured groups comes from results gathered by Osgood, Suci, and Tannenbaum (1957) using a technique known as the *semantic differential.* Basically, subjects are asked to rate sets of words on different rating scales defined by words opposite in meaning at each end (e.g., *good–bad; fast–slow,* etc.). When Osgood and his associates examined these ratings, they found that if a word were rated as "good," it also tended to be rated as "pleasant," or "light," or "beautiful," and so on. If a word were rated as "hard," it also tended to be rated as "strong," and "male"; whereas if a word were rated as "active," it also tended to be rated as "hot," "fast," and "excitable." The first set of adjectives (*good, pleasant*) was considered to define what Osgood has called an evaluative group, the second set (*hard, strong*), a potency group, and the third set (*active, fast*), an activity group. Here again the data clearly imply that adjectives cluster into regularly occurring groups, and these groups are intuitively meaningful to users of the language.

Although Osgood and his collaborators feel that the total population of adjectives, both those that refer to direct sensory experience as well as those that refer to emotional states, can be divided into a small number of regularly occurring clusters (between two and three), Deese (1965) has shown that such a reduction is not always possible. For his analysis, Deese selected a group of 280 different frequently occurring adjectives in English and then collected word associations to these adjectives. On the basis of his results, Deese concluded that there were slightly more than 40 primary adjectival contrasts in English, and that many of the remaining 240 or so adjectives could be described by their relationship to one or another of these fundamental contrast pairs. For example, the words *few* and *many* seem to represent a fundamental contrast: they provide the reference point for adjectives such as *entire, total, all, various, numerous,* and *several.*

The only serious exception to a grouping scheme for adjectives based on contrasts is provided by the color words (*red, blue,* etc.). One reason why this may be is that color names tend to produce word-association patterns similar to those produced by nouns rather than to those produced by adjectives. Although Deese's work suggests that the number of basic adjectival groupings is larger than the three described by Osgood, his results still lead to the conclusions that adjectives form stable clusters and that in English these clusters include both literal and figurative uses.

Do similar effects also apply in non-English language groups? Although data on this point are scattered and sparse, those that have been collected are novel both in conception and execution. Asch (1955), for example, examined adjectives describing sensory qualities in a number of different—and historically unrelated—languages such as Biblical Hebrew, Homeric Greek, Chinese, Thai, and a few others. Just as English does, all of these languages employ words or phrases that can be used to describe both a physical and psychological quality. For example, the word *straight* in English implies, in addition to its literal meaning, honesty or trust (in addition to heterosexuality), while *crooked* implies the opposite characteristics of dishonesty and untrustworthiness. This same situation is found to apply in various other languages considered by Asch. Far from being specific to English, metaphorical usage is common in historically unrelated languages.

This tendency to metaphorical extension is general enough that when Osgood and his co-workers (Osgood, 1962) examined the way in which adjectives comprising semantic differential scales were grouped in non-English languages, such as Japanese, Flemish, and Kannady, they discovered groupings similar to those found in English. In all the languages considered to date, results invariably produce an evaluative factor, a potency factor, and an activity factor. To be sure, there are some groupings peculiar to an individual language (for example, in Japanese *thankful–troublesome* is a member of the evaluative group; while in Kannady *red–black* is a member of the activity group), but these idiosyncratic groupings in no way detract from the overall similarity found to apply across different language communities.

Further, informal anthropological analyses reported by Osgood, Suci, and Tannenbaum (1957) indicate that in a number of primitive cultures—such as Aztec or Pueblo Indian or Australian Bushman—good events such as gods or places are almost always characterized as *up* and *light* or *white,* while their evil counterparts are characterized as *black* and *down.* The folklore of these cultures is rich in myths describing how the *light* gods help primeval man arise from the *dark, cold, wet*, and *sad* world below to the *light, warm, dry*, and *happy* world above.

All in all, such data are quite consistent in documenting both within the confines of a culture as well as across cultural boundaries that sensory experiences often provide psychologically significant descriptions of internal states (metaphor) and that inter-sensory matching is a relatively common event. Given these facts, two questions arise: (1) How do such effects come about? and (2) what function does nonliteral usage serve?

When one is answering the first question, it seems possible to draw on the concept of mediated associations or some derivative explanation. Take the case of the word *warm*. As Asch's data indicate, a *warm* person is thought of in a considerably more favorable light than a *cold* person. It seems characteristic of the physical world that things that are thermally warm (not hot), such as kittens, embraces, coats, blankets, soup, and so on, almost universally make the person feel better; whereas thermally cold (not cool) things, such as freezing metal, icy rains, cold winds, etc., make the person feel unpleasant. Given this correlation of *warm* with *pleasant* and *cold* with *unpleasant*, it is easy enough to imagine how a *warm* person would be regarded as more kindly than a *cold* one.

Even when different languages show that a given word, such as *hot*, does not stand for identical characteristics in different languages, such cross-language use is not incomprehensible. For example, *hot* means rage or wrath in Hebrew, enthusiasm in Chinese, and sexual arousal or worry in Thai. There is a clear compatibility among these metaphorical extensions if we keep in mind that *hot* refers to emotional arousal or heightened activity. From this starting point the difference in these uses, while probably not predictable in advance, does make very good sense. If we take slang into account, all these meanings also occur in English.

Perhaps the most extensive associationistic analysis of metaphor and metaphorizing has been offered by Osgood, Suci, and Tannenbaum (1957), and it runs somewhat as follows: Consider the relationship between auditory pitch and visual size; it is characteristic of the physical world that large-sized objects produce low-pitched tones, and that small-sized objects produce high-pitched tones (think of a series of organ pipes and bells, or the voices of men and boys, large dogs and small dogs, and so on). This means that large objects are often paired with low-pitched tones, and vice versa for high-pitched tones and small objects. On this basis, a number of different stimuli come to evoke a common mediational response. Any overt responses associated with this mediator, such as "large" movements or saying the word *large*, should transfer to a stimulus eliciting this mediator. Thus, when a deep tone produces "large" drawing movements, we call this synesthesia; when the word *deep* is associated with the word *large*, we call this metaphor. When a story teller speaks of the Big Daddy Bear in a bass voice, the Mother Bear in a normal voice, and the Little Baby Bear in a soprano voice, he is using culturally based metaphorical extensions. Clearly, metaphorical tendencies such as these expand the scope of mental operations in ways that can be made completely comprehensible to an *S–R* analysis of thought.

A slightly different—although clearly related—associative explanation has been offered by Koen (1965). For Koen the phenomenon of metaphor always involves at least two terms: the figurative term used in a given context and the literal term which might be expected in that context. In order for a metaphor to be understood, the reader or hearer must know what literal term is implied and must be able to sense the relationship (the similarities and differences) between the literal and figurative terms. When a metaphor is substituted for a literal term, the content of the sentence is changed, so that the concept used is different from (but overlaps with) that of the literal word.

In order to test this hypothesis, Koen asked subjects to select one of two words in completing a sentence of the following general form: "The sandpiper ran along the bench leaving a row of tiny $^{STITCHES}_{MARKS}$ in the sand." Three different groups of subjects were tested: Group I was presented with the target sentence and a set of words containing word associates (*prints, dents*, etc.) to the literal response word (MARKS); Group II was presented with the target sentence and a set of words containing word associates (*thread, needle*, etc.) to the metaphorical response (STITCHES); while Group III was presented with a mixed set of words derived from Sets I and II (*dents, thread*, etc.).

Koen's results showed that subjects in Group I chose the literal word (MARKS) for 8 of 12 sentences; that subjects in Group II chose the metaphorical word (STITCHES) for 9 of 12 sentences; and that subjects in Group III chose the two response words equally often. On the basis of these results, Koen concluded that a metaphor and its literal term are related by word-association connections. In addition, the choice of a metaphor or a literal term seems to depend not only on literal meaning but also on the unique linguistic context of the situation.

The answer to our second question about metaphor (What function does it serve?) is a good deal more difficult than the first. Probably the simplest explanation has been offered by William J. J. Gordon (1961): Metaphor serves to make the strange familiar and the familiar strange. That is, metaphor (as well as other figurative language) is always meant to be taken as a somewhat strange or different way of stating a familiar idea, or as a familiar or ordinary way of stating a strange idea. The poet-critic, Elizabeth Sewell (1964) has argued more formally that metaphor must not only serve to exemplify some event in different terms, but must also work as a model in furthering our understanding of one or both of the ideas joined in metaphor. Speaking in terms of poetic metaphor, Sewell has noted:

[A certain metaphor] though exact will take me no further. I cannot think with it; merely note its exactness and leave it there. A certain amount of metaphor met with in poetry is of this kind. It gives its own pleasure, as Rilke does when he compares the sound of a peal of carillon bells, lingering momentarily in the sky and then vanishing, to a bunch of grapes hanging, with Silence eating them off, one by one. It is fitting but not fertile. In greater poems, and in great poets for the most part, it is harder to find metaphors of this partial sort. All the figures work, have energy or lend the mind energy to work and to work further. That is to say, ... they are beautiful, beauty being considered as just such a dynamic heuristic, whether we meet it in the figures of science, those of poetry, or elsewhere. It is exactly such a forward-moving or prophetic energy that the chosen metaphor, within the method in use, has to supply. [From *The Human Metaphor*, 1964, University of Notre Dame Press]

If a metaphorical or nonliteral usage is meant to help "the mind do work," it should be possible to demonstrate the role of nonliteral thinking in solving problems. Although the psychological literature is almost non-existent on this topic, two small trends do appear: One of these is concerned with demonstrating the role of metaphoric thinking in creative problem solving, while the second is concerned with showing its role in psychotherapy. In Gordon's phrase, both problem setting (making the familiar strange) and problem solving (making the strange familiar) should involve metaphoric thinking.

In the case of problem-solving groups, Mewardi (1959, 1961) has shown that metaphoric usage is a common part of such group problem solving. For the group studied by Mewardi—an industrial consulting group—fully one quarter of all the communications involved metaphorical usage, whereas only 50% consisted of direct, realistic attempts, and 25% consisted of group process statements such as jokes. The specific problem attempted by this group required the construction of a novel closing device to be used on men who load missiles. This closing device was to protect them from the fumes of red foaming nitric acid. Some of the metaphors used prior to solution were quite ingenious: One member said, "Think of the frightening aspects of being shrouded in a thick fog," while another produced "Hydrogen fur coat," and still a third produced "This thing is going to turn out to be a big fat woman getting into a girdle in the middle of an air raid ...," and so on. All in all Mewardi's results showed these metaphors to be an intrinsic part of problem solution.

A different type of problem-solving situation is represented by psychotherapy. Here too, scattered data show the importance of metaphor in psychotherapy. Consider for example the following excerpt of a case reported by Goldiamond and Dyrud (1968):

A suicidal adolescent who is currently under therapy has dropped out of school, and does no work. He watches the late show on TV, and gets up in the morning at 11:00. He can be considered a loser. One of the discussions centered around the fact that there was very little communication between the boy and his father. When either spoke, the other made some comment which terminated the conversation. The therapy had reached the point where it was possible to analyze this transaction and to suggest that the boy might try to respond to his father in some manner which would continue the discussion and perhaps move it in a direction of interest to him. The boy commented that he did not wish his father to control him, but wished to maintain his own autonomy and would not engage in such extended conversation. The metaphor of a tennis game was then brought up by the therapist. If one wished to control the other player in tennis, one had to put oneself under the control of the oncoming ball. Hitting the ball left made the opponent run left. Then hitting it right made him run again, and so on. But, said the young man, I can choose not to hit the ball back. Then you lose, was the answer. You're a loser. This discussion continued with vigor, and the patient has raised it several times since.

In this way a therapist can communicate an understanding of some condition that could not be communicated by ordinary literal means. Like the poet, therapists encounter people who want to know about love, suffering, mortality and fear of failure; and like the poet, they sometimes provide answers by appeal to metaphor. In this way, metaphors serve both to concretize the ephemeral and to open new possibilities for people whose possibilities are momentarily blocked.

## SUMMARY

The philosophy of associationism provides the conceptual framework for much of contemporary psychology. In its most basic form, associationism stresses the role of the environment in bringing about the content of human mentality. Initially, events or their internal representations—ideas—are brought together solely on the basis of having occurred contiguously in the experience of the subject. With the passage of time, tracing the contiguity between two events occurring in adjacent positions in thought or behavior becomes extremely difficult, for early undifferentiated contiguity gives rise to mediated contiguity. Mediation tremendously enlarges the scope of associative processes in that it allows for connections between two events even if these events never have, and never will, occur in temporal or spatial contiguity.

But this is all philosophy—background—and in order to translate associationism into a viable psychology, certain adjustments have to be made, the most important of which is to "externalize" thought. Ideas are fine; responses better. With this as an orienting attitude, the psychology of thought becomes a psychology of responses; responses which occur in situations that seem—often on an intuitive basis—to involve thinking.

Although overcoming some of the basic difficulties of philosophical associationism, this strategy still seems to miss the mark: Thought is a covert process that is often not directly reflected in behavior. To take care of this consideration, objective responses go underground with the important methodological requirement that these underground, or fractional mediation responses, obey the same rules as the manifestly overt responses that parade around at the periphery. If overt responses fatigue or generalize, so too do covert ones.

Experimentally, mediation effects have been studies in terms of both overt stimulus–response connections (the Shipley–Lumsdaine paradigms) and in terms of assumed verbal connections. The results of a number of studies indicate that mediation effects do occur even over as many as four different steps. Although associative response strength (i.e., the probability with which one word produces another word as an associate) does not predict mediation effects in any simple way, results involving children in simple situations, and adults in highly constrained ones, do provide support for the hypothesis that associative–response strength can predict the ease and extent of mediated learning.

If mediation serves to bring St. Andrew and St. Peter together, then the processes involved in synesthesia and metaphor greatly augment this ability. Although cross-modality matching, of the type found in synesthesia, is relatively rare, metaphor is relatively common. Although the estimate that 25% of all verbalizations during creative problem solving involve metaphor seems a bit high, it is still true that nonliteral usage occurs quite frequently in human speech. Metaphors seem to have two primary properties: (1) They enable the speaker to relate ideas to one another and (2) they serve as a model for what to do in future situations. This latter property is best illustrated by the role of metaphor in problem-solving and in psychotherapy.

# CHAPTER 4

# MEMORY AND FORGETTING

If human beings are to be able to think at all, it is clear that the effects of past experience must somehow or other remain with us. Without this assumption the appropriate response to every stimulus would have to be learned anew each time it was encountered and each new instance of a problem or a concept would have to be relearned. Without memory, the past vanishes.

Now this manifestly is not the case: Organisms from earthworms to human beings are consistently able, to a greater or lesser degree, to show what they know after having once learned a maze or solved a problem or mastered a concept. Indeed, one theoretical analysis of the memory process (Melton, 1963) starts out by assuming that the only way in which to infer that learning has occurred on a given trial is to test for an occurrence of the appropriate response on a subsequent trial. If this next trial is not delayed for too much time (and here definitions vary) and if external conditions remain relatively constant (and here definitions vary as well), both trials can be considered as part of the acquisition phase of an experience; if the external situation remains constant, but the time interval between any two exposures is long (however defined) we have conditions appropriate for testing human memory or forgetting. If, on the other hand, there are systematic variations in the external situation, or in the response required of the subject between the $N$th and the $N + 1$ trial, we then have procedures appropriate for studying transfer.

All these experimental niceties are important to keep in mind, for an associationistic analysis assumes similar principles are involved in transfer and memory. Consider, for example, the following three words: *Borborygym*, *androcephalic*, and *prorogue*. Assume you don't know what they mean. In an attempt to define these words, subjects generally begin by breaking each word down into syllables or into other meaningful units. *Borborygym*—not too much there ... *androcephalic*—*andro* and *cephalic*, where *andro* may mean "man" and *cephalic* could mean "head" or "headlike"; therefore *androcephalic* may mean "having a man's head like the Sphinx." *Pro-rogue*—*pro* means "for" and *rogue* means "thief"—could the word possibly mean: "for a thief?" Or perhaps it means "doing something like a thief," "in a sneaky manner," and so on. In each case, the subject first uses a general strategy—breaking the word down into units—and then sees if any responses are evoked by each unit.

It is the second part of this process, however, that is particularly important for an analysis of transfer and ultimately of forgetting. In terms of an $S-R$ analysis the syllable *rogue* serves as a stimulus to evoke the identifying response of *rogue* or perhaps the defining response, *thief*. As it turns out, however, both these are incorrect and consequently produce negative transfer. An inappropriate response has been evoked by the stimulus *rogue*. If the subject were asked to learn that *prorogue* means "to postpone" or "to delay" and that it had nothing to do with thieves, the resulting situation could be diagrammed as follows:

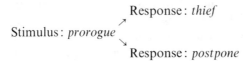

Response: *thief*

Stimulus: *prorogue*

Response: *postpone*

Given this pattern of stimulus–response relations, after the passage of some time a subject asked to define *prorogue* might reasonably be expected to do one of three things: (1) He would pause for awhile, but would finally say: "Prorogue means to postpone"; (2) he would pause for awhile, but would finally say: "Prorogue means 'for thieves';" or (3) he would say: "Sorry, old chap, I really can't remember." All three alternatives show the effects of competing response tendencies, although only under the first alternative would the subject demonstrate what we would be willing to call memory.

This situation is not altogether artificial or uncommon; it happens all the time in trying to learn deceptive cognates in a foreign language. For example, *chair* in French is something to sit on only if we stretch the meaning of the word greatly; while *but* is a purpose and not a pause. The reason there is so much difficulty in remembering that *chair* means "flesh" and that *but* means "purpose" may be diagrammed for the *chair* case as follows:

"chair"

*Chair*

"flesh"

with the English response (primarily one of identifying the stimulus) the more dominant. With enough repetition, however, *chair* (French) is discriminated from *chair* (English), and the correct response *flesh* thereby strengthened.

## Competition and Unlearning as Factors in Forgetting

Is there any evidence for this view of memory? An early study by Melton and Irwin (1940) was concerned with exactly this problem. In their experiments, subjects were first exposed to an 18-item list of nonsense syllables for 5 presentations. During this time the subject's task was to anticipate each of the items in the list. With only 5 trials, no subject was able to anticipate correctly all items in the list. After this initial learning experience, subjects were asked to learn another series of items. Some of these subjects were exposed to this second list for 5 trials, some for 10, some for 20, and some for 40 trials. Another group of subjects served as a control group and was not exposed to the second list at all.

Melton and Irwin's results were quite clear in showing that subjects recalled fewer List 1 items as the number of trials on List 2 increased from 0 to 40 trials. This means, they reasoned, that as the number of List 2 trials increased, the total amount of interference of List 2 items on List 1 items also increased, thereby producing poorer recall of items from the first list.

But what is the nature of this interference? Melton and Irwin noted that there are two things a subject can do in *failing* to recall: He can produce items from List 2 and think they are from List 1 (so-called *competing responses* or *response intrusions*) or he can fail to produce any List 1 responses at all. The results of their experiment showed that the number of competing responses from List 2 reached a maximum when the number of trials on List 1 and List 2 were about equal (at 5 trials). After this point competing responses underwent an almost catastrophic decline. This decline, they argued, was due to the competition of List 2 response with List 1 response. After a sufficient number of trials (20–40), the now better-learned List 2 items are clearly discriminated from the less-well-learned List 1 items, and so no further intrusions occur. If all interference is due to response competition, however, any decrease in overt competitions should also produce a drop in total interference. Since such a drop did not occur, Melton and Irwin cautiously postulated that a new factor, *Factor X*, must account for the difference.

Using instrumental conditioning procedures as their basic model, they proposed that Factor X was *unlearning* the responses from List 1 during the learning of List 2. Specifically, if a subject produces responses from List 1 while learning List 2, these incorrect responses are not reinforced and consequently extinguish during this period. Once extinguished, they are not available during the relearning of List 1. Under the logic of this argument two different factors account for forgetting: competition between responses at the time of recall and unlearning of initial responses.

*Fate of List 1 responses.* If this type of analysis is correct, it seems reasonable to ask about the fate of first list associations during the learning of the second list. A number of theorists (Melton, 1961; Postman, 1963) assume that extinguished List 1 responses show spontaneous recovery in strength with the passage of time and that there is a progressive shift in the balance of strength in favor of List 1 responses. Given this further analysis, interference effects should vary markedly both as a consequence of the number of List 2 trials and the amount of time between List 2 learning and the recall of List 1 responses.

If the number of List 2 trials produces a dramatic reduction in the availability of List 1 responses relative to List 2 responses, this would be strong evidence for an unlearning factor; if the length of the interval following List 2 learning leads to an increase in the number of List 1 responses produced, this provides evidence favoring the hypothesis of spontaneous recovery; and if both these predictions are verified, the analogy of forgetting to extinction rests on a somewhat firmer base than ever before.

### Competition and Unlearning in Paired Associates

Although Melton developed the concepts of competition and unlearning in the context of learning lists of nonsense syllables, it remained for later investigation to study these factors in the more appropriate context of a paired-associates task.

Perhaps the most direct evidence for the effects of List 2 practice on the relative availability of List 1 and List 2 items is provided in a paired-associates study by Barnes and Underwood (1959). In the critical portion of this study, subjects first learned a set of paired items such as *WEM-tall* and then learned a second set of items such as *WEM-book*, for either 1, 5, 10, or 20 trials. After the appropriate number of trials, all subjects were asked to write down and distinguish the appropriate List 1 response (*tall*) from the appropriate List 2 response (*book*). Figure 4.1, which presents these results, indicates remarkable

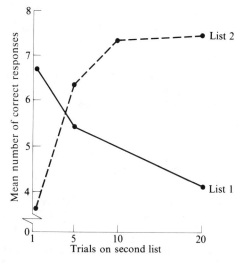

**Fig. 4.1** The number of responses correctly recalled as a function of degree of practice on the second list. The more practice on the second list, the fewer responses subjects could recall from the first list. (From Barnes and Underwood, 1959)

agreement between theory and data. List 1 responses systematically decrease in availability (are extinguished), while List 2 responses progressively increase in availability.

A further test of this hypothesis (Goggin, 1963), in which subjects were not asked specifically to identify whether the response came from List 1 or List 2 but were asked to "List as many items from both lists you can remember," also yielded similar results: List 1 items are just not available after a number of trials on List 2.

The particular design used in both experiments can be represented by the following pairwise notation: List 1, Pairs $A-B$; List 2, Pairs $A-C$; or more simply this design is represented as $A-B$, $A-C$. It is also possible to use a design other than an $A-B$, $A-C$ design in order to find out what types of unlearning might occur. In an attempt to clarify the mechanisms responsible for unlearning, McGovern (1964) actually tried out 4 different pairing procedures. She began her analysis by asking what kinds of associations need be considered to talk meaningfully about unlearning. She concluded that three different types of connections were established in original $A-B$ learning:

1. Forward associations between words of the form $A \rightarrow B$.
2. Backward associations between words of the form $A \leftarrow B$.
3. Contextual associations between response term(s) and the experimental situation of the form $S_{\text{situation}} \rightarrow B$.

McGovern argued that in the case of $A-B$ only learning (that is, when no List 2 response was learned), all 3 types of associations should remain intact and that under this condition little or no unlearning should occur. For this reason she used this condition as a baseline against which to evaluate any unlearning effects that might occur in the other conditions. In addition to the $A-B$ only condition, she also set up 4 other conditions, two of which she believed would lead to the extinction of 2 of the 3 associations possible in this situation, and two others which she believed would lead to the extinction of only 1 of the 3 possible associations.

McGovern tested her predictions by using two 8-item lists, and by asking subjects to recall all the paired-response terms they could after List 2 learning was completed. Table 4.1 (see next page) presents a summary of McGovern's results, along with a brief explanation of which associations were thought to be unlearned.

The condition $A-B$, $A-Br$ refers to the case in which the same stimulus and response terms were used in both List 1 and List 2, but in which the pairings were changed for List 2:

| List 1 | List 2 |
|--------|--------|
| *WEM–table* | *WEM–love* |
| *PIV–love* | *PIV–table* |

All other List 1–List 2 pairings are reasonably obvious if the letters are interpreted properly.

**Table 4.1**  A summary of McGovern's experiment

| Training list 1 | Condition list 2 | Mean number of correct responses after interpolated learning | Nature of associative connections extinguished |
|---|---|---|---|
| A–B | A–C | 4.79 | Forward and contextual associations |
| A–B | A–Br | 4.75 | Forward and backward associations |
| A–B | C–B | 6.42 | Backward associations |
| A–B | C–B | 6.54 | Contextual associations |
| A–B | — | 7.71 | — |

The results in Table 4.1 show that for Training Conditions 1 and 2 (where presumably two associations were unlearned) subjects recalled far fewer items than for Conditions 3 and 4 (where only one association was unlearned). All 4 conditions, however, are considerably poorer than the control condition under which subjects produced almost perfect recall (7.7 out of 8 possible). As in prior studies, these data offer strong support for the role of unlearning in forgetting.

### Spontaneous Recovery in Paired-Association Learning

A second hypothesis suggested by an unlearning analysis of memory—that extinguished List 1 items might be expected to show spontaneous recovery— was tested in an early experiment by Underwood (1948) and in more recent ones by Adams (1962) and by Postman and his associates (Postman, Stark, and Fraser, 1968; Postman and Stark, 1969). In these studies, subjects were first required to learn an initial pair, and then a second pair in which the same A-term was used, i.e., subjects were run under the A–B, A–C procedure. Recall tests occurred at varying time intervals after the second set of pairs was learned; generally recall was asked for immediately after A–C learning, after 20 minutes, after 24 hours, after 48 hours, and after one week. These procedures obviously parallel to some degree those used by Barnes and Underwood and McGovern, and indeed results do show the expected unlearning of B responses to A stimuli.

More relevant to the present point, however, was the finding that, with the passage of time, B responses show an increase in frequency of occurrence ("spontaneous recovery"), while C responses show a decrease. In Underwood's study, for example, the total number of B and C responses was about equal after 24 hours. This result occurred despite the fact that subjects tested for recall immediately after A–C learning were able to recall many more C than B responses. Under these conditions it seems as if there is some fixed level to which both B and C responses fall, and after that there is no further loss in memory. In the Adams study (1962), A and B words were paired for 19 trials and A and C words for 10 trials. Recall for A–B pairs was equal to 2.8 pairs on immediate recall and 4.5 pairs after 48 hours. This compares favorably with 5.6 pairs and 5.0 pairs for a control group given only 19 A–B trials.

## THE REEMERGENCE OF COMPETITION

In all these experiments, the increase in recall of List 1 responses relative to List 2 responses has been described in terms of concepts clearly borrowed from the conditioning literature. That is, unlearning is equated with extinction and the increased recall of List 1 responses is equated with spontaneous recovery. If this analogy is correct, what it is that gets unlearned, and what it is that gets recovered spontaneously, is a specific associative connection between a given stimulus word (A) and a given response word (B). Recently, however, Postman—one of the leading theorists in this field—has questioned whether it is appropriate to regard unlearning and spontaneous recovery as the only, or even as the major, factor involved in forgetting (Postman and Stark, 1969). His newer work suggests that competition may be an even more important factor than unlearning.

In this more recent series of experiments, subjects are asked to go through the usual paired-associates learning and memory designs, similar in all important respects to those used by McGovern. The only difference between these experiments and those reported by McGovern was that Postman and Stark used a multiple-choice rather than a free-recall procedure after List 2 learning. During this phase of the experiment subjects were shown 4 different words and asked to pick the correct one; that is, the one occurring in List 1. The three incorrect choices were other items from the list.

Contrary to much of the research done prior to this experiment, none of the subjects tested under multiple-choice procedures showed significant losses in their ability to recognize responses from List 1. Although there was some small loss for the A–B, A–Br condition, this loss amounted only to about 1 item out of 10. The classical procedure for demonstrating unlearning— A–B, A–C—failed to show any significant losses at all. What all of this means is that specific stimulus–response pairs show very little unlearning (and therefore very little spontaneous recovery) if the subject is asked to select the correct response rather than produce it spontaneously.

These data suggest that subjects don't lose specific $S-R$ pairs, but rather the entire set of responses appropriate for the first list. Postman has explained this in the following terms: Seeing and saying responses from List 1 during original learning increases their tendency to be evoked by stimuli in the situation (what McGovern called contextual cues). During the learning of List 2, responses appropriate to this second list also become strongly attached to the present experimental situation. This means that two different sets of responses are associated with the same cue. In order to produce the correct response in recall, the subject must adapt a "selection criterion" which serves to differentiate the set of responses appropriate to List 2 or List 1. Since in the standard $A-B, A-C$ procedure the final test of recall involves $A-B$ pairs, selection criteria appropriate to $A-C$ still operate during this recall phase, thereby serving to make all $B$ responses equally unavailable, but *not necessarily unlearned*. If responses are again made available, as in a recognition test, subjects show no unlearning—precisely the results reported by Postman and Stark.

What is important about this new version of interference theory is that interference is brought about not as a result of unlearning, but rather by the (inappropriate) dominance of a List 2 selection criterion. If unlearning is seen as only of secondary importance, this means that competition must be the single most important type of interference and that most forgetting is the result of response competition rather than the result of $S-R$ unlearning. Such competition is no longer between specific responses ($B$ and $C$) but rather between alternative sets of responses connected to the same experimental situation.

*Proactive factors in forgetting.*   All in all, most of the data presently available are very much in accord with this new analysis of memory if we extend our notion of interference to include competition between sets of responses. What need not be changed, however, is the view that interfering events occur in the period following initial acquisition and final recall. But a moment's reflection indicates that initial learning itself could properly be considered as interpolated learning, with all 18–20 years of the college student's pre-experimental life providing the conditions of initial learning. Simple interference views of memory consider learners as "*tabula* more or less *rasa*"—that is, as having no relevant prior history with present materials. This, of course, is in accordance with the associationistic view of memory and learning and in the best experimental and theoretical tradition dating back at least as far as Ebbinghaus (1885). Unfortunately, such an assumption is no more tenable now than it was then, for Ebbinghaus early discovered that his nonsense syllables differed considerably in meaning, and more importantly in terms of how easily they were learned and remembered.

Ebbinghaus' experimental legacy also gave rise to another problem, a problem that made no sense until Underwood critically analyzed the effects of prior learning on contemporary recall.  Although Ebbinghaus was certainly a "master memorizer" if ever there was one, his results produced the surprising conclusion that he was able to recall only about 35 % of the material he had just learned.  This is in marked contrast to what would be expected intuitively: "Certainly we don't forget 65 % of the material we have just learned."

Underwood (1957), in analyzing this peculiar "lapse of memory," reasoned that Ebbinghaus showed such poor recall not because he had a poor memory, but because he was not a *tabula rasa* in each new experiment; that is, items from all prior lists he had learned must be interfering with his recall of material from the present list.  The evidence marshaled for this purpose was ingenious: Underwood sorted through all previous experimental literature, paying particular attention to the number of lists experimental subjects had learned prior to the one they were presently being asked to recall.  After examining 14 different experimental reports (see Fig. 4.2), Underwood felt confident that the number of previous lists learned adversely affected recall of the present list, with memorizers having learned and recalled only one list showing between 75 % and 85 % recall and with subjects having learned 15 or more lists showing less than 20 % recall.

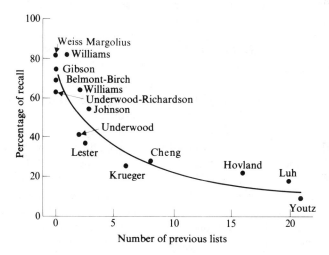

**Fig. 4.2**  The effects of proactive interference on recall.  Each dot represents the data obtained by a different investigator.  (From B. J. Underwood, *Psychol. Rev.* **64**, 49–60, 1957, page 53)

*Extra-experimental sources of interference.*  How, in terms of interference theory, should such proactive experience affect memory?  The logic of this argument proceeds in much the same way as the argument developed to explain the effects of interpolated activity.  All that need be done in the proactive case is to ask what effect an already existing $A–B$ connection has on the recall of another, as-yet-to-be-learned, $A-C$ pair. Perhaps the most elaborate attempt to conceptualize the effects of prior habits on subsequent learning was undertaken by Underwood and Postman in 1960. Basically their argument was made, and appropriately so, in terms of the verbal materials, mainly words and nonsense syllables, characteristically used in experimental studies of memory.

For example, compare the verbal units *jqr* and *boy*. The first purely formal property which is obvious, as Underwood and Postman remind us, is that *boy* is really a single unit and *jqr* is not. This means that the memorizer does not have to integrate the separate letter units in *boy*; such integration is given by his experience with the language. The sequence of *b*, followed by *o* (as in *boy*, *bottle*, *boat*, etc.) and the *o* followed by *y* (*boy*, *joy*, *toy*, etc.) occur very frequently in the language. On the other hand, *q* never follows *j*, nor does it ever precede *r* in normal usage; therefore, the strongest response given *q* as a stimulus is probably *u*, with *r* having no prior connection with *q*. If a subject has to learn a list in which *jqr* is a response element, Underwood and Postman assume two different consequences: (1) It will be difficult to learn (relative to a meaningful unit, such as *boy*, or to a statistically more frequent bit of nonsense, such as *est*) because of the low frequency of occurrence of the constituent letters; and (2) With the passage of time, as in a recall task, a more usual sequence (such as *q*, *u*) will show spontaneous recovery and make the production of *jqr* quite difficult (this is an obvious application of the interference analysis described previously).

According to Underwood and Postman, all is not completely kosher with *boy* either: if *jqr* is subject to letter-sequence interference, then *boy* should be subject to an entirely different type of interference called unit-sequence interference. What this means is that in ordinary language usage *boy* is frequently preceded by an article and followed by a verb, and these prior patterns of occurrence should serve to establish preexisting connections between *boy* and other words in the language. Since this pattern of connections is different from the one embodied in the random collection of words used in laboratory studies, such preexisting connections should cause interference. Thus, if a memorizer has trouble overcoming letter-sequence interference with *jqr*, he will also have trouble overcoming unit-sequence interference with meaningful units such as *boy*.

One of the more interesting studies of letter-sequence effects was done by Coleman in 1962. In this experiment Coleman first presented one subject with a series of about 30 scrambled letters. This subject was asked to memorize this sequence, although he was stopped before he could reach 100% accuracy. He was next asked to recall as many of these letters as he could, which the experimenter then typed on another card and handed to a second subject. This process went on for 11 subjects, all of whom were shown the output of the immediately preceding subject.

If the general tenor of Underwood and Postman's hypothesis is correct, then the order of letters in successive recalls should come to approximate English letter order more closely than did the original list of stimulus letters. Coleman's results were quite consistent in showing that letter sequences were much more similar to English after the last subject's recall than after the first subject's recall, although none of these outputs showed the sequential properties characteristic of English. In this regard it is well to remember that increases in approximation to English letter sequences means poorer memory for the sequence actually presented. The results of this experiment provide good confirmation for the view that over a series of recalls, extra-experimental habits do affect recall adversely in much the manner required by the Underwood-Postman hypothesis.

So much for letter-sequence effects. What about unit-sequence effects? Here the hypothesis is that subjects show better long-term recall for words having fewer extra-list connections than for words having a great many extra-list connections. Although the direct test of this hypothesis has not been impressive, the "other side" of this hypothesis does seem to imply that if subjects are asked to recall a series of words having strong unit-to-unit connections with each other, they should be able to do so more readily than if asked to recall a series in which such connections were weak or absent. Stating it differently, the more closely a to-be-recalled series of words approximates subjects' normal linguistic sequencing, the more likely it is they will produce an extensive recall.

The first experiment on this topic was done more than 20 years ago by Miller and Selfridge (1949). What they were interested in showing was that as a sequence of words came to resemble English prose more closely, subjects would be able to recall it that much better. In order to do this experiment, Miller and Selfridge first needed to construct stimulus materials differing in the degree to which their sequences approximated normal English. For a zero-order approximation (that is, for the sequence least resembling English) they chose words randomly from the dictionary, while for a first-order approximation to English they scrambled words appearing in other sentences in the experiment. For a second-order approximation, they gave one word to a subject, such as *is*, and asked him to add another word to it as if he were writing a sentence, e.g., *is this*. A different student was then presented only with the word *this* and asked to add another word as if he were writing a sentence, e.g., (*is*) *this is*, and so on until "sentences" 10, 20, 30, and 50 words long were constructed.

Higher-order approximations to English were created by a similar procedure. Thus, if Miller and Selfridge wanted a fifth-order approximation, they might present a given subject with the sequence: *Great people are humble*, to which the subject might respond *because*; and so on until a sequence such as the following might be produced: "Great people are humble because they have no electricity but we made it is too and always will be."... Not great poetry, but certainly more like English than zero- or first-order approximations. After 8 different orders of approximations to English were constructed, 20 students were asked to recall the materials they had just heard. Results of this experiment showed that as the order of approximation to English increased, there was a corresponding increase in the percentage recalled, with this increase reaching its maximum by about the fifth-order approximation.

In terms of the Underwood–Postman hypothesis, these results support one ancillary aspect of their hypothesis: It is clear that unit-sequence characteristics exert a strong effect on recall in a way completely compatible with the original hypothesis. A specific analysis of what does go on when subjects learn higher-order approximations of this type must await Chapter 15.

### Recent Theoretical Developments

Despite these obviously supportive results, the analysis of extra-experimental sources of interference has not produced impressive results. Since the associationistic tradition in research on memory involves a strongly self-critical component, it is not at all surprising to find that the most severe analyses of this hypothesis have been offered by associationistic psychologists: namely, Postman (1963), and more recently, Keppell (1968) and Adams (1968). Basically, Postman argues that the original conception of unit-sequence interference was much too simple, and that while words that occur frequently may be expected to produce unit-to-unit interference effects, they should also produce co-varying facilitation. On this basis, then, the same factor—frequency of occurrence of a unit in natural language—should have both facilitating and interfering effects. For example, Postman (1962) performed an experiment involving pairs of items, A–B, in which he varied stimulus frequency. If the frequency-interference hypothesis was correct, then items of medium frequency should be acquired more easily than items of either high or low frequency. Although such results were found in this particular experiment, the conclusion to be derived from this kind of work has been aptly stated by Postman: "Interference theory predicts too much forgetting, because the same factors that bring about forgetting also serve to bring about recall." A fair conclusion seems to be that frequency of items both facilitates and interferes with rote learning and recall.

This emphasis on co-variation is an attempt to maintain interference as a primary principle, while recognizing that a particular research strategy—i.e., varying the frequency of the items used—may sometimes produce side effects which mask the relationship of frequency to interference. In short, studies that vary item frequency may not test the interference hypothesis in a completely adequate way.

Adams, who is also an interference theorist, maintains (1968) that most experiments designed to test the Underwood–Postman hypothesis have been confounded by not taking the memorizing subject into account. Thus, he argues, if a memorizer were presented with the stimulus letters $XV$ as in a study by Underwood and Keppell (1963), these should be rapidly forgotten because $V$ very infrequently follows $X$ in normal language usage. However, if the subject simply considers XV as a single Roman numeral and changes it to 15, this same $XV$ pair, far from being a difficult one, becomes an extremely easy one. Adams argues that the process within a subject can be best represented by the following interior monolog:

"Hm—let's see—$X$ then $V$—I know that's 15, so next time I see $X$, all I have to remember is $X$ leads to 15 and 15 means $XV$. No problem with that one—bring on the next one."

On this basis Adams is led to conclude that subjects must make use of naturally occurring language mediators and that the use of such mediators helps explain why many of the expected differences fail to occur.

But is there any evidence that a process such as natural language mediation ($NLM$) does in fact occur? The best experiment on this topic is by Montague, Adams and Kiess (1966). In this experiment subjects were presented with 96 pairs of 3-letter nonsense syllables, such as $WEM–PIV$, and asked to write down any word or phrase that they thought would help them remember the pair, e.g., *Wembly–Pivot*. The word or phrase produced was called the natural language mediator ($NLM$). Over all the various conditions of the experiment (the specific details of which need not concern us here), about 50% of the pairs did produce $NLM$'s during the time that the pair was presented. While this is of interest in and of itself, the effects of $NLM$'s on recall are even more important for the present discussion.

During the recall portion of the experiment, the first nonsense syllable of each of the 96 pairs was presented, e.g., $WEM$; and the subject was required to write down both the $NLM$, *Wembly–Pivot*, and the response actually correct, $PIV$. The recall results obtained in this experiment were broken down into 3 groups depending on the occurrence or nonoccurrence of a $NLM$ at the time of recall: One group contained pairs in which the $NLM$ was given in essentially the same form as it had been produced during original learning; a second group contained pairs in which the $NLM$ produced during recall was different from the one produced during the learning phase; while a third group consisted of words not producing any $NLM$'s during initial acquisition. After only one presentation of the total list, subjects were able to recall about 15% of all the response items seen, for a total of 1621 items over all subjects. Of these 1621 items recalled, 77% were recalled in conjunction with their appropriate $NLM$, while only 5% were recalled when the $NLM$ was different from the one produced during acquisition. Only 18% were recalled when no *NLM* had been produced.

These results provide quite strong support for the view that when subjects are actually able to recall items, they do this by using some sort of covert process that is not related in any simple or direct way to the properties of the stimulus. What this means is that the laws of interference may account for a significant portion of forgetting only where the situation and/or the materials are so impoverished as to deny the subject an opportunity to use covert or mediational processes. When these conditions of experimental control are in operation, however, an interference analysis of memory does offer great explanatory power in explaining why people forget.

Words, however, do not exhaust the types of events that can mediate learning and recall. Normal experience indicates that we often use mental imagery in recalling some event or other. If, for example, you are asked to recall how many pictures there are in your living room, you would begin by picturing the layout of the whole living room. "Let's see, over there's the couch, there's the brown leather chair and the black leather chair and then the fireplace and the door from the hall and the door to the dining room. Let's see, there are pictures over the fireplace, and near the doorway and . . . ." No amount of purely verbal description seems to suffice—what is necessary is a vivid mental image of the room.

Now associationistic psychology has always been pretty wary of images, yet if the data of everyday and laboratory experience seem to demand images and imagery, then the *S–R* psychologist is obliged to provide as exact and careful a definition as scientifically possible.

In order to tackle this problem experimentally, Paivio (1965, 1968, 1969, Paivio and Medyan, 1968) began by attempting to define imagery as precisely as possible. In order to do this, he started with the rather common-sense (and, as it turned out, quite correct) notion that concrete nouns such as *tree* or *house* would evoke imagery much more easily than abstract ones such as *health* or *truth*. Students were asked to rate words on a 5-point scale ranging from "image aroused immediately" to "image aroused only after long delay or not at all." Paivio's original results (1965) showed that for the 32 words he used, the 16 concrete words aroused images significantly more easily than the 16 abstract words.

Of more importance, however, was the finding that when students were asked to learn word pairs, Paivio found that two concrete words—*tree* and *house*—were easier to learn than two abstract words—*health* and *truth*. In addition, pairs having concrete stimulus words were more easily learned than pairs having abstract stimulus words, regardless of whether or not the response words were abstract or concrete.

Since most of the earlier work on mediation in paired-associates learning had shown that verbal events predicted such learning quite well, it seemed reasonable to wonder if noun imagery was really the effective mediator, or whether it might not be some other verbal property of concrete nouns. One obvious contender was the *m*-value of words, i.e., the number of words evoked by a stimulus word in 60 seconds (see Noble, 1952), since in an earlier study Paivio (1965) found that concrete nouns produced significantly larger *m*-values. This hypothesis, however plausible it seemed to be, was laid to rest in a series of studies by Paivio and his associates (Paivio, Yuilles and Smythe, 1966; Paivio and Madigan, 1968; Paivio, 1969) in which it was found that rated imagery was considerably more important than *m*-value.

The theoretical analysis of exactly what's happening in this situation hinges on the important observation that stimulus imagery is more important than response imagery in facilitating paired-associates learning. Earlier work by Lambert and Paivio (1956) found that pairs consisting of adjectives and nouns were more easily learned when nouns served as the stimulus term than when adjectives served as the stimulus term. Thus it was easier to learn the pair *house–large* than *large–house*. Although this is contrary to usual language habits, Lambert and Paivio assumed that nouns function as "conceptual pegs" for their associated adjectives. Paivio has extended this analysis by assuming that nouns are better able to serve as conceptual pegs because they arouse imagery much more easily than adjectives. If this is true, then the ease of learning a paired connection between two words should depend on the image-arousing capabilities of the stimulus term. This is true because at recall the stimulus element is presented alone, and the ease with which it serves to cue the response term predicts recall of the total pair. Concrete nouns provide more solid conceptual pegs than abstract ones.

All in all, the series of experiments described by Paivio and his collaborators justifies his recent assertion (1969) that "It is clear that imagery has established itself as a scientifically useful concept, even in an area long dominated by an emphasis on verbal mechanisms."

## SUMMARY

At the very heart of an associationistic analysis of symbolic activity is the topic of memory. Memory, however, is not considered as a special faculty, but rather as part and parcel of the larger topics of transfer and interference. Given this emphasis, it is not surprising to find that most associationistic theories of memory are actually theories of forgetting, with memory defined as what is left over after forgetting. To be sure, positive transfer effects are also assumed to occur, but just as surely, an associationistic theory of memory is largely concerned with negative transfer, or forgetting. Given this emphasis on forgetting, the essential postulate used is that of interference among and between $S–R$ connections. Forgetting occurs in accordance with the degree of incompatibility between two responses evoked by the same stimulus. If this incompatibility is strong, but one habit is stronger than the other, the relevant principle of interference is *response competition*; if one habit is reinforced considerably more frequently than the other, the relevant principle is *unlearning*. Both concepts can be specified with great precision in the laboratory and for this reason the laws of memory interference are well worked out and, in most instances, provide a firm empirical base for future prediction.

Interference, however, results not only from experience interpolated between original learning and recall, but also from experience taking place prior to original learning. The first type of interference (or facilitation as the case may be) is called *retroactive* interference; the latter is called *proactive* interference. For a long time after Ebbinghaus, retroactive interference was the more strongly stressed of the two (largely because of its use in experimental situations) although a recent shift in emphasis by Underwood and Postman to preexisting habits has brought proactive effects back into prominence. This certainly seems reasonable in that the normal experimental subject brings the results of 18–20 years of experience into the memory laboratory, and this certainly must be more important than the actual half-hour spent in learning laboratory itself.

Unfortunately, however, the attempt to describe proactive factors in terms of extra-experimental sources of interference has not been entirely successful; consequently, recent attempts have shifted to an analysis of what McGovern first called contextual associative connections. In a recent statement of interference theory, Postman has directed his attention from an analysis of forgetting based on unlearning and competition between specific S–R bonds to an analysis based on competition between alternative sets of responses connected to the experimental situation. This competition is seen to result from the subject's inability to select the proper set of responses for a particular set of experimental stimuli.

If this new emphasis on selection mechanisms represents a departure from classical interference theory, so too do attempts to describe facilitative memory factors. By and large, such mnemonic aids are described in terms of mediational events. By far and away the most usual event thought to mediate recall is the word, or some combination of words. Adams, for example, has stressed the role of natural language mediators (*NLM*) in recall, by which he means to emphasize the role of a subject's creative verbal processes in augmenting recall. In general, his results show that if a subject is able to recall his own *NLM*, he is able to recall the experimenter's response term for a particular S–R pair.

Words, however, do not exhaust the list of potential mediators. Paivio has argued that imagery evoked by a word should significantly mediate learning and later recall. In a series of experiments, Paivio has been able to show that imagery provides a good conceptual peg capable of facilitating recall. Since a concrete stimulus is better able to arouse imagery, it is not surprising to find that concrete words are better recalled than abstract words. In addition to these findings, Paivio's work has done much to make imagery a respectable psychological concept that can now be used without trepidation by a proper associationistic psychologist.

# CHAPTER 5

# CONCEPT FORMATION

Right at the beginning it is important to emphasize how difficult a concept is the concept of a concept. Take a seemingly simple one, such as the concept of dog. How do we know something is a dog? Well, we could begin by saying that it has four legs and a tail, and we would probably be happy to let it go at that. Yet this clearly won't do, for sheep, cows, llamas, and an almost infinite variety of other beasts also have four legs and a tail. Okay then, suppose we extend the list of characteristics: A dog is a four-legged animal, which is of a certain size and is friendly. Well and good; but a toy poodle and an English sheepdog are certainly not within the same "certain size," unless we allow that certain size to cover a good deal of ground, perhaps more than necessary to provide an unequivocal definition of "dogness." As for friendly, well, the limits here are as broad as in the case of size. What is even worse in this case is that the same dog—a mongrel watchdog for example—can be both friendly and hostile depending on the circumstances.

At every turn then, what seems to be obvious—we as humans do know what a dog is—becomes increasingly more obscure as we attempt to define it abstractly. Perhaps part of the trouble is that our whole approach may be wrong; perhaps we shouldn't try to define a dog in terms of critical aspects, but look instead at how and when human beings find the need to call something a dog. To make matters even worse, there is some evidence (Herrnstein and Loveland, 1964) that it is possible to teach pigeons concepts at least at the level of complexity of dogness. In this experiment, pigeons were trained to behave as if they had the rather amorphous concept of people. Let us not pursue this matter any further, except to note that the concept of people for the pigeon seemed to include all the complexities that we humans would and are willing to include by use of the term: children, older people, men, women, tall people, short people, people standing, people sitting, and so on.

If the problems raised by the foregoing discussion were described in terms of philosophical concepts, they would be termed an attack on essentialism. *Essentialism* is the tendency to assume that some word or concept has a unitary meaning and that it can be rigidly defined by a finite set of characteristics. On what basis can we say the word "dog" has no unitary meaning? The reason is this: There is a group of characteristics $X_1, X_2, X_3, \ldots, X_n$ that dogs typically have. Perhaps some of the characteristics described above meet these criteria, e.g., four-legged, friendly, tailed, etc. If all dogs had all these characteristics, and no other animal had any characteristics of this particular set, it would then be possible to say dog equals (is defined by) characteristics $X_1$ through $X_n$. But this is clearly not the case; not all dogs have all $n$ characteristics. All that is really required for an animal to be considered a dog is to have some dog characteristics; no dog need have them all. To be sure, not all characteristics will do; i.e., four-leggedness ($X_2$) is not enough to specify an animal as a dog, for the animal in question may be a sheep or an elephant, or God knows what. What seems to be true is this: There is no way of specifying in advance and in the abstract just how many characteristics are enough to specify something as a dog. In certain situations any three might do; for other purposes we might require more.

Although there doesn't seem to be any quick and easy way to resolve these problems, perhaps a recognition of its existence is of some import, and perhaps such a recognition might serve to clarify for us the very difficult term *concept*. The philosopher Wittgenstein, after a similar analysis, expressed his conclusion as follows:

> And the result of this examination is: we see a complicated network of similarities overlapping and criss-crossing: sometimes overall similarities, sometimes similarities of detail.
>
> I can think of no better expression to characterize these similarities than 'family resemblances'; for the various resemblances between members of a family: build, features, colour of eyes, gait, temperament, etc., overlap and criss-cross in the same way.
>
> And for instance . . . numbers form a family in the same way. Why do we call something a 'number'? Well, perhaps because it has a—direct —relationship with several things that have hitherto been called number; and this can be said to give it an indirect relationship to other things we call (by) the same name. We extend our concept of number as in spinning a thread we twist fibre on fibre. And the strength of the thread does not reside in the fact that some one fibre runs through its whole length, but in the overlapping of many fibres.*

But science progresses not by philosophical analysis alone, but by empirical results as well. The best a scientist can do with respect to philosophical strictures is to pick out a few that he can agree with, and then get on with his experiments. If he happens to be an $S-R$ or, more precisely, an associationistic psychologist, he does have available a collection of orienting attitudes that clearly color the direction of his enquiry. For one, he is likely to begin an analysis of concepts, insofar as he is able, in terms of events in the

---

* From *Philosophical Investigations*, Sections 66–67, by Ludwig Wittgenstein, Oxford, England: Basil Blackwell, 1963.

environment that are public and observable. For another, he is likely to stress the role of learning (no innate ideas for him) as of great significance. For a third, he probably begins with a vigorous experimental analysis of a concept-learning task. Such an empirical analysis should provide theoretical guidance when and where his common-sense notions fail him.

One of the earliest experiments on concept formation, done by Clark L. Hull in 1920, conforms nicely to this description of how an associationistic psychologist approaches concept formation, and indeed forms the starting point for most subsequent analyses of this phenomenon. Hull began by considering how a child might learn the concept of dog. He assumed that a child comes to this concept by hearing the word *dog* pronounced in conjunction with a particular object in the environment; in this case some variety of dog. The pairing of the word *dog* with dogs, so Hull's analysis goes, continues on a number of different occasions, sometimes involving $dog_1$, sometimes $dog_2$, sometimes $dog_3$, and so on. Ultimately, these experiences allow the child to abstract the common property or properties of dogs 1 through $n$; and from then on the child is able to name without error most new instances of the concept—dog $n + 1$, for example.

The crucial aspect of this analysis is clearly carried by the term *abstracts*. For Hull, the child abstracts his concept of dog on the basis of a property common to all the specific instances presented. In other words, the child develops what Vinacke (1952) has termed a composite picture of the object based on a common perceptual property.

But for Hull, as for all scientists, hypotheses are not enough: Such hypotheses must be put to experimental test before any stock can be placed in them or in their implications. In order to do this, Hull prepared a series of 36 cards composed of 6 groups of 6 cards. For each group all cards had a common meaningless symbol such as $+$ or $S$, camouflaged by other crisscrossing lines, e.g., $\$$. Each of these card groups was randomly assigned a nonsense syllable name, and the subject's job was to learn which nonsense name went with which particular symbol.

Since subjects were not told to look for common elements, it is possible to assume they treated the experimental situation as a simple paired-associates task in which they had to learn to pair nonsense names with nonsense figures. After all subjects were able to give a correct response for each of the 36 cards (a task they were able to complete after about 30 trials), they were tested on a new set of stimulus materials. This new set of 36 items was constructed so as to embody the same common element in each of 6 sets as applied to the earlier set of cards. If Hull's analyses of concept learning were correct, then subjects should show good transfer of nonsense names from the first set of stimulus materials to the second set of similar materials.

The results, for the second set of cards, indicated that subjects were able to give about 27% correct responses on the first trial of this transfer set, with

the percentage of correct anticipations rising to about 40% on Trial 2 and to 55% by Trial 6. These results showed that subjects were able to learn the appropriate responses for the second set of materials much more rapidly than they learned correct responses for the first set. This was true despite the fact that when subjects were questioned as to how they had managed to accomplish the task, most did not talk about "common elements," nor did they give any indication of the fact that they recognized any similarity among the elements. Hull interpreted these results to mean that concept acquisition, in principle, was no different from any other kind of complex discrimination learning.

As a consequence of this type of experimental demonstration, Hull seemed able to push aside many of the difficult philosophical problems and to reduce the matter to a simple combination of two well-known processes—generalization and discrimination. That stimulus generalization is an important component of an associationistic analysis of concept formation should come as no surprise, for in order to infer that someone "has a concept," what is required procedurally is that he be able to give the same response, $R_1$, to a variety of different stimuli. For example,

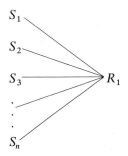

This analysis, multiple $S$: single $R$, is an exact prototype of the generalization experiment; that is, the situation in which the same response occurs to a wide variety of different stimuli.

However, if we analyze the situation further, as Hull did, it is clear that another behavioral process is required: This, of course, is the process of discrimination. In the early studies of animal learning, such as one by Fields (1932), it was possible to show that rats could be trained to choose triangular forms when such forms were contrasted during acquisition with other geometrical forms such as squares and rectangles. This occurred despite the fact that the size and position of "triangular" stimuli changed from trial to trial. In order to establish the animal's ability to select triangles, however, triangular stimuli first had to be discriminated from other geometric shapes. Indeed, early in training, the rats often showed generalization to (actually chose) other geometrical configurations. With continued training, such responses were not rewarded and dropped out of the animal's repertoire. Under Hull's definition, the behavior exhibited by the rat in this experiment should be called *concept acquisition.*

The essence, then, of early associationistic analyses of concept learning involved the familiar behavior processes of generalization and discrimination. These two processes were taken by Hull as the basis on which to build his analysis of abstraction, with such abstraction taking place in terms of the perceptual overlap of stimuli presented to the subject. Concept formation depended on abstraction, which in turn depended on physical identity among elements, which in turn depended on the very ordinary processes of generalization and discrimination. Given this analysis, such learning should, and did, proceed in a manner similar to ordinary multiple discrimination learning.

But such an analysis based primarily on the purely physical properties of a stimulus, could not stand for too long, for, as Osgood (1953) correctly noted, Hull was not studying concept acquisition but something Osgood has termed *labeling behavior.* The exact criticism of Hull's approach was perhaps best stated by Smoke (1932), who asked the following question of an identical-element analysis:

> If an exact drawing were made of all the dogs now living, or even of those with which any child is familiar, would they contain certain strokes in common which could be easily embedded in each?

This, of course, was just Smoke's way of stating the philosopher's criticisms of essentialism presented earlier. Hull's insistence on direct physical similarity among different exemplars of the same concept is a difficult, if not impossible, condition to achieve in concept learning in real-life situations. In order to get around this problem, Smoke proposed that concept formation is not so much a matter of identical elements, but of the pattern of relations existing among these elements. According to his view, there need be no physical identity among examplars, only a common pattern of relations capable of inducing a common symbolic reaction.

In order to make this analysis more explicit, Smoke spelled it out in terms of an experiment involving geometrical figures as stimuli. One of Smoke's concept classes, the concept of $DAX$, was defined as any circle with two dots in it. The size of the circle, the size of the dots, the specific location of the dots inside the circle—all these aspects of the stimulus were allowed to vary; the only thing that remained constant was the relation of two dots to the circle; namely, that they be inside it. As in Hull's case, subjects were able to learn the concepts and were later able to pick out $DAX$s when presented with novel examples. Also in agreement with Hull's results, Smoke found that many subjects showed the correct "conceptual" response in the absence of being able to define precisely what were the essential characteristics of a concept such as *DAX*ness.

The upshot of this experiment, as well as Smoke's critical analysis of Hull's composite-picture hypothesis, has been to acknowledge that an identical elements theory, couched solely in terms of physical similarity of examplars, is inadequate and that some provision must be made to account for similarity that does not depend on physical factors. Although Hull himself was the first to attempt such a theoretical extension, the clearest statement of what such an approach might look like was provided by Osgood (1953) in terms of his theory of mediational responses. As a starting point, Osgood took an experiment by Reed (1946) in which subjects were required to learn a nonsense syllable name as a response to a 4-word stimulus unit. So, for example, a subject might be presented with the 4 words *horn, leaf, monkey, debt* to which the correct response might be *BEP*. He would next be presented with another 4-word set, *fame, ought, tiger, saucer*, to which the same response *BEP* would be correct. Further examplars of the *BEP* category might be *answer, lion, highest, red*, or *elephant, anywhere, club, picnic*, and so on. All *BEP* cards contained one animal name, and the subject's job was to respond with *BEP* when one of these cards was presented. In a similar fashion other nonsense syllables were associated with other concepts: all *DAX* cards contained a color name; all *MIB* cards had a vegetable; all *KUN* cards, a fruit; and so on for 6 different concepts.

In his analysis of this situation Osgood assumed 3 overlapping processes. (a) The subject must first discriminate which of the 4 items on a card is the critical one—is it *horn*, or *leaf*, or *monkey*, or *debt*? (b) Once this is done, the second part of the problem is to apply pre-experimental response connections to the stimulus array. A word such as *leaf* is assumed to arouse a family of responses, as do all other words on the card. In the case of *monkey*, for example, the series of responses might look something like this:

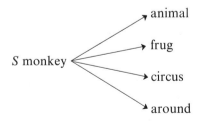

If the response *animal* is aroused easily, that is, is a high-probability response to *monkey* as well as to *tiger* and the other concept examplars, then all these words are classified as belonging to the same concept because they all evoke the same response. This bridging or mediation then goes on until the responses common to all members of a family have been isolated. Osgood's diagram of this hypothesis is presented in Fig. 5.1, where the third and final aspect of the process is also shown: (c) After the mediational response, $r_m$, of *vegetable* has been evoked and identified, this response must next be associated (connected) with the correct nonsense syllable, *MIB*.

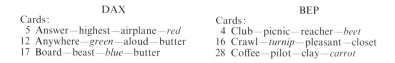

| DAX | BEP |
|---|---|
| Cards: | Cards: |
| 5 Answer—highest—airplane—*red* | 4 Club—picnic—reacher—*beet* |
| 12 Anywhere—*green*—aloud—butter | 16 Crawl—*turnip*—pleasant—closet |
| 17 Board—beast—*blue*—butter | 28 Coffee—pilot—clay—*carrot* |

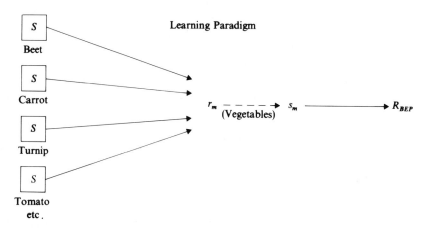

**Fig. 5.1** Sample materials in an experiment on concept formation, and a mediational model suggested as the learning paradigm involved. (From Osgood, 1953)

What this implies is that once a concept mediator is discovered this eases the strain of remembering all preceding sets of 4 words appropriate to the *MIB* response. Once the correct $r_m$ has been discovered (*vegetables*), instead of retaining specific pairings, the subject has to remember only a small number of connections: "Vegetables are *MIBs*, fruits are *KUNs*, colors are *DAXs*," and so on; and then apply this bit of learning whenever the stimulus card evokes one or the other of these mediating responses. The memory task is thereby considerably reduced, even to the point of saying it no longer exists: Once a subject learns the crucial mediating element, he could presumably give the correct response to any and all examplars of the concept.

The development of the mediation hypothesis to account for concept formation is no small achievement, for it permits the derivation of complex conceptual behavior in terms of simple and potentially observable responses.

One important reason for insisting that the mediational element be considered as a response is that it is then assumed to follow the same functional laws as manifestly observable responses. By the expedient of mediational responses, the covert becomes overt, and the principles of overt behavioral laws can be applied to complex mental phenomena.

Although this type of analysis has moved away from Hull's emphasis on physical similarity, the essential nature of the mediational hypothesis differs little in many important respects from Hull's initial analysis. The focus of attention, however, has now shifted from how a concept is learned by a naive organism to how a concept is learned by an organism which comes to the concept-learning task with a full repertoire of prior learning. This is simply a recognition that subjects are not blank organisms when they participate in a psychological experiment. Similarly, it represents an attempt to include, if we may paraphrase the same development in work on memory, extra-experimental sources of concept facilitation.

### How Shall a Mediator be Measured?

Once we agree that mediational responses—that is, explicit prior learning—are important in dealing with conceptual behavior, it then becomes necessary to provide a reliable and public procedure for measuring such responses. In order to make the analysis of mediational responses an experimentally viable one, experimenters have often used verbal materials. Verbal materials make extremely good stimuli largely because many of their associated mediational responses can be easily assessed. As an example of this type of approach, consider the data in Table 5.1 (overleaf).

This table presents 21 different nouns and their 3 most common responses under conditions in which subjects had been asked to give their first sensory impression to each word (e.g., "Is the word *sharp, open, soft, circular*, etc.?"). Although there are obvious percentage differences in each column, i.e., 32% for *big* as a response to *zoo* as compared to 72% for *white* as a response to *teeth*, each word clearly does produce a collection of sensory impressions. Many of these sensory impressions apply to more than a single word. For example, the sensory impression "white," even from the limited sample of material presented in Table 5.1, occurs as a dominant response to *ivory, linen, rice*, and *teeth*, and as a response of second-level dominance for *onion, paste*, and *sheep*.

These materials suggest an obvious experiment. To determine whether the ease with which a concept is learned depends on the dominance level of the correct response, Underwood and Richardson (1956) went about testing this assumption in the following way. They first prepared a series of 24 cards, each containing a single noun. Subjects were told that there were 6 different concepts in the list and that their task was to find each of these concepts and

to guess what the concept was. Of the 6 concepts, two were of high dominance, two of medium dominance, and two of low dominance. In this experiment dominance was defined in terms of nouns such as those provided in
Table 5.1.

**Table 5.1** Illustrative material from the Underwood–Richardson (1956a) cali-
bration

| Stimulus Word | | | Associates | | | | |
|---|---|---|---|---|---|---|---|
| | Word | % | Word | % | Word | % |
| Anchor | Heavy | 57 | Metallic | 15 | Hard | 7 |
| Badge | Shiny | 32 | Metallic | 27 | Round | 21 |
| Cabin | Small | 39 | Woody | 28 | Brown | 11 |
| Diamond | Shiny | 65 | Hard | 15 | Clear | 9 |
| Eye | Round | 32 | Small | 10 | Brown | 8 |
| Forest | Green | 52 | Dark | 14 | Big | 12 |
| Ginger | Strong | 40 | Brown | 15 | Sweet | 11 |
| Head | Round | 66 | Hard | 9 | Small | 5 |
| Ivory | White | 65 | Hard | 14 | Smooth | 12 |
| Jellyfish | Slimy | 49 | Soft | 31 | Small | 5 |
| Kitten | Soft | 41 | Small | 25 | Hairy | 13 |
| Linen | White | 59 | Soft | 14 | Smooth | 9 |
| Moss | Green | 52 | Soft | 22 | Wet | 6 |
| Needle | Sharp | 53 | Pointed | 15 | Small | 9 |
| Onion | Smelly | 49 | White | 15 | Strong | 14 |
| Paste | Sticky | 64 | White | 16 | Slimy | 7 |
| Rice | White | 54 | Small | 24 | Hard | 6 |
| Sheep | Fuzzy | 49 | White | 23 | Soft | 14 |
| Teeth | White | 72 | Sharp | 8 | Hard | 5 |
| Waist | Small | 43 | Round | 24 | Narrow | 12 |
| Zoo | Big | 32 | Smelly | 30 | Noisy | 7 |

Column one presents the stimulus nouns given to each subject. The remaining
columns show the three most frequent (most dominant) responses, along with the
percentages of subjects making them. It should be noted that some stimulus words,
not appearing in this tabulation, elicited fewer than three distinctly different
responses.

The results were not surprising: High-dominance concepts were learned
fastest, followed in order by medium- and low-dominance concepts. The
procedure used in this particular experiment was quite similar to a standard
paired-associates learning task, except that subjects were required to provide
their own response words. In terms of their actual performance, not only
were high-dominance concepts learned more readily than low-dominance
ones, they were also the occasion for fewer interfering responses.

In order to extend the plausibility of a mediational analysis further, Coleman (1964) used the same type of stimulus materials. Instead of requiring subjects to guess the correct concept name, Coleman asked each subject to produce a descriptive adjective for each name. The results not only indicated that subjects could give the "correct" adjective more often to high-dominance pairs but that they were able to do it much more rapidly (9 seconds for high-dominance problems as compared to 16 seconds for low-dominance problems).

An examination of the pattern of sensory mediators aroused by the nouns contained in the Underwood and Richardson list indicates that not only do such mediators differ in terms of their probability of occurrence but also in terms of the number of different sensory responses they evoke. That is, both the probability of the primary response as well as the number of different responses produced vary. In order to determine whether the absolute probability of the mediator is of primary importance (i.e., its actual percentage of occurrence) of whether its rank is of primary importance (i.e., whether it is the first, or second, or nth response regardless of percentage), Mednick and Halpern (1962) presented subjects with concepts whose average rank varied (Rank 1 versus Rank 2) but whose absolute value was constant. Using the Underwood and Richardson guessing paradigm, results showed that rank was a significant variable independent of, and probably more important than, absolute percentage. Subjects learned Rank 1 concepts considerably more rapidly than Rank 2 concepts, despite the fact that their absolute probabilities were equal.

The results of all these experiments are clear in supporting the view that mediational responses (as indexed by the Underwood and Richardson technique) do have profound and predictable effects on concept acquisition. The critical problem now remains. How is this effect to be understood, and will such an analysis give rise to novel experiment predictions?

Perhaps the easiest way in which to conceptualize the process is to reconsider Osgood's initial analysis, that each stimulus word evokes a mediating response, and these responses tie together originally separate stimuli. If this analysis is correct, it should be possible to vary certain aspects of how the material is presented, and these variations should affect the ease with which a concept is learned.

One factor that Underwood (1952) early specified as of importance in concept learning was contiguity of instances; that is, all things being equal, the closer together in time two examplars are in initial presentation, the more likely it is that a common concept will be recognized. In order to test this prediction, Schulz, Miller, and Radtke (1963) presented subjects with 6 concepts: two of high dominance, two of medium dominance, and two of low dominance. Three levels of contiguity were also defined, with high-contiguity lists prepared so that all 4 instances of a given concept occurred in succession, with medium-contiguity lists having 2 of the 4 instances occur together, and with the low-contiguity list having no 2 instances of the same concept occur together. Schulz, Miller, and Radtke's results were exactly as expected on the basis of Underwood's hypothesis; both increases in dominance and in instance contiguity were shown to have obvious and significant effects on concept recognition.

One of the real tests of whether a subject has a particular concept or not is to test his ability to solve new problems involving that concept. This is exactly what Greeno and Scandura (1966) did with the Underwood–Richardson materials. In their experiment they had subjects first learn a 12-item list containing only 3 different response terms. Each term was the correct response for a different set of 4 stimulus words. One of the sets contained 4 words representing a single concept such as *earthworm, freckle, tweezer, grasshopper* —(*small*). A second set contained two words representing a single concept, *paste, sheep* (*white*), while a third set contained a single word representing a single concept, *globe* (*round*). In order to make up the 12-item list, subjects were given one presentation of each item in the 4-item concept, two presentations of each item in the 2-item concept group, and four presentations of each item in the 1-item concept group. All subjects were told that all stimulus items were related to one another because they often produced similar descriptive adjectives such as *white* or *big*, etc.

After each subject was able to give 3 correct recitations of the training list, he was next asked to learn a second list containing 6 items. Three of these items involved stimulus terms from the same concept as occurred in the training list, while 3 did not evoke any concept contained in the training list. The first set of 3 pairs was tested for concept transfer, while the remaining set of 3 pairs served as a control. All subjects were tested until they reached a criterion of 5 correct recitations of the list. During this phase of the experiment, subjects were told that some of the pairs in the test list might be related in the same way that pairs in the training list were related.

The results showed that the 3 transfer items were learned more rapidly than the 3 control items. The greatest amount of transfer occurred for the 4-item concept pairs, whereas the least amount of transfer occurred for the 1-item concept pairs. The most important aspect of Greeno and Scandura's results, however, was that there were marked differences between those transfer pairs subjects were able to get correct on the first transfer trial and those transfer pairs subjects were unable to anticipate on the first transfer trial. Basically, Greeno and Scandura argued that two hypotheses are possible concerning transfer concepts: a first-trial hypothesis and a continuing-opportunities hypothesis. The first-trial hypothesis assumes that a subject will produce transfer to the degree that he recognizes a common aspect between learning and transfer on the first trial. If a common aspect is not recognized, then no transfer occurs and subjects show similar learning rates for transfer and control items. A continuing-opportunities hypothesis assumes that transfer pairs are learned more readily than control pairs largely because they have certain subthreshold connections with the concept mediator that will be strengthened more readily than control pairs which have no such connections.

The results of this experiment strongly favored the first-trial hypothesis. When Greeno and Scandura divided up the transfer pairs into those that were correctly anticipated on Trial 1 and those that were not, they found that the second group of transfer items produced learning results identical to those produced by control items. That is, if a subject failed to show positive transfer on Trial 1, his learning statistics were exactly the same as if he had not had experience on the training list. In this situation then, it seems that when concept transfer does occur, it occurs in an all-or-none fashion on the first transfer trial. Either the subject recognizes the appropriate mediator during transfer or he does not; if he does, he shows positive transfer, and if not, he shows no concept transfer at all.

## Mediation and Creativity

The results of many of these earlier experiments led one of Underwood's former students (Mednick, 1962) to propose a theory of creativity based on a mediational analysis of thinking. As an illustration of the type of task used by Mednick, consider the following three sets of items and see if there is one word that "makes sense" in conjunction with all the members of a given set.

| | | | |
|---|---|---|---|
| Set 1 | *railroad* | *girl* | *class** | _____ |
| Set 2 | *surprise* | *line* | *birthday* | _____ |
| Set 3 | *wheel* | *electric* | *high* | _____ |
| Set 4 | *out* | *dog* | *cat* | _____ |

What Mednick argues, and quite persuasively at that, is that creativity can be defined as the ability of a subject to produce novel connections among originally disparate or remote elements. Mednick's test, the Remote Association Test (abbreviated *RAT*), meets this criterion in part by requiring subjects to come up with a novel response that ties together three seemingly unrelated words. This sort of technique was suggested to Mednick both by a mediational analysis of concept formation and by some informal statements made by acknowledged creative scientists on how they go about "training" for creative thought. One of the scientists, a physicist, said that he found it particularly helpful to pick terms at random from the back of an introductory physics book and attempt to relate items selected on this basis to some single

---

* The correct responses for Sets 1–4, respectively, are *working, party, chair* or *wire, house.*

common idea.  If Mednick's analysis of the associative basis of the creative process is correct, what this physicist was trying to do was to find a mediating element capable of making a novel combination of concepts.

But what factors are involved in solving $RAT$ word problems?  Here Mednick assumes that one of the major factors involved is the degree to which a subject can provide a large number of uncommon word associations in response to a particular stimulus word.  If a subject is able to provide only a few stereotyped responses, then the probability is quite small that he will be able to come up with a single element capable of fitting any set of 3 words.  In general, Mednick believes that the $RAT$ provides "stimulus items from two mutually distant realities and asks the subject to 'draw a spark from their juxtaposition.'"  (Mednick, 1962, page 227.)

Since Mednick's approach is an extremely attractive one, it seems reasonable to ask whether there are any data supporting this analysis of the creative process.  The best confirmation is provided by an early piece of research done by Mednick at the University of California.  A group of graduate students in architecture and psychology were rated by their professors as to their "creative potential" and subsequently given an extended form of the $RAT$ described earlier.  Since intelligence (particularly verbal intelligence) may be expected to correlate with $RAT$ performance, the correlation between these two factors was first determined before correlations between ratings of creativity and $RAT$ performance were carried out.  In the case of intelligence and creativity, correlations were small and insignificant, while in the case of $RAT$ scores and creativity, correlations were substantial and impressive.  All in all, these results lend some plausibility to Mednick's analysis: People who are able to solve $RAT$ problems are often rated as highly creative by their supervisors.

A slightly different way of looking at creativity—although one that has much in common with Mednick's approach—is described by William J. J. Gordon in his book, *Synectics*.  The word *synectics* is a neologism based on the Greek, meaning the fitting together of diverse elements, and it is this process, according to Gordon, which is at the heart of a creative act.  Synectics theory is also a practical theory, and as such is concerned with the integration of diverse individuals into a problem-stating, problem-solving group under the assumption that it is possible to make "conscious use of the psychological mechanisms present in man's creative activity."  (Gordon, 1961.)

With this assumption in mind, Gordon and his coworkers examined the biographies and autobiographies of a number of creative people, as well as reports of people in the process of invention.  With this analysis as a starting point, the synectics group has gone on to develop procedures designed to help groups come to creative solutions.  Basically, these procedures involve making the strange familiar (understanding the problem as given, with all its various ramifications) and making the familiar strange (taking the problem and distorting, inverting, and transposing it so that it can be viewed from a new angle). A number of procedures are suggested in order to make the familiar strange; the most important are:

1. *Personal analogy*, in which the inventor tries to become one of the objects looked at so that he can feel, think, and act as that object. This goes beyond mere role-playing, in that the inventor is encouraged to be an inanimate, as well as an animate, object or being.
2. *Direct analogy*, in which the inventor attempts to compare parallel facts, knowledge, or technology. In problem-stating, problem-solving situations, analogies from the biological sciences appear to be the most fruitful.
3. *Symbolic analogy*, in which the inventor tries to develop a compressed description of the function or elements of the problem. It is the poetic response that sums up what has been said in the personal- and direct-analogy phases.

Actual problem solving is done in a group, with different group members entering into the different mechanisms at any or all points. The account of creative problem solving involves nine phases.

1. *Problem as given* (assuming the problem is given)
2. *Making the strange familiar*
3. *Problem as understood*—isolating for examination all the various bits of the problem
4. *Operational mechanisms*: The analogies or metaphors described above are evoked and related to the problem as understood. This phase pushes and pulls the problem as understood out of its rigid form of impregnable regularity into a form that offers some conceptual fingerholds. These fingerholds open up the problem as understood.
5. *The familiar made strange*: The problem as understood is seen as though never seen before, i.e., as something foreign.
6. *Psychological states*: The psychological states described above are reached, so that the proper psychological climate for creative activity is brought into being.
7. *States integrated with problem*: The most pertinent analogy is conceptually compared with the problem as understood.
8. *Viewpoint*: The comparison in the preceding step is analyzed to see whether this viewpoint is leading to a technical insight into the problem.
9. *Solution or research target*: The viewpoint is reduced to practice in terms of testing the underlying principle.

Although the whole synectic process sounds like a magical, ritualistic incantation designed to summon the goddess Creativity, it nonetheless has been shown to work in industrial and business settings. In these settings the standard of evaluation was the development of a new or improved product or invention, and in most cases, synectic groups have provided superior solutions. Whether or not the entire process sounds strange (or familiar), it does seem to produce creative results, and that, after all, is the name of the game.

### Reversal and Nonreversal Shifts

Another way in which mediational processes have been investigated involves reversal and nonreversal concept shifts in animals and human beings (Kendler and Kendler, 1962; 1964). Perhaps the simplest way of explaining the differences between the two is in terms of Kendler's own diagram, presented in Fig. 5.2 on the opposite page.

Basically, Kendler's experiment requires the subject (rat or human) to learn two successive discriminations involving stimuli that vary in at least four different ways. Thus, in Fig. 5.2, for example, the stimuli vary in terms of being large or small and black or white. In the initial discrimination task, experimental subjects are required always to pick the larger object in each set of pairs. If the second task involves a reversal shift, the required discrimination is exactly the reverse of what it was in the first problem; that is, the small stimulus is now correct in each set of pairs. If the second task is a nonreversal shift, the other dimension, irrelevant to the task up to that point, now becomes the basis of a correct solution. For a nonreversal shift, black is now correct, whereas size (large or small) is now irrelevant. In the nonreversal case, one of the previously correct stimuli, the large black square, is still correct, while one of the previously incorrect stimuli, the small white square, is still incorrect. On this basis, nonreversal shifts involve a change in response to only 2 of the 4 stimuli, whereas reversal shifts require a change in response to all 4 stimuli.

In absolute terms then, nonreversal shifts seem to require a smaller change in behavior than complete reversal shifts, and perhaps might be thought of as easier to accomplish. Although the type of problem described in Fig. 5.2 is an extremely simple one, reversal-shift problems can be arranged at any level of difficulty. In practice, Kendler and his associates have employed a wide variety of stimuli and a wide variety of organisms, with the latter variation producing rather interesting results. In this latter case, results indicate a striking difference between humans and animals: Humans find reversal shifts relatively easier than nonreversal shifts (Kendler and Kendler, 1962); whereas animals find nonreversal shifts relatively easier (Tighe, 1964).

The reason for this difference seems to be that rats are able to learn only direct, one-level connections between stimulus properties and responses. Therefore, when they are required to perform in a reversal shift, 4 habits must

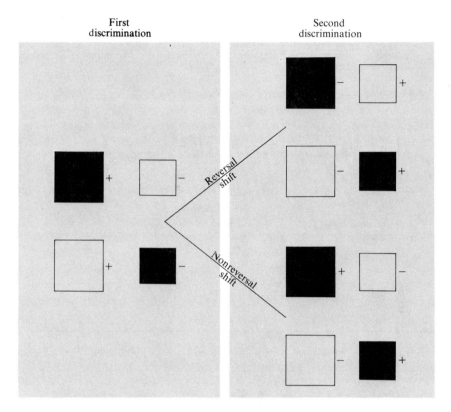

**Fig. 5.2** Examples of reversal and nonreversal shifts in discrimination learning. In a reversal shift, after learning to select the large stimuli in the first discrimination, the subject is reinforced for selecting the small stimuli in the discrimination. In a nonreversal shift, he is required to respond to another dimension (brightness) in the second discrimination. (From *Basic Psychology*, second edition, by H. H. Kendler, New York: Meredith Corporation, 1968.)

be extinguished and 4 new ones acquired. This is in contrast to a nonreversal shift condition in which only 2 of the 4 responses must first be extinguished and then relearned. Human subjects, on the other hand, find reversal shifts easier because all they have to do in this case is reverse the connection between the internal mediator $r_m$–$s_m$ and the overt response $R$. In the case of a non-reversal shift, an entirely new mediator has to be learned and the old one abandoned. If we take the large-small, black-white example already described, a diagram of the ongoing processes in an adult subject might look something like the table on the following page.

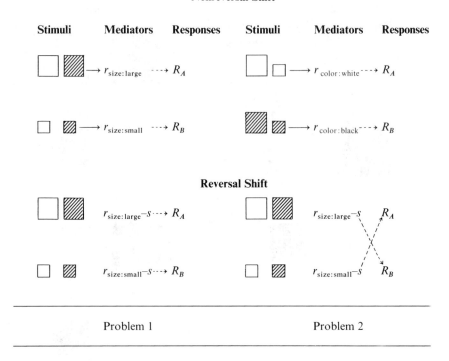

Problem 1                                    Problem 2

On this basis, then, it is possible to see that the reversal shift simply requires a switch of S–R (actually (r–s)—R) connections, while the non-reversal shift requires a complete change in mediators and the establishment of an entirely new set of S–R connections.

If this analysis is correct, and if the crucial mediational event is the ability to provide a label for the relevant dimension, we should expect differences in performance between young children (who are unable to label dimensions easily) and older children (who have little difficulty in defining dimensions). This conjecture has been tested experimentally (Kendler, Kendler, and Learnard, 1962). Results indicate that up to about the age of 5 children perform more efficiently on nonreversal shifts, but that from 6 on, their behavior more closely approximates that of adult subjects. It is also true that when kindergarten children, ages 4–6, are told to try to use words describing the stimuli in the experiment, their ability to execute a reversal shift increases (Kendler, 1964). This seems to suggest that the critical mediating event in this type of task is a verbal label of some sort, probably one capable of reflecting the salient properties of the stimulus.

## Stimulus Factors, Mediational Responses, and their Interaction

One obvious aspect of concept-formation studies is that they involve different types of stimulus materials, and for this reason it is necessary to determine the relationship of the exemplars used to the ease with which a concept is learned. The classic set of studies dealing with this problem was done by Heidbreder (1946a, 1946b, 1947) and the particular stimuli employed in her experiments are presented in Fig. 5.3.

**Fig. 5.3**  Drawings used in experiments on concept formation.  Each drawing is an example of a concept.  The concept itself is named by a nonsense word.  The concept "manks" (sixes), for example, is exemplified by the six stars or six wavy lines.  (After Heidbreder, 1946)

In this experiment each picture represents a concept exemplar to which a nonsense-syllable label had to be attached. The nonsense names, as in the original Hull study, were attached to a group of pictures all having a common characteristic. All *relks*, for example, were faces, whether these were full-face or side-view or whatever. The dependent measure used in this particular experiment was the average number of repetitions required before a subject could provide an appropriate concept name to a newly presented picture. Since new exemplars of a class were always being presented, the only way this problem could be solved was by learning some response (concept) that did not depend on a specific concept exemplar. In terms of the materials used, Heidbreder found that it took the smallest number of trials to learn "object concepts" such as *birds*, *hats*, and *faces*, that it took a somewhat greater number of trials to learn "form concepts" (circles, V forms, and T forms), and an even greater number to learn "number concepts" (6, 4, and 3 items). Heidbreder interpreted these results to mean that subjects find it easiest to form concrete concepts, and more difficult to form abstract ones.

Now although this is an extremely interesting hypothesis—that concrete concepts are more easily acquired than abstract ones—a number of experimenters (Dattman and Israel, 1951; Osgood, 1953; and Baum, 1954) have disagreed with this interpretation, suggesting instead that Heidbreder's results could be more easily interpreted in terms of the explicitness of the exemplars used as well as in terms of the relative dominance of the mediational responses evoked by these exemplars. Dattman and Israel, for example, presented subjects with concrete concepts (such as *birds*), in which the individual exemplars involved either a picture of a bird alone or a picture in which a bird was presented in conjunction with other distracting items. Subjects were then run through a procedure similar to Heidbreder's and showed considerably more rapid acquisition for *bird-alone* than for *bird-plus-distractors*. By this same procedure Dattman and Israel were able to show that subjects learned numerical concepts much more easily if the items used involved concrete objects rather than meaningless forms.

From the mediational point of view, Osgood (1953) has argued that although a picture of a face (such as those used in the original Heidbreder experiments) is quite likely to arouse the response *face* or something similar to it, a picture of six stars is more likely to arouse the (incorrect) response *star* or *stars* than the (correct) response *six*. In other words, Heidbreder's results are probably best accounted for in terms of the immediacy or dominance of the mediational response evoked by the specific exemplars used.

There is still another way in which to consider the interaction of stimulus factors and mediation in concept learning. This involves an attempt to describe the role of relevant and irrelevant stimulus attributes in concept attainment. In the usual concept-formation task involving nonword stimuli, such items often differ in a number of ways. For example, stimuli can be red or green, large or small, triangular or square, and so on. Each of these characteristics defines an attribute or dimension of the stimulus—color, size, and shape, respectively, in the examples presented above—and each specific characteristic (large or small, red or green, etc.) defines a value ($V$) of that dimension ($D$). If there are 3 dimensions with 2 values for each dimension, there are eight possible patterns, with the general form of the equation: number of patterns $= V^D$. If some of the possible patterns are missing, as for example in the case where there are no small, red triangles, 1 of the 8 possible alternatives is removed and the total number of possible patterns reduced by one. Similarly, if all red objects are always large and all green objects are always small, then large green patterns and small red ones do not exist. This, in turn, implies that the size of the stimulus is perfectly predictable from its color (and vice versa, of course). Under this latter condition it is possible to say that either color or size is redundant; that is, extra or not required for concept solution.

Given the use of such stimuli, redundancy can be defined in two ways: either in terms of the number of missing (nonexistent) patterns or in terms of the number of redundant attributes such as size and color. Thus redundancy increases both as the total number of patterns decreases and as the number of overlapping attributes increases.

In his book on human conceptual behavior, Bourne (1966) has organized and summarized much of the research done on the role of redundant and nonredundant stimulus attributes and their effects on concept formation. Figure 5.4 presents such results as there are.

The $X$-axis in the figure is to be understood as the number of different relevant (redundant) dimensions used in a particular task. What this means, in the present context, is that as the number of relevant and redundant dimensions increases, subjects make fewer errors in sorting specific exemplars into concepts. Figure 5.4, however, also presents a family of four curves, with each of these curves representing the role of nonredundant, irrelevant dimensions in concept attainment. As these later results clearly indicate, subjects have considerably more difficulty in sorting stimulus items into conceptual groupings as the number of irrelevant dimensions increases.

How might these results be interpreted? In terms of the mediational analysis offered earlier, it is clear that a large number of irrelevant dimensions produces a large number of irrelevant mediational responses. Because of this, subjects have great difficulty in discriminating among relevant and irrelevant dimensions and their associated mediators—hence difficult concept attainment. A similar analysis (in reverse, of course) accounts for the facilitative role of relevant, redundant dimensions in concept formation. As the number of correlated dimensions increases, more of the pool of mediating responses aroused are correct; therefore fewer discriminations need be made. In this case, any correlated dimension (or mediator) is correct, and only a small

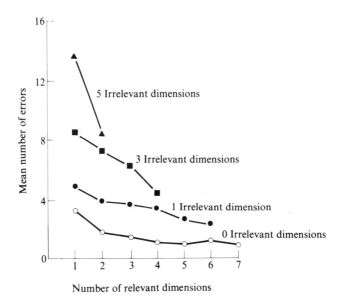

**Fig. 5.4** Mean number of errors made by subjects prior to solving the problem. Performance improves as number of redundant relevant dimensions increases and number of nonredundant irrelevant dimensions decreases. (Data from Bourne and Haygood, 1959, 1961.)

number of discriminations are required.  Hence rapid concept attainment.

These results, on the role of relevant and irrelevant nonverbal dimensions in concept formation, offer some point of comparison with similar studies involving words and similar materials.  In these earlier studies by Underwood and his associates (1957), verbal materials were used in which the relevant mediators aroused by concept exemplars were to some extent ambiguous; that is, they did not allow the subject to distinguish among the to-be-learned concepts.  For example, if a subject saw the words *baseball, snow, teeth,* and *rock,* there are at least two and perhaps three different sensory dimensions that could apply: *white, hard,* and *round.*  Since these particular words produce so many "irrelevant" responses, i.e., white exemplars may/may not be either hard or round, subjects should have more difficulty in learning these concepts than in learning concepts that do not have a great many irrelevant or confusing aspects.

In order to test this hypothesis, Underwood constructed three different lists, each containing 11 exemplars of 4 different concepts.  For List 0 there was no overlap in mediators; for List 1 all exemplars had exactly one confusing mediator; while for List 2, the average overlap was equal to about 1.9

mediators. Subjects were tested under the Underwood–Richardson procedure (see p. 105ff for a description of this procedure) and results indicated that List 0 was considerably easier to learn than either List 1 or 2, although there were no significant differences between these latter lists.

These results, taken in conjunction with those on irrelevant dimensions in nonverbal tasks, provide a consistent family of data. In all cases, increases in the number of irrelevant dimensions serve to make the concept-learner's task that much more difficult, and thereby retard successful performance. In all cases, this difficulty is one of deciding which of the many mediators evoked is the correct (most useful) mediator for that task. Once the learner is able to discriminate the correct mediator, he is well on his way to successful concept attainment.

## Response Factors and the Problem of Awareness

One of the most frequently used experimental procedures followed in studies of concept learning requires the subject to sort cards into one, two, or more different groupings. That is, a series of cards is shown to the subject one at a time and he is required to indicate whether this card is or is not an example of a particular concept. In principle, this is no different from the Hullian situation, except that in the Hullian case the subject is required to learn a nonsense syllable as a discriminative response to each stimulus. Indeed, in one experiment (Richardson and Bergen, 1954), subjects spent most of their time remembering which nonsense syllable went with which concept instance and very little time in mastering the concept. In some cases, then, it would seem easier and better to use the simpler sorting procedure so as to reduce this irrelevant aspect of procedure.

If we accept the card-placing procedure as a good one for studying concept formation, it seems reasonable to ask what the subject is doing while the experimenter is presenting the cards. One obvious thing that subjects do during the course of an experiment is to "talk to themselves." They try to figure out either what the task is about, or what the experimenter wants, or what they plan to do with any given card. If, however, the subject only talks to himself, then the experimenter is left out, and may miss some of the more significant determiners of the subject's behavior, conceptual or otherwise. When verbal reports are used in an experimental situation, the experimenter is not usually interested in them for their own sake, but rather because they provide some insight into whether the subject is aware of the purpose, nature, or aims of the procedure or experiment.

In an attempt to explore the area systematically, Verplanck and his students (Verplanck, 1962; Oskamp, 1956; Rilling, 1956) tried to determine the relationships of one measure of concept attachment—correct placement of concept cards—to the verbal statement—the hypotheses—of the bases on which subjects said such placements were accomplished.  Since these studies were done under the aegis and guidance of research growing out of the operant-conditioning laboratory, a good deal of the terminology used to describe what goes on in simpler situations (rats pressing bars and pigeons pecking keys) was transferred to concept learning in the hope of showing that many of the same variables operating in simpler situations also operate in more complex ones.  For this reason, telling a subject "right" or "wrong" after his response is equated with reinforcement, and telling a subject "wrong" four times out of ten when he is in fact right is equated with a "partial reinforcement" schedule.  Whether or not such transfer is justified can be evaluated only in regard to the results produced.  For this reason, let us now look at these experiments in some detail.

In the major experiment done by Verplanck *et al.*, subjects were given a set of 110 children's playing cards as stimuli and their job was to place the cards, one at a time, either to the right or left.  After the placement had occurred, student subjects were told "right" or "wrong."

There were three different groups of subjects: Group $P$; Group $Ph$ and Group $pH$, with the letters $P$ and $H$ standing for the words *placement* and *hypotheses*, respectively.  Before testing each subject, the experimenter decided on a "concept," i.e., all cards with one object on them go to the left and all cards with more than a single object go to the right, and subjects in the $P$ group were told "right" or "wrong" on each trial according to whether the card was placed correctly.  Subjects in the $Ph$ group were also treated in accordance with this procedure, except that they were asked to tell the experimenter, on each trial, the rule followed in placing the card.  Such statements of hypotheses were to be made prior to card placement.  Subjects in the $pH$ group were treated in exactly the same manner as subjects in the $Ph$ group, except that they were told "right" or "wrong" for their statement of the hypothesis rather than for their placement of the cards—hence $H$ for this group and $h$ for the other group.  For all groups, reinforcement ("right" or "wrong") was administered after card placement.

The experiment was broken down into two phases: In Part 1 all subjects under all conditions were run to a criterion of 10 correct placements and always received reinforcement for each correct response.  This was true for all groups.  In Part 2, the subjects were still told "wrong" when, in fact, they were wrong, but were only told "right" 6 times out of every block of 10 correct responses, and were told "wrong" for 4 of 10—in other words, subjects were put on a "partial-reward schedule" during Part 2.  All reinforcements were of the criterion response: That is, in Groups $Ph$ and $P$, rewards were contingent on placements, not hypotheses; while for Group $pH$, rewards were contingent on hypotheses, not placements.

For all groups, there was no significant difference in trials to acquisition during Part 1.  The more important data, however, concern the subjects' performance during Part 2. All three groups during Part 2 produced about 73 % correct placements, and did not differ in this regard. Table 5.2, however, presents the results for hypothesis-making behavior.

**Table 5.2** Percent correct hypotheses produced during part 2

| Category of rule | Group | |
|---|---|---|
| | *pH* | *Ph* |
| Correct | 94 % | 48 % |
| Incorrect | 6 % | 52 % |

The results presented in this table make it quite clear that subjects in the *Ph* group were able to state the correct hypothesis, or some acceptable variation thereof, only about 48 % of the time, while subjects in the *pH* group stated the rule correctly about 94 % of the time. What this means, when we take these data in conjunction with those on correct placement (about 73 % for both groups), is that about 25 % of the time (73–48) subjects in the *Ph* group were able to place the card correctly but were unable to state the correct rule, while subjects in the *pH* group found themselves able to state the correct rule 21 % of the time (94–73) more than they were able to place the card correctly.

Now these are most interesting results, for they show that subjects are able to dissociate their statements of intention (i.e., their rules) from their actual performance, and this leads, of course, to the question of whether or not the verbal report is a valid index of a subject's intentions, or, more generally, whether or not the verbal report is a valid experimental indicator of the presumed underlying state of "awareness" which presumably guides a subject's performance. The results of this work led Verplanck to conclude somewhat dramatically: "As an experimental strategy, then, let us remain unaware of awareness, but let us diligently ask the subject what he is or 'thinks' he is doing, and let us ... determine how such verbal statements behave, and, in turn, how they are related to—sometimes control—other ongoing activities." (Verplanck, 1962, page 157.)

The upshot of this experiment seems to be that awareness and verbal report can not be considered synonymous in all contexts. In many cases, they may be; but this is not always necessarily so. Although under some circumstances it may be profitable to remain unaware of awareness as Verplanck suggests, his own strategy seems more sensible: Examine the conditions under which verbal and nonverbal behaviors are correlated, and accept neither the placement response nor the verbal statement of the background conditions as *the* more critical event. Experimentally, both placements and hypothesis are responses of a single subject, and their correlation or lack of correlation is an empirical rather than a definitional problem.

Although Verplanck's arguments concerning the haphazard use of the term awareness seem well taken, it remained for Dulaney and O'Connell (1963) to clarify what was going on in the original Verplanck and Oskamp studies. Basically Dulaney and O'Connell argued that some of the cards used by Verplanck and Oskamp were not completely unambiguous. For example, if the correct rule (hypothesis) was that "pictures with one item go to the right and pictures with more than one item go to the left," a picture containing a vase with a bunch of flowers in it is ambiguous. That is, there is only one object in the picture (the vase with flowers) but there are many flowers—hence it is unclear whether or not the picture contains one or many items. If a subject were to consider the vase and flowers as more than a single item and state the correct rule: "Pictures with one item go to the right," and then place the item to the left, they would show a correct hypothesis and an incorrect placement (since by Verplanck and Oskamp's criteria the vase with flowers was considered a single item).

Of the total cards used, Dulaney and O'Connell were able to show that about 15% of the cards were ambiguous in precisely this way. Since subjects in the group reinforced for correct hypothesis produced 92% correct hypotheses but only about 75% correct placements, this difference could be accounted for just about perfectly by the 15% discrepancy, that is, $92\% - 15\% = 77\%$, which is close to the 75% value actually observed.

Dulaney and O'Connell then turned their attention to the group reinforced for correct placements. For this group, results again showed about 75% correct placements, but only 50% correct hypotheses. Here Dulaney and O'Connell argued that on 50% of the cases in which subjects misstated the rule, they should still be able to get half the placements correct by chance alone. Therefore 50% (for correct hypotheses) $+ \frac{1}{2} \times 50\%$ (for incorrect placements) $= 50\% + 25\% = 75\%$, or only 2% different from the value of 73% actually observed in both experiments.

There is one additional conclusion that can be drawn from these studies, particularly where they bear on a theory of awareness: Subjects who were reinforced for hypothesis-stating (Group $pH$) were extremely careful (correct about 92% of the time) about their hypotheses, while subjects who were not reinforced for hypothesis-stating (Group $Ph$) were not very careful (correct only about 50% of the time) about their hypothesis. Conversely, subjects who were reinforced for correct placements almost never misplaced an ambiguous card, whereas subjects who were not reinforced for correct placements misplaced ambiguous cards about 17% of the time. Subjects paid attention to (were aware of?) those responses that produced reinforcement, whether such responses were placements or hypotheses. To be sure, people do what they say they intend to do, but the correlation is perfect only if reinforcement depends on both responses, or if there is no ambiguity in the task. Where there is ambiguity, selective reinforcement can serve to emphasize one or the other response, seemingly to the detriment of the noncontingent response.

## SUMMARY

Psychologists, like philosophers, have always found concepts a difficult concept to work with. Although we all have, or seem to have, a clear common-sense notion as to what is or is not a concept, our sureness vanishes if the matter is pursued critically. It turns out to be quite difficult to specify why we categorize yon animal as dog and not as cat, llama or furry child.

Despite the fact that a completely satisfactory definition of a concept is difficult to come by, theoretical and empirical principles are available to tackle this problem in an experimentally meaningful way. Concept formation is generally inferred from procedures wherein the subject is required to place certain stimuli in the same group, or to exclude certain stimuli from certain groups to which they might otherwise go. At the operational level, the first type of placing operation has much in common with studies of *stimulus and response generalization*, while in the latter case it has much in common with studies of *discrimination*.

Now there are two complementary ways in which to treat generalization and discrimination: One assumes that generalization among stimuli occurs because of physical similarity among exemplars, while the second assumes that such similarity can be expressed in terms of acquired or learned equivalences among items. The first of these depends on directly observable dimensions, while the second depends on covert mediational links among items. With verbal or conceptual materials, learned equivalences are obviously more significant.

Given this emphasis on mediational events in concept formation, an important next step concerns the measurement of these covert responses. One approach to this problem has been pursued by Underwood and Richardson. In these experiments, subjects have been asked to provide sense impressions for a number of different words. Some of the words produce similar mediating words (i.e., *tooth, snow, rice—white*) quite easily, and a good deal of research work has shown that the relative dominance of these mediating words has a strong effect on how easily a subject is able to come up with the required concepts. In other cases, however, the occurrence of a mediational response is purely hypothetical, although the conceptual and empirical network describing these relationships is quite well known. Much of this work concerns reversal and nonreversal problems studied so extensively by Howard and Tracy Kendler. For the reversal problem, subjects must be able to produce a verbal mediating response which describes the relevant dimensions of the problem. Research on children confirms the importance of these implicit verbal mediation responses in reversal problems: Where children have appropriate verbal responses available, they solve reversal shifts more readily; where children do not have appropriate verbal responses available, they solve nonreversal shifts more readily.

But there is still much to be learned about the verbal regulation of concept behavior, and this problem, although peripherally raised by the Kendlers, has been considered carefully by both Verplanck and Dulaney and their students. Verbal reports have often been taken, in and of themselves, as indications of a general mental state of awareness, with such "awareness" presumed to serve a regulating function in concept behavior. Although this is the usual case, both Dulaney's and Verplanck's experiment make it clear that under certain experimental conditions this correlation can be broken. Although the conclusion that hypotheses and placements can be dissociated seems too strong given Dulaney's reanalysis of the original Verplanck and Oskamp studies, it nonetheless is plausible to feel that reinforcement can come to emphasize verbal or placement responses differentially. Given this possibility, it is probably best not to use the general purpose term "awareness." Rather it seems much wiser to use the term "aware of" where this is always followed by a specific referent.

# CHAPTER 6

# PROBLEM SOLVING

If the major problem for an organism who would form concepts is to discover an appropriate mediator, then the major problem for an organism who would solve problems is to get the goal to occur at the start rather than at the finish of a behavioral episode. The logic of an $S-R$ analysis requires that behavior occur only in response to some stimulus or stimulus situation, and this poses a major problem for problem solving: How can the goal object or goal stimulus be both at the start and finish of a behavioral episode? Obviously, the goal object itself can only occur at the completion of a complicated behavior pattern and what is required at the start of the sequence is something like the "idea" of a goal. This then is the crux of the problem: How shall an anticipating and guiding idea be described in $S-R$ theory?

As is true of many concepts employed in contemporary associationistic analyses of mind, the original hypothesis concerning "anticipatory ideas" arose in connection with studies of a simpler organism, the rat. For the rat, the problem of anticipation, or goal direction, is seemingly simple, and it is extremely unlikely that an investigator would ask the rat for an introspective report. It is probably for this reason—the fear of being misled by an introspective report—that the maze proved to be so crucial in defining the psychological equivalent of a "guiding idea." In this enterprise the earlier classic work on conditioning by Pavlov was seen to provide guidance, for, after all, didn't Pavlov himself call the conditioned response a "psychic secretion?" From here it is but a short step to develop the more complete concept of an antedating goal response as the $S-R$ counterpart to the philosopher's guiding ideas.

The attempt to describe human problem solving in terms of processes first described in the rat has a long history. For example, John B. Watson, the founder of Behaviorism, often described human problem solving as conceptually similar to the trial-and-error behavior of a rat in a maze. But let's let Watson talk for himself:

> A colleague of mine came on a visit to stay in an apartment in which I had rooms. In a passage leading from the shower bath was a peculiar piece of apparatus standing near a sink. The essential features were a curved shallow nickel pan about twelve inches wide by twenty inches long; at

one end the pan had been bent in the form of a half circle, while at the other end the side pieces did not extend for the full width. The pan was mounted on a stand adjustable in height. Furthermore the pan itself was attached to the stand by a ball and socket joint. My friend had never seen anything like it and asked me what in the world it was. I told him I was writing a paper on thinking and pleaded with him to think his problem out aloud. He entered into the experiment in the proper spirit. I shall not record all of his false starts and returns but I will sketch a few of them. "The thing looks a little like an invalid's table, but it is not heavy, the pan is curved, it has side pieces and is attached with a ball and socket joint. It would never hold a tray full of dishes (*cul de sac*). The thing (return to starting point) looks like some of the failures of an inventor. I wonder if the landlord is an inventor. No, you told me he was a porter in one of the big banks down town. The fellow is as big as a house and looks more like a prize-fighter than a mechanic; those paws of his would never do the work demanded of an inventor (blank wall again)." This was as far as we got on the first day. On the second morning we got no nearer the solution. On the second night we talked over the way the porter and his wife lived, and the subject wondered how a man earning not more than $150 per month could live as our landlord did. I told him that the wife was a hairdresser and earned about eight dollars per day herself. Then I asked him if he did not see the sign "Hair-Dresser" on the door as we entered. The next morning after coming from his bath he said, "I saw that infernal thing again" (original starting point). "It must be something to use in washing or weighing the baby—but they have no baby (*cul de sac* again). The thing is curved at one end so that it would just fit a person's neck. Ah! I have it! The curve does fit the neck. The woman, you say, is a hairdresser and the pan goes against the neck and the hair is spread out over it." This was the correct solution. Upon reaching it there was a smile, a sign and an immediate turn to something else (the equivalent of obtaining food after search).*

In terms of contemporary problem-solving theory, however, the straight runway has been found to be more useful than the *T*-maze in providing theoretical principles. In a typical study involving a straight runway, the rat is started from one end of the alley with food placed at the other. Usually the rat is unable to see the food from the start box. Since the start box is small and confining, there is really no way for the rat to go but forward. Occasionally, the rat doesn't move forward but remains within the confines of the start box, where he either continues to be quiet or goes to sleep. Since the rat has usually been deprived of food for from 24–48 hours, he is not likely to sleep for long, and consequently he soon ventures out of the start box and

* From J. B. Watson, *Psychology from the Standpoint of a Behaviorist*. Philadelphia: J. B. Lippincott, 1924, pages 349–50.

down the alley. Although there are presumably all sorts of stimuli in the alley part of the runway, the only stimuli that are radically different from these occur in the vicinity of the goal box. These include both stimuli associated with the goal box and the goal stimulus object ($S_G$) itself. If deprivation has been sufficiently extended, and even if not, the goal object is "relevant" for the animal, and while under the influence of deprivation he may first sniff the food and then eat it. In a nondeprived state, however, he may only sniff it.

The act of consuming the $S_G$ is temporally coincidental with a rather circumscribed set of cues in the maze. These are the cues of the goal box itself: $S_{GB}$. Given these two sets of stimuli, $S_{GB}$ and $S_G$, with the second of these evoking eating behavior ($R_G$), the situation is ideal for classical conditioning to occur:

$$S_{GB} \searrow R_G$$
$$S_G \rightarrow R_G$$

After a number of pairings, $S_{GB}$ should come to evoke $R_G$ as a classically conditioned response; that is, $S_{GB} \rightarrow R_G$.

Although $R_G$ can be treated as a unitary response for some purpose, it really consists of a number of parts: grasping and moving the food object, chewing, salivating, swallowing, and so on. Some of these components require the actual presence of the stimulus object—i.e., grasping and moving—while other fractional components can be detached from the presence of the food object, with anticipatory salivation the most obvious example. Any one of these sets of fractional response components is often called a *fractional, detachable, antedating goal response*; *fractional* because it is a fractional component of the total *goal response*, *detachable* because it can be separated from the total complex aroused by the goal object, and *antedating* because as a conditional response it moves forward in time to precede an encounter with the goal object. The usual notation used for a fractional antedating response is $r_g$ to symbolize its intimate relationship with $R_G$ (the goal response itself). The lower-case letters simply indicate that such responses are hypothetical and not subject to direct observation.

The $r_g$ mechanism enters into problem solving in the following way: When the rat is returned to the start box on Trial 2, the pattern of available stimuli may be represented as in Fig. 6.1.

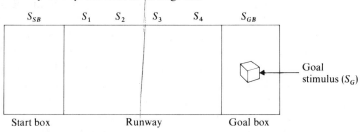

**Fig. 6.1**    Hypothetical pattern of stimuli available in a straight runway on Trial 2.

All the stimulus components in the situation, from start-box stimuli ($S_{SB}$) to goal-box stimuli ($S_{GB}$), as well as all those in between ($S_1$–$S_4$) are presented at the top of the figure. By Trial 2, $S_{GB}$ has been conditioned to produce both $R_G$ and $r_g$; therefore, $S_{GB} \rightarrow r_g$. On the basis of trace conditioning, stimuli $S_{SB}, S_1, S_2, S_3$, and $S_4$ are also weakly connected to $r_g$. Thus $S_{SB}$ also has a weak connection with $r_g$. More important than this, however, is the fact that $S_{SB}$ is similar in many important ways to $S_{GB}$. On the basis of stimulus generalization, $S_{SB}$ and $Ss_{1-4}$ also come to evoke $r_g$. Thus the actual chain of behavior includes the following connections:

$$S_{SB} \rightarrow r_g\text{--}s_g \rightarrow R_{run}, S_1 \rightarrow r_g\text{--}s_g \rightarrow R_{run}, S_2 \rightarrow r_g \cdots$$
$$S_3\text{--}r_g \cdots S_4\text{--}r_g \cdots S_G \rightarrow R_G.$$

That is, the stimuli of the start box evoke $r_g$'s and these in turn are cues for running; such running then brings about the next set of alley stimuli, $S_1$–$S_4$, which in turn evoke $r_g$ and overt running, until the rat is finally in the goal box; and there, large as life, is the food reward, $S_G$, which in its turn serves to evoke the consummatory response and a consequent increase in the strength of both $R_G$ and $r_g$. The picture can be complicated considerably with the inclusion of drive stimuli, although these are of little or no concern in human problem-solving situations.

Through the $r_g$–$s_g$ mechanism, the apparent goal-directedness of human behavior is handled in complete accord with the usual principles of conditioning and association. In more complex experimental situations this $r_g$ hypothesis, developed in the context of the maze, can be complicated, although its underlying logic remains essentially unchanged.

Given all this conceptual machinery, an analysis of problem solving is most conveniently treated in terms of problem situations and how previous responses transfer to these situations. The most comprehensive statement of this approach has been provided by Dashiell (1949) and Melton (1950), and we would do well to follow their outline. Melton begins by noting that a problem situation arises only under those conditions in which there is some definite goal state or object relevant to a performing organism. For a hungry rat, food could represent such a goal, whereas the correct solution would work for a human subject. In either case, some aspect of the behaving organism serves to define an element of the environment as relevant or not; and it is this relationship that is critical.

For a problem situation to exist—given the existence of an organism–goal relationship—there must be some barrier between the organism and the goal. In some cases the barrier may be a palpable, physical aspect of the environment such as a hurdle or a block; in other cases the idea of a barrier is used metaphorically to include incorrect response dispositions on the part of the performing organism. In the face of such barriers, the organism will try out habitually correct responses. If this is a genuine problem situation, such responses fail to attain the goal. The production of responses which do not lead to overcoming the barrier induces a motivational state in the organism ("frustration") which then leads to extinction of the originally dominant response and to trying out initially less frequent responses. Variable behavior of this type continues for a while—the subject keeps trying out a whole family of responses—until either one response proves successful and the barrier and the problem are overcome, or until the organism has no more alternative responses available and retreats from the situation. Figure 6.2 presents a diagram of this process, including a happy ending; namely response $R_c$, or that response capable of leading to a successful solution.

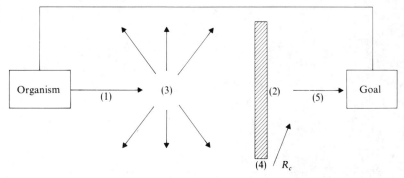

**Fig. 6.2**  The readjustive process. (From Dashiell, 1949, page 26.)

Is the diagram really far removed from reality? Enter Michele, aged 3, onto the scene. The scene involves Michele, a cookie jar, and a shelf. The cookie jar is on the shelf, and the shelf is 4 feet off the ground. Michele, stretched to her longest (tiptoes, arms stretched, all that) is only 3 feet 6 inches high, even giving her a few inches. Michele on the ground sees the cookie jar —goal object is now relevant—and so she walks over trying the direct approach. She raises her right arm $(R_1)$; it won't do; she raises her right arm and gets up on tiptoes $(R_2)$, no luck; she grasps some wall molding with her left hand, raises her right arm and jumps $(R_3)$. Almost, but no cigar. She goes to the corner of the room, brings a step stool, climbs up and gets her reward $(R_4$ or $R_c)$: Happiness is a newly filched cookie.

This situation and its accompanying diagram demonstrate a number of important principles in problem solving. Perhaps the most important concerns the period of variable behavior. During this period the subject (child, adult, or rat) tries out a variety of responses, some occurring early in the situation and others later. The fact that some responses appear more probable than others in a given problem situation suggests the hypothesis of a habit-family hierarchy; namely that the same situation is differentially likely to evoke responses $R_1$ through $R_n$. Such a situation, in which many different responses are given to a single stimulus, results in what is sometimes called a divergent hierarchy, and, in combination with its opposite number (the condition in which many different stimuli evoke the same response—the convergent hierarchy) is of great theoretical import for an $S$–$R$ analysis of problem-solving behavior.

Maltzman (1955) attempted to show how convergent and divergent habit mechanisms provide an underlying structure for many of the extremely complex habit-family hierarchies involved in human problem solving. An example of an extremely complicated hierarchy (although actually highly simplified) is presented in Fig. 6.3.

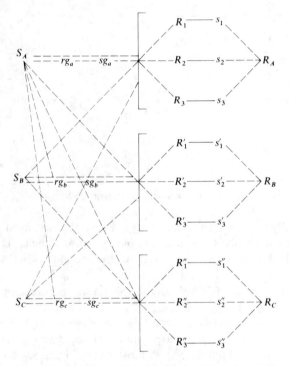

**Fig. 6.3** A compound habit-family hierarchy produced by a combination of habit-family hierarchies. (From Maltzman, 1955)

In this figure, $S_A$, $S_B$, and $S_C$ (external components of the problem situation) all give rise to their separate habit-family hierarchies as a divergent mechanism, while at the same time serving to evoke elements in two other convergent hierarchies. When such a compound hierarchy is formed, as by stimulus events $S_A$, $S_B$, and $S_C$, response $R_A$ (originally only elicitable by $S_A$) is also potentially elicitable by $S_B$ and $S_C$, as well as by their associated fractional anticipatory goal responses. If we, or Maltzman, are willing to make the diagram complicated enough, everything will have a potential connection with everything else, be these connections direct or mediated.

The consequence of this analysis is to show that there is a complex network of habits that serves to interconnect, to a greater or lesser extent, any one response with any other response. Thus, if a subject has available even one response that could solve a particular problem, there is always a potential network of interconnections between the present stimulus event and the required response. If the connection is direct, that is, $S_A \rightarrow R_{criterion}$, no problem exists; if there are a great many intervening steps capable of producing distracting "paths," then the problem is a difficult one and its solution often beyond the reach of the performing subject.

Armed with this type of analysis, we can consider problem solving—in principle—to be no different from other simpler kinds of stimulus–response processes, and, as in the case of memory, can view it as depending on transfer of response principles. In order to examine this approach in any detail, we must describe certain experimental situations in some detail. These situations, which were considered extremely difficult for association theory to handle when they were first proposed, can be categorized under three headings: *insight* problems, *water-jar* problems and *functional-fixity* problems.

## Insight Problems

In 1915 Wolfgang Kohler, then a young Gestalt psychologist, was visiting an anthropological field station on the island of Tenerife when the First World War broke out. Although Kohler had done work only on perceptual phenomena, his enforced vacation gave him an opportunity to study the mentality of apes in a variety of situations. The most useful of these involved an investigation that has come to be known as the two-stick problem: A banana is put behind a set of bars well out of reach. Although there are a number of usual implements in the problem environment, two hollow but firm bamboo sticks are the most important. These sticks have been selected so that one is larger than the other and so that the smaller of the two can easily be fitted into the larger. The banana, however, is well beyond the reach of even the larger of the two sticks, so that in order to get the banana, the subject has to put the two sticks together to form a single longer pole. Given this problem-setting and Kohler's smartest ape, Sultan, the scenario runs as follows:

> This time Sultan is the subject of the experiment. His sticks are two hollow, but firm, bamboo rods . . . . One is so much smaller than the other, that it can be pushed in at either end of the other quite easily. Beyond the bars lies the objective, just so far away that the animal cannot reach it with either rod . . . . Nevertheless, he takes great pains to try to

reach it with one stick or the other, even pushing his right shoulder through the bars. When everything proves futile, Sultan commits a "bad error," or, more clearly, a great stupidity . . . . He pulls a box from the back of the room towards the bars; true, he pushes it away again at once as it is useless, or rather, actually in the way. Immediately afterwards, he does something which, although practically useless, must be counted among the "good errors": He pushes one of the sticks out as far as it will go, then takes the second, and with it pokes the first one cautiously towards the objective . . . he pushes very gently, watches the movements of the stick that is lying on the ground, and actually touches the objective with its tip. Thus, all of a sudden, for the first time, the contact "animal-objective" has been established, and Sultan visibly feels (we humans can sympathize) a certain satisfaction in having even so much power over the fruit that he can touch it and slightly move it by pushing the stick.*

Kohler leaves the scene and the thread of the narrative is picked up by Sultan's caretaker:

Sultan first of all squats indifferently on the box, which has been left standing a little back from the railings: then he gets up, picks up the two sticks, sits down again on the box and plays carelessly with them. While doing this, it happens that he finds himself holding one rod in either hand in such a way that they lie in a straight line; he pushes the thinner one a little way into the opening of the thicker, jumps up and is already on the run towards the railings, to which he has up to now half turned his back, and begins to draw a banana towards him with the double stick. I call the master: meanwhile, one of the animal's rods has fallen out of the other, as he pushed one of them only a little way in the other: whereupon he connects them again.

There are two salient points that have been made in interpreting these (and other similar) results. The first of these concerns the role of perceptual organization in problem solving, while the second deals with the concept of insight. In his observations of Sultan and other apes, Kohler was struck by the fact that the animal often moved around a bit first and seemed to survey the perceptual field before making any overt movement. Thus Sultan sat on a box after failing in his first attempt to get the banana. Only after he inadvertently inserted one stick into the other did he act vigorously in attempting to go after, and, of course, secure the goal.

Kohler then goes on to suggest that when this happens the complex components of the total task have suddenly been seen in a new light—quite unpredictable from prior responses to the component elements—and that this

---

* From *The Mentality of Apes*, by W. Kohler, New York: Humanities Press, 1925.

new perspective (in both its perceptual and cognitive sense) allows for rapid and smooth attainment of the goal object. The unobservable cognitive condition that accompanies (indeed underlies) this dramatic shift in the direction of behavior is termed *insight*, and is thought to be the critical element in solving a problem.

Now these are significant observations and daring speculations which seem to challenge many of the basic tenets of $S-R$ association theory. For one, they see behavior as emergent; that is, not predictable from a knowledge of Sultan's responses to constituent parts of a situation. For another, the role of prior experience (learning) is minimized in favor of the hypothesis of an immediate reorganization of the perceptual field. And finally, the suddenness of the final correct performance is seen as evidence for this drastic perceptual cognitive reorganization. In short these results pose—and were meant by Kohler to pose—an explicit challenge to any associationistic interpretation of problem solving.

How did association theory respond to this challenge? The major experimental thrust of this response was aimed at showing the role of experience in problem solving and of uncovering the factors involved in the suddenness of problem solution. The major theoretical thrust was concerned with developing an appropriate extension of mediational principles to cover this situation. Perhaps the study most directly relevant to the role of past experience in problem-solving situations involving apes was performed by H. G. Birch in 1945. Birch, at that time, was associated with the Yerkes Laboratory of Primate Biology in Orange Park, Florida, and had on many occasions prior to the experiment observed his 6 chimpanzee subjects in their normal daytime activities. Only one chimp, Jojo, had ever been observed to play with sticks prior to the onset of the Kohler experiment; all the other chimps ordinarily never used sticks.

Birch made use of two different testing sessions, both employing a variety of tasks conceptually similar to those used by Kohler. In the first session, only Jojo was able to solve the problem set to him; all the other animals were unable to solve it in the time allotted (30 minutes). Following this initial experience, all the other chimps were allowed to play for three days with short straight sticks placed in their cage. During this play, chimps were observed to use the sticks in order to poke other chimps, to use them as prying instruments, and in many other situations. After this experience, all 5 chimps and Jojo were again exposed to the Kohler insight problem, with the result that all 6 were now able to solve the problem easily on their first try.

Although this certainly does argue against the view that past experience is irrelevant for problem solving, it does not necessarily refute Kohler's analysis. It is always possible to argue that a perceptual–conceptual reorganization occurred during the chimp's play with the sticks and that this reorganization transferred to the problem-testing situation. It is not so much a matter of transferring specific responses to the test situation as it is a matter of understanding the limits and uses of sticks. Given this new perspective, transfer to new situations is inevitable.

A different line of approach, however, has also been taken in analyzing the "sudden solution" aspect of insightful behavior. Stripped of all its complexities and connotations, insight is inferred whenever an organism exhibits a dramatic upswing in his ability to solve a particular problem or class of problems. In other words, an organism unable to solve the problem on Trial 1 is perfectly able to do so on Trial 2. In a two-choice problem, an insight analysis implies 50 % responding on Trial 1 and 100 % responding on Trial 2. A naive reading of association theories might suggest a gradual increment in the percentage of responses correct on Trial 2, with further progressive, but small, increments on Trials 3 and 4.

Perhaps the most significant attack on the problem of insight and its relationship to prior learning has been carried out by Harry Harlow and his associates at the University of Wisconsin under the general topic of learning-set formation (see Harlow, 1959, for a review of his earlier work). In these experiments a chimpanzee is presented with a pair of stimulus objects differing on a number of dimensions. These objects cover two foodwells of a test tray containing rewards such as raisins. These covering objects are shifted from left to right in a random but predetermined order for a single problem series of 6 trials. After this set of 6 trials, a new problem is introduced for another 6 trials, and so on for as many as 300 or more different problems. In some experiments monkeys have been able to complete as many as 14 problems a day, and this is kept up every day, sometimes for several months.

Harlow's justifiably famous graph of his early findings is presented in Fig. 6.4, in which results are plotted for each of the 6 within-problem trials after each of the monkeys had experienced a different number of problems.

The lowest curve (labeled Problems 1–8) traces the monkey's performance over 6 trials of the first 8 problems; while the topmost curve (Problems 201–312) traces the monkey's performance over the 6 trials of the last 111 problems. The most striking difference is, of course, in terms of the shape of the curve; the bottom curve exhibits a gradual and roughly S-shaped form, while the top one exhibits a dramatic upsurge between Trials 1 and 2.

These data give an empirical result of wide generality: Insightful solutions to a class of problems develop gradually as a consequence of repeated experience with a wide variety of problem situations. The point made by Kohler—that under certain circumstances sudden and dramatic solutions are possible—is not denied or contradicted by these data; what *is* suggested is that, if the past history of an organism is controlled, then the "nonpredictable" and "emergent" solution to a problem is neither nonpredictable nor emergent. Quite the contrary, insight builds cumulatively.

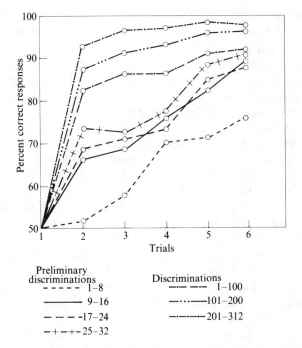

**Fig. 6.4** Family of learning set curves. (From Harlow, 1949)

But if it is not sudden perceptual reorganization, what sort of learning is involved, and is such learning interpretable in associationistic terms? Here again, Harlow's analysis is cogent and to the point: What the organism learns is not *how to respond* but rather *how not to respond* to irrelevant properties of the stimuli presented. That is, if oddity is the criterial attribute for problem solution, the monkey has to learn to inhibit his responses to such specific and irrelevant attributes as size, color, shape, etc. Suppression of these irrelevant dimensions then leaves the organism's choice of behavior solely under the control of the correct (relevant) attribute. Contrary to many other associationistic theories, which stress the incremental or growth aspects of habit formation, Harlow stresses the gradual elimination of inappropriate responses which compete initially with the correct or problem-solving response.

### Water-Jar Problems

Gestalt psychologists often see their role as that of gadfly. No sooner has the diligent S–R psychologist been able to resolve, at least to his own satisfaction, a problem set by Gestalt psychology, than another demonstration is produced designed to cause embarrassment. With the insight problem somewhat out of the way (or at least tucked into a familiar side corner), the difficult problem of set, as embodied in water-jar problems, comes into focus. Is there no end to the problems of $S-R$ psychology?

Water-jar problems are deceptively simple in appearance. The subject is presented with a series of problems, either physically or symbolically, involving 3 different water jars, $A$, $B$, and $C$, each of known capacity. All the problems contained in a given set of problems are presented in the same way: Given that jar $A$ has a capacity of 21 quarts, jar $B$ a capacity of 127 quarts, and jar $C$ a capacity of 3 quarts, how is it possible to use the jars so as to obtain 100 quarts? The solution to this problem is presented by the equation: solution $= B - A - 2C$. After 6 problems are presented, which can be solved in exactly this way, subjects are presented with the following seventh problem: Jar $A$ holds 23 quarts; jar $B$, 49; and jar $C$, 3; and the required solution to 20 quarts. Obviously the $B - A - 2C$ solution will work here as well, but so too will the much simpler solution, $A - C$.

In Luchins' (1942) demonstration experiment—an experiment which has been repeated an almost infinite number of times in introductory psychology classes—the usual result is that at least 55% of the subjects tested solve the seventh problem by the rather laborious procedure $B - A - 2C$. In Luchins' experiment, four of his subjects were given the phrase "Don't be blind" to write down just before they tried the seventh problem. In 5 of 8 cases, that is, on two different sets of problems, some subjects did in fact use the simpler solution. Luchins felt on this basis that his suggestion reduced the tendency to use a habitual mode of response. Similarly, if a subject was presented with Problem 7 as his first problem, he would tend to use the simple $A - C$ solution and not the more complicated $B - A - 2C$ one.

This then is the classic demonstration. How is it to be interpreted in terms of association theory? Schulz (1960) has argued that these results can be explained in terms of negative transfer of training. The basis of this negative transfer, so Schulz argues, is in the sequence of events to which subjects in these experiments were exposed, and in the particular responses they learned. Thus Schulz argues that the total sequence, $B - A - 2C$, constitutes a single response in the sense that any movement on the part of an organism is a response; and it is this compound response that is acquired during initial learning (Problems 1–6). Such a response, or, more appropriately, such a response chain, interferes with the more efficient, and simpler, solution possible for the seventh problem.

If this analysis is correct, then a number of predictions can be made: One is that as the number of set-inducing problems increases, so too should the tendency to produce the habitual $B - A - 2C$ response. This has been demonstrated to be the case for the water-jar problem (Tresselt and Leeds, 1953), as well as for short arithmetic problems (Youtz, 1948) and anagram problems (Maltzman and Morrisett, 1952).

A second and perhaps experimentally more useful way in which to show that procedures which affect simple responses also affect the more complicated $B - A - 2C$ responses required by Luchins' problems is provided in an experiment by Gardner and Runquist (1958). In this experiment, 3 different groups of subjects were presented with either 6, 11, or 21 different water-jar problems that could be solved only by the $B - A - 2C$ solution. After the predetermined number of problems had been successfully completed, a new problem was introduced which could not be solved by the usual solution. Following this problem, a final $B - A - 2C$ problem was presented to all three groups.

In terms of $S-R$ transfer theory, the original experience of 6, 11, or 21 problems was considered the equivalent of acquisition training under normal circumstances, while the novel problem was considered equivalent to extinguishing the sequential response evoked by problems of this type. If this analysis is correct, then subjects should be able to perform the $B - A - 2C$ response more quickly as a function of the number of prior problems experienced, and should be slower in their response to the single problem presented during extinction. By the same analysis, the absolute amount of time taken to produce a response in "extinction" should be longer than during any of the acquisition problems. Similarly, if the second problem serves as an effective extinction procedure, there should be no difference in speed of reapplying the $B - A - 2C$ response for the 6, 11, or 21 acquisition groups. An analysis of Gardner and Runquist's data showed that all these predictions were confirmed, and, taken in conjunction with Schulz's analysis of this task, lends support to the view that water-jar problems can be described in terms of response transfer, subject to the same constraints as other simpler responses.

## Functional-Fixity Problems

In the case of water-jar problems, persistent and interfering responses are learned during the course of the experiment itself. In the case of experiments on functional fixity, the experimental subject was thought (by Duncker, 1945) to have become so "fixed" or "set" in his perception of certain objects and their use that it would have been impossible for him to use the object in a novel way if a particular problem required it. In the original experiments by Duncker, five different tasks involving five different tools were used; each in one of two versions. One version of the task (the control version) required only the novel use of the tool, while the second or experimental version required that the tool first be used in its normal way and then in some new way. The conjecture being tested was that if the subject first used the tool in its usual way, it would be more difficult to perceive a new meaning—that is, to use it in a novel way appropriate to the present task.

As an example, consider the so-called "pliers problem." Here the subject's task was to make a stand, when only the following objects were available: a pair of pliers, a board, a wooden bar, and two iron joints (these were actually irrelevant to the solution). Figure 6.5 shows these materials, as well as the correct solution.

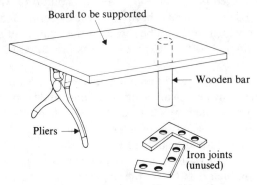

Solution of the "flower stand" problem

**Fig. 6.5**  When the subject is presented with the objects shown, the problem is to construct a flower stand using any of the items given, not necessarily all of them. The best result is obtained by using the pliers in an unusual way, as shown.

In one version of the problem (the experimental version), the wooden bar was nailed to the board and had to be freed by using the pliers. In the control version, the bar was tied to the board and easily removed without using the pliers. Results in this demonstration experiment were clear: Of 51 subjects in the control group, 50 were able to solve the problem; while of 49 subjects in the experimental group, only 31 were able to solve the problem.

Similar results have also been found in further studies making use of different materials. Thus Birch and Rabinowitz (1951) tested subjects on the two-string problem in which the subject's job was to tie together two strings suspended from the ceiling. The distance between the 2 strings was sufficiently great that it was impossible for subjects to hold one and grasp the other at the same time. The only way to solve this problem was to tie a weight to the end of one rope, and then, treating the rope as a pendulum, swing it across the room so that the subject could grasp it while he held on to the other string.

Birch and Rabinowitz ran two groups of subjects, both of whom had the same objects available—an electric switch and an electric relay. The only difference was that Group *R* (relay) was asked to install the relay in an electrical circuit before trying to solve the problem, while subjects in Group *S* (switch) had to install an electrical switch before trying to solve the problem. The results indicated that all 10 subjects in Group *R* used the switch in solving the problem, while 7 of 9 subjects in Group S used the relay. A control group given no previous training split 50–50 in use of the switch and the relay. Thus, even when alternative solutions are equated, functional fixity seems to be a factor in problem solving.

A subsequent experiment by Adamson and Taylor (1954), in addition to providing still another confirmation of the Duncker effect, was also interested in determining what role the passage of time might have in reducing functional fixity. The procedure used duplicated Birch and Rabinowitz's study in all important respects: The only difference was that 5 different groups of subjects were used. Half the subjects in each of these groups first performed in either Group R or Group S, and then were allowed a period of time before being tested on the two-string problem itself. One group waited 1 minute; the second group, 30 minutes; the third group, 60 minutes; the fourth group, 1 day; and the fifth group, 1 week. The results of this experiment indicated that functional fixity—the tendency to use the object *not* used in the pre-test—decreased to a chance level only after 7 days.

How can functional fixity be understood in terms of an $S-R$ analysis? Schulz (1960) has suggested that functional fixity should be considered as a case of negative transfer. His analysis of this problem begins with a description of still another of Duncker's original problems; namely, the box–candle problem. In this problem the subject is given a few thumbtacks, three small paper boxes, 3 candles, a few matches, and a vertical board. The subject's task is to mount the candles on the vertical surface so that they will be in an upright position. The problem is solved first by tacking the boxes to the wall, and then by using a bit of the wax melted from the candles to mount the candles at the top edge of the box. The experimental manipulations consisted either of presenting all the materials, i.e., the candles, matches, and tacks, within each of the three boxes, or of presenting all the materials completely separated from each other; that is, three empty boxes, 3 separated candles, a vertical board, and a few matches. The effects of these were quite dramatic: Only 12 of 29 subjects solved the problem when all objects were presented within the box, while 24 of 28 subjects solved the problem when the various materials were kept separate (Adamson, 1952).

The reason for this result, so Schulz argues, is to be found in considering the responses potentially evocable by each of the various stimulus objects, and the boxes in particular. When the boxes were used as a container, the $S-R$ sequence could be diagrammed $S_{box} \rightarrow$ *Implicit Verbal Response*: "Use as a container." Since this connection was probably strongly established prior to the experiment, using the box as a container in the present situation served only to rearouse the connection and thereby to produce a condition of functional fixity. Instead of considering functional fixity as *an ability to change perspectives*, Schulz feels that the crucial event is reactivating an already established implicit verbal labeling response.

Is there any direct evidence as to the role of labeling responses in problem solving of this type? Perhaps the most convincing demonstration has been provided by Glucksberg (1964, 1966). In the first of his experiments, subjects who solved the box–candle problem, when asked to recall the objects involved, reported "the box" earlier in the list of recalled objects than did non-solvers. Perhaps even more important, solvers recalled the box as a separate entity, e.g., "a box," rather than as a container of something or other, such as a "box of tacks" or a "tack box," etc.

In a further experiment, Glucksberg and Weisberg (1966) presented subjects with a line-drawing illustration of the box–candle problem under one of three conditions.

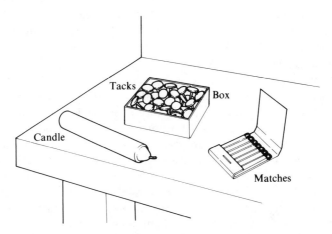

**Fig. 6.6** Candle problem illustration used in the three experiments. The all-labeled form is the one shown. [Adapted from Glucksberg and Weisberg, Verbal behavior and problem solving, *J. Exp. Psych.* **71**, 1966, p. 660]

For Group *A*, all objects in the picture were clearly labeled (see Fig. 6.6); for Group *T* only "tacks" were labeled; while for Group *N*, none of the objects were labeled. In one experiment subjects were asked to write out their solutions to the problem, while in a second experiment they were asked to manipulate the actual objects. In the written case, Group *A* produced 95% correct solutions; Group *N*, 65%; and Group *T*, 54%. Considered statistically, only Group *A* differed from the other two. In the manipulation part of the experiment, a time-to-solution measure was used, with the result that Group *A* took a median of 0.6 minutes; Group *N*, a median of 10.9; and Group *T*, a median of 5.0. All these values differ significantly.

The interpretation of functional fixity suggested by these experiments is radically different from that offered by Duncker. In essence, Duncker argued that functional fixity in the box–candle problem is the result of a subject's inability to perceive the "platform properties" of the box, seeing instead only its "container properties." Glucksberg on the other hand argues that providing a subject with a verbal label for a functionally fixed object makes that object more readily available for use. In other words, "if a particular functional fixity effect results from a lack of perceptual signaling of the fixed object, then the name of that object eliminates that effect." (Glucksberg and Weisberg, 1966, page 664)

## Anagram Problems

A favorite experimental procedure used to study problem solving is verbal anagrams. In these problems, the subject is presented with a series of letters in scrambled order, and his job is to rearrange the letters so as to make a meaningful English word.

Consider, for example, the following set of problems in which the subject's job is to rearrange each of 5 letters so that they make a meaningful English word.

NELIN

YNPEO

NEDOZ

SDLEN

HCWHI

WOALL

ESTHE

KLSTA

NOLEM

DLSCO

Now some of these are easier to do than others. For example, many students find it much easier to solve *linen* from NELIN than *peony* from YNPEO. This is consistent with experimental work reported by Mayzner and Tresselt (1958), who found that anagrams whose solution words occur with great frequency in the English language are solved about four times as fast as anagrams having low-frequency solutions.

A second property of the anagrams presented above is that if an anagram has more than a single solution (*stalk* and *talks* from KLSTA), the more-frequent solution is more likely to occur than the less-frequent one (Mayzner and Tresselt, 1966). In the case of the examples presented above, this tendency can be counteracted by a Luchins' type set induced by the first seven anagrams, which made the responses *stalk*, *lemon*, and *scold* more likely than *talks*, *melon*, and *colds*.

Probably the most coherent attempt to understand and analyze anagram construction as an associative problem-solving activity was presented by Carl F. Duncan in his presidential address to the Midwestern Psychological Association in 1966. Although, as he noted, Maltzman and other $S-R$ psychologists discussed problem solving in terms of a number of rather complexly patterned stimulus and response hierarchies, Duncan felt it best to limit his discussion only to response hierarchies; or to what Maltzman called a *divergent hierarchy*. Although Duncan did consider the role of word associations and concept hierarchies in his analysis, for purposes of the present discussion, we shall consider the frequency of occurrence of items as most important.

The obvious starting point for Duncan's experiments is a result described earlier: that frequent words are produced as anagram solutions more readily than infrequent ones. Mayzner and Tresselt interpreted their results to imply that the letters of an anagram problem serve as a stimulus for implicit responses, with the more frequent of these implicit responses produced sooner. Considering letters as stimuli raises the possibility that letter variables such as position or order of individual letters might affect problem solution. In order to assess such effects, Duncan (1966) presented subjects with two letters (actually the first and last letters of a 5-letter word) and asked them to think of a 5-letter word. The results of three different studies, all variations on this type of procedure, showed that the majority of words produced were indeed words having a high frequency of occurrence in the language.

But frequency can operate in still another way in the usual anagram problem situation: in terms of the pattern imposed by the scrambled letters. For example, the anagram TIRFU looks, potentially at least, something like an English word, whereas the anagram *iufrt* does not. Given that *iufrt* does not look even remotely like an English word, there is less hesitancy in moving around the letters to produce the solution *fruit* than there would be given the sequence *tirfu*. If this is correct, then some measure of how closely a sequence of letters approximates English should predict the speed of solution of an anagram. Such a measure is called *bigram frequency*, or the frequency with which two letters follow each other in written language. For the example presented, *t* and *i*, and *i* and *r*, and *r* and *f*, and *f* and *u* follow each other much more frequently than the comparable pairs derived from *iufrt*.

Perhaps an even better example of how letter order affects anagram solution is provided by the following pair of stimuli: *eanoc* and *canoe*, when *ocean* is the correct solution. The obvious difference in the ease with which such anagrams are solved arises from the fact that *canoe* is a meaningful word, whereas *eanoc* is not, despite the fact that their respective bigram frequencies are about equal. Under these circumstances, as Beilin and Horn (1962) and Ekstrand and Dominowski (1968) have demonstrated, it takes much longer to produce a solution to anagram stimuli which are words. Although Beilin and Horn have described their results in Gestalt terms—that is, meaningful letter groups such as words are organized units and therefore resist reorganization more than nonsense units—it also seems possible to argue that a word is a different sort of stimulus unit from a nonsense syllable, and then to point out that this is not necessarily the result of perceptual factors alone. Perhaps, instead, a word resists reorganization more strenuously because it has been used as a meaningful unit in its own right in verbal behavior. This implies that in seeing a word such as *canoe*, the subject tends to produce a response hierarchy at the same level as the stimulus word; i.e., by producing other words such as *boat, water, paddle*, etc. If, on the other hand, *eanoc* is presented, the subject will probably not respond with any other words; *eanoc* is not a unit, but simply a collection of letters. In practice, the Gestalt statement that a word resists being broken down into its constituent letters is correct; the associationist would argue, however, this in no way offers any explanation as to why such resistance should occur. Saying that a stimulus resists reorganization because it resists reorganization does not add anything in the way of a further analysis of this problem.

All in all, results involving anagram problems can be interpreted on the basis of describing problem solving in terms of transfer-of-training principles. The concepts of response frequency and response hierarchy, coupled with certain specific assumptions about natural language habits, allow for an analysis of anagrams in familiar $S-R$ terms. Once again, simple associative principles have been successfully extended to a new task domain.

## PROBLEM SOLVING AND HUMAN LEARNING

The associationistic analysis of problem solving sees it as continuous with, and dependent on, lower-order behavioral processes such as are involved in classical and instrumental conditioning. The learner, or problem solver, comes to each of these situations with a lifetime of prior experience and tasks or behavioral processes can be ordered in terms of how much the human subject has to know (i.e., have already available) before he can function effectively in a given situation. In the case of classical conditioning, for example, the subject is required to bring only a sensitive receptor–effector system; no real prior learning is required. In the case of forming a concept, the subject must come with certain previously learned connections among stimuli and responses, whether these responses be directly related to the situation at hand or whether they be covert mediational responses capable of establishing stimulus equivalences where none existed before. In short, as the focus shifts from relatively simple $S-R$ connections, such as occur in conditioning, to more complex behavioral processes such as occur in problem solving, the controlling variables become farther and farther removed from the stimulus situation and tend to exist as previously acquired capabilities of the individual.

Thus, for various higher-order behaviors, the experimenter is wise to look both to the subject and the environment rather than simply to the environment itself.

One psychologist who has done the most to stress the ordered arrangement of learning tasks is Robert Gagné (1964, 1965). For Gagné, the ability to solve a particular problem always depends on an accumulation of lower-order response dispositions. If, for example, the solution to a problem requires the subject to sort different-sized cubes into one group, and different-sized pyramids into another, the subject must first learn, or have pre-available, the respective concepts of cubes and pyramids before he can even attempt a general solution to this particular problem.

The type of order Gagné has in mind is perhaps best represented by his own table, which presents a suggested ordering of what subjects must learn in various learning situations. (See Table 6.1 on the opposite page.)

The column labeled "Paradigm" shows only the presumed *S–R* connection and not the specifics of the procedure itself. Beginning with concept learning, only the central portions of the chains involved are shown.

In this table, Gagné identifies a type of learning falling somewhere between concept formation and problem solving, which he calls *principle learning*. As an example, he chooses a principle that could be learned by a kindergarten child: "Round things roll." (Gagné, 1965, pages 142–144.) There are two parts to this principle: (1) "round things" and (2) "rolling." Both of these the child knew (had learned) before the new principle was taught to him. So, for example, if the child has only a relatively incomplete concept of roundness, he may end up with a restricted principle—*wheels roll*—but will not learn the more extended one: plates, balls, discs, cylinders, etc., all also roll. In the same way the child must know the concept "roll" and be able to distinguish it from "sliding," "tumbling," and so on.

How would a kindergarten teacher attempt to get such a principle across? Let Gagné present this hypothetical example:

> Having these prerequisites accomplished, the remainder of the situation for learning is contributed by a representative set of stimulus objects and by a set of verbal instructions to which the learner responds. The stimulus objects might include a set of unfamiliar blocks, some of which are round, some not, and an inclined plane. The instructions might go like this: "I want you to answer the question, what kinds of things roll?... You remember what *roll* means (demonstrate with one round object)... Some of these objects are *round*. Can you point them out?... (Student responds)... Do all *round* things roll? (Student answers "Yes.")... Show me... (Student responds by rolling two or three round objects.)... Good! ... What kind of things roll? (Student responds "Round things roll.")... Right!" With the completion of this exercise, it is reasonable to conclude

that the principle has been learned. However, to test this, a new and different set of blocks may be presented to the student, and he is asked to answer the question, "Which of these will roll?"*

**Table 6.1**  A suggested ordering of the types of human learning

| Type | Paradigm† | Description |
|------|-----------|-------------|
| Response learning | $S-R$ | Establishment of a response-connection to a stimulus specified along physical dimensions |
| Chaining | $S-R \sim S-R$ | Establishment of chains of response connections |
| Verbal learning (paired associates) | $S - r \sim \{\, s - R\,]$ | Establishment of labeling responses to stimuli varying physically within limits of primary stimulus generalization. Previous "response learning" assumed (as indicated by brackets) |
| Concept learning | $S - r \sim\sim s$ <br> $S - r \sim\sim s \rightarrow$ [Concept] <br> $S = r \sim\sim s$ | Establishment of mediating response to stimuli which differ from each other physically ("classifying") |
| Principle learning | [Concept] [Concept] → (Rule) | Establishment of a process which functions like a rule "If $A$, then $B$," where $A$ and $B$ are concepts |
| Problem solving | (Rule) (Rule) → [Higher-order rule] | Establishment of a process which combines two or more previously learned rules in a higher-order rule |

† The paradigms shown have been designed to depict what is learned, and not the learning situation which leads to this result. In addition, note that beginning with concept learning, only the central portions of the inferred chains are shown.

This analysis reaches its logical conclusion in problem solving, or, as Gagné puts it, in the ability to establish a new rule based on lower-order rules, where such rules are to be considered as "if–then" $S-R$ chains. Although much of the research considered in this section probably does not reach this

* From *The Conditions of Learning,* by Robert Gagné, New York: Holt, Rinehart, and Winston, 1965.

level of complexity, it is probably well to keep such processes in mind, particularly if we want to understand how a student in elementary algebra is able to solve the problem: Show that $21(a + b) = (21 \times a) + (21 \times b)$. In order to do this for the first time, the student has to make use of a number of previously learned principles; principles such as the commutative and distributive properties of addition and multiplication, and so on.

If there is one overall implication to Gagné's thoughtful analysis, it is that, as we move from lower-order behaviors, such as are involved in rote learning and memory, to concept formation and finally to problem solving, our focus of emphasis must shift from an analysis of the formal properties of the environment to an analysis of the role of subject capabilities and its interaction with task requirements. In a sense, this is the essential problem set by higher mental processes for any associationistic analysis of mind.

## SUMMARY

The crucial problem involved in problem solving is to get the idea of a goal to occur at the start of a behavioral episode without having to accept all the philosophical connotations of the idea of an idea. In order to get around this problem, $S-R$ psychologists have developed the concept of a fractional anticipatory goal response as the response equivalent of the philosopher's guiding idea. This response, symbolized $r_g$, is learned on the basis of the contiguity of environmental stimuli with consummatory responses that can occur only in the presence of the goal object. Certain of these consummatory responses can be detached from the actual presence of the goal stimulus, and on this basis are able to move forward in time to the start of an instrumental sequence. In this way instrumental, or goal-directed, behavior occurs with appropriate goal direction provided by these fractional $r_g$'s.

Once the problem of guiding ideas has been solved, the next step is to describe how complex response sequences arise which lead to successful performance. Here, as in the case of concept formation, recourse is taken to principles of stimulus and response generalization and discrimination in the form of hypothetical *divergent and convergent response hierarchies*. This concept provides for potential connections among any collection of stimulus and response elements. Any stimulus can cue any response and thereby lead to the solution of any given problem.

A particularly important aspect of problem solving is encompassed in the term *insight*. Descriptively, insight is said to occur if there is a dramatic upswing in the ability of an organism to solve a particular class of problems. The original analysis of this problem proposed the hypothesis that insight was the result of a perceptual–cognitive reorganization of the stimulus field; although subsequent work has indicated the significant role of experience in producing behavior that could be described as "insightful." The series of experiments undertaken by Harlow on the development of *learning sets* serves, however, to provide firm and conclusive evidence on the role of practice in bringing about insightful solutions. Harlow has subsequently generalized this earlier work, so that he now views learning as the elimination of erroneous responses to noncriterial aspects of the problem. In his hands, this approach seems to have wide applicability to the domain of discrimination learning and problem solving.

In addition to Harlow's analysis of insightful behavior in discrimination tasks, other problem situations originally proposed by Gestalt psychologists have also been examined in an attempt to develop $S-R$ principles capable of explaining experimental results. Here, the major thrust has been to show that set and functional fixity effects are the result of negative transfer, and that under appropriate conditions such effects can either be magnified or eliminated. Psychologists armed with this analytic approach have been able to show that the processes involved in such special situations depend on principles occurring in simpler and more clearly understood stimulus–response situations.

Associationistic analyses of problem solving have also made a good deal of use of anagram problems. Although such problems have a number of advantages, probably the most significant one is that they allow for an assessment of the preexisting response hierarchies involved in the solution of a particular anagram. In general, these preexisting response factors have been shown to predict the speed and reliability with which a particular anagram is solved.

Finally, Gagné has attempted to order learning tasks in terms of the amount and variety of prior learning required to do a particular task. These requirements range from simple $S-R$ connections, as in the case of paired associates, to considerably more complex $S-R$ chains involving "if–then" rules, as in the case of algebra. In general, problem solving of the type usually accomplished in the classroom requires the use of a number of previously learned $S-R$ connections, and the difficulty of a particular task can be described in terms of the number and complexity of these prior $S-R$ connections.

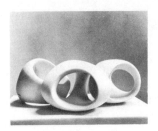

# CHAPTER 7

# THE DEVELOPMENT
# OF THOUGHT

If there is any one topic on which association theory should have a lot of say —and does—it is on the topic of the development of thought. One of the basic premises of early associationism was that the mind of an infant is a blank tablet (*tabula rasa*) on which the environment writes its message. All rationality was seen ultimately as the result of a contiguous occurrence of events in the environment, with these events giving rise to internal representations; that is, to ideas.

If the child is viewed as a receptacle of the environment's wisdom, then a careful consideration of how the infant and child interact with their environment should be particularly rewarding. But there are a number of ways in which to view this person–environment interaction, with the differentiating property of each view having to do with the presumed "natural state" of the child and how this is shaped or modified by the world of fact. One possible form of this relationship assumes that the child is essentially noble at birth— totally moral in a primitive and uncomplicated sort of way—and that the environment (society in this case) deflects this original nobility. For this view, the environment corrupts the innate morality of the child as it goes about educating him to the ways of people and symbols.

A second theory reverses this perspective entirely and views the child as a seething hodgepodge of aggressive and sexual instincts which somehow or other must be brought under control if the child and the society are to survive. Just as society attempts to produce a balance among destructive, sexual, moral, and rational constituents, so too the individual must be taught to regulate his assertive instincts on the basis of cognitive and moral constraints. For this view the environment tames an originally asocial beast and makes him fit to live in the society of other men.

There is also a third tradition, and this is essentially a pragmatic one. The child comes to the world as a relatively unfit organism. He can't stand, talk, think, control his bowels, etc., yet somehow or other, by age 4 he can do either all or most of these things. Somehow these skills must be taught to him, and the agency of such teaching is obviously in part outside the child, or in the environment. Building on these seemingly common-sense notions, it is possible to view the environment as neither corrupting nor taming, but simply as there. If this view is taken, some psychologists have argued that there is no need to talk about internal representations of the environment (for after all why talk about ideas and their development when these can't be seen, but the environment can). In addition this pragmatic view reemphasizes the environment as an agent for change, with the direction of such change necessarily guided by extra-environmental considerations. In order to teach the child requisite skills, look to the world of fact and design better learning environments. Behavior no longer need be viewed in terms of its moral properties, and almost any and all kinds of behavior and behavioral changes are possible, given a society's desire to produce them.

## Victor and Dr. Itard: A Test of the Noble-Savage Hypothesis

The philosopher Jean Jacques Rousseau was probably the most articulate spokesman, if not the originator, of the hypothesis that society corrupts the natural nobility of man. That is, if a human being were freed of the stultifying and immoral constraints imposed by society, he would be not devious, but direct; not acquisitive, but generous; not hostile, but gentle; and so on. How seriously an older Rousseau would have taken this extreme view is hard to say, although, given his emphatic early statement of the theory, it is scarcely possible to imagine the excitement caused by the discovery in 1797 (some scant 40 years after Rousseau's initial description of the noble-savage hypothesis) of a 12-year-old boy wandering around the woods near Paris behaving as if he had been raised by animals. Here certainly was the natural experiment to test Rousseau's hypothesis.

Unfortunately, the precious hope aroused by this discovery was short-lived, for when the boy was examined by Pinel, the great French psychiatrist, all evidence seemed to indicate that the savage child was probably of subnormal intelligence, and probably had been left by his parents in the woods to die. While it was true that he moved about with an animal gait—on all fours —and that his knuckles and knees had calluses capable of supporting his body, and that he ate his food by bringing his mouth down to it rather than by raising it up to his mouth, and that he responded attentively to the rustling of leaves and bushes, and that his body bore the scars of a number of wild-animal attacks—while all this was true, the savage boy still proved a great disappointment to the Parisian elite, and as is the wont of beautiful people, they saw fit to consign him quickly to a cage in the zoo. There the savage boy, except for his anthropomorphic form, was considered a subhuman animal and was placed on exhibit for the enjoyment and enlightenment of the general public.

The story would end here, a sad indictment of a presumably enlightened society, and would have no psychological relevance at all, if it had not been for the intervention of a young non-Parisian doctor by the name of Itard. Itard, on the basis of a number of philosophical notions, reasoned that the child only appeared subnormal and that this subnormality had been caused by the boy's lack of interaction with an educating and supportive environment. If this were true, Itard reasoned further, it should be possible to rehumanize and reeducate the boy by exposing him to a more normal human environment. In order to accomplish this, Itard asked for, and received, permission to put the boy in a special room at the Institute for the Deaf in Paris. There, for five years, Dr. Itard worked with Victor in an attempt to teach him to speak, to read, to think—in short, to behave like a civilized young man.

Unfortunately, Dr. Itard never really succeeded in bringing Victor to human estate, most probably because Victor was, in fact, of subnormal intelligence. However, despite his seeming failure, Itard did succeed in teaching Victor to do an elementary form of reading and to form certain relatively simple concepts. All this learning was accomplished through the use of procedures quite easily described in contemporary S–R terminology. Almost all that Victor learned involved a contiguous pairing of a symbol and an object. In one of Itard's games, the word *pen* was paired with the appropriate object, until, when he saw the word-card, Victor—in a manner reminiscent of laboratory paired-associates learning—would respond by getting the object, a pen. In order to see if this sort of response could be evoked when a time interval intervened between the presentation of the stimulus card and the required response, Itard placed the pen some distance away. The card was first presented, and, even under these conditions, Victor was able to find the pen.

Although Itard was able to teach Victor these rudimentary cognitive skills, and although Victor came to wear clothes and assume the posture and manners of a civilized child, by the time Victor was about 17 it was apparent to Itard that they both had gone about as far as they could; and Itard terminated his observations and training. Unfortunately, despite the tremendous changes brought about, Pinel's original diagnosis was probably correct—that Victor did have subnormal intelligence—and this limited the ultimate level Victor could attain.

Although an analysis of this particular case did not provide any information as to whether the environment does or does not corrupt a noble savage, it did show that associationistically based procedures could be used to teach new skills even to a subnormal child. Itard's interest in, and his success with, Victor were derived from the view that ideas and knowledge are not innate, but rather develop as a result of the interaction of a naive organism with his environment. Although Itard didn't use contemporary concepts or terminology, his results are perfectly compatible with the tenets of this position.

### Freud on the Development of Thought: The Unnoble-Savage Hypothesis

One of the great methodological inventions of psychoanalysis is free association. Although Freud borrowed the technique originally from his co-worker

Breuer, it was he who carried it forward as one of the primary tools of psycho-analytic therapy. Largely through the analysis of his own and his patients' adult free associations and dreams, Freud was led to reconstruct a theory of how a human being develops from a senseless infant to an articulate adult. Although this process was viewed as a constant interaction between the unfolding biological drives of an organism and the demands of his environment, the psychoanalytic tradition at base always presupposed a rather straightforward associationistic model.

Consider, for example, the following stream of association as it occurred in a psychoanalytic interview (Knight, 1950). The patient is speaking.

> "You've asked me about my father . . . . He wasn't a particularly large man, as I think about him as an adult . . . . He was more distant than anything else . . . . Oh I must tell you about an incident that I'm now thinking of that occurred a few years ago.
>
> "While driving downtown I met a policeman . . . . I became tense and trembled with fear even before he spoke to me . . . . He merely asked for a ride down the street . . . . The officer turned out to be one of our company guards who had recognized me . . . .
>
> "On a few occasions when I happened to be present in the same restaurant as a uniformed officer, I preferred to leave rather than stay and struggle with my acutely painful and nervous feelings . . . .
>
> "It is important to remember that ever since childhood I had been uncomfortable in the presence of policemen. I had no real reason to fear the police, yet a simple warning from a traffic officer was enough to set my heart pounding . . . .
>
> "Let's see, where were we before I started talking about policemen? Oh yes . . . , we were talking about my father . . . ."*

The significant aspect of this fragment is the seeming discontinuity between the content of the association and the ideas that precede and follow it: First Knight talks about Topic *A*, his father, and then suddenly he talks about Topic *B*, his feelings of anxiety in the presence of uniformed officials. With that out of the way, he resumes his narrative on Topic *A*. It is precisely this kind of seemingly chaotic topic-jumping that is extremely important in analyzing the stream of free association, as well as the content of dreams and slips of the tongue.

In this case the switch from talking about his father to talking about anxiety aroused by an anonymous policeman seems plain enough: Both the father and the policeman represent authority (perhaps of an anonymous and incomprehensible kind). It is this link with authority that cements the two topics together: Father → authority → anxiety → Policeman → authority →

---

* From *The Story of My Psychoanalysis*, by J. Knight, New York: McGraw-Hill, 1950.

anxiety → father again.    The mediating elements (authority + anxiety) are common to both, and the seemingly chaotic leap in the stream of association is given coherence by the relationship of Topics *A* and *B* to the same mediating element.

But how do such connections occur, and why are they not as obvious to the patient as to the therapist? There are a number of answers to this question, but in one way or another they all involve the assumption of an unconscious —unverbalizable—process and its associated mental maneuvering that keeps events and ideas out of awareness.  These maneuvers are usually thought of as defensive reactions and mechanisms so characteristic of neuroses and lesser neurotic states.  Such defensive maneuvers develop in the history of a child in accordance with an innate biological timetable: the so-called psychosexual stages.  Without going into detail about these stages, we can describe the development of thinking as a change from primary to secondary process.

This change from primary to secondary processes, from wish fulfillment to goal-directed behavior, represents the growth of rational intelligence and thought.  Although Freud was also concerned with how the moral code of society is introjected in the form of the Superego, this is of no real concern in characterizing the developmental trends that take the child from autistic, timeless thinking to directed, reality-oriented thinking.  There are, however, in adult life a number of significant functions still motorized by primary process: slips of the tongue, dreams, and neurotic symptoms all give an adult some insight as to the *modus operandi* of primary process.  The dream, in which the past and the present exist coterminously; in which the logical flow of time and space need not appear; and in which all wishes can and are fulfilled, represents the interjection of primary-process thinking into adult rationality.

But not all messages in adult life from primary process are nonproductive: primary process is ideally suited to breaking down patterns of usual thought. If this is true, then an individual who can occasionally "dip down" into such thinking, and not get lost in its labyrinth, is precisely that person who might be able to come up with a new insight, or a new work of art.  Such dipping into the unconscious under the guidance and control of rational adult processes should lead to creative and novel thought.  If such regression to early modes of thinking is not subject to Ego control, however, neurotic symptoms and bizarre thought result; if such regression is in the service of the Ego (Hartman, Kris, and Lowenstein, 1957), genuinely novel and creative thoughts are possible and indeed likely.  Thus creative thought involves the development of a new perspective unclouded by prescriptions as to "the usual way of doing things"; and to accomplish this, the creative thinker or artist must often break the bonds of contemporary practice and establish new ones.  In order to do this, he "regresses" to a time when all things are possible and none impossible, reverting back to secondary process only after new combinations have been established. Once such new combinations have been formed, secondary-process thinking is required to fill in the details of this new recombination.

*Freud and academic psychology.* The Freudian hypothesis was derived from clinical practice. It is natural that nonclinicians should attempt to recast Freud's analysis in terms more congenial to experimental psychology. Miller and Dollard (1950) have made perhaps the most detailed attempt to translate the complexities of Freudian theory, into the complex (but hopefully better understood) language of the learning laboratory. It is easy to see why associationistic psychology would find this a viable possibility: Both academic psychology and Freudian psychoanalysis considered organisms to be driven by biological forces which cease to be effective when removed; i.e., when tension, from whatever source, was reduced. Similarly, both the clinic and the laboratory spoke about learning, one rather more vaguely and the other more precisely, and both saw the organism as a closed and finite energy system.

Although a great many cross-theory extrapolations and translations have been made, the one that is of most significance for the analysis of thought *per se* involves the concept of a cue-producing response and its relationship to primary and secondary processes. A cue-producing response is similar to what in other contexts has been termed a mediating response. The change in terminology, however, does reflect a change in emphasis: Whereas mediational elements tie together originally disparate responses or response systems, cue-producing responses are postulated solely as cues for further behavior; that is, responses which are themselves cues.

The most obvious of these cue-producing responses are words, where such words are considered primarily as labels for bits of experience. Labeling serves its most significant function in the processes of generalization and discrimination. If, for example, there are two individuals, both blonde, both tall, and both good-looking, and one is labeled an Englishman and the other a Nazi, these differential labels serve to evoke entirely different behavioral responses to these otherwise similar individuals. Labels for objects, events, or people serve either to extend or curtail generalization.

For Miller and Dollard, the unconscious is largely the "unverbalized" or the "unverbalizable." Such mental inarticulateness arises in one of two ways, both of which depend for their theoretical analysis on the development or use of speech and labeling. The first major area concerns all those drives, responses, and cues which occurred prior to the advent of speech, while the second involves an analysis of repression in terms of the response of "not-thinking" about something.

Miller and Dollard relate the conscious–unconscious dimension to the activity of labeling, particularly in terms of its role in restricting symbolic trial and error as well as in terms of producing inappropriate generalization and discrimination tendencies.  If thinking of a particular word (or the reality it labels) arouses anxiety, rational responding becomes difficult and inappropriate responses, either overt or cue-producing, result.  These restrictions on the organism's secondary process succeed in bringing about a much more "childlike" organism, dominated by the immediate environment and unable to do long-range, rational planning.

Now although Freudian and S–R traditions do make contact in Miller and Dollard's theory, it is clear that much of this relationship depends on accepting as valid the Freudian description of certain mental processes, and then showing how these processes can be construed as learned on the basis of ordinary associative principles.  Although Freud's analysis is strongly associationistic in character, the specifics of these two traditions are widely different.  At best, Miller and Dollard's "translation" made Freud's analysis more acceptable to academic psychology, although the change in terminology really reflected a change in the specific processes involved in thinking about thought.  For Freud, thought represents an interaction of a prearranged series of stages with environmental frustrations, while for Miller and Dollard the prearranged stages are of much less importance and the whole of thinking (including repression, creativity, autism, etc.) is construed as a complicated type of stimulus–response process, subject to the same constrains as simpler forms of learning.

### Cue-Producing Responses, Words, and Thinking

If the laboratory tradition views labeling as of critical importance for the development of thought, then it is reasonable to expect that studies done within this orientation should be concerned with the role of words—considered as cue-producing responses—in children's thought.  One of the earliest studies of this topic was performed by Kuenne (1946) who studied the relationship of a child's ability to verbalize a concept with his ability to solve transposition problems.  In transposition experiments in general, and in this one in particular, subjects were trained to choose the smaller (38 inches) of two squares (larger, 68 square inches) and were then presented with another pair of stimuli, 21 and 38 inches, respectively.  The child or animal was said to show transposition if it chose the 21-inch square rather than the 38-inch square in the second test.

The result was that both animals and children usually showed transposition in response to the 21-inch square.  However, if the transposition test was carried to still smaller stimuli, say 2 and 4 inches, most lower-order organisms (rat, monkey) tended to show only chance responding to both stimuli.  Given these results on infra-human subjects, Kuenne argued that if children were able to verbalize the reason for their choice, "the *smaller* one is right," they would show transposition for both near and far sets of stimuli, whereas children unable to verbalize the reason for their choice would respond on a purely chance basis.

In order to examine this hypothesis, Kuenne tested children on the "near" and "far" transposition problems, where these children ranged from 3 to 6 years of age. Results of Kuenne's experiment were quite clear and quite consistent with her original hypothesis: Younger and older children do equally well on "near" transposition tests, while only older children do well on "far" transposition tests. So far so good. Kuenne also recorded spontaneous verbalizations, and in those cases in which the child did not talk during testing Kuenne questioned him at the end of the experiment. On the basis of these spontaneous or prompted responses, she was able to divide the children into 4 different verbalization groups, which for our purposes can be collapsed into two. One of these groups contained children who, although they might be able to see the size dimension (i.e., "what a nice *little* block"), never verbalized the correct principle. All children in the second group were able to verbalize the correct dimension and the correct rule, e.g., "the toy is always in the little one." Using this division of subjects, results showed that although performance on the near test was at 100% for both groups, none of the children in the first group solved the "far" problem, while 73% of the children in the second (verbalization) group were able to solve the problem. On the whole, results support the hypothesis that verbalization aids correct responding in this task.

These results demonstrate the cue function of words in the transposition experiment. Another test situation in which verbal labeling has been found to facilitate performance involves the reversal-shift problem extensively studied by the Kendlers (1962). In a previous discussion of this procedure (see Chapter 5, pages 112 ff), we noted that older and presumably more verbal children were better able to perform reversal than nonreversal shifts. However, in the course of one experiment, Kendler and Kendler noted that it was not uncommon for children to verbalize the correct solution as they made an incorrect response. In order to account for this result, the Kendlers hypothesized that at a certain level of development verbal responses and overt response sequences may represent parallel response processes which do not yet interact with one another.

In order to investigate the cue function of words for children at two different age levels, Kendler and Kendler tested 4- and 7-year-old children with reversal shifts involving the dimension of size (large versus small) and brightness (black versus white). One-third of the children at each age level were induced to say "large" or "small," depending on conditions, by being asked to tell the experimenter whether the large or small object was correct. A second group of children learned to say "black" or "white" on the basis of the same procedure, while subjects in a third and final group were not required to say anything. After initial training, all subjects were presented with a reversal shift. Some of the verbalizations prompted during learning were relevant, while others were irrelevant (for example, if the shift was on the basis of size, those children who said "large" or "small" made relevant verbalizations, whereas those who said "black" or "white" made irrelevant ones).

The first result of interest was that for all subjects the relevant-cue groups showed the fastest reversals, while the irrelevant-cue groups showed the slowest reversals. For 7-year-old children, subjects in the *None* and *Relevant* conditions had an equally easy time in performing reversal shifts. Seven-year-old children in the irrelevant-verbalization condition were markedly interfered with in performing reversal shifts. This condition reduced their performance to the point at which it was worse than that of 4-year-old children under the same condition. By contrast with these results, 4-year-old children showed a facilitation of *Relevant* over *Irrelevant*, and more importantly, a facilitation of *Relevant* over *None*. The later results, of course, are in complete agreement with those found in the Kuenne study described earlier.

Perhaps the most systematic analysis of the regulatory role of speech in voluntary behavior has been made by the Russian psychologist, A. R. Luria (1961). In terms of relating speech to voluntary behavior, it is quite apparent, as Luria correctly notes, that *"the accomplishment of a simple action on verbal instruction* can be regarded as the core of voluntary behavior regulated by speech."* In order to investigate just how verbal instructions affect the subject —whether these instructions were delivered by an experimenter or by the person himself—Luria and his colleagues made use of a very simple response in a very simple situation. The basic procedure involved a ball which the child was asked to squeeze in response either to a verbal command or to some other stimulus condition specified by prior verbal instruction.

If we go through Luria's results chronologically, let us begin with a description of this behavior in children 18–24 months. Figure 7.1 presents the performance of a Russian child named Katya who was instructed to "squeeze" a balloon.

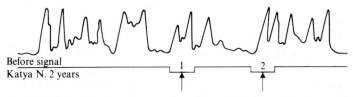

Before signal
Katya N. 2 years        1        2

**Fig. 7.1** Unregulated motor reactions in a child of preschool age. Generalized action on verbal order or instruction. (Experiments by S. V. Yakovleva; from Luria, 1964)

Looking at the behavior following each of the arrows (which represent the experimenter's instructions), we see that the word "squeeze" was sufficient to initiate balloon pressing (i.e., this is recorded by an upward deflection of the record) but that the child wasn't able to stop at a single press. In this case Katya continued to press as many as four times after the instruction had been given. Luria interprets this to mean that the first effect of verbal instructions for a child is to impel action and that at two years of age the child is unable to regulate behavior sufficiently to inhibit the action after a single response. Speech can initiate behavior (i.e., "clap your hands"; "play patty-cake," etc.), but the behavior is not under direct verbal control insofar as offset is concerned.

In order to induce the child to press only once, Luria instructed children of this age (20–24 months) as well as older children (24–36 months) in the following way: "When a light comes on, squeeze the balloon; when there is no light, don't squeeze." This problem was considerably beyond the younger age group under all verbal instructive conditions (and this is not surprising), but inhibition was also beyond the ability of the 2–3-year-old child, except under the condition in which the child's response of pressing to the light also served to turn out the light after the press. Although at 3 years of age the child can understand the task, he is able to inhibit his response only when increased feedback is provided. He needs more than a single verbal cue to inhibit his behavior.

There is yet another way in which to augment feedback, and this is through the use of a single word occurring at the moment the child presses the balloon. In this case the regulating function of the extra feedback shifts from the physical environment to the child's own verbal behavior. Figure 7.2 presents a record of balloon-pressing for a $3\frac{1}{2}$-year-old child under conditions of silence, as well as under the condition in which the child says "go!" at each response. The qualitative changes in his response are indicated by the greater precision and regularity of the response when it occurs, concurrent with increased feedback resulting from saying the word "go." This is contrasted with its much less regular occurrence under conditions of silence.

It is clear that, at about 4–5 years of age, verbal behavior now can do all that is required in the way of regulating behavior: It can initiate, terminate, and regularize the occurrence of a voluntary response, as well as coordinate this response with complex environmental stimuli. In general, further development of the regulating role of speech continues beyond 5 years of age, but with a dramatic upsurging in the ability to follow instructions voluntarily between the ages of 5 and 7. As the child grows older, the regulating role of words ceases to require overt verbalization and the child comes to internalize such responses and make the overt, covert.

In reviewing these studies dealing with the development of verbalization and its role in regulating behavior, the obvious trend has been from the externalization of speech to the internalization of speech. Where speech is spontaneously produced by children, the usual finding is that it aids the child in performing the required task, as results by Kuenne, Luria, and the Kendlers show. However, in all these observations there is a persistent trend that is difficult to reconcile with the view that mental processes can be identified with the verbalizations that presumably control these bahaviors. Thus, in Kuenne's experiment, many of the children who were unable to do the "far" transposition were able to talk about the stimulus, "what a nice *little* block"; whereas the Kendlers noted that it was "not uncommon for children to verbalize spontaneously the correct solution while simultaneously making an incorrect choice."

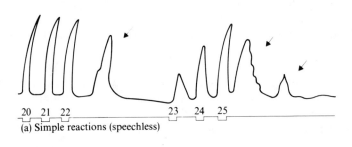

(a) Simple reactions (speechless)

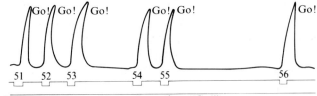

(b) Simple reactions with speech reactions "Go!"

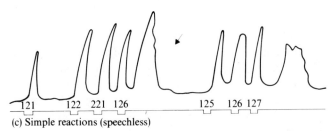

(c) Simple reactions (speechless)

Lena P. 3 years 6 months

**Fig. 7.2** Behavioral record for balloon pressing under three different conditions. (From Luria, 1964)

Luria (1957) has attempted to explain this lack of correlation in terms of what function speech performs for children at various age levels: At first, Luria argues, the child uses speech (verbalization) simply as a means of communicating with adults. There is no attempt to apply speech to problem solving or other processes involving only the child. Subsequently, however, the child develops the ability to regulate his own voluntary behavior on the basis of speech, and, consequently, his actions and planning come to be dominated by overt and covert verbal planning. It is only under this latter condition that the usual correlation between saying and doing comes about.

## The Environment: Benevolent or Tyrannical?  Neither

If the noble-savage and Freudian hypotheses attribute value judgments to the role of the environment in the development of mind, it is because they have prejudged the biological—or at least the innate—morality of the human infant. The objective, behaviorist view of the environment makes no prejudgment as to the moral or biological nature of man; it simply assumes that "something" has taken place to make the organism the particular type of organism he is at the present moment. In other words, just as the environment is morally neutral, so too is the behaving organism. If this is true, then the first job of psychology is to assess the current behavioral repertoire of the child with an eye toward determining what is and is not possible at the moment. The child is considered from the perspective of "where's he at" and not from some "ought" or "where he ought to be."

What this means pragmatically is that once a child's current behavioral repertoire is assessed, the behavior analyst's job is to take the child from "where he is" and get him to some determinate, well-defined end point. In a nutshell, this is the problem of education. It is not surprising that such a view of the organism–environment relationship should give rise to educational technology in the form of programmed instruction.

Since this approach takes its starting point in part at least from the operant conditioning laboratory, the concepts used in educational programming also come from this source. Of all the procedures and concepts used in operant conditioning, perhaps the most significant one for programmed instruction is that of *shaping*, or of describing how you get a nonoccurring, or infrequently occurring, response to occur more frequently.

Take the case of teaching a child to speak more softly. The important empirical concepts here are reinforcement, extinction, and response distribution. In accord with the view that an appropriate opening move in any sort of training is to assess the initial behavioral potentialities of the subject, a baseline level of "noisiness" is first required. In this hypothetical example, suppose that Fig. 7.3a represents the number of sentences Michele talks at varying degrees of loudness. Point *a*, then, represents Michele's usual loudness level. In order to get Michele to speak more softly, the experimenter would tend to reinforce (say "good" to, or simply pay attention to) all soft sentences, and not reinforce any loud sentences. In terms of Fig. 7.3a, this implies the establishment of a new point such as indicated by line *b*. All sentences louder than *b* would not be reinforced, and consequently their probability of reoccurrence would decrease; all sentences softer than *b* would be reinforced, and hence their probability of reoccurrence would increase. Under this circumstance, a new distribution of responses such as the one presented in 7.3b would occur with its average value now at point *b*. By applying a new criterion, line *c*, the distribution of loudness could be moved further toward the soft end, and so on until the desired terminal distribution, 7.3c, is established.

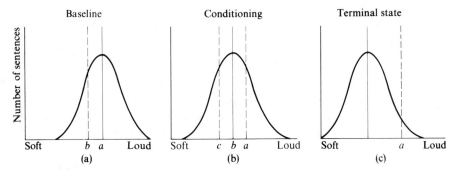

**Fig. 7.3** Shaping Michele to talk quietly: some hypothetical data.

If one wishes to accomplish this change in behavior, a number of points are worth noting; one, the desired terminal behavior must be decided on in advance; two, the progression of patterns must make gradual approximations to this terminal distribution—the jump not being made in one step; three, reinforcement is of extreme importance. Although an intermediate value (such as represented by line *b*) may be implicit in most shaping experiments, it is nonetheless significant for the occurrence of the desired end behavior. In order to program material for instructional purposes, one requires these same properties, but in different form.

Consider the following three frames from an introductory physics program.

The program begins with Frame 1 describing a familiar situation that all high school students would certainly know about. This is equivalent to producing a current response because it is assumed to be part of the learner's preexisting repertoire of knowledge. In a sense this question is comparable to an initial distribution, with the learner receiving immediate reinforcement for his correct response. Frame 2 requires the same response (whose probability of occurrence has been increased in Frame 1), and not surprisingly the learner has it available and is able to produce it without difficulty. As in Frame 1, reinforcement is immediate. Frame 3 takes up the cues provided in the first two frames and asks a slightly different, but quite clearly related, question, and again the response is obvious and reinforcement immediate.

---

1. The important parts of a flashlight are the battery and the bulb. When we "turn on" a flashlight, we close a switch which connects the battery with the_____.

   *Response: bulb*

---

2. When we turn on a flashlight, an electric current flows through the fine wire in the_____and causes it to grow hot.

   *Response: bulb*

---

3. When the hot wire glows brightly, we say that it gives off or sends out heat and _____.

   *Response: light*

---

(From DeCecco, 1968, page 493)

How far can you go with such a program? Consider Frame 29.

---

29. A nearly "dead" battery may make a flashlight bulb warm to the touch, but the filament may still not be hot enough to emit light—in other words the filament will not be _____ at that temperature.

   *Response: incandescent*

---

31. When raised to any temperature above 800 degrees Celsius, an object such as an iron bar will emit light. Although the bar may melt or vaporize, its particles will be _____ no matter how hot they get.

   *Response: incandescent*

---

(From DeCecco, 1968, page 494)

Here the common-sense term, such as "fine wire" in Frame 2, is replaced by the more technically correct term "filament," and the technical term "incandescent" has been introduced and responded to correctly.

In all this discussion the principles of initial response distribution, reinforcement, and response are obvious; but what about the implicit criteria we spoke about in regard to shaping Michele's speaking more softly? As in the loudness case, these are not explicit, but rather implicit in the progression of frames presented. Technically, these criteria are embodied in both the composition of individual items and in the flow of the program.

One of the most significant first principles of shaping in the animal laboratory, and by extension, of programmed learning, is to make sure the animal never learns anything that he has to unlearn—that is, make the successive approximation genuinely approximate the desired terminal behavior. In the case of programmed frames this involves the use of a technique that has come to be called *prompting*. There are really two different kinds of prompts: thematic prompts and formal prompts. Since the formal is the easier of the two to illustrate, let us begin with it.

Skinner (1958) illustrates the role of formal prompts in the following example.

---

Frame 1  Manufacture means to make or build.   Chair factories manufacture chairs.  Copy the word here.

_ _ _ _ _ _ _ _ _ _

Frame 2  Part of the word is like part of the word factory.  Both parts come from an old word meaning make or build.
m a n u _ _ _ u r e

Frame 3  Part of the word is like part of the word manual.  Both parts come from an old word for hand.  Many things used to be made by hand.
_ _ _ _ f a c t u r e

Frame 4  The same letter goes in both spaces:
m _ n u f _ c t u r e

Frame 5  The same letter goes in both spaces:
m a n _ f a c t _ r e

Frame 6  Chair factories _ _ _ _ _ _ _ _ _ _ chairs.

---

This example is also important because it illustrates a special type of prompting technique called *fading*. Fading involves the use of a number of stimuli which gradually vanish as the learner is assumed to develop mastery over the material. As the response is more firmly established in a particular context, the number of supporting contextual stimuli is reduced until the behavior occurs in the complete absence of these supports.

Although it is easier to demonstrate vanishing or fading within the context of formal prompts, thematic prompts can also be faded. There are a number of different types of thematic prompts such as antonyms or synonyms or a total meaningful context. For example, in a biology text it is possible to use a thematic prompt such as: "*Canis familiaris* is man's best friend. *Canis familiaris* is a technical name for the animal called a____." In this case *man's best friend* serves as the thematic cue to produce the word *dog*, which is, of course, the correct answer.

The second major type of consideration involved in leading the learner to a correct response involves the progression of material presented to him. Here again there are two major types of programs: the linear program and the branching program. Linear programming is most true to its laboratory origins. In this type of programming the learner does one frame at a time, progressing in small units from one segment of material to another. Most of our previous illustrations were of this type. It views the acquisition of knowledge as a sequential, linear process—as a chain—in which progressively more difficult information and concepts are attached to simpler ones. Given one of the basic attitudes toward programming,—namely, that the learner's initial response repertoire needs to be assessed prior to actual training—it is possible to hold the view that linear programming is best, yet still allow for certain variations on this basic process. In one variation on this type of program, the learner is presented with a criterion frame (i.e., one that assesses the present level of knowledge); if the learner is able to complete this frame (say Frame 90) successfully, he is allowed to skip the next few frames and is told to progress to Frame 110, skipping Frames 91–109.

This change in the logic of linear progress is quite consistent with intuitions derived from the laboratory, and actually provides a bridge with the second major type of program, the branching program. In one of the best-developed versions of this technique, Crowder (1960) presented the learner with an extremely long selection of prose (a paragraph or even as much as a page), after which the learner was asked to answer a series of multiple-choice questions. Each of the (usually three) alternatives directed the student to a different subsequent page.

Although it would be nice, at this point, to say that one type of program is better than the other, the issue is not easily resolved, for some topics are more quickly learned under linear programming, while other topics are better under branching programs. The discussion of programming types is, however, of wider significance, for it asks basic questions about the optimum sequencing of steps for producing the fastest and best learning. One interesting result of this concern is the finding that small steps are best early in learning, while larger steps are better as mastery of a substantive domain is approached (Maccoby and Sheffield, 1961).

But programmed instruction also offers a change of answer to complaints such as: "I don't know why my boy won't learn" or "She's just not well motivated," and a wide variety of others. What these complaints by parents and teachers express is the basic philosophy that if a learner doesn't learn somehow or other, he—and he alone—is responsible; that is, he's a bad pupil. Programmed learning takes the opposite point of view: If the student fails to learn, the programmer and his program are "bad," not the student himself.

Parenthetically we should note that this change in direction—that the expert and not the novice is to blame if proper learning doesn't take place—has also been applied to psychotherapy. In more classical forms of psychotherapy, if patients refused to talk about their problems or failed to improve, they were told they were "resisting" or "bad" patients. The onus for improving was put on the patient and not on the therapist. The newer therapies, arising largely out of the operant learning laboratory (see Krasner and Ullmann, 1965, for example), accept full responsibility for changes to be induced in their patients. The only problem here is that such therapies focus directly on changing behavior and not on changing underlying attitudes or concepts of self.

## Associative Brain Mechanisms and Symbolic Activity; Hebb's Views

Psychologists who study symbolic activity only rarely concern themselves with the role of the brain in such processes. Associative principles can be applied directly to brain processes if we take a definite stand on certain issues: (1) That we want to do it, (2) that our theoretical connections between stimulus and response be translated into functional connections between neurons, and (3) that we do not violate known psychological, physical, or psychophysical facts.

One of the most puzzling of these psychophysical facts has, in fact, provided Donald Hebb with the impetus to develop a fully consistent associative theory of the interaction between the human brain and human symbolic activity. The paradoxical observation giving rise to Hebb's theory (1949, 1966) concerned the problem of why certain types of brain lesions produced astonishingly small behavioral and intellectual deficits. For example, Hebb reports two cases: one of a man with an IQ of 160 after a prefrontal lobotomy, and another of a woman with a post-operation IQ of 115 despite surgical removal of the entire right side of her cortex. As Hebb put it: Either most of the cortex has nothing to do with intelligence, or present conceptions of how the cortex operates are completely inadequate.

Another property of human cognitive activity that Hebb felt had to be handled by any adequate psychophysiological theory was set by Gestalt psychology; namely, that in most aspects, adult and child perception has a unitary property considerably in excess of what might be expected on the basis of associationistic principles. This then is Hebb's problem: to account for the development of intelligence (including perception, reasoning, memory, etc.) on the basis of associative growth principles, where such principles provide for the possibility of wholistic perceptions and emphasize the role of cortical connections in behavior.

Hebb's answer to these problems took the form of a neuropsychological theory in which he made use of two primary theoretical mechanisms: cell assemblies and phase sequences. For Hebb, learning involves the growth of cell-to-cell connections called *cell assemblies*. These cell assemblies develop on the basis of repeated contiguous firings of the neurons involved. For example, if Neuron *B* was usually active right after Neuron *A* had been stimulated, Hebb assumed that these cells would develop into a stable unit, *A–B*. This unit would then come to form a cell assembly containing (at least) one of these two neurons. Once this cell assembly was established, it would be evoked in its entirety when stimulated by appropriate environmental events. This is Hebb's basic associative learning postulate, and involves nothing more than the Law of Contiguity in physical form.

After an initial period of growth, these lower-order cell assemblies develop into more flexible higher-order units known as *phase sequences*. These phase sequences are "assumed to coordinate and organize the lower-order assemblies in functional units for specific problem situations." Phase sequences form the major units in what was termed the semi-autonomous central processes. In order to understand how such units work, let us turn to a sample analysis of a simple (but really complex) problem: the nature of the central processes involved in adding 8 + 2. Figure 7.4, with its associated text, explains how this might occur according to Hebb's theory. Both the addition and subtraction reverberating loop would qualify as phase sequences —or higher-order mental processes—with their role essentially one of determining how the subject would deal first with 8 and then with 2.

For purposes of the present chapter, however, it seems best to concentrate on only one aspect of Hebb's approach: that dealing with the growth of intelligence. Perhaps the key observation here is related to one made earlier: Damage to the cortex of an adult seems to have little or no effect on his intellectual performances, whereas comparable, or even less-extensive cerebral lesions, when they occur in childhood and infancy, produce considerable retardation, particularly in regard to verbal IQ tests. This seemed to Hebb to imply, in accordance with the theoretical views previously described, that brain tissue needed for the *development* of intelligence was different from that required for the *maintenance* of intelligence. It is as if

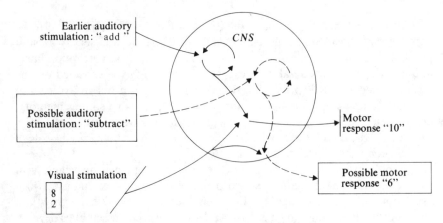

**Fig. 7.4** Diagram of a possible mechanism of a set to add. The excitation from the prior stimulus, "add," is held in a reverberatory loop. The second stimulus (8, 2) is connected with two motor paths, and can evoke "10" or "6." But the reverberatory activity supports only one of these, and the response is "10." If the prior stimulation had been "subtract," a different reverberatory circuit would have been active, and would have determined the response "6." (This diagram is of course schematic.) (From D. O. Hebb, *A Textbook of Psychology*, third edition, Philadelphia, Saunders, 1972)

during childhood and infancy the development of intelligence is highly localized in specific cortical areas, but that as intelligence develops, phase sequences and cell assemblies become sufficiently multiply interconnected (i.e., have a great number of mediational connections) so that damage to a specific part of the cortex is not as debilitating to the adult as to the child.

These notions give rise to two analytic and experimental trends: (1) the concept of an $A/S$ ratio and (2) an intensive study of the role of early experience in the development of intelligence. By the $A/S$ ratio Hebb simply means to contrast the amount of cortex given over for ($A$) associative functions with the amount used for ($S$) sensory processes. Presumably the higher the ratio the greater the possible development of autonomous central processes; i.e., those processes which underly symbolic activity. This, in turn, implies less control of the organism by his immediate environment during adulthood and more control by organism-produced processes. The fact that an organism comes to be controlled more by internal than by external events implies that the child has a great deal to learn. Coupling this fact with a large $A/S$ ratio in children suggests relatively slow initial learning in infants and children, and relatively rapid learning in older children and adults. Many facts— even common-sense ones—do seem to fit the theory and Hebb has summarized the pertinent subhuman facts as follows:

(1) More complex relationships can be learned by higher species with large $A/S$ ratios at maturity; (2) simple relationships are learned about

as well by lower as by higher species; and (3) the first learning is slower in higher than lower species (Hebb, 1949, page 116).

If intelligence results from the development and profusion of cell-to-cell and assembly-to-assembly linkages, it should then be possible to retard or accelerate such development by special early experiences and thereby alter the final level of intelligence attained. If the early environment is restricted, a less intelligent animal will result than if an animal were raised in a more normal environment, or in a particularly enriched one. An early series of exploratory studies were done by Hebb, who compared the performance of rats on a series of complex maze problems where different groups of these rats had been raised in restricted, normal and enriched environments. The results of these studies indicated that the rats raised in restricted environments performed least well, and those raised in enriched environments performed best (Hebb, 1949, page 292 ff). A variety of studies supporting this conclusion have been ably reviewed by Hunt (1961, pages 100–106) and also by Hebb (1958, 1965), and the conclusion in almost all cases agrees with the original hypothesis and data presented by Hebb. Although Hebb was primarily interested in presenting a neurophysiological theory of behavior, these results suggest that his analysis applies quite well to the development of thought in children and adults.

## SUMMARY

Association theory is largely a theory of growth. Historically, one of its primary assumptions was that the mind of an infant is a blank tablet, extraordinarily receptive to change on the basis of experience. All human mentality comes about because of the contiguity of events in experience, whether such contiguity is the result of contiguity in the environment or is mediated by prior learning.

When we turn specifically to the development of thought, the major task for association theory is to specify the critical role of the organism–environment interaction as it affects thinking. Freud, whatever the other influences on his theory, was clearly influenced by an associationist bias. Indeed one of the primary therapeutic procedures introduced by Freud was free association. In this technique, the psychoanalyst focuses on the sequence of responses produced by the patient, particularly at those points at which the associative stream seems to take an unpredictable turn. The reasons for such unpredictable turnings are then sought in the developmental history of the adult, particularly in regard to unconscious or primary-process thinking. Primary-process thinking, in contrast to the more reality-oriented secondary-process thinking, is not bound by the restraints or logic of time and space. Anything is possible, and any bizarre alteration in the associative sequence is assumed to represent primary-process thinking.

Primary-process thinking is not always regressive; there are times when a creative thinker needs to break contemporary frames of reference, and a controlled regression (in the service of rational, creative processes) provides such a possibility. Here the very "illogical" properties of primary process are more likely to lead to a novel juxtaposition of ideas necessary for the creative act. It is not at all uncommon in the history of creative discovery for dream sequences to provide raw material for wake-a-day elaboration. Such phenomena are perfectly consistent with this hypothesis.

Because psychoanalytic theory grew largely out of clinical observation, many of its words and concepts were unfamiliar to most laboratory psychologists. For this reason, Miller and Dollard translated many of the Freudian concepts into the language of the learning laboratory, with the most important of these dealing with labeling behavior and cue-producing responses. For Miller and Dollard the unconscious is largely the unlabeled, and as such it is not surprising to find that strange combinations (generally actions) occur among such unlabeled bits of experience.

But human rationality advances because we are able to label our experience, and such labels provide us with cues for responding. One of the major lines of developmental research evolving out of this concern for the cue-producing properties of labels deals with the role of verbalization in regulating children's nonverbal behavior. From a wide variety of studies, the most general conclusion that can be drawn seems to be that labeling serves a different function for children at different ages: At first, it is simply a means of communicating with adults and only later does it come to help in regulating further behaviors.

If laboratory principles have helped make Freud accessible to the laboratory psychologist, then operant conditioning principles have helped make the learning laboratory accessible to education in the form of programmed learning. The various problems associated with programming (*linear* or *branching*, size of step, the role of *fading*, etc.) all deal with the very significant problem of determining the optimum way in which to sequence the presentation of knowledge so as to achieve maximum learning. This is one of the main problem areas of educational psychology, and research on programmed learning brings these problems into sharp focus.

In addition to Freud's work, perhaps the most broad-ranging attempt to understand the development of thought and intelligence has been provided by Hebb. Beginning with the surprising observation that widespread cortical damage in adults leaves their intellectual ability relatively unimpaired, Hebb went on to develop his neuropsychological theory of the cell assembly and phase sequence. On the basis of this analysis, Hebb was led to the conclusion that the tissue giving rise to intelligence is probably different from the tissue sustaining intelligence. The former seems to be highly specific, while the latter seems to be more diffuse.

Hebb's theory has also provided the impetus for an exploration of the role of early experience on later intelligence. The results of a great many animal and naturally occurring human studies give some support to the general statement that enriched environments during infancy lead to more "intelligent" adult performance, whereas impoverished environments give rise to less intelligent performances when both are compared to more normal conditions. Such data are consistent with the Hebbian view that the development of intelligence involves freeing the organism from direct sensory domination and that intelligent organisms have highly developed autonomous mental processes. As a corollary to this, organisms able to achieve freedom from environmental dominance pay for it in terms of an increased period of pre-adult learning. Thus some organisms more directly responsive to the environment display adaptive behavior almost immediately after birth, whereas human offspring always require a more extended infancy. In any event, this longer period of childhood is predictable from Hebb's theory and completely consistent with an associationistic analysis of mind.

# PART III

# INFORMATION-PROCESSING
# APPROACHES TO THINKING

# CHAPTER 8

# THE RULE'S THE THING:
# THE LOGIC OF
# COMPUTERS
# AND COMPUTATION

Once upon a time, in the land of Crete, there lived a king named Minos. Now this king had a rather sordid history: When the god Poseidon sent a bull to him so that he could offer it as a sacrifice to the gods, Minos found the bull such a glorious animal that he substituted another in its place and kept the god's gift for himself. Gods, then as now, are not to be crossed; because of Minos' greed, Poseidon caused Persephae, the king's wife, to fall in love with the stolen bull. The union of Minos' wife and the bull produced a half-man, half-bull creature called the Minotaur, who was confined by Minos to a specially constructed labyrinth. Every 9 years, or thereabouts, the Minotaur was fed 7 youths and 7 maidens transported from Athens. These 14 young Athenians were exacted as a tribute by Minos after he had defeated the Athenians in a prior battle.

So there the situation stood: every 9 years the Athenians were required to provide 14 young men and women as a sacrifice to the Minotaur. The King of Athens at the time of the present tale was Aegeus, protector of the warrior Theseus. Theseus, in spite of Aegeus' opposition, volunteered to be one of the group sent as a tribute to Minos and to do what he could to rid Athens of her horrible burden. Upon their arrival in Crete, Theseus and the 13 other youths were presented to King Minos and his daughter, Princess Ariadne. In order to save the others, Theseus offered himself as the first sacrifice to the Minotaur.

Here the story changes a bit, for while Theseus was in prison awaiting his encounter with the Minotaur, Princess Ariadne came secretly to him at night. It seems she had fallen in love with him at their first meeting when he stood before her and King Minos. Ariadne then told Theseus all that she knew about the Minotaur and the labyrinth. She next supplied him with herself and a ball of twine. The ball of twine was to be used in order to mark out an exit path from the labyrinth should Theseus be successful in killing the Minotaur. To anticipate and summarize a bit: In the endeavor of the Minotaur and Ariadne, Theseus was successful, and upon killing the Minotaur he, Ariadne, and the other Athenian youths escaped from Crete and sailed home to Athens....

The story goes on for a good bit more, telling in its leisurely way how Theseus abandoned Ariadne on the Island of Naxos and how she was befriended by Dionysus and so on..., but for present purposes enough of the story has been told. The crucial matter of interest is: How did Theseus use the ball of twine supplied by Ariadne to find the Minotaur and effect his escape from the maze?

Consider, for a moment, the scope of the problem: an unknown maze consisting of an unknown pattern. Some of the corridors end in blind alleys, while others simply go round and round, leading the searcher back where he started. In the maze: a fierce monster at an unknown position, and Ariadne at a point near the entrance holding onto one end of Theseus' life twine. How should Theseus proceed in this matter?

It is possible to represent the problem (and the labyrinth) geometrically as a series of choice points having one or more corridors at each juncture; such as, for example, the one depicted in Fig. 8.1, with Ariadne located at point $A$, and the Minotaur at point $E$.

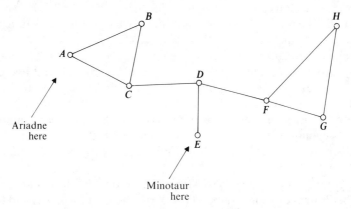

**Fig. 8.1**  Ariadne, the Minotaur, and a labyrinth.

Each corridor of the labyrinth can be specified by its end points. Thus $DE$ represents the corridor leading to the Minotaur. Stating the situation most abstractly, Theseus' job is to find the Minotaur by whatever route possible and return to Ariadne by the most direct path from that point.

In order to solve the search problem involved, Theseus needs to distinguish among three types of corridors: those through which he has never passed (call these *Zero corridors*), those through which he has passed once

(*One corridors*), and those through which he has passed twice (*Two corridors*). Obviously *One Paths* are those he has gone through right from the beginning; *Two Paths* are those he has to double back through; while *Zero Paths* represent possible new directions. Whenever Theseus moves from one junction to another, he can do so in one of two ways: He can unwind the thread thus provisionally marking the corridor a *One Path*, or he can retrace his steps through an already traveled path, rewinding the thread as he goes. In this latter case he needs to make a special mark on the wall so as to tell him which is a *Two corridor* and which is a *Zero corridor*. On this basis then, Theseus need never go through a *Two corridor* more than twice; that is, in and back. Given these constraints, Theseus is likely to find one of the following five conditions at each choice point:

1. The Minotaur
2. Ariadne
3. An unmarked corridor (a *Zero corridor*) meaning there is a new (never traversed) corridor leading away
4. A loop—Ariadne's thread already goes through both corridors (or Theseus has been here before). In other words, there are at least 2 *One corridors* leading away from that point
5. Anything else: possibly some combinations of conditions, or a clearly marked *Two corridor*

Given these five conditions, the Russian mathematician Trachtenbrot (1963) proposed that Theseus use the following procedures in order to find his way out of the labyrinth.

| Condition | Move |
|---|---|
| 1. Minotaur | Stop |
| 2. Ariadne | Rewind the thread |
| 3. Zero corridor | Unwind the thread |
| 4. Loop | Stop |
| 5. Anything else | Rewind the thread |

Let us now consider an actual search pattern using this table of instructions as a guide. If (referring back to Fig. 8.1) Theseus starts at Point *A*, the condition of corridor *AB* is *Zero* and therefore Theseus unwinds the thread and progresses on. This condition also applies at choice point *B* leading down corridor *BC*. At the end of this corridor, Theseus has a choice, with corridors *CD* and *CA* available. If he chooses *CA*, he ends up at Ariadne and a loop condition (both corridors *One*). At this point he would follow Rule 5, and therefore rewind the thread and go back down *CA* marking that point as *Two*—not to be entered. He is thus once again at point *C*; with *CD* the only remaining *Zero* corridor at this point. On this basis he unwinds the thread, and progresses down corridor *CD* until choice point *D*. Here he has two choices: He can either go down *DE* and face the horrible monster at *E* (which is what he wants to do) or continue down *DF* and go on without finding the Minotaur. If he goes along *DF*, he will ultimately go around the loop *FG*, *GH*, *HF* and be led by his search rules back to point *D*, at which point he will then have only one choice, *DE*, which will lead him to the lair of the Minotaur.

Instead of following Theseus through the *F–G–H–F* cycle, let us assume that he traverses corridor *DE* at this point and comes face to face with the Minotaur and (since we know the outcome already—no real need for suspense now) slays him on the spot. At this point Theseus still has the problem of getting out of the labyrinth. If, however, he followed the search rules previously described, Ariadne's thread should cover the following path: *AB*, *BC*, *CD*, *DE*, and thus provide a direct route from the Minotaur to the exit of the labyrinth. All's well that ends well.

The success of this entire adventure depends on the list of instructions used by Theseus in searching the labyrinth. Technically, such a formalized list of instructions—which tells the user what to do under any and all conditions—is called an *algorithm*. Algorithms form an important part of the logic of electronic computers, as well as some psychological models of symbolic activities that view the computer as an appropriate analogy on which to base their analysis. Before, however, we can move on to strictly psychological considerations, it will be necessary to examine some further concepts in the mathematics of computers as well as to describe how these abstract problems relate first to automatic computing machinery and then to psychological analyses of thinking.

*The concept of a tree.* One of the most significant properties of an algorithm is that it works. That is, a procedure is considered an algorithm to the degree that it provides a successful solution to a class of problems. Naturally, the desired solution is one that solves the problem best. In order to uncover how to approach a problem of a given type, it is best to begin by asking a relatively simple although often involved question: What are the alternatives, and how may they be represented?

Consider the following admittedly simple game involving two players *A* and *B*: These players are required to make alternate moves. There are six matches on the table, and each player is allowed to pick up one or two matches. The loser is the one who has to pick up the last match.

The best way in which to catalogue all the possibilities is by drawing a *tree* of the game, or by enumerating all possible moves by each player under any and all conditions. Figure 8.2 presents a tree for this game, with the two players labeled *A* and *B*, respectively.

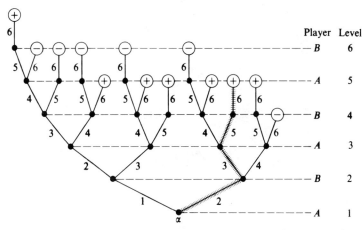

**Fig. 8.2** Tree diagram of the six-matches game for two players, *A* and *B*. (From Trakhtenbrot, 1963)

The bottom *vertex* of the tree, point α, represents the conditions at the start of the game, while other vertices represent various conditions of the game after a varying number of different moves. The first two paths leading away from vertex α are called *branches* and represent the possible choices of player *A* at the start of the game. Branches further up the tree have similar meaning. In this tree the left branch of any vertex represents picking up one match, while the right branch represents picking up 2 matches.

The hatched path running from vertex α upward represents one complete game in which Player *A* first picks 2 matches, followed by *B*'s choosing 1, then *A*'s choosing 2; with this sequence of choices, *B* is left holding the last match and thereby loses the game. Thus, in a simple game of this sort, it is possible to represent each and every move and thereby derive a general picture of the game from an analysis of its tree.

It is also possible to go the other way, and say that a particular tree defines a game. The importance of this is that for a great many different games, given the tree of the game, it is possible to specify a winning algorithm for one of the players. For example, if we extend the 6-matches game to one involving 11 matches: and if we allow each player to pick up 1, 2, or 3 matches: and player *A* makes the first move; then the following rule specifies a winning strategy for *A*: If *B* picks up *K* matches (where *K* can be 1, 2, or 3), then *A* is to pick up 4 *minus K* matches on his next move. A rule that always leads to victory is called a *strategy*—that is, a list of instructions for playing a game completely specified in terms of the other player's responses. (If this game is to be used for fun or profit—that is, at home, in school, or at the beer hall— it is probably best to reduce the game to 9 matches, and allow your opponent to go first. It's much more impressive that way.)

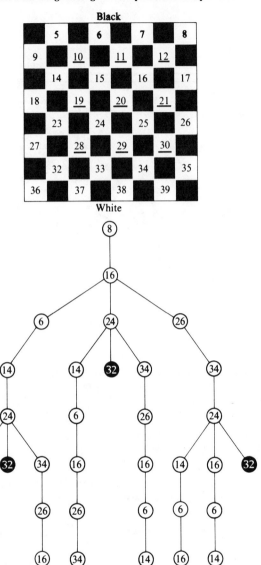

**Fig. 8.3** Capture tree depicts all the possible partial-capture moves for a given piece after the first such move. In checkers, a move is not complete until no more captures can be made. It is possible to make, at most, nine captures in a single move, as shown here. (From C. Strachey, "System Analysis and Programming." Copyright © 1966 by Scientific American, Inc. All rights reserved.)

As should be clear, trees are quite useful in leading to the development of winning strategies or algorithms in perfectly fixed games. But as should be clear, the size of the tree is related to the complexity of the game. An example of the complexity involved in even as simple a game as checkers is presented in Fig. 8.3, for only a single move of a "white king" and for a single rather remarkable constellation of black checkers on the board at one given time.

Obviously, a different sort of approach is needed for games that have extremely complicated tree structures. As one author put it with respect to checkers: "The complete exploration of every possible path through a checker game would involve perhaps $10^{40}$ choices of moves, which at 3 choices per millimicrosecond, would still take $10^{21}$ centuries to consider." (Samuel, 1959, page 212)   In the case of chess, the total number of paths through the chess tree has been estimated to be on the order of $10^{120}$, give or take a few powers.

Given these staggeringly large numbers, it is obvious that the complete enumeration of all possible consequences of a given move is well beyond the possibility of even the largest computer, mechanical or human. How then has it been possible to develop procedures that allow computers to play a reasonably good game of chess, or to play a game of checkers sufficiently well so as to beat a checkers champion? The answer usually given involves the concept of a *heuristic*, or a partial and highly selective search of the tree of a game. Generally, this partial search consists of an examination of a limited number of paths for only a few moves in the future, and repeats this process after each move made by the opponent.

The relationship of algorithms to heuristics should be clear: An algorithm guarantees the solution of a class of problems, whereas a heuristic does not always provide the predicted payoff. In heuristics, on the other hand, the search procedure is much reduced, but the best solution (however that may be defined) or for that matter any solution, may not be found. In terms of the types of problems that machines are called on to solve, an algorithm represents the optimum choice and is the more desirable of the two for "telling" a machine how to do a particular problem.

At this point we probably need to sound a small warning alarm so as to avoid possible misunderstanding. We do not want to give the impression that information-processing models apply only, or even primarily, to algorithmic behaviors, or for that matter that such models force behavior into an algorithmic straightjacket. As a matter of fact, algorithmic behaviors are not the only or even the most important basis for the man–computer analogy, and most cognitive activities are probably better represented in terms of heuristics than in terms of algorithms.

Why talk then about algorithms? Primarily because computers solve problems on the basis of such algorithms, and only if we understand how algorithms work will it be possible to describe, even superficially, how computers work. The purpose of this description is to allow you, the reader, an opportunity to see if computers really represent an appropriate way in which to think about substantive human processes, such as remembering, or problem solving, or concept formation. Only if we spell out some of the details will it be possible to see how far, and how seriously, psychology should go in pursuing computers as an appropriate analogy for human thinking. However, before specific connections can be made between algorithms, heuristics, computers, and minds, we need first describe modern computational procedures and devices.

## Some Words on Computer Software

The difficult part of an algorithm is its construction. Once an algorithm is known, it requires very little additional knowledge to apply it. In a sense, a person in possession of an algorithm can use it "mechanically"—that is, as a machine, without really worrying about why it works. Consider for example a student doing a series of separate addition problems with the aid of a desk calculator. First of all, all the problems (say 10) are written down on a piece of paper. Also say the student is using a new calculator—that is one he has never used before and therefore one he doesn't really know how to use. In order to do the problems, he has to make use of the handbook that gives him instructions on how to do addition: "First pick the keys representing the first number, then press the + bar, then press the second number, and press the + bar again. The answer will appear in the upper register." If the student can find the appropriate keys, the answer to each problem appears in the upper register. This he then writes down in the appropriate place on his paper and moves on to the next problem.

This rather simple situation illustrates many of the major components of any piece of computing machinery: a *memory unit* which keeps track of information and instructions (i.e., the paper on which the problems are written, and the instruction book telling him how to work the machine); a *control unit* that keeps track of the order of processes (in this case, the student who punches the numbers and records the answers); and an *arithmetic unit* that performs the actual computations (in the present case, the desk calculator). Any computation involves both the *storage* and *processing* of material, as well as some procedure to *control* the entire process. Each process is usually represented by a separate mechanical component. In the case of machine computation, two further components are needed: an *input device*—to code the material into the machine—such as a card reader for Punched Cards, and an *output device*—to code the material for the human user—such as an output printer giving off endless reams of perforated paper.

All of these pieces represent the mechanical parts of the system: the so-called *hardware* of computation. If the computer is to serve as an analogy, or metaphor, for human information processing, then it seems apparent that the hardware of a machine—tubes, circuits, wires, cards, etc.—must be different from the hardware of the human—nerves, muscles, cells, blood, etc. —and that at this level the analogy is not only inappropriate but downright wrong. However, the part of computer technology that is most significant for the psychological analysis of symbolic activity is not the physical properties of computation, but rather the plan, or program, that controls the operation of the computer: in other words, its *software*.

## Computer Alphabets and Operations on These Alphabets

One of the first prerequisites of computer software is that it have a symbolic alphabet available to it capable of representing, at the very least, logical decisions, numbers, and words. For a number of reasons, some of which have to do with the capabilities of electronic tubes and wire cores, the simplest alphabet capable of doing the job consists of only two terms: 1's and 0's. The basic unit of this system is a bit: that is a given component can be in one of two states. If there are two such components, there are two states for each component or a total of 4 states ($2^2$). If there are three components, the total number of states is $2^3$ or 8 states. The number of bits, therefore, represents the number of states that can be specified as 2 raised to some power equal to the number of components. For 5 components, there would be $2^5$ or 32 states. A machine with 5, two-state (binary) components could therefore accommodate the 26 letters of the alphabet plus a few marks of punctuation in addition to providing for spaces between letters.

At this level—the level of bits—the primary operations are the logical ones; "and," "or," and "not," which are represented logically as $\cdot$, $+$, and $-$. Computer designers work in terms of the logic of these three functions. An example of the type of "software" considerations involved at this level is presented in Fig. 8.4. Each of the 3 circuits represents one of the logical systems together with its respective table of values. This table of values lists all possible input states and their correlated output states.

The next level above that of a simple two-valued "yes" or "no," or "true–false" decision is the level of numbers, and here the basic operations involved are the same as in the case of ordinary $base_{10}$ numbers used in everyday counting. In this connection, it is well to remember that the number 111 in our ordinary number system represents $1 \times 10^2 + 1 \times 10^1 + 1 \times 10^0$ or $1 \times 100 + 1 \times 10 + 1 \times 1$ or one hundred and eleven (ten + one). In binary numbers, where the base is 2 not 10, the number 111 represents $1 \times 2^2 + 1 \times 2^1 + 1 \times 2^0$ or 7 in $base_{10}$. The important part of translating $base_2$ numbers into $base_{10}$ numbers is to remember that only the base is changed and therefore the number of places goes up astronomically in $base_2$ relative to $base_{10}$. The reason for using $base_2$ numbers has to do with the basic unit of the computer, that is, each individual element has only a two-state capacity: it is not something intrinsic to computer software.

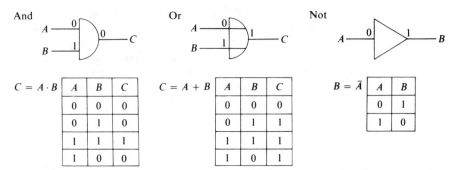

| $C = A \cdot B$ | $A$ | $B$ | $C$ |
|---|---|---|---|
| | 0 | 0 | 0 |
| | 0 | 1 | 0 |
| | 1 | 1 | 1 |
| | 1 | 0 | 0 |

| $C = A + B$ | $A$ | $B$ | $C$ |
|---|---|---|---|
| | 0 | 0 | 0 |
| | 0 | 1 | 1 |
| | 1 | 1 | 1 |
| | 1 | 0 | 1 |

| $B = \bar{A}$ | $A$ | $B$ |
|---|---|---|
| | 0 | 1 |
| | 1 | 0 |

**Fig. 8.4** *And, or,* and *not* constitute a set of binary logic elements that is functionally complete. The three symbols represent circuits that can carry out each of these logic functions. Input signals, either 0 or 1, enter the circuits at the left. Output signals leave at the right. Below each circuit is a "truth table" that lists all possible input states and corresponding output states. (From D. C. Evans, "Computer Logic and Memory." Copyright © 1966 by Scientific American, Inc. All rights reserved.)

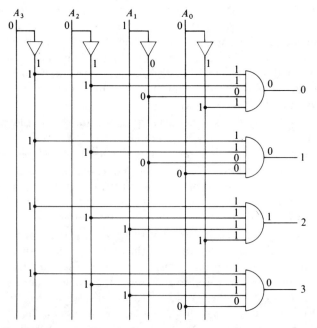

**Fig. 8.5** This circuit, made up of four *not* circuits and four *and* circuits, converts binary to decimal digits. (It carries the decoding only as far as decimal digit 3.) The signal at each of the numbered outputs is 0 unless all the inputs are 1. This is true for the third *and* circuit from the top, labeled 2. Thus the binary digits 0010 are decoded to yield the decimal digit 2. Table 8.1 shows the binary equivalent for the decimal digits from 0 to 9. (From D. C. Evans, "Computer Logic and Memory." Copyright © 1966 by Scientific American, Inc. All rights reserved.)

How are such operations as the conversion of $base_2$ numbers to $base_{10}$ numbers carried out by the logic of the computer?  Figure 8.5 presents a portion of a circuit designed to accomplish such conversions.

If we let terminals $A_3$, $A_2$, $A_1$, and $A_0$ represent input nodes and use the notation developed earlier for "not" and "and" circuits, then the fragment of the network shown in Fig. 8.5 indicates how an input to $A_1$ alone comes to be transferred into the output response of "2."  The total table for this type of logic circuit is presented in Table 8.1, which presents the circuitry required to produce the numbers 0–9 in $base_{10}$.

**Table 8.1**

| Decimal | Binary | | | |
|---|---|---|---|---|
| | $A_3$ | $A_2$ | $A_1$ | $A_0$ |
| 0 | 0 | 0 | 0 | 0 |
| 1 | 0 | 0 | 0 | 1 |
| 2 | 0 | 0 | 1 | 0 |
| 3 | 0 | 0 | 1 | 1 |
| 4 | 0 | 1 | 0 | 0 |
| 5 | 0 | 1 | 0 | 1 |
| 6 | 0 | 1 | 1 | 0 |
| 7 | 0 | 1 | 1 | 1 |
| 8 | 1 | 0 | 0 | 0 |
| 9 | 1 | 0 | 0 | 1 |

**Computer memory systems.**  One important part of any computational process involves what is called information storage or memory.  In many instances, access to memory has been a stumbling block for many operations.  Physically, information may be stored on registers in the operational memory units of the computer, or may be stored on auxiliary tapes, magnetic drums, magnetic cores, or on some combination of these.  In some of the more modern machines, photographic means are often employed which are quite economical in terms of cost per bit (see Evans, 1966, for a discussion of the state of the art).

There are really three main considerations involved in discussing computer memory: "word length," storage capacity, and access time.  Each memory unit is called a *word* and may contain a varying number of bits/word.  Large scale computers may have as many as 32,000 or more storage (or word) cells in the memory unit of the computer and a considerably larger store available on slower-access media such as tapes, cards, etc.

How is a memory unit stored for later use?  Access to a particular memory cell is usually accomplished by providing the cell with an "address" or location (i.e., Cell 23).  This address is included in any description of this particular piece of memory content.  As is obvious, the address must ultimately be coded on the basis of a binary number so as to enable the machine to process it. Addressing memory cells or content is accomplished either by more-or-less arbitrary numbering as described above, or in terms of content. Content addressing is the less common of the two, but it is the type most often used in commercial computers for locating such things as a person's airline reservation or bank statement. In this latter regard, the odd-shaped numbers used on the bottom of many bank checks represent the check-writer's code, and all information about that person is content-addressable under that number.

Storage or computer memory comes in a number of different types. As we have noted, there is external storage in the form of magnetic tape with very slow access time. Internal storage is contained in the processing unit itself and consists of two types: static and dynamic storage. In static storage, information is always held in a fixed location and is instantantaneously available. Dynamic storage, on the other hand, contains addressable items that may be moved around in the course of calculation, even to the extent of being put into external storage should the need arise.

Perhaps the most complete, and at the same time, one of the most straightforward accounts of storage and the operations on stored material is provided by Reitman (1965) in a simple information processing language known as *IPL-V.*

As in his example, consider a rather small memory of 35 cells as diagrammed in Fig. 8.6. Although it would be differently realized in hardware, let us assume a rectangular array for ease of presentation. The first problem is to assign an address or name to each cell. This is accomplished by going from left to right across each row so that the uppermost left-hand cell is 0 and the bottom-most right-hand cell is 34.

| | | | | | |
|---|---|---|---|---|---|
| (Cells 0–4) | | | | | |
| (Cells 5–9) | | | | | |
| (Cells 10–14) | | | | | |
| (Cells 15–19) | | | | | |
| (Cells 20–24) | | | | | |
| (Cells 25–29) | | | | | |
| (Cells 30–34) | | | | | |

**Fig. 8.6** A sample matrix of cells used in computer programming.

In order to make the job of storage easier, it is often convenient to set up memory regions by labeling all the input of a particular type with the same symbol, and having all the constituent items occupy adjacent or nearly adjacent memory locations called memory regions. Obviously, any cell can be selected as a starting point for a region, and all other elements will occupy adjacent positions. Such regions are usually defined in terms of a letter and a number, such as $A2$; which would mean the item in the second cell in Region $A$.

In order to facilitate further the retrieval of stored materials, the contents of each cell can be expanded into a *link part* and a *symbol part*. The symbol part is entered as in Fig. 8.7, in a number of different memory cells.

| Symb | Link | Symb | Link | Symb | Link | Symb | Link | Symb | Link |
|------|------|------|------|------|------|------|------|------|------|
|      |      |      |      | SO   | 0    |      |      |      |      |
| FO   | 6    | GO   | 21   |      |      |      |      |      |      |
|      |      |      |      |      |      |      |      |      |      |
|      |      |      |      |      |      | AO   | 33   |      |      |
|      |      | IO   | 30   |      |      |      | 18   |      |      |
|      |      |      |      | NO   | 2    |      |      |      |      |
| MO   | 27   |      |      |      |      | CO   | 5    |      |      |

**Fig. 8.7**   Circled cell, cell 23, is the head cell of an alphabetically ordered list. See text for explanation. (From Reitman, 1965)

In this example, symbols and links have been entered in Cells, 2, 5, 6, 18, 21, 27, 30, and 33. In Cell 23 we have included only the link symbol 18, with the SYMB part of the cell left open. Cell 23 serves the function of organizing the other 8 cells into a single list. Suppose we want all these items to be arranged alphabetically, it is then possible to see that the LINK numbers serve to select the appropriate next cell. Starting at 23 go to 18 ($AO$) then to 33 ($CO$) then to 5 ($FO$) and so on until Cell 2 ($SO$). On this basis a list is constructed with 23 as the lead access symbol that serves to define the list. In this way the memory can be organized and searched given the single instruction: List 23 (or Cell 23).

**Control processes.**   With this last analysis we come to the third major component of computational procedures: the control function. In terms of psychology, the control function represents probably the single most important area for it is here that intelligent action or planning is carried out. Control serves the function of directing and even of modifying all of the other components, as well as determining the sequencing of processes within both the arithmetic and memory units.

How is such control achieved? The heart of the control process is contained in the program as a series of fixed steps to be done by the arithmetic and memory units in order to produce a solution. To write a successful program requires a number of steps, the most important of which are an analysis of the process to be undertaken as well as the construction of a specific program. In preparing a computer program, one first makes an organizational chart showing the order in which computations have to be done in order to achieve the desired result. Generally these charts, indicating the flow of the process, begin at a relatively imprecise level, and only subsequently are the subcomponents specified in any detail.

Consider, for example, the sequence of *flow charts* presented in Fig. 8.8.

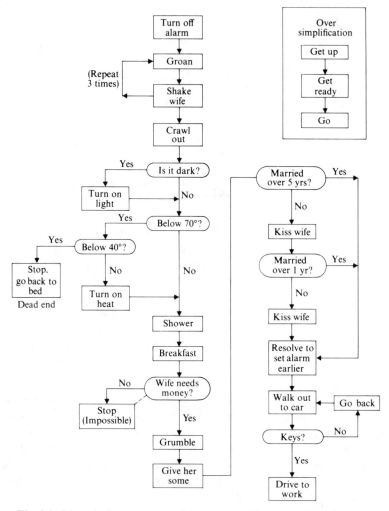

**Fig. 8.8** Flow chart: How to get to work in the morning. (Adapted from Borko, 1962.)

The figure labeled "oversimplification" segments the process into three components: getting up, getting ready, and going. At some level of description, these three categories might do—for example, in describing your morning routine to a friend. The second figure, which presents the situation in much greater detail, provides a much fuller—if somewhat facetious—specification of the total process. Note that the behavior at any one level is not necessarily linear, as might have seemed to be the case if only the over-simplified flow chart were considered: Certain parts of the sequence require loops, e.g., if the answer to the question "Is it dark?" is "Yes," then a light has to be turned on before the rest of the behavior can proceed. Sometimes a part of the behavior is to be repeated or looped a number of times such as "groaning" and "shaking" your wife.

Even this second diagram is not really sufficiently precise: The segment of the behavior near the end labeled "Keys?"—"drive to work" is not quite as simple as it appears. For one, there are three keys on Mr. Mits' (Man In The Street) key ring, the smallest of which is for the car. How might a computer come to pick the correct one? Figure 8.9 presents a flow chart for the key problem, in which the solution is based on finding the smallest key.

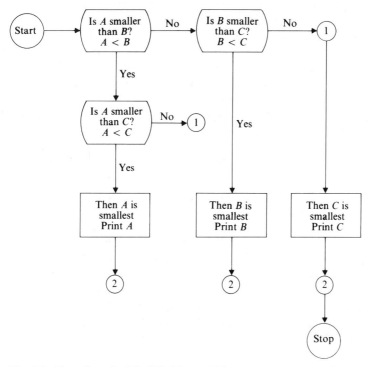

**Fig. 8.9** Flow chart for Mr. Mits' key problem program.

There are a number of different ways in which to accomplish recognition of this sort: One is to provide the computer with a plate of the exact size and try out all of the keys until one matches exactly. This is called a *template* approach. Another way in which to do it is to compare each of the keys against each of the other keys, and pick out the smallest, as in a sequential processing operation. A third way is to provide a set of distinguishing characteristics that seem to define one and only one key as correct. In this case the computer "recognizes" the key on the basis of its relative agreement with a list of *distinctive features.* The two terms—*template matching* and *distinctive features* analysis—represent the usual ways in which computers go about recognizing patterns and as such form the basis of most psychological analysis of pattern recognition.

This brief and necessarily sketchy excursion into flow charts and programming has a number of important implications for psychology which need be emphasized. For one, it is possible to describe behavior at a number of different levels. That is, "getting up" may be a perfectly acceptable description of what Mr. Mits does between 7 and 8 o'clock in the morning, although at another level of precision the behaviors involved have to be specified further. As is also obvious from the preceding example, each specification can be further specified to a next lower or microscopic level, as in the key problem. The question of how to represent this levels-within-levels problem has been discussed before, when the notion of a hierarchy was emphasized. Any act can be considered as containing certain subcomponents, each of which can be analyzed into further subcomponents.

In this connection it is obvious that the tree diagram explored in connection with an analysis of all possible moves in simple games provides an appropriate tool for analyzing a hierarchy of components. In order to enable a computer to perform a particular control operation, the hierarchical nature of the task must be recognized, and a structural representation produced (such as a tree or flow diagram) to specify all of the constituent parts. The tree diagram has still another property; namely, that an entire sequence can be represented at once, with the recognition that a description at the highest or most macroscopic level automatically contains implicitly (and explicitly if the tree is drawn) all the more microscopic components. The sequence of appropriate substeps is thus available from the very beginning.

Another implication of this type of programming becomes apparent from an analysis of certain loop properties in the diagram; namely, that at points in the flow of behavior the outcome of a particular piece of behavior is fed back to the system and determines the future direction of the process. In the case of turning on the stove, for example, there are a number of test phases (such as: Is the temperature below 70°?) that need be met before the ongoing "behavior" can progress. We have already come across feedback notions in Miller, Galanter, and Pribram's concept of the TOTE (see

Chapter 2 for a discussion) and, as will become apparent, a good deal of effort has gone into determining the role of various types of feedback in concept formation and problem solving.

## More Mathematics: the Turing Machine

The existence of computer hardware, particularly in terms of the arithmetic and memory units, indicates the close connection between algorithms and computational procedures. If a process can be represented by an algorithm, it is possible to construct a device to put the algorithm into operation. In many cases, however, although an algorithm is potentially "do-able," the capacity of the machine (memory or arithmetic) may be exceeded in carrying out the operation. This is analogous to the case in which a human calculator runs out of ink or paper before a problem is completely solved, although he could solve it if enough external memory and computational space were provided. Some algorithms are realizable only if a machine has infinite memory.

Why should the problem of infinite memory be of any concern to mathematics? For one thing, it relates to a rather famous speculation by the German mathematician and philosopher Leibnitz, who seriously considered the possibility of constructing an algorithm capable of solving any and all mathematical problems. The refinement of this problem came to be known as the *deducibility problem*, that is, is it possible to construct an algorithm for a particular class of problems, even if the problem were as large as all mathematics? Prior to Leibnitz, the term algorithm was applied only when a concrete algorithm was already in existence; stating the deducibility problem in its general form raised the problem to one of utmost importance for the logical bases of mathematics. Not to postpone the answer unduly, the answer to Leibnitz's question is *no*; there are a great many problems for which not only are there no known algorithms, but for which algorithms are impossible to construct. Thus, it is not possible to construct an algorithm for every class of problem.

This conclusion implies that it is possible to demonstrate not only that there is not an available algorithm at present, but that the construction of such an algorithm is an impossibility. The precise formulation of this class of proofs, however, had to wait until a rigorous definition of algorithm had been developed. As it turns out, the most important of these definitions was developed from a consideration of how a computer (human or machine) translates an algorithm into a set of mechanical operations. The definition of algorithms by machine operations was first proposed by Turing in 1937, and the class of "machines" derived from his definition have come to be called *Turing machines*. Turing machines, however, are not machines in the hardware sense of the term—rather they are defined by their table of operational procedures; or, what has come to be called, their functional matrices.

One important property of Turing machines is that they require infinite memory; with such memory usually described in terms of an infinite tape. The reason for developing a Turing machine was to provide a logical procedure for analyzing problems of deducibility, and one component of deducibility is potential realizability, even if such realizability is only theoretical. This necessity then provides the logical reason for assuming that Turing machines have an infinite memory tape.

Before proceeding further, let us consider one specific Turing machine as represented by John Kemeny in *Scientific American* (1955). Kemeny endows his Turing machine with the potential to do six things: (1) Write the letter $X$, (2) write the digit 1, (3) erase either of these marks, (4) move the infinite tape one place to the left, (5) move the tape one place to the right, and (6) stop. The tape is considered to be infinitely long and divided into a series of squares, which are scanned one at a time.

In terms of construction and function this is a very simple machine, much simpler logically than any of the binary machines considered thus far. Kemeny's machine reduces the chain of possible operations to the simplest form possible, indeed to the limit. Although Kemeny's alphabet is reduced to a single element, namely 1, this reduction necessitates an increase in the number of steps required in calculation. Despite this increase it simplifies the logical structure of the task enormously. This latter simplification is necessary in order to provide for the definitions of algorithms and deducibility. In terms of the previous discussion, it is clear that the Turing machine uses a one-address format: Only a single memory cell (the scanned cell) is involved in any computation.

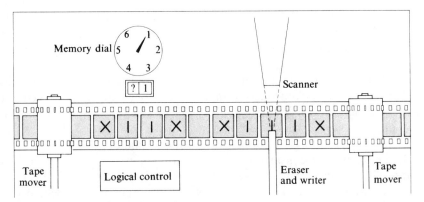

**Fig. 8.10** Kemeny's Turing machine, designed for simple addition. (From J. G. Kemeny, "Man Viewed as a Machine." Copyright © 1955 by Scientific American, Inc. All rights reserved.)

Figure 8.10 presents the hardware of Kemeny's Turing machine designed to perform simple addition. In the particular problem presently in the machine, the task is to add 2 + 3. The $X$'s serve as "punctuation" in order to define the limits of a number (11 or 111), while spaces are inserted between units enclosed by $X$'s. There are obviously only three things that can be on the tape at any one scan: a 1, an $X$, or □ (a blank space). The moves of the machine are $E$ (erasure); $X$, write an $X$ on the tape; $D$, write the digit 1 on the tape; $R$, move the tape one frame to the right; $L$, move the tape one frame to the left; $S$, stop; ?, something is wrong; and !, the operation is finished. The machine has two other components in addition to the tape movers and the writer-eraser, and these are the memory dial with numbers 1 through 6, and its logical control. The memory dial can be set by the logical control to have any one of the six numbers showing. The logical control is contained in the functional matrix of instructions presented in Fig. 8.11.

| | □ | X | \| |
|---|---|---|---|
| 1 | D6 | E2 | R1 |
| 2 | R2 | E3 | ?2 |
| 3 | R3 | E4 | E5 |
| 4 | L4 | ?4 | R6 |
| 5 | L5 | ?5 | R1 |
| 6 | X6 | I6 | R3 |

**Fig 8.11** Matrix of instructions needed to operate Kemeny's machine. (From J. C. Kemeny, "Man Viewed as a Machine." Copyright © 1955 by Scientific American, Inc. All rights reserved.)

In this matrix, each column heading stands for one of the states of the tape, either blank, with a 1 on it, or with an $X$ on it, while each of the row headings stands for the present state of the memory dial on the machine. For example, the matrix cell produced by the intersection of □ and 1 tells the machine to write the digit 1 in the space on the tape and then to move the memory dial to 6. By the same token, the expression $E4$ in $X3$ means "erase the number presumably on the tape, and move the memory dial to 4."

Let us see how the machine would work in the case of adding 11 and 111 with the setup presented in Fig. 8.10. The cell scanned contains a 1 and the memory dial is set at 1. By reference to the functional matrix, the appropriate instruction is $R1$ or move the tape one square to the right, and leave the dial at 1. The same 1–1 result is produced by the scan, so the tape is moved over one more cell to the right. By the third move the cell scanned has an $X$ unit, while the memory dial is set at 1. The appropriate instruction here is $E2$ or erase the $X$ and set the memory dial to 2. The next constellation is □2, where the appropriate instruction is $R2$. Performing this operation produces another □2 scan and the same $R2$ instruction. Now the situation is $X2$, with an $E3$ instruction and so on. Figure 8.12 presents the state of the machine and tape after 10, 20, 30, and 36 trials, at which time the process ends. The operation consists essentially of moving all of the 1's to the same general area of the tape and then stopping the process when $X$'s enclose the new number. Reference to Fig. 8.12 makes it clear that the machine does get the correct answer.

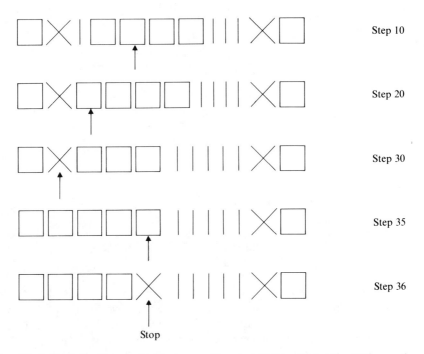

Fig. 8.12 State diagram for Turing machine designed to do simple addition problem.

From these considerations it is clear that a Turing machine is completely specified by its *functional matrix of instructions*. If two Turing machines have the same matrices, they must be regarded as equivalent machines. The functional matrix is that point at which Turing machines make contact with the theory of algorithms, for the functional matrix of a Turing machine represents the definition of a particular algorithm. Indeed this forms the basic hypothesis for the theory of algorithms: "All algorithms can be given in the form of functional matrices and executed by the corresponding Turing machine." (Trakhtenbrot, 1963, page 77) In short, the search for an algorithm becomes the search for the appropriate Turing machine.

**The Universal Turing Machine.** In analyzing the operation of Kemeny's addition algorithm for a simple Turing machine, the process was first represented in terms of a machine with a certain configuration, and then by a series of state diagrams (more accurately tape configurations) of what the machine could and did do. In the case of Kemeny's machine, the "machine" or mechanical part was concretized by a particular piece of hardware capable of following the appropriate functional matrix. But this particular piece of hardware does not exhaust the way in which this functional matrix could be realized. As is clear, a human operator would also be capable of doing the work of any given Turing machine if he were supplied with its functional matrix. More generally, the process of imitating a machine by following the properties of its functional matrix can be given algorithmic form, and as such the original matrix is "do-able" in the form of another Turing machine. This algorithm, which enables one machine to mimic another, is called the *imitation algorithm* and forms the basis of a *Universal Turing Machine*, or a machine capable of executing the functional matrix of any other Turing machine.

Now it is obvious that human beings represent one type of Universal Machine; that is, they can do any problem for which an algorithm exists; but what is not clear is whether or not a nonhuman Universal Machine can be developed. In order to do this, two considerations need be kept in mind: (1) Functional matrices have at least two dimensions (one representing the memory state and the other the present element scanned), whereas Turing machines have only unidimensional elements; and (2) a Universal Machine needs a fixed alphabet capable of encompassing functional matrices that might contain an infinite number of elements. The handling of both these problems is interrelated: First of all a simple code capable of defining any functional matrix in terms of a single element is needed, and second the Universal Machine must be able to handle this code. Although there are a number of codes which are able to meet these criteria, perhaps the simplest one makes use of integers.

Consider, for example, the table of commands presented in connection with Kemeny's example. Each row has 3 possibilities 1, $X$, or □, and there are 6 possible moves. If we let the numbers 1–6 represent the 6 internal elements $E$, $X$, $D$, $L$, $R$, and !, in order, then the first line would read 3–6, instead of $D6$, 1–2 instead of $E2$, and 5–1 instead of $R1$. After this, each row of the table can now be represented by a single integer. The best way to do this is to treat these numbers as an exponent for the prime numbers and multiply these out to obtain a single product. Such a product turns out to be unique for any particular set of numbers and therefore is able to specify the row unambiguously. After each row has been reduced by this procedure to a single number, all 6 rows (now 6 single numbers) can be reduced by the same trick, and the entire table uniquely specified by a single number. Given this reduction, a Universal Machine can now be designed to treat the functional matrix of the addition algorithm as appropriate input, and then proceed to utilize these instructions in further computations.

The result of all this maneuvering is that Universal Machines are always a possibility, and that anything any given Turing machine can do, so too can the Universal Machine. Similar to its human counterpart, anything that is algorithmetically possible for any particular Turing machine is possible for the Universal Machine.

Here, contact is again made with modern computing machinery. The logical existence of a Universal Machine implies that any Universal Machine may be given the program of any particular Turing machine, and on this basis the Universal Machine will be able to handle the corresponding problem. This line of argument further implies that the essential part of computation is not the hardware, but rather the particular program of instructions that guides it, and given these considerations it is possible to view electronic computing machines as but one type of Universal Turing Machine. If computers meet this status (which in fact they do) there is no need to develop a new computer for every problem; all that is required is a change in program.

Here then is certainly a significant implication for the psychology of symbolic activity: If both human and electronic computers can be viewed as Universal Machines—keeping in mind that the important part defining such a machine is its program, and not its mechanical form—then one of the most important problems to be considered in analyzing symbolic activity is the role of rules in behavior; how they are acquired, under what conditions they operate, and how they interact.

## Psychology and the Computer

The introduction of computers into psychology has brought with it a number of new concepts. Some of these, such as feedback, were congenial to existing concepts such as reinforcement, and so were adopted into psychology without any problem or hesitancy. Other concepts, such as functional matrices, or trees, or any of a great many others, have been incorporated only with great difficulty (see Berlyne's 1965 attempt in this direction) and the implication of others is still unknown.

What seems somewhat obvious is that in order to use computers as an analogy or metaphor for human cognitive activity, many existing concepts have to be discarded or at least reconsidered. Certain dearly held beliefs, or opinions, or prescriptions, may no longer be useful or even valid. For example, in more traditional psychological analyses of problem solving, one of the more difficult conceptual problems to be handled concerned goal direction—or how was it that an organism knew in advance what to do in a particular situation? In the case of associationistic psychology, it just wouldn't do to say "the animal is hungry, therefore he runs down the maze," if we had first defined "being hungry" in terms of an animal running down a maze. Such definitions were entirely circular: He is hungry, therefore he runs; we know he is hungry, because he runs.

Yet is this, in principle, any different from the key problem posed and solved in the case of Mr. Mits? How was it possible to get him to pick the correct key for his car? Because he had prior information as to which was the correct key. On the other hand, we were sure that he had such information because he picked the key correctly. If we knew nothing about Mr. Mits' internal logic (that is, his program), this definition would be just as circular as that of the hungry rat. The important point, of course, is that we do know something else about the mythical Mr. Mits, and this extra knowledge allowed us to describe his behavior as goal directed in terms that previously would have been forbidden to most associationistic analyses. This type of description escapes circularity because there is independent evidence (in terms of the program presumably guiding his behavior) to indicate that Mr. Mits does in fact know the correct key.

Given that it is possible to specify internal states with some degree of precision suggests that it may be possible to discuss symbolic activity in an entirely different way. If it is possible to specify these internal states independently of behavior, it may no longer be necessary to consider them as internal responses. Similarly, if it can be shown that computational machines are able to learn new programs and develop new algorithms for the solution of old problems, it may also be possible to reconsider the role of the organism in obtaining information from the environment. For associationism, the organism is essentially passive and receives almost all its useful information from the environment. Only the principles of stimulus and response generalization enable the organism to "go beyond" the present sets of stimuli and responses, and in many instances this may not be quite enough in and of itself. For the information-processing approach, on the other hand, the organism may be considered as much more aggressive in dealing with the environment: It knows from the start what information is required, and sniffs it out as required. Information is acted upon rather than reacted to.

This suggests that information-processing analyses of symbolic activity belong to a different psychological tradition from associationism. Although there is no single dominant philosophical group—say as the British Empiricists are for S–R psychology—the rationalist movement in philosophy would seem to be the most applicable. Without singling one out for detailed examination, such views usually assume a strong inherent endowment in the form of inherited mental categories. Given the existence (postulation) of these capacities, the organism largely constructs a mental world for himself rather than having the world structure itself for him.

All these considerations—philosophical and mathematical—provide the informational (sometimes called cognitive) psychologist with a certain new freedom in postulating the structure of mental events which underly behavior. Prior to the advent of machine computation, cognitive psychology was often considered "soft" and "unscientific" by those psychologists who wanted to view raw behavior—responses—as the only appropriate data for psychology to consider. With the recognition that brute machines can behave intelligently, the stigma attached to mentalistic concepts has abated somewhat and cognitive psychologists have felt a new surge of interest in their work and a new feeling of freedom in their conceptualization of underlying process. What they have done with this interest and freedom forms the content of the following four chapters.

## SUMMARY

Starting with Theseus, we have followed a long and somewhat involved path in going from the beginning to the end of the present chapter. We have gone through trees and algorithms, not to mention *binary arithmetic* and *Turing machines*. In almost all phases of this trip we have been guided by the assumption, taken by most people involved in computer applications, that intelligent machines and intelligent humans may operate on the basis of similar procedures and that computers provide appropriate models for describing human thinking.

The most important aspect of computer technology for psychology, however, is not the machine itself but rather the program that guides it. The use and production of such software depends ultimately on developments in mathematics, and for this reason the early portion of the present chapter explored such topics as algorithms, heuristics, trees (complete with branches), flow diagrams, and perhaps most critically, the abstract properties of Turing machines—be these particular or universal. All these concepts relate to the more general problem of deducibility: Can a given class of problems be solved by algorithmic procedures?

In order to answer any deducibility problem, it was first necessary to define algorithm unequivocally. This was accomplished by Turing, who viewed the deducibility problem in terms of how computation gets done, and on this basis suggested it was easier to examine the logical structure of simple computational procedures than more complex ones. In its turn, this led to the development of a Turing machine, or a single-element machine capable of executing simple programs. As is true of all computers, the mathematically significant aspect of a Turing machine is not its embodiment in mechanical hardware, but rather its list of procedures or its functional matrix. Given Turing's approach, a particular algorithm is defined by its functional matrix, and the search for a particular algorithm then becomes the search for an appropriate computational procedure.

But specific Turing machines are of little general interest precisely because they are so specific: In order to make contact on the one hand with existing computers and on the other with human cognitive processes, the idea of a Turing machine has to be generalized to the universal case, or to the case of a general machine capable of performing the operations of any specific machine. The theoretical development of a Universal Machine along the lines of its simpler counterpart is possible only if it is programmed with an imitation algorithm phrased in terms of elements no more complex than those required by simpler machines. Both mathematically and practically it turns out that universal or all-purpose machines can be constructed and that such machines are capable of turning appropriately specified algorithms into effective operational procedures.

Obviously, both the general commercial computers now in operation and any human subject capable of following a particular set of instructions can be considered a Universal Machine: Given a program both can execute it. While at some abstract or philosophical level this is certainly comforting, psychology has not in any real sense made use of this insight except as a way of justifying simulation as a valid procedure. What psychology has taken from computer technology are a few general concepts and procedures and a general orientation toward intelligent behavior. This general orientation has then been used as a model for human cognitive activity.

The very concepts of information and information processing obviously arise from computer technology. Computer inputs pass through a series of transformations beginning with an initial step which codes them into machine language. From here, the now-coded input goes either into temporary or long-term storage. After various operations have been performed, input is transferred to an output unit which serves to transform it back into a code suitable for use by another machine or human observer. Over and above the input, storage, and output units are control processes—processes which direct the transformation and storage of information in accordance with pre-written instructions known as a program.

One author (Neisser) has coyly termed what goes on in human information processing as the "vicissitudes of information," and has gone on to suggest that cognitive activity is properly considered a series of transformations operating on information from point of entry to point of exit. Put less dramatically, this means that human beings in deriving their information from the environment first code it into acceptable neurophysiological form, next store it in some memory system, then perform various operations on its stored form, and finally use this newly transformed information in complex patterns of behavior. Since these same operations seem to describe mechanical, as well as human, information-processing systems, this insight forms the bridge linking men and computers.

# CHAPTER 9

# SOLVING PROBLEMS

*Question*:  In what way are understanding a joke and solving a problem the same?

*Answer*:  (after some delay).  Well . . . I really can't see how the two are very similar at all . . .

Despite the fact that most of us would probably answer in the same way, the distinguished Gestalt psychologist Kurt Koffka (1935) began his analysis of problem solving with precisely this question.  Consider for a moment the following joke situation:

London Lottie asks Cockney Jim: "What did Noah say when he heard the rain patter on the roof?"  Since Cockney Jim can't figure it out for himself, London Lottie tells him "'Ark!"

A short time later Cockney Jim runs into Michigan Bill and asks: "What did Noah say when he heard the patter of rain on the roof?"  Michigan Bill doesn't know and so Cockney Jim tells him: "Listen!"

According to Koffka (1940) this old burlesque joke comes about (let us assume for Koffka's sake and for the sake of our future discussion that it does) because Cockney Jim failed to understand London Lottie's answer completely.  Jim clearly understood the word *ark* as having something to do with listening or hearing but failed to see that the same word could also apply to the Noah–flood–boat situation.  Instead, the meaning of *ark* stayed solely within the context of "hear–listen" and, therefore, when Cockney Jim told the joke to Michigan Bill, he could only use the *hear–listen* meaning leaving poor Michigan Bill with a strong feeling of "What's that all about?"

Cockney Jim's retelling of the joke didn't work mainly because he failed to see the connection between *ark* and the Noah–flood–boat meaning.  It would also have been possible for this joke to misfire if the word *ark* had made contact only with the Noah–flood–boat meaning but not with the hear–listen meaning. In this case, Jim probably would have said "Boat," again leaving poor Bill mystified.

This type of analysis can be applied to almost any and all puns and implies that there are at least two parts involved in understanding a pun (and, as we shall soon see, in solving a problem):

1. Making contact with the appropriate part meanings
   (a) ark–boat
   (b) 'ark–listen, and
2. Combining these meanings in such a way as to achieve a novel synthesis, i.e., tying both prior meanings together with a single phonetic knot.

These components, however, are not (and should not) be considered as completely independent in the case of a joke (or for that matter, in the case of a problem). As a matter of fact, the joke comes about not only because 'ark means *boat* and *listen*, but also because it fits both the Noah story and a cockney accent. It is this latter property that makes the joke, a joke.

But jokes are not problems, and the nature of this difference sets an important problem for Gestalt psychology. One way in which Maier (1932) long ago tried to resolve this dilemma was by assuming that in humor the subject must step outside his ordinary logical or quasi-logical analysis of a situation and evaluate it instead in terms of a special attitude called a *joke attitude*. By joke attitude, Maier simply meant that it was necessary for a person to accept certain assumptions about the nature of the world that would be contrary to fact in other, more ordinary, situations. Only if a subject were able to accept or generate these extra-real possibilities would it be possible for him to laugh, say, at an old lady slipping on a banana peel or at some other antisocial incident of this sort. Such events evoke laughter only if the listener is willing to respond to them in terms of the extra-real mental attitude set up by jokes and joke situations. Only in such extra-real contexts do jokes seem funny.

For Gestalt psychology then, humor and reasoning have a good deal in common. The essential aspects of seeing a joke, and seeing the solution to a problem, involve a type of perceptual–conceptual reorganization leading to a novel, or at least unexpected, conclusion. Understanding a joke in contrast to solving a problem, however, requires a special mental attitude in which the listener suspends his ordinary ways of evaluating reality and does not empathize with the butt of a joke, choosing instead to maintain a degree of noninvolvement uncharacteristic of tragedy or ordinary life. Within this attitude, however, there must be some internal, sensibly nonsensical, progression of events and ideas, and it is at this point that problems and jokes make direct contact.

Arthur Koestler (1964), the well-known author and essayist, has also noted a strong similarity between seeing a joke and solving a problem. For Koestler, laughter arises whenever two different frames of reference are abruptly brought into contact with one another and one or the other or both of these arouse self-assertive emotions such as accompany aggressive or sexual activities. These self-assertive emotions provide the drop of adrenalin required to produce the large-scale bodily response involved in laughing. Scientific problem solving involves the same mental act as occurs in humor—the only difference is in terms of the motivational systems aroused. In order to solve a problem, the scientist needs a particular blend of emotional states, not only those subsumed under self-assertive emotions. As Koestler put it:

> "The creative act of the humorist consists in bringing about a momentary fusion between two habitually incompatible frames of reference. Scientific discovery can be described in very similar terms—as the permanent fusion of thought previously believed to be incompatible. . . ." "When witticism is transformed into epigram, and teasing into challenge, the overflow reflex for primitive emotions is no longer needed . . . (and) . . . the roar of Homeric laughter is superseded by Archimedes' piercing cry or by Kepler's holy ravings."*

## OPEN AND CLOSED SYSTEMS

The analyses of humor and problem solving, provided both by Koffka and Koestler, involve situations in which the subject has to go beyond the data in order to come to some resolution of the joke or problem. But there are other problems that require much less of a subject. For example, if the sequence $3, 5, x, 9, 11 \ldots$ is presented, and the subject asked to fill in the missing number, he will have very little trouble in completing the sequence with the number 7. In this situation the problem as presented seems to contain all the pieces needed for solution, if the subject recognizes the properties of the sequence. In a sense, this type of problem—as well as many other obvious (and more complicated) extensions—presents the subject with all the pieces, and all he need do is recognize it as a problem and then supply the missing element.

It is largely for this reason that Bartlett (1958) has come to distinguish between thinking in terms of "closed" and "open" systems. By *closed systems* Bartlett means to suggest mental systems characterized by a finite number of identifiable units which do not change as thinking progresses. In closed-system thinking, a problem is presented in such a way that all the elements for solution are available and what the problem solver has to do is to fill in the appropriate element, e.g., as in an anagram task. In *open-system,*

---

* From *The Act of Creation*, by Arthur Koestler, New York: Macmillan, 1964.

or adventurous thinking, the problem solver must go beyond the units immediately given in order to "close the gap."

It is important to distinguish between open and closed tasks and open and closed-thought systems, although in actual practice the distinction is difficult to make. In the usual meaning, open and closed tasks refer primarily to environmental situations actually presented to a subject. In talking about open and closed systems, however, Bartlett has in mind a more "mental" system that may or may not have direct correspondence to a particular task situation. A subject may in fact deal with an "open task" by using a closed-systems approach or deal with a "closed task" by an open-systems approach. In general it is probably helpful to think of open-system thinking as somewhat equivalent to inductive reasoning, and closed-system thinking as somewhat equivalent to deductive reasoning.

### Thinking in Closed Systems

One of the most important parts to closed-system thinking is that the problem solver must know how to deal with "evidence in disguise," and then to develop a systematic plan of attack. One of Bartlett's problems leading to this conclusion involves the following addition problem in disguise:

$$\begin{array}{r} \text{DONALD} \\ + \text{ GERALD} \\ \hline \text{ROBERT} \end{array} \quad \text{where } D = 5.$$

This problem was all that subjects were presented with, and their task was to find the correct number for each letter so that the spelling (addition) came out right. After analyzing a number of protocols, Bartlett concluded that no subject who haphazardly assigned numbers to letters was able to solve the problem, and that once a subject discovered the critical move (namely that $E = 9$) the entire problem fell easily into place. Thus the critical step involved rearranging previously "disguised" elements, rather than developing new ones.

The more general topic of deductive reasoning is an old one in psychology, and a number of conclusions seem fairly well established. One of the more important of these has come to be called the *atmosphere effect* (Woodworth and Sells, 1935; Sells, 1936). In general, the atmosphere effect applies most strongly to the syllogistic form of argument. In this type of argument there are generally three assertions of which one—the last one—is said to follow from the other two. As an example, consider:

> All $A$ is $B$
> All $C$ is $B$
> therefore: All $A$ is $C$.

If the student agrees that the last statement follows from the other two—that is, says the conclusion is "true"—then he has fallen victim to the "atmosphere effect." Every syllogism seems to have a characteristic tone, such as the word *all* in both statements, and the inclusion of this word often leads the subject to an incorrect conclusion. What is wrong with this syllogism can be seen in the following example:

All (*A*) members of the weight-lifting team are (*B*) students.
All (*C*) sorority sisters are (*B*) students.
Therefore, all members of the weight-lifting team are sorority sisters.

Very interesting—but not necessarily true.

The occurrence of errors in syllogistic deductive reasoning is of considerable importance for a rather long-standing debate: Are the laws of logic equivalent to the laws of thought? Many early philosophers and mathematicians considered this to be true, although more recent analyses (both psychological and nonpsychological) have tended to reject such an assumption. These analyses argue that if the laws of a syllogism were the laws of thought, then subjects should never draw improper conclusions, e.g., should never make errors in reasoning. Indeed Lord Russell argued that "The existence of (a) human . . . mind is totally irrelevant (to logic); . . . the subject matter of logic does not presuppose mental processes, and would be equally true if there were no mental processes." (Quoted in Henle, 1962)

This is also the conclusion that seems most generally accepted by psychologists: Thinking in closed systems might involve syllogistic or other logical forms *only* if the thinker is familiar with these forms (i.e., has been taught or has learned them). If the thinker is not familiar with them, such forms seem relatively useless in describing how problems are approached. The principles brought to bear on thinking in closed systems vary in accordance with whether the psychological analyst uses associationistic or informational analyses, but in neither case would the theorist assume the laws of logic describe the laws of human problem solving.

Henle (1962) has argued, however, that rejecting the laws of logic as equivalent to the laws of thought because subjects make errors in deductive reasoning may not be defensible. More specifically she asks: "Does the occurrence of an error mean that the syllogism is a bad one, or can the error be accounted for otherwise? Is it possible that a process that would follow the rules of logic, if it were spelled out, is discernible even when the reasoning results in error?" (Henle, 1962) In order to carry out such an analysis, Henle suggests that subjects are unable to use syllogistic reasoning correctly because they often fail to accept the experimental task as a logical one. Instead they tend to interpret such tasks as dealing with attitude judgments. It isn't that subjects can't use a syllogistic form; rather they refuse to accept the task as dealing with logical reasoning. Even when subjects do argue on a deductive basis, they frequently come to "incorrect" conclusions not because of any inability to handle the logical form, but rather because they have restated a premise or conclusion so that the intended meaning is changed. Within the context of the now-changed problem, a subject's reasoning may be perfectly accurate. Such changes often include omitting one of the premises, or slipping in an additional one. In both cases an analysis of what a subject says as he reasons about a problem (i.e., his protocol) indicates his grasp of the logical form even if he does come to an erroneous conclusion, where erroneous is defined in terms of the task as set by the experimenter.

Henle's analysis suggests that syllogistic reasoning in particular and logical reasoning in general can be done by human subjects, but that it is often difficult to assess the subject's competence in such reasoning because the specific test problems used by an experimenter often lead the subject to view the problem not as one of logic but rather as one of agreement or disagreement. In many instances, as Woodworth and Sells (1938) long ago demonstrated, certain aspects of how a problem is worded affect its solution profoundly. The conclusion that subjects can use deductive reasoning in the formal sense seems true, although this should not be taken to imply that such reasoning is the primary or even the most usual form of directed thinking in closed systems.

Actually, Henle's analysis also raises a larger issue which, when stated most directly, comes out as follows: How should we, as psychologists, relate a subject's competence with a formal system (say, such as syllogistic reasoning) to his performance on a particular task involving that system? Although a complete, or even a beginning, answer to this question would take us well beyond the present topic, it is important to recognize—as Henle has done— that the task of relating competence in a formal system to actual behavior involving that system is a formidable one, and one that is significant for many different areas of human symbolic activity. We will stub our theoretical toes on this issue again (in Chapters 14 and 16) when we will have to spell out the relationship of human language behavior to formal grammatical systems such as have been proposed by many contemporary linguistic theories.

## Thinking in Open Systems

Most problem solving, however, does not take place within rigidly defined systems such as those of logic or grammar, but rather within the context of much less structured tasks and situations. Solving problems in the "real" world is not so much a matter of rearranging already existing elements, as one of developing new and different modes of attack. Sometimes it is necessary to develop new systems or to revise old ones before a problem can be solved. In any sort of genuinely novel or creative work—be it artistic or scientific—the usual feeling of the artist or scientist is that some act of

imagination is required, or at least some act which requires the thinker to go
beyond the constraints immediately imposed by the problem.

One stage of creative problem solving that is very evident in the work of
scientists involves a process often referred to as induction: the ability to
derive a general principle from a number of exemplars. Consider a be-
havorial scientist attacking a genuinely novel problem. He begins by
observing what the subject of his investigation does, be this subject a child,
an animal, or an adult. Since he assumes that the behavior of his subject is
not random, that it has some pattern, he is particularly sensitive to recurring
regularities in the behavior. If the subject turns right—to take a simple
example—is he more likely then to continue going right, or is he more likely
to turn left or to do something entirely different? The process of scientific
induction begins by searching for regularity. Often the regularity is apparent,
or seems to be apparent, before any really numerical analysis is done. At
other times, such regularity emerges only after a quantitive analysis of what
the scientist has observed.

Now regularity can emerge in a real-life setting only to the degree that an
observer agrees to define certain occurrences as events or units. The first job
of discovering regularity is dependent on recognizing events in the stream of
observation—in short, of segmenting the flow of incoming observations into
events. Once this has been done, the job of determining regularity remains as
a next step.

In studies of inductive problem solving, this first stage of segmentation is
often omitted from experimental analysis. The subject is simply presented
with a series of readily discernible events and then asked to discover the
pattern characterizing them. Perhaps the simplest experiments of this type
involve two stimuli which are each presented a differential number of times,
and the subject is required to guess which of the two stimuli will occur,
and how often. For example, there may be two lights, with the left one
blinking on 25 % of the time and the right one 75 % of the time. The subject
receives a reward only if he picks the light that actually blinks on at that time.
This type of task has been called a *probability matching* task, and results
uniformly indicate that organisms from goldfish to human beings give every
indication of responding to the relative probabilities of occurrence of each
light.

But this type of induction is still far removed from the regularities that
have to be discovered by scientists and laymen alike. In order to provide a
slightly more complex task, Bruner, Wallach, and Galanter (1959) asked
subjects to predict whether a light would appear to the left or right of an
apparatus, with reward dependent on correct prediction. The basic sequence
was of length three and involved a repeating pattern of the form *LLR*. Each
subject was exposed to this pattern for 13 repetitions of the pattern. Although
there were many different conditions in this experiment, the most important

ones for the present discussion concern a comparison between subjects exposed to a perfectly regular sequence, i.e., where all trials followed the *LLR* sequence, and ones exposed to a schedule in which the *LLR* cycle was disturbed on the fifth and ninth cycle. This type of occasional "off-pattern sequence" is very similar to inductive discoveries in more naturalistic settings. Once the scientist describes a pattern based on his understanding of prior observations, he is still likely to encounter certain off-pattern events that do not agree with his analysis. The results of the Bruner, Wallach, and Galanter study indicate that such pattern disruptions cause profound changes in the subject's ability to predict the pattern; it took as many as three additional cycles for them to predict again the correct *LLR* pattern after the first disruption, and as many as two cycles after the second disruption.

One implication of this study is that in most tasks subjects seek to provide the incoming flux of information with some sort of structure or organization. That is, input—even if completely novel—is not taken in without some attempt at organizing it in some way. In order to analyze this "ordering" aspect of problem solving, Shipstone (1960) proposed the following game to his subjects: "Imagine you are the officer in charge of a code information center during the war. Your job is to receive and store (sort) the incoming coded information so that it can be easily retrieved."

For the actual task Shipstone presented his subjects with a series of cards one at a time, each containing a sequence of nonsense syllables such as: *ZIR PAG ZIR ZIR PAG NEN* and *ZIR PAG NEN PAG NEN PAG NEN PAG NEN PAG NEN PAG NEN PAG ZIR NEN*. If we let *Z* stand for *ZIR*, *P* for *PAG* and *N* for *NEN*, it is possible to see that the first two messages consist of three "nonsense words" arranged in different orders. The third and fourth cards presented to the subject were *ZPZN*, and *ZPZZZZZZZZZZZZZPN*, respectively.

Now on what basis is it possible for a subject to sort these cards? In this type of task, it turned out that there were only 20 different strategies, with some sufficiently similar to others so as to allow Shipstone to categorize them into five primary and one residual category. The five most common categories were: *Length*—subjects sorted sequences of the same number of words into the same category. *Alphabet*—all messages were treated as a single category and filed alphabetically. *Initial Word*—words were sorted by initial items only, i.e., does it begin *ZZP* or *ZPN* or *PNZ*, etc. *Initial–final* —words were sorted by both initial and final orders. And *Rule*—words were sorted according to the rule used by the experimenter in producing the orders in the first place.

Of the 54 *S*'s employed under all conditions of the experiment, 18 *S*'s (33%) actually used some variety of the rule used by the experimenter, whereas only 5 subjects failed to use any rule that could be described easily.

The initial–final group—the most strongly structured of the other categories —provided the next most frequent approach and produced 12 cases. In other words at least 30 of the 54 $S$'s attempted to develop an obvious coding system based on self-produced patterns; only 5 did not attempt any really obvious scheme. The major point of this study is perhaps best given by the observation that no subject ever handed the cards back to the experimenter saying: "Are you kidding?" Instead all took the task seriously, and all attempted to impose order onto a seemingly disordered input.

## PROBLEM SOLVING AND THE STRUCTURING OF PROBLEMS

What mental processes occur when a human subject solves a problem? Although there are all sorts of problems in using introspective data, some-times it is none the less possible to learn something interesting by questioning the "right thinker." In one case the "right thinker" was A. C. Aitken, a distinguished professor of mathematics at the University of Edinburgh, and the right questioner was I. M. L. Hunter of Keele University. Professor Aitken's remarkable calculational skill may be illustrated by asking him to express the fraction $\frac{4}{47}$ as a decimal. Let Hunter's record speak at this point.

> He is asked to express as a decimal the fraction $\frac{4}{47}$. He is silent for four seconds, then begins to speak the answer at a nearly uniform rate of one digit every three-quarters of a second. 'Point 0851063829787234042553191 4, that's about as far as I can carry it.' The total time between the presentation of the problem and this moment is twenty-four seconds. He discusses the problem for one minute and then continues the answer at the same rate as before. 'Yes, 191489, I can get that.' He pauses for five seconds. '361702127659574458, now that is the repeating point. It starts again at 085. So if that is forty-six places, I am right.'*

How *was* Aitken able to perform this rather astounding bit of calcula-tion? He began by changing the form of the problem slightly; instead of dividing 4 by 47, he transformed the whole fraction into $\frac{68}{799}$, and thereafter changed 799 to 800, making sure to allow for the $\frac{1}{800}$ correction required at each step. The entire process of computation is presented in Fig. 9.1 (see next page), the legend of which explains it in some detail.

The conclusions arising from this protocol are of some interest: For one, an initial decision must be made concerning the overall approach to a

---

* From "Mental Calculation," by I. M. L. Hunter, in *Thinking and Reasoning*, edited by P. C. Wason and P. N. Johnson-Laird, London: Penguin, 1968.

**Fig. 9.1**  Unconventional step-sequence followed by an expert calculator*

| Dividend | Answer | Remainder | Next dividend |
|----------|--------|-----------|---------------|
| 680 ÷ 8 | 0.085 | none | 85 |
| 85 ÷ 8 | 10 | 5 | 510 |
| 510 ÷ 8 | 63̇ | 6 | 663 |
| 663 ÷ 8 | 82 | 7 | 782 |
| 782 ÷ 8 | 97 | 6 | 697 |
| 697 ÷ 8 | 87 | 1 | 187 |
| 187 ÷ 8 | 23 | 3 | 323 |
| 323 ÷ 8 | 40 | 3 | 340 |
| 340 ÷ 8 | 42 | 4 | 442 |
| 442 ÷ 8 | 55 | 2 | 255 |
| 255 ÷ 8 | 31 | 7 | 731 |
| 731 ÷ 8 | 91 | 3 | 391 |
| 391 ÷ 8 | 48 | 7 | 748 |
| 748 ÷ 8 | 93 | 4 | 493 |
| 493 ÷ 8 | 61 | 5 | 561 |
| 561 ÷ 8 | 70 | 1 | 170 |
| 170 ÷ 8 | 21 | 2 | 221 |
| 221 ÷ 8 | 27 | 5 | 527 |
| 527 ÷ 8 | 65 | 7 | 765 |
| 765 ÷ 8 | 95 | 5 | 595 |
| 595 ÷ 8 | 74 | 3 | 374 |
| 374 ÷ 8 | 46 | 6 | 646 |
| 646 ÷ 8 | 80 | 6 | 680 |

680 which is the original dividend

The problem is to express the fraction $\frac{4}{47}$ as a decimal. First, he transforms $\frac{4}{47}$ into $\frac{68}{799}$. Then he proceeds to divide 68 by 800 (in effect, by 8) with a recurring correction to allow for the difference between 799 and 800. Each line represents the same cycle of events. The dividend is divided by 8 to give two digits of the answer and a remainder; then the next dividend is formed by combining this answer and this remainder, e.g., from answer 10 and remainder 5, the next dividend is 510. Repetition of this cycle generates the answer to $\frac{4}{47}$, two digits at a time.

* From I. M. L. Hunter, "Mental Calculation," in *Thinking and Reasoning*, edited by P. C. Wason and P. N. Johnson-Laird, London: Penguin, 1968.

problem. In this case Aitken chose first to change $\frac{4}{47}$ into $\frac{68}{800}$, and then carry out the requisite manipulations. This step is viable or usable only to the degree that our human calculator has a store of effective numerical algorithms available to him. Exactly how these get built up is not clear, yet what is clear is that Aitken does have a distinctive set of available subsystems appropriate to this type of problem. All these processes require that the results of prior calculations be retained and reused. In the case of Fig. 9.1, for example, about 46 elements need be retained in order to solve the problem.

But memory is involved in problem solving in still another way: Human subjects seem to be limited in the number of things they can do at the same time. This limitation forces the calculator to a serial processing approach. That is, instead of doing all 23 divisions at the same time, Aitken must do them in series, always making sure to store the preceding answer and the preceding remainder.

From this protocol a number of general principles are possible: The first aspect of problem solving, at least for the skilled practitioner, is deciding how to solve the problem. The number and quality of the available procedures set obvious limits on both the mode of approach and speed of completion. Following this original decision, there are practical problems of memory, both in terms of processing operations, as well as in terms of holding subanswers in memory. From the present case study it seems clear that even highly skilled problem solvers use sequential rather than parallel processing for involved operations.

The first step to solving a problem requires the subject to decide how to approach the problem in a particular way. This implies that a given problem will always be organized or structured in terms of some goal decided on at the outset of the problem-solving situation. In Aitken's case, the initial stage of problem solving was one of selecting among the large number of computational subroutines he already had at his disposal. This suggests that the development and organization of subroutines is one of the most important general aspects of problem solving considered from an information-processing point of view. Such organization is possible whenever we are dealing with a family of related subproblems, all of which are clearly related to the final solution of the major problem at hand.

But Aitken is obviously a special case: Is there any other evidence showing that such overall structuring actually takes place when less-special problem solvers solve problems? An early experiment by Duncker (1945) provides further evidence on this point. In this experiment, subjects were asked to solve a number of problems, the most instructive of which was the following: "Given a human being with an inoperable stomach tumor, and rays which destroy organic tissue at sufficient intensity, by what procedure can one free him of the tumor by these rays and at the same time avoid destroying the healthy tissue which surrounds it?"

Figure 9.2 presents a diagram showing the respective solutions proposed by one subject.

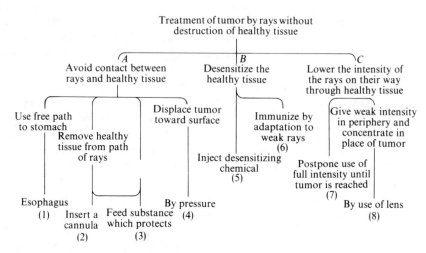

**Fig. 9.2**  Solutions proposed to solve the x-ray, cancer problem. (From Duncker, 1945.)

The numbers which have been added to this protocol represent roughly the order in which each of the proposed solutions was produced by this subject. In general, this subject felt that there were three main types of procedures (*A*, *B*, and *C*) that would meet the overall requirement of the problem.

This diagram has much in common with tree diagrams described in connection with the solution of logical problems. Each solution, prior to Number 8, involves some dubious element, which in this particular experiment was pointed out to the subject by the experimenter. For example in Solution 3, the subject proposed that "One should swallow something inorganic (which would not allow passage of the rays) to protect stomach walls," to which *E* replied . . . "It is not merely the stomach walls which are to be protected." Here the subject tried out a solution, with the adequacy (or inadequacy) of the solution evaluated by the experimenter. Duncker feels that any solution containing an unacceptable element causes the subject to go back up the tree, incorporating this newly discovered insight in the next provisional solution. Each of the proposed solutions thus serves to recast the problem so that a new and different approach will be tried.

This analysis can, and should, be related back to the Dashiell–Melton Diagram of Adaptive Behavior (see Chapter 6, page 129), which described problem solving in terms of trial-and-error principles. One aspect of their analysis was that subjects often engage in variable behavior if they are unable to solve a problem at the first attempt. Although their description was essentially neutral with respect to the causes of this variation in mode of attack, Duncker's analysis makes it likely that each sequence attempted is under the control of a single idea and that as a solution fails to resolve the problem, the subject backs up to the next-highest level of his understanding of the problem and begins again. Thus all attempted solutions can be considered under the control of a single overall plan. In slightly different terms, what the subject does is to conceptualize the problem first and then produce a series of hypotheses as to how to solve it. As he progresses through the task, however, the subject comes to understand the task differently at various pre-solution stages and on this basis modifies his original hypothesis in accordance with his new understanding of the task still remaining to be done.

In an attempt to understand the reciprocal relationship between the changing structure of a problem and a subject's response to this changing structure, J. W. Whitfield (1951) presented subjects with a deceptively simple task. In this task, the subject was required to match 8 objects to 8 different squares drawn on a piece of paper. On the first trial there are 8! (or some 40,000) possible arrangements which may or may not meet the arbitrary contraints of the task. In order to make our analysis of this situation somewhat easier, consider a 4-item case where there would be only 4! or 24 possible matchings. Of these 24, one is completely correct; 6 allow only one possible move on the second trial; 8 leave 2 moves on the second trial; and 9 are totally incorrect. However, each of these first moves does provide some information: if all the objects are correctly sorted, the problem is solved; whereas if all are incorrectly sorted, they still give information of a sort— don't do that again. Although there were other conditions of the experiment, the results for the 8-into-8 situation showed that subjects did take advantage of the changing structure of the problem and that the number and pattern of their correct choices was virtually indistinguishable from that given by a logical analysis of the problem.

Peter Wason (1960, 1968), in a series of studies concerned with how subjects behave in an open-ended task such as Whitfield's, has argued that there are differences in a subject's ability to seek out and use positive and negative information. In one of Wason's simplest tasks, subjects were told that a series of numbers, 2, 4, 6 . . . , obeyed a simple rule which they were to discover by producing a numerical series of their own. The rule actually followed in this task was the general one of "numbers in increasing order of magnitude." Subjects were told whether or not a particular sequence they produced did or did not conform to the rule.

Now it might be argued that the subject's job in this task is misleading in that the rule actually followed is a general one. As Wason points out, however, the purpose of his experiment was not to determine if a subject would get the "right" rule, but rather what he would do in order to find evidence for his rule in a situation that admitted of a great many possibilities. For example, some subjects tried out the sequence: 6, 8, 10 and assumed the rule to be "numbers increasing by 2"; others produced sequences such as 8, 54, 98 and assumed the rule to be "increasing even numbers," and so on. In all cases the incorrect rule was obviously correlated with the correct rule, but the "incorrect" rule was far too specific in its formulation.

The most important aspect of this task is that the production of a large number of positive instances, all derived from a single hypothesis, does not necessarily increase the correctness of that hypothesis. This is of course true of scientific work where the scientist attempts to discover a "rule of nature," and here the same constraint holds true. As Karl Popper, the eminent philosopher of science, put it: "It is easy to obtain confirmations or verifications . . . if we look only for confirmations" (as quoted in Wason, 1968). This suggests that the general strategy scientists should use is to try to falsify a hypothesis rather than confirm it. Note that this procedure refers to *testing* hypotheses, not *forming* them.

In the context of Wason's experiment, if a subject produced only the series 8, 10, 12, 14, etc., and none other, he was likely to conclude that the rule was: "increase each number by two." If, however, the subject used the principle of falsification, he was led to try out a series that did not conform to the rule, such as 8, 51, 98, before he would conclude that he had the right rule. In the case of the increase-by-two hypothesis, it is clear that trying out this latter series (which is also correct) would serve to exclude the original hypothesis.

What are the facts? Do subjects attempt only to confirm their hypotheses or do they also attempt to refute them? Of 29 subjects tested by Wason (1960), 22 produced at least one incorrect rule (even though they were told not to give the rule until they were fairly certain of it), while 9 of these 22 produced a second incorrect rule, and two of these 9 produced three incorrect rules. Seven subjects produced only the correct rule. When the protocols of these 7 "successful" subjects were examined, results indicated that they were able to give up their earlier hypotheses more easily and that they tended to falsify rather than confirm hypotheses.

In another similar study, one of Wason's students asked subjects after they had announced an overly specific and wrong rule how they would go about finding out if they were wrong. Of 16 subjects asked this question, only 2 said they would try to falsify their hypothesis in some way, while 3 said essentially "I can't be wrong . . . If you were the subject and I the experimenter then I should be right . . . (Very annoyed) Rules are relative." On the basis of these and similar results, Wason was led to conclude that seeking negative instances (refutation, or falsification) does not represent a usual approach to testing one's hypotheses.

In summary then, problem solving can be construed as an active process in which the problem solver provisionally structures the task as he attempts to provide a solution. Each partial solution serves not only to test the presently held hypothesis, but if incorrect, to restructure the problem so that future solutions can be attempted. Subjects generally seek further information to confirm their hypotheses, and only infrequently do they seek to falsify them. In tasks that require the subject to invent hypotheses as he goes along, and in which he is prevented from testing the correctness of his hypothesis unequivocally, falsification seems a particularly unlikely strategy for subjects to use.

## COMPUTER SIMULATION OF PROBLEM SOLVING

Much research on human problem solving has been guided, in part, by an analogy: the analogy that human problem-solving behavior involves processes similar to those found in computers. Thus the concepts of strategy, rule, algorithm, and so on figure very strongly in these analyses. There is, however, another way in which to make use of the computer as an aid in analyzing problem-solving behavior, and that is to invoke Turing's game. If the computer provides a suitable metaphor for human problem-solving activities, it should be possible (once the limits of certain human problem-solving processes are known) to program these into a computer, give the registers a whirl, and on this basis stimulate problem-solving behavior in the human problem solver himself.

This is precisely the logic employed by Simon and Newell and their associates at the Carnegie-Mellon Institute of Technology and elsewhere in attempting to simulate human problem solving. Their analysis began with a purely formal problem: to see if they could develop a computer program capable of discovering and formulating a logical proof. This original model was called the Logic Theorist (LT) and was thought to provide a rudimentary program resembling how a human subject might go about proving mathematical theorems (Newell, Shaw, and Simon, 1958). As they noted in this relatively early paper, their concern was not so much with a theory that would prove theorems, but rather with an attempt to determine general processes involved in problem-solving situations both similar to, and decidedly different from, those involved in proving theorems.

In general, LT was composed of such all-purpose processes as searching for possible solutions, producing these possible solutions from already existing elements, and evaluating partial solutions and cues. Problem solving was seen to depend on an original analysis of the problem which then determined how LT would go about solving it. If LT did not have available any procedures capable of solving a problem directly, it then was forced either to break the problem up into subproblems that were manageable, or to devise new procedures based on ones already available.

The program incorporated into LT was not designed to simulate human problem solving directly; instead it was set up to show that it was possible to provide a computer with heuristic (rather than algorithmic) solution processes, and on this basis solve problems which previously only humans had been able to solve. Its track record in regard to proving theorems is a pretty good one: Of a possible 52 theorems solved by Russell and Whitehead in Chapter 2 of their *Principia Mathematica*, LT succeeded in solving 38 of them. Half of these proofs were produced in less than a minute, with the longest proof requiring no more than 75 minutes. The important point to this early work was that Newell, Shaw, and Simon found it possible to develop more or less general programs that were capable of solving difficult logical problems where these solutions depended on heuristic rather than algorithmic methods.

This emphasis on time-saving heuristics characterizes the major assumption made by Newell, Simon, and Shaw in their attempt to extend results from the Logic Theorist to a genuinely more general problem solver called logically enough the General Problem Solver; or more simply, GPS. In the context of GPS, heuristics which aid discovery are defined in terms of their ability to do three things: (1) to suggest an order in which to examine possible solutions, (2) to rule out an entire class of solutions previously thought possible, and (3) to provide "a cheap test" of likely and unlikely solutions.

In general, GPS begins to solve a problem by detecting a difference between the location of a desired goal state and the present location of the subject with respect to that goal. If there is no discrepancy, there is no problem. If, however, a discrepancy does exist, the exact nature of this discrepancy has to be determined and a suitable plan formulated to remove the discrepancy. If this plan can't be formulated directly, GPS must first formulate some subgoal that can in fact be met. Thus any problem is first analyzed to discover whether a discrepancy exists between "where an organism is now" and "where he would like to be." This analysis gives rise to a series of subgoals, each one of which may require reformulation into further, less difficult subgoals. This tree, or hierarchy, of subgoals is then attacked in order of difficulty—beginning with the most difficult and proceeding through to the least difficult. Once all subproblems have been solved, the solution of the original and major problem can then take place.

Does this sound hopelessly abstract? In order to make the process a bit more concrete, consider the following problem set by Newell, Shaw, and Simon (1960):

"I want to take my son to nursery school. What's the difference between what I have and what I want? One of distance. What changes distance?

My automobile. My automobile won't work. What's needed to make it work? A new battery. What has new batteries? An auto repair shop. I want the repair shop to put in a new battery; but the shop doesn't know I need one. What is the difficulty? One of communication. What allows communication? A telephone ... And so on."

This then is the basic heuristic used by GPS: Classify things in terms of what functions they serve and then develop means to bring about the function required. This strategy is called a *means–end heuristic* and has at least three major components: (1) determining the difference between two objects, *A* and *B*, (2) developing operations that change some features and leave others unchanged, and (3) eliminating differences in order of difficulty.

The actual working parts of GPS consist of two primary components. One of these, the *core*, contains an executive decision-making unit involving heuristic processes which permit the executive to set up and evaluate goals. This unit is assumed to be the *general* part of GPS. The second component is called the *task environment* and contains all the information necessary for a specific problem domain, e.g., the rules of logic, if a problem involves proving theorems.

The GPS involves a task environment populated by specific objects that can be changed by various operations. It is sensitive to differences between objects and sets up goals to modify these differences. In this scheme there are three basic types of goals: simply transforming *A* into *B*; reducing the difference between *A* and *B*; and transforming *A* into *B* through the application of Operator *Q*.

This then is how the means–end heuristic proposed by Newell, Simon, and Shaw works. If the program employed only means–end heuristics, however, it would have to proceed one step at a time, and would therefore not have any overall direction to it. An overall grasp of the problem is provided by the so-called "planning-heuristic" which consists primarily of changing an originally complex problem into simpler ones. This simplification is carried out by first abstracting the specific problem to more general terms, and then by simplifying the overall structure of the problem so that it can be subject to a more direct means–end analysis. Since the abstracting process serves to simplify the problem, this increases the likelihood that any proposed means–end solution will be successful.

An appropriate question to ask at this point is how well does GPS match the performance of flesh-and-blood subjects involved in solving similar problems. Data appropriate to answer this question are provided by comparing protocols obtained from subjects working on problems with a *trace* of the computer's (more accurately, the program's) mode of approach to the same problem. Subject protocols are obtained by having a subject talk about what he is doing as he attempts a problem. This method is an old one in psychology and often goes under the name of the "thinking-aloud" method. A careful line by line comparison of a subject's protocol with the computer's trace indicates very good correspondence: sufficiently good, in fact, to enable Newell and Simon (1963) to conclude that "If the mechanism of the program (or something essentially similar to it) were not operating, it would be hard to explain why the subject uttered the remarks that he did."

Despite the strong general and specific agreement between a subject's protocol and a program's trace, there are a number of differences that seem to be of some importance. For one, GPS is designed to process each problem (or subproblem, actually) in sequence, where there is evidence that human subjects often do subproblems in parallel. For example, in transforming an equation, GPS considers a transformation of the right-hand side as one subproblem and a transformation of the left-hand side as a second problem. Human subjects are able to apply both transformations at the same time. A second difference involves what might loosely be called hindsight. It shows up in human protocols in statements such as "I should have (applied Rule 6) . . . earlier (so that I wouldn't be in the fix I'm now in)." These continuing evaluations often lead the subject back to a revision of his earlier decisions. Although Newell and Simon acknowledge the occurrence of hindsight as a serious problem, they do feel that it can be corrected by the addition of a new series of general routines (even if they are unwilling to specify them as yet).

A final problem with GPS is its "single-mindedness." It never gets distracted by a pretty girl or a handsome boy, or by an emotional crisis or a distended bladder as do many human subjects in the course of solving a problem. If the problem is a short one, then a "single-minded" description may be adequate. When, however, sustained effort is required, distractions can and do take over, with the result that problem solving is often interrupted. Given that such distractions occur, how is it that human subjects return to a problem after a period of distraction with little loss of efficiency; or conversely, how is it that in some situations humans may never return to the problem if the distraction is attractive enough (e.g., the pretty girl)?

It was in response to questions and problems of this sort that Reitman and his associates (1965; Reitman, Grove, and Sharp, 1964) produced a cousin to GPS called *Argus*. Argus contains a number of major components, the most important of which are a *sequential executive* (similar in description and function to the serial executive found in GPS) and a *network of active semantic elements*. This latter component operates with a good degree of independence from the central executive, and in many instances is able to bring about changes capable of disrupting the ongoing activity of the executive. This "disruption" takes place largely on the basis of signals sent by the semantic network to the central executive. Argus is programmed to take account of "local" disturbances in the semantic network. In this way interference in the parallel-processing semantic network is conveyed to the sequential central executive.

Figure 9.3 describes the operation of a simplified executive cycle.

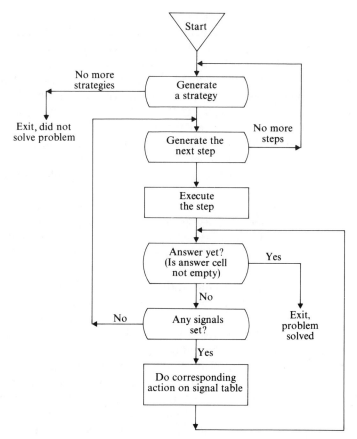

**Fig. 9.3** Executive cycle (slightly simplified). Subject and problem are specified beforehand. This gives the executive a set of strategies and rules for their use. The signal-action pairs in the signal table at any given time are a function of the rules. (From Reitman, 1965.)

The executive cycle starts with the generation of a strategy for the solution of a problem. After the strategy is chosen from those available for the task at hand, the program continues to perform the steps of the program until the problem is solved or until the executive routine is interrupted by a signal from the semantic network. Whether these signals will "distract" the executive depends on the current level of distraction produced in the semantic network, as well as on the decision rule provided to the executive program for "taking account of" local disturbances. If the signal is effective, the executive switches his "interest" to the new problem; if not, it continues with the old problem until it is solved, or until distractor signals become sufficiently strong.

For Argus to function, the computer must operate in a dual capacity: in one case permitting interaction of network and executive elements, and in another, attending to sequential problem-solving aspects. This latter function must be carried on in more or less complete ignorance of any parallel processes which may be ongoing in the semantic system. At the present time, Reitman's newer model has been tried out primarily on analogy problems of the form $A:B::C:?$ ($L$, $M$, $N$, or $P$), with results indicating that it works quite well on these problems. As Reitman has indicated, the purpose of Argus is not only to stimulate human problem solving, but also to explore as completely and systematically as possible a reasonable set of assumptions about processes involved in problem-solving activities of this type.

Generally it is possible to view Reitman's model as an attempt to introduce less goal-directed activity into the single-minded stream of computer thought. In order to do this, Reitman has made operational an earlier suggestion offered by Neisser (1963), namely, that there are at least two main categories of thought—one that is rational, goal-directed, and routine, and one that is irrational, constantly uncontrolled, and surprisingly novel. Neisser has proposed that each of these may be dependent on a different mode of information processing, with the first involving strictly sequential processes (such as described by Newell, Simon, and Shaw) and with the second involving multiple, parallel processing (such as found in Reitman's network of semantic elements). In this second case Neisser assumed that inputs derived from parallel processes would interact both among themselves and with the more routinized sequential processing. This orientation to thinking seems to be well embodied in the Argus program developed by Reitman and represents an attempt to simulate both the directed and unconstrained flow of thought, as well as their reciprocal, and often interfacilitating, interactions.

## SUMMARY

A pun such as: "I'm descended from a very old line that my mother fell for" works largely because the subject is able to identify both relevant meanings of the word *line* and combine these into a novel synthesis encompassing both. Both Koffka and Koestler have noted that similar processes seem to operate in understanding a joke and in solving a problem. The major difference between solving a problem and understanding a joke has to do both with the subject's attitude and the motivational systems aroused: Problem solving of the type found in scientific work seems to involve a blend of emotional states, whereas jokes always seem to involve self-assertive emotions of the type usually associated with aggressive or sexual activities. When these emotions are channelled as in the case of problem solving, "the roar of Homeric laughter is superseded by Archimedes' cry of 'Eureka.'"

In order for any analysis of problem solving to get into high gear, it is necessary to distinguish between thinking in open and closed systems, with the correlated thought operations described as open or closed thinking. An open system is one in which the elements of a system are not fixed and unchangeable and therefore one in which the solution to a problem is not necessarily contained in the initial system. A closed system is characterized by a finite number of identifiable units which do not change markedly as thinking progresses. Closed-system thinking is involved in problems such as occur in number sequences, anagrams and logical reasoning, while open-system thinking appears in inductive tasks such as occur in scientific research.

Henle has argued that psychology may have been misled in concluding that logical reasoning, as involved in the syllogism, is of little or no interest to the psychology of problem solving. She feels, instead, that most subjects can use syllogistic reasoning if they view the experimental task as one dealing with logic rather than one dealing with attitudes. If, however, we look at how a subject (rather than an experimenter) understands a particular experimental problem, it is possible to see that subjects can and do reason logically, even if their conclusions are not those intended by the investigator.

But most problem solving takes place under considerably less structured conditions. In laboratory studies, such as those described by Duncker, subjects were required to solve complicated verbal problems dealing with such issues as destroying a cancerous stomach tumor without destroying the surrounding healthy tissue. On the basis of Duncker's results, it seems reasonable to conclude that subjects attempt to solve problems by using a series of provisional hypotheses related to the overall flow of the problem. With the refutation of an early hypothesis, the subject comes to understand the task differently at various pre-solution stages and, on this basis, continually modifies his present hypothesis in accord with his newly developed reanalysis of the task still remaining.

Duncker's analysis and the analyses of those who have followed his approach feel that it is proper to represent the structure of a problem situation in terms of a tree diagram. A similar analysis is implicit in the General Problem Solver (GPS) developed by Newell, Simon, and Shaw. In the program used to motorize GPS, the problem tree involves a series of subgoals that must be solved in getting the subject from "where he is now" to "where he would like to be" (i.e., from problem situation to problem solution).

After GPS analyzes a situation in this way, a number of subgoals are developed, which in turn allow for an overall development and solution of the problem. Considered in the light of Duncker's earlier work on creative problem solving, each subgoal represents one aspect of a problem to be solved, with the general solution at the apex of the tree and subsolutions at each of the lower-order nodes. Each subgoal also enables the subject to gain a new perspective into what it is that is required to solve the problem.

Unlike GPS, however, human subjects are not free of distractions as they attempt to solve problems. In order to loosen up GPS, Reitman and his co-workers have developed a general problem solver called Argus. Unlike GPS, Argus can be distracted, and once distracted will first take care of the disruption and then return to the problem at hand. Argus attempts to simulate both goal-directed and reverie thinking, and the degree to which it accomplishes this is the degree to which it simulates human thinking effectively.

# CHAPTER 10

# FORMING AND
# USING CONCEPTS

Human beings excel at putting things into categories. This is true whether we talk about little boys sorting baseball cards, little girls cataloging stamps or coins, big boys describing automobiles, or big girls describing big boys. The tendency to sort and categorize on the basis of some concept or other is nowhere more obvious than when we are introduced to someone we don't know. One of the first things we usually do in this situation is to ask a series of questions: Where are you from? What do you do for a living? How old are you? What kinds of things do you like to do? And so on. These questions are meant to help put this new and unknown somebody into a comfortable and known category. Without such categories, each new person would have to be responded to as a completely new entity. Categorizing each new person as part or not part of some specific set of concepts (I'm from Texas, I work as a copy editor, I'm 29 years old, I like to travel, etc.) helps us enormously in knowing what to say and how to behave with respect to that person.

In getting to know someone new, we try first of all to describe them in terms of a series of important properties or attributes. We apply this same strategy to strange experiences or objects; our aim is always to describe the strange in terms of familiar concepts and qualities. In "psychologese" (psychological jargon) it is possible to consider an unknown person, or a strange object, as an example of some unknown concept or concepts. In order to describe this unknown, we first have to supply a set of relevant characteristics and then describe the unknown on the basis of these characteristics. Such an approach defines a concept in terms of a set of characteristics or attributes, with the concept specified by its pattern on these attributes.

Once we define concepts in terms of attributes, it is clear that each attribute may itself be a concept, which in turn must also be defined in terms of other concepts, and so on. Thus *copy editor*, which served to define one important property of our friend from Texas, can itself be defined in terms of further properties, and this is true for any and all of the other attributes as well. In addition we would have to consider our copy-editor friend as only one instance (or example) of a straightforward, but nonetheless complex concept: 29-year-old copy editors from Texas.

But our new friend can also be an instance of additional concepts as well, for there is a very large if not an infinite number of ways in which to categorize any given case. The way we actually choose to do it often reflects what it is we are trying to do, or the particular context we find ourselves in. So, for example, all of the attributes used to describe our friend would be useless if we needed a car driven, or a diaper changed, or any of a number of other rather specific things. No reasonably small set of factors or attributes considered independently of a given context would seem able to exhaust the universe of characteristics that might be used to define various different people considered as instances of one, or another, or yet another, concept.

It is largely for this reason that psychologists studying concepts in the laboratory have often made use of easily specifiable attributes such as color, size, shape, and so on, and have embodied these qualities in easily defined objects such as small, green cubes, etc. With this done, the experimenter simply asks a subject to tell whether a particular object is or is not an example of some concept or other, e.g., large objects, green objects, or large, green objects, etc.

Sometimes, however, experiments on concept learning have been concerned with more complex cases that would seem to relate more directly to concept learning in the real world. One such example is provided in a study by Pollio and Reinhart (1970) in which they were interested in finding out how college-age subjects learned to count in non-base$_{10}$ number systems, i.e., the type of learning required to understand the arithmetic operations of a computer (see Chapter 8).

In usual base$_{10}$ counting, the appropriate sequence of numbers is given by the series: 0, 1, 2, 3, 4, 5, 6, 7, 8, 9, 10, ... 20 ... 99, 100 ... 1000, ...; whereas in non-base$_{10}$ systems such as base$_2$, the appropriate sequence is: 0, 1, 10, 11, 100, 101, 111, ... 1000, 1001, 1010, 1011 ... Considered from a mathematical point of view, each subject has to learn the concepts of place and place value if he is to be able to count in non-base$_{10}$ number systems.

The meaning of these concepts can be best explained in terms of analogy; the analogy of a simple desk calculator—or more specifically, the wheels of this calculator. Each wheel of such a calculator has the numbers 0–9 on it, and the calculator may have as many as 10, or 15, or even 20 wheels. Counting, which is nothing more than adding by 1, involves starting on the wheel at the extreme right and progressing by 1's from 0 through 9. Every number indicates how many units on that wheel have been used up. The tricky part of the procedure comes when 9 is reached and another 1 has to be counted.

The wheel continues to follow the same rule as before: Turn one more space. On this basis it comes around again to 0. If this wheel were somehow not connected to the wheel one over to the left, 0 would appear in the register and that would be that. (This is of course what happens in a clock; there is no number past 12 so that when all the numbers are used up the clock is "reset" back to 1, the original number.)

Since, however, the right wheel on a desk calculator is connected to the next one on the left, this connection causes the left wheel to turn from 0 to 1, thereby producing the numbers 1 and 0 (10) which now come to fill the first 2 registers. Note the rule for turning the second wheel (the one to the left) is a complete cycle of 0 through 9 on the wheel at the right. The occurrence of a 2 on this wheel means that two (2) complete 0–9 cycles have been passed on the right wheel.

What happens now if the base system is switched—that is, if the admissible numbers on each wheel run only from 0 through 1 rather than from 0 through 9? Exactly the same procedure will work—turn the "wheel" at each place, always shifting to the wheel on the left any time the right wheel has gone a complete cycle.

Coming back to experiments now, Pollio and Reinhart (1970) found that in order to be able to count in new base systems subjects had to learn two different things: (1) the acceptable numbers in the new system, e.g., in binary counting, subjects had to learn to use only 0 and 1, but not 2 through 9, and (2) an operational rule that would allow them to add by 1. These two aspects of learning to count in a binary number system represent general processes that seem to be at work in almost all concept-learning studies—laboratory or otherwise: namely, that a subject has to identify relevant elements (i.e., the relevant parts of a dimension or attribute) and then to learn, develop, or apply an appropriate rule capable of manipulating these elements so as to solve a concept problem (Bourne, 1968). Most experiments require a subject to accomplish both of the processes at the same time and for this reason Bourne (1966) has suggested that there are few "pure" studies of rule learning or attribute identification. Rather, many different procedures have been used with the implicit emphasis occasionally on identifying relevant elements, occasionally on learning to develop or apply appropriate rules, but most often on some combination of both.

## ATTRIBUTE IDENTIFICATION, RULE LEARNING AND CONCEPT LEARNING: SOME COMPARISONS

If we accept the idea that a concept can be described in terms of a set of relevant attributes and a rule which serves to describe the relationship among these attributes (see Bourne 1966; Bourne, Ekstrand, and Dominowski, 1971), it then is of some interest to see whether subjects differ in the ease with which they learn to identify attributes or parts of attributes as compared to the ease with which they learn to develop or apply rules.

But how can such an experiment be done? For the sake of convenience, experimenters have often used stimuli that differ on two dimensions; for example, whether or not instances are red ($R$) and whether or not they are shaped like a star ($S$). Using such simple materials it is possible to see how subjects learn to apply a number of different rules, some of the most important of which are presented in Table 10.1.

**Table 10.1**  Conceptual rules describing binary partitions of a stimulus population†

| Rule name | Symbolic description* | Verbal description | Real-life examples |
|---|---|---|---|
| Affirmation | $R$ | Every red pattern is an example of the concept | Any attribute will do; a *copy editor, short, blonde,* etc. |
| Conjunction | $R \cap S$ | Every pattern which is red and a star is an example | A *volume*: *large and bookish* |
| Inclusive disjunction | $R \cup S$ | Every pattern which is red or a star or both is an example | An eligible *voter*: a *resident and/or* a *property owner* |
| Conditional | $R \rightarrow S$ | If a pattern is red then it must be a star to be an example; if it is nonred then it is an example regardless of shape | A *well-mannered male*: *If* a *lady* enters, *then* he will *stand* |
| Biconditional | $R \leftrightarrow S$ | A red pattern is an example if and only if it is also a star; any red nonstar or nonred star is not an example | An *appropriate piece of behavior*: wearing a *cummerbund if and only if* it is a *formal occasion* |

*$R$ and $S$ stand for red and star (relevant attributes), respectively.

†Adapted from *The Psychology of Thinking*, by Lyle E. Bourne, Bruce R. Ekstrand, and Roger L. Dominowski, Englewood Cliffs, N.J.: Prentice-Hall, 1971.

In one study designed to evaluate the relative ease of rule learning and attribute identification, Bourne (1967) had subjects solve a series of problems, each of which involved the same rule for a different pair of attributes, or a different rule for the same attributes. The specific rules studied were: conjunctive, disjunctive, conditional, and biconditional (see Table 10.1 for a description of these rules); while the specific attributes used were: size, color, shape and number of objects. Four groups of subjects were used, with each group asked to learn how to use one of these four rules. All four groups were subdivided into two parts, so that for half of the subjects in each group the relevant attributes were known and the rule was not, while for the other half the rule was known and the relevant attributes were not. All subjects were required to learn nine different problems.

The results of this experiment showed that except for the very first problem, attribute identification and rule learning were about equally difficult. In addition, early trials showed that rule learning was more difficult for certain types of rules (biconditional and conditional) than for others (conjunctive and disjunctive), although these differences washed out as the number of trials increased.

Since there was little or no difference between how fast subjects learned to apply rules and identify attributes, it seemed reasonable to wonder if subjects in both of these groups were able to solve concept problems more readily than subjects who were given neither the relevant attribute nor the correct rule; in other words, subjects who learned under conditions usually found in most studies of concept learning. One experiment designed to answer this question was done by Bourne and Haygood (1965). In this study, subjects were required to learn five different problems, with a different group of subjects required to learn one of the different logical rules presented in Table 10.1. Some subjects simply had to learn to apply the rule; others had only to learn to identify the correct attributes, and others had to solve these problems without any hint as to the relevant attributes or correct rules. The results of this experiment showed that subjects solved the rule-learning and attribute problems significantly faster than the concept-learning problems, with no significant differences between attribute-identification and rule-learning groups.

All in all, these results suggest that concept learning involves two sub-processes: identifying relevant attributes and learning combinational rules. What we really need keep in mind, however, is that although these processes can be analytically separated in the laboratory, most extra-laboratory concept learning requires us to handle both processes at the same time. Outside of the laboratory there are few "pure" cases of either process, and before we as psychologists can say we understand how human beings form and use concepts we will have to resynthesize, if possible, what we have analytically pulled apart.

## Concept Problems and Subject Strategies

As a start in this direction, let us evaluate critically one procedure often used in laboratory studies of concept formation. Most often, this involves presenting the subject with a series of items which he is required either to label with a single concept name, or to sort into one of two (or more) categories. Now this is certainly a peculiar arrangement considering the case from a more naturalistic, or if you will, from a more naive viewpoint. When human subjects learn or develop a new concept in extra-laboratory settings, the instances are not usually presented to them by Nature one at a time. Although it is true that concept learning in nonlaboratory situations may begin with the occurrence of recurrent regularity in certain events, it simply is not true that the human learner passively waits for the next instance to show up of its own accord. In most cases, whenever a concept dawns, however dimly, one strong reaction is to look for other events that might fit that concept or category. Although it is equally possible to seek out instances that do not fit, and thereby define a category on the basis of what the concept is not, Wason's results described earlier (see Chapter 9, pages 211 ff) indicate that human subjects seek confirming information and actively solicit their environment so as to find appropriate exemplars to confirm or modify newly discovered concepts.

This idea of an active search was first described and given experimental implementation in a series of studies by Bruner, Goodnow, and Austin (1956). In these experiments subjects were given a wide variety of examples and allowed free choice in picking out what further information they needed so as to feel secure in knowing that they really did know a given concept. In these "selection" studies, the subject was told that the experimenter had a particular concept in mind and that the subject's job was to discover what it was. This approach is quite different from "reception" studies, in which the order of instances is fixed by an experimenter, and the subject simply has to classify each instance into one or another category. Undoubtedly, concept discovery or invention in the "real" world involves some combination of both reception and selection procedures, although little attention had been paid to selection procedures prior to Bruner's studies.

**Subject strategies in selection studies.** How might (and indeed how does) a subject behave when confronted with a concept task in the selection procedure? In one series of studies done by Bruner, Goodnow, and Austin, 81 now-famous cards were presented to each subject (see Fig. 10.1). The figures on these cards differ in 4 respects: (1) in shape, (2) in number, (3) in color, and (4) in having 0, 1, or 2 borders.

For this particular experiment the correct concept (as defined by the experimenter's arbitrary choice) consisted of a combination of more than one of the attributes, i.e., involved a conjunctive rule such as "red squares," or "green circles," and the like. Let us now pick up a sample protocol, with the first card shown by the experimenter containing two red circles on a non-border card. The subject has already been told that this card embodies a particular concept and that he is to pick out other instances that will help him find out what the concept is.

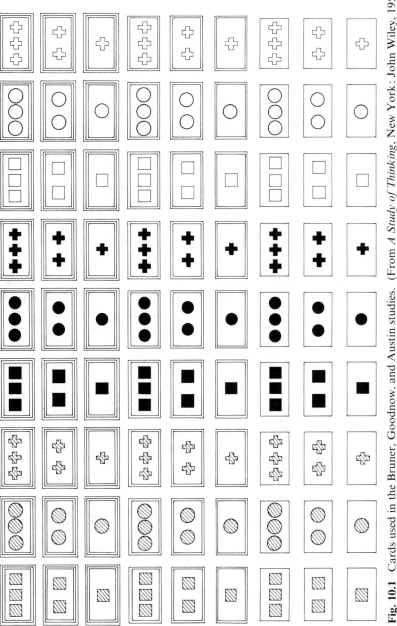

**Fig. 10.1**  Cards used in the Bruner, Goodnow, and Austin studies.  (From *A Study of Thinking*, New York: John Wiley, 1956)

Assume the subject picks out the following cards (where cross-hatching means red).

| *Order of cards* | | *Running commentary* |
|---|---|---|
| 1. First card shown | | After this the subject makes his first selection. |
| 2. First card selected | | The experimenter's response to this card is "incorrect" and so the subject then makes another choice. |
| 3. Second card selected | | Experimenter's response, "correct." Subject then selects third card. |
| 4. Third card selected | | Experimenter's response, "correct." Subject selects fourth card. |
| 5. Fourth card selected | | Experimenter's response, "wrong." Subject selects fifth card. |
| 6. Fifth card selected | | Experimenter's response, "correct." |

Following this, the subject says he knows the concept and tells the experimenter: "It must be *red circles*," which is in fact correct.

If we follow what this particular subject did, it is clear that his behavior is quite systematic and that it follows some sort of plan, or what Bruner and associates termed a *strategy*. What might this strategy sound like if put in words? The first card shows two red circles on a card with no border. It may be a correct exemplar either because it is red and circular, or because it is red without borders, or any combination of these factors. The subject begins perhaps by assuming that the concept is "two objects on a non-border card." On this basis he picks his first card. Since this card turns out not to be correct, "twoness" or a "blank border" does not serve to define the correct concept. Given this information, the subject goes back and chooses a card having all the same correct attributes as the experimenter's card with the exception of number of circles. At this point the subject has probably formed some provisional hypothesis (such as red circles) but he still has to rule out certain other properties, such as the number of borders. This he does with his next selection. He continues using this approach until he is convinced his provisional hypothesis is correct.

In this type of task there are a number of strategies that could be used, either singly or in combination with each other.  Bruner, Goodnow, and Austin feel that their results imply four different types of strategies.  The first type, *simultaneous scanning*, assumes that the subject holds all possible concept combinations in mind simultaneously and that he tries to eliminate incorrect possibilities by his choice of cards.  Such an approach, however, is a very difficult one, for the subject must deal with all the possible hypotheses at the same time.  Although some subjects do in fact attempt this strategy, the memory problem becomes sufficiently demanding that some subjects shift to the second major type of strategy, *successive scanning*.  In successive scanning, the subject develops a specific hypothesis on the basis of the card presented to him by the experimenter, e.g., red circles are correct, and then goes about securing evidence to confirm or refute the particular hypothesis under consideration at the moment.  The advantage of this method is that it greatly reduces memory strain, since the subject need remember only his present hypothesis and not all possible hypotheses.  It is unfortunately not completely economical in terms of errors, for often some aspects of previous (rejected) hypotheses may be part of the "correct" concept, and a subject will often have to go back and reconsider these previously rejected dimensions.

The obvious disadvantage to successive scanning is that a subject is not really searching for relevant dimensions in a completely systematic or focused way.  Some subjects, however, do attempt a systematic approach that has come to be known as *conservative focusing*.  In this strategy the subject begins by using the first instance presented as a focus, and then makes a series of decisions which either eliminate or confirm a certain aspect of the card as relevant.  The only real drawback to this type of strategy is that if cards are presented randomly (that is, not arranged according to attribute), the task of searching out appropriate exemplars becomes rather forbidding.  Under conditions of a random array, a subject will probably resort to a less restricted or mechanical mode of focusing, one called *focus gambling*.  In focus gambling, the subject uses the first card (or any subsequent positive instance) as his focus, but rather than changing only one attribute at a time he tends to change more than a single attribute with each choice.  The obvious value of this type of strategy is that if the subject "jumps" to a correct conclusion, this jump may save him the trouble of having to try out each attribute separately.  The disadvantage of this method is also obvious: If a wrong conclusion is jumped to, the subject has wasted his time and has to revert back to a more conservatively focused strategy.

In general, scanning strategies require the subject to remember a good deal more than focus strategies.  For the so-called successive-scanning strategy, the subject has to remember all previously tested and rejected hypotheses, while for the simultaneous-scanning hypothesis he has to remember not only hypotheses that have been successful and unsuccessful in the past, but also has to keep track of hypotheses that are still possible but have as yet not been confirmed or refuted. Focus strategies, on the other hand, provide the subject with an excellent bookkeeping device: On every trial his hypothesis is a composite which includes all tested and untested possibilities. All that the subject has to remember is one specific card (i.e., as representing a specific set of attributes) and this card serves as a continuously updated record of what has been successful and of what remains to be done.

Given these strategies, what factors seem to favor the use of one or the other? One such factor has already been mentioned—ordered versus random displays. In actual tests of this factor, the results of Bruner *et al.* show that under conditions of disorganized stimulus array, subjects not only tend to require considerably more choices to learn a concept (10.4 to 6.1), but also tend to use a strategy most closely approximating the one described as successive scanning. By contrast, subjects presented with an orderly array tend to be not only much more systematic but also tend to use a combination of the two focus strategies, concentrating primarily on conservative focusing.

Memory load also affects the type of strategy employed. In one experiment subjects were asked to solve three different concept problems: For the first and second of these problems, all 81 concept cards were always available to the subject, while for the third problem none of the cards were available. About half the subjects used some type of modified focus strategy on Problems 1 and 2, while the remaining subjects used a slightly modified scanning strategy. In the crucial third problem, in which memory became a consideration, the focus group (that is, subjects who used a focus strategy during Problems 1 and 2) required a median of 5 choices, whereas the scanning group required a median of 13 choices. Other indices also produced similar results under the more demanding third problem: Focusers made a median of 1 redundant choice during Problem 3, whereas Scanners made a median of 6; performance deteriorated from a medium of 3 choices to 10 choices on Problems 2 and 3 for the Scanners, while it remained at about the same level of 5 for Focusers. Increased memory strain seems to interfere more with scanning than with focus strategies.

**Subject strategies in reception studies.** Bruner and his associates, however, were not content to analyze the role of strategies in selection tasks only; they also examined the role of such strategies in reception tasks. In reception tasks, the subject has no control over the order of instances; all he can really do is vary his hypotheses. In the case of conjunctive concepts presented by a reception procedure, Bruner, Goodnow, and Austin found two different classes of strategy: a whole-hypothesis and a part-hypothesis strategy. For the wholist strategy, the subject uses a correct instance (perhaps the first card) as his hypothesis. If the next card is not an example of the concept, the subject still uses Card 1 as his hypothesis about the concept. If, however, the second card is also an example of the concept, he alters the first card in such a way as to include only those factors that appear on both ends. In a sense the first card provides a rough summary of what the concept might be, whereas the second card eliminates noncritical aspects of the hypothesis. In this way, the subject need never recall specific past exemplars for his present hypothesis, as embodied in a particular card, is a concise summary and distillation of all prior alterations of the initial concept. It is, in fact, a continuously updated summary.

The subject who attempts concept attainment on the basis of a part strategy tends to pick out some part of the first card (rather than the whole card) as his hypothesis. If he is lucky in his original choice, then further instances only reinforce his conviction that he has the correct hypothesis. If the subject is only in part correct, or if he is dead wrong, memory strain soon becomes a problem for him, as he must go back and recall all preceding exemplars he has seen and decide whether or not they were correct. The results of a number of studies confirm what seems obvious from either a logical or psychological analysis: More conjuncture concept problems are solved correctly under whole, as opposed to part, strategy, and more subjects tend to prefer a wholist to a partist strategy.

This same concern has also come up in a series of reception studies done by Hovland and some of his students. Hovland's focus, however, was slightly different. What he was interested in determining was the role of positive and negative instances in concept learning conducted under the reception paradigm. Hovland (1952) based his experiments on a reanalysis of an earlier experiment done by Smoke (1932). In this experiment (see Chapter 4), Smoke's subjects were presented with a series of items that *did* or *did not* serve to define a particular concept. These were called *positive* and *negative* instances, respectively. Although Smoke's experiment was set up to show that concepts could be learned on the basis of abstract relationships, Hovland was interested in the unexpected finding that negative instances were of little help in bringing about the development of a correct concept. Given this result, Hovland wondered whether subjects had difficulty in learning concepts because negative instances carry low information, or because subjects simply have difficulty in handling negative information. By low information, Hovland simply meant that telling someone that an item is not an example of some concept doesn't really help him figure out what the concept might be.

In order to consider this problem experimentally, it is first necessary to define a particular problem in terms of the total number of possible stimulus exemplars. This, in turn, means that the experimenter has to tell the subject both the relevant dimensions and the number of values each of these dimensions has. For example, if an experiment involved square and circular objects, that could be either small or large, and white or black, there are 3 relevant dimensions (shape, size, and color), each having 2 values, for a total of 8 possible combinations ($2^3$). If the subject is not provided with any relevant information, there are 256 possibilities. These 256 possibilities include the one extreme case in which all 8 patterns define the concept (i.e., "any geometric shape") to the other extreme in which none of the 8 define the concept (i.e., "a triangular-shaped object"). Intermediate to these extreme values are concepts defined by the combination of 2 (28), 3 (56), 4 (72), 5 (56), 6 (28), and 7 (8) factors, where the total number of possible exemplars for each combination is presented in parentheses. Adding up all the figures in parentheses gives a total value of 248, which in conjunction with the case in which all 8 are correct, produces the grand total of 256 possibilities.

Thus part of the problem for a subject in Smoke's experiment was its unclear structure; the subject was never told which factors (dimensions) were relevant and which were not. If, however, the subject were given prior information about the relevant dimensions, then each item presented, whether positive or negative, would serve to reduce the number of possibilities defining the correct solution.

Armed with this analysis, Hovland and Weiss (1953) presented some subjects with all positive instances, some with all negative instances, and some with a mixture of positive and negative instances. The results of their experiment revealed that although positive and negative instances are logically equivalent, subjects had most difficulty in solving problems when only negative instances were used. In the mixed series, in which positive and negative instances were used and which turned out to be of intermediate difficulty, presentation order was found to have no effect. That is, it didn't matter whether the positive or negative instances were presented first—problem difficulty remained at the same level.

Huttenlocher (1962), however, felt that presentation order should have had more of an effect than was found in the Hovland and Weiss study. In order to examine such effects, she set up a situation in which positive and negative instances were equated for information per instance. She did this by defining all her concepts in terms of two examples, the first of which eliminated half the possible hypotheses and the second of which eliminated all others except for the correct answer. When this was done, Huttenlocher found that under the condition, in which both instances were negative, subjects made fewer correct responses than under the condition in which a negative instance was followed by a positive instance. These results both agree and disagree with Hovland and Weiss: Negative–negative remained the most difficult; but the sequence negative–positive produced more correct responses than either positive–negative or positive–positive.

Both these experiments were concerned with describing how information is used as a subject progresses through a problem. Hovland assumed that subjects have to remember all possible hypotheses about a correct solution and check all tentative hypotheses against each new instance. Each new example, therefore, provides confirming or rejecting information about one or many of the hypotheses presently being considered. Huttenlocher, however, assumed that subjects continually refer to the content of a specific example, e.g., a black square, and then change or update this example on successive trials. It is not so much that subjects entertain several hypotheses at once, but rather that they retain highly specific instances and subject these to continued analysis with further input. Under this hypothesis the negative–positive condition is ideal, for all the subject need know to solve the problem is that the dimension that changes is relevant, and that the value shown in the final exemplar is correct. In agreement with Bruner's interpretation, Huttenlocher feels that subjects tend to use wholist strategies in concept-formation tasks done within a reception paradigm. Such strategies require the use of a continuously updated hypothesis summarized in the form of a single card embodying the hypothesis.

A different approach to specifying subject strategies in a very circum-scribed concept-formation task was taken by Levine (1966).

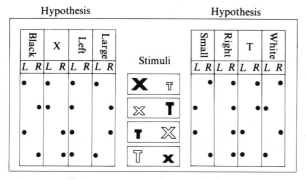

**Fig. 10.2**  Eight patterns of choices corresponding to each of the eight hypotheses when four stimulus pairs are presented. *L* and *R* refer to subject choices, and serve as the basis on which to infer the subject's hypotheses. (After Levine, 1966.)

In this experiment, subjects were presented with stimulus materials such as are presented in the middle two columns of Fig. 10.2; that is, either the letter *T* or *X*. These two letters differed in color (black or white), position (left or right), and size (large or small). Given these 3 dimensions, there are 8 possible hypotheses as to the correct response. The 8 possible hypotheses are specified to the right and the left of the sample stimuli presented. Figure 10.2 also shows the pattern of choices a subject would have to make in order to allow Levine to decide which of these 8 hypotheses the subject was testing. So, for example, if the subject's hypothesis was that *black* is correct, he would alternate his choices on each of the 4 sample cards presented. This is shown by the pattern of dots under the column labeled "black." If the subject's hypothesis was that the large item is correct, his choices would be left, right, right, left (see the columns labeled "Large"), and so on for all the other hypotheses.

On the first trial of the experiment, the subject was shown a card with 2 items on it and was told which one was correct. After this, Levine presented a subject with 4 new cards (see Fig. 10.2) and asked him to pick the correct one. For these 4 additional cards (Trials 2–5), subjects were not told whether or not they had picked the correct item. By observing the pattern of choices, Levine could decide which hypothesis was presently being used by the subject. If we assume, along with Levine, that subjects will use the same hypothesis on Trial 6 as they did on Trials 2–5, it should be possible to predict the subjects' choices on this trial almost without error. In terms of actual data, Levine did find that he could predict Trial 6 choices with about 98% accuracy. All in all, Levine's results show that it is possible to describe hypotheses with great precision if the task is simple enough and if the subjects' choices are exhaustively limited by the constraints of the concept task itself.

### Concept Learning: Some Selected Experimental Findings

However much we may be interested in processes which underlie the formation and use of hypotheses, all our conclusions must be based ultimately on an analysis of how human subjects perform on particular tasks under particular conditions. For this reason it seems a good idea to examine briefly some of the major experimental results emerging from research on concept formation, in the hope that these results will be useful in evaluating what must be included in any informational account of how human beings form and use concepts.

**Task factors.**    One very obvious place to begin is with an analysis of the tasks that have been set for experimental subjects. Since these vary in a number of different ways, let us take up some of the major task factors, one at a time, and see what conclusion we can come to about each of them.

1. *Number of dimensions.*    One factor that should, and does, have an obvious effect on concept attainment is the number of relevant and irrelevant concept dimensions. The usual result here is that as the number of both relevant and irrelevant dimensions increases, concept attainment becomes progressively more difficult. With respect to irrelevant dimensions, these findings are best interpreted in terms of the amount of information that has to be ignored: With many irrelevant dimensions there is more information to be ignored than with fewer irrelevant dimensions (Bulgarella and Archer, 1962; Walker and Bourne, 1961; Kepros, 1965). In the case of relevant dimensions, these

results are best interpreted in terms of information condensation or reduction: The greater the amount of information reduction required by a task, the more difficult it is to achieve this task.

2. *Contiguity of instances.* All things being equal, the closer together in time two or more instances of a particular concept occur, the easier it is for the subject to attain the concept (Kurtz and Hovland, 1956; Bourne and Jennings, 1963; Schulz, Miller, and Radtke, 1963). Perhaps the simplest explanation for this is in terms of memory load. Under conditions in which all instances of a single concept are presented together, the subject is able to form a hypothesis as to what constitutes the essential properties of the concept and then check it immediately against the next item. This is to be contrasted with a mixed presentation condition in which a number of different hypotheses, about a number of different concepts, need be held in memory at the same time. This makes the development of a clear hypothesis more confusing. Any presently held hypotheses should in fact interfere with each other, thereby making concept attainment quite difficult. Alternatively, a mixed presentation may produce too many different hypotheses to be held in temporary memory span (see an experiment by Hunt, 1961, for partial confirmation of this view).

3. *Use of negative instances.* In general, subjects are less likely to use negative instances in concept tasks and when such are used, they often cause the performing subject a good deal of difficulty. One probable reason was first pointed out by Hovland (1952), who noted that defining an item as not being an example of a concept really provides the subject with very little information as to what the concept might be. In this type of situation, unless the subject knows the relevant attributes of the concept, there is no way in which he could know which attributes were ruled out by a given negative example.

Another reason is that there is an infinite number of things that are not instances of a given concept, but instead are examples of other, different concepts. In the laboratory many of the possible non-examples are ruled out by the way in which the task is presented and, on this basis, negative examples can sometimes be used. Since restrictions in the real world are undoubtedly very much less than in the laboratory, negative examples are not very helpful in ruling out other concepts. To put it another way, knowing that something is "not-$X$" only helps us if the set of possible hypotheses is reasonably small. In a sense, coming to the laboratory from the real world—in which negative instances are not very useful—may imply a change in the rules of the hypothesis-forming game. If this is true then it is not surprising that subjects seem to use strategies appropriate to the real world (positive instances only) and to ignore negative examples.

Freibergs and Tulving (1961) stated this point in somewhat different but related terms: Subjects may have difficulty in using negative instances in the laboratory largely because they have very little experience in using such instances. So, for example, we seldom define things negatively: The usual procedure is to say: "Look, there's a doggie," and only when the child makes a mistake are we likely to say, "No, that one isn't a doggie." If this is true, then allowing a subject to practice solving restricted laboratory problems on the basis of negative instances should lead to an improvement in his ability to use negative instances, and this ability should come to equal the forming of concepts on the basis of positive instances.

Experimentally, this meant providing different groups of subjects with a series of 20 all positive or 20 all negative instance problems and observing any change in the subject's ability to produce the correct solution. The results of Freibergs and Tulving's experiment showed that subjects who had not attempted and solved previous concept problems in the laboratory were far better on positive-instance problems. With practice, however, there were only slight differences in the speed at which subjects in both groups solved concept problems.

A second aspect to the use of negative instances in forming concepts has been described by Wason (1959, 1961) who found that human subjects almost never attempt to negate an hypothesis but prefer instead to confirm it. In Wason's task, contrary to results provided by Freibergs and Tulving, subjects still had difficulty in using negative information after extended practice. Whether this inability (or really impoverished ability) to use negation for evaluating the adequacy of an hypothesis is a general property of human information processing cannot be said for sure at present. What can be said with some confidence, however, is that subjects prefer not to do it, and whenever possible actually avoid doing it.

**The role of feedback in concept attainment.** One important aspect of concept attainment for any informational analysis concerns the process by which a subject evaluates his own hypotheses. In experimental terms this problem concerns knowledge of results; or, said more fashionably, *informative feedback*. In any concept task, the subject either chooses items as representative of a concept, or makes a series of responses that serve to define an item as an example of a particular concept. In both cases he is subsequently told whether or not his choice was correct. The nature of such feedback can vary along a number of dimensions, some of the more important of which are described below.

1. *Completeness of feedback.* In concept-attainment tasks (as in simpler tasks such as drawing a line of a specified length when blindfolded), the completeness of post-response information serves to reduce the number of errors made in learning the desired concept (Cason, 1931). In an experiment

by Bourne and Pendleton (1958), for example, subjects were required to sort geometric patterns into four conjunctive categories. Results indicated that simply telling the subject that categorization of a particular pattern was either right or wrong was inferior to the condition in which subjects were actually shown the correct categorization for that pattern. From an informational point of view this implies that more specific feedback produces more information about ruling the hypothesis wrong, and probably helps the subject in formulating a new one. Thus, if a subject is told that his choice is wrong, the correct category can still be any one of the other three. If, on the other hand, he is given complete feedback, not only is his prior analysis evaluated as to its correctness, but the correct categorization is specified precisely and the formulation of a new hypothesis made that much easier.

The results of the Bourne and Pendleton study also showed that continuous feedback on every trial was superior to feedback presented on 90%, 80% or 70% of the trials. This result is probably due to the relatively longer time period between successive "correct" exemplars. For the 70% feedback condition, subjects have to experience a greater number of instances before receiving an equivalent amount of positive (and negative) feedback when compared to the 100% case. This increase in intervening time may make it more difficult to remember and evaluate the exact properties of the positive or defining exemplars.

2. *Delay of feedback.* The obvious prediction here is that as the delay between the occurrence of a particular response and its associated feedback gets longer, the attainment of the concept will be made more difficult. Although the original study on this topic (Bourne, 1957) did show that concept attainment was most rapid under 0 time delay and, slowest under progressively longer delays up to and including 8 seconds, this study confounded two factors—delay of informative feedback and post-feedback interval. Consider what this means: In any experiment on concept attainment, the subject first makes a response and then waits until the experimenter tells him "right" or "wrong." This is the feedback interval. Following this evaluation, another period of time intervenes before the next exemplar is presented. This is the post-feedback interval. In Bourne's original experiment the situation was set up so that, as the delay of feedback time increased, post-feedback time decreased. This was done in order to maintain an equal time interval between the completion of one instance and the presentation of the next.

What sorts of things might happen during the two different time intervals? The post-response, or feedback delay interval, would seem to involve the subject's specific response to the instance just shown him, whereas the post-feedback interval is probably used to assimilate the new information gained on that trial to other aspects of the task. The post-response delay is relevant only to the present instance, while the post-feedback interval gives the subject time to evaluate his hypotheses as to the correct concept. If this is the case, delay of feedback should have very little overall effect on the total course of concept attainment, while various delays in the post-feedback interval should have much more widespread effects.

In an attempt to evaluate the relative contributions of post-response and post-feedback delays, Bourne and Bunderson (1963) combined three post-delay intervals (0, 4, and 8 seconds) with three post-feedback intervals (1, 5 and 9 seconds). In this experiment it is important to note that 3 of these arrangements produce identical total times: 0 and 9, 4 and 5, and 8 and 1, where the first value refers to the post-response delay interval and where the second value refers to the post-feedback interval. For a complex concept task, Bourne and Bunderson's results indicate a total of about 17 errors for the 0–9 condition, 53 errors for the 4–5 condition, and 68 errors for the 8–1 condition. These results, taken in conjunction with results found for the other 6 conditions of the experiment, indicate that the post-feedback interval is considerably more important than the post-response interval in determining the speed of concept attainment. Even in those cases in which the total time between exemplars is controlled (as in the 3 conditions above), whether or not more time is available after feedback has the greatest effect on ease of concept attainment. This suggests that the post-feedback interval is the more important source of delay, with efficiency of performance increasing as this interval gets longer. Such a result naturally suggests that the post-feedback interval is probably taken up with an evaluation and possible revision of existing hypotheses.

**Transfer Across Problems**

No adult subject ever comes to an experimental situation completely free of past experience, and for this reason many concept problems can be seen to involve transfer of prior learning. For experimental purposes, an analysis of transfer does not in general involve determining what skills a subject brings to the experiment in the way of relevant prior experience; rather it involves an attempt to determine the effects of different types of prior practice on concept learning. Perhaps the best perspective from which to view these studies is provided by Harlow's (1949) studies dealing with the acquisition of learning sets. Recall that Harlow and his co-workers followed the individual performances of single monkeys as they attempted and solved as many as 600 different concept problems (see Chapter 7 for a discussion of this work). The major result was that as the monkey (and in subsequent studies, the child) experienced and solved a wide variety of problems, he became able to solve rapidly any new (or similar) problem.

Adams (1954), in building on this early work by Harlow, was interested in finding out how subjects who have varied experience in concept-learning tasks would compare in performance on a new task with subjects who had a great deal of experience in a single task. In his experiments, there were two primary groups: One of these groups—the Constant Experience Group—was trained for 192 trials on problems requiring the same conceptual rule—i.e., the card with the square over the circle is in Category 1, etc. The second group—the Variable Experience Group—was given 24 different sorting problems, each requiring a different rule for its solution. Since each problem was presented for only 8 trials, this made a total learning experience of 192 trials. After these 192 trials, all subjects were presented with a transfer task involving new stimulus materials, but following the same rule as that learned by the Constant Experience Group. The results of this experiment indicated that subjects in the Constant Group did better during both acquisition and transfer than subjects in the Variable Experience Group. The only point at which the Variable Group showed superior performance was during the first few transfer trials, with the Constant Group overcoming this advantage when all 24 trials of the transfer task had been completed.

These results are certainly paradoxical if taken at face value—that is, subjects who have broader experience in concept-attainment tasks do worse in transfer tasks than subjects having more restricted experience. A little reflection, and a subsequent experiment by Morrisett and Hovland (1959), however, resolved this difficulty and led to a less paradoxical conclusion. In this experiment three different groups of subjects were used: One of these was the exact equivalent of the Variable Experience Group (that is, 8 trials on each of 24 problems). A second group was the exact equivalent of the Constant Experience Group (that is, they worked on a single problem for all 192 trials), while a third group, which could be called the Variable Constant Group, required subjects to work on three different problems for 64 trials each. All subjects were then given the same problem as a transfer task for 24 additional trials.

In terms of acquisition, results showed that subjects in both of the groups that had extensive practice on a single concept-sorting problem (the Constant and Variable Constant Groups) did better than subjects whose problems varied every 8 trials. In terms of the transfer task, similar to Adam's results, the Variable Group did more poorly than the Constant Group. The group that did best, however, was the Variable Constant Group which showed almost perfect and immediate transfer on the final or test task.

How then are these results to be interpreted? They suggest that Adams failed to find maximum transfer for the Variable Group because subjects in this group were unable to learn very much about solving any one particular problem if they were only allowed 8 trials on that problem. If a subject is not permitted to solve any one problem completely, he never really has a chance to develop general concept-problem skills that might serve him in cross-problem tasks. If, however, a subject is allowed both to attain a fair degree of proficiency in solving one particular problem and is also allowed to shift to other problems, he then seems to be able to learn not only how to solve particular problems but also tends to develop more general rules of procedure, rules that are relatively indifferent to the particular requirements set by any given problem. Perhaps subjects come to develop higher order or more general problem-solving skills only to the degree that they have already attained a complete and satisfactory solution to any one particular problem.

## Information Processing and Concept Learning: An Attempt at Simulation

In preceding sections we have assembled many of the available empirical pieces—the facts, if you will—and what now remains is to summarize them succinctly and then use this summary as a guide to what we might aspire to for a simulation model. If we take the data and our discussion of it seriously, such a model would have to include at least the following four properties:

1. It must form and use provisional hypotheses.
2. It must continuously evaluate and change these hypotheses on the basis of either scanning or focusing strategies, or some combination of both.
3. It must be differentially sensitive to positive and negative instances except in highly circumscribed situations.
4. It must take account of changes in context, e.g., whether or not we care if a new friend can correct copy or change diapers.

While small in number, these, nonetheless, represent a formidable set of criteria, and we should not expect any correct simulation model to fulfill all or even most of them. But we do have a right to see how well any attempt in this direction does do against this admittedly high standard.

Perhaps the most extensively developed simulation model of human concept learning has been presented by Hunt and his co-workers (Hunt, 1962; Hunt, Marin, and Stone, 1966). This analysis represents a development of work begun initially by Hovland (1962) and concentrates primarily on decision processes involved in concept learning. Basically, Hunt's model assumes three phases: perceiving concept items, defining positive instances, and finally developing decision trees.

In perceiving any given instance, the model assumes that each instance can be described by its value on a list of attributes, e.g., the *color* (attribute) is *green* (value). That is, any given item is defined by a set of attributes which are immediately recognized by the concept learner.

In order to define concepts once an instance has been perceived (i.e., its set of attributes noted and stored), Hunt's program assumes that subjects search only for positive (confirming) instances, although it does take note of negative instances as well. The psychological grounds for this postulate have been reviewed earlier, and this aspect of the program seems quite reasonable. Hunt's program is assumed to know neither the relevant attributes nor the concept rule as it goes about trying to learn a concept.

Given this orientation, the major contribution of Hunt's approach is its description of how subjects develop decision trees; or how his program goes about deciding on a concept. For Hunt, a decision tree is a plan for producing and evaluating a series of decisions. One example of such a decision tree is presented in Fig. 10.3.

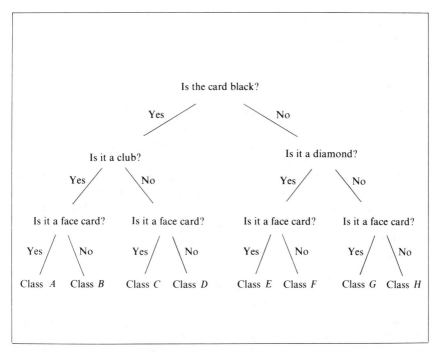

**Fig. 10.3** A concept tree. Each of the classes at the bottom can be identified by a sequence of guesses and yes-no answers. (From *Concept Learning: An Information Processing Problem*, by E. B. Hunt, New York: John Wiley, 1962)

Here the subject is required to classify objects into one of eight classes (*A–H*): actually the face and non-face cards for each of the four suits in a deck of cards, with this particular tree showing one possible order in which to test the attributes. The strategy employed in this case is conceptually similar to that of conservative focusing in selection studies, and that of a wholist strategy in reception studies. Obviously, the tree would have a different form if the order of decisions began with a determination of whether or not the present card were a face card, rather than if it were black or red.

Each node or vertex on the decision tree represents a decision, and the depth of the tree (the number of vertices) is taken as a measure of concept difficulty. For this model each decision is binary and so has only two outcomes: yes or no. This means that each exemplar ultimately gets judged as a positive or negative instance.

As an example of how this program might go about forming a concept —say, the concept of a legal automobile driver—we have to describe the sequence of binary decisions required. Suppose that all persons who apply for a driver's license can be described by the attributes:

1. Sex (male, female)
2. Height (short, medium, tall)
3. Criminal status (no record, misdemeanor, felony)
4. Driving skill (passed test, failed test)

Further assume that the definition of a legal driver is: "Any person not a felon who has passed a driver's test." Under this definition, there are a great many positive cases, e.g.: male, short, no record, passed test; male, short, misdemeanor, passed test; female, tall, misdemeanor, passed test.

Actually the concept of "legal driver" could be specified much more easily by using the following two decision rules in sequence: Question 1. Has the person passed the test? (yes or no). Question 2. Has the person committed a felony? (yes or no). These decisions could obviously be represented as a tree, with Question 1 as the top node and Question 2 as a lower node.

This problem (and Hunt's solution of it) deals with concepts defined by the joint presence of two or more critical attributes. Hunt and Hovland (1960), however, have also tackled the more difficult problem (both for human subjects as well as for computer programmers) of disjunctive concepts, which are concepts defined by the presence of $A$ or $B$, or both, or by some other combination. For this type of problem, concept learning again depends on "growing" a decision tree capable of defining some terminal nodes as correct and others as incorrect. For example, a particular concept might have two attributes, 1 and 2, with each having two values, $A$ and $B$. If the correct disjunctive concept were "$A$ or $B$" but "not $A$ and $B$," then the first decision to be made might run something as follows: Is the first attribute $A$—yes or no? Following the same general plan, the second decision to be made then would be: Is the second attribute $A$ or $B$—yes or no? Under these conditions there are four possible outcomes:

1. *A*–yes, *B*–yes
2. *A*–yes, *B*–no
3. *A*–no, *B*–yes
4. *A*–no, *B*–no

In this case, both (2) and (3) define the disjunctive concept "*A* or *B* but not both," while (1) defines the conjunctive concept "*A* and *B*" and (4) defines the case in which neither attribute is relevant, "not *A* and not *B*."

These then are fragments of the Hunt–Hovland approach: How well does it stack up against our criteria? It obviously meets our first criterion—concept learning is seen to involve the development and use of provisional hypotheses. The model does a little less well on our second criterion, for although it does evaluate its own hypotheses, it does so primarily on the basis of only one strategy (focusing) and not really in the same way as Bruner's flesh-and-blood subjects did it. While it is true that many subjects did use focusing strategies, many did not and a simulation program might be expected to take this into account. In addition, Hunt's program has to remember any and all past instances, a requirement clearly beyond any human subject.

Although it is possible to fault this program for its all-too-rational rationality, for its all-too-large memory, and for its all-too-inhuman ability to use a complex focusing strategy, Hunt has been the first to acknowledge the provisional nature of this class of program. Hunt feels that the future generation of programs will have to be set up so as to "humanize" them by making them less rational, somewhat more subject to distraction, and somewhat more subject to what might best be termed "pure habit factors."

But the heart of Hunt's analysis is not to be found in any of these areas; rather it is concerned with the idea that concept learning can be described as a sequential decision process. Probably the most important point to be made in this regard concerns the notion of a decision tree: Since there is an almost infinite number of attributes that could be relevant to a particular problem, which attributes the subject actually picks must depend on some hypothesis, or preknowledge, on the subject's part as to which attribute would be appropriate for a particular concept. Because of this, concept learning depends in many instances on a process of sampling selected attributes from a total pool of possible attributes. Such sampling often produces unique and idiosyncratic decision trees for individual subjects faced with the same problem and implies that no general solution is possible. In terms of the fourth of our criteria, Hunt's program has some difficulty in its ability to take context (both in terms of subject and environmental demands) into account. Until some provision can be made to handle concepts with a more open-ended set of attributes, simulation models will have to fall short of simulating real human concept learning.

## SUMMARY

Although it is not clear whether any meaningful distinction should be drawn between solving a problem and learning a concept, it is clear that human beings do have concepts. Without concepts, each new stimulus instance would have to be responded to anew. The functional significance of conceptual grouping is clear: Categorizing a particular event (an animal or a chemical) as part or not part of a particular concept (cat or poisonous) gives the person helpful guidelines as to how to behave with respect to that object. If something were categorized as "poisonous," a subject would certainly behave differently toward it than if it were categorized as "delicious" or "aromatic."

Although *concept* is a diffuse and difficult term, a number of different investigators have tried their hand at definition. For information-processing analyses, these definitions stress cognitive economy and cross-situation utility as of greatest significance. Only a few emphasize the rather obvious fact that there is almost (if not actually) an infinite number of ways in which to categorize any given concept instance, and that *which* category is chosen often depends on context. Thus a *grapefruit* is an example of a *fruit*, a *round object, something that grows in Florida, food*, and so on, depending on context. No reasonably small set of factors, considered independent of a particular context, seems able to exhaust the universe of dimensions that might give rise to different concepts.

The most usual description of what is meant by the term *concept* defines it in terms of attributes and values of these attributes. So, for example, we might characterize a given person in terms of a series of questions: Where are you from? What do you do for a living? How old are you? And so on. In terms of laboratory procedures, concepts have been defined on the basis of simple attributes such as color or size or shape, etc., and presented to subjects under either *reception* or *selection* procedures. In the reception procedure, subjects are shown a series of items and their task is either to give a category name to that item, or say "Yes, it is an example of some concept," or "No, it is not an example of some concept." In the selection procedure, the subject is usually told that the experimenter has some concept in mind that is exemplified by the card, and that the subject's job is to select other cards he thinks represent that concept. In reception studies, the experimenter controls the order of instances, while in selection studies the subject does.

Although most studies have been done using reception procedures, early work by Bruner, Goodnow, and Austin using selection procedures gave strong support for an analysis of concept learning in terms of hypotheses and strategies. These authors inferred the use of a particular strategy (as indeed of any hypothesis) from the consistency of a subject's behavior—if a subject *always* does behaviors $a_1, a_2, \ldots, a_n$, then he is following Strategy $A$; if he does $b_1, b_2, \ldots, b_n$, then he is following Strategy $B$, and so on.

The results of Bruner, Goodnow, and Austin's studies seemed to imply that subjects use a number of different strategies, the most important of which were termed *scanning* and *focusing*. The essential difference between these two is whether or not the subject chooses to scan all exemplars in coming to a decision, or whether he chooses to focus on one attribute of a concept at a time. As Bruner *et al.* were able to show, certain specific task and response constraints forced subjects to modify both these strategies in predictable ways, sometimes even requiring them to switch from one to the other.

Bourne and his co-workers attempted to describe concept learning in terms of two constituent subprocesses: attribute identification and rule learning. In terms of a series of experiments, Bourne was able to show that both these subprocesses are equally difficult for subjects, although both are accomplished considerably more rapidly than concept learning which requires simultaneous attribute identification and rule learning.

One concept derived from the logic of computer operation, that of a hierarchical tree, has figured prominently in Hunt's simulation of concept learning. This program builds on an earlier logical analysis of problem solving and concept attainment undertaken by Hovland which was primarily concerned with the seemingly wide difference of positive and negative exemplars to lead to adequate concepts. His argument was that positive and negative exemplars should be equally useful when all relevant attributes are specified, but that positive exemplars should be more useful when attributes are not specified in advance. Although empirical results suggest that human subjects sometimes have great difficulty in negating hypotheses, specifying relevant attributes does tend to make negative instances more useful to the concept learner.

In Hunt's model of concept learning, decision trees are used in simulating how human subjects decide whether or not a particular stimulus element is (or is not) an example of a particular concept. For Hunt's program it is necessary for the subject to be told, in advance, the significant attributes serving to define the concept. For this model, concepts are discovered on the basis of a sequential decision process modeled after the strategy of perfect focusing. Although this simulation does not handle a good deal of the empirical results having to do with concept learning, it nonetheless does call attention to the role of decision processes in concept learning.

# CHAPTER 11

# REMEMBERING
# THINGS PAST

The best way to go about a discussion of remembering is to invite you to remember. Think of a fairy tale from your childhood—say *The Emperor's New Clothes* (or *Candy* if you come from a more permissive family)—and try to tell it to yourself right now. Don't be so sophisticated—go ahead and try. If you attempt the task honestly, you'll find that you can remember a few significant facts—an Emperor, some crooked tailors, a naked ride through town, a pesky little boy, and perhaps a few others. One of the things you're likely to notice is that the story is a good bit shorter than you remember it as being when you first heard it and that you are unable to produce a good deal of detail that was in the original story.

If you tell the story aloud, you may find words like *retinue, courtiers, mendacity, vanity,* and a few others cropping up. Words that certainly never occurred in any child's fairy tale in the first place. Similarly, if you are asked, or somehow feel obliged, to fill in some of the missing details, you can weave a perfectly reasonable story even if you don't really "remember" it. Then too, if the original story had some unusual details—if for example, in the original story the King rode on a donkey—you probably will change it to a more likely animal such as a horse.

Now at this point you have every right to protest: "This is only a single example; how do you know that under strict laboratory conditions these same phenomena would occur?" Well, the answer is simple. Someone (Bartlett, 1932) did a similar experiment many years ago and found that if subjects were asked to tell the experimenter a story they had heard a few minutes, or weeks, or months before, they tended to compress and abbreviate the original story and tell it in their own words rather than in the original words of the story. If a detail in the original was unfamiliar to them, many subjects simply made up their own version of it or altered the story to fit their own view. Subjects tended not so much to recall the exact wording or style of the story, but tended instead to paraphrase according to their own vocabulary and experiences.

These results led Bartlett to conclude that memory is an extremely active process that involves the reception, categorization, and reconstruction of material on the basis of highly personal and highly idiosyncratic factors. He went on to propose that in remembering, as in other cognitive tasks, the subject first attempts to make sense out of the material presented to him by referring it to what he already knows about the topic, or one similar to it. This pre-existing knowledge, which selectively alters and categorizes past and present experience, Bartlett termed a *mental schema*. Bartlett believed that such schema served as a basis not only for memory, but also for concept learning, problem solving, attitude formation, as well as a great many other cognitive activities.

The act of remembering occurs, according to Bartlett, as the subject attempts to reconstruct a story from his stored representation of it (i.e., from its schema). Since any schema is in part personal and therefore highly idiosyncratic, different subjects reconstruct the same story differently. One subject emphasizes this detail, a second that detail, and a third still another detail. If all subjects had exactly the same schema and followed exactly the same rules of reconstruction, all would produce exactly the same story.

Although such a state of affairs seems highly unlikely with material such as Bartlett used, there is one well-studied experimental situation in which such inter-subject agreement can be reached and in which, after sufficient practice, all subjects can and do produce exactly the same recalls. This procedure involves the recall of strings of 1's and 0's, when subjects have been taught to code them into a different form. The original experiment was performed by Smith and reported in detail by Miller (1956) (see Chapter 2, pages 47–48). A description of the procedure and what it implies for a theory of memory should provide us with a working model of what goes on when subjects attempt to recall meaningful material.

As a precondition for remembering 1's and 0's, the subject is first taught to code them into more economical units, usually $base_{10}$ numbers. So, for example, 000 is coded as 0; 001, as 1; 010, as 2; and so on up to 111, as 7. Obviously, once the subject knows this code, he tends to break up or segment the continuous input of 1's and 0's into groups of three. After such initial segmentation, each group of 1's and 0's is recoded into a more economical form such as: $010 \rightarrow 2$. As this recoding goes on, the subject must also segment the next set of items into groups of three, again coding them into an appropriate $base_{10}$ number. The subject continues in this way until all 1's and 0's have been segmented and coded.

How then does the subject remember in this situation? Once all the coded numbers have been held in memory, the subject next has the job of recoding them back into acceptable 1–0 form. This is accomplished by reapplying the same rule which will decode the stored base$_{10}$ number back into 1's and 0's. The actual process of producing the response (i.e., of remembering 1's and 0's) can be construed as involving reconstruction rather than rote recall. In this case, as in the case of *The Emperor's New Clothes*, the subject never really need store any specific details of the material as they were presented to him. Rather, in the 1–0 case, a subject's output protocol depends on a reconstructive process—a process governed by a sufficiently exact coding rule which does not permit distortion of the original material.

Is there any evidence that such reconstructive processes actually go on in memory tasks? Perhaps the first piece of evidence in support of this view was provided by Smith. In his original demonstration, Smith not only taught himself to code 1's and 0's into groups of three (that is 3 into 1 coding), he also taught himself 2 into 1 coding ($1, 0 = 2 + 0$ or 2); 4 into 1 coding ($1, 0, 1, 0 = 8 + 0 + 2 + 0$ or 10) and 5 into 1 coding ($1, 0, 0, 1, 0 = 16 + 0 + 0 + 2 + 0$ or 18). Once he achieved a high level of proficiency in the various coding systems (no small task, by the way), Smith determined his span for a 1 into 1 condition and used this as a basis on which to predict his 2:1, 3:1, 4:1, and 5:1 memory spans. If Smith were able to remember 12 items in the 1:1 condition, he reasoned that 12 unrelated numbers would be worth 24 items with 2:1 coding ($12 \times 2$) and 36 items with 3:1 coding ($12 \times 3$). For reasons that are not altogether clear in the original report, a slightly different coding schema was used for 4:1 and 5:1 coding which produced expected recall values of about 40 digits for these coding systems. The important point, however, is that Smith's memory span was increased from 12 binary digits to 40 binary digits simply by using an appropriate coding procedure.

These results suggest that a memory task has a great many points in common with a concept-formation or problem-solving task. It seems fair to say—although perhaps a bit too strong—that for information-processing analysis, the division of cognitive tasks into concept formation, memory, and problem solving is not only artificial but misleading. In all cases the organism attempts, as far as possible, to reduce his task to a manageable size; and in all cases this involves a continuous interplay among the various subprocesses involved in problem solving ("How am I going to remember this stuff?") and concept formation ("Let's see if I can find any way to categorize the stuff.") What this means is that a subject scarcely if ever attempts to categorize items on the basis of contiguity; rather he begins the process of recall by searching through the material presented to determine its "categorizability." Subjects don't seem to be too fussy about what kinds of principles they use: Sometimes if materials permit, they group them according to meaning; other times according to pre-existing categories; other times according to some sort of coding rule; and if all of these and other strategies fail, they may revert to the simple strategy of rhythm or contiguity alone.

If this is how recall works, how is it that so many studies show contiguity and interference to be significant factors in memory performance? Here the answer has something to do with the experimental procedures used to study memory.

To take two extremes: In Bartlett's experiments the subject was presented with highly meaningful material and allowed to progress through it at his own rate. Similarly, his recall was not timed and he was not forced to do a simple repetition of the story but, rather, was allowed to retell it as near the original as he could manage. Contrast this with an experiment on memory and forgetting that might be done by an associationistic psychologist. In this type of study the subject is presented, one at a time, with a series of perfectly meaningless items (or as near that ideal as possible). The rate of presentation is rapid—no item for more than 2 seconds—with recall also paced and rapid. The subject is not only required to recall nonsense material exactly, but usually in a perfectly arbitrary and meaningless order. Given these two extremes, it is possible to see how informational analyses come to emphasize the rational, problem-solving aspect of a rather extended memory ability, whereas associationistic approaches stress the rote, interference-prone aspects of a much more restricted memory capacity.

This obvious difference in task also reflects an obvious difference in theoretical emphasis. As we have noted many times before (see Chapter 2), an associationistic approach assumes an essentially passive organism who learns and remembers on the basis of the law of contiguity, while an information-processing approach assumes a much more active organism who learns and remembers on the basis of plans and strategies. This difference in theoretical assumptions led to clear differences in how each approach tested and developed its theory in the laboratory. Given these background considerations, it is clear that if an experimenter puts the subject under rigorous time conditions involving materials that are not easy to code, he can then analyze the role of contiguity and interference in memory. If he puts the subject under more relaxed conditions and encourages him to code the material presented, he can then analyze the role of information-processing capacities in memory.

Consider what the differences mean in an experiment done by Bower and Clark (1969) which compared rote and reconstructive procedures directly. In this experiment, one group of subjects was given a list of ten unrelated nouns and told to fabricate any story including all ten words. On the average, subjects took about 2.5 minutes to think up a story. A second group of subjects—a control group—was simply given 2.5 minutes in which to memorize all ten words. When both groups were asked for immediate recall, subjects in both groups were able to recall all ten words. Following this initial list both groups were asked to go through the same procedure for 11 more lists. After the twelfth list, subjects in both groups were asked to recall all 120 words. Subjects in the control group were able to recall only about 17 words, whereas subjects in the story group were able to recall well over 100 words. What subjects in the story group seemed to do was first recall the theme of the story, and then reconstruct almost all the words they had used in that particular story. When subjects are given equal time for memorizing, those who "package" the words around a single theme produce considerably superior recall.

## CATEGORY CLUSTERING IN RECALL

Some of the earliest work hinting at the role of informational capacities in recall involved highly codable materials presented under fairly rigorous task conditions. In an early study, Bousfield (1953) presented subjects with 60 nouns so selected as to involve four categories of 15 words each. None of the subjects, however, was told about these categories. All the categories used were easily recognizable ones such as *men's names*, or *animals*, or *vegetables*, etc., and each of the words used was an obvious exemplar (*Robert, weasel, spinach*). All 60 of the words were randomized so that no two words from the same category appeared in adjacent positions in the list as presented. Presentation was oral, at a rate of about one every three seconds, with subjects required to write the words in any order during recall.

The result of most interest was the sequential order of items during recall relative to their order during presentation. Almost without exception subjects tended to recall items by category, despite the fact that the original input order had been completely random. In order to evaluate the degree of non-randomness in output records, Bousfield developed an index of repetition which measured the degree to which items from the same category occurred in adjacent positions in recall. In his analysis, the ratio of repetition was higher for output lists than for input lists, implying that subjects produced categorized recalls.

The first interpretation Bousfield put on his results (he subsequently changed his mind not once, but twice) was that during the course of presentation each item cued a conceptual category, and this category served to organize recall into higher order units. Since the concept category was cued by each item (or at least by most of the constituent items—some, such as *orange*, may be ambiguous with respect to category membership), a concept must be the dominant response to the situation and therefore the one recalled most easily. Recall of the concept, however, not only organized the input during presentation, but also served to cue the appropriate category members during recall. The recall of any category member served to cue the category again, and so the process proceeded until no more category items were cued. At this point, the subject moved on to the next category.

This hypothesis is a rather curious beast: On the one hand, Bousfield considered that memory for clusterable material involved concept utilization; yet, on the other hand, his description of how the process actually works was couched in terms of an *S–R* mediational process, with a concept name serving as the mediating element. For this reason it is not surprising to find that a few years later Bousfield abandoned his emphasis on the role of concepts in mediating category clustering and came instead to view such recall completely in terms of pre-existing connections among the words comprising a category. In this revision, he argued that a category (or concept) could be defined as a strongly interconnected set of words; and given this definition, there was no reason to postulate the separate existence or operation of what previously he had called a super-ordinate category or concept.

Bousfield undoubtedly was helped to this revision by some early data reported by Jenkins and Russell (1952), and Jenkins, Mink, and Russell (1958) and by subsequent data reported by Deese (1959, 1961). The most important aspect of these studies, leading to Bousfield's change of heart, was the demonstration that items which produce each other as word associates also tend to cluster in recall. In the earliest of these studies (Jenkins and Russell, 1952) subjects were presented with a list of 48 words, in which this list consisted of 24 pairs of word associations such as *bread–butter, king–queen*, and so on. The 48 items were in random order, as in the Bousfield procedure, and subjects were asked for a written free recall. Results showed that in most cases, subjects tended to put the pairs back together again during recall so that mutual associations appeared in adjacent positions in recall. Deese's studies (1959, 1961) only further emphasized this trend. His results showed that collections of words in which the constituent words produce each other as word associations were recalled better than sets of words not having these connections. This result led to the general conclusion that free recall, categorized or not, could be described in terms of the pattern of word associations existing among all words to be recalled. No further theoretical need was seen to invoke the concept of a category.

The first series of experiments questioning the conclusion that category factors were of no importance in predicting recall clustering was performed by Marshall and Cofer in a series of experiments beginning in 1961 (Marshall and Cofer, 1961; Cofer, 1965). The critical aspect of their procedure was to compare clustering for category words with clustering for non-category words, where the number of word-association connections between pair members was equal. Equating the number of associative connections was based on the number of word associates two stimulus words had in common. For example, if the two words *bed* and *dream* both elicit *sleep, night*, and *nightmare*, these response words would figure in the degree of associative overlap between *bed* and *dream*.

In the basic experiments in this set, each of a number of different subject groups was presented with a list of 24 words composed of 12 pairs of words. For 6 of these pairs, both words were members of the same category, while for the remaining 6 pairs, the words were not members of the same category. On this basis, it was possible to determine the degree of pair clustering in free recall, where input materials had equal association strengths, but where half the pairs shared membership in the same category and the other half did not. In all cases the results were clear: Category pairs tended to cluster more in recall than non-category pairs. Cofer interpreted this to mean that not all clustering in recall could be accounted for in terms of word-association connections. Membership in a conceptual category also seems to exert a strong effect on recall clustering over and above that accounted for by associative interconnections.

Another problem for Bousfield and Jenkins' attempt to describe recall clustering in terms of word associations is that the process by which one word produces another as an associative response is not a completely settled topic. Although older views tended to describe the process in terms of word-to-word connections (see Osgood, 1953; or Pollio, 1966), other more recent analyses have attempted to describe word association in terms of concept-utilization factors (Deese, 1966; Johnson, 1968). Although the details of this controversy must be delayed until a subsequent chapter (see Chapter 16, page 433 ff), what is important in the present context is that an explanation of clustering phrased in terms of word-association processes poses difficulties of its own. We still really don't know for sure why it is that one word produces another as an associative response.

The phenomena of category clustering has still further implications for an information-processing analysis of memory. If memory involves some sequential combination of information-reducing and information-expanding processes, then the nature of the material to be recalled should strongly affect clustering. One way to vary input material is to select category items that are often given as exemplars of a category (e.g., *sports–baseball, basketball*) and compare the clusterability of such items with items given less frequently (e.g., *sports–rugby, croquet*). In order to determine the frequency with which different items are given as responses to different category names, Bousfield, Cohen, and Whitmarch (1958) asked groups of subjects to give them examples of items from each of a number of different categories such as "a piece of furniture," "an animal," "a vegetable," and so on. What their compilation revealed was that some items were given by a much larger number of subjects than other items. The total number of people giving a particular item was called its *taxonomic frequency of occurrence*. Armed with these norms, it was then possible to find out if high-frequency exemplars are recalled more readily than low-frequency ones. Here the overwhelming bulk of evidence (Bousfield, Cohen, and Whitmarsh, 1958; Pollio and Gerow, 1968) does indicate this to be the case: Subjects have more extended recalls, involving greater clustering, when high-frequency rather than low-frequency items are used. Again, these data seem to suggest that what the subject actually stores in memory is some representation of a category, with the overt process of recall essentially one of getting from the category to the individual word.

In an attempt to examine this hypothesis more directly, Pollio, Richards, and Lucas (1969) presented subjects with five high-frequency items from each of five different categories, and asked for an oral free recall. Oral, rather than written, recall was used because it seems reasonable to assume that if subjects were in fact recalling categories and reconstructing items as needed for recall, there should be much longer inter-response times (IRT) between two exemplars of different categories than between two exemplars of a single category.

Figure 11.1 presents a highly schematic, but quite realistic example of what such recalls looked like.

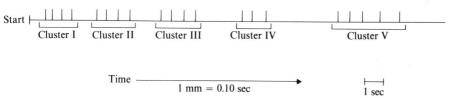

**Fig. 11.1** Schematic drawing of a typical record, revealing distribution and temporal properties of free recall of categorized word lists. (From Pollio, Richards, and Lucas, 1969.)

The first burst of responses—the first four "blips" on the record—all come from the same category. Where there is a slightly longer inter-recall time, the subject has shifted to the words of a different category. This same pattern holds for the entire record—a sequence of very fast responses is followed by a single longer IRT, which in turn is followed by another rapid burst of responses, and so on.

This pattern, which was found to characterize the results of almost all records, reveals that subjects do collect items into categories (with these categories defined both by pre-existing norms and by a break in recall output) and that items from the same category are produced extremely rapidly. Intuitively, such a process is reflected by the subject thinking: "Let's see, I've already recalled all the sports and furniture items; now let's try the fruits . . ." "Let's see, I've already recalled sports, furniture, and fruits . . . , how about men's names" . . . and so on.

This analysis of category clustering in particular, and of recall in general, assumes that in a recall experiment the subject really does two different jobs during presentation and during recall. During presentation, he searches the input material in an attempt to find some sort of order, or better, some sort of schema such as a category. During recall, his job is to retrieve the now organized materials and then reconstruct individual items comprising each category. If such an analysis is correct, then helping the subject to discover the organizational properties of input materials should help him in recall. Since there seem to be two different places at which such help can occur—namely before presentation and/or before attempted recall—giving subjects instructions as to how the materials are organized at either point should augment both recall and clustering.

An experiment by Pollio and Gerow (1969) is relevant here. Basically, their subjects were presented with a 25-item list containing five categories of five items each. Some of these subjects were given the hint before items were actually presented that the materials were organized into five categories (which were then named) of five items each. For obvious reasons this group was called the *Hint Before* Group. A second group of subjects saw the items without any hint at all. However, just after presentation was finished (and just before the subjects were to attempt recall), they were given essentially the same hint as the Hint Before Group. For obvious reasons this group was called the *Hint After* Group. A final group of subjects was not given any hint (*No-Hint* Group) and served as a baseline condition against which to compare the other two groups. Results were quite clear: Both of the hint groups recalled substantially more items than the No-Hint Group, with little or no difference between the Before and After Groups. This latter point is important, for subjects in the After Group obviously were treated in exactly the same way as subjects in the No-Hint Group until they were told the appropriate hint prior to recall. Given these conditions, whatever advantage they had in recall must have had to do with getting material out of storage and not with the way in which it was stored in the first place.

Probably the best way to interpret these results is to assume that the Before Group has an advantage at both the initial coding stage and at the recall stage, whereas the After Group has an advantage only at the recall stage. What this might mean is that getting information out of storage is the difficult part of memory and that any hint given before presentation probably was effective only during the process of recall itself. Parenthetically, it should be noted that Pollio and Gerow collected word-association norms for all the items used in their experiment and failed to find any relationship between inter-item, word-association connections and either the pattern or extent of recall.

Ference Marton (1970) of Goteborg University, Sweden, has also attempted to describe what subjects do in a memory task involving highly codable materials. He presented his subjects with a list of 48 names that could be categorized in a number of different ways. All subjects were read the same list for 16 trials, with the order of names put into a different random order on each trial. As might be expected, most subjects were able to recall at least 45 names by the end of about 13 trials. In addition, when Marton examined the degree to which items from the *same* category occurred in adjacent positions in recall over all 16 trials, he found that subjects imposed very few sequential constraints on recall order for the first few trials (1–8) but did tend to impose such constraints very strongly on the last nine trials. When, however, he examined the degree to which *subject-defined* categories occupied adjacent positions, he found that such constraints reached their maximum by about the ninth or tenth trial and then remained relatively constant. In other words, the subject spends most of his time on the early trials in planning how to retrieve categories, and only once this is achieved does he begin to concentrate on setting up a rigid order for item retrieval.

These data imply that category constraints precede individual word constraints in recall. Marton has generalized this finding in the following way: "My general impression is that more flexible modes of organization precede less flexible ones; that is, hierarchical constraints precede sequential ones . . . and that the structure develops toward greater rigidity." Thus the increase in speed and skill characteristic of highly practiced retrieval performance is the result of learning a specific sequential structure, a structure purchased at the price of a decrease in flexibility and generality.

## RETRIEVAL PROCESSES

If one major problem in memory is to be retrieval, how is this process to be understood? Mandler (1967, 1968) has discussed this problem within the context of accessibility rules and their role in recall. His analysis begins with a distinction between *item availability* and *item accessibility* which he illustrated by way of an analogy: Think of a house on an island in the middle of a lake. The house is available because it can be seen from the shore, but is not accessible in the absence of boats or similar devices. The more such devices are available, the greater is the accessibility of the house. None of these, however, affects the availability of the house. It is not that the house (a particular memory) is not available—the subject just can't get to it.

In general, Mandler proposes that there are three major classes of rules involved in remembering:

1. *Associative-cue rules*: Largely equivalent to contiguity-based connections between stimulus and response items. For example, saying *Ping* may help the subject recall *Pong* because these two often have been paired contiguously in the past.

2. *General accessibility rules*: Specify a general solution to a class of problems. For example, the use of a category structure to organize memory falls under this general heading.

3. *Generative rules*: Designed to produce novel material from the input such as creative elaboration of a remembered sentence. This seemed to have occurred in Bartlett's reconstructive memory task—"*The Emperor's New Clothes* Phenomenon."

Although Mandler divides accessibility rules into three categories, they could comfortably be considered in terms of two classes: Those that are reproductive (associative rules) and those that are reconstructive (general and generative rules). The reproductive rules are those that depend on the exact properties of the input—stored items are not changed in any way and are recalled as presented. In this case, the organism is a passive medium who in no way attempts to transform the input at presentation nor to decode it at recall.

For the information-processing theorist, there is no such thing as pure reproduction: All cases involve at least one transformation at input and another at output. Here, the argument goes, the fact that output maps input is hardly grounds for claiming that no transformation has occurred in the interim. If this view is pursued to its logical conclusion, then there are no such things as reproductive rules; rather such rules can and should be treated as special limited cases of reconstruction rules.

The operation of reconstructive rules can be seen at work in category clustering: Once a category is developed from the input (or heard as in the Before Hint Condition), it is stored and subsequently retrieved essentially in its untransformed state. An entirely different process seems to operate at the level of individual items: Not only need these be marked as to category membership but, in many cases, as in 1–0 coding, the individual item probably never even gets into storage. Under this latter condition, retrieval involves re-expanding the category at the time of recall so that items are produced as responses that need never have been stored in an untransformed state.

The discussion of reproductive rules has been pursued most carefully by associative analyses of memory and has been described in great detail in Chapter 3. The description of reconstructive rules in memory is nowhere near as far advanced, and about all that can be done is to describe some general considerations that seem relevant. One important aspect concerns the "determinability" of the rule by which some input has been coded. Consider the following cases: If a subject is asked to recall binary digits and he has coded a set of three of them into the number 5, given that he knows the appropriate expansion rule, the response "101" is perfectly determined. The same analysis is also true of an exhaustive category, for if a subject remembers the category—directions of the compass—the responses "North," "South," "East," and "West" are perfectly determined. Of lesser determinability are items in a nonexhaustive category. If the subject remembers the category as "sports," he still has the problem of deciding which particular sports were in the input list and which were not. If the items were of high frequency, he should be able to reconstruct them with some degree of success. If, under similar conditions, low-frequency items were used, these will be much more difficult to reconstruct and consequently will lead to poorer retrieval and poorer recall.

Obviously, even low-frequency-category items are still quite high on any scale of *generatability*, for, given the coded form, the output is still reasonably well specified. But what of other less-structured materials—do they show similar organizational and recall trends? Although undertaken for a different purpose, an experiment by Pollio, Kasschau, and DeNise (1968) is relevant here. In this experiment, subjects were presented with a number of different sets of 22 words each. Some sets were mutual word associations, while others were simply a random collection of words. All subjects were presented with the words, one at a time, and asked for an oral recall after presentation was completed.

Similar to results described earlier, an examination of output protocols revealed a good deal of variation in output rate as subjects produced oral recalls. Since there was no *a priori* way to decide which words went with which other words to form a meaningful category, an attempt was made to determine when subjects changed their rate of recall significantly. Such significant changes in rate were defined by a fivefold difference in the interword response time separating any two words. Without going into great detail, there was an average of about 4.5 rate changes in individual records, thereby indicating that, in terms of time between items, recall was quite episodic. These alterations were taken to indicate the existence of an underlying cluster; and, in accordance with the view that recall is augmented to the degree that input materials are coded, it was expected that subjects who showed a great many alterations would also show the best recall. Correlations computed over individual subjects between number of recall alterations and total recall were all positive and seem to support the view that alterations in rate may be used to specify the boundaries of a memory unit. In addition, these results seem to show that subjects will code items no matter how "uncodable" the items might appear to be at first glance.

## SUBJECTIVE ORGANIZATION IN RECALL

The most striking evidence for the role of organizational processes in memory is provided in a series of studies done by Tulving and his associates (Tulving, 1962; 1964; 1968). The basic procedure used in these studies is quite simple: Subjects are presented with a list of 16 different, and randomly selected, words for 16 trials. After each trial, subjects are asked to recall the words in any order they choose. The words are then put in a different random order for the next trial.

There are two primary measures in these experiments, the number of words recalled and a measure Tulving defined as SO or *subjective organization*. Basically, SO is a measure of the degree to which two words appear in adjacent positions in recall across trials. If input materials are arranged so that no two words ever follow each other on more than a single trial, then the degree to which these words follow each other in an individual subject's recall record on many trials must indicate that the subject has recalled the words in a rearranged order. If words are recalled in the same order on successive trials (as might be the case for category materials), then SO is complete; if they reflect input completely, then SO is nonexistent, with recall completely governed by input properties.

In Tulving's experiment the average SO value was about 0.30 (SO values can range from 0.00–1.00), indicating that subjects did tend to establish reasonably regular word clusters despite the complete absence of such clusters in input materials. Furthermore, the correlation between the mean number of words recalled and the mean SO over all 16 trials of the experiment was 0.96. Similar correlations for individual subjects were high and positive, and together these results suggest that increases in amount recalled are strongly related to increases in subjective organization. In terms of an informational analysis, the more the subject organizes the material, the better he is able to recall it.

Another aspect of these data—of some theoretical importance—is that correlations between performance and subjective organization were lower on the first eight trials than on the last eight. Similarly, the mean SO score was found to increase over successive trials. From these results it seems that subjects do impose a subjective structure to recall, that this subjective organization develops over repeated exposures of the materials to be recalled, and that there is a strong correlation between organization and recall.

In most of the studies described so far, input materials were presented in such a way as to make the subject's job of devising or discovering organizational properties for the input extremely difficult. That is, words were presented one at a time, and with the exception of the Pollio and Gerow (1968) study (and a similar one by Mandler, 1967), subjects were never given any idea as to the nature of the input list. If memory is facilitated by the formation of categories, then providing subjects with a specific opportunity and instructions to categorize materials prior to recall, should aid recall. Probably the first experiment in recent times to tackle this problem was done by Mandler and Pearlstone (1966). In this experiment, subjects were presented with a number of unrelated items written on cards and were told to sort the cards into from 2 to 7 categories on whatever basis they chose. Afterward, subjects were asked for a free recall of these materials. This experiment produced two interesting results: (1) Items sorted into the same category tended to occur in adjacent positions in recall, and (2) there was a positive correlation between the number of items in recall and the number of categories in sorting.

In this experiment the first thing the subject did was to sort items into categories in a way very similar to that used in the study of concept learning. Following this, subjects then attempted recall, with the best categorizers producing the best recall. Mandler (1967) has argued that the use of many rather than few categories facilitates accessibility (retrieval) and therefore better recall. It is also possible to interpret these results in terms of re-constructive processes: the subject who sorts into more categories forms more coherent and less diffuse categories, and on this basis has little difficulty in generating or reconstructing the constituent words.

Whichever of these interpretations is correct cannot be determined with certainty at present. What is important about the Mandler experiment is that it demonstrates the role of self-produced categories in memory. In a more extensive analysis of this problem, Pollio and Foote (1970) had subjects first sort a wide variety of words into categories. Since subjects were told that they were participating in a concept-formation task, they were quite sur-prised when, at the end of the sorting task, they were asked to recall the words they had just sorted. The subjects produced their recall onto a tape recorder so that inter-word recall times could also be examined.

As in the results found by Mandler, subjects tended to recall words in their own idiosyncratic groupings. That is, they tended to produce items together in recall to the degree that they grouped them together during sorting. Further results revealed that when the average inter-recall time between items from the same subject-defined category was compared with the average inter-recall time separating items from different categories, these latter values were two to three times as large. In agreement with results found to hold in the case of obvious category materials (see Pollio, Richards, and Lucas, 1969), between-category, inter-response times were much longer than within-category, inter-response times.

## TIP-OF-THE-TONGUE PHENOMENA

In our discussion of reconstructive processes in memory, the word *concept* has been used in a relatively loose and common-sense fashion. Perhaps one of the most ingenious attempts to describe how concepts and memory interact has been made by Brown and McNeill (1966) in their analysis of tip-of-the-tongue phenomena.

We are all familiar with this phenomenon, as for example when you are asked for the name of your third-grade teacher, you say: "Was it Hill, Hilman, Hillian, Gilmon?... no, it's Gillian."

In the tip-of-the-tongue phenomenon, the person attempting recall has a definite feeling that he knows what the word is he is looking for, yet is unable, at least initially, to produce it. Instead, he recalls either words of similar sound (*Hillian*, in the present case) or words of similar meaning. Such a sequence of events: the foreknowledge that the word is known but cannot be retrieved, the retrieval of words similar in meaning or sound to the target word, and the recognition that some of these are, or are not, correct defines a tip-of-the-tongue, or TOT state. If specific recall of the word fails to occur but similar-sounding or similar-meaning words are produced, such recall is called *generic recall*. Brown and McNeill (1966), in their analysis of the TOT state, provide the following description: "The signs of it (TOT state) were unmistakable; he (the subject) would appear to be in mild torment, something like the brink of a sneeze, and if he found the word his relief was considerable."

In order to precipitate such arrested sneezing, Brown and McNeill read their subjects definitions of a number of low-frequency words such as *sampan, apse, cloaca* and so on, and asked them to produce a word fitting the definition. If the subject could not provide the word, he was asked to tell the experimenter the number of syllables (1 to 5) he thought the word had, its initial letter, and any other words similar in either sound or meaning that he (the subject) thought of in his attempt to produce the correct word. Although this procedure was not uniformly successful in inducing TOT states for all subjects or for all words, several hundred such states were precipitated. An examination of the responses produced during these states (before recall occurred) revealed that subjects had some knowledge of the correct number of syllables, the correct initial letter, some noninitial letters, and the location of the primary stress. Similarly, and not surprisingly, subjects were able to produce words similar in meaning to the target word. In looking at their data in a slightly different way, Brown and McNeill found that if a subject was eventually able to recall the correct word (was able to resolve the TOT state), his presolution information (number of syllables, pattern of stress, etc.) was more accurate than if he failed to produce the word correctly.

These results are really not surprising for anyone who has ever experienced a TOT state, or who has resolved it either with an unsatisfactory generic recall, or with recall of the correct word. But this very plausibility makes their solution an important problem—and in order to do this, some description of how a subject stores words is required. Brown and McNeill began by assuming that each word can be represented as a collection of characteristics, such as might be found on an IBM key punch card— that is, the word is written at the left and the significant characteristics occupy all the remaining columns.

| Word | Characteristics | | | | | | | | |
|------|---|---|---|---|---|---|---|---|---|
|      | 1 | 2 | 3 | 4 | . | . | . | $10\ldots n$ |
| BOY  | + |   | + | + |   |   |   | + |
| GIRL | + | − | + |   |   |   |   | + |

In this case the word BOY is stored as a list of $n$ characteristics. But what might some of these characteristics be? From Brown and McNeill's work it is possible to argue that the list or collection of characteristics (or attributes) contains some of the same information as given by a dictionary definition. In their example, if the subject is to retrieve the word *sextant*, and is given the appropriate definition (a navigational instrument used in measuring angular distances, . . . etc.), then all cards presently in long-time storage are sorted out to the degree that their characteristics have something to do with "navigation," "instrument," "geometry," etc. A first attempt at retrieval might fish up words such as *astrolobe, compass*, etc. This first retrieval obviously depends on semantic factors and will not explain any of the similar-sounding words that were retrieved. Note too that this way of describing semantic characteristics is very similar to the attribute-value analyses of more general concepts such as were described in Chapter 10.

There are a number of possible outcomes to this first retrieval. One possibility is that the word retrieved matches the definition as given. A second is that the word retrieved does not match the word defined, but the subject thinks it does. A third is that the subject is unable to produce any word at all and therefore says "I don't know." In none of these three cases (correct production, incorrect production, no production) has a TOT state been precipitated; this occurs only when the subject fishes up a card that matches the characteristics of the definition, but where the left-hand entry (equivalent to BOY in the example described above) is incomplete. On the basis of Brown and McNeill's data, an incomplete entry for *sextant* might be $s\_\_t$, or one that provides a correct initial and a correct final letter and one which specifies the correct number of syllables. If this type of card is retrieved, the subject is in a TOT state.

What should he do now? Try another retrieval; only this time use all the defining semantic characteristics, in addition to word-form information (begins with *s*, ends with *t*, has two syllables), and then attempt another retrieval on the basis of this new pool of information. Using all this information might now lead to the (erroneous) retrieval of *secant* and *sextat* in addition to *sextant*. The analysis goes on for a bit more, but enough of the general details have been presented to make further description unnecessary. What is extremely important about Brown and McNeill's analysis is that it provides for a clearer specification of how reconstructive memory might work.

Gordon Bower (1967) has attempted to use a model of this type to derive certain well-known memory phenomena. Bower begins by assuming that subjects code words into memory storage on the basis of a number of attributes in much the same manner as Brown and McNeill described for the word BOY. Once the word or any other memory unit is stored in this form, there are two alternatives as to what gets lost in forgetting: the total set of attributes, or individual attributes of the set. On the basis of comparing purely mathematical derivations from both these assumptions with actual recall data, Bower concluded that attributes are probably lost one at a time, rather than all at once.

Bower has also attempted to derive the effects of repeated presentation on recall, given an attribute model. Repetition effects, such as those reported by Hellyer (1962), not surprisingly show that forgetting is retarded by repeated exposures. In order to accommodate this finding, Bower assumes that each repetition serves to produce another copy of the total attribute set. If we assume that the several copies of each component fade out randomly and independently of other copies, then the more copies made, the greater the likelihood that any given component will be available for retrieval after repeated presentation. This scheme is called *multiplexing*, and assumes that when one represents an attribute component by multiple indexing and by pooling many unreliable units the total memory system becomes very reliable. As Kintsch (1970) has noted: Bower's analysis is an attempt to "find some kind of a solution to the problem of how to make performance reliable when every component is inherently unreliable."

## CATEGORY CLUSTERING REVISITED

Take again the case of category clustering. In this task the subject is presented with a series of words one at a time. If each word is represented by a list of characteristics in the manner described by Brown and McNeill and by Bower, then each word should arouse its "card of attributes" as it is presented to the subject. Since these words come from different categories, certain regularly recurring characteristics will be aroused, with these characteristics serving to define a category. If the categories are reasonably distinct, and if the words used are reasonably good instances, this recurrent regularity will be noted by the subject. If the category is one already known to the subject, he may at this point retrieve the appropriate category card, using subsequent "trials" only to confirm that he in fact has the correct category. If the subject is convinced he has the correct category, individual cards will be dropped back into the general long-term storage file with the subject only holding onto the category cards.

If the experiment is such that there are not too many categories that need be retained without further higher-order coding, recall will consist essentially of reconstructing the individual word cards which are now in long-term storage. This would seem to involve a process exactly opposite to that used in recovering the category in the first place: The subject begins with the category card and undertakes his sorting on this basis. He then goes through the equivalent of a matching process in which he tests words in his vocabulary against the characteristics of the concept card and pulls out only those that match. The ones that match best are those that gave rise to the category in the first place and these, therefore, are the ones that will most probably be retrieved.

Is this account consistent with what is known about category clustering? For one thing, it does explain why the order of recall output seldom follows the order of input—during recall subjects tend to produce items in clusters. Second it explains why category items of low taxonomic frequency are not as well recalled, or clustered, as high-frequency ones—they do not form as consistent clusters as high-frequency items and therefore are harder both to code and reconstruct. In addition they are often of lower frequency of usage in the language and their "card" may not have as sharp outlines on the word side of the card.

This type of hypothesis also offers some explanation for a number of other findings dealing with the role of input organization in category clustering. Here a most important finding is that when items from the same category are presented in blocks rather than randomly, both clustering and recall are strongly augmented (Cofer, Bruce, and Riecher, 1966). In terms of the analysis just described, blocked presentation (which involves presenting all items from a single category one after the other) serves to make concept discovery easier than under conditions of random presentation. This result also agrees with results obtained in concept-formation tasks (see Chapters 5 and 10, for examples). In one sense blocked presentation may be equivalent to instructing the subject about the specific categories involved in an input list.

The role of frequency of experience, that is, the effect of repeating a list more than once, also has specific and predictable effects that can be interpreted in terms of a category-attainment analysis of recall: Repeating a list gives the subject a chance to check his categories if these were available, or an additional opportunity to develop categories if input categories were unclear. On this basis, in agreement with Tulving's analysis, increases in amount recalled are a direct consequence of the subject's ability to organize the material, with repeated exposure providing for this possibility.

There is, however, another type of frequency that can be studied experimentally; this involves presenting the same types of material for a number of different trials. Such a procedure is quite similar to those used in studies of learning set phenomena, where repeated experience with similar concept problems produces faster subsequent acquisition. The question to be asked here is: Will subjects show better recall of organized material (say categorized lists) after they have recalled such material a number of times, or will their recall always be at the same level for this type of material? Here there are really only a few relevant studies (Bousfield and Cohen, 1956; Roberts and Smith, 1966), and the general result is that subjects who have had previous experience with categorized recall show better recall on later recalls than subjects who never had this experience.

Roberts and Smith (1966) suggest an interesting limitation to this conclusion. In their experiment, subjects were asked for as many as ten different recalls of categorized lists. There were two main types of lists: In one type, *Same Lists*, the categories remained the same over all ten recalls, while individual words varied. In the second type, *Different Lists*, both categories and the items varied on successive recalls. Figure 11.2 presents a portion of their results.

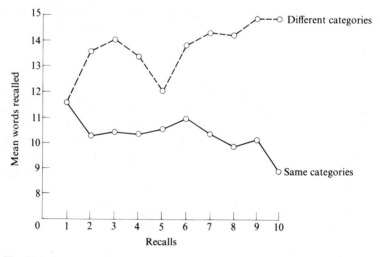

**Fig. 11.2** Mean number of words recalled for ten different recalls, when categories were the same or differed over all ten recalls. (Adapted from Roberts and Smith, 1966.)

It shows that with Different Lists, recall improved with increasing experience, whereas with Same Lists, recall decreased with experience. Roberts and Smith explained that with experience both groups got better at finding the categories. Unfortunately, subjects in the Same Lists group had no difficulty in finding appropriate categories, but according to Roberts and Smith, proactive interference among items seems to have caused a decrement in the number of specific items recalled.

Now proactive interference is really a descriptive term—that is, it describes the condition in which something that was learned before interferes with what is now being recalled—and the real question in this case as in others must remain one of providing some explanation for the amount and type of proactive interference observed. As we shall see, an answer to this question will not only handle the case of proactive interference; it will also suggest something new about recall processes in general.

If we continue on the assumption that memory for categorized materials is a reconstructive process, then one big problem for the subject is that of having too many items to produce in recall rather than too few—an embarrassment of riches. This implies that somewhere prior to overt recall, subjects first produce a response that is appropriate to a particular category, and then test to see if they recognize it as one presented during presentation. If recognition of the subject's own responses prior to overt recall is the crucial problem affecting how much subjects will recall, it should be possible to produce a profound increase in recall performance if we change the incentive for correct responses and decrease the penalty for incorrect ones. What this means is that if subjects were told that they would get a dime for every correct response and there would be no penalty for guessing, it seems reasonable to expect that the total number of items (both intrusions and correct responses) would increase, and on this basis the absolute number of correct responses would probably also rise. Contrariwise, it should be possible to depress recall by charging the subject a dime for every intrusion, and giving him only a penny for each correct recall.

This approach suggests that somewhere prior to overt production, the subject goes through a process of monitoring his own responses, and this monitoring or recognition process is sensitive to incentives—be these positive or negative. Given the occurrence of such a recognition-decision process, it is possible to allow for a reintroduction of "motivational" effects in memory at this point. Certain events may not be produced overtly simply because the cost of an error is too great at that time, whereas certain events may intrude at other times because there is no penalty for error. In the usual experimental task, subjects are probably geared not to produce errors— their "embarrassment" cost is too high—hence, in most experiments, subjects tend to produce very few intrusions in recall.

Decision processes of this type have been studied in recognition tasks. Unfortunately, none of these prior analyses has been concerned specifically with the effects of costs and payoffs in recognition experiments. Instead most have been concerned with describing the role of a number of purely formal properties of the stimulus input on memory. Thus Shepard and Teghtsoonian (1961) showed that the probability of a subject recognizing an old item (i.e., an item already presented) decreased as a function of the number of intervening items since the last presentation of the stimulus. Although there are a good number of other studies using this type of recognition methodology (see Kintsch, 1970, for a detailed review), these studies are concerned primarily with providing an elegant mathematical treatment of relatively simple decision processes in recognition memory tasks and not with the role of motivational variables in these same tasks.

## ONE MEMORY PROCESS, OR TWO, OR MORE?

Although some memories may be accessible for minutes or days or years, others are extremely transitory. There is, for example, the telephone number you just looked up and forgot; and looked up, and forgot; and looked up, and forgot. There is the unfamiliar street name you just saw and don't remember; there is the watch face that just told you the time, even though you can't tell what time it is, should someone ask you "What time is it?" All these observations suggest that some information is available for an extremely short period of time, but somehow or other never makes the trip to a more permanent sort of memory storage.

Information-processing analyses of memory usually describe two different types of short-term memory. One is assumed to involve perceptual processes and is usually called something like *visual short-term memory* or *iconic memory* or *perceptual trace memory*, while a second type of short-term memory is assumed to involve a somewhat more elaborate, but nonetheless, immediate-memory capacity and is usually called *short-term memory*, *immediate storage*, or *primary memory*. In the present discussion let us adopt the terms *perceptual short-term memory* for the first, and *primary memory* for the second.

*Perceptual short-term memory.* Much of the information that is available about perceptual short-term memory involves the visual modality and comes from experiments by Sperling (1960, 1967) and by Averbach and Corriell (1961). In Sperling's original experiments, subjects were exposed to a rectangular array of letters something on the order of

$$X \quad N \quad B \quad J$$
$$L \quad K \quad G \quad Z$$
$$M \quad G \quad H \quad P$$

and then asked to report how many of these letters they saw. Under these conditions, the usual report contained about four or five letters. This seems an unusually small number of items, and subjects often reported that they had the distinct feeling of seeing more than they could report. This sort of feeling was taken by Sperling to imply that perhaps the process of actually producing letters interfered with producing other letters, and if some procedure could be devised that did not require an extensive overt recall perhaps subjects would remember a larger number of letters, or one more commensurate with what they felt they had seen.

In order to get around this problem, Sperling presented subjects with an array of letters similar to the one described above (that is, three rows of four letters) and then presented them with either a high, medium, and low-pitched tone. If the tone was high-pitched, the subject's job was to report letters in the upper row; if medium-pitched, the middle row; and if low-pitched, the bottom row. This procedure made sure that subjects couldn't concentrate on any given row during presentation and eliminated the interfering effects of the recall output by requiring the subject to produce only four items.

The results found by Sperling support the view that subjects actually see more than they report, for under Sperling's partial-recall procedures, subjects were able to recall between 75 and 100% of the row they had just seen even if instructions specifying which row to recall were delayed for 0.15 second. When, however, Sperling delayed the onset of the tone for slightly longer intervals up to and including 1.0 second, he found that, even under his extremely favorable row-by-row report conditions, the number of letters subjects reported decreased as a consequence of time. Sperling interpreted these results to mean that a brief visual presentation provides a large amount of information, but that this information decays rapidly.

On the basis of these experiments Sperling argued that there are probably three components to memory: The first of these contains a rapidly decaying sensory image which is quite rich in detail; the second involves the more limited information we are able to extract from this transitory image; and the third is a permanent long-term memory with extremely large capacity. Assuming this is so, Sperling suggests that auditory rehearsal probably plays an important part in relating these components. For Sperling, the sequence is thought to run something as follows: The $3 \times 4$ pattern of letters is presented to the subject and recorded by the visual trace system. Depending on the tone presented, part of this image is scanned and if the appropriate letters are still available they are converted into a program of motor instructions geared to produce auditory rehearsal. After such a program has been set up (by this time, the visual image has disappeared) the now transformed letters are turned into auditory patterns capable of going to a component called *auditory memory storage*. In order to prevent the decay of this input now in auditory storage, further internal production (rehearsal) of the letters occurs, and continues to occur, until it is time for an overt report. In this approach, important emphasis is given both to the transitory nature of the initial visual image and to the role of auditory rehearsal in short-term memory.

Is there other evidence for the primary visual memory? In an experiment similar to the one Sperling reported, Averbach and Corriell (1961) presented subjects with an array of letters for about 50 milliseconds and cued recall with one of two probes. The first was a single dark line that appeared over the letter to be reported, and the second was a circle that went around the letter to be reported. When the bar was used, the decay results were entirely consistent with those reported by Sperling: very good reporting of letters for up to about 1.0 second. When, however, the letter to be reported was indicated by circling it, subjects reported that the letter disappeared, or —as Averbach and Corriell put it—was erased. Thus, a second stimulus appearing in the visual field in exactly the same location and immediately after a first stimulus caused the image of the first to disappear. These results may mean that an initial memory image is entirely visual in nature.

But what about the role of auditory factors in recall, factors which play such an important role in Sperling's analysis? Here the earliest experiments were performed by Conrad (1964). In the first of these experiments, subjects were presented with letters recorded on tape against a background of noise. These letters were presented at the rate of one every five seconds and subjects were asked to write down the letters they thought they heard. The most significant result was that letters which sound alike when spoken—*B, V, D,* etc.—were frequently confused with one another, whereas letters that only look alike, *B, R,* etc., were scarcely if ever confused. In a second experiment, subjects were presented with six-letter sequences visually and then asked to recall them immediately. When Conrad examined errors in recall under visual-presentation conditions, he found that subjects tended to confuse letters on the basis of sound (*B* and *V*) rather than on the basis of visual similarity (*B* and *R*). In fact the correlation across letters used in both experiments was 0.64, indicating that auditory errors predicted recall errors for visually presented materials. Subsequently work by Wickelgren (1965, 1967) on the nature of errors for visually presented letters fully supports the conclusion that, for short-term memory, acoustic similarity accounts for most of the errors found.

*Primary memory and rehearsal.* In terms of Sperling's model these two sets of results offer some support for the view that there is a short-term perceptual storage (primarily visual in his experiments) that can easily be interfered with (erased) by subsequent visual stimuli, and that rehearsal which allows for subsequent reproduction is probably largely a matter of auditory rehearsal. This emphasis on rehearsal is also central to a further analysis of short-term memory proposed by Waugh and Norman (1965). Their basic contention is that the span of immediate memory is limited by an inability to rehearse items. Without rehearsal, newly presented items are unavailable and hence incapable of entering long-term memory. Following William James, Waugh and Norman use the terms *primary memory* and *secondary memory* for short- and long-term storage, respectively, with the general schema they propose presented in Fig. 11.3.

According to their analysis, every verbal element that is attended to

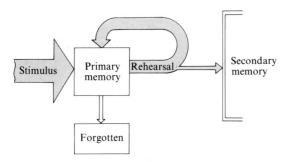

**Fig. 11.3**  The primary and secondary memory system.  All verbal items enter PM, where they are either rehearsed or forgotten.  Rehearsed items may enter SM. (From Waugh and Norman, 1965.)

goes into primary memory.  Because this system has a very limited capacity, new items replace old ones with displaced items forgotten.  In order to prevent such displacement, items must be rehearsed, which serves both to maintain the item in primary memory as well as to make its subsequent entry into long-term storage that much more likely.  Once an item has passed into long-term memory, an entirely different set of factors govern its ultimate reappearance.  There is a good deal of evidence (such as that reported by Bousfield, 1953; or Brown and McNeill, 1966, and so on) to suggest that retrieval from long-term memory is more a matter of meaning than of auditory confusability.

## SUMMARY

In agreement with an informational analysis of both problem solving and concept attainment, informational analyses of memory also assume an active subject, actively organizing his world.  In the case of remembering, as George Miller has noted, the crucial problems concern information reduction and information retrieval.  Since human memory has obvious limits, it is necessary to code stimulus inputs into information-rich "chunks" so as to minimize the absolute amount of information to be stored.  Once, however, information has been contracted or chunked, it has to be reconstructed in order to be of any use when retrieved.  This then gives rise to a view of memory in which retrieval processes play a significant role.  Retrieval may be facilitated by arranging incoming chunks into a storage system involving already existing retrieval rules.  Mandler has suggested that such a system is organized hierarchically, with successively higher levels using successively more abstract rules of categorization.  Once the chunk is retrieved, it still needs to be expanded. Depending on the initial contraction rule, the chunk may either be very easy to reconstruct, or the task may not be possible at all.

The idea that memory involves an act of reconstruction was first proposed by Bartlett. In his initial studies he showed that highly regular and highly predictable memory omissions and distortions took place when subjects were asked to recall unfamiliar materials. More generally, Bartlett proposed that subjects refer all incoming stimuli to a highly organized, but constantly changing, mental structure known as a *schema* and that recall is a joint function of the characteristics of the input and the composition of the subject's pre-existing schema. In short, input information is changed under the influence of the schema, with the nature of this induced change accounting for mnemonic omissions and distortions.

All these analyses obviously deal with material the subject wants to hang onto for a relatively long time. Yet it is also true that sometimes information is needed only for a short period of time and is best forgotten immediately after use. The existence of the short-term memory operations involved in recalling telephone numbers, addresses, shopping lists, and so on, leads to the assumption of a short-term memory system having properties different from that of long-term memory. One fact that is known for sure about short-term memory (STM) that differentiates it from long-term memory is that how a stimulus sounds is just as important as what it looks like or means. Most errors in STM are the result of auditory rather than semantic confusions.

There is, however, another type of memory also postulated by some, and this is perceptual short-term memory. Since this type of memory has been investigated primarily in terms of visual materials, the effects that occur have been described in terms of highly unstable visual images that fade rapidly with the passage of time. Visual short-term memory also seems highly affected by other interfering visual stimuli. Erasure phenomena represent one type of such interference.

In order to cast these theories into a form that can usefully be simulated on a computer, materials that are to be recalled—particularly words—are often described in terms of a list of attributes or characteristics. Experiments on *Tip-of-the-Tongue phenomena* (TOT) offer some support for the psychological reality of these attributes, and the present chapter has tried to show how such attribute patterns might lie behind category clustering and related phenomena. In general, such an analysis bears a good deal of similarity to one proposed initially by Mandler and substantiated by series of studies in his, and in other, laboratories. All in all, these results suggest that memory is often a reconstructive process, and Bartlett was probably right in naming his book *Remembering* rather than *Memory*, as Ebbinghaus had done some 50 years before.

# CHAPTER 12

# THE DEVELOPMENT OF THINKING

Information-processing analyses of human cognitive activity see it as an extremely complicated affair, far too complicated, in fact, to be determined by the coincidental comings and goings of environmental events. Instead, the growth of mind is seen to depend on the unfolding of genetically determined predispositions, predispositions that develop at a fairly regular rate during the life history of the child and adult. Part of the evidence on which this hypothesis is based involves the relatively narrow age limits within which certain major cognitive activities occur: For most normal children the ability to recognize the identity of an object occurs between the ages of 6 and 18 months; the ability to speak in a way that is understood by one's peers and parents between the ages of $2\frac{1}{2}$ and 4 years; the ability to demonstrate conservation of quantity or number—that is, the ability to recognize that changing the container in which a liquid is stored does not change its quantity—occurs between the ages of 5 and 7, and so on throughout the entire range of complex cognitive activities.

The most highly developed genetic theory of this type has been presented by Jean Piaget and his associates in Geneva. Over the course of the last 50 years or so, they have examined the development of various cognitive skills as these progress from childhood through adolescence. The present chapter, however, will deal primarily with only one of these skills, numerical ability. In this way our discussion will be more manageable and serve as an introduction to more general aspects of Piaget's thought.

## ASPECTS OF THE THEORY OF COGNITIVE GROWTH

It is important to realize at the outset that Piaget's analysis of how numerical concepts develop is but one specific application of a more general and comprehensive theory of intelligence. Although a summary of the total system is beyond the scope of the present chapter (see Flavell, 1963, or Ginsburg and Opper, 1969, for a comprehensive presentation and analysis), a few significant facets of theory do need to be spelled out in detail.

Standing behind, and in fact motivating, much of Piaget's work on cognitive growth is the view that intelligence is an *epigenetic* process. That is, intelligence involves a constant interchange between an organism having certain potential capacities for cognitive growth and the nature of an environment which sets problems and impels actions. It is epigenetic in that certain solutions or even certain modes of approach to a problem are impossible for a child before he is at a particular stage of development. Intelligence develops when the existing or potential capacities are appropriate to the environmental problem at hand—neither before nor, perhaps, even after.

The division of intellectual growth into stages is meant to imply some discontinuity among these stages. So, for example, children in the earliest stages are not only unable to do certain problems, they are even unable to understand why these are problems. To state the matter more generally, children and adults are not only differentially skillful in cognitive functioning, they also think differently. The child's thought is not the adult's thought, and this assumption lies behind Piaget's analysis of developmental stages. Once, however, a particular intellectual stage is reached, the achievements of all prior stages are carried forward. Intelligence is cumulative: What can be done at an earlier stage can be done more efficiently and with more understanding later.

If intelligence progresses as a stage-wise interchange between a developing organism having certain pre-set capacities and a problem-setting environment, then the nature of this interchange between organism and environment must hold an important place within the theoretical system. For Piaget, the crucial concept here is *adaptation*. In common with biological connotations of the term, cognitive adaptation implies a modification of the child so as to make him more successful in future interchanges with the environment. Adaptation involves two separate but complementary processes; the first of these is *accommodation*, and the second *assimilation*. As is true of biological assimilation and accommodation, cognitive adaptation presupposes and builds on preexisting organization. Given this precondition, accommodation refers to the process by which an interchange with the environment leads to a change in cognitive organization. Any encounter with an object in the environment is either referred to some preexisting category (assimilation) or comes to induce the development of a new category so as to make possible its assimilation. But each specific object also has specific properties, and the special properties of the object always require some change on the part of the system which encompasses it. As Flavell put it, "Cognitive incorporation of reality implies both an assimilation *to* structure and an accommodation *of* structure (to reality)."

## The Developmental Stages

Now this is all very complex and abstract—as indeed it is meant to be. For Piaget the development of mind is a complicated affair, and only a highly abstract system is capable of describing it in all its complexity. In order to make discussion a bit more concrete, however, Piaget describes the development of intelligence in terms of a series of specific stages during the course of which the complementary process of assimilation and accommodation are at work. For Piaget, the growth of all intelligence is defined as a form of equilibrium toward which all cognitive functions move.

But the focus and objects of this equilibrium process are different for each of the great stages of intelligence and Piaget's theory divides this development into four major periods: *sensori-motor* (roughly from birth to 2 years); *pre-operational* (roughly from 2 to 7 years); *concrete operational* (7 to 11 years) and *formal operational* (12 years and onward). All these age ranges are approximate and meant only as a guide to the stage under discussion.

The first general stage makes its appearance before the advent of language and concerns the construction of schemas (organized patterns of behavior) for dealing with objects. Infants are not convinced, as many of Piaget's early observations showed, that when an object disappears from view, it can ever again be found. In the development of this particular ability, behavior progresses from earliest infancy—where an infant continues to look at the place where an object last appeared—to the point at which a child is able to search actively for a now-removed object. The very young infant maintains a constant orientation toward the last place at which an object was seen, yet will not attempt an active visual or motor search for a missing or removed object. It is only with subsequent experience that the child is able to institute a search for hidden objects. The critical point in this development is that objects are now seen as having an existence apart from the child. Although the child has as yet not learned very much about the invariant properties of objects, he has at least learned of their substantiality and this, in itself, is quite an achievement.

Once the child has mastered the permanence of objects, he is next concerned with the development of symbolic representations. The second of the so-called development stages is called the *Pre-Operational Stage*. The great achievement of this period (from ages 2–5) is language. Up to this point, the child has been capable of intelligent reactions primarily in response to the immediate, or relatively immediate, filled space which surrounds him. The development of language makes it possible for the child to invoke objects not present, to reconstruct the past or plan the future, to think of objects not present, and so on—in short, language gives the child greater mastery of both time and space.

But this new mastery, which is superimposed on the sensori-motor stage, is not a simple extension of what was learned in the past. It is quite clear that behavior in words is different from behavior in action. Because a child knows how to move about in his house or play yard by following the cues which surround him, does not mean that he is capable of representing abstractly the total pattern of his house or play yard. This latter ability, which is not yet attained, will enable the child to detach his behavior from the immediate environment and represent it in a much more abstract way.

So as to demonstrate that children even in this stage are unable to represent events independent of direct motor action, Piaget and Szeminska (Piaget, 1962) asked 4- and 5-year-old children who went to and from school by themselves to trace out their route in a special kind of construction game. In this game, they provided children with a concrete set of houses and streets. Even given this very concrete situation, the children were unable to represent the route successfully. To accomplish this job, Piaget feels the child must not only remove himself from the center of his perceptual world (a process Piaget calls "decentering"), but must also reconstruct his world from this new perspective.

This inability to represent "from above" ultimately has to do with the child's inability to perform transformations. In the case of spatial representation the child is unable to transform his "walked-through space" into a conceptually articulated visual space. The child reasons on the basis of what he sees and not on the basis of what he thinks or thinks he knows about what he sees. In general, if the child can do anything by way of representing transformations, he is tied to his own direct manipulations of the objects involved and this ability occurs only in the latter parts of preoperational thought.

If language is the major intellectual achievement of preoperational thought, numbers and elementary logical relations are the major achievements of the *Stage of Concrete Operations*. So that we keep some track of time, this next stage occurs at about the seventh step of life and continues roughly until the child is 11 years of age. The simplest logical achievement learned by the child in this stage is concerned with classifying objects according to similarities and differences. In the extreme case this gives rise to the concept of identity—a thing is itself—while in more complex form it gives rise to classes and subclasses, or to the idea of logical inclusion.

The recognition of similarities and differences also gives rise to a very important concept, that of series or sequence whereby individual items can now be arranged according to some ordering principle such as size, amount, or whatnot. This is the rudimentary skill on which natural numbers rest, particularly counting.

But the development of logical and mathematical abilities implies not isolated fragments, but tightly organized systems. As Flavell (1963) put it:

"These systems are equilibrated, organized affairs in the sense that one action may annul or otherwise compensate for another previously performed; two actions can combine to produce a third, and so on. That is to say, the system these actions form is truly a system, with definite structural properties; it is something quite other than a simple concatenation or colligation of juxtaposed terms."

These newly developed and developing systems are called cognitive *operations*, and indeed it is in this sense that the term appears in *preoperational*, *concrete operational* and the like.

In one sense Piaget feels that mathematical structure is a good model (perhaps an ideal one) of the cognitive structures which underly successful ability in adult thinking. This means that if a child or adult is able to use numbers constructively, it is quite possible that he has some internalized, highly organized structure, perhaps congruent with or even identical to formal mathematical postulates. Although Piaget has never directly made this particular assumption, it seems a reasonable extrapolation from his general view that logical and mathematical structures provide excellent models for cognitive structure.

Although developments occurring during the stage of concrete operations take the child a long way on the road from perceptual dominance to a more balanced perceptual–conceptual type of intelligence, the child is still limited in certain ways. To be sure, he has now escaped domination by the environment, but just as surely he is still tied to relatively concrete situations and problems. He has also as yet not begun to coordinate the various operational systems which he has acquired.

The major achievement of the last developmental stage of intellectual growth, the *Stage of Formal Operations*, is the ability to reason not only about objects, but also about hypotheses and propositions. It is the beginning of true scientific, mathematical, and logical reasoning. One major difference between this stage and the Stage of Concrete Operations is that the content of an argument (its concrete form) can now be overlooked so as to make possible an analysis of its logical form (its abstract form). This represents a further movement from the *real* to the *potential*.

Another formal, content-free procedure that characterizes this stage is the use of hypothetico-deductive reasoning. Such procedures are tried out by the adolescent in a great many more contexts than those dealing only with scientific investigation. Piaget feels that the emergence of this mode of thought may be what accounts for the adolescent's taste for theorizing about himself and his world. In his newly found world of "if $p$, then $q$," all propositions—no matter now radical or bizarre—are given a fair run for their theoretical money and may result in action different from his parents'. Although this fourth stage is a developmental possibility, not all thinkers come to it—and indeed most probably make very little use of it. Actually this last fact is of little importance, for Piaget is really talking about an underlying capacity, whether or not it ever gets used.

This then is Piaget's system, a most ambitious program to specify and detail the growth of intelligence. It stands in stark contrast to associationistic analysis of mind, in that it refutes the significance of strict contiguity for mental development except at very elementary levels. It is not strictly *a priori*, however, in that intelligence cannot progress without an interchange between a developmentally tuned organism and an appropriate problem-setting environment. Each successive stage of intellectual development does not invalidate those that went before—rather each provides a new and previously impossible perspective from which to understand and use the achievements of earlier stages.

## The Developmental Course of Numerical Ability

When we think, even naively, about numerical ability it is clear that we can mean one of two things: how well a person does the various computations of arithmetic and higher mathematics, or how well he understands the basic ideas that lie behind these computations. To be sure, we would hope for some degree of correlation between the two, but it is clear that it is possible to perform many computations by rote without really understanding at some deeper level why $2 + 2$ must equal 4. Actually Piaget is interested only in the latter question: What must the child know in order for us to say that he understands the concept of number? All his work has been done with this question in mind. Before we can review this work, however, we will have to present evidence on what is known about what children know (computationally and otherwise) about number at various age levels.

*Some significant aspects of number.* When we think of numerical ability, one of the simplest skills would seem to be counting. Although counting from 1 to 10 or even a bit higher seems a rather rudimentary skill—anyone who watches *Sesame Street* can do it—what is obvious is that in order to count efficiently the child or adult must be able to produce an infinite number of responses if called on to do so. Counting from 1 to 10 may do well enough for some cases, but the critical aspect of "really knowing how to count" is the ability to produce an infinite set of responses from a finite number of elements ($0–9$ in our own base$_{10}$ system) founded on a few simple rules. Normal counting depends on a creative use of these simple rules. Anyone who has ever studied a foreign language knows that if you know how to count in your native language, then a few key number words (*zero* through *twenty* inclusively, *thirty, forty, fifty ... hundred, thousand, million*, etc.) will enable you to transfer your counting ability directly. In this case, knowing both the number names and their sequential patternings is all that is required for successful counting.

But skill with numbers surely involves more than just counting. It also involves the ability to apply the sequence of numbers produced to objects, events, or ideas. In most instances, the objects, events, etc., are in the environment, and the subject must somehow or other generate the series of numbers on his own. This type of coordination seems to involve two separate although perhaps complementary aspects: the first of these is called *enumeration*; the second, *conservation*. By enumeration is meant the ability of a child or adult to establish a one-to-one correspondence between the numbers freely counted and the objects to which they apply. If there are two, four, or ten apples, enumeration means using the correct number name for the correct set of 2, 4, or 10 apples. When a number is used in this way, it is called a cardinal number, which really means the number is applied to a set in such a way as to describe the number of things in that set.

Cardinal numbers need, of course, be distinguished from ordinal numbers, or numbers that describe an ordered sequence. Generally speaking, the names of the more common cardinal numbers occur as nouns (one, two ...) in a language, whereas ordinals occur as adjectives (first, second ...) except that for many counting purposes, the cardinal nouns are used. Thus the child will undoubtedly learn one, two, three ... much earlier than first, second, etc.

Actually, the mathematical concept of cardinality implies more than just enumeration; and this something extra is best described in terms of the psychological concept of *conservation*. By conservation is simply meant the ability of a number user to maintain the cardinality of a set despite wide variations in either the physical properties or arrangements of the objects enumerated. For example, it makes no difference mathematically whether 5 objects are spaced 2 inches or 20 inches apart when they are presented; they are still 5 objects. As we will see, at some point during the developmental sequence that takes a child from a limited rote counter to a fluent number user, the physical properties of objects and their arrangement does determine whether or not the child senses the equality of equal sets. This effect is called *nonconservation* and, although surprising when first described, now seems a well-established and significant aspect of numerical thinking in children.

## Numerical Ability in Children: Some Facts

So that there can be no doubt as to what we mean by numerical ability, let us set our sights at least as high as the corner grocer. That is, let us say that our grocer can perform, skillfully and successfully, all the various arithmetic operations; that he can do fractions; and because we have a particularly classy grocer in mind, let us assume that he can even take various roots. Mathematically, this means that he has knowledge of numbers extending at least as far as what are called the rational numbers. When we talk about numerical ability, keep the grocer in mind.

But how are we to find out what children, let alone grocers, know about number? One line of attack on this problem is very down to earth in its approach and is concerned primarily with finding out what it is that a child can do with numbers when he comes to school so as to enable a teacher to begin instruction at an appropriate point. Very much in this tradition is an early investigation by McLaughlin (1934). What she attempted to do was to determine how much children between the ages of 3 and 6 years knew about counting, recognizing number aggregates, and combining number aggregates. A summary of her counting results indicate progressive increases in the number counted correctly from a median value of 5 at age 3 to a median value of 33 at age 6. When these self-generated sequences had to be used to enumerate how many blocks there were in a line of blocks, results indicated only slightly lower enumeration scores, i.e., the median number of items enumerated at age 3 was 4 while at age 6, it was 28. All the children, with the exception of those exhibiting a good deal of number sophistication, were completely unable to count backward. As later results will show, backward counting is an extremely difficult skill not really appearing until the child seems to have a good deal of additional knowledge about numbers and their uses (Wohlwill, 1960; Pollio and Whitacre, 1970).

Further results by McLaughlin showed regular and progressive increases in the child's ability to respond appropriately to the numerical properties of groups of objects (i.e., being able to form a group of 5 objects on request, or to pick out the larger from the smaller group, etc.). In general, the order of development is from the perception of simple spatially organized collections of objects toward a more specific numerical analysis of these collections, first by counting single objects, and later by recognizing small aggregates of 2 and 3 and then by combining these newly recognized sets into a single larger set. The third aspect of numbers investigated by McLaughlin—that of combining aggregates of numbers—proved quite difficult. Those children who were able to accomplish this feat generally did it by first recognizing one of the aggregates and then by counting the aggregate remaining so as to reach a final sum. Most of the younger children found these tasks well beyond them.

Perhaps the most complete study of what the preschool child knows about number is contained in a report by Brace and Nelson (1965). As in previous studies, the children had not been to school and ranged in age from 5 years 4 months to 6 years 5 months. All subjects were tested individually on a 55-item test. After all children had been tested, scores on all tests were inter-correlated and a factor analysis performed to determine whether these

55 tests could be considered as representing a smaller number of significant groupings. Seven factors were recovered as involved in number usage in preschool children (the specific factors uncovered are listed along with a test exemplifying what type of underlying knowledge is required to assume the presence of that factor):

*Factor 1*   *Ordinal number, one dimension.* The child is asked to find the first (fifth, eighth) soldier in a row of toy soldiers.

*Factor 2*   *Ordinal number, two dimensions.* The child is asked to find the third card in the fourth row.

*Factor 3*   *Conservation of number.* The child is asked if two rows of blocks are equal if the same number of blocks are spaced differently so that one row takes up more space than the second row.

*Factor 4*   *Place value.* The child is presented with bundles of 10 sticks and several single sticks and asked to make groups of 11, or 19 or 25, etc. If he had the concept of place he would use one bundle of 10 and a single stick; if not he might use 11 separate sticks.

*Factor 5*   *Group cardinality* (up to groups of 5 items). 2 to 5 items were presented on a card and the child is required to tell the number of items that are on the card.

*Factor 6*   *Group cardinality* (groups of more than 5 items). Same as above, but more than 5 items per card.

*Factor 7*   *Comparisons.* The child is presented with a group of horses and a group of riders and asked to determine whether there is a horse for each rider, and so on with other toys.

These results indicate that the test items used seemed to be tapping seven different areas of number competence and that competence in all these areas served to define the preschool child's knowledge of number. Although Brace and Nelson do not present the data in this form, their results show that comparison was the easiest factor, while conservation was the most difficult.

The general picture that emerges from these results is that as numerical skill develops, the child's dependence on the direct perceptual experience of objects decreases. Low-level enumeration, consisting largely of counting a number of objects, seems to precede any concept of cardinality, although the ability to talk about a "first," or "second," or "third" *thingumabob* is not achieved until the child can recognize cardinals easily. Surprisingly, Brace and Nelson's results show that there were two types of cardinality: one dealing with a small number of objects (less than 5; see Factor 5); and a second dealing with a larger number of objects (see Factor 6). The ability to recognize the cardinality of sets having more than 5 items seemed to depend on the child's ability to combine the cardinality of smaller sets, while the cardinality of smaller sets (less than 5) seemed to depend on the child's immediate grasp of the number of objects. So, for example, a set of 3 items was immediately called "three," whereas a set of 7 items was named only much more slowly, and then only if the child were able to combine two smaller sets say of 5 and 2 or of 4 and 3.

One important problem still remaining to be disentangled concerns the relationship of cardinals to ordinals. In a survey approach similar to that of Brace and Nelson, Holmes (1963) employed a series of problems, the most novel of which attempted to see if children could coordinate ordinal numbers with cardinal numbers. The test involved ten cards $A, B, C, \ldots, J$, with each succeeding card larger than the preceding one by a constant amount. Card $A$ was 1 inch, while all other cards were constant multiples, such that $B$ was 2 inches (i.e., $2A$), $C$ was 3 inches ($3A$), and so on. Children were asked a question roughly of the form: "How many $A$ cards do you need to make a card as big as card $C$?" The original number of the card, of course, gives the cardinal number.

This was a surprisingly difficult task. Only about 12% of the oldest group of kindergarten children were able to solve it correctly, despite the fact that 66% of these children had no trouble in finding ordinal numbers and 40% had no trouble in giving the appropriate number name to a collection of objects. Even though this is a particularly difficult task, it is clear that combining ordinal and cardinal number concepts involves a higher level of abstraction than either of the other two considered separately.

The general trend of number-skill development, from direct perceptual influence to relatively little perceptual influence, is similar to general trends observed in the development of all types of symbolic usage. It is possible to view the development of symbol usage as involving a progressive lessening of direct perceptual influences on thinking. True symbol usage often implies an ability to "get away from" the influence of an immediate environment and to depend instead on constructed internal systems.

## Piaget's Analysis of Numerical Abilities

A second major approach to the development of numerical skills—that undertaken by Piaget and his coworkers—attempts to place these attainments within the larger context of more general cognitive growth. The original work on this topic was summarized in Piaget's early book, *The Child's Conception of Number*, which appeared in 1952. Although there is a good deal of interesting theoretical analysis as to how number concepts develop and what these are, perhaps it is best to begin with a description of one of the main empirical results—that of conservation—and see what sorts of general implications can be drawn from it.

**The idea of conservation.** The overriding discovery of this early work had to do with conservation in its various forms. The simplest experiment in this early series involved two equal lots of beads. These were counted out into two similar containers and obviously reached the same level in each container. One set of beads was then put into a different container, first into a short, fat one, and then into a tall, skinny one. Following this, the children were asked whether there were the same number of beads in the original jar and in either the short fat one or in the tall skinny one.

The original results indicated that children could be divided into three distinct groups which were somewhat dependent on age. In so-called Stage 1, the children (mostly 4–5 year-olds) thought that there were more beads in the tall skinny container than in the comparison container primarily because "it was taller." Even if the beads were then returned to their original container, shown to the child, and then again put into the tall skinny container, the child still said that there were more beads in the skinny container. If the child were also asked whether the numbers would be the same if the beads from the taller container were poured out on the table, he replied: "No, there would be more because they came from a taller glass."

Similar experiments were done in which liquids were poured from jar to jar, and these experiments produced exactly the same results: When liquid was transferred to a taller, thinner container, the child said there was more. The children were so sure that such was the case that when the experimenter asked the child to guess how high he thought the liquid from both jars would reach if they were poured into similar larger glasses, the child unhesitatingly indicated two different levels and was quite astonished when he found them to be the same. Some children even went so far as to accuse the experimenter of fooling them, saying that some liquid must have been added to the comparison glass.

The children in Stages 2 and 3 exhibited quite different behavior in these (and other) situations. Stage 2 is clearly a transition stage: Children sometimes solve the problems (conserve number or quantity) and sometimes not. With help and guidance, they ultimately are able to see the nature of the problem and its solution in most cases. Stage 3 children usually express amazement or condescension or both at an experimenter even asking the silly questions he does: "Why everybody knows," "It's always the same thing," or "There only seems to be less in this glass because it's wider, but it's the same," or "This is skinnier, so it fills up more," and so on in an appropriately indignant tone.

The most interesting aspect of these data on conservation is that many children who are capable only of Stage 1 conservation answers are perfectly well able to count when asked to do so. Here then is the crux of the problem: Children who can count, and even perform simple feats of enumeration, are completely unable to see that number or quantity is conserved despite transformations in its outward appearance. This observation suggests that counting in the young child may represent a piece of rote behavior or one that is essentially unrelated to other aspects of number, such as the ability to map numbers on to some sort of physical array.

*1. Conservation of number.* Since the original discovery of nonconservation was so unexpected, a number of other investigators not directly associated with the Geneva laboratory have attempted to replicate and extend Piaget's results. One of the most extensive of these was reported by Dodwell (1960, 1962) who gave a series of five different Piagetian tasks to a group of 250 children ranging in age from 5 to 8 years. Unlike Piaget, Dodwell developed a standard series of questions to ask each child about each of the situations. In the typical Piagetian investigation the experimenter is free to ask the child whatever seems appropriate in a particular situation, and in most cases the specific form of the questions asked are idiosyncratic to a particular child. The argument given in favor of this unstructured approach is that it is the only way of gaining insight into the mental processes of the child. Only by careful individual questioning is it possible to find out how and what the child knows about a particular topic. Dodwell argued that idiosyncratic questions, presented in an idiosyncratic order, might prejudice the results and therefore he settled on a well-specified set of questions to be asked in a prearranged order.

In general, Dodwell's results showed marked similarity to those obtained by Piaget and his collaborators under less stringent test conditions. Dodwell's children showed remarkably little conservation in beads and containers tasks, but had little difficulty in coordinating two series of objects such as eggs and egg cups, etc. In Piaget's original analysis he distinguished among three levels of ability in number tasks, with children at the third level showing complete familiarity and easy success in conservation tasks, and with children at the first level showing complete unfamiliarity and confusion in conservation tasks. In Dodwell's experiments the degree to which a child gave answers indicating Level 1 knowledge was called his "*A*-Score." Such *A*-Scores provide a measure of the degree to which a child gives evidence of *not* understanding the principles of conservation but of relying instead on direct perceptual factors.

The results for kindergarten children (5 years old) indicate a relatively normal distribution, with most children showing a good degree of non-conservation (maximum possible *A*-Score = 10) and only a very small percentage showing complete conservation ($A = 0$). By the time children reach the first grade (age 6–7) numerical abilities fall into two distinctly different levels: One group knows no more than the kindergarten children, while a second group—roughly 35%—has the concept well in hand. By the time the children are in the third grade (7–8 years) almost all are "in the know" and only a very small proportion of the children produce large *A*-Scores.

Although Dodwell and his associates experienced no difficulty in classifying any given answer as an *A*-answer or not, they had great difficulty in specifying whether or not a particular child was at a Stage 1, Stage 2, or Stage 3 level of numerical competence. As Piaget had shown a number of years before (1941) children often exhibit behavior characteristic of a given stage for only a given problem, but seem unable to cope with all problems at that level equally well. Even when Dodwell considered specific tasks, these results did not provide an unequivocal ordering for all tests, as required by a stage hypothesis; for example, some subjects who were able to give Stage 3 responses on matching eggs with egg cups gave Stage 1 responses on con-servation tasks. This may mean that a child acquires procedures appropriate for dealing with a specific task at a specific level and does not always have these same high-level skills for other tasks presumably involving the same skills.

This raises the problem that task factors may interact strongly with how advanced we should consider a child in terms of numerical concepts. In order to determine whether numerical tasks do, in fact, produce a specific ordering, Wohlwill (1960) gave a series of tasks embedded within a learning situation to determine the level of difficulty for each. Each task was supposed to tap a critical aspect of number development. So, for example, to test for conservation, subjects were first trained to perform in a three-choice problem situation. In this type of task the subject was shown a card—say one with 3 squares arranged randomly on it—and then asked to match a second card with this one. For this particular example, one of the choice cards might have 2 dots arranged in a line on it, a second might have 3 dots arranged in a triangle on it, while a third choice card might have 4 dots arranged in a diamond. The correct response for this task would be the card containing the 3-dot triangle.

In Wohlwill's conservation test, choice cards contained 6, 7, and 8 dots. The subject was presented with a collection of buttons, say 6, and was asked to select the correct choice card. If the subject was unable to make the correct choice, the experimenter guided him to it. After this initial choice, the buttons were scrambled and the subject prevented from recounting them. If, when asked to pick the correct choice card again, the subject chose the 6-dot card, he was thought to exhibit conservation; if he made the wrong choice, he was thought to exhibit nonconservation.

The basic objective of Wohlwill's investigation was to see whether an ordering for tasks would develop paralleling Piaget's various stages of development. On the basis of results for seven different tasks, Wohlwill concluded that the order of difficulty for his tasks was consistent with Piaget's stages. Qualitative examination of the results, however, indicated that various tests did not form a scale having equal intervals between tests; rather there seemed to be three distinct task groupings. For the initial grouping the child responded to number wholly on a perceptual basis; for the intermediary grouping the child responded to number in more conceptual terms, but failed to exhibit conservation; while for the final set the child was able to conceptualize the relationship among individual numbers in addition to exhibiting conservation of number.

Another study designed to determine the order in which numerical abilities are acquired was done by Kofsky (1966). In this experiment 122 children, aged 4 to 9 years, were given 11 different tests presumed to measure various aspects of classificatory behavior. These tests were constructed to determine whether mastery of later tests implied mastery of simpler tests. When the data were analyzed by scaleogram analysis—which attempts to determine the degree to which subjects who pass Test 4 also passed Tests 1 through 3—a constant order was *not* found. This occurred despite the fact that there were significant correlations between the age of the child and the number of different tasks mastered. Although age trends did appear, it was impossible to describe a single order for all tests. Similar to results found by Dodwell, increases in the number of tasks children can complete successfully does not seem to proceed through an invariant sequence of steps. The specific nature of the task strongly determines the child's ability level.

To take a simple conservation example: If a child is presented with a rubber band and the rubber band is stretched, most children will not see the stretched rubber band as having properties different from the unstretched one. Yet these same children when tested on more usual conservation tasks will fail to show conservation. The inescapable conclusion is that the specific nature of a task strongly interacts with the concept under consideration, and different tests of presumably the same abstract concept may well yield different results.

The real problem, however, is what we mean by the term "the same abstract concept." Actually, because adult experimenters think that two tasks tap the same ability does not mean that the child will see it that way at all. Rather, there seems to be a necessary distinction between a stage, say concrete operations, and a concept. The stage seems to set some upper limit on the kinds of operations that can be performed on concepts. Entering a given stage is a necessary condition for some kinds of conceptual performance, but it is not by itself a sufficient condition. So, for example, to deal in a concrete operational manner with either number conservation or volume conservation, the child must be capable of concrete operations. In addition, however, volume conservation is a more difficult concept because it requires a more complex physical theory. On this basis we would not necessarily expect a child who could solve number conservation tasks successfully to solve volume conservation tasks equally well.

Returning again to rubber bands and beads, it is possible to argue that a child is able to "conserve" rubber bands, but not beads, because he has had sufficient experience with rubber objects to have learned that rubber bands can and do change their shape without altering their essential size. If this is so, then specific experience with a given task should lead to improved conservation for that task and presumably for other related tasks as well. Here, as Flavell (1963) notes, the general experimental procedure is to give a large group of children tests in order to identify a group of nonconservers. After such a group has been identified, the next step is to subject some of these children to a specific training procedure and then compare their performance with a nontrained group on some post-test measure of conservation.

One of the earliest of these training studies following this general procedure was done by Wohlwill and Lowe (1962). In their experiment, 72 children who failed both verbal and performance conservation tasks were divided into four groups. One of these groups served as a control and received no specific training. The first training group was required to count the number of stars before and after their spatial arrangement had been changed. This training was designed to reward an invariance of number response, despite a clear change in how items were displayed. A second experimental group had stars taken away in an attempt to get across the idea that addition and subtraction change numerical value but that changing direct perceptual properties does not. The third group was shown that despite the fact that the stars could be bunched up into a short line, they still had the same number of elements as they did when they were widely spaced.

The results of this experiment were rather surprising: For all four groups, the control included, there was a significant increase in conservation from the pre-test to the post-test; but (and this is the important point) the three experimental groups did not differ from the control group during the post-training test. In short, *none* of the three training procedures significantly affected the child's ability to conserve number.

Using essentially similar procedures, Gruen (1965) did succeed in bringing about some improvement in conservation, but results were far from impressive. Of 60 subjects exposed to training, only about 30 showed any improvement in conservation. Although this improvement is certainly greater than that reported by Wohlwill and Lowe, it is certainly not very impressive after about 32 training trials designed specifically to induce conservation on a particular task. One other interesting aspect of these results was that training children on number conservation did little to increase their ability to conserve on other tasks. Children who learned to conserve in a particular task were not readily able to conserve on other tasks.

*2. Conservation of quantity.* All these studies have been concerned primarily with the conservation of number. However, in order to discuss factors involved in conservation generally, it is necessary to discuss an integrated series of studies done by Smedslund at the University of Oslo on the conservation of quantity. In Smedslund's first experiment, children were trained by one of two procedures on a task involving conservation of substance. The particular task used involved a ball of plasticine clay which was rolled out into a sausage-shaped object. Children were then asked if the ball or the sausage weighed more. For one of the training procedures, children actually weighed the two objects on a scale. A second group was treated somewhat differently; these children were asked to estimate the weight of the ball either when some of the plasticine had been removed from one ball, or alternatively, when some plasticine had been added. They were then allowed to test their predictions by means of the scale. The results of this first experiment were remarkably similar to those reported by Wohlwill and Lowe: Both training groups and the control group showed some improvement from pre- to post-test, but none of the groups differed significantly on the post-test.

Why do children get better at doing conservation tasks? Smedslund argued that there are really two alternative ways to view any improvement taking place in conservation tasks. One of these he calls the reinforcement position, and describes it as follows:

> "The subjective validity and necessity of the inference of conservation derives from an empirical law ... Children discover empirically that as long as nothing is added or taken away, objects maintain the same amount of substance and the same weight irrespective of changes of shape."

The second alternative is called the Equilibration Theory and is derived from Piaget's approach. Smedslund characterizes this position as follows:

> "(a logical structure) develops as a function of an internal process which is heavily dependent on activity and experience.... Practice is not assumed to act through external reinforcement, but by a process of mutual influence of the child's activities on each other. Logical influences are not derived from any properties of the external world, but from the placing into a relationship of the subject's own activities."*

In order to distinguish experimentally between these hypotheses, Smedslund focused his second experiment on the processes of extinction. Two groups of children were employed. One group was derived from his first study: 11 children who failed the conservation task in the pre-test, but

---

* From "The acquisition of conservation of substance and weight in children," by J. Smedslund, in *The Scandinavian Journal of Psychology* **2**, 1961, pages 11–20.

who gave correct responses in the post-test. These children were considered to represent an "acquired" conservation group. Presumably they had learned on the basis of reinforcement that in the present task a "conservation response" leads to reward. The second group consisted of 13 children, of equal age and intelligence, who unequivocally passed the pre-test, thereby demonstrating conservation. Although the antecedent conditions under which these children acquired conservation are unclear, Smedslund felt that the reinforced group may have acquired "a pseudo concept" of conservation, based on different properties from one acquired "normally"—presumably based on equilibration processes.

This experiment consisted of showing the subject two balls. One of these, as in the earlier experiment, was changed to a sausage; but, unlike the situation in the earlier study, the experimenter actually did remove a small piece, thereby making the sausage lighter than the remaining plasticine ball. Two other surreptitious and sneaky manipulations were also performed, and for all three tasks the child was to predict whether the two objects weighed the same and to explain why the ball was heavier than the sausage. Under these conditions children in these two subject groups behaved quite differently. All 11 children in the Reinforcement Group quickly reverted to a nonconservation approach, offering such statements as: "The ball weighs more because it's rounder and fatter," etc. Of the 13 children in the Normal Conservation Group, six rejected a nonconservation explanation of why the ball was heavier, using arguments (depending on how nice the child was) such as: "We must have lost some on the floor" to "I think you took away some of the clay." On this basis, Smedslund argued that the responses acquired during training were much less resistant to extinction than responses dependent on equilibration processes.

But how do such processes work? In a later experiment, Smedslund (1961c) described them in terms of cognitive conflict. Basically, the procedure involved in this experiment pitted two different types of transformations against each other: a deformation transformation and a subtraction transformation. For example, if a child thought that turning the ball into a sausage increased its quantity, Smedslund would just elongate the ball and then take a piece from the newly elongated sausage. After both transformations had been done, the child was asked to explain which object, the ball or the subtracted sausage, had more clay. Smedslund argued that pitting these two expectations against each other would induce conflict and hopefully bring about a resolution as to how transformations affect quantity.

Of 13 subjects used in this experiment, only five came consistently to ignore the deformation and to respond only to the subtraction aspects of the procedure; the remaining children continued to respond in accord with their initial deformation strategy. In this experiment, the experimenter provided the subjects with no information as to whether they were correct or not in their answers—training was simply designed to induce conflict between two transformations. Results showed that four of the five children who adopted the addition–subtraction strategy in arriving at their answers showed conservation during the post-test when they had not done so during their pre-test, while none of the eight children answering on the basis of a deformation strategy alone revealed any post-test change. They still failed to exhibit conservation.

Although the number of subjects was small, Smedslund felt sufficiently encouraged by these results to perform another similar study (Smedslund, 1961d). The first result of interest here was that children who are able to use an addition–subtraction strategy are also more likely to do conservation problems successfully. Perhaps the ability to see an object as potentially alterable (being either diminished or increased by subtraction or addition of material) is a necessary condition for conservation. In order to test this hypothesis further, Smedslund presented children with a training program similar to the one used in connection with his last study. An attempt was made to induce cognitive conflict without telling the child whether he was right or wrong. The results of this experiment were consistent in showing that significantly more children subjected to this type of experience showed conservation on a post-test when compared to a control group not having such experience. A qualitative analysis of these protocols indicated that the development of conservation seems to depend on the prior acquisition of an addition–subtraction strategy.

**The Harvard Approach**

Another way to train children in conservation has been reported in a series of studies done at Harvard University under the general direction of Bruner, Olver, and Greenfield (1966). The first novel training procedure employed to teach conservation was developed in an experiment by Frank (see Bruner, Olver, and Greenfield, page 193 ff), who argued that part of the young child's inability to conserve is based on his inability to overcome perceptual immediacy. If children could be shielded from such perceptual factors, it should be possible to train them in conservation that much more easily.

In order to reduce the attraction of immediate perception in a water-conservation task, and force the child to see the conflict between his prediction and the ultimate level of the liquids in an altered container, Frank first hid the standard and comparison beakers behind a screen and then asked the children to make a mark on the screen where they thought the water would reach in the comparison jar. As in most prior experiments, systematically different comparison jars were used, ranging from ones that were tall and thin to ones that were short and fat.

Contrary to results found elsewhere, the screening procedure seemed to bring about changes in the direction of conservation for 5-, 6-, and 7-year-old children, but not for 4-year-old children.  As in the Smedslund experiment, forcing the child to make a judgment and then having this judgment produce cognitive conflict seems to be a good way of inducing cognitive growth. These experiments seem to bring about such changes by forcing the child to come to terms with the difference between "how things look" and "how things really are."

Although screening worked quite well in inducing conservation in this experiment, a subsequent experiment by Sonstroem (1966) failed to find any effects due to screening.  Instead, she found that the most successful procedure leading to conservation involved the joint operation of two factors: manipulation and labeling.  In this experiment some of the children were allowed to manipulate the plasticine clay by themselves, while others were only allowed to observe the experimenter do it.  Similarly, some children were given verbal help in describing what they had been doing while playing with the clay, while others were not.

In contrast to results found in the prior study, screening had little or no effect in bringing about conservation : The only condition of the experiment regularly serving to induce conservation was one involving a combination of manipulation and verbal labeling.  Both factors alone failed to have significant effects.  In attempting to evaluate these results, Bruner drew on his own hypothesis of mental growth, which assumes three different stages of cognitive representation.  The first of these is called *enactive representation*, whereby an object is represented in terms of the action or reaction evoked by that object; the second is called *ikonic representation*, whereby an object is represented by an image that is relatively independent of overt or covert action; while the third is called *symbolic representation*, whereby an object is represented in terms of some specifiable symbol system, such as language or mathematics, with this representation relatively independent of either its action or image properties.

Given these three modes of representation, combining manipulation and labeling brings about conservation largely because only in combination can enactive and symbolic representations effectively oppose the pull of immediate perceptual experience.  By allowing the child to manipulate the clay, the experimenter encouraged the child to use enactive representation; by giving him labels for both length and width, he encouraged him to use symbolic representation.  In this situation, and at this particular age, ikonic (image) representation is dominant.  In order to overcome this dominant mode, one must augment any conflict induced by the enactive mode against the ikonic mode if the child is to recognize the conflict at all.  It is only when a child is "saying" and "doing" that he learns not to believe fully what he is "seeing."

## A Final Word on Conservation

What then can we say in summary about these experiments on conservation? For one, conservation acquired "naturally" is not subject to experimental extinction, as is true for conservation responses acquired under laboratory conditioning procedures.  The recognition of this difference lends some plausibility to the conclusion that laboratory procedures are not very effective in speeding up the development of conservation. The few procedures that are effective involve an attempt to discredit immediate perceptual experience and to substitute instead a rethinking of what is given by such experience.   The successful procedures of screening and labeling plus manipulation are both this type of approach.  Similarly, the procedures used by Smedslund in putting two different strategies into conflict and thereby forcing some sort of rethinking of the problem are also successful training procedures.  Conservation, when it is learned, is learned by disregarding the immediate perceptual properties of the situation and relying instead on a conceptualization of the metric or mathematical properties of the objects perceived.  Conservation is a property of the thinker, not of the object.

This, however, should not be taken to mean that the child simply ignores the immediate perceptual situation, for if it is ignored there is nothing for concrete operations to operate on.  Instead it is better to speak more in terms of the concrete operational child not being bound by the perceptually given (i.e., not considering only that).  In a loose sense, the difference between pre- and post-operational thinking is like the difference between responding to input versus evaluating the input.  In any event, the operational child does not ignore the perceptually given; he uses it differently from the preoperational child.

But what sorts of cognitive operations could be involved in bringing about conservation?   Piaget (1952) has suggested that two important cognitive operations involved in conservation are reversability and logical multiplication.  By reversability, Piaget simply means that a child may come to see the amount of liquid in two different beakers as equal because he is able to consider performing a reverse operation such as pouring the water back into its original beaker.  More generally, it may also make the ability to consider what $X$ was like before it was transformed (i.e., to compare present with past status).  In terms of the clay experiments, he can see re-rolling the sausage back to the ball, or vice versa.  Logical multiplication is a much more complicated process.  In its simplest form, it implies that a child can come to compensate for changes in width by recognizing co-occurring changes in length: If the clay gets longer, it also gets skinnier.  In the case of the width and height of water jars, the tradeoff is perhaps somewhat more obvious.

Attaining conservation sets the major hurdle before a child can pass from an early intuitive stage of numerical ability to the more advanced stage of concrete operations. This latter transition marks the child's emancipation from the purely "here and now." At this point, the child's ability to handle numbers and mathematical operations exhibits many of the hallmarks of adult number usage: He is able to count constructively, he achieves conservation, and in general, he exhibits stable and self-consistent operations, including those of reversability and logical multiplication. At this stage such operations can be performed only on concrete objects—the child is still unable to perform them in the abstract.

In our original discussion, we set the limit of our aspirations at the level of the corner grocer. By the time the third stage is achieved, the corner grocer is about to be superseded. But it is also quite obvious that the corner grocer and other adults can and do go on to display more advanced levels of thinking if appropriate problems are put to them. The ability to consider numbers as an abstract system is always a possibility; and it is this possibility that defines a last stage in the development of numerical ability. This specifically numerical stage is, of course, coordinate with the more general last stage of intellectual development, that of Formal Operations.

## SUMMARY

The order of topics covered in Part III—Information-Processing Approaches to Thinking—is exactly opposite to that of Part II—Associative Approaches to Thinking—and this is as it should be, for information-processing analyses generally assume an element of problem solving in almost all aspects of human cognitive activity. If rational, or at least planful, problem solving is the major process involved in forming concepts and remembering things past, then the development of these processes requires an organism ready and able to learn highly complex procedures. Since the growth of mind shows a good deal of regularity in terms of when certain critical facilities develop, a theory such as Piaget's seems inevitable.

For Piaget, the human child passes through a series of intellectual stages, with each stage requiring the attainment of a particular cognitive skill. Thus the earliest stage, that of *sensori-motor intelligence*, concerns the attainment of perceptual constancy—when an object acquires "thingness" for an infant. The great achievement of the preoperational or second stage is that of language. With the development of language the child begins to escape some of the perceptual "here and now." The major achievement of the *stage of concrete operations* further removes the child from concrete perceptions and allows for the fully fledged growth of numerical ability. One major intellectual stumbling block that must be overcome by the child between the ages of 5 and 7 is that of nonconservation. A good deal of research has still not yet uncovered the "heart of conservation," although, Lord knows, not for lack of trying. The fourth and final stage, that of *formal operations,* leaves the child free to "talk about talk," or "reason about reason," or "moralize about morality," and so on. Operational intelligence allows for the development and use of inductive and deductive reasoning and allows the thinker to dabble in realms that are often justly described as abstract thought.

Piaget's theory is essentially an epigenetic one—that is, in order for the child to develop certain critical intellectual skills, he must be mature and experienced enough for them. Complex skills can only develop in a biologically "tuned" and receptive organism. Although Piaget would not claim, as Freud did, that "biology is destiny," he certainly would view the development of intelligence as dependent on some unfolding biological plan: a plan selectively ready to learn the lessons of the environment and to assimilate those of preceding intellectual stages.

# CHAPTER 13

# REPRISE: THE DAYDREAMER AND THE FISHERMAN—A BRIEF EPILOG

Both daydreams and directed thought are representative operations of mind. In one—daydreaming—the flow of thought seems haphazard and strongly determined by the immediately preceding thought or action. In directed thinking, the flow of thought appears very much under some sort of central control so that the sequence of ideas and behavior produced seem to be guided by some overall consideration or plan. Any particular thought or idea is determined as much, or more, by the initial decision as to what needs to be done as by the immediately preceding thought or action.

The primary factor involved in daydreaming and other types of seemingly nondirected thought is that of contiguity: Events occur together in thought because they have been experienced together in that order in the past. Although this basic principle can be complicated by the laws of similarity or contrast, or by mediated contiguity, etc., all ultimately can be derived as arising from some form of contiguity. Now this analysis would be of limited interest if it accounted only for reverie or daydream; but as we have seen, it can, and has been, extended to account for more directed thought functions such as problem solving and concept formation. The associative analysis of thought is clearly meant as a general theory.

Over and against this view is the hypothesis that thinking is guided by hierarchically organized plans. For this view—the hypothesis-testing view—the way in which thinking progresses is to be found in a careful and detailed analysis of directed thought. Unfortunately, this still leaves as unexplained the less constrained and more free-flowing types of mental activity captured in dream or reverie states.

The most significant aspect of these differences is not set by determining who is right or wrong in any absolute sense, but rather by noting that both approaches fail to make meaningful contact with one another. As results presented in Parts II and III indicate, both contiguity and hypothesis-testing views have produced two quite different traditions of theory and experiment, with very little overlap. The strange fact is that both views have been able to generate reasonable and extensive research programs which make sense not only to the proponents of a particular view, but also to anyone who has a less prejudiced stake in the matter. There are times when the mind functions as if it were guided by perfectly rational plans, and there are other times when it seems to function strictly on the basis of contiguity.

But which times are which? Here it seems appropriate to recognize that what an organism is required to do often determines how he will do it. As we have seen in the case of memory, if task constraints do not permit the memorizer to use coding procedures easily, his recall will be minimal and strongly affected by interference and contiguity factors. If, however, the situation is right (highly codable materials presented with few presentation constraints), the memorizer will behave as a planful organism. In a less strictly experimental case, a thinker will often relinquish his ability to plan and simply let autonomous central processes proceed "on their own." This may be done voluntarily as in the case of a daydream, or involuntarily as in a dream state. In either state the classical laws of association seem to apply.

Another, and perhaps even more significant, determiner of directed versus associative thought has to do with the developmental level of a particular piece of thinking. The occurrence of learning set phenomena, documented so well by Harlow and his coworkers, indicates that with limited experience an organism is strongly tied to the immediate stimulus properties of the environment, whereas he is easily able to overcome this domination after more extensive experience. The development of a general-purpose concept of oddity, for example, allows an organism to disregard particular stimuli and respond instead on the basis of an environment-free rule.

This analysis is also congruent with the line of argument developed by Piaget—the growth of intelligence involves freeing an organism's concepts from his immediate perceptual environment. To generalize, it seems possible to conclude that the developmental level of either an organism or of a concept determines whether the organism's behavior will look primarily as if it were determined by associative or by hypothesis-testing factors. One other aspect of Piaget's analysis also deserves mention: Mental capacities are hierarchically organized so that whatever mental ability was available at first is incorporated into ever-higher levels of skill. Thinking is a cumulative activity, both across ages and concepts.

Freud also considered thought to develop according to this general scheme. The infant is guided largely by the demands of the immediate environment, whereas the adult is guided by long-range considerations. Freud captured this difference by distinguishing between primary and secondary process. In the language of the present discussion, primary process operates on the basis of associative factors regarding both its development and its current mode of operation in dreams, slips of the tongue, and neurotic symptoms. Secondary process operates in terms of long-range plans designed to escape the domination of immediate stimuli. Together, Freud and Piaget have mapped the origin and operation of primary and secondary processes, respectively, and their attempts should be seen as complementary, rather than competitive.

Perhaps this, then, is the clue: Thought progresses either in terms of contiguity or of hypothesis testing, with the limits set only by the task and developmental levels of the thinker. Perhaps the sequence is as Freud, Piaget, Harlow, and Gagné have proposed, one of development from associative to directed thinking.

Although this seems a reasonable, and reasonably well-supported, generalization, there do seem to be some higher-order processes in which directed thinking precedes associative thinking. Consider the case of a child learning to add the numbers 3 + 2. The first thing that occurs is that 3 is shown to equal 1 + 1 + 1 and 2 is shown to equal 1 + 1. This is usually done by showing the child 3 and 2 fingers respectively. Next the child is asked to count up the fingers, one by one, so as to produce the correct answer of 5. Although the child may continue to use this type of procedure for a short while, after sufficient experience he no longer need go through it in order to produce a correct answer. Instead what seems to happen is the words "three plus two" become a stimulus in the associative sense of the term, and the word "five" becomes the response. What started out as a complicated rule-governed problem ends up a much more simplified stimulus–response chain. Sometimes thinking goes from information processing to stimulus–response.

Neisser, in analyzing the distinction between associative and information-processing approaches, has argued that thinking always contains a number of more or less independent "trains of thought." Ordinarily one of these involves the motor system, and ordinarily this is the one a subject would describe if questioned: "What are you thinking about?" Other trains of thought also seem to go on at the same time—operating perhaps on the basis of associative mechanisms—but unless these become particularly insistent, the mainstream of thought continues until it is brought to a successful conclusion, the solution of the problem.

This analysis then envisions two complementary thought processes, one operating in a fixed, planful way on the basis of a systematic program(s), and another operating on the basis of element-to-element contiguity-based associative connections. The specific nature of how these processes get along with one another in the adult thinker is probably best captured by Reitman's *Argus* program. As may be remembered, associative elements operate autonomously, and only when certain elements reach a critical value do they impinge on the rather straitlaced and highly sequential central processor or executive. In this analysis, associative processes dominate precisely when central processing is at a minimum. This occurs in sleep, or when such autonomous processes exceed a critical threshold value and "distract" executive routine.

Under this further analysis it is possible to accede to the human thinker what is characteristic of human thought: Associative processes operate autonomously, and often develop historically prior to central, rule-governed cognitive activities. Highly planful, rational adult thinking seems to grow out of an original matrix provided by associative connections in a manner described by Freud and given experimental plausibility by Harlow in his work on learning sets. The ultimate achievement of this growth is a highly organized and a highly flexible pattern of intellectual abilities capable on the one hand of highly planful activities as is Hemingway's fisherman, and capable on the other of seemingly episodic reverie characteristic of Proust's daydreamer. With this the cycle closes.

# CHAPTER 14

# THE STUDY OF LANGUAGE

Anyone who has ever thought or written about language has a favorite sentence or phrase. These bits of language are treated with the same respect that one affords a good set of china—they are brought out only on a strictly limited number of occasions and then only to impress someone or to clinch some important deal. Although the list of these sentences and phrases is quite large, there are a number that stand out as of singular importance:

1. Colorless green ideas sleep furiously. (Chomsky)
2. Visiting relatives can be boring. (Chomsky)
3. Sir Walter Scott is the author of *Waverley*. (Russell)
4. Light lights lightly light light lights. (Osgood)
5. The boy hit a ball. (Miller, Galanter, and Pribram)

and perhaps, a more extended one from Lewis Carroll:

6. "Who did you pass on the road? the King went on. . . .
   "Nobody," said the messenger.
   "Quite right," said the King, "this young lady saw him too. So of course Nobody walks slower than you."
   "I do my best," the messenger said. . . . "I'm sure nobody walks much faster than I do."
   "He can't do that," said the King, "or else he'd have been here first."

## BOYS, BALLS, RELATIVES, AND GREEN IDEAS

So much for the sentences; considered separately or in a set, they don't seem terribly impressive. Yet looks are deceiving, for each of these sentences, in its own way, represents a summary of some problem confronting anyone who would attempt to analyze language and language users. Consider some of the problems captured by the least exotic sentence: *The boy hit a ball.*

If the sentence is written, it seems reasonable to feel that it contains five words, with the beginning of the sentence marked with an upper-case letter and the end marked with a small dot known as a period. This extremely simple observation is not without implication: A string of words known as a sentence, even in its written form, contains at least two different types of units: individual words and the complete sentence itself. For some purposes —say communicating the idea of who did what with what—the sentence is an appropriate unit, while for some other purpose—say talking about a *boy* or a *ball* in a different context—the word would be an appropriate unit. For still other purposes, certain collections of words called phrases, such as *the boy, a ball, hit a ball*, etc., provide appropriate units of description. Pushing our analysis a bit further, we see that each word can be decomposed into letters, and for purposes of teaching someone to spell, letter units would be most appropriate. If we are interested in teaching someone to write, it is apparent that letters may be broken down into movement patterns—as for example in combining a vertical line with a crossbar to make the letter T.

Even in the case of simply writing a very simple sentence, we come smack up against what can only be called the "units problem"—that is, what is *the* appropriate unit for an analysis of language? If we consider the sentence "The boy hit a ball" in its spoken form, the problem is even more complex, for here there are no spaces between words. So, for example, the phrase *the boy* may be spoken without any pause between the two words, as indeed may the whole sentence. Here then certainly is our unit—the sentence. But no, it is still possible and likely for a speaker to treat the words, the phrases, the sounds, the articulatory movements required to make the sounds, and so on, as individual and indivisible elements in different contexts, and so, on this basis the units problem still remains for speech.

If an attempt is made to coordinate a written sentence with a spoken sentence such as in reading, there are still further problems. Each letter has to be correlated with a particular sound, and the same letter need not have the same sound twice. For example, the final *e* in *the* is pronounced in some Eastern American pronunciations as a type of *u* or *uh* (*thu* or *thuh*) whereas the *a* in *arrive* is pronounced in the same way: *uh*rive. This would be easy enough to accept if the *a* in *ball* weren't pronounced *aw*, as in *bawl*. In the first case the *e* and the *a* yield the same sound (*uh*), whereas the first and second *a*'s (in *arrive* and *ball*) yield discriminable different sounds (*uh* and *aw*, respectively). Now although this is not as overwhelming a problem such as might be *phound* in *farmacy*, it nonetheless does require further discrimination of *a*'s into $a_1$ and $a_2$, and as later examples will show into $a_3, a_4$, and so on.

The general problem of relating letters to sound is particularly difficult in English. Consider the following excerpt from a poem written to a young girl who is learning English (for best effect read the poem aloud).

Lines on the Pronunciation of English

> Dearest creature in Creation,
> Studying English pronunciation,
> I will teach you in my verse
> Sounds like corpse, corps, horse and worse.

It will keep you, Susy, busy,
Make your head with heat grow dizzy;
Tear in eye your dress you'll tear.
So shall I! Oh! Hear my prayer!

Just compare heart, beard and heard,
Dies and diet, lord and word,
Sword and sward, retain and Britain.
(Mind the latter, how it's written!)

But be careful how you speak,
Say break, steak, but bleak and streak;
Previous, precious; fuchsia, via;
Pipe, swipe; recipe and choir;
Cloven, oven; how and low;
Script, receipt; shoe, poem, toe.

From "desire," desirable,—admirable from "admire";
Lumber, plumber; bier, but brier;

This phonetic labyrinth
Gives moss, gross, brook, brooch, ninth, plinth;
Billet does not end like ballet;
Bouquet, wallet, mallet, chalet;
Blood and flood are not like food!
Nor is mould like should and would.
Banquet is not nearly parquet,
Which is said to rime with "darky."

And your pronunciation is O.K.
When you say correctly croquet;
Rounded, wounded; grieve and sieve;
Friend and fiend; heave and heaven;
Rachel, ache, moustache, eleven.

and so on, for 80 more lines until the last four!

Finally; which rimes with "enough,"
Though, through, plough, cough, hough or tough?
Hiccough has the sound of "cup"...

My advice is—give it up!*

---

* I have written several letters trying to track down the author of this poem. It came to me through a friend of a friend of a friend, who got it from a teacher of English in an evening class in Geneva, Switzerland, in 1960.

But the units problem does not begin with sound nor end with sentences, for sentences usually do not occur alone; they are usually produced in the company of other sentences which, in written form, serve to define a paragraph, or in spoken form, a segment of fluent speech. The same problems apply here as before: For some purposes, one or another element may be considered an independent unit, whereas for other purposes it clearly cannot stand alone, but must be viewed in a larger context. There are units within units within units, and any analysis of language must take this fact into account. Some analyses solve the units problem by concentrating on a single unit such as the word, while others are more ambitious and try to handle all levels at once.

**The ambiguity of visiting relatives.**    Sentence 2: *Visiting relatives can be boring*, depends for its effectiveness on a "grammatical pun." Actually there is nothing very special about this sentence and, as a matter of fact, there are a great many other sentences—such as, *They are cooking apples* or *The shooting of the hunters was terrible*, to mention only two—which work on exactly the same principle. To take the simpler of these sentences, *They are cooking apples*, the critical thing is how we treat the word *cooking*. For one interpretation of the sentence—say the one given in response to the question "What kind of apples are those?"—*cooking* and *apples* form a single unit. So on this basis, the sentence can be broken as follows: (*They*) (*are*) (*cooking apples*). For a second interpretation of this sentence—the one given in response to the question "What are they doing with the apples?"— the sentence would be broken up as (*They*) (*are cooking*) (*apples*). A purely semantic pun can also be made—"What are the natives doing to Mr. Apples?" but this need not concern us now because such an interpretation would be covered by the second case, i.e., where *are cooking* would be treated as a phrase.

Using parentheses to tell us how to understand a sentence is only one way in which to divide a sentence into meaningful units. Another way in which to do this is to use a tree diagram. For this type of analysis the first sentence would be diagrammed as:

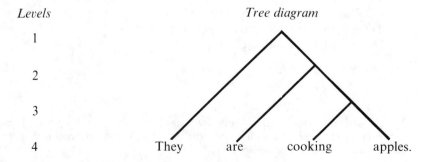

Levels          Tree diagram

  1

  2

  3

  4          They      are      cooking      apples.

with the topmost level, 1, representing the sentence as a unit; the second level representing a verb phrase; the third level a noun phrase; and the fourth, a series of words.

In order to capture a second meaning, the sentence would have to be diagrammed as follows:

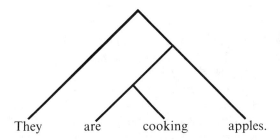

They     are     cooking     apples.

The difference between the two sentences is then one of *sentence structure*. Chomsky has argued that syntactical ambiguity of this type arises only because human speakers not only respond to the structural aspects of language, but indeed often require it in order to understand a particular sentence. Any analysis of sentences or language at the level of the word alone must be incomplete, for syntax is independent of specific words and their specific meanings.

In order to reinforce this latter point—namely the independence of syntax and meaning—consider the very first sentence, *Colorless green ideas sleep furiously.* The importance of this sentence is twofold.

 1) In all likelihood, prior to Chomsky, none of the constituent words ever preceded or followed one another in spoken or written language. That is, it is very unlikely that *green* ever was preceded by *colorless*, or followed by *ideas.*

 2) All speakers of English are quite capable of recognizing this sentence as syntactically well-formed even if they are unable to provide a consistent meaning to it. That is to say, they can see this sentence as a sentence, whereas a different order for the same words—*Sleep colorless furiously ideas green*, for example—would not give us this same impression. It is this latter point that Chomsky considers of theoretical significance. Speakers can recognize a sentence as being well-formed even if they are unable to provide any meaningful interpretation for it.

**Some problems about the learning of language.** After these two sentences, *The boy hit a ball* must seem a bit tame, but there is still more to be learned from it. If we consider that a speaker has a vocabulary consisting of only these five words, of which one is a verb, two are articles, and two are nouns, and we consider only simple declarative sentences of the form: Article, Noun,

Verb, Article, Noun, there are 16 word strings that yield acceptable English sentences:

| Articles | Nouns | Verb | Articles | Nouns |
|----------|-------|------|----------|-------|
| A | boy | hit | a | boy |
| The | ball | | the | ball |
| 2 | 2 | 1 | 2 | 2 |

This figure, 16, is derived from multiplying all the column sums in the above example. Looking at these words in this way shows that they will yield 16 perfectly acceptable sentences such as: *A boy hit a ball*, or *A ball hit a boy*, . . . and so on. If we increase any one of the classes—say that of nouns by the inclusion of a word like *club*—the column totals go to 2, 3, 1, 3, 2, thereby increasing the total number of perfectly acceptable sentences to 36.

Now all this poses particularly tricky problems for describing how children learn to recognize or produce grammatical sentences in their native language. One version of such an analysis might be that the child is rewarded for correct word combinations and not rewarded for incorrect combinations. If this is true, then for a vocabulary consisting of 6 words (*the, a, boy, ball, club, hit*) there are 36 sentences that have to be reinforced. But how many are there that need to be extinguished?

The most unrestricted upper estimate would allow each word to occur in every position, or would allow 6 words in 5 positions, producing a total of 7776 possibilities ($6^5$). A more restricted estimate which would not allow repetitive combinations such as *The the the the the*, would still produce 720 combinations ($6 \times 5 \times 4 \times 3 \times 2 \times 1$). Even this lower estimate (which is really too low because it would exclude perfectly good sentences such as *The boy hit the boy*) still requires the subject to discriminate 36 "correct" word combinations from 684 incorrect ones. This is no small learning task, particularly since we are only considering a child with a 6-word vocabulary and only requiring him to produce simple declarative sentences. The problem obviously becomes incredibly more complex if we allow a child a 500-word vocabulary, and allow him to ask questions, or talk in the passive voice, and so on. Miller, Galanter, and Pribram have perhaps overstated the case in the following quote, but the learning problem, under anybody's description, is still prohibitive. "In short, the child would have to hear about $3 \times 10^{20}$ sentences per second in order to be exposed to all the information necessary . . . to produce sentences according to these left to right rules, and that is on the assumption of a childhood 100 years long with no interruptions for sleeping, eating, etc., and perfect retention of every string of twenty words after one presentation!"*

* From *Plans and the Structure of Behavior*, by G. A. Miller, E. Galanter, and K. H. Pribram, New York: Holt, Rinehart, and Winston, 1960.

But speech does not take 100 years to develop in the normal child; quite the contrary, most children are able to produce perfectly good, understandable sentences by the time they are 3 or 4 years of age, and many are able to talk at 18 months. Although estimates of vocabulary size are notoriously unreliable, one set of figures runs something like this: At age 1 the average child can use 3 words; at age 2, 272; at age 3, 1500; and so on (Smith, 1921). If an analysis similar to that performed on the 6-word vocabulary described earlier is performed on vocabularies of this size, the learning problem assumes critical proportions. Children undoubtedly do not learn language on the basis of a principle as simple-minded as the one proposed above.

There are, however, various way in which to increase the power of a learning explanation so as to make it appear more reasonable. For one thing, it is possible to argue that once a particular string of words such as *The boy hit a ball* is reinforced as a correct sentence, the child will tend to repeat, on the basis of generalization, parts of it as appropriate in new situations. Thus *the boy* referred to in *The boy hit a ball* can be referred to as *the boy* (same response) when and if he hits *a stick*. In short, *the boy* becomes integrated into a single unit and can be so used when necessary. Presumably, transfer could be complete from *The boy hit a ball* to *the boy hit the boy*, after but a single reinforcement for the first sentence. Such word units do occur quite frequently in English ("In reply to your letter," "Give me liberty or give me death," etc.) and their occurrence as total units does make the language-learning problem a bit more manageable. Even given this extended analysis, the child still does have to cram a lot of learning into three years.

One suggestion that has gained a good deal of support in regard to what it is a child learns when he learns to speak a language, is that he learns the construction rules of the language, or a set of rules that allow him to create or generate sentences as these are needed. What might these rules look like? For the sentence, *The boy hit a ball*, the following set will do the trick.

> *Rule 1.* Any sentence, S, can be rewritten as a Noun Phrase (*NP*) and a Verb Phrase (*VP*): $S \rightarrow NP + VP$.

> *Rule 2.* Any Noun Phrase (*NP*) can be rewritten as Article (*A*) plus Noun (*N*): $NP \rightarrow A + N$.

> *Rule 3.* Any Verb Phrase (*VP*) can be rewritten as Verb (*V*) plus Noun Phrase (*NP*): $VP \rightarrow V + NP$.

> *Rule 4.* All vocabulary items must be assigned to one of the grammatical classes: Noun, Verb, or Article. In the present case (*a, the*) = *A*; (*hit*) = *V*; and (*boy, ball*) = *N*.

In order to see what these rules can do, let us simply follow the rules for producing a sentence.

$$S \rightarrow NP + VP \qquad \text{by Rule 1}$$
$$NP \rightarrow A + N \qquad \text{by Rule 2}$$
$$V \rightarrow V + NP \qquad \text{by Rule 3}$$
$$NP \rightarrow A + N \qquad \text{by Rule 2}$$

Therefore

$$S = A + N + V + A + N,$$

or exactly the description of a simple declarative sentence. If the child learns rules rather than responses, he has a good deal less to learn (three rules and a few grammatical class markers for each vocabulary item). Note that if an extra word such as *girl* is added, no new sentences need be reinforced or extinguished; the only new learning that has to take place is the grammatical class of the word, i.e., *girl* is a Noun. On this basis, the acquisition of language does seem a bit more easily interpretable.

**Alice, Sir Walter Scott, and light lights.** Up to this point, we have been considering *colorless ideas, visiting relatives,* and *boys and balls,* but "The time has come," said the Walrus, "to consider nobody." By this of course we mean the classic passage from *Alice in Wonderland* dealing with the King, his messenger and Nobody (or nobody, if you prefer).

The problem that arises in connection with the King's analysis of the Nobody Situation is partly grammatical, and partly related to the more general problem of meaning. The King's problem (actually the messenger's, for Kings are never wrong) is to treat *nobody* as if it were a proper noun such as *Alice* or *King,* etc., and use it in a sentence in accordance with such an interpretation. On the basis of a description phrased solely in terms of syntactic rules (see the preceding section), the King has improperly marked the word *nobody* as to grammatical class. In one sense, the King's mistake is grammatical.

There is, however, another sense in which the King erred, and this is in terms of meaning. But what has the King's error to do with meaning? A number of contemporary philosophers, chiefly Wittgenstein, have argued that it is futile to try to describe the meaning of a word in abstract terms and categories; what is required instead is an analysis of the situations in which people use a particular word. "Don't look for the meaning, look for the use" is the way the theory runs. According to the Wittgensteinian view, the King also erred with respect to meaning: He used the word *nobody* in a manner completely at odds with our normal use, and recognition of this fact makes this situation funny.

When, however, we talk about meaning from a non-Wittgensteinian point of view, we usually assume that meaning has something to do with the relationship of words to the objects they stand for. In its simplest form such a referential view of meaning assumes a relationship between a word and some piece of reality. This simple form of the referential theory has been discussed by Bertrand Russell in terms of the sentence: *Sir Walter Scott is the author of* Waverley. This sentence is not repetitive nor redundant, for historically, the author of *Waverley* was not identified when the books first appeared. Because of this, the phrase *the author of* Waverley simply meant: "whoever he is." At that same time, Sir Walter Scott was well known as a poet, but his identity as *the* author of *Waverley* was unknown when the books first appeared. Thus, when the identity of the author of *Waverley* was revealed to be Sir Walter Scott, Russell's sentence becomes completely understandable and completely meaningful. The nub of the problem set by the sentence is that two phrases refer to the same man, but both have different meanings.

Recognizing this difficulty, but still wanting ultimately to define meaning in terms of reference, Russell went on to state a more sophisticated form of the referential theory as follows: "When we ask what constitutes meaning... we are asking, not who is the individual meant, but what is the *relation* of the word to the individual which makes the one man mean the other." (Russell, 1921, page 191) Here the focus has shifted: No longer do we ask to what does the word refer, but rather what is the relationship between word and referent. If the referent is the same (i.e., the person, Sir Walter Scott) but the relation is different (a poet or the author of *Waverley*), we are free to say that the meanings differ.

Although this argument meets Russell's objection, it runs into rough sailing with words such as *and, but, if*, etc., which really do not refer to anything at all. This objection could be met if we argued that some words don't really have meaning in and of themselves, but depend for their meaning on being included in sentences which ultimately do have referential existence. Even if this argument is granted, there is still a more profound difficulty with such a view. Generally speaking, a word such as *apple* is assumed to have a fairly obvious referent. But to what exactly does it refer?—certainly not to any specific apple—but rather to a class of objects. Hence even for apples there are no obvious referents.

Over and above all this is the view that meaning is an entity of some sort—something to be looked for and found. W. P. Alston (1963) has argued that this view arises from an uncritical analysis of a defining sentence, as for example: "The meaning of procrastinate is *put things off*." If not considered carefully, such a sentence is likely to be considered as equivalent to *The author of* Waverley *is Scott*." In the second sentence a specific person (entity) is specified by the sentence, whereas in the first sentence what is implied is: Use the word *procrastinate* as you would use the phrase *put things off*. Alston argues that the glib identification of the first sentence as being equal in intent to the second is wrong and surely leads to unreliable results.

The consequences of this discussion are easily summarized:

The referential theory is based on an important insight—that is, language is used to talk about things outside (as well as inside) language, and that the suitability of an expression for such talk is somehow crucial for its having the meaning it has. But in the referential theory this insight is ruined through oversimplification. ... Some of the meaningful components of the sentences we use to talk about the world can be connected in semantically important ways to distinguishable components of the world, but others cannot.*

If we return for a moment to our earlier analysis of the *Waverley* sentence, there is still more to be learned. The simple referential theory fails because the same object can be referred to by two different words both of which have different meanings. But the opposite case can also be true; that is, where the same word has the same meaning but for different referents. Consider the word *I*. When I utter it, it means *me*; when you utter it, it means *you*; when he utters it, it means *him*—yet in all cases *I* means the speaker, whether it be *me*, *you*, or *him*. The meaning of *I* is always the same (a speaker), but the referent can be, and often is, quite different. (A similar example is to be found in the use of the word *it* in the sentence immediately preceding the last one. In some cases it refers to the word *I*, whereas in the last clause it referred to *me*, *you* or *him*. Hence index words such as *it* need not have any observable object as their reference. Some, such as *I*, *he*, etc., do; others, such as *it*, do not.)

All this, of course, raises the question: How do we know what an index word such as *I* refers to, even granted all the difficulties involved in a simple reference theory? The most obvious consideration is that words such as *I* are understood because of the communication situation in which they occur. This is the essential insight involved in a behavioral analysis of meaning such as the one offered by Osgood and his associates (Osgood, 1953; 1963; 1968; Osgood, Suci, and Tannenbaum, 1957). Although we will have much more to say about this specific theory in a later chapter, let us now consider the last of our sentences.

**Light lights lightly light light lights.** The essential point of this sentence, as Osgood sees it, is that it is very difficult to interpret, or at least to paraphrase, when it stands alone; that is, out of some situational context. The reason is that in the absence of context, it is extremely difficult to know which of the lights is "turn-onable," which light does the turning on, which tells what kind of light it is, and so on. The word *light* can be coded as a noun, a verb, or an adjective, and the appropriate grammatical class for any of the *lights*

---

* From *Philosophy of Language*, by William P. Alston, Englewood Cliffs, N. J.: Prentice-Hall, 1964.

is not immediately apparent from the sentence when it stands alone. In the context of a balmy summer evening in a Japanese garden, Osgood softly says: *Pale flames gently illuminate airy lanterns*, or more ambiguously, *Light lights lightly light light lights*, and the meaning is suddenly clear. In short, the structure of the sentence is illuminated not only by syntactic structure and the referents of its constituent words, but also, and in this case, by the particular context within which it is used.

But surely this is an extraordinary case; more usual sentences don't have this difficulty with meaning—or do they? Consider a further example: *The man hits the colorful ball*, a prosaic example if ever there was one. Yet as Osgood points out, it is open to no less than four different interpretations:

1. *The man strikes the colorful round object with a blow* (very high probability).

2. *The man collides with the colorful round object* (conceivable, but it would have to be a pretty big ball).

3. *The man strikes the colorful solid missile with a blow* (conceivable, but not probable in this day and age).

4. *The man collides with the colorful solid missile* (What, is Tom Thumb drunk again?).*

As it stands, a simple sentence such as *The man hits the colorful ball* is capable of four different interpretations, and if multiple interpretations are the rule rather than the exception, communication seems impossible. The reason that speakers are able to communicate with each other is that speech always occurs in a context, and the specific nature of the context, the speaker, as well as the person spoken to, all help to provide a relatively clear interpretation to a given sentence. On this basis, Osgood argues that any adequate theory of meaning should not, and cannot, be concerned only with sentences in the abstract, but must also consider both the situational and environmental context within which they occur.

Everywhere we turn, the problem of meaning deepens, and seems incapable of solution; yet the obvious fact is that words do have meaning, do refer to objects, and do correlate with ideas. The problem with all these statements is that once the essential insight of the view—say, that words refer to objects—is agreed on, this simple statement turns out to be not quite so simple. Exactly what is meant by *refer* and *objects* is not clear, except in an informal and intuitive sense. What is clear is that meaning is an essential aspect of language, even if the precise way to consider it has eluded us for more than 1000 years.

---

* From "On understanding and creating sentences," by C. E. Osgood, in *American Psychologist*, **18**, 1963, page 738.

The upshot of this introductory discussion is that language, however it is characterized, has two primary components. One is a purely formal, or structural, component, while the second has to do with how these patterned structural components convey meaning. Structure and references are the essential aspects of language that must be handled by any analysis.

**Some informal but important definitions.** The term *language* refers to an abstract system, never directly observable, and must be distinguished from the term *speech*, its observable counterpart. The structure of language generally appears only on analysis—it is not necessarily what speakers do in using the language at any given time in any particular situation. Speech can be most simply defined as the totality of verbal behaviors that the speakers of a given language commonly use, whereas language is an abstract system of elements governed by rules describing the permissible and non-permissible combinations of elements which occur in speech. The properties of a language system are always inferred from an analysis of speech.

Perhaps an example will clarify the difference. Every time a Frenchman speaks, he is adding to the total of verbal behavior (speech) that has gone on in his language community—he is not, however, adding to the French language itself. Language then is an abstraction derived from an analysis of behavior, and as such is not subject to the same factors that affect speech. For example, language is indifferent to the social relationship of the speaker t ) the listener, yet it is quite clear that grammar, word choice, and even pronunciation are often profoundly affected by moment-to-moment factors, as when a student talks to the principal of his elementary school, or when a junior executive talks to his boss. Speech, considered as behavior, is subject to the same factors in both the environment and the person that affect other behaviors, be these other behaviors linguistic or not. In short: Language is a system. Speech is behavior.

Given this division of language behavior into language (the formal system encompassing structure and reference) and speech (behavior governed by factors similar to other nonlanguage behaviors), it seems inevitable that different disciplines would concern themselves with one or the other of these domains. *Linguistics* is a descriptive science that seeks to describe the code of any language as economically and elegantly as possible. Since linguistics in its modern form arose from an attempt to specify and record languages not having a written form, it has been primarily concerned with spoken language. In line with our analysis of the levels problem, this implies that an acceptable description of language requires procedures for analyzing the sound aspects of the language as well as grammatical and semantic ones. These three linguistic subspecialties are called *phonemics* (including phonetics, *morphemics* (including syntax) and *semantics*. As is obvious, an analysis of the sound system is closest to the raw, unanalyzed behavior that goes on in speech acts, whereas an analysis of words, sentences, and meanings is further removed from the data and involves a good deal more analytic inference. For this reason the most significantly developed aspect of linguistics (or at least the one least in dispute) is that dealing with the sound system itself.

Although the "behavior" part of language behavior is thought to depend on quite general principles of behavior, very few psychologists (Skinner, 1957, being the notable exception) are willing to attempt an analysis of such behavior independent of some sophistication in linguistics. For this reason, a border discipline, *psycholinguistics*, has developed which attempts to analyze linguistic behavior both in terms of its psychological and linguistic components. As Osgood (1963) put it in an introductory survey of the field: "Psycholinguistics is concerned, in the broadest sense, with relations between the structure of messages and the characteristics of the human individuals who produce and receive them..." (page 248). The title itself—with the *psych* part preceding the *linguistics* part—indicates that psycholinguistics is a specialty more cultivated by psychologists than by linguists.

Since in the next two chapters we will be concerned primarily with what Osgood has called the "psych" in psycholinguistics, the remainder of the present chapter is devoted to an elementary description of linguistics and linguistic problems. Specifically, it will describe first the phonological or sound component of language and then move on to the morphological and grammatical components. Finally, we will present some attempts to describe how these structures interrelate in order to see how language might convey meanings.

## LINGUISTICS: THE SCIENCE OF LANGUAGE

The problems that face the linguist in his attempt to describe language are very much like those that face a traveler who goes to a country where he doesn't know the language. The sounds that strike him as he steps from the airplane seem entirely indistinguishable and strange; so strange, in fact, that the speaker has very great difficulty in dividing the rush of sound into smaller units such as words. Instead, what he hears is an indistinguishable blur of noise with pauses or hesitations of greater or lesser duration.

If he is a resourceful traveler (or an experienced one) he knows that he can get along by using a very graphic and obvious sign language, but that ultimately he must learn some of the sounds and meaningful words of the language. Accordingly, he starts out by pointing and gesturing. Some things are easy to convey, as for example, when he points to his shoe and looks around questioningly.

The linguist is regularly faced with problems of this type in his attempt to analyze an unknown language. The difference, of course, is that the linguist wants to describe the formal properties of an unknown language, while the traveler wants to learn how to communicate with it. While it is true that the speaker's problem is to achieve the sort of knowledge that the linguist wants to express, they both tend to seek such knowledge in quite different ways.

The linguist begins with a small sample of the language (a corpus) and then tries to determine what are the significant sounds of that language. In order to analyze a given language, some method of recording is needed. While tape recorders are extremely useful for this purpose, ultimately some provision must be made to record these sounds in writing.

As we know from our previous discussion, the ordinary alphabet of English won't do: Remember the pronunciation of *thuh* (*the*), *uh*rive (*arrive*), and *bawl* (*ball*). In this example, two different letters, *e* and *a*, yield the same sound, while the same letter *a* yields two different sounds. In order to overcome this difficulty, a list of speech sounds, the international phonetic alphabet (I.P.A.), was developed to provide a separate symbol for many of the sounds that occur in a number of different languages. For example, the vowel sound in the word *the* is symbolized [ə] while the vowel sound in *ball* is symbolized [ɔ]. Thus the word *the* would be written as [ðə], while *ball* would be written as [bɔl]. In general, the sounds normally denoted by the consonants have roughly the same symbol as in standard writing, whereas the vowels, because of the large numbers of individual sounds associated with each written form, generally require a more extended list of symbols. For example, all the following words spelled with an *a* in standard writing take a different phonetic symbol: [ey] as in *date*; [æ] as in *man*; [a] as in *father*; [ɔ] as in *ball*; and [ə] as in *arrive*. The number of different phonetic distinctions required for the usual five English vowels jumps to about 14 or 15 or more when these are considered phonetically. In field work, the linguist often makes up new symbols as these are needed for a particular language.

One obvious fact about the sounds of a language is that the speaker or listener seldom finds all the phonetic distinctions that he is capable of making important. For example, if a speaker is asked to produce the same sound on a number of different occasions, he tends to vary in his pronunciation on many or all of these occasions. Even more to the point, certain vowels often serve to change the nature of a particular sound in a given language. For example, the [k] sound in *ski* is slightly different from the [k] sound in *king*. Another example is the pronunciation [p] in *pin* and in *nip*. In this latter case, the [p] in *pin* is aspirated (produced with a "breathy" quality), while the [p] in *nip* is not, or at least not as much. Although these distinctions are not immediately apparent, a little practice serves to make the difference a bit more obvious.

On what basis then does a linguist conclude that two discriminably different sounds really are only unimportant variations on a single sound?

Consider a fragment of an example provided by Gleason (1961) for the two Spanish sounds [b] and [v] both of which are considered as variations on a single higher-order sound symbolized by /b/. In order to facilitate this discussion, two technical terms, *phoneme* and *allophone* need to be defined provisionally. Considered most loosely, a *phoneme* is a significant unit of sound in a particular language. The phoneme never really exists—it is a scientific fiction used as a summary term for a great many observations of sounds as these function in a language. Thus when a linguist is asked to produce a /b/ phoneme, all he can do is provide a sound that approximates his *concept* of the phoneme. No phoneme is ever displayed directly, only specific examples are.

Similarly, since the phoneme is a theoretical fiction, there are a number of different examples of it. Some of these are similar to each other, while others are not. Two examples of a single phoneme may be different because of the immediately preceding or following sounds (i.e., as in *nip* and *pin*). These variations in the sounds which comprise a phoneme are called *allophonic variations*, and any sound or subclass of sounds grouped as members of the same phoneme are called *allophones* of that *phoneme*.

The following list of words are a small hypothetical example of a language sample secured by a linguist trying to determine the phonemes of Spanish. For purposes of the present discussion, we will consider only the /b/ phoneme.*

| | | | | | |
|---|---|---|---|---|---|
| [aʋana] | Havana | [durař] | to endure | [peřo] | but |
| [bala] | ball | [ganař] | to earn | [peřo] | dog |
| [baɣa] | rope | [gato] | cat | [pipa] | pipe |
| [beso] | kiss | [gola] | throat | [ponderoso] | heavy |
| [boða] | wedding | [gosař] | to enjoy | [poŋgo] | I put |
| [buřo] | burro | [kasa] | house | [siɣařo] | cigar |
| [damos] | we give | [kuʋa] | Cuba | [teŋgo] | I have |
| [dios] | God | [laɣo] | lake | [toðo] | all |
| [deveř] | to owe | [naða] | nothing | [taʋako] | tobacco |
| [donde] | where | [nuðo] | knot | [uʋa] | grape |

**Figure 14.1**

In this specific example, the first thing we notice is that the sounds [b] and [v] seem to occur in different parts of the word. If this conjecture is tabulated, the following results appear: Of the five occurrences of [b], all five occur in the first position, whereas of all five occurrences of [v], none occur in the first position and all five occur in middle positions. On the basis of this corpus (sample) of words it is possible to conclude that [b] and [v] do

---

* In ordinary notation the phonemes of a language are denoted by a letter enclosed in slash marks, /b/, whereas phonetic transcriptions are denoted by brackets [b].

not occur in the same position in the word. In a sense, their occurrences complement each other; that is, where one sound occurs the other does not. This pattern of occurrence is called *complementary distribution*, and is used as one condition serving to assign two sounds to the same class. On the basis of this analysis both [b] and [v] are considered allophonic variations of the /b/ phoneme.

But how did we come to consider the distribution of [b] and [v] in the first place—why, for example, didn't we compare the distributions of [b] and [a] or [b] and [S]? The reason [b] and [v] were chosen is fairly obvious: Considered as sounds, both [b] and [v] are similar in terms of their articulatory properties. *Articulatory similarity* is then a good way in which to begin the search for phonemes, but it alone never defines the properties of a phoneme. For example, the sounds [p] and [b] are actually more alike in terms of articulation than [b] and [v], yet they are not allophones of the /b/ phoneme—this can be shown by considering a few words having a [p] sound in them: [pe̯ro], *but*; [pe̯ro], *dog*; [pipa], *pipe*; [ponde̯rosa], *heavy*; and [poŋgo], *I put*.

Let us begin by assuming a position preference as distinguishing between [p] and [b]; but an examination of [p] and [b] words immediately dispels this hypothesis, for both sounds do occur in an initial position. A more complicated hypothesis is that the vowel sound following [b] and [p] leads to the difference. When the data are tabulated here, both [b] and [p] occur before [e], before [a] and before [o]; therefore no hypothesis based on the subsequent vowel sound is tenable. If we take the alternative hypothesis, namely that [p] and [b] are in complementary distribution with respect to their following consonant, we find that both are followed by [r̄]. On this, and other more complicated hypotheses, the test for *complementary distribution* fails and we are led to the conclusion that [b] and [p] are not allophones of the same phoneme, but define different phonemes.

The important aspect of this [b]–[p] analysis is that although [p] and [b] are acoustically more similar than [b] and [v], they are not in complementary distribution and therefore cannot be considered as allophones of the same /b/ phoneme. For the definition of a phoneme both criteria, *acoustic similarity* and *complementary distribution*, are required. One is not defining without the other.

So far, phonemes have been defined by similarity, but as we have seen, similarity is not always critical to the definition of a phoneme. One quick way in which to search for different phonemes involves the techniques of *minimal pairs*. In this technique, all the sounds in a pair of words are kept constant with the exception of one. So, for example, minimal pairs used to distinguish between [m] and [n] might be *moon* and *noon* and *mine* and *mime*. In this case, examples were chosen so that the minimal contrast would occur in both the initial and final positions.

In order to make a complete inventory of the phonemes of a language, it is generally more helpful to use more than pairs of words. For the class of consonant sounds, sets of words are often used to define consonant phonemes. As a starting point, Gleason (1961) presents the following set of 17 "ill" words, all of which differ with respect to a single sound.

| pill | paul | pet | ville | | vet |
|------|------|-----|-------|--|-----|
| bill | ball | bet | sill | saul | set |
| till | tall | | hill | haul or hall | |
| dill | | debt | mill | maul or mall | met |
| chill | | chet | nil | | net |
| jill | | jet | rill | | |
| kill | call | | Lil | | let |
| gill | gaul | get | will | wall | wet |
| fill | fall | | | | yet |

On this basis each of the 17 initial sounds can be taken to define an English consonant phoneme. In order to discover the list of phonemes characteristic of a language, it is necessary to produce other sets of minimal pairs and coordinate these with the "ill" set presented above. For this purpose, consider the "all" set and the "et" presented in combination with the "ill" set. All the "all" items confirm the existence of 10 of the 17 "ill" initial phonemes, while 12 of the "et" set agree with 14 of the "ill" set and 6 of the "all" set. The "et" set, however, provides a possible new phoneme in the initial sound of *yet*. Although this example does not establish the existence of the /y/ phoneme as independent of /r/, a different minimal pair such as *rung* and *young* delimits the phonemic independence of /r/ and /y/.

This discussion has been somewhat abstract, and to see what it is all about in a concrete case, consider the following anecdotal study of a child learning to pronounce the two English phonemes /t/ and /k/. Four words in the child's vocabulary caused most of the difficulty: *Kate, Tate, take* and *cake*. For this child both [t] and [k] were mutually substitutable, so that any of these words could and were pronounced alike, e.g., *cake* was pronounced as /teyt/, /keyt/, /teyk/, and even sometimes (although rarely) as /keyk/. For this child, both [t] and [k] were allophonic variations of a single phoneme that could be denoted /K̄/. The existence of /K̄/ is best indicated by the fact that either [t] or [k] was accepted as the same sound, and that *take* and *cake*, instead of defining a minimal pair, were considered as acceptable variations of the same word. For this child, the sentence *Take cake to Kate Tate* came out sounding like Osgood's *Light lights lightly light light lights*; no word was different from any other in terms of pronunciation.

## The Phoneme as Concept

Since linguistic analysis views the phoneme as an abstraction (or a concept) rather than as strictly observable, it seems natural to seek a further description of the phoneme in terms of defining attributes. This approach follows closely the usual strategy used in talking about concepts of any sort, namely, that a concept be defined in terms of its pattern over a set of attributes. In the case of the phoneme considered as concept, there are a number of different factors that could serve as these attributes, with the two most likely being the articulatory process used to produce a sound, or alternatively the acoustic properties of the sound as produced. Many textbooks (Gleason, 1961; Hall, 1964, etc.) attempt to describe phonemes in terms of articulatory process. For example, it is well known that English vowel sounds are produced by variations in the size and shape of the various cavities through which the stream of breath passes while consonants, on the other hand, are produced by blocking the air stream by various structures in the mouth such as the lips, or teeth.

The most highly developed attempt to describe phonemes in terms of distinctive attributes or features uses essentially a combination of acoustic and articulatory processes, although we must be careful to realize that such attributes are, in most cases, as abstract as the phonemes they serve to define. Although distinctive features appear in acoustic and articulatory properties, their justification ultimately rests on their theoretical role in the total phonological system.

A distinctive-feature approach to the phoneme (such as the one developed by Jakobson, Fant, and Halle (1952), proposes that English phonemes can be characterized in terms of a set of some nine distinctive features. A list of these features is presented in Table 14.1.

The table has a key to help in the pronunciation of each of the phonemes listed, and for a better definition of what is meant, it is probably best to actually make the sounds presented as examples. Thus Feature 7, Tense/Lax, is found in consonant sounds such as /f/, /p/, /θ/, /t/, but absent in /v/, /b/ and /d/. If these two sets are said aloud, and /f/ is contrasted with /v/, and /p/ with /b/, and so on, it should be clear that the first sound of each pair does not require voicing for its production, whereas the second set does.

One of the more important aspects of this table of distinctive features is apparent in the first two lines: All the vowels (o–i) are positive (+) on Feature 1 and negative (−) on Feature 2, whereas all but two of the consonants are negative (−) on Feature 1 and positive (+) on Feature 2. Since this table is too large to be considered all at once, let us consider instead only a fragment of the total table. For this purpose the sounds /f/, /p/, /v/, /b/, /θ/, /t/, /th or ð/ and /d/, will prove most helpful. From an examination of Table 14.1, we can see that these eight sounds all have identical values on

**Table 14.1**  Distinctive-features pattern of English phonemes as proposed by Jakobson, Fant, and Halle. From Neisser, 1966; adapted previously from Lindgren, 1965.

| | o | a | e | u | ə | i | l | ŋ | ʃ | ʃ̂ | k | ʒ | ʒ̂ | g | m | f | p | v | b | n | s | θ | t | z | ð | d | h | # |
|---|---|---|---|---|---|---|---|---|---|---|---|---|---|---|---|---|---|---|---|---|---|---|---|---|---|---|---|---|
| 1. Vocalic/nonvocalic | + | + | + | + | + | + | + | − | − | − | − | − | − | − | − | − | − | − | − | − | − | − | − | − | − | − | − | − |
| 2. Consonantal/nonconsonantal | − | − | − | − | − | − | + | + | + | + | + | + | + | + | + | + | + | + | + | + | + | + | + | + | + | + | − | − |
| 3. Compact/diffuse | − | + | + | − | − | − | − | + | + | + | + | + | + | + | − | − | − | − | − | − | − | − | − | − | − | − | | |
| 4. Grave/acute | + | + | − | + | − | − | − | + | − | − | + | − | − | + | + | + | + | + | + | − | − | − | − | − | − | − | | |
| 5. Flat/plain | + | − | | + | − | | | | | | | | | | | | | | | | | | | | | | | |
| 6. Nasal/oral | | | | | | | | + | | | | | | | + | | | | | + | | | | | | | | |
| 7. Tense/lax | | | | | | | | | + | + | + | − | − | − | | + | + | − | − | | + | + | + | − | − | − | + | |
| 8. Continuant/interrupted | | | | | | | + | − | + | − | − | + | − | − | − | + | − | + | − | − | + | + | − | + | + | − | + | |
| 9. Strident | | | | | | | | | + | + | | + | + | | | + | | + | | | + | − | | + | − | | | |

Key to phonemic transcription: /o/—pot, /a/—pat, /e/—pet, /u/—put, /ə/—putt, /i/—pit, /l/—lull, /ŋ/—lung, /ʃ/—ship, /ʃ̂/—chip, /k/—kip, /ʒ/—azure, /ʒ̂/—juice, /g/—goose, /m/—mill, /f/—fill, /p/—pill, /v/—vim, /b/—bill, /n/—nil, /s/—sill, /θ/—thill, /t/—till, /z/—zip, /ð/—this, /d/—dill, /h/—hill, /#/—lll.

Features 1, 2, 3, 5, and 6, and that Feature 9 is irrelevant for defining /f/, /p/, /v/, and /b/. On the basis of this information we can now prepare a new table, Table 14.2, which considers only Features 4, 7, and 8.

**Table 14.2**  Reduced table of distinctive features for eight selected English sounds

| Feature | Sound | | | | | | | |
|---|---|---|---|---|---|---|---|---|
|  | f | p | v | b | $\theta$ | t | ð | d |
| 4 | + | + | + | + | − | − | − | − |
| 7 | + | + | − | − | + | + | − | − |
| 8 | + | − | + | − | + | − | + | − |

Even a superficial glance at this table indicates a remarkably symmetrical pattern, a pattern that progressively divides these eight sounds into three groups of four each, e.g., Feature 4 separates /f/, /p/, /v/, /b/ into one group and /θ/, /t/, /ð/, and /d/ into a second group; whereas Feature 7 places /f/, /p/, /θ/ and /t/ in one group and /v/, /b/, /ð/ and /d/ into a second group, and so on for Feature 8. These partitions end up by producing a unique pattern for each sound. Thus /f/ is defined as (+, +, +), whereas /d/ is defined as (−, −, −).

Given this unique pattern for each sound, it is tempting to describe the difference between any two sounds in terms of the number of features they have in common. In the case of /f/ and /d/, there are no features in common, whereas /f/ and /p/ [/f/ = (+ + +) and /p/ = (+ + −)] have two features in common. One obvious hypothesis that emerges from an analysis of this sort is that under less than optimum listening conditions, a subject will be more likely to confuse /f/ with /p/ than with /d/. Generalizing this expectation a bit implies that phonemes sharing two distinctive features will be confused with each other more often than phonemes having only one feature in common. This, in turn, implies that phonemes having only a single feature in common will be confused more often than phonemes having no features in common.

Miller and Nicely (1955) have actually carried out such a test. In their experiment, highly trained subjects were presented with one of 16 phonemes (eight being the particular phonemes described above), and asked to make a judgment as to which of the 16 they had heard. What this means is that if the phoneme /f/ were presented, the subject was asked to try to identify it. Under certain conditions—where these phonemes were played against a background of noise—subjects often made errors. A detailed examination of these errors showed that subjects often confused phonemes that differed only in terms of a single distinctive feature (that is, /f/ and /θ/, /p/ and /t/,

/v/ and /ð/, etc.), and only rarely confused phonemes having no features in common (/f/ and /d/, /p/ and /ð/, /v/ and /t/, etc.). Such a result provides good support for Jakobson's hypothesis, at least insofar as auditory confusions are concerned.

In a previous chapter (Chapter 11), results of a number of experiments showed that many errors in short-term memory seemed to involve acoustic confusions (e.g., see work by Conrad, 1964, and Wickelgren, 1965, 1966, etc.), and it seems reasonable to ask how well a distinctive-features analysis describes these results. Murdoch (1967), who examined the effect of distinctive features on memory confusions, has found that such an analysis also predicts intrusion errors in short-term recall quite well. Specifically, he found only a small number of recall confusions between letters having a few distinctive features in common as compared to many recall confusions for letters having a great many features in common.

But what about a more detailed analysis of confusion errors in recall? Here we must turn to results presented by Wickelgren (1966) which provide recall confusions for the same pairs of sounds tested by Miller and Nicely. In general, Miller and Nicely's results showed that Feature 7 led to fewer auditory confusions than Feature 4. If, however, we look at Wickelgren's data dealing with recall intrusions for pairs of sounds, we find that pairs separated by Feature 7 produced a total of 230 confusions in recall, while pairs separated by Feature 4 produced only 168 confusions in recall. On the basis of these results we can see that subjects are less likely to confuse sounds in recall when these sounds differ in Feature 4 than in Feature 7, and that the reverse is true for auditory recognition errors.

If we look again at what distinction is captured by Features 7 and 4, we note that 7 involves "voicing," whereas 4 involves a tonal quality of sound related to the place in the mouth at which the sound is produced. It seems that when the stimulus is physically present, voicing provides for fine discriminations, while in the case in which the subject does not say the phoneme aloud but simply says it "inside his head," Feature 4 is more important. In terms of the distinction captured by each of these features, Feature 7 seems to describe one primarily based on acoustic properties, while Feature 4 seems to describe one primarily based on articulatory properties. If this is true, then it is not too surprising to find that Feature 7 is more discriminating in perceptual tasks and Feature 4 is more discriminating in "internally produced" sounds such as occur in a recall task.

## Morphemics

In just the same way that a linguist seeks to define a minimal sound unit for a language (its phonemes), so too would he like to define a minimal unit of meaning. These minimal units of meaning or minimal units of grammatical structure (see Lyons, 1968) are called *morphemes*, although their explicit definition is nowhere near as precise as that used in the definition of phonemes.

If it were not for the existence of morphemes, or minimal units of meaning, vocabulary acquisition would be beyond the ken of most adult speakers. A short look at any standard dictionary gives some indication of the magnitude of learning required. To be sure, most speakers do not know all or even most of the words in a dictionary, but just as surely they do know at least as many as 5000 words, with estimates running as high as 50 to 100,000 different items for college-aged speakers (see Miller's 1951 discussion of this problem, pages 148–150). Even at its lower limit, there is still a lot to be learned.

Some factors which serve to reduce the size of this job are suggested by Fig. 14.2. This figure presents a set of words, all related, in one way or another, to the nuclear unit, *act*. Such a nuclear unit is usually called a *base*. Generally speaking, a base is a relatively independent minimal unit of meaning (i.e., a morpheme) which when combined with *prefixes* and *suffixes* (jointly called *affixes*) forms different words in the language.

**Fig. 14.2** Vocabulary growth on the basis of morphemic changes. (From King, 1967)

One thing that is apparent from this type of chart, and indeed from morphemic analysis in general, is that words have structure and that the linguist's job must be to develop a method capable of representing this fact. Consider the word *reenactment*. One way in which to diagram the structure of this word is to break it up (segment it) by means of dashes: so *reenactment* becomes *re–en–act–ment*. But this method of diagramming makes it appear as if all elements were of equal value and that all have the same meaning-giving function. Intuitively, a more satisfactory diagram would have to indicate that a word at one level is a single entity, yet at other levels, it contains components that are more closely interrelated than others; for example [[*re* + [*en* + *act*]]*ment*]. Such segmentation indicates that the primary or core element is [*en* + *act*] and that the order of attaching other elements is *re* + *enact*, and then *re-enact* + *ment*.

But we have already noted in the context of sentence structure that tree diagrams provide a very useful technique for describing the priority of unit formations, as well as the overall integrity of a particular collection of units. In terms of a tree diagram, reenactment could be represented best as:

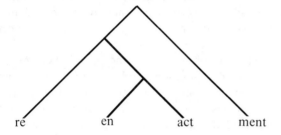

re      en      act      ment

This method of diagramming agrees with our intuitive feeling as to how this word has been built up (i.e., with a description of its significant morphemes) and with our more general analysis of the levels problem as discussed previously.

But not all suffixes have the same function. For example, the change from *active* to *actively* is given by the suffix *ly*. From our knowledge of English, this suffix informs us that *actively* will be used in a sentence so as to tell us something about (i.e., to modify) a verb, as in the sentence: "He supported the motion actively." In the case of an *ly* ending, we can also usually tell that a particular adverb was probably derived from an adjective. For example, *slow* → *slowly*; *inactive* → *inactively*; *rapid* → *rapidly*, etc. Such a suffix, which helps to describe the route by which one word was derived from another, is called a *derivational suffix*. If we reexamine the structure of the word *reenactment*, the last component, *ment*, meets the criterion of a derivational morpheme. In general *ment* is used in English to imply a state of something or other, such as in the words *enjoyment* (the state of enjoying) or *recruitment* (the state of being recruited), etc.

Derivational endings obviously lessen the amount of learning required in building up a vocabulary. For example, if an adult speaker's vocabulary consists of say 15,000 words, many of these elements are probably the result of derivational endings. All that really has to be learned is a base morpheme and the rules of use and meaning for derivational suffixes.

A complete description of derivational endings is beyond the scope of the present discussion. A few further examples should, however, make the concept a bit clearer. For example, the suffix, *tion* (pronounced /shun/) as used in such words as *addition, construction, flirtation*, etc., implies a derivation from verb to noun, whereas *ize*, as in *specialize, finalize, italicize*, etc., implies an adjective-to-verb derivation. There are many such derivational morphemes in English, and, as is obvious, these provide a relatively small base vocabulary with a good deal of growing room.

Suffixes such as *tion* and *ize* often necessitate a phonological change in the base morpheme. For example, the pronunciation of *-ure* (as in *behavior* or *failure*) is often altered or conditioned by the final phoneme of the base. After a /t/ sound, *ure* /yar/ becomes /char/ as in *departchar*, whereas after a /z/ sound as in seize it changes to /zhar/ (*seizhar*). Similar phonetic changes produced by /d/ (*proceed → procyjar*) and /s/ (*press → preshar*) also occur in connection with the *ure* morpheme.

These examples indicate that the phonemic and morphemic elements of a language often interact, and in combination produce highly regular and predictable changes. Changes in pronunciation that are induced by, or correlated with, morpheme changes are called *morpho-phonemic* for obvious reasons. Generally speaking, small changes as occur in a single morpheme (such as the *ure* morpheme), are considered to represent phonemically determined changes on a single morpheme. This means that [ure] defines a family of morphemes (yar, shar, char, shar, . . . etc.) all of which are pronounced in a slightly different way depending on the phonemic properties of the base. The elements of such a family are called *allomorphs* (by analogy to allophones in the sound system of the language), with the entire family usually symbolized by a single symbol such as [ure]. The use of such a symbol implies that the morpheme will have different pronunciations according to its specific base element.

If we return again to the Morpheme Family [Act] presented in Fig. 14.2, there is still more to be said. It is possible to add the letter s to each of the following three words: *action, act* and *actress*. When this is done, each of these words is changed in the same way; each now refers to more than one *action, act,* or *actress*. The letter s in this case has the force (meaning) of changing certain words from singular to plural and for this reason is called a *pluralizing morpheme*, and is denoted as $[Z_1]$. The main reason for using the letter Z as a symbol for this particular morpheme has to do with certain morpho-phonemic changes conditioned by the sound preceding [Z]. Returning to *acts, actions* and *actresses*, it is clear that $[Act] + [Z] = actz$ whereas $[action] + [Z] = actions$ and $[actress] + [Z] = actresses$. In some cases the $[Z_1]$ morpheme is realized as a /z/, in others as a /iz/ or /ez/, while in still other cases as /s/. In some few rarer cases the entire word is changed: $[man] + [Z_1] \rightarrow men$; $[tooth] + [Z_1] = [teeth]$. In still other cases, the plural is pronounced as $[en]$; for example, $[ox] + [Z_1] = [oxen]$. Considered linguistically, all these different phonemic patterns represent allomorphic variations on a single morpheme, variations that are phonemically determined in some cases but not in others.

All of this might explain the use of the $Z$, but why $[Z_1]$? Largely because there is still another $Z$ morpheme, which when attached to base morphemes significantly changes their meaning. To take an example already used: the $s$ in *acts*, when *act* is considered a verb, indicates the third person singular. It occurs in other places as, "it *occurs*," or "he *acts*," etc. This use of the $Z$ morpheme (as an indication of third person singular) is symbolized $[Z_2]$ and is to be understood as changing the meaning of the word; or at least of specifying it to a greater degree.

There are other suffixes in addition to $[Z_1]$ and $[Z_2]$ that also have broad generality. Among the more useful of these are: $[D_1]$ (*ed* indicating past tense), $[D_2]$ (*ed* indicating past participle), $[ing]$ (indicating present participle), $[er]$ (indicating comparative) and $[est]$ (indicating superlative). Without being overly specific about any of these five additional suffixes, the important point to note about them is their great generality. They serve to modify an extremely large number of bases. These seven suffixes are sufficiently important to constitute a separate class of morphemes called *inflectional suffixes*.

In addition to their range of usage, inflexional suffixes also have the following properties: (1) They do not change the part of speech of their base morpheme, i.e., *action* and *actions* are both nouns; (2) they may be added to words already containing a derivational suffix, i.e., *reenactment—reenactments*; and (3) they show a high degree of correlation between form and function, e.g., in most places where a plural noun occurs (as signaled by $[Z_1]$), almost any other plural noun can serve in its place without destroying the grammatical structure of the sentence.

Of these seven inflectional endings, four have to do with the class of morphemes usually called verbs. Anyone who has ever learned to speak a language other than English is painfully aware of tables of declension. The ability of such declensions to increase the size of an adult speaker's vocabulary is probably nowhere better illustrated than in Hebrew. In modern Hebrew, which is a highly inflected language, most verbs are composed of three major phonemes. When these three phonemes are combined with a variety of prefixes, suffixes, and infixes (i.e., affixes that break into the base morpheme), not only do they give an indication of *who* (*I*, *you*, *he*, *she*, etc.) *is* (*was* or *will be*) doing *what* to *whom* (*him*, *her*, etc.), they also can change the meaning of the root verb in predictable ways. For example, /K/ /t/ /V/

are the root phonemes of a form usually translated as "to write." By appropriate substitutions, [$K$ o $t$ ay $v$], it can mean "I am writing," "I will write," "I wrote," and so on.

As in English, these various affixes are used to define tense. So far so good. Hebrew, unlike English, has certain other characteristic verb constructions which are capable not only of reflecting person and tense, but can also change the meaning of the base, [ktv], significantly. One such verb construction is called the *intensive*. This construction serves to intensify the action of a particular verb; thus *write* becomes *inscribe* when inflected in this construction. Similarly there are constructions such as the *reflexive* which change "write" to "write oneself a note" (i.e., "to memorandize") and the *causative* which change "write" to "cause someone else to write" or "to dictate." Although there are further verb constructions (essentially concerned with passive descriptions), the point has already been made: These constructions strongly supplement an original vocabulary in ways that are easily and regularly predictable.

So far, English vocabulary seems to grow primarily on the basis of derivational and inflectional suffixes. There is still one further way in which an increase in vocabulary power can occur, and this is by means of *compounding*. For example, *houseboat*, *teamwork*, *newspaper*, *skyscraper*, etc., all represent words constructed from two distinctly different words. Often these new words arise as a consequence of new things coming into existence that demand a new term.

In French, for example, the word for *skyscraper* is *gratte-ciel*, which literally means "scrapes the sky." In this instance obviously both skyscrapers and the word *skyscraper* occurred first in a different language community— English—and both the object and then the word were exported intact. Such new forms constructed from two already existing words are called *compounds*, and represent another way in which new elements come into a language. It should be noted that in languages such as German compounding is a regular and frequent part of standard usage.

So far, we have used two terms rather casually in this discussion of morphology: *morpheme* and *word*. As is quite obvious, the two are not identical (as the discussion of affixes indicates), yet a clear distinction between the two is difficult to come by. Similarly, no consistent distinction has been made between a *syllable* and a *morpheme*. This latter distinction is relatively easy to make if either definition of morpheme is considered seriously: that it is (1) a minimal unit of grammatical structure (Lyons, 1968); or (2) a minimal unit of meaning (Gleason, 1961). In either case, a form such as *mahogany* or *Connecticut* contains more than a single syllable, while forms such as [$Z_1$], [$Z_2$], [$D_1$], and [$D_2$] often contain only a single syllable. The size of a morpheme in English usually varies from 1–6 syllables, with most morphemes falling toward the smaller values.

Although the distinction between a *word* and a *morpheme* is intuitively apparent (*ly* is a morpheme and not a word; whereas *reenactments* is a word containing five different morphemes), it is quite difficult to describe this difference abstractly. Part of this has to do with our well-learned habits of reading; we are used to seeing certain strings of letters bounded on both sides by a space. Although this is not true of all orthography (i.e., classical Hebrew contained in parchment scrolls does not have spaces between words), it is sufficiently true to make it appear that "words" don't really need to be defined at all.

But the ability to understand a request such as "Say that to me word by word" is characteristic not only of languages having a written form but also of those that do not. Lyons (1968) in his discussion of this problem notes that speakers of languages not having an alphabet can also comply with this type of request. In other tasks preorthographic peoples are also able to isolate "words" in spoken discourse, again indicating the psychological reality of a word even if its unambiguous definition escapes the linguist and the psychologist.

How then shall a word be defined? One definition is based on the idea of a "potential pause"—that is, a word can be defined as any part of a sentence at which it is possible to pause. This definition is analogous to defining words by spaces in orthography. Unfortunately, spaces occur between all words in their written form, but the distribution of pauses (see Goldman-Eisler's work, pages 341 ff) in spontaneous and continuous speech is often uncorrelated even with word borders. While potential pausing could serve as a methodological procedure, it does not seem adequate as an abstract definition.

Another approach involves the semantic definition of a word. For this type of approach a word is defined in terms of a particular complex of sounds, having a particular meaning, which is capable of functioning as a single unit in a particular grammatical usage. Even granting that it is possible to define each of these three criteria precisely, a comparison of *unacceptable* with *not acceptable* indicates that both meet all three requirements, yet *unacceptable* is usually considered a single word, whereas *not acceptable* is clearly two words. On the basis of this example alone, the semantic definition just won't do.

Perhaps the most satisfactory approach is provided by Lyons (1968) who analyzes the following sentence:

(a) *The – boy – s – walk – ed – slow – ly – up – the – hill.*

  1    2    3    4    5    6    7    8    9    10

If each of the numbers is taken to refer to a morpheme, it is possible to see that other orders will also produce acceptable sentences: (b) 6 7 1 2 3 4 5 8 9 10

(*Slowly the boys walked up the hill*), (c) 8 9 10 6 7 4 5 1 2 3 (*Up the hill, slowly walked the boys*). Although these sentences are not stylistic masterpieces, they do not violate our feeling of the grammatical.

Now for the definition of *word*. In terms of sentences (b) and (c), some of the morphemes seem to move around freely, while others always seem to remain together. So, for example, 3 then 2 (*s* then *boy* or *sboy*) is an impossible form; if 2 and 3 are to be moved around they must be moved around together. This observation provides the crux of Lyons' definitional procedure: "One of the characteristics of the word is that it tends to be internally stable (in terms of the order of the component morphemes), but positionally mobile (permutable with other words in the same sentence)." (Lyons, page 203). In order to follow the implications of this analysis, it now becomes necessary to examine a further property of grammar, namely that of syntax, or sentence structure.

## The Structure of Sentences

The May 6, 1968, issue of *Newsweek* devoted an entire section to a topic they called "New Peak for Newspeak." Essentially, it concerned the dangers involved in jargon and euphemisms. "As a forlorn slum-dweller in a Jules Feiffer cartoon put it: 'First I was poor. Then I became needy. Then I was underprivileged. Now, I'm disadvantaged. I still don't have a penny to my name—but I have a great vocabulary.' "

Of more direct relevance to the issue of sentences and making sentences is a game called the Systematic Buzz Phrase Projector developed by Philip Broughton, an official of the U.S. Public Health Service. Essentially it involves three columns of carefully chosen words, words which enable the user to sound knowledgeable on any technical topic. As Broughton says, "No one will have the remotest idea of what you're talking about, but the important thing is they're not about to admit it."

Table 14.3 presents Broughton's sure-fire, never miss, selection of 30 carefully selected words.

The procedure is simple: Think of any three-digit number and then select the appropriate buzzword from each column. For example, 5, 2, 4 turns out to be "responsive, motivated programming"—a perfectly plausible phrase if ever there was one.

The importance of the Broughton Effect is that it shows how it is possible to produce perfectly grammatical phrases by a simple linear chaining of words. If certain words in a language can be assigned to morphemic classes such as adjectives or nouns, etc., there seems to be some regular order capable of producing grammatical phrases and sentences. Unfortunately, unlike the situation that exists in English, order is not always the most important determiner of a meaningful phrase (as for example in German), and sometimes even within English, the meaning of a phrase is often unclear even if the order is perfectly regular. Here the sentence *They are cooking apples* is again relevant. The meaning of this sentence depends completely on how the speaker or listener understands the phrase *cooking apples*. More than simple linear order is involved in sentence structure.

**Table 14.3**  How to win at wordsmanship (from Broughton, 1968)

| Column 1 | Column 2 | Column 3 |
|---|---|---|
| 0. integrated | 0. management | 0. options |
| 1. total | 1. organizational | 1. flexibility |
| 2. systematized | 2. monitored | 2. capability |
| 3. parallel | 3. reciprocal | 3. mobility |
| 4. functional | 4. digital | 4. programming |
| 5. responsive | 5. logistical | 5. concept |
| 6. optional | 6. transitional | 6. time-phase |
| 7. synchronized | 7. incremental | 7. projection |
| 8. compatible | 8. third-generation | 8. hardware |
| 9. balanced | 9. policy | 9. contingency |

There seem to be three distinct ways to treat the grammar of a language, each somewhat more powerful than the one preceding it. At the lowest level is what might be called the pattern-production approach, in which a sentence can be described in terms of a specific pattern such as Article + Noun + Verb + Article + Noun for what is usually called a simple declarative sentence. The components of this pattern are not individual words or morphemes, but rather abstract grammatical classes sometimes called *parts of speech, form classes* or *morpheme classes*.

Given these form classes, a reasonable question is to ask how such classes are to be defined. Traditional grammar-school grammar used a combination of semantic and inflectional rules. Thus a noun is the name of a person, place or thing, whereas an adverb is "a word that modifies a verb," etc. The difficulties with this approach are reasonably obvious, and hinge largely on the ambiguous use of such terms as *thing* or *modifies* and so on.* Similarly, words refuse to stay forever put in a particular form class: *Table* can be construed either as a noun or a verb, with more than a single interpretation for each class.

How then, if not on the basis of meaning, can parts of speech be defined rigorously? One of the earliest attempts (Fries, 1952) tried to do this in terms of an analysis of form classes. The crucial concept for this type of approach is called *distributional analysis* and consists of an examination of the privileges

---

* For a critique of this view, as well as an excellent introduction to the analysis of English, see H. A. Gleason's book, *Linguistics and English Grammar* (New York: Holt, Rinehart and Winston, 1965). Indeed, much of the present discussion follows the outline presented in this book.

of substitution for words in what can best be called an empty-sentence technique. For example, the frame:

The ——————— was good.

allows only some words and not others. By using an appropriate set of frames, Fries was able to set up word classes based on this "substitution-in-frames technique." Although explicit definitions are not provided, some measure of differentiation between two classes is provided by contrasting pairs in each of the two classes; between *delivery* and *deliver, acceptance* and *accept*, and so on.

All classes, then, are defined by position within a sentence, and these classes must be derived from an inductive examination of a great many sentences. Unfortunately, this is not completely satisfactory, for many classes are open ended, and therefore it is impossible to produce a complete classification on the basis of a purely inductive approach. There are certain classes that can be completely specified (say pronouns), but many of the more interesting classes can be defined only in terms of positional equivalence and mutual substitutability. These must be described in terms of contrasts rather than in terms of absolute distinctions.

What sort of grammar is implied by these considerations—that is, how would such a grammar suggest sentences are produced? Here it is possible to describe the grammar of a language either at the level of the word or at the level of the form class. In both cases the resulting grammar is largely a probabilistic one. In the case of form classes, this implies that certain form classes are more likely to occur at the beginning of a sentence (article) and others at the end of a sentence (noun). Similarly, certain form classes are more likely to follow others, and so on. If we take a declarative sentence as an example, a simplified fragment of the grammar might look something as follows:

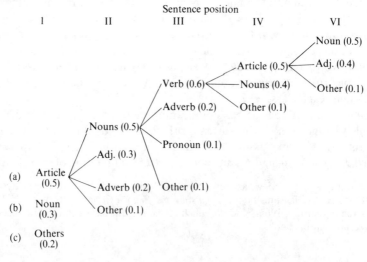

In this figure, parenthetical entries indicate the probability of choosing a particular form class after a specific choice has been made at an earlier stage. For example, the Noun (0.5) at Sentence Position II means that, given there is an article in Sentence Position I, the probability is 0.5 that a Noun will be chosen for Position II. Further, this figure indicates that the most likely sentence form is Article + Noun + Verb + Article + Noun— or the pattern of a simple declarative sentence.

Each sentence position generates a series of possibilities, each with its associated probability, and the production of an entire sentence is viewed as a left-to-right process controlled by the probabilities at each point. To be sure, this is only a fragment—a more complex pattern could be derived from a more extended analysis of the actual probabilities occurring over a sample of sentences.

Consideration of specific sentences makes it apparent that further constraints also operate at the word level. For example, the last word in the sentence, *The boy closed the* ———, is likely to come from a relatively small subset of all of the words in a person's vocabulary—words such as *door*, *window*, *drawer*, the things that are "closable by a boy." In terms of the model of grammar being considered, this indicates that word choice is determined not only by form class but also by content. For this type of analysis, selection of a word in a sentence is determined by some combination of all the events that precede the particular choice.

Technically, this model of a grammar is called a *finite-state grammar*. For this type of grammar, sentence production depends largely on the state the grammar is in at any position in time. Its "memory" is exhausted by its present state, and each momentary state poses a number of possible alternatives, each having an associated probability. Such a model seems reasonable because sentences, after all, do have a specifiable beginning and end state, as well as a number of specifiable states in between. To take a simple case, consider a finite-state grammar capable of producing the two sentences *The boys play* and *The boy plays*. This grammar can be represented by the present state and each momentary state poses a number of possible alterna- the grammar is in at any position in time. Its "memory" is exhausted by its following diagram.

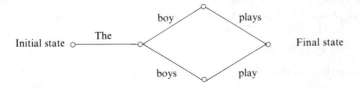

This grammar can be expanded by adding loops that need not be used in any sentence. For an example, see the top of the next page.

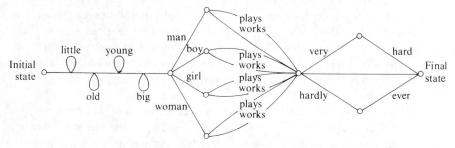

or by adding states and transitions that also need not necessarily be used:

This last diagram, which is quite a bit more complex than the two preceding ones, will produce a great many perfectly grammatical sentences and no ungrammatical ones. Unfortunately, for a finite-state grammar phrased either in terms of words or form classes the complexity of the underlying-process diagram increases staggeringly as the to-be-produced sentences become more complicated, or even just longer.

If this were the only problem with finite-state grammars it still wouldn't be so bad. Previously we have noted an even more serious problem in terms of sentences such as *They are cooking apples*, etc. The essence of this problem is that the same string of words (sentence) can be interpreted in two entirely different ways depending on how the string is structured. There is still one further problem with a finite-state grammar, and this has to do with how words are chosen to complete a given sentence. For example, in the sentence: *The plan which was thought up by the students is now complete*, there is no way for a probabilistic left-right model to account for the transition between *students* (plural) and *is* (singular). The verb *is* is appropriate only because it relates to *plan* rather than to *students*. The more general problem, then, is that there are many cases in language in which the choice of a particular word depends on words that occurred much earlier in the sentence, and that the only way to see this dependence is to recognize the syntactical structure of the sentence. In order to do this, we need to consider phrase-structure grammars which provide the wherewithal for accurate syntactical description.

*Immediate constituents and phrase-structure grammars.* The solution to the problem posed by *They are cooking apples* involved diagramming this sentence in two alternative ways. As we noted previously, two different tree diagrams easily capture this difference in intention. Considered from the standpoint of linguistic analysis, such diagrams present the *phrase structure* of the sentence or divide the sentence into its *immediate constituents*.

One further purpose for this type of division is to help discover which sentence or clause patterns occur regularly within a given language. Sometimes the discovery or description of these patterns helps to interpret ambiguous sentences, but this is not the main purpose of a phrase-structure grammar. Rather, its main purpose is to provide a description of a language that is capable of being used to develop a *generative grammar*. Now *generate* is an extremely tricky concept to get hold of: *generate* often seems to imply that a man or machine should be able to use the so-called rules of a language to generate (create) any given sentence. Actually, the reverse is true: A generative grammar must allow for the description rather than the creation of any and all sentences actually or potentially produced by a fluent speaker. A generative grammar is one that serves *to define* a given sequence of words as a sentence in that grammar. As Gleason put it, "A generative grammar does not generate one sentence now and another at another time. Rather it generates all the sentences it is capable of at all times." (Gleason, 1965, page 247) Such an analysis indicates that it is important not to confuse the problem of providing rules which will generate ("accept") word strings in the logical sense, with the problem of providing an algorithm which will generate ("produce") strings in the psychological sense. For the linguist, the "accept" sense is the more important of the two.

But some linguists, such as Victor Yngve, hope to use generative phrase-structure grammars for both purposes: as a descriptive logical device, and as an algorithm describing how the human subject produces sentences. In order to do this, he makes extensive use of the concept of a rewrite rule. In terms of simple declarative sentences, the instruction: $S \rightarrow NP + VP$ represents one example of a rewrite rule. This rule is usually read: "$S$ is to be rewritten as $NP$ plus $VP$." In his approach Yngve places one further restriction on the form of these rewrite rules: namely, that each rewrite rule involves only a single binary decision. On this basis no construction can be expanded into more than two other subconstructions at any given time.

Given this initial analysis, Yngve assumes that each sentence is produced by successively expanding constructions. This expansion continues until every construction is completely specified so that words occupy all final slots. Ordinarily, Phrase-Structure Grammars also contain a morpho-phonemic component which translates these word choices into phonological form, such as a speaker might do. Yngve does not proceed to this level of analysis simply because he is primarily interested in machine translation, in which specification at the level of the printed word is completely acceptable.

In order to give a feel for this type of analysis, Fig. 14.3 presents the constituents of a grammer sufficient for the first ten sentences of a child's book, *The Little Train*, by Lois Lenski.

(a)

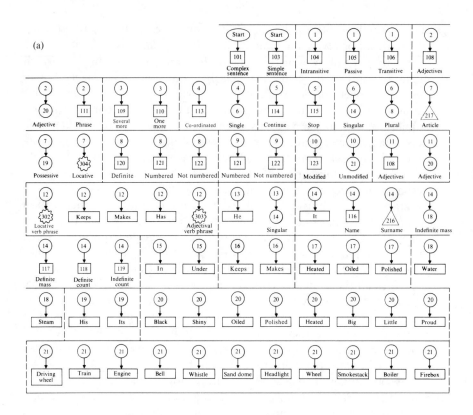

(b)

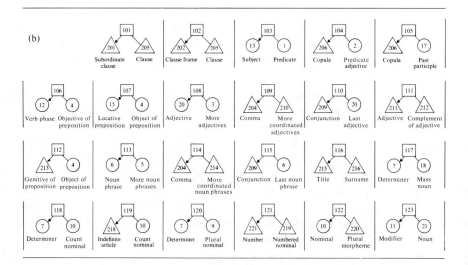

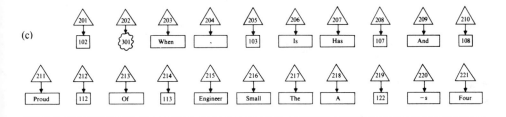

(c)

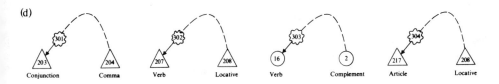

(d)

**Fig. 14.3** Simple grammar sufficient for the first ten sentences of a children's book. Each arbitrarily numbered shape is a potential node, controlling one step in the sentence-building process. Part (a) shows the nodes at which the computer can choose among several possibilities. Part (b), the constituents of various grammatical constructions. Part (c), the nodes at which the computer has only one choice. Part (d), discontinuous constructions. (From V. H. Yngve, "Computer Programs for Translation." Copyright © 1962 by Scientific American, Inc. All rights reserved.)

As an example of how the grammar presented in Figs. 14.3a–c works, consider the sentence *The steam makes it black*. The derivation of this sentence in terms of the grammar presented above would look like Fig. 14.4.

At Step 1, the sentence is the unit. Since the shape at this step is a circle, we are free to choose either square 101 or square 103, both of which represent different sentence types. Now the process is begun in earnest: Moving to section (b) of Yngve's grammar, 103 is expandable into two components (this is in accord with the binary decision made earlier), 13 and 1. This is presented as Step 3, which also presents the first level of phrase structure. Since sentence production proceeds in a left-to-right direction, 103 is expanded into 13 and 1, and the next step involves a further development of 13 into 14, 14 into 117, 117 into 7 and 7 into 217, at which time the terminal word *the* is finally produced. The production of *steam* is somewhat simpler, arising directly from 18.

After this expansion has occurred, the next choice involves the as-yet-unexpanded 1. Here further choices are carried out, with the final result presented as Step 9. If we disregard all the intervening numbers (which are really instructions for the computer) the final structure is very similar to one that would arise from a more traditional Immediate Constituents analysis, with the major partitions at (*The steam*) (*makes it*) (*black*).

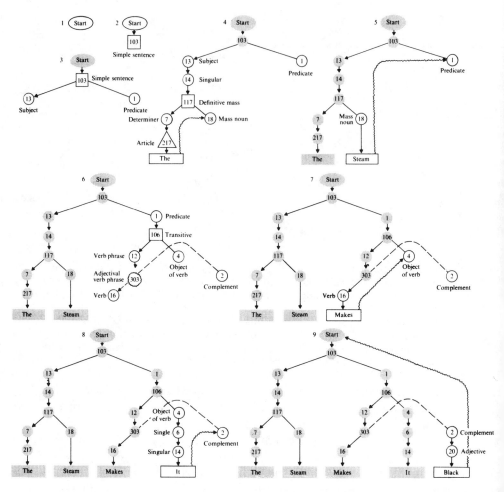

**Fig. 14.4** The computer constructs a sentence by working its way from node to node, as shown in the numbered sequence of steps. There is always a "current node" which controls the next step. You can follow the computer's procedure by noting the shape and number of the current node, referring to that node in the proper part of Fig. 14.3, and choosing the corresponding lower node, which becomes the new current node. If the node is a circle, a choice is available; the machine makes this choice at random. If the node is a triangle, only one choice is provided. If the node is a square, the lower left-hand node under it becomes the new current node and the one at the right a "remembered node." If the node has a wavy line around it, the procedure is the same, except that the remembered node must be delayed until later in the sentence. Each word in a rectangle is a word in the sentence; after it is in place, the next current node is found by moving up and to the right (wavy lines) until the next remembered node is encountered, or back to START to begin a new sentence. (From V. H. Yngve, "Computer Programs for Translation." Copyright © 1962 by Scientific American, Inc. All rights reserved.)

There are a number of significant implications of a model of this sort, and these are worth noting. Some of the rewrite rules (those in square boxes) involve transfer of controls; others (those set in circles) provide the grammar with a choice of next step; while still others require memory (those surrounded by wavy lines) or provide only a single choice (those set in triangles).

One problem that Yngve has noted in his attempt to work out the details of this procedure concerns a general problem occasionally found in immediate-constituents analysis, the problem of discontinuous constituents. For example, *called up* can be considered a single constituent. In its usual use, such as in the context of the sentence *He called the girl up*, the component words are separated; in other words the constituents are discontinuous. In traditional phrase-structure grammar, such constructions were noted but not handled in any systematic way. As we will later see, discontinuous constituents are much better handled by transformational grammars, or grammars having greater generality than the phrase-structure grammars presently under consideration. Yngve's handling of discontinuous constituents is shown in part (d) of this original grammar. For the specific example presented in Fig. 14.3, *it* comes between *makes* and *black* and this discontinuity is handled by Rules 301–304, which skip the intervening words or phrases.

The description of sentence production as dependent on a successive expansion of subconstructions has certain important implications for memory. For one thing, Yngve distinguishes between two types of sentences, those that require a good deal of memory and those that do not. The phrase: *very much more clearly projected pictures of Rome* (Carroll, 1964) requires a very heavy memory load, as indicated by its immediate-constituents diagram (see Fig. 14.5).

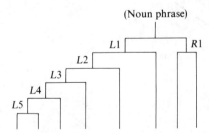

Very much more clearly projected pictures of Rome

**Fig. 14.5** Immediate-constituents analysis for the sentence fragment: very much more clearly projected pictures of Rome. (From Carroll, 1964.)

According to Yngve's rules, all left-hand words have to be remembered before the entire phrase can be produced. This property of left-branching sentences (so-called because their tree "branches" to the left) is termed the depth of a sentence, and gives an estimate of the memory load. The sentence presented above has a depth of five and is considered to place fairly strong demands on short-term memory.

Since short-term memory is limited, language structure must provide ways around these limitations. In order to meet these limitations, many languages, English included, "prefer" right-branching sentences to left-branching ones. For example, the nonsentence *What what what he wanted cost in New York would buy in Germany was amazing* can be made understandable by changing its structure to *We were amazed by what could be bought in Germany, for the cost in New York, of what he wanted.* Not brilliant syntax, but certainly more understandable.

Another device used to get around right-branching sentences is to postpone a long phrase on the right-hand side of the sentence. For example: *He gave her the candy he got in New York while visiting his parents between Christmas and New Year's* is easer to understand than *He gave the candy he got in New York while visiting his parents between Christmas and New Year's to her.* Similarly, many grammatical constructions, such as passives, also help to reduce memory load considerably.

One further psychological problem illustrated by Phrase-Structure Grammars has to do with the locus of control in sequencing overt speech. In the case of a Finite-State Grammar described earlier, each preceding word serves in part to control each succeeding word. This means that a sentence is considered a chain, something on the order of $A \rightarrow B \rightarrow C \rightarrow$ etc. A hierarchical model of the Phrase-Structure variety assumes that $B$ follows $A$ not necessarily because there is any immediate connection between the two, but because both are produced at a "higher" level.

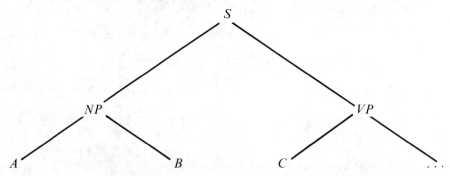

Similarly, the general flow of words in a sentence, $A, B, C, \ldots$ is not a consequence of any specific $A$ to $B$ or $B$ to $C$ or $C$ to $\ldots$ connection, but rather the result of hypothetical mechanisms which allow for sentence production all at one shot. For such a view, the sequencing of words is not controlled by word-to-word linkages, but rather by some more central process capable of producing extremely well-coordinated word strings. For this type of description, it makes sense to deal with grammar independent of meaning, for the skill involved in producing a sequential string of words is independent of the constituent words. A sentence can be a melody without words.

*Transformational grammars.*   The essential aspects of a Phrase-Structure Grammar involve three types of rules: *P*-rules, *L*-rules and *MP*-rules. The structure of any sentence can be defined in terms of rules for forming phrases (*P*), rules for making lexical choices (*L*), and rules for transforming the abstract strings so produced into phonetic patterns conforming to the morphology of a given language (*MP*). Transformational grammars add still another component, which is not surprisingly called the *transformational* or *T*-component of a grammar.

In order to get an intuitive feel for this additional grammatical component, consider the following set of sentences.

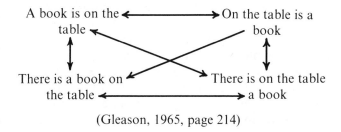

(Gleason, 1965, page 214)

Each of these sentences is related to each of the other sentences in an easily specifiable way. For example, going across the top and bottom lines, the change involves a reordering of the components *a book* and *the table*. If we let *A* = *a book* and *B* = *on the table*, the relationship can be expressed as *A is B* ↔ *B is A*. This indicates that not only are the two sentences related, but they are related in a very specific way having to do with word order.

This type of relationship, whereby one sentence can be transformed into another, is to be distinguished from sentence-to-sentence relationships analyzed in the context of Fries' empty-frames technique. These sentence-to-sentence relationships were specified in terms of direct substitution of words, where such substitutions were done in order to discover form classes. In the present case, pairs or quadruples (or more) of sentences are not related by word-to-word substitution, but rather by order of transformation.

Returning again to the four sentences presented above, there are still other transformations possible, and these can also be expressed quite easily. For example, going down the two sides of the figure, the sentences are related in the following way (again letting *A* = *a book* and *B* = *on the table*; *A is B* ⇔ There is *A*, *B*; and *B is A* ⇔ There is *B*, *A*. The cross-diagonal transformation, that is, *A book is on the table* ⇔ *There is on the table a book*, may be expressed as *A is B* ⇔ There is *BA*. This last expression is of further interest for it can be expressed more elegantly in terms of two successive transformations.

$$A \text{ is } B \Leftrightarrow \text{There is } B, A$$

or

(1) $AB \leftrightarrow BA$

$+$

(2) $[\ldots is \ldots] \leftrightarrow [There\ is \ldots, \ldots].$

Although this is a relatively simple example, there is really no need to be any more complex in order to describe the essential points of transformations. The important aspect of the $T$, or transformational, part of a grammar is that it specifies relationships among a number of different sentence types in ways that are not possible with any of the less-powerful methods described as Finite-State or Phrase-Structure Grammars.

Originally Chomsky (1957) took the occurrence of transformations as evidence for the view that generative grammars need be concerned with the production of a few simple or prototype sentence structures and subsequent transformations on these sentence structures. The best example of a prototype (or kernel sentence structure) is given by the simple declarative sentence consisting of an $NP$ and a $VP$. Given this view, linguistic ability involves the use of various transformations on kernel structures. The power of a grammar, however, is in its ability to transform these kernel structures into other sentence types.

The economy achieved by this approach is remarkable: Families of sentences are related by obvious links which can be described in terms of relatively simple transformational rules:

| | |
|---|---|
| *The boy hit a ball.* | *The boy didn't hit a ball.* |
| *The ball was hit by the boy.* | *The ball wasn't hit by the boy.* |
| *Who hit a ball?* | *Who didn't hit a ball?* |
| *What did the boy hit?* | |

and so on. On this basis the rules of the language are enormously reduced.

Transformations are important for other reasons as well. The need to develop a Phrase-Structure Grammar arose in order to handle "grammatical puns" (*Visiting relatives, . . .* etc.); that is, different phrase structures for sentences containing the same string of words. It is also clear that sentences may also have the same phrase structure and still be grammatically ambiguous. Here, consider Chomsky's sentence, *They were made by the machine*, which tells either *how* "they" were made (*by the machine*) or *where* "they" were made (*by the machine*). In both cases, the phrase structure of the surface sentence is identical. No tree diagram can capture this distinction—what seems to be needed is some understanding of the speaker's intention in uttering the sentence.

One way in which to examine a speaker's intention is to consider the transformational possibilities of the sentence. A paraphrase or transformation capable of interpreting the "how meaning" of the sentence would differ from a paraphrase capable of interpreting the "where meaning" of the sentence. In short, the *surface* structure of a sentence is not always a good guide to its underlying meaning structure, or what Chomsky has called the sentence's *deep structure.*

The more general point is perhaps better understood in terms of a few more specific examples. The following three sentences all present the same surface or tree structure (Chomsky, 1968): (1) I told John to leave, (2) I expected John to leave, (3) I persuaded John to leave.

If these sentences are all paraphrased in the same way, only Sentence 1 produces an acceptable sentence: (1) *What I told John was to leave* (Acceptable), (2) *What I expected John was to leave* (Unacceptable), (3) *What I persuaded John was to leave* (Unacceptable).

Further transformations are also possible that would serve to specify the points of difference between Sentences (2) and (3), but there is no reason to consider these in detail. What this example indicates most clearly is that identical surface structures do not necessarily imply identical deep structures. Transformational rules distinguish surface structures that are truly identical from those that are not.

Any overt speech production, then, involves three different components: a semantic component, a phonological component, and a syntactic component, each of which operates and interrelates deep and surface structure. This pattern of interrelationships can best be described in terms of Fig. 14.6.

As Fig. 14.6 indicates, the syntactic component is viewed as central largely because its output is operated on by the semantic and phonological components, but not *vice versa.* The syntactic component likewise is a generative system in the sense that each sentence is considered to be a theorem derived from a particular set of abstract rules.

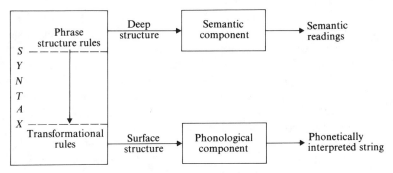

**Fig. 14.6** Components of a linguistic description. (From Garrett and Fodor, 1968)

The syntactical component of the grammar contains two further diversions, complete with their associated rule systems: a *base* component and a *transformational* component.   The base component consists of phrase-structure grammar and a dictionary.   The phrase-structure grammar, although similar in many respects to those considered previously, differs in one important respect: It never makes direct contact with words in the dictionary.   Instead it produces an abstract structure which is considered complete when the final level of its tree contains what Chomsky (1965) has called *dummy symbols* (*DS*) (that is, terminal symbols free of any specific word).   So, for example, a context-free, phrase-structure grammar might produce the following type of tree (where *DS* stands for Dummy Symbol):

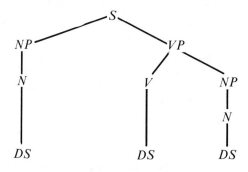

The base component also contains a "dictionary," which in addition to providing an ordinary "dictionary definition" also contains syntactic information.   This information determines the positions that a word can occupy in a sentence as well as rules which apply to phrases containing that word as it will ultimately appear in a "surface" sentence.   In this latter case, it might contain information such as "this is a transitive verb," with such information capable of specifying the ways in which this word can and cannot be used in a sentence.

On the basis of transformational rules, the transformational component of the syntax works largely on the structures generated by the base.   Usually such rules do things such as substitute, delete, or rearrange the elements provided.   For example, transformational rules would replace a Dummy Symbol with an appropriate word by taking into account the complete derivational history of a particular sentence.   In contrast to base operations, which are context free, transformations are always context dependent.   In addition, transformational rules do the routine operations required to rearrange sentences from one grammatical form to another; as, for example, from active → passive, and so on.   The ultimate destination of these derivations into sound form is then done by a special type of rule which fleshes out surface structure into a phonetically interpretable form—into the sounds of the sentence as produced.

To summarize and simplify the matter: A generative grammar is a system of rules relating sound patterns to meanings· Such a grammar has three components (syntactic, semantic, and phonological) and each has its own job. The syntactic component is responsible for both deep and surface structure. Deep structure ultimately provides information relevant to meaning and derivational history, whereas surface structure ultimately leads to a phonetic interpretation. Thus the primary component involved in relating sound to meaning is the syntactic one—all others are more directly related to the overt response.

If all this sounds abstract and deterministic—it should, for Chomsky and his coworkers are interested in providing an abstract and deterministic description of language systems: Abstract, because they would like it to describe all languages; and deterministic, because they would like it ultimately to run off like a mathematical system with nary a slip between linguistic intention and phonetic production.

This then completes a rather limited survey of grammar as described by linguistic analysis. In general, the problems discussed relate primarily to the structure of language and only incidentally to how human beings actually use language in speaking to one another. Before we can complete our preliminary discussion of language and language uses, we must move from this somewhat lofty and abstract level of analysis and get down down to the "nitty gritty" of language usage, and how she is spoke.

## SPEECH AS SHE IS SPOKE

The usual metaphors for speech imply that verbal output is a continuous *stream*; a skilled speaker is said to be *fluent* in his production of speech. We all have the feeling that if pauses occur in speech they are likely to be brief and highly regular; something on the order of spaces occurring between words in their written form. Actual records of spontaneous speech such as the one presented in Fig. 14.7 indicate that speech is neither regular nor continuous, but rather better described as episodic, composed of irregular "fits and starts." The continuity of speech is in the ear of the listener rather than on the tongue of the speaker.

Some of the facts gathered by Frieda Goldman-Eisler and her collaborators at the University of London (see Goldman-Eisler, 1964, 1968, for a review of this work) indicate how discontinuous the "verbal stream" actually is. For one thing, about half of all our speech time involves continuous phrases of fewer than three words, with only 10% involving phrases of ten words uttered continuously. Speech phrases are short, seldom exceeding five or six words at any one shot.

Considered from a different perspective, about 40–50% of all the time used in producing spontaneous speech involves pauses, with individual speakers pausing from a low of about 4% of their total speech time to a high of about 67%. Even highly skilled speakers—those who produce an overall value of less than 30% pauses—tend on occasion to balance pause and speech time equally. In spontaneous speech, the duration of these pauses varies between 0.5 and 0.8 second, with the vast majority (99%) usually less than 2 seconds. Only for the most difficult sorts of spontaneous speech, i.e., the speech of patients undergoing a psychiatric interview, do mean values fall at about 1.0 second duration.

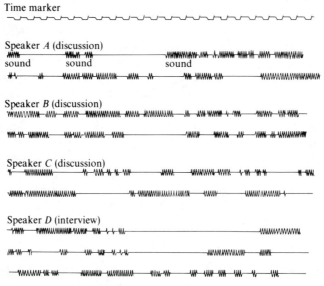

**Fig. 14.7** Graphic transformations of spontaneous speech by four speakers. Straight lines indicate periods of silence, while vertical lines represent periods of speech. Each line represents a period of 10 seconds. (From Goldman-Eisler, 1968)

But what about differences in speech rate—the number of words produced per unit time? Here too, the matter seems to depend on the proportion of time taken up by hesitation pauses: Variation in speech rate seems largely a matter of variation in pause time. In one study (Goldman-Eisler, 1956), for example, the correlation between speech rate and pauses equaled −0.94, indicating that speed of talking and the percentage of pauses in a given speech sample are inversely related. In this same analysis, articulation rate (how fast the speaker was able to produce sounds) was unrelated to speech rate.

All these results seem to indicate that the vocal properties of speech are subject to only slight variation, and that most of the variability which occurs in speech production is a consequence of the pauses that occur. If this is the case, it seems reasonable to ask where such pauses occur in the spontaneous flow of speech. Ideally, such pauses might be thought to help in communicating the meaning of an utterance. If this is the case, then we might expect pauses to be strongly correlated with the grammatical structure of the utterance—that is, pauses would occur at the end of phrases, or at the end of sentences, or at other "natural" grammatical points such as parenthetical remarks, or after "therefores," and so on. In the case of spontaneous speech, results (Goldman-Eisler, 1958; Henderson, Goldman-Eisler and Skarbek, 1966) indicate that only 55% of all pauses occur at these natural grammatical junctures, and that about 45% occur at nongrammatical points such as: *We have* (pause) *taken issue with them, and they are* (pause) *resolved. . . .* This distribution of pauses in spontaneous speech is to be compared with the case of reading from a prepared text, in which the overwhelming majority of pauses do take place at obvious "grammatical junctures." As Goldman-Eisler has noted: "What seems clear is that a large proportion of pauses in spontaneous speech does not fit in with linguistic structure and does not seem to serve communication; indeed, it may at times impede . . . (it)." (Goldman-Eisler, 1968, page 14)

If pauses do not serve communication ends, and if they make up about 45% of most utterances, how are they to be understood? The assumption usually made in this context is that speech consists of two component processes: one involving well-learned or well-integrated word sequences, and a second involving verbal planning such as word selection, syntactical construction, or comprehension of content.

In terms of word selection, some early studies are relevant. In these studies (Goldman-Eisler, 1958a; 1958b; 1958c) a comparison was made between words that were uttered fluently and those that were preceded by a pause. The general finding was that words preceded by a pause were much more difficult to guess than words uttered fluently. This conclusion, however, needs to be modified in terms of the guessing procedures used. In one case, a group of 15 subjects were presented with a group of sentences which had various words deleted from them and were asked to guess what words the person producing the sentence might have had in mind when he said the sentence. For this first group, guesses were always given in the left-to-right direction, that is, in the direction of the flow of speech. For a second group, guesses were always made in the right-to-left direction, or from the end of the sentence to the beginning.

One of the interesting results of both these analyses was that the same words *did not* turn out to be equally difficult in the forward and backward guessing directions. Some of the blanks that were easy (hard) to fill in in one direction were easy (or hard) in the opposite direction. There were relatively few words that were difficult to fill in in both directions. Of most importance for the present discussion was the finding that only those words difficult to guess in *both* directions were correlated with pauses in speech; neither strictly left–right nor right–left guesses predicted pauses on their own; only their joint probability was able to do so. To say it more meaningfully: Pauses are jointly affected both by what has been said before and by what is yet to be said.

In another experiment designed to test the relationship of word choice to pauses in previously recorded spontaneous speech, subjects were asked to read incomplete sentences aloud and to fill in the blanks as they read. Some of the blanks in these sentences were located at places at which the speaker had paused, while others were placed during periods of fluent speech. For some of the sentences, subjects were almost always able to fill in the missing words correctly, while for others they were usually unable to do so. Results indicated that subjects took longer to fill in the blanks for low-probability words than for high-probability words, but that delays in reading were proportional in length to original pauses only in those sentences in which the subject was able to fill in the blanks correctly. What this means is that only in those cases in which the reader was able to "conjecture the original speaker's intention" did he tend to pause in exactly the same place as the original speaker.

This seems to imply that pauses in the free flow of speech are correlated with difficulty of word choice, and more generally may be taken as an index of the degree of planful activity required in the production of a given sentence. In order to pursue this later hypothesis further, subjects in another experiment were presented with a series of cartoons and asked first to describe the content of the pictures and then to formulate the general point of the cartoons.

All subjects in this experiment were asked not only for an initial description and interpretation, but also to repeat their descriptions and interpretations six times so that the effects of repetition on pauses could be determined. Figure 14.8 presents these results for the first description and interpretation offered, as well as for all subsequent repetitions.

The important point about these results is the large difference in pausing between description and interpretation on the first attempt, and the rapid decrease in pauses for subsequent repetitions of the interpretation. This seems to indicate that pausing is related to—is an indicator of—the spontaneous act of producing novel information, and that once this production becomes automatic or habitual, the correlation between hesitation and information disappears.

This analysis of speech as she is spoke implies that pauses in spontaneous, creative speech are related both to the uncertainty of choosing a particular word and to the complexity of the idea embodied in that utterance. It seems natural enough at this point to ask whether grammatical complexity is also related to pauses in speech and by inference to complex cognitive operations as well.

In order to do this experiment, speech produced in response to cartoons was further analyzed in terms of the complexity of its grammatical structure. In order to determine grammatical complexity, an index called the *Subordination Index (SI)* was defined for each of the utterances produced. The index is a percentage obtained from comparing the number of subordinate clauses to the total number of clauses, where a clause was defined simply as a subject plus a predicate. For verbal outputs produced in the cartoon task, *SI* was equal to 19 % for description and 49 % for interpretation.

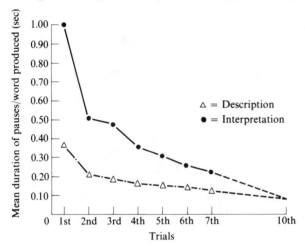

**Fig. 14.8**  Hesitance at two levels of verbal planning, and its decrease with repetition. (From Goldman-Eisler, 1968)

If these were the only speech samples available, it would be possible to conclude (erroneously) that syntactic structure and pausing are interrelated. Unfortunately description and interpretation also differ in the difficulty of the task required of the subject—in one case he is simply describing a picture and in the other he is interpreting it. In order to disentangle this aspect of the task, a further sample of speech was examined. This sample was taken from psychiatric interviews and yielded an *SI* of 48 % and a pause time per word (p/w) ratio equal to 0.12, in other words, syntactically complicated speech containing few pauses. The comparable p/w values for descriptions was 0.17, and for interpretations, 0.34. This means that pause time and sentence complexity are unrelated in psychiatric interviews, and confounded in interpretations. It also implies that speakers can produce complex sentences without a great many pauses, and that this in fact is what seems to happen in psychiatric interviews.

Considered in this light (psychiatrists please take note) it is possible to argue that in certain situations (i.e. an unstructured interview) the subject may use well-prepared and habitual phrases of reasonable grammatical complexity, but may not in fact be producing genuinely novel speech. Only in those situations in which preparation is impossible and the task difficult (cartoon interpretation) do complex structure and pausing co-vary. In this case their co-variation is probably related to the difficulty of the idea to be expressed, rather than to the difficulty of the syntactic structure used.

On the basis of those results, Goldman-Eisler was led to conclude that syntactical processes operate as a skill requiring little or no cognitive activity, whereas word selection and interpretation require relatively difficult cognitive activity. Further support for the view that pausing (cognitive activity) and syntactical complexity are unrelated was found in a further examination of 15 new samples of spontaneous speech. More than 142 sentences were examined and in no case did Goldman-Eisler find a relation between pausing and sentence structure: "In other words, syntactical operations as such, however complex the result, were not reflected in the time of hesitation pauses. Lexical choices, as well as the semantic complexity of intellectual content, on the other hand, are functions of the capacity... for delaying speech action." (Goldman-Eisler, pages 76, 78) Of the three possible determiners of pausing, only syntactical complexity seemed not to require extra production time. Once a sentence is under way it seems as if it can be "run off" without any further cognitive activity on the part of the speaker, a condition clearly not true of selecting words or interpreting content.

## SUMMARY

Beginning with a very small bag of sentences, the present chapter has attempted to sort out some of the problems involved in a formal analysis of language. The primary problems raised by the study of language divide themselves into two categories: those that have to do with meaning and those that have to do with structure.

The problem of meaning is a particularly difficult one, and although a number of different approaches have been taken, none is completely satisfactory. The simplest and most direct approach assumes that it has something to do with words and the things they stand for; i.e., seems to suggest a reference theory of meaning. Almost immediately the sentence *Sir Walter Scott is the author of* Waverley, comes to mind, posing the problem of paraphrase (where two phrases have the same referent, but different meaning) and thereby setting an insurmountable problem for any simple referential theory. Similarly, any attempt to provide a more elaborate version of this theory also runs into trouble and leads to the conclusion that although language is used to talk about things, some of the things we talk about cannot be related to the referential world in any simple or direct way.

As a corrective to a strict referential analysis of meaning (or even to a modified referential view), a number of contemporary philosophers have suggested that what is required is an examination of how specific words are used in specific contexts. Although the stricture "Look for use, not for meaning" presents a useful methodological orientation, it has not as yet given rise to a consistent analysis of meaning. The best it has been able to do is to provide an analysis of a few specific words or concepts (pain, truth, etc.) which had been hopelessly mishandled in earlier theories. It has not yet produced a coherent analysis of meaning—and perhaps this is as it should be, or more strongly, as it must be.

When, however, our attention turns to the structured aspects of language, we find linguistics on much surer ground. Although different problems arise, solutions do seem within reach. For a starter, there is the problem of levels—that is, any utterance is at one and the same time a structured collection of phrases, words, sounds, and perhaps ultimately, a structured set of articulatory movements. Sentences such as *Visiting relatives can be boring* indicate important ways in which grammatical structure can be ambiguous, and have initiated attempts to explain these ambiguities in rigorous terms.

There are essentially three different ways in which to describe the grammar of a language. One of these views language as a simple left-to-right process and therefore stresses its sequential aspects. *Finite-State Grammars* view the production of a sentence as dependent on a number of choices made by a speaker at a number of critical points. Linguistically, such points can be interpreted as words (in which case sentence production is described in terms of sequential word-to-word probabilities), or as grammatical form classes (in which case sequential class-to-class probabilities are stressed). In any event, the surface structure, either at the level of the word or at the level of the form class, is considered of primary importance.

Although a good deal of sentencing can be accounted for in terms of sequential or probabilistic factors, certain linguistic facts (*Flying planes . . .*, *Visiting relatives . . .* etc.) indicate that the same sequence of words is open to two distinctly different meanings, or more accurately, to two different phrase patterns. Such considerations undoubtedly led to the development of a grammar phrased in terms of the immediate constituents of a language—the so called *Phrase-Structure Grammar*. In a grammar of this sort, the essential unit is not a word or form class, but rather the sentence. Word choice and even phrase choice is determined by a system of rules used to generate acceptable sentences. For Phrase-Structure Grammars, sentence production is viewed as a hierarchically organized act of great complexity, requiring highly skilled performance for its use.

Despite the fact that Phrase-Structure Grammars provide a much more powerful analysis of grammatical structure than Finite-State Grammars, one crucial problem still remains: Sentences having the same pattern of phrases still may have different meanings. Thus surface structure (words or phrases) is still equivocal; what is required is an analysis of sentences in terms of their deeper significance—an analysis of their *deep structures*.

By its very nature, deep structure is a theoretical concept; strictly speaking, it is only inferable, never directly observable.

But language involves not only syntax; it also has to do with sounds. This branch of linguistics is called *phonemics*, and deals with the specific pattern of sounds used in all languages as well as the sounds specific to a particular language. The analysis of sound and sound patterns often begins with a phonetic transcription of all the distinctively different sounds that can be distinguished by the trained ear of a linguist. On the basis of a variety of well-specified procedures, this collection of sounds is reduced to a smaller set encompassing only those sounds that "make a difference" to a native speaker. These sounds are subject to further examination in terms of their distribution of occurrence in speech, and a minimal set of sounds—the phonemes of the language—are developed for a given language.

Since the phoneme is really a child of analysis—a concept—rather than an immediately given fact, it seems reasonable to try to reduce it to more fundamental attributes or features. Such an attempt has been undertaken by Jakobson and his collaborators. The outcome of this work has been to provide a set of about eight distinctive features capable of dividing the sounds of a language into more homogeneous sound families. This partition is achieved by analyzing the pattern of feature similarity and difference found to apply across a set of phonemes. In general, the structure of these sound families is strongly related to how often the specific sounds are confused in well-controlled psychophysical experiments as well as in field observations.

The sound pattern of the language is not altogether independent of the meaning of the language—what has been called its morphemic structure. If the phoneme is defined as a minimal unit of sound, the morpheme has been defined analogously as the minimal unit of meaning or as the minimal unit of grammatical structure. The morphemic structure of a language is described in terms of bases (or words) and their inflectional and derivational affixes. Inflectional affixes are usually small in number, yet do powerful work in the language. For example, the $[Z_1]$ morpheme is capable of pluralizing any and all words in the English language. A careful examination of the pluralizing morpheme indicates that like a phoneme, it does not consist of a single element always articulated in the same way, but rather of a series of allomorphs. Although the number of inflectional affixes is quite small in English (consisting of about seven specific cases) other languages, such as Hebrew, are highly inflected. In Hebrew, for example, a single verb base is given a number of significantly different meanings as a result of different inflections.

All these linguistic categories—phonemics, morphemics, morphophonemics, syntax—provide descriptions that are relatively static or at least nondynamic. But what does speech look like as it is spoken? Here we need turn to a series of studies undertaken under the direction of Goldman-Eisler. Using pauses which occur in spontaneous creative speech as an indication of underlying cognitive activity, Goldman-Eisler was able to show that word choice and semantic interpretation seem to require ongoing planning for their operation, whereas syntactical operations do not. Only in the first two cases does pausing relate systematically to the ongoing process, whereas it is completely unrelated to the ongoing processes involved in producing different grammatical constructions. This has been interpreted to mean—in agreement with a good deal of psycholinguistic theory—that syntax is probably best considered as a skilled performance rather than as involving ongoing planful activity.

This work by Goldman-Eisler provides a convenient bridge to the chapters that follow. In much of the present chapter, we have been concerned with a formal analysis of language, and have to a great extent neglected the language user. The next two chapters will try to remedy this by describing the processes presumed to go on in the production and reception of language by a language user. As in the case of other cognitive activities, two different types of theoretical approaches have been taken; one stemming from the empirical tradition of associationism and the other arising from the more *a priori* tradition of rational philosophy. Chapter 15 deals with the empirical tradition, while Chapter 16 deals with the rational tradition.

On your mark, ready, set, Go!...

# CHAPTER 15

# THE LEFT-TO-RIGHT APPROACH: ASSOCIATIONS IN LANGUAGE

If you step on someone's toe in a crowded bus you say, "Excuse me," or "Sorry"; if someone does something you particularly like, you say "Thank you"; if a stuffy businessman writes a stuffy business letter he usually begins with "In reply to your letter," and just as often ends up with "Very truly yours"; and if you have a particularly tired instructor he is likely to begin his lecture with "In last week's discussion we considered the problem of . . . ." All these phrases may vary in their specific detail from time to time, but in general, they—and many others like them—represent highly stable and highly stereotyped modes of verbal behavior.

Even more complicated social situations also call forth their own regular brand of verbal behavior; for example, at the end of a party, "Oh what a lovely party" or at the beginning of a party, "Haven't I met you somewhere before?" There seems to be no end to these stereotyped phrases, either in terms of the situations they apply to, or in terms of the people who apply them. They also include a wide variety of grammatical constructions, ranging from sentence fragments right through to more complicated sentences such as questions and the like.

Many of these bits of verbal behavior either are, or become, so well known that they can be used as jokes in and of themselves. For example, continuing television programs such as Rowan and Martin's *Laugh-In* are able to make good (?) use of the following highly predictable bits of verbal behavior:

1. *Did I tell you what my aunt said when she . . .*
2. *Blow in my ear and I'll follow you anywhere.*
3. *It's sock-it-to-me time.*
4. *Say goodnight Dick . . . Goodnight Dick.*

and so on for about an hour's worth.

Much of what passes for ordinary verbal behavior is remarkable for its predictability and its lack of novelty. People seem to say the same things over and over again. The regularity with which certain phrases or sentences occur within the same speaker or within the same context provides a common starting point for almost all associative analyses of speech and language.

350

Even if the specific words vary from time to time in the same speaker or across different speakers, there seems to be enough commonality to permit (or even encourage) a discussion of language in terms of stimulus and response factors.

The advantage to be gained from considering language behavior in stimulus and response terms is quite considerable: For one thing, this approach implies that ordinary behavior principles will do for language; while for another, it emphasizes the learned nature of such behaviors. Both these advantages, of course, are quite dear to the hearts of empirical and tough-minded psychologists. If a tough-minded psychologist feels that a particular topic such as language can be covered by existing principles developed in the learning laboratory, he is then ready to step in and undertake a thorough-going analysis.

Even the early history of learning research itself seemed to imply that language could be handled as a learned $S-R$ phenomenon. It was Pavlov who felt that the conditioned response was a symbolic act ("a psychic secretion" as he called it), and from here it is but a short step to view conditioning as an overt analog of symbol development such as might occur in word meaning. The development of an associative analysis, first by Mowrer (1959, 1962a, 1962b) and then by Osgood (1953, 1957, 1960, 1968), is a formal attempt to apply the conditioning paradigm to language directly.

One of the most obvious characteristics of speech or verbal behavior is its sequential flow, and the psychological concept of response chaining seems to provide an appropriate model of how such behavior might be learned. If an animal can be trained to perform a sequence of responses in order to obtain a particular goal, why couldn't the same principles apply to a child learning a sequence of verbal responses? Both serial rote-learning and response chaining in the Skinnerian sense certainly seem relevant here.

Thus the laboratory tradition of $S-R$ psychology provides ready models for an assault on the two major problems of language: structure and meaning. If structure can be described in terms of response sequences and meaning in terms of classical conditioning, then an $S-R$ analysis of language could develop as a logical outgrowth of more general association principles. Taken in conjunction with the obvious fact that different cultures teach their children different languages, such an approach places learning principles at the very center of language development. It is indeed in this tradition that Osgood begins his analyses of what it means to say that a word has meaning.

## MEANING IN THE ASSOCIATIVE MODE

Anyone who has ever had anything to do with children knows that two of the most important words in the English language are *good* and *bad*. Many of the things you want a child to do, or not do, can be controlled by appropriate use of these words. *Good* and *bad* are multipurpose words, they require no specific or unique situations for their use: "Good boy, Jono"; "bad boy, Jono"; "good, ya did that very well"; "bad, don't touch the stove"; etc. They can be used with great effect across a number of different situations. This trans-situationality should make them particularly difficult for the child to learn: yet this is not usually the case. How then is it that a child does learn the "meaning" of words such as *good* and *bad*?

Psychological analyses assume that *good* is learned on the basis of classical conditioning procedures. Consider how this might occur: Jonathan, aged 18 months, picks up a toy and carries it across the room to his mother. When he gives her the toy she says "*Good*, Jono," and hugs him. Let us assume this is the first time she has used the word *good*. In learning terms, what Jono's mother is doing is pairing an originally meaningless stimulus, that is, the sound *good*, with the response of hugging Jono. In terms of the usual classical conditioning diagram, the situation can be represented as follows:

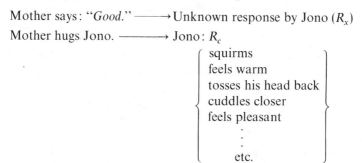

Mother says: "*Good*." $\longrightarrow$ Unknown response by Jono $(R_x)$

Mother hugs Jono. $\longrightarrow$ Jono: $R_c$

$$\left\{ \begin{array}{l} \text{squirms} \\ \text{feels warm} \\ \text{tosses his head back} \\ \text{cuddles closer} \\ \text{feels pleasant} \\ \vdots \\ \text{etc.} \end{array} \right\}$$

In this case, *good* is paired with a hug, which gives rise to a whole complex of responses $(R_c)$ that can be conditioned to the occurrence of *good* as a conditioned stimulus, or *CS*. Some of the abovementioned responses are quite specific to the condition of being hugged, such as squirming, or cuddling; others can also occur in response to other stimulus situations as well. The fact that most stimuli give rise both to highly specific and to highly general subresponses is an essential component of $S-R$ analyses of meaning. The more general response patterns (such as "feels pleasant") are "detachable" from specific stimulus situations, and can and do occur in reduced form even when the instigating event is not present. These detachable components of the response evoked by the paired stimulus (what is usually called the *unconditioned stimulus* or the *UCS*) are the least effortful and least interfering (that is, with other overt responses) of the response components evoked by the *UCS*.

Since Osgood (1953, 1957) and Mowrer (1962a, 1962b) specifically identify these detachable, lightweight, fractional components of the response compound evoked by the *UCS* as responses in their own right, it seems reasonable to ask what properties such fractional responses might have. In the case of *good* it is reasonable to assume that they would include an emotional feeling of well-being, or, said less dramatically, a pleasant feeling. In terms of possible behavioral effects, stimuli evoking fractional "pleasant" responses are approached rather than avoided, are reinforcing rather than punishing, and tend to induce a reasonably rapid response.

In the usual notation, fractional responses such as the pleasant feeling now conditioned to the word *good* are symbolized $r_m$ (lower case *r* because they are internal and unobservable, and subscript *m* because they carry the meaning function in behavioral terms) and are thought to have the same status as other mediational responses. In terms of a conditioning analysis, the sequence of events initiated by the word *good* would look something like this.

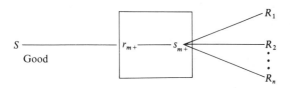

*Good* considered as a stimulus evokes the newly conditioned $r_{m+}$ (a pleasant feeling), which in turn evokes its distinctive stimulus pattern, $s_{m+}$, which is then selectively attached to environmental responses, $R_1, R_2, \ldots, R_n$.

By the same type of conditioning analysis, *bad* would come to evoke an unpleasant implicit response ($r_{m-}$). This implicit meaning would be established in the context of $UCS$'s which arouse unpleasant feelings in the child (e.g., hitting or restraining him while saying the word *bad*). The specific properties of unpleasant $r_m$'s can be specified as exactly opposite to those evoked by pleasant $r_m$'s; namely, they produce avoidance rather than approach, they are punishing rather than reinforcing, and they tend to induce slow responding.

In the case of both *good* and *bad*, it is possible to pinpoint a specific class of environmental events capable of producing the appropriate $r_m$ (and before it, $R_c$). Some words, such as *truth* or *Communism*, however, do not have specific situations or events regularly associated with them, so that it is impossible for direct word–$UCS$ pairings to occur so as to bring about the conditioning of an appropriate $r_m$. As a matter of fact, there are very few words that really have highly specific environmental referents; therefore, for most words, meaning (considered as an $r_m$) must develop on the basis of a slightly different procedure. If we take a naive view and ask how a child might learn the meaning of the word *Communism*, the answer is plain enough: by seeing it or hearing it paired with other words.

Fragment of a conversation:

*David*:   What is Communism?

*Enlightened Social Studies Teacher*:   Communism is Bad.

*David*: Is it Bad like Measles?

*Teacher*: In a way—it's sort of a Disease.

*David*: Is it worse than Mumps?

*Teacher*: Yes, it's very Bad, more like a Cancer.

*David*: Oh, that's funny—I thought it was an economic system.

The point of this conversation is that in order to convey the meaning of a word such as *Communism*, the teacher paired it with a series of other words already evoking specific $r_m$'s. In all cases these preconditioned $r_m$'s were negative, presumably because the teacher wanted to convey an emotional attitude rather than a precise description. The essential properties of this situation can be diagrammed in classical conditioning terms with the proviso that each of the paired words be considered as a *UCS* and the word *Communism* as a *CS*. Thus,

Trial 1.    Communism  
            Bad         $\longrightarrow r_m(-)$

Trial 2.    Communism  
            Ugly        $\longrightarrow r_m(-)$

Trial 3.    Communism  
            Disease     $\longrightarrow r_m(-)$

Trial 4.    Communism  
            Mumps     $\longrightarrow r_m(-)$

Trial 5.    Communism  
            Cancer     $\longrightarrow r_m(-)$

By the end of five conditioning trials, it is reasonable to suppose that a negative $r_m$ had been conditioned to *Communism*, although it is not necessary for any of the specific words (*bad*, *ugly*, etc.) to have been connected to the *CS* word.

## The Conditioning of Meaning

Now this further type of analysis has a certain plausibility to it, and, even more important, it can be tested experimentally. The experimental procedures are given almost exactly by the above conversation: Take an originally neutral or meaningless term and pair it with a series of words all of which produce characteristic $r_m$'s, be these positive or negative. In order to get an appropriate set of *UCS* items it is first necessary to have a collection of words rated as either *good* or *bad* and then systematically pair the "good" words or the "bad" words with the originally meaningless term.

This is in fact exactly the procedure used by Staats and Staats and their associates in a series of experiments concerned with what has come to be called the conditioning of meaning (Staats and Staats, 1957; 1959; see Staats, 1963, 1968, for a review of work on this topic). In one of the Staats' experiments, the nonsense syllable $XOF$ was paired with 18 positively rated words and the syllable $WEM$ was paired with 18 negatively rated words. Another group of subjects had $XOF$ paired with negative words and $WEM$ with positive ones. The subjects were told they were taking part in a study of pronunciation and that it was not necessary for them to learn the specific pairings (other later studies did not use this same instruction and still produced exactly the same result). The results of an entire series of experiments were quite consistent in showing that the same nonsense syllable (say $XOF$) when paired with unpleasant words tended to be rated as unpleasant, and when paired with pleasant words tended to be rated as pleasant. Pairing an originally neutral stimulus with emotionally loaded words does produce changes in meaning; changes predictable on the basis of a conditioning analysis.

Staats and Staats and their associates then went on to show that similar procedures could induce positive and negative ratings toward the names of national groups (Staats and Staats, 1958) and that many of the variables found to be effective in ordinary classical conditioning also apply to conditioned meaning. In this later context, they showed that as they increased the number of $UCS$-nonsense-syllable pairings, the ratings of the paired nonsense syllables became more extreme (Staats and Staats, 1959). Similarly, if they paired a nonsense syllable or word with an unpleasant noise and electric shock, the nonsense syllable so conditioned came to arouse a galvanic skin response ($GSR$) and that the intensity of its rating was related to the size of the evoked $GSR$. The stronger the $GSR$ evoked by a given word, the more negative it was rated (Staats, Staats, and Crawford, 1962).

These results establish the plausibility of a conditioning analysis of how meaning is acquired. Since conditioned meaning, once acquired, is thought to function as a response, it should be possible to make some predictions as to how pleasant and unpleasant words would function in specific tasks. This is exactly what Solarz (1960) did. In his particular experiment, subjects were required to learn one of two antagonistic movements when a word was presented on a movable platform. One of these required the subject to move the platform toward himself, while the other required him to move it away. Some of the words used had previously been rated as "pleasant" while the remaining words had been rated as "unpleasant." In Solarz' experiment there were four possible combinations of word type and movement pattern: pleasant words–toward; pleasant words–away; unpleasant words–toward; and unpleasant words–away.

In terms of Osgood's analysis of response dispositions associated with pleasant and unpleasant words, two of these patterns represented compatible combinations (pleasant–toward; unpleasant–away), while the remaining two represented incompatible combinations. Although there were many different dependent variables recorded, the most interesting one concerns the amount of time taken to perform the appropriate movements for each of the four categories. Basically results showed that the average latency for unpleasant words was longer than for pleasant words and that compatible movements (negative–away; positive–toward) were initiated more rapidly than comparable incompatible movements (negative–toward; positive–away). On the basis of these results it is possible to argue that positively rated words induce rapidly initiated approach tendencies, while negatively rated words induce avoidance tendencies which delay overt responding.

In an attempt to carry this analysis somewhat further, Pollio and Gerow (1968) studied the effects of positive and negative contexts on the speed with which subjects were able to give word-association responses. Basically, they argued that if negative words induce avoidance tendencies, negative contexts should serve to delay an associative response, whereas if pleasant words induce approach tendencies, such contexts should serve to speed up an associative response. As in the Solarz case, Pollio and Gerow presented four different types of context-target word pairings: +, +, a pleasant target word preceded by a pleasant context; −, +, a pleasant target word preceded by an unpleasant context; +, −, an unpleasant target word preceded by a pleasant context; and −, −, an unpleasant target word preceded by an unpleasant context. Each of the target words was preceded by a context of either zero, one, or two words. This means that in the −, + context, length 2 condition, the following set of words was presented: *rough, hungry, faith*, with the subject required to produce an association in response to only the last word of the set, that is, *faith*.

The results of this experiment are presented in Fig. 15.1.

They reveal that the longest associative reaction times ($RT$'s) occurred in response to unpleasant words in unpleasant contexts, and that the shortest $RT$'s occurred in response to pleasant words in pleasant contexts. Of more crucial importance for the fractional meaning hypothesis are results occurring in the mixed cases; that is, +, − and −, +. The data obtained under these conditions fit snugly, as they should, between those obtained for the unmixed conditions, and show progressive changes in the predicted directions. Thus associative reaction time for unpleasant words embedded in pleasant contexts, [+, −], (*house, baby, anger*) decreases as context increases, whereas associative reaction time for pleasant words embedded in unpleasant contexts [−, +], increases as contexts lengthen.

Taken together, these results indicate that words rated as pleasant produce associative responses more quickly than words rated as unpleasant, and that contexts consisting of pleasant words increase response speed, whereas contexts composed of unpleasant words decrease response speed. All these results are in complete agreement with Osgood's analysis of the behavioral implications of pleasant and unpleasant word ratings.

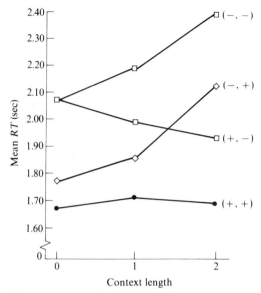

**Fig. 15.1** Associative *RT*'s to pleasant and unpleasant stimuli as a function of context length and context type. (From Pollio and Gerow, 1968)

The fractional meaning response, $r_m$, which does so much of the work in S–R analyses is not to be confused with other responses potentially evoked by a word. Most usually, these "other responses" are words, or as they are usually called, word associates. Although it is not necessary, strictly speaking, to provide anything other than a purely formal definition of the $r_m$ (that is, a definition couched in terms of antecedent characteristics and consequent behavioral effects) it is helpful to provide an intuitive feel for $r_m$'s that are not words. For an example, consider Fig. 15.2 (see next page).

The first column presents six different "squiggles," while the second column presents six different adjectives. In this demonstration the subject's job is to match up each squiggle with one of the adjectives that seems appropriate. Although students often complain "This is mad" or "You've got to be kidding" or the more unkindly *ad hominum* "You're out of your mind!" over a sample of about 2000 students, agreement on which squiggle goes with which adjective runs at about 90%. Since nothing is perfect, 90% ain't bad. This being the case, no "correct" answers will be provided—you are invited to try it for yourself.

Although it is possible to make an analysis of this task in terms of word factors— e.g., ⋀⋁ is *jagged* and *angry* is *jagged*, the way this task is usually done seems much less verbal than that. Most students report that it involves a series of pairwise impressions such as: Is ᴍᴡ more similar to *angry* or to *tranquil*, or to *hopeful* or to *sorrowful*, etc.

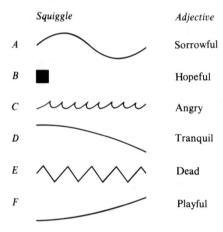

Fig. 15.2  The famous squiggle test.

It is precisely at this point—in defining similarity—that the $r_m$ hypothesis comes into play. It is possible to argue that each squiggle evokes some internal response (an $r_m$) and that each word also evokes some internal response (another $r_m$). Given this assumption, similar nonverbal $r_m$'s come to serve as mediating elements which tie the squiggle and the word together. Although it is hard to specify precisely what such an $r_m$ might be like, it is possible to see that a squiggle such as ᴍᴡ involves a series of sharp, episodic motions; first up / and then down \. This type of fractional motor response is certainly more similar to the emotional meaning associated with *angry* than with the emotional meaning evoked by *tranquil* or *hopeful* or *sorrowful*. A similar analysis, comparing the motor responses required to produce a given squiggle and the emotional meaning evoked by a word, will show how this type of explanation would work for the remaining cases.

Now that meaning has been identified as a mediational response—the $r_m$—and hopefully given some intuitive significance, how shall this response be measured as objectively and conveniently as possible? In order to accomplish this task, Osgood and his collaborators (Osgood, 1952, 1960, 1961; Osgood, Suci, and Tannenbaum, 1957) developed a measuring instrument known as the *semantic differential* (*SD*). The semantic differential consists of a series of rating scales having opposite-meaning words (such as *good–bad*, *active–passive*, etc.) as anchor points, with the subject required to rate a word(s) or concept(s) on a series of these scales.

For example, in 1952, the word *Socialism* was rated by a group of Midwestern voters as follows:

Socialism

| | 1 | 2 | 3 | 4 | 5 | 6 | 7 | |
|---|---|---|---|---|---|---|---|---|
| fair | . | . | . | . | . | ✓ | . | unfair |
| strong | . | . | . | . | ✓ | . | . | weak |
| active | . | . | ✓ | . | . | . | . | passive |

For these subjects, the word *Socialism* was rated as strongly unfair, somewhat weak, and somewhat active. If we assign numbers, Socialism produces the triple of values (6, 5, 3); values which define its semantic profile exactly. For purposes of comparison, these same voters voted *Universal Military Training* (the draft) with the following triple (3, 3, 2), or as somewhat *fair*, somewhat *strong*, and strongly *active*.

In some instances it may be important to know how two words differ in their pattern of semantic differential ratings. In order to evaluate this, Osgood, Suci, and Tannenbaum (1957) suggest that semantic differential scales be considered as defining a linear space of three dimensions. They also suggest that the difference in meaning between two words be calculated in terms of the following formula:

$$D_{w_1 - w_2} = \sqrt{(R^{[1]}_{w_1} - R^{[1]}_{w_2})^2 + (R^{[2]}_{w_1} - R^{[2]}_{w_2})^2 + (R^{[3]}_{w_1} - R^{[3]}_{w_2})^2}.$$

In words, the distance between word$_1$ and word$_2$ ($D_{w_1 - w_2}$) is equal to the square root of the rating of $w_1$ on semantic differential scale 1 ($R^{[1]}_{w_1}$) minus the rating of $w_2$ on the same scale ($R^{[1]}_{w_2}$) squared, plus the squared differences on Scale 2, $(R^{[2]}_{w_1} - R^{[2]}_{w_2})^2$ and on Scale 3 $(R^{[3]}_{w_1} - R^{[3]}_{w_2})$.[2]

In terms of the two words used above, their difference would be

$$D_{w_1 - w_2} D_{s\,unit} = \sqrt{(6 - 3)^2 + (5 - 3)^2 + (3 - 2)^2}$$

or 3.74 semantic differential units.

So far so good. The only remaining problem is to determine which adjectives should be used to define which semantic dimensions. In order to accomplish this task, Osgood, Suci, and Tannenbaum (1957) decided to look for redundant dimensions. What this means is that, if you know someone has rated a given word as *good*, will he also be likely to rate it as *pleasant*, or *nice*, or *sweet*, or any of a number of other adjectives? Similarly, if a word has been rated as *weak*, is it also likely to be rated as *feminine* or *smooth* or *soft*, and so on for other seemingly related adjectives?

In order to answer these questions experimentally, Osgood and his collaborators asked a great many different subject groups to rate a great many different words on a great many different oppositional scales (see Osgood, 1961, for an indication of "how many" is a "great many"), and in almost all cases found that these scales segregated themselves into three major, and a number of minor, word groupings. By far and away the most important of these three major groupings involved scales such as *good–bad*; *pleasant–unpleasant, positive–negative, nice–awful*, etc., scales which Osgood has taken to define the Evaluative Dimension of the semantic differential. The other two major dimensions, Potency and Activity, were defined respectively by scales such as *strong–weak, hard–soft, large–small*, etc., and *fast–slow, active–passive, young–old*, etc.

What these analyses suggest is that a word can be construed as a point within a three-dimensional space defined by factors such as Evaluation, Potency, and Activity. The word *Socialism* is given its specific location in semantic space on the basis of its triple of ratings (6, 5, 3) and Universal Military Training is likewise defined by its triple of ratings (3, 3, 2).

These then are two analyses of meaning—one couched in terms of implicit response properties, and the other in terms of a structured model of three dimensions. Can these descriptions be coordinated? In order to do this, Osgood argues that the $r_m$ evoked by a meaningful word is composed of at least three major components, each identified with one of the three major semantic dimensions. Thus, for the word *Socialism*, the coordination would be as follows:

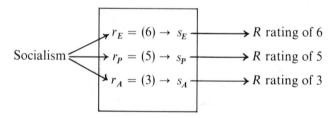

$$Socialism \begin{cases} r_E = (6) \rightarrow s_E & \longrightarrow R \text{ rating of } 6 \\ r_P = (5) \rightarrow s_P & \longrightarrow R \text{ rating of } 5 \\ r_A = (3) \rightarrow s_A & \longrightarrow R \text{ rating of } 3 \end{cases}$$

By this logic the response model is tied to the structural model, and a set of procedures provided that allows for unambiguous placement of words in semantic space. Predictions of behavior can be made on one or both of these grounds. For example, if a given rating is 2 (*good*) it seems reasonable to propose, on the basis of evidence presented earlier, that a subject is likely to approach such an object more readily and rapidly than one rated a 7 (*bad*). Similarly, it is possible to predict that if two words are separated by three semantic differential units, they are more likely to be confused or give rise to generalization effects than would be the case for two words separated by ten semantic differential units. Confusion or generalization should be inverse to the distance separating two words.

All this research originally took place in the absence of any real connection with linguistics or linguistic analysis. More recently, however, Osgood (1963, 1968) attempted to relate his analysis more closely to other linguistic theories of meaning. In this specific regard Osgood has proposed that each dimension of the semantic differential be viewed as a semantic feature, and that meaning be defined "as a bundle of simultaneous semantic features." (Osgood, 1963.)

For this type of analysis, there are three possible outcomes when and if words are combined in a phrase or sentence: (1) If the features associated with two words show opposite signs (+ and −) on any one feature, then the combination is semantically anomalous (e.g., *green thoughts*) and the meaning is given as some averaging of the shared features. (2) If the word codings show the same sign on any given feature, then the condition is of semantic consequence (e.g., *hopeful sign*) and the meaning of one or both is intensified. (3) If the word codings show no overlapping signs on any feature, then the condition is semantically permissible (e.g., *sad face*), a condition that comes closest to the usual condition of modifying meaning. (Osgood, 1968.)

If the semantic differential provides a procedure whereby it is possible to distinguish among the various meanings of a word, it should also be possible to go the other way round, and recover a word given a set of semantic differential ratings. If a subject is able to "put" a word into semantic space on the basis of ratings, he should be able to "take" a word out given the appropriate ratings. In order to test whether or not this is possible, Gerow (1968) presented subjects with a series of three semantic differential ratings (one for each major dimension) and a set of five different words. The subject's job was to select which of the five words was best represented by the specific ratings presented.

One obvious factor that Gerow varied was the degree of similarity of the four incorrect words to the word that was actually correct. In terms of the procedures used to measure semantic similarity, he varied the average inter-set semantic distance, with those sets having large distances composed of dissimilar words and those having small distances containing similar words. Gerow's results were quite clear in showing that subjects could do this task with a good deal of accuracy, and that the subject's accuracy depended on the average distance among all noncorrect words.

For two additional groups, Gerow went on to vary the precision of semantic information provided. For one of these groups, semantic differential (*SD*) ratings were dichotomized so that subjects were told a word was "good," "active," and "fast" (but not 1.3, *good*; 4.67, *active*; and 2.74, *fast*), while a second group of subjects was told simply to "pick out the word that is different." By comparison with subjects given full information, subjects in both these groups were less able to select the unique word, but—and this is the important point—they were still able to select the unique word when the word sets contained words that differed markedly. Over all conditions, then, subjects were able to pick out the unique item, with the major difference among groups being the exact value at which they were able to do this with 75% accuracy. To answer the original question: Under appropriate conditions, subjects are able to translate a set of *SD* ratings into a specific word. Further, even in the absence of specific values, they are still able to pick out as different a word selected as different on the basis of specific *SD* ratings.

Although Osgood's analysis and its subsequent refinements have taken the associative analysis of meaning a long way, a number of pesky problems still remain—as even Osgood himself admits. For one thing, there is the problem of denotation, what words refer to in the real world. While it is true that *nurse* and *sincerity* (words producing about the same *SD* ratings) are similar in some respects, it is perfectly clear that no one would ask "sincerity" for a bedpan. This objection has, of course, been realized and has forced a distinction between cognitive and emotional meaning, with the semantic differential considered as appropriate only for emotional meaning. Even if the semantic differential is restricted to emotional meaning, it is not at all clear how the mediational approach could be extended to cover the denotational aspects of meaning (although both Staats, 1961, and Mowrer, 1962, have tried their hand at it).

Of perhaps more significance is the fact that certain *SD* scales are simply irrelevant for judging certain words—"Is a boulder sweet or sour?" (Brown, 1959.) What this may mean is that it is impossible to find a perfectly general set of semantic dimensions, and that the semantic dimensions described by Osgood are highly specific to the particular materials he used in developing them. It may not be possible to describe a general theory of meaning, but rather any analysis of the semantic relations which exist among a set of words must be specific to that set of words. Words or concepts seem to travel in limited families; and while any given word may have membership in a number of different concept families, the same dimensions may not be appropriate across families. In any event Osgood has provided a usable set of dimensions for some of these families, and has done psychology a good service by showing how these dimensions can be assimilated into existing *S–R* theory.

### Word Associations and Meanings

Word association is clearly a legitimate empirical child of classical association theory. Present the subject with a word and his task is to produce the next one that comes to mind. In terms of classical theory, the mind can move from one mental element to another on a number of bases, the most significant of which are described by the classical laws of association, laws such as contiguity, similarity, and contrast. Essentially, the Law of Contiguity states that mental event *A* will produce mental event *B* because the environmental counterparts of *A* and *B* have occurred contiguously in the experience of the organism. The other two laws are self-explanatory.

Ever since the first use of word associations by Galton, it was felt that word associations must surely have something to do with meaning. If we take the Law of Contiguity seriously, then the least that could be said was that words which occur as word associations have probably occurred in similar contexts, and this is not an improper starting point for an analysis of meaning. Both the Law of Similarity and the Law of Contrast imply meaningful relations between the stimulus and response members of an associative pair, and suggest word association as an appropriate vehicle by which to approach word meaning. Even simple consideration of the fact that most words are defined in terms of other words (*Communism is bad*, etc.) lends plausibility to a word-association analysis of meaning.

What then do word associations look like? As an example, consider the words evoked by the stimulus *liquor* as taken from a fairly recent collection of association norms (Gerow and Pollio, 1967).

**Table 15.1**  Word associates given in response to the stimulus word liquor (from Gerow and Pollio, 1967)

| | |
|---|---|
| 30 drink | 1  intoxicating, Cutty Sark, smell, |
| 12 whisky | relief, drunkenness, money, brown, |
| 8 good | party, distasteful, warm, great, |
| 6 drunk | beverage, gin, evil, Scotch, rum, |
| 4 bad, alcohol | amber, bottle, happiness, good mood, |
| 3 store, bourbon, booze | fine |
| 2 wine, beer | |

The first thing to note in this collection is that over a group of subjects many of the response words occur a different number of times. This simple fact is very comforting and useful to $S-R$ theory, for it implies that associates form a response hierarchy of the type usually considered to be involved in problem solving and concept formation. (See Chapter 5 for a discussion of the role of response hierarchies in problem solving, etc.)

Given this pattern of probabilities across a group of subjects, it seems reasonable to ask whether a similar hierarchy also applies to an individual. That is, if it were possible to ask one subject to give 10 or 15 or 50 responses, would his order of production correlate with the order derived from a group pattern? Although there are a number of practical problems involved in asking a subject for more than a single response (i.e., earlier responses may contaminate later ones) there is another indirect way in which to do this. If the distribution of response probabilities obtained across a group of subjects is representative of the response hierarchy of an individual, and if these differing probabilities indicate $S-R$ connections of differing strength, then a high probability response, or alternatively, a stimulus word having a single dominant response, should produce associative responses more rapidly than a lower probability response, or than a stimulus word not having a dominant response.

The first experiment to demonstrate this relationship was done by the German psychologist, Karl Marbe (Thumb and Marbe, 1901), and although a much more refined analysis was accomplished by Schlosberg and Heineman (1954), the general result is still called Marbe's Law. Basically, Marbe's Law says that the group probability of a given associative response predicts the speed with which that response will be produced by an individual.

So far an associative analysis of word association may be summarized by the following diagram.

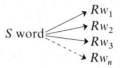

Here $S$ word is the stimulus word and each response is hierarchically ordered on the basis of its probability of occurrence. But one thing must be remembered: Each response is itself a word, and as such can be used as a stimulus in a different and further word-association task. In order to determine what types of effects can occur, consider Fig. 15.3.

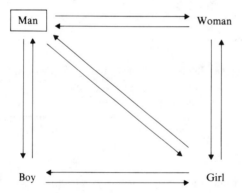

**Fig. 15.3** Interrelationships among the first three associates to the initial stimulus word *man*. (From Pollio, 1966)

This figure presents the pattern of inter-item association which occurs among the words *man*, *woman*, *boy*, *girl*. In this particular case, *man* was the initial stimulus word, and *woman*, *boy*, and *girl* were associative responses. The arrows, which occur among all four words, indicate the existence of an associative connection. For this set, only *boy* and *woman* are not mutual associates.

While it is easy to represent associative interconnections among a small number of words in terms of network diagrams of this type, it turns out to be more useful mathematically, and practically more convenient, to present the same data in terms of matrices. In these matrices, each row represents a stimulus and each column a response. If a row word produces a column word as a response, this fact can be indicated in one of two ways: Either the actual probability can be entered in the appropriate cell, or a 1 can be entered to indicate the presence of a relationship and a 0 to indicate the absence of such a relationship. For example, the pattern presented in Fig. 15.3 can be represented in a 1–0 matrix as follows:

| | Response words | | | |
|---|---|---|---|---|
| Stimulus words | Man | Woman | Boy | Girl |
| Man | $x$ | 1 | 1 | 1 |
| Woman | 1 | $x$ | 0 | 1 |
| Boy | 1 | 0 | $x$ | 1 |
| Girl | 1 | 1 | 1 | $x$ |

Now there are a number of measures that can be derived from a matrix of this sort. For one thing, it is possible to count up all cells containing a 1 (which in this case equals 10) and in this way develop an index of cohesiveness for this group of words. Similarly it is possible to add up each of the columns and in this way determine the number of stimulus words that cue a particular response word. Such an index is called a word's $N_c$ or cue number: for *man*, $N_c = 3$, for *woman*, $N_c = 2$, and so on. Finally, there is the sum across each row, which indicates the number of other words in the set evoked by a particular stimulus word. This is comparable to, although not identical to, what has been called a word's association value, or its meaningfulness value. For a further discussion of how graphs and matrices have been used in word-association procedures, see a series of articles by Kiss (1967, 1968, 1969).

All three of these indices, or ones conceptually similar to them, have been shown to have significant effects on standard laboratory tasks of recall. Thus Deese (1959) was able to show that word sets which have high cohesiveness values are better recalled than word sets having lower values; Rothkopf and Coke (1961) were able to show that more subjects recall high $N_c$ words then low $N_c$ words; and finally, it is a well-known fact that word meaningfulness is strongly related to ease of learning. (See McGeoch and Irion, 1951, for a review of early studies, and Noble, 1961, for a review of later ones.)

While all these relationships are interesting in and of themselves, the most significant work on the problem of word meaning from an associative point of view has been undertaken by Deese (1962, 1965). According to Deese's analysis, the relationship between two words is given by the number of word associations they have in common. For example, the words *moth* and *insect* have the following words in common—*moth* [2], *insect* [1] and *fly* [9], with the bracketed numbers indicating how many subjects gave that particular response. Since 50 subjects produced responses to *moth* and 50 to *insect*, the maximum overlap possible in this case is equal to 100, if all 50 subjects in both groups produced the same responses. Given this procedure, the degree of relationship between these two words can be expressed as a proportion involving the number of overlapping associations over the total number possible, which in the present case equals $\frac{12}{100}$ or 0.12. In terms of the *man-woman-boy-girl* set presented before, Table 15.2 presents the appropriate data.

**Table 15.2**  Intersection coefficients for *woman, man, girl,* and *boy\**

|         | Woman | Man  | Girl | Boy  |
|---------|-------|------|------|------|
| Woman   | 1.00  | 0.68 | 0.16 | 0.12 |
| Men     |       | 1.00 | 0.08 | 0.04 |
| Girl    |       |      | 1.00 | 0.73 |
| Boy     |       |      |      | 1.00 |

\* 100 Johns Hopkins University undergraduates.
*Source*: *The Structure of Associations in Language and Thought*, by James Deese. Baltimore, Md.: The Johns Hopkins University Press, 1965.

The next step in this analysis consists of partitioning a group of words into component subclusters. In order to do this, Deese assumes that overlap coefficients are equivalent to correlation coefficients and once this identification is made, it is possible to look for word clusters through the use of factor analysis. Basically, this consists of putting groups of words that have high intercorrelations with words in the group, and low correlations with non-group members, into the same cluster. As an example of the type of groupings achieved, the results of this procedure used on a set of 16 words evoked by the stimulus *butterfly* showed that these words partitioned themselves into four groups. The first group contained the words *moth, butterfly, insect, bug*; the second, *bird, wing, bees, fly*; the third, *blue, color, sky, yellow*; and the fourth, *sunshine, summer, garden, spring*.

The purpose of this demonstration, at least at this point, is to indicate that a collection of words produced as associates by a single word can be partitioned into meaningful subgroups; and further, that these groups define the meaning of that word.    In the case of *butterfly*, for example, Deese's analysis suggests that butterflies are flying organisms (be these birds or insects) who appear in pleasant weather.    Really not a bad definition of *butterfly*.

## Word Associations and the Semantic Differential

By and large, the word-association and semantic-differential approaches to word meaning have been pursued in relative independence of one another. Yet it is clear that both are derived from an associative analysis of meaning and that they complement rather than compete against each other.    Even at the simplest level, such a combination produces novel predictions if we rediagram the responses evoked by a stimulus word in the manner shown in Fig. 15.4.

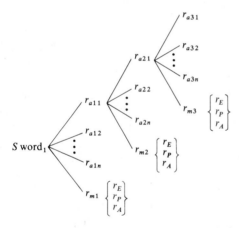

**Fig. 15.4** Hypothetical pattern of associative ($r_a$) and meaning ($r_m$) responses evoked by a single stimulus word ($S$ word$_1$).  Word associates to all but the first $r_a$ are omitted.

Given this analysis, it seems reasonable to expect a relationship between the $r_m$'s of the various words evoked by a stimulus word.  In terms of experimental procedures, such an analysis would predict a positive correlation between the *SD* rating of a stimulus word and the *SD* ratings of its associated responses.  In support of this, Staats and Staats (1959) found that the rank-order correlation between the *good–bad* rating of 10 different stimulus words and the mean *good–bad* rating of each of these word's first 20 associates was equal to 0.90. Considering only the first associate, Pollio (1964) found correlations between *SD* ratings of stimulus words and their primary associates to range between 0.26 and 0.69, with a general average around 0.50.

Now although these later results indicate that word associations $(r_a)$ and mediating responses $(r_m)$ are related, the correlations are relatively small, largely because of a rather special quality of primary associates: They tend, wherever possible, to be opposites. This is particularly true of adjective stimuli such as make up semantic differential scales, but it is also true of some nouns as well (*sickness–health*). There is, however, one additional property of oppositional associates that is of some interest, and that is that children, unlike adults, hardly ever give them. On this basis, it is possible to argue that for children the process which produces one word as an associate of another depends more strongly on the properties of the mediational response evoked, rather than on the strength of direct word-to-word correlations such as occur in the adult.

If this is true, how does the child come to use opposites? Originally, let us assume, the child has very few word-to-word connections and tends to produce associates on the basis of similarity in meaning. With repeated experience with words, certain contiguity-based verbal habits develop between pairs of words such that when the subject is asked to produce an associative response the mediational response is not evoked, but the subject simply makes use of an already established link. In the training history of a child, opposites often occur in the same situation so that oppositional words may come to form strong word-to-word habits. For example, in order to tell the child to keep away from a *hot* stove, it is likely that a mother might say, "Stay away from the stove—it's *hot* . . ." "It's all right to go near it when it's *cold*, but stay away when it's *hot*. . . ." or "It's *dangerous* to use *sharp* scissors—here, use these—it's *safe* to use *blunt* scissors . . ." or "Don't be a *bad* boy—do try to be a *good* boy until Daddy comes home . . ." etc.

In all these cases, oppositional words (pairs of adjectives) are put in contiguity with each other in order to convey a contrast in its simplest form: Scissors are *dangerous* when *sharp*, but *safe* when *blunt*. There is a good deal of economy and information in such a statement and it is not surprising, therefore, to find oppositional words occurring in the same context. If they occur in the same context, in a repetition of almost the same sentence, it is not improbable for the child to think the word *blunt*, when the word *sharp* is used, and to come on this basis to develop a strong word-to-word connection between the two.

Such direct verbal habits prove advantageous to the adult. For example, it is easier to dichotomize the weather into *nice* or *nasty* (rather than into a specific description of the *temperature, precipitation, prevailing winds*, etc.) in order to decide whether or not to put on a raincoat and boots. For the adult, opposites serve a simplifying function, and on this basis the existence of strong word-to-word connections between opposite words is neither surprising nor at variance with an associative analysis.

The upshot of this discussion is that one word can produce another as an associative response on a number of bases, with the two most important being similarity of $r_m$ and contiguity of prior occurrence. In many cases these two are correlated, although it is not impossible for an adult to produce an association completely on the basis of a word-to-word habit, or alternatively, completely on the basis of similarity of $r_m$.

## The Structure of Meaning and Continuous Association

Now this is an interesting hypothesis, namely, that word association can depend on two different but related associative principles but is there any way in which to test it directly? In 1944, Bousfield and Sedgewick asked subjects in a word-association task to produce not a single associate but rather a group of associative responses. What they found first of all was that after some variable time period, most subjects ran out of words. This was interpreted to mean that each stimulus word was connected only to a finite number of other words, and that when the subject exhausted his response hierarchy he was unable to produce further responses. When Bousfield and Sedgewick made a fine-grained analysis of individual output rates, however, they found an even more important result. In general, subjects did not produce their associates at a constant rate (e.g., 1 or 2 per second) but tended to produce a string of responses very rapidly (say with an inter-word response time of about 0.3 seconds), then paused for a while (say 5–10 seconds), and then went on to produce another rapid burst. Sometimes after the subject had produced an extremely rapid burst, he wouldn't stop altogether, but would tend to produce a slow output sequence, in which the individual words were separated by 2.0 sec or more, to be followed again by a burst of rapidly produced responses.

When Bousfield and Sedgewick examined these bursts, they found that the constituent words seemed to "belong together." So, for example, if the subject were asked to produce pieces of furniture, his first two bursts might look like this: *table, chair, sink, dishwasher, buffet* ... (pause) *bed, dresser, night table, lamp*, ... etc. Such a protocol suggests that a subject might first name objects found in the kitchen, then name things found in the bedroom, and so on. Although all the associates given were presumably connected to the same stimulus word, the behavioral output indicated that words were produced in certain meaningful subgroupings.

This fact suggested that perhaps rapidly occurring output sequences might define the limits of conceptual clusters associated with a particular word. In terms of meaning, alternations in output rate might define the significant factors giving a particular word its distinctive meaning. In terms of an associative analysis, this would mean that sets of words which are produced in a continuous association with extremely short inter-word response times ($IRT$'s) might have more word-to-word connections in common than words produced more slowly. Further, these rapidly produced word sequences would have more similar $r_m$'s than word sequences produced more slowly.

In order to test these predictions, Pollio (1964) had subjects associate continuously for four minutes to the words *house, trouble, justice,* and *thief.* After all subjects had produced their associative responses orally, two different sequences were selected: One of these was called a *Fast Sequence* (i.e., a burst) and was defined as the longest sequence of words where the inter-word response times ($IRT$'s) were in the fastest 25 % of all the $IRT$'s produced by that subject. The second of the sequences was called a *Slow Sequence,* and consisted of that sequence of words whose $IRT$'s fell in the slowest 25 % of all $IRT$'s produced by that subject.

After a Fast and Slow sequence had been selected, and a month had gone by, subjects were recalled to the laboratory and asked to rate the words in these sequences on Evaluative, Potency, and Activity scales, and then to produce word associations to them. After these ratings had been gathered, semantic distance scores were computed between all words in Fast and Slow Sequences. In addition, inter-word association matrices of the type described earlier were also established for Fast and Slow sequences.

The results of this analysis confirmed the original prediction: For all subjects, Fast Sequences had more word associations in common, and had smaller average within-sequence semantic distances than was true for Slow sequences. On this basis, the more closely related words are either in terms of associative ($r_a$) or emotional ($r_m$) meaning, the more likely they are to appear together in response bursts.

If the associates evoked by a single word regularly clusters into cohesive verbal subgroupings, such subgroupings should also be involved in other cognitive processes such as recall. It is possible to argue that if a subject is presented in a recall task with a set of well-structured words he will tend to recall them in terms of associative subgroupings. In order to test this prediction, Pollio, Kasschau, and DeNise (1969) presented subjects with two different word lists. One of these lists contained 22 word associates given in response to the word *music,* while the other list contained 22 words evoked by *command.* All lists were presented in a different random order to each subject and an oral free recall was then asked for.

As in the case of continuous free association, recall outputs were quite episodic, with periods of extremely rapid response intermingled with periods of slower response. When the semantic and associative properties of Fast sequences were compared to those of the Slower sequences, results indicated that words in a Fast sequence were associatively more interconnected and semantically more similar than words in a Slow sequence. This seems to mean that stimulus words regularly evoke the same verbal subclusters and that subjects make use of these subclusters in free recall.

There do seem to be situations, however, in which the cluster pattern of a set of materials might interfere with the ongoing task. In one such experiment using Deese's *butterfly* list, Weingartner (1963) asked subjects to learn all the items on the list in a specific serial order. For one group of subjects, all the words of a given subcluster remained together (i.e., *moth, butterfly, insect, bug,* then, *bird, wing, bees, fly,* etc.). For another group of subjects all the words were randomly ordered, so that any word from any given subcluster could and did follow any other word from any other subcluster, and so on. Results indicated that it took subjects about nine trials to learn the *butterfly* series when the clusters were left intact, but about 15 trials when words were randomly ordered.

All these results indicate that individual words do produce regularly recurring word clusters, and that subjects are able to make use of these verbal clusters in various ways. In general, where such pre-existing structure is appropriate to task demands, subjects make use of it; where such pre-existing structure is inappropriate to task demands, subjects find it quite difficult to disregard, often finding that such structure interferes with their performance in the ongoing task.

Meaning for the associative or *S–R* theorist is seen to be a complicated, compound response. Included in this response are a number of components that can be grouped into two separate categories: those having to do with affective states and those having to do with other words. In recent work Osgood has tended to identify meaning as a bundle of semantic features, with the meaning of any given word defined in terms of its featural pattern. Word-association approaches, on the other hand, stress that any given word functions as an element in a network of other words and that this network serves to define the word. Although such networks seem to involve a number of purely word-to-word connections, their general pattern is compatible with a semantic-features hypothesis. Each subcluster evoked by a given word may in fact exemplify one of the significant semantic dimensions evoked by that word.

## SYNTAX IN THE ASSOCIATIVE MODE

The associationistic analysis of the sentence stresses two of its most obvious components: first, that it is designed to convey information, and second, that it progresses from left to right. One of the earliest analyses of the communicative function of language was undertaken by Mowrer (1954), who viewed the declarative sentence as a simple conditioning device. For his example he took the sentence: *Tom is a thief.* In this case Mowrer assumed that the listener already knew the meaning (considered as an $r_m$) of both the main words, *Tom* and *thief*, and all that was really novel was the assertion of a relationship between them. What Mowrer assumed was that *Tom* (the word to be modified) served as a *CS* in the classical conditioning sense, and that *thief* functioned as a *UCS*. Since the $r_m$ evoked by *thief* is essentially a negative one, the function of the sentence was to condition the negative $r_m$ evoked by *thief* to *Tom*.

This type of analysis has a great many problems connected with it: How can a conditioned response be established in a single trial? How can we understand a sentence even if we don't believe it? Why isn't simple contiguity the whole story, as in classical conditioning? For example, if the sentence *Tom is a thief* were followed by the sentence *Virtue is its own reward*, why isn't the $r_m$ evoked by *Virtue* conditioned to *thief*? However, these problems in no way vitiate Mowrer's major point: Sentence meaning is a dynamic interaction in the mind of the listener. It is not that words convey meanings from one mind to another; rather that they make combinatorial use of already existing response potentialities.

The left-to-right aspect of the sentence is very congenial to an associationistic analysis of the sentence, for it suggests that sentencing may be nothing more than a complicated serial response. In the case of nonlanguage behavior, serial responses are thought of as a chain of stimulus–response elements, with each element capable of serving both as a stimulus and a response. One simple chaining hypothesis has been well described by Osgood (1953) in connection with the problem of learning a skill such as tying one's shoelaces. As Osgood notes, the standard, garden-variety shoe salesman is able to continue his line of patter (or salesmanship) as he swiftly and unerringly ties up the shoe he has just put on your foot.

If, however, we look at a young child attempting the same task, the complexity of this seemingly trivial act becomes somewhat more apparent. The child presumably begins to tie his shoes in response to some stimulus—either just putting on his shoes, seeing open shoelaces, or some combination of the two. This stimulus (open shoelaces) then gives rise to the child grasping the laces in a certain way. By so doing he has changed the stimulus pattern from one simply of "open shoelaces" to one in which both his hands and the shoelaces are in a new position. This second stimulus (hands and shoelaces in new position) then gives rise to the next response of crossing the shoelaces over, which then presents the third stimulus pattern and its associated response (e.g., making a bow), and so on until the sequence is completed.

For this sort of analysis, the major connections are between points of the observable situation (stimuli) and movements of the subject. Yet it is quite clear that the skilled behavior exhibited by the shoe salesman does not depend on environmental stimuli of this sort, for if it did he would have to pause occasionally in his sales pitch—a condition completely contrary to the behavior of shoe salesmen. What this means is that external cues come to "lose" their controlling function and that serial acts come to progress on an "internal" basis alone. In order to effect this translation from "external" stimulus control to "internal" stimulus control, the usual assumption is that each response produces a unique pattern of movement feedback, and that this feedback comes to serve in a stimulus role.

## An Excursion to Information Theory

If the flow of sequential behavior is viewed as a series of chained elements, it is then possible to consider the selection of each word in a sentence as representing some kind of choice or decision. Sentences, no less than other sequential behaviors, obviously do not have equally likely choices at each point—there must be limiting factors. In terms of a sentence, it seems reasonable that the selection of a specific word must lie somewhere between completely random and completely determined. Now in the specific such a hypothesis is surely a fiction, but nonetheless it is a useful fiction, for it allows, even encourages, an intensive statistical analysis of language behavior in order to discover what these probabilities might be.

In order to undertake a statistical analysis of language behavior, some precise way of talking about choice is required before we will be able to understand our data. One way of doing this is given by a procedure developed by the mathematician Claude Shannon (1948) and used by Miller and Selfridge in their analysis of the role of sequential dependencies in recall (see later sections of this chapter for a description of this approach). Suppose we wanted to define a perfectly random sequence of $n$ words. The simplest thing to do would be to go to a list of words and select $n$ different ones at random. If these were 64 different words, then the probability of getting any one word would be equal to $\frac{1}{64}$. If we wanted to find out which of the 64 words was actually selected, there are a number of possible strategies, the most efficient of which is to get rid of the most alternatives at each choice. In the present case, if there are 64 words, and if we divide them into two equal groups of 32 each and ask, "Is the word in Group 1?" then the number of alternatives will be reduced to 32 regardless of the answer.

By this same technique it is possible to continue halving each of the remaining sets (32, 16, 8, 4, and 2) until the unique word is specified by this procedure. In order to specify one particular word in a group of 64, six yes–no decisions are required. In general the number of alternatives is related to the number of decisions by the following formula: $A = 2^D$, where $A$ is the number of alternatives and $D$ is the number of decisions. In the present case, $D = 6$ and $A = 64$ or $2^6$. Thus, for a vocabulary of 64 items, it requires 6 binary (yes–no) decisions to specify a given word exactly, and the probability of any given word is equal to $\frac{1}{64}$ or $\frac{1}{A}$. For practical reasons it is helpful to reduce the equation $A = 2^D$ to logarithmic form and solve for $D$:

$$\log_2 A = \log_2 2^D = D \log_2 2$$
$$D = \log_2 A$$

In words, the number of decisions required to select a given item in a set of *equally likely* items is equal to the logarithm to the base$_2$ of the number of alternatives from which the choice is made. In most discussions of statistical factors in language, $D$ is taken as a definition of the amount of information per symbol (be the symbols letters, words, or whatnot) and is usually given the letter $I$. Regardless of which letter is used, it is important to keep in mind that $I$ (or $D$) is always defined in terms of the total number of alternatives in a given situation.

But not all alternatives are equally likely, and somehow this needs to be represented. In order to do this, remember that the probability of a given alternative, $P_i$, is defined as $\frac{1}{A}$. Since the basic formula so far has been defined in terms of $A$, and since we want to get some probability into this definition, all we need do is solve for $A$ in the equation $P_i = \frac{1}{A}$. The answer here is $A = \frac{1}{P_i}$. Substituting this into the equation produces the following results: $I = \log_2 A = \log_2 \frac{1}{P_i} = \log_2 1 - \log_2 P_i = 0 - \log_2 P_i$; therefore $I = -\log_2 P_i$. What this means is that the definition of information has been shifted from one that was based on the number of alternatives in a situation to one based on the probability of occurrence of individual alternatives.

This way of stating the basic equation has a number of implications. For one thing, as the probability of any alternative $P_i$ increases, the amount of information given by that alternative decreases. What this means is that if we know something is going to happen and it does, we are not surprised— that is, it doesn't convey much information. In the extreme case, in which there is only one alternative, the amount of information conveyed is equal to zero.

If a set of alternatives is not equally likely, then the best statistic designed to convey how much information is likely in this situation is given by the average information across the entire set of alternatives. Garner (1962) has suggested the term *average uncertainty* $U$, in place of average information, and defines this value as $U = \Sigma P_i I_i$, which means that the average uncertainty across a set of alternatives is given as the sum of the individual uncertainties weighted by their respective probabilities of occurrence. If we substitute for $I$, the general equation for the average uncertainty in a given set of alternatives can be written: $U = -\Sigma P_i \log_2 P_i$.

In order to consider what these equations mean in a specific situation, let us consider two sets of alternatives. For the first set assume that all the alternatives are equally likely, whereas, for the second set, assume that they are unequal. If we assume four alternatives, Table 15.3 presents the appropriate values for the equal-probability case.

**Table 15.3** Equal-probability case*

| Alternative | Probability $(P_i)$ | $-\log_2 P_1$ | Weighted uncertainty $-P \log_2 P_i$ |
|---|---|---|---|
| 1. | $\frac{1}{4}$ or 0.25 | 2.00 | 0.5 |
| 2. | $\frac{1}{4}$ or 0.25 | 2.00 | 0.5 |
| 3. | $\frac{1}{4}$ or 0.25 | 2.00 | 0.5 |
| 4. | $\frac{1}{4}$ or 0.25 | 2.00 | 0.5 |

$$-\Sigma P_i \log_2 P_i = 2.0$$

Each alternative occurs with a probability of 1 in 4, and therefore its associated $P_i$ value is 0.25. Looking up the value of $-\log_2 P_i$ in a table of such values we find it equals 2.00. Since the equation specifies that $P_i$ serves to weight each alternative, these values are presented in the fourth column. The sum of all of the values in this fourth column represents the total amount of uncertainty (or information) in this particular set, and it turns out to be equal to 2.00. If we go back and check this against an analysis based on decisions and alternatives—that is, the number of decisions required to specify one alternative in four—the results are identical: It takes two decisions to specify one alternative unequivocally, given four alternatives.

**Table 15.4** Unequal-probability case*

| Alternative | $P_i$ | $-\log_2 P_i$ | $-P_i \log_2 P_i$ |
|---|---|---|---|
| 1. | 0.50 | 1.00 | 0.50 |
| 2. | 0.25 | 2.00 | 0.50 |
| 3. | 0.125 | 3.00 | 0.375 |
| 4. | 0.125 | 3.00 | 0.375 |

$$-P_i \log_2 P_i = 1.75$$

* Adapted from *Uncertainty and Structure as Psychological Concepts*, by W. R. Garner. New York: John Wiley, 1962.

If we look now at Table 15.4, a similar analysis is done for a four-alternative case, except that these alternatives are not equally likely. In this case, Alternative 1 occurs 50% of the time, whereas Alternative 4 occurs only

$12\frac{1}{2}\%$ of the time.  In comparing the total information or uncertainty in this second case with the equal probability of the first case, the first difference that is obvious is that the average value is higher in the equal-probability case (Example 1), yet the highest individual value occurs in the unequal case for the third and fourth alternatives.  The average uncertainty for each alternative is given in the third column, and by examining these values, we see that the single most frequently occurring case ($P = 0.5$) has an information value of 1.00, whereas the least likely case ($P = 0.125$) has the highest value, 3.00.  This simply illustrates what was said before: More information is gained when an unlikely event occurs than when a likely event occurs.

So far we have talked only about information in a single choice—but it is also apparent that any given choice must be constrained by preceding choices.  In a very real sense, these sequential dependencies reduce the amount of information that can be conveyed by any given symbol (word?) that occurs in a sequence of symbols.  Such a situation is technically called a *Markov process*; i.e., a process defined in terms of a finite number of states, each with a fixed number of alternatives at each state.  Since each state involves a fixed number of alternatives, it is possible to calculate the amount of information at each state.  In the same way that it was possible to calculate the average uncertainty at a given state, it is also possible to calculate the total uncertainty across all states.  In general this situation is defined by the following equation: $I = \Sigma P_j I_j$, where $I$ is the average information over all states, $I_j$ the average information in any state, and $j$ and $P_j$ the probability that state $j$ will occur.

This discussion of sequential states concerns the rather important concept of *redundancy*.  Redundancy has to do with the degree of corelationship between successive states.  To the degree that there is sequential constraint, the next state will have a highly probable response.  By definition, then, a state that has a very likely response is one which has less total information than one which has equally probable alternatives (see Tables 15.3 and 15.4).  Given this reduction in the amount of possible uncertainty (information) in a given constrained state, redundancy can be defined quite simply as the difference between the total uncertainty possible and the uncertainty actually in the situation.

As Garner (1962) points out, the nominal uncertainty of the 27-element English letter alphabet (26 letters + 1 space) is the $\log_2 27$ or 4.75.  If we calculate the actual uncertainty, it turns out to be 4.10.  The difference of 0.65 represents redundancy for individual letter distributions.  In general, predictability increases as the length of a sequence increases.  What this means practically is that the choice of a letter is much easier to predict if the stem is *bottl_*, than if only a single letter, e.g., *b_____*, is presented.  Similarly, the last word in a sentence is considerably more constrained, that is, easier to predict, than the first or second or third word.

## THE STATISTICAL DESCRIPTION OF LANGUAGE

An information-theory approach to language suggests that we will get the most mileage out of our statistical data if we examine them with the following two questions in mind: (1) What are the probabilities of occurrence of individual items such as letters, sounds, words, etc., in the language? (2) What is the role of sequential constraints in changing such probabilities? Let us take up each of these questions in order.

*Individual-item probabilities.* Although a good deal is known about the probabilities with which certain letters and sounds occur in written and spoken language (see Miller, 1951, Chapter 4, for a review of this early work, and Garner, 1962, Chapters 7 and 8 for a review of later work), we will concentrate primarily on the word as our unit of analysis. In general, most frequency counts have been done on samples of written language. The most famous of these was by Thorndike and Lorge, done in the late 1930's (under the auspices of a Government public works program). This word count involved a listing of some 30,000 words in order of their frequency of occurrence in popular magazines, children's books, and other such printed sources. *In toto* Thorndike and Lorge (1944) counted 20 million words of text.

What are the properties of words which occur very frequently? Miller, Newman, and Friedman (1958), in attempting to answer this question, plotted the relationship of word length (in letters) to frequency of occurrence and found that most of the frequently used words contained 2, 3, or 4 letters. This agrees rather well with earlier findings of Zipf (1935) who showed that the most frequently used words were monosyllables. This is true both of written language (where *the* is the most frequent word) and of spoken language such as occur in telephone conversations (where *I* is the most frequently occurring word).

Because frequency of occurrence is such an obvious variable, a good deal is known about how it works in different psychological tasks. For example, it is well known (Solomon and Howes, 1951; Howes and Solomon, 1951, and many others) that the speed with which an individual word is recognized in a tachistoscope is affected by its frequency of occurrence in the language. In the absence of any context, more frequently used words are reported more rapidly than less frequently used words. Although it is not altogether clear that subjects actually see the words more readily (see Goldiamond and Hawkins, 1958, for evidence on this point), subjects certainly are able to produce them more readily as responses. Whether or not the effect is a perceptual one is relatively unimportant; what is important is that frequency of occurrence does have a marked effect on the use of a word as a response.

A more recent experiment by Oldfield and Winfield (1965) concerned the speed with which people could name objects where the appropriate object names differed in Thorndike–Lorge frequency; e.g., *clock* versus *anvil*. In general, their results showed a very strong relationship between how frequently a particular word occurs in English and the ease with which it is used to name an object. This was true despite the control introduced by Oldfield and Winfield that all words be of equal length.

One other aspect of simple frequency of occurrence is mentioned by Miller (1951), and this concerns the relative degree of occurrence of the various parts of speech. Table 15.5 presents some empirical results obtained by French, Carter, and Koenig (1930), who gathered these data from recorded telephone conversations.

**Table 15.5**  Occurrence of parts of speech in telephone conversation

| Parts of speech | Number of words | | Type token ratio |
|---|---|---|---|
| | Tokens | Types | |
| Nouns | 11,660 | 1029 | 0.086 |
| Adjectives and adverbs | 9,880 | 634 | 0.064 |
| Verbs | 12,550 | 456 | 0.036 |
| Auxiliary verbs | 9,450 | 37 | 0.0039 |
| Prepositions and conjunctions | 12,400 | 36 | 0.0029 |
| Pronouns | 17,900 | 45 | 0.0025 |
| Articles | 5,550 | 3 | 0.00054 |
| Totals | 79,390 | 2240 | 0.028 |

* From "The words and sounds of telephone conversation," by N. R. French, C. W. Carter, and W. Koenig, *Bell System Tech. J.*, **9**, 2, 1930; quoted in *Language and Communication*, by George A. Miller, New York: McGraw-Hill, 1951.

The heading *tokens* simply means the number of times a particular category occurred, whether or not it was the same word whereas *types* means the total number of different words excluding repeats. The type–token ratio then is a measure of speech novelty; if the rating is high, then few of the words were repeated; if the value is low, it means that a small number of different words occurred relatively frequently. For example, of the 79,390 different tokens, 17,900 involved pronouns and 11,660 nouns. If we look at the *types* column, it is possible to see that 1029 different nouns were used, while only 45 different pronoun or pronounlike words were used, thereby yielding a type–token ratio of 0.086 for nouns and 0.0025 for pronouns. Considered from a form-class point of view, this difference in ratio represents the difference between open and closed form classes.

As Miller (1951) has noted in regard to these data:

"The articles, prepositions, conjunctions, pronouns and auxiliary verbs determine the general form of our statements, while the nouns, adjectives and adverbs contribute to the context. The different forms repeat themselves more often than do the different contexts, and so the minor parts of speech compose the major part of our utterances."*

*Sequential constraints.* Although it is clear that human subjects are aware of, and able to make use of, the frequency properties of words, it is much more important for a discussion of the sentence to consider how sequential constraints operate in language. As Garner (1962) has noted: "The total amount of redundancy which is due to distributional constraints (how frequently one or another word occurs) is relatively small compared to that due to sequential constraints." It is to these sequential constraints that we now turn.

One of the earliest studies on the problem of sequential constraints was done by Chapanis in 1954. Since written language generally makes for easier experimental procedures, Chapanis presented subjects with reasonably extended passages of prose (about 50 words) and randomly deleted from 10% to 66% of the letters in the passage. The results of this experiment showed that subjects were able to replace letters with 90% accuracy even when every fifth letter was removed. It was not until about one of every two letters was deleted that letter guessing dropped to a significantly low level (about 20%).

But aren't some types of deletions easier to replace than others? For example, there are advertisements on trains and buses for speedwriting that read something like this: *Lrn to tk shrthnd at* 120 *wpm & mk wndrfl frnds.* If all the words (except 120) were spelled out in full it would take 62 letters and numbers. The message presented above involves only 33 letters, so that in terms of Chapanis' procedure, about 45% has been deleted. If we estimate the replacement accuracy from Chapanis' results, we would expect it to fall at less than 20%, yet it is clear that accuracy for the above sentence is probably closer to 100%. This casual observation was borne out experimentally by Miller and Friedman (1957), who found that certain types of deletions are easier to fill in than others. In terms of the example given above, as well as in terms of Miller and Friedman's results, the best sort of deletion is one which leaves out the vowels. This is only another way of showing that the informational value of individual letters is unequal, with vowels having much lower information value than consonants. Deleting a vowel is much less influential in reducing word coherence than deleting a consonant, particularly when these words occur in meaningful sentences.

---

* From *Language and Communication,* by George A. Miller, New York: McGraw-Hill, 1951, page 94.

Given this finding with letters in words, a logical next step is to examine the effects of word deletions in sentences. One of the earliest experiments in this regard was done by Morrison and Black (1957), who randomly deleted words in 11-, 12-, and 13-word sentences. Their results were quite similar to those reported for letters, except that the general level of prediction was much poorer. For example, when 10% of the letters were deleted, 90% guessing accuracy was still possible; with 10% of the words deleted, the best a subject could do was 50%.

In a slightly different sort of word-guessing task, Howes and Osgood (1954) used words such as *dark*, *beautiful*, etc., which produce both opposite and synonymous associations. What they were able to show was that if a word such as *dark* were preceded by appropriate context words (*Hell, fearful, sinister*), it was possible to increase the probability of occurrence of words like *devil* from about 7% to one of 25%. This is reminiscent of other similar work reported by Pollio and his associates (Pollio and Gerow, 1968; Pollio, Sundland, and Wilcox, 1967, etc.), who were also able to get particular words to occur by increasing the length and appropriateness of preceding context.

In information-theory terms, such results imply that as the context increases in length, a small number of responses become very likely, and all other responses become less likely or completely impossible. In an experimental test of this analysis, Shepard (1962) had subjects produce as many words as they could in five minutes in response to a sentence containing an omitted word. His results indicated that as context increased in length, the total pool of responses produced decreased dramatically. When 40 words of context were presented, subjects were able to come up with fewer than ten words. Since all words to be guessed were in the middle of the passage, sentence position did not play any significant role. Shepard's results indicate that an increase in context length serves to reduce the uncertainty of a particular word. If we assume that uncertainty is related to speed of a response, it is possible to argue that response speed (words/minute) is faster when there is more uncertainty, exactly the result obtained.

This conclusion is, however, in contrast to one found by Goldman-Eisler (1958b) and described in Chapter 14. Her results showed that when subjects attempted to replace words in text that had preceded a pause in its original spontaneous production, they took longer to produce the word if they produced it correctly. Since pauses in spontaneous speech were associated with points of maximum uncertainty, it might be possible to argue from Shepard's data that subjects should have been able to replace words faster at these points. This apparent contradiction can be understood in terms of the subjects' tasks in both experiments. Although it is true there are more responses available at points of maximum uncertainty, subjects will be able to respond quite rapidly if all they were asked to do is to produce words, but will respond more slowly if they are asked to produce a particular word.

In both cases, points of uncertainty imply that a large word pool exists—if no selection is required, the size of the pool favors speed; if selection is required, the size of the pool implies a longer search, and hence, longer reaction time.

We have, as yet, not reached the level of the sentence—yet it is quite clear that sentences also impose their own forms of constraint and these must surely be reflected in certain aspects of verbal behavior. One obvious test of sentence effects is to compare how accurately subjects can report words presented in noise, when these words are presented in random order or in sentence form. Miller, Heise, and Lichten (1951) have done such an experiment and their results are as expected: Subjects are much better able to report words correctly when these occur in a sentence than when these are presented randomly. As in much of the preceding discussion, this improved ability to recognize words in a sentence is undoubtedly the result of a reduction in the number of possible alternatives. A sentence provides a number of signals (both word-to-word and grammatical) as to the type of word required (adjective, noun, pronoun, etc.), as well as to its specific nature (*The_____ rolled down the street after being hit by the bat*). Under these powerful forms of constraint, it is not surprising that subjects are more accurate in reporting what they heard, when what they heard was a sentence rather than a random collection of words.

## SEQUENTIAL VERBAL BEHAVIOR: AN ANALYSIS OF APPROXIMATIONS TO ENGLISH

If grammar is nothing more than a highly probable sequence of words and form classes, it should then be possible to explore this habit system in terms of how such habits influence memory and transfer. This is the general strategy taken with regard to the most obvious associative analysis of grammar—that it reflects a probabilistic sequence of word-to-word connections. The reference experiment here is by Miller and Selfridge (1951), who constructed passages of various length (10, 20, 30 and 50 words) and then examined the number of words recalled as a consequence of how closely the sequence approximated English. The general findings were that as the order of approximation to English increased, the number of words recalled also increased and that the greatest effect occurred at lower-order approximations. They also found that there were essentially no differences between fifth-order approximations and connected textual material. (Miller and Selfridge, 1951; Sharp, 1958; Richardson and Voss, 1960.)

Now this increase in recall is not surprising from anybody's point of view, though it is difficult to specify why in any detail. Johnson (1968) has suggested that two different types of associations may be involved in this case: (1) As sequences increase in their order of approximation to English, there does appear to be an increase in the relative meaningfulness of the material. (2) There is also an increase in the degree to which these materials duplicate the grammar of the language. In short, both grammar and meaning may make their own contributions to the results obtained, and these are not necessarily of the same order of importance for high and low levels of approximation.

Consider the difference between zero and first-order dependencies in terms of an experiment by Deese (1961). Also remember that a zero-order approximation is constructed by taking words randomly from a dictionary (and hence an approximation contains mostly low-frequency words), whereas a first-order sequence is constructed by randomly selecting high-frequency words. What this means is that words in the 0-order list are extremely rare, and in addition will not be repeated in a short passage of 50–100 words. Words in the first-order list, in addition to occurring quite frequently in the language, also tend to appear more than once in short passages. In this latter regard, words such as *is, and, the*, etc., tend to reappear quite frequently.

In Deese's experiment, subjects were required to recall zero- and first-order word sequences. The difference between the two means was about 4.5 items (roughly 8.0 to 12.5 words for the zero and first order, respectively). When Deese examined the structure of the two sets of material he found that they differed in the number of repetitions by about 4.5 items: In other words, the difference in recall between zero- and first-order approximations could be accounted for by the subject's ability to guess repetitively words such as *the, and*, etc. No if's, and's, or but's about it—the difference in recall between zero- and first-order dependencies is accounted for solely by an increase in the number of *if*'s, *and*'s, *but*'s, contained in first-order approximations.

If we move on to the middle range of approximations (second-order through fifth-order), an examination of these materials shows the possible effects of word-to-word linkages such as occur in the case of inter-item associations. That is, for sequences of varying length, the content of the sequence seems to contain words that would occur as word associates (i.e., represent more usual verbal habits) and that these associates are connected by relatively simple declarative sentence or phrase structure.

If this is the case, it seems possible that increases in recall at the middle levels are dependent on word-to-word linkages, as well as on the occurrence of regularly recurring response sequences such as: *What is being said* (fifth order), *Go back home* (second order), etc. In order to examine this possibility, Tulving and Patkau (1962) scored recall protocols not in terms of the actual numbers of words recalled, but rather in terms of the number of words recalled in an unbroken sequence. Using this measure, they found that at all levels of approximation to English, subjects were able to recall between five and six sequences; the only difference at the various levels was in terms of sequence length.  At first order, the size of the sequence was a single word, whereas at higher orders the length of these sequences was considerably longer, and up to four or five words in some cases.

In a more extended analysis of this same problem, Coleman (1963) examined the properties of recall for all orders of approximation, including running text.  He made changes in the material used, the most important of which were that he controlled for the frequency of occurrence of words in the text passages (in most of the earlier studies, the text passage had tended to use relatively rare words) and the number of syllables in these words.  When this was done, Coleman was able to show significant differences between fifth-order approximations and connected texts; something not found by previous investigators.

Coleman also examined his data in terms of unbroken response sequences in much the same way that Tulving and Patkau had.  When he examined one-word sequences (essentially total number words recalled) the results were identical with earlier studies in showing a negatively accelerated curve—that is, the greatest increases in recall were at the lower orders of approximation.  When, however, Coleman plotted the number of two-word, three-word, and, . . . , up to 17-word unbroken sequences, the shape of the curve changed markedly, so that when longer sequences are considered, the curve is positively accelerated, with the greatest effect occurring for higher-order approximations.

These results indicate that left-to-right habits do occur and do have striking effects on recall.  Although the original demonstration by Miller and Selfridge seemed to show that there was a limit to this effect, more recent studies by Coleman and others indicate that when materials are equated for certain properties across various levels, further increases in recall do occur beyond fifth-order approximations.  Selected analysis done at various orders of approximation indicate that different factors are at work at different levels.  For example, Deese's work seems to show that guessing habits account for much of the increase in recall found between zero- and first-order approximations to English.  Similarly, more analytic studies of what happens during the recall of passages at various levels of approximation (by Tulving and Patkau, and by Coleman) indicate that subjects are able to make better use of longer sequences at higher levels, but that the absolute number of unbroken sequences remains constant at about five or six.  Presumably these longer sequences represent well-integrated response units that can be transferred to the present recall task.

## Grammar and Verbal Learning

But these studies are still a long way from what ordinarily would be called grammar.  As a point of departure, consider instead a study by Marks and

Miller (1964), which attempted to separate the independent contribution of grammar and meaning in sentence recall. In this experiment, four different groups of subjects were run. Each group learned a number of different verbal sequences: One group learned meaningful English sentences; a second group learned the same words, except this time they were presented in scrambled order; two other groups learned meaningless sentences, with one of these groups learning meaningless material in grammatical order and the other learning meaningless material in nongrammatical order. For this experiment then, each group represented one of the four possible combinations of meaningful versus meaningless, and grammatical versus ungrammatical. The results of the experiment were clear in showing that meaningful and grammatical sentences were learned most rapidly, and meaningless ungrammatical sentences were learned most slowly. For present purposes, however, the most interesting finding was that meaningful ungrammatical material was learned at about the same rate as meaningless grammatical material.

The conclusion which emerges from this study is similar to that arising in connection with work on order of approximation to English: Habits involving both grammar and meaning transfer to new recall situations. When both are present, as in text or higher-order approximations, learning and recall are maximal; where neither is present, as in a series of disconnected words, learning and recall are poorest. In this latter case, the frequency of occurrence of constituent words is a reasonably strong determiner of learning and recall.

If we take Deese's (1961) analysis as a starting point, both grammar and meaning have their effect by promoting appropriate guessing tendencies and by retarding inappropriate ones. If a subject recognizes material as grammatical and meaningful, certain noncontent words—*the*, *a*, etc.—as well as certain specific content words, become very likely. Given the increased availability of these words, the subject is well able to offer good guesses as to what the entire passage must be, and thereby is able to produce better learning and recall performance.

The Miller–Marks study really represents an extension of earlier work by Epstein (1961, 1962, 1963) on the facilitative effects of grammar in learning. In these earlier experiments, subjects were presented with nonsense syllables tagged with the grammatical inflections of normal English, e.g., *The Yigs war virmly rixing* ... etc., and then asked to recall such sequences. For this condition it took about 5.8 trials to achieve perfect recall. A second group was presented with a series containing the same nonsense syllables, but in this case, no inflections were provided; e.g., *The Yig war vum rix,* ..., etc. Under these conditions, it took about 7.6 trials to achieve perfect recall. Although there were other conditions (for example, where inflectional suffixes were included that violated usual grammatical order), the point seems well taken that grammatical structure can and does facilitate sequential recall.

In one of Epstein's later studies, subjects were required to learn structured and unstructured lists by the method of serial anticipation. If these syllables were presented at a 2-second rate, that is, where syllables were presented separately and were separated by 2 seconds, there were no differences among the various types of materials. Under single-word presentation conditions the influence of sentence structure is much reduced. Further studies by Rosenberg and Moran (as described by Johnson, 1968) have shown that grammatical structure does facilitate recall under certain conditions and that there are other conditions under which its effects are minimal. The important point to these early studies is, of course, that even with nonsense materials grammar can facilitate recall if subjects are cued to treat the material as analogous to sentences in some way.

A different way in which to relate grammar and rote learning was adopted by Glanzer (1962). In the first part of his study, subjects were required to learn a series of paired associates, in which for some pairs the stimulus term was a nonsense syllable and the response term a content word such as a noun, verb, adjective, or article (e.g., *YIG-food*, *MEF-think*, etc.), while for other pairs the stimulus term was again a nonsense syllable and the response term was a function word such as a preposition, pronoun, or conjunctive (e.g., *TAH-of*; *KEX-and*, etc.). The results of this experiment were clear in showing that content words were easier to learn in this situation than function words.

This conclusion had to be modified by Glanzer's next experiment. In this experiment subjects were required to learn word triples consisting of a nonsense syllable, a word, and a final nonsense syllable. Under these conditions, when the word was a function word (*of, and,* etc.) the triple was learned more readily than if the word component was a content word (noun or verb). Thus, *TAH-of-ZUM* was learned more easily than *LIG-food-SEP*. Glanzer explained this result as follows: Since function words are normally used to tie together other elements in a sentence, this function is exploited in the context of a learning task and easier learning results. Glanzer's results seem to demonstrate the different status of content and function words and their respective roles in a sentence: Content words carry the major burden of communication, whereas function words serve to form syntactic constructions.

While Glanzer was concerned with words as units of analysis, Rosenberg (1965, 1968) concerned himself with larger constructions such as clauses and phrases. In general, Rosenberg has argued that grammar facilitates verbal learning on the basis of two associative factors, one having to do with the particular sequence of words used, and the other with the sequence of form classes employed. The strength of the word-to-word or associative habit is indexed by tables of word association, particularly for those associative pairs in which the stimulus and response words are from different grammatical form classes, e.g., *dark–night*. Grammatical habits are indexed by the normal order of form classes in simple sentences: e.g., adjective–noun.

In order to provide some special support for this type of analysis, Rosenberg (1965) compared the recall of the following pairs of items: adjective–noun; noun–adjective; adjective–adjective and noun–noun. After eight presentation trials, subjects were asked for a free recall of the pairs. Results were quite convincing in demonstrating that adjective–noun pairs were better recalled than any other combination, although the recall of noun–adjective pairs was considerably better than either of these other comparisons.

In order to extend these findings, Rosenberg has gone on to gather controlled word-association norms in which subjects are asked to produce word associates of a specific grammatical form class. Making use of these norms, Rosenberg has examined the joint contribution of grammatical and associative habits in verbal learning. In general, results suggest that both word-to-word and class-to-class habits strongly determine the learning and recall of words.

Perhaps the most ambitious attempt to relate grammatical structure to verbal learning has been undertaken by N. F. Johnson (1965a, 1965b, 1968). In these experiments, the basic procedure is to have the subject learn a series of seven paired associates in which the stimulus terms are single-digit numbers and in which the response terms were complete seven-word sentences such as: *The tall boy saved the dying woman*, as well as *The house across the street is burning*. Each subject learned eight number-sentence pairs presented on a memory drum. The reason for using such sentences can be seen by looking at the tree diagrams in Fig. 15.5.

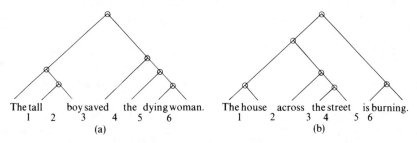

**Fig. 15.5** Tree diagrams for both experimental sentences. (From Johnson, 1965)

The important aspects of both sentences are numbered 1 through 6, which represent word-to-word transition points. The basic hypothesis of the Johnson studies was that if grammatical structure has any effect at all, it will show up in the pattern of errors made by subjects at these six points as they learn this particular type of paired associate.

Johnson measured errors in these studies in terms of an index he developed, called a *transitional error* or a *TE*. Transitional errors were scored every time an incorrect word followed a word that had been correctly recalled. For example, if in response to the sentence, *The tall boy saved the dying woman*, the subject produced, *The tall man went*, the first transition point (between *The* and *tall*) would show no error, the second transition point would show a *TE* (since *tall* is correct and *man* is not), whereas the third transition (between *man* and *went*) would not be counted as a *TE* since the preceding word had been incorrectly produced. Given this scoring procedure, the results for both "the tall boy" and "the burning house" sentences are presented in Fig. 15.6a and 15.6b.

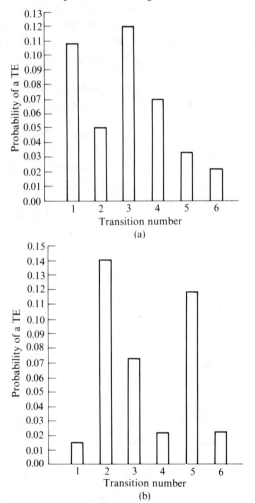

**Fig. 15.6** (a) Pattern of transitional error probabilities obtained when subjects learn the sentences in Fig. 15.5(a). (b) Pattern of transitional error probabilities obtained when subjects learn the sentences in Fig. 15.5(b). (From Johnson, 1965)

For the "tall-boy" sentence, the major break in clause pattern is between *boy* and *saved*, (transition point 3) whereas for the "burning-house" sentence the major breaks are at 2 and 5. In both cases, the greatest number of *TE*'s occur at these points, indicating the psychological reality of phrase structure.

One further significant finding was that *TE*'s within clauses were of unequal value. An examination of this pattern indicated, however, that the pattern of such errors was meaningfully related to the structure of the phrase. for example, in the phrase, *saved—¹the—²dying—³woman*, there are three different transition points and the pattern of transition errors was consistent with an immediate-constituents analysis of the clause. That is, [*dying woman*] forms a basic constituent with the word [*the*] added onto this core. This further analysis makes the general point that the pattern of *TE*'s obtained reflects the total phrase structure of the sentence, not only its division into major constituents.

Another approach to the problem of relating surface structure to memory has been pursued by Martin and Roberts (1966; Martin, Roberts, and Collins, 1967; Roberts and Martin, 1968). They take as basic Yngve's analysis of sentence construction (see Chapter 14 for a discussion of this model) particularly insofar as it relates to a structural analysis of the sentence. According to Yngve, in order to generate a sentence the speaker has to hold certain parts of the sentence clause in memory as the sentence is being produced. Sentence production is viewed as dependent on the expansion of successive rewrite rules. To take Martin, Roberts, and Collins' (1967) example, consider the structure of the sentence diagrammed in Fig. 15.7.

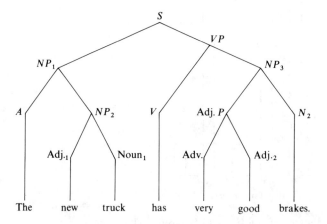

**Fig. 15.7** Phrase-structure analysis of a sample sentence. (From Martin, Roberts, and Collins, 1968)

According to Yngve's analysis, the necessary rewrite rules and memory components are presented in Fig. 15.8.

| | | |
|---|---|---|
| * $S \longrightarrow NP_1 + VP$ | $[-]$ | |
| * $NP_1 \longrightarrow A + NP_2$ | $[VP]$ | |
| $A \longrightarrow$ The | $[NP_2, VP]$ | 2 |
| * $NP_2 \longrightarrow Adj_1 + N_1$ | $[VP]$ | |
| $Adj_1 \longrightarrow$ new | $[N_1, VP]$ | 2 |
| $N_1 \longrightarrow$ truck | $[VP]$ | 1 |
| * $VP \longrightarrow V + NP_3$ | $[-]$ | |
| $V \longrightarrow$ has | $[NP_3]$ | 1 |
| * $NP_3 \longrightarrow Adj\ P + N_2$ | $[-]$ | |
| * $Adj\ P \longrightarrow Adv + Adj_2$ | $[N_2]$ | |
| $Adv \longrightarrow$ very | $[Adj_2, N_2]$ | 2 |
| $Adj_2 \longrightarrow$ good | $[N_2]$ | 1 |
| $N_2 \longrightarrow$ brakes | $[-]$ | 0 |

**Fig. 15.8** Rewrite rules necessary to produce the sentence, *The new truck has very good brakes*. (From Martin, Roberts, and Collins, 1968)

In this figure each of the rewrite rules required to generate the sentence is preceded by asterisks, whereas operations not preceded by an asterisk select specific words. Each bracket contains the nodes to be held in memory during the operation of a rewrite rule.

In this type of analysis, an important concern is with the number of nodes in memory as a specific word is being written out. For example, when *The* is being written, there are two as-yet-unexpanded nodes, $NP_2$ and $VP$, whereas when *has* is being produced, only $NP_3$ is still in memory. Given these considerations, Martin and his collaborators have defined a measure of sentence complexity in terms of what they have called a sentence's Yngve number. An *Yngve number* is simply the mean number of nodes held in memory during the expansion of a structural marker into a word. In the case of the sentence presented in Fig. 15.7, these values are 2, 2, 1, 1, 2, 1, and 0. The arithmetic mean of these values ($\frac{9}{7} = 1.29$) yields an estimation of the sentence's structural complexity.

Perhaps the most important aspect of this analysis to keep in mind is that Yngve numbers are concerned only with sentence structure—not with the likelihood of occurrence of a given word. Psychologically this means that the phrase-structure grammar of sentence production represents the habits a speaker might use in producing a sentence, or a listener in understanding that sentence. Once the speaker decides at the highest level which type of sentence to use, his ability to develop that sentence—and to have it understood—depends primarily on memory limitations. If this is the case, then sentences differing in complexity (as defined by Yngve numbers) should differ in the degree to which they are recalled.

A test of this prediction was made by Martin and Roberts (1966), and results support the expectation: Sentences having low Yngve numbers were better recalled than sentences having high Yngve numbers. In this particular experiment, Martin and Roberts also varied the type of sentence (declarative, passive, negative, etc.) in an attempt to see if this factor would affect recall. An example of a passive sentence, producing a low Yngve number is *They were not prepared for rainy weather*, whereas an example of a comparable passive having a high Yngve number is *Children are not allowed out after dark*. Sentences of the first type were recalled significantly better than sentences of the second type.

In a further experiment (Martin, Roberts, and Collins, 1967) this conclusion had to be modified. These results showed that low Yngve number produced good recall for passive but not for active sentences. In addition, it was also found that certain word classes (adverbs, adjectives and auxiliaries) were most often either omitted or changed. These results indicate that, in attempting to recall sentences, subjects probably focus both on key words (largely content words) and on sentence type (active versus passive, etc.), and using these two components as a guide, generate anew the sentence during recall itself. During presentation the form of the sentence serves to direct attention to key elements, whereas during recall these key elements guide the type and content of the sentence produced in recall.

The issue, however, is still open at present as to the exact role of sentence complexity in sentence recall. Some investigators, such as Martin and his coworkers, have found some effect of Yngve number on recall, while other investigators such as Perfitti (1969a, 1969b) have failed to support this earlier work. Although it is true that some sentences are easier (or more difficult) to recall than others, Yngve number does not seem unequivocally to predict the relative difficulty of different sentences.

## An *S–R* Model of How Sentences are Generated

Most of the experiments reviewed indicate the psychological reality of units derived from grammatical analysis. Although it may be possible to describe stimulus materials in terms of probabilistic connections among words or form classes, it does seem highly unlikely that subjects produce sentences on this basis.   Generating material for experiments is one thing; generating sentences for communication quite another.

It was largely with these considerations in mind that Osgood (1963; 1968) twice set himself the task of describing how speakers and listeners understand and create sentences.   At the outset he assumed that a simple linear model (that is, a simple Markov chain) was inadequate for the job. After some further consideration he proposed that a grammar at least as complex as one embodied in a phrase-structure grammar is required; but with one difference—and this difference is crucial for his argument.   Perhaps the best way to present Osgood's hypothesis is in terms of his own (1963) diagram (Fig. 15.9).

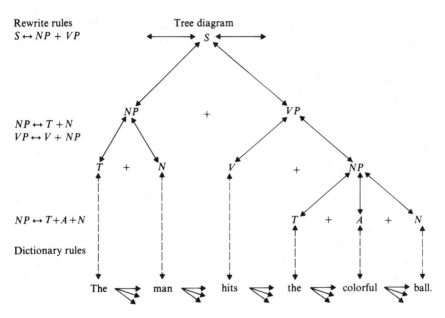

**Fig. 15.9** Phrase-structure analysis used by Osgood. (From "On understanding and creating sentences," by C. E. Osgood, *Amer. Psychologist,* **18,** 1963)

At the left of the figure are the usual sentence-rewrite rules, by now exhaustingly familiar to us all.   There is, however, one difference between Osgood's version of these rules and their more standard canonical form; and that is in terms of the double-headed arrow, i.e., $S \leftrightarrow NP + VP$.   This is true at all levels of the diagram and is meant to imply that rewrite rules are reversible.   Similarly, the tree diagram includes bidirectional arrows at each level.   At the level of the sentence, for example, these are included in order to suggest that most sentences—except those produced by linguists for purposes of analysis—are usually preceded and followed by other sentences.

A range of possibilities is also included at each level, and these are indicated by the three left-going arrows such as are specifically presented at the word level. Considering only this lowest level, that of the word, the model is essentially probabilistic: that is, a linear hierarchy of responses given *the* as an initial stimulus word. If no further constraints operate (as for example is true in a word-association task), then the subsequent response of *man* would occur on the basis of a simple probability-based linkage between these two words.

But other constraints do exist—and they exist at each and every level of the sentence. In producing connected discourse there are two different sets of constraints that operate in selecting the final string of words known as the sentence. Some of these constraints are sequential or linear or probabilistic at a given level, while others are unitizing or hierarchical or deterministic over the entire sentence. What this means is that the word *man* is produced on the basis of its sequential connection with *the*, on the basis of its hierarchical connection as a *noun* within the *NP* constituent, as well as on the basis of the constraint imposed on *NP* by the intent of the total sentence itself.

All this is quite formal—what are its psychological implications? By this type of analysis Osgood means to suggest that speech is both planful and adventurous and that speakers are able to provide sentences that are both genuinely novel and genuinely grammatical, as well as sentences or phrases they have uttered many times before. And this seems to be true at all levels. For example: A speaker may begin by generating a novel sentence and find that he has available as a total response sequence a clause which will serve to complete the sentence accurately and well. At each level, then, the production of a sentence may involve novel word or phrase sequences intermingled with old, well-rehearsed phrases, words, or even sentences. A model of sentence production which allows for control both from top to bottom as well as from left to right seems to Osgood to describe the way in which speakers go about creating sentences.

The most important aspect of Osgood's analysis is that it attempts to tie linguistic analysis to well-known psychological processes. If this specification is successful, then all the data gathered in support of general association theory are relevant to sentence production. This is no small achievement. What this implies is that the analysis of meaning as an implicit response (either an $r_m$ or an $r_a$ or some combination of the two), as well as the analysis of cognitive interaction in terms of some type of congruity or matching hypothesis are reasonable and viable hypotheses, and that the data used in support of these processes apply to sentence creation as well.

The best single piece of evidence directly relating to Osgood's analysis of sentence creation is provided by Johnson's experiments on transitional errors in paired-associate learning. As Osgood points out:

"Note (in regard to these experiments) first that ... major error peaks ... occur (between phrase boundaries). ... But note, second, that within each phrase there is an almost linear decrease in transitional errors running from left to right. These data appear to confirm rather strikingly the idea that simultaneous and sequential hierarchies combine in the understanding and creating of sentences."*

## LANGUAGE LEARNING: THE SKINNERIAN APPROACH

In the case of language, as in the case of other behaviors, there are two approaches that can be taken by a tough-minded associationistic psychology. One of these takes as crucial a careful description of both the implicit and explicit system of habits that go into the production of a particular piece of behavior, and so far in this chapter we have followed the intellectual peregrinations of this assumption. A second group of empirically minded psychologists, however, sets itself a different task, and that is the precise and accurate description of environmental factors which encourage and promote the acquisition and use of language behavior.

Speech, the overt aspect of language, is a motor response. In his book, *Verbal Behavior* (1957), Skinner explicitly set himself the task of analyzing how speech behavior or speech responses occur. He assumed that the principles involved are the same as those found to apply in the learning of any motor response. This analysis, therefore, takes account of the original level of the response (its operant level), the conditions under which it occurs (its discriminative stimulus conditions), and the consequences of performing a verbal response (i.e., its reinforcing contingencies).

Basically, Skinner distinguished three different ways in which speech responses can be made to occur. The first and perhaps the simplest of these is the *echoic verbal* response. Echoic verbal responding is involved in direct imitation. For the development of an echoic response, there are two discriminative stimuli: One of these is an adult who provides reinforcement for the appropriate response, while a second is the specific sound pattern to be imitated. Obviously, a single adult can and often does provide both stimuli. The appropriate response is obviously the repetition of the sound pattern. As an example, consider the case of a mother with a young child (Barry); the mother says: "Eugene Ionesco—say Eugene Ionesco, Barry." If Barry then says "Eugene Ionesco," momma will promptly respond with a reinforcing event such as saying "good" or smiling at Barry. If this occurs a number of times, it will increase Barry's tendency to say "Eugene Ionesco," and also his general tendency to imitate his mother's verbal behavior.

---

* From "On understanding and creating sentences," *Amer. Psychologist*, **18**, 1963, page 743.

Verbal behavior is often developed when the child wants to ask for something or to demand something. This type of verbal behavior is called a *mand* response, and again is learned on the basis of a simply specified set of events. This situation is usually one in which a quite specific motivational state is aroused: The speaker wants something (such as a glass of water or milk) or wants someone to do something for him. Since mands occur in *demand* or *command* activities, the obvious prerequisite for learning to use mands is another person—in the case of a child learning to speak, probably his parent. The response again is a verbal one—"*Tastee Freeze*" or if the child is older "Get me some *Tastee Freeze*"—which brings about the desired object, namely, *Tastee Freeze*.

Whereas mands benefit the speaker, the final type of verbal response, *tacts*, often benefit both listener and speaker. Tacts are comments about things that the speaker has come, or is coming, in con*tact* with: "This is a table," "an apple," etc. Tacting responses are naming responses, and again one obvious component of the situation in which such responses are learned must include an object to be named. Also included must be a listener (actually a sympathetic listener in the case of a very young child) who can understand that the verbal response "hap" uttered by a child in the presence of an apple is meant to be *apple*, and who will reward the child for this type of verbal approximation.

Occasionally some parents push their children toward *tacting* with such vigor as to produce bizarre behavior episodes: Consider the case of Michele (age $2\frac{1}{2}$), a strong-willed child, who occasionally pushes her father too far. When this occurs, her father gets a particular look on his face (roughly describable as "the urge to kill" look) which is easily recognizable. This look serves as warning (discriminative stimulus) that bodily harm is about to occur. At this particular time in Michele's and her father's life, he was anxious to have her learn to speak, but child that she is, she would speak only when it was to her advantage. Assume now the following situation: For some reason or other her father has that "urge to kill" look on his face and he is approaching Michele menacingly. What does Michele do at this point? She retreats slowly and starts to name objects in the room. "See table, Daddy," ... "lamp," "chair, ... etc." And what does the poor trapped father do? "Good, Michele, that's a table, a lamp, etc." Once the father is on the "good" trail, his anger drains away, and Michele for the 4621st time has carried the day. In this situation the father's anger serves as a discriminative stimulus for the child to name objects. To be sure, most tacts don't develop in precisely this way, but this situation does demonstrate, with some vigor, most of the requisite elements at work in more normal tacting situations.

Skinner distinguishes two further classes of verbal response which occur at more advanced levels of verbal behavior: *textual* responses and *intraverbal* responses. Textual responses are reading responses to written stimuli, and Skinner considers their development as largely analogous to verbal echoic response. Intraverbal responses are roughly equivalent to word-association responses, and are assumed to be learned on the basis of contiguity between words in experience. This class is included by Skinner for much the same reason that Osgood has included them in his analysis of meaning: Much of what we talk about (truth, democracy, God, historical persons, etc.) can never be experienced directly, and we therefore come to learn when and how to use these terms on the basis of their connections with other words.

Skinner's analysis has often been criticized on the grounds of being incomplete, and of overstressing the environmental (including prior verbal) control of all verbal behavior (see Chomsky, 1957). To make this simple negative criticism of this approach is to miss much of the impetus behind Skinner's analysis. He is not trying to describe the processes that go on within the head of the speaker; quite to the contrary, he is trying wherever possible to describe those specifiable conditions (insofar as these are specifiable) under which a given piece of verbal behavior occurs. The only justifiable complaint then is one that shows that much or all adult speech is unrelated to stateable conditions in the physical or verbal environment. If this step is taken—as Chomsky (1957) has done—then not only is Skinner's analysis of language called into question, but so too are all *S–R* analyses. More of this, however, in Chapter 16.

By way of summary, we can say that the developmental course of speech seems to involve learning procedures familiar to anyone who has worked in a psychological learning laboratory. The production of speech is a motor response and therefore subject to an operant-conditioning analysis of how it develops and is maintained. As part of this development, words and objects, and words and words, must occur contiguously, and on the basis of classical conditioning, word meaning develops in the child. To be sure, this type of conditioning is different from Pavlovian conditioning, in that the conditioned responses ultimately of interest are covert and unobservable, but all the functional properties are assumed to be the same. Grammar—or at least word strings—presumably begins to develop on the basis of some combination of classical and operant-conditioning principles that give rise to verbal chains. Since the sentences of a language are infinite, grammar alternatively comes to involve not only word-to-word dependencies, but also form-class-to-form-class and phrase-to-phrase dependencies. With sufficient experience, an organism comes to acquire more generalizable habits that allow for the production of grammatical and novel sentences. At this stage the speaker has incorporated the rules of a grammar at least as complicated as that implied by a phrase-structure grammar.

In order to round out this developmental analysis, what is needed is some evidence showing that speech sounds can in fact be conditioned by an operant conditioning paradigm, and that children can learn grammatical rules on the basis of a straightforward extension of familiar learning principles. The first of these considerations has been attempted by Harlan Lane (1965) in the context of second-language learning, whereas the second has been attempted by Martin Braine (1963; 1965), in the context of the learning of grammar by very young children.

Lane's basic procedure is quite simple and straightforward: An adult subject (college student) is presented intermittently with one of two stimuli. Say the student is to learn to distinguish between a Spanish /r/ and an English /r/. In this case, whenever the Spanish phoneme is presented and the subject responds by depressing a key he scores a point; if he responds to the English phoneme he loses a point. Using this sort of procedure, Lane was able to demonstrate that most subjects are able to master this task to a criterion of eight correct after only a single trial. In this case, as in many others, Lane and his associates were able to show that ordinary operant-conditioning procedures work as well for the learning of phonemes in humans as they do for the learning of lever pressing in rats.

Martin Braine, in a series of papers (1963a; 1963b; 1965), has also attempted to show that ordinary learning principles can be used to account for how children learn simple grammatical constructions. His analysis begins appropriately enough with an examination of the utterances produced by a child between the ages of 19 and 22 months. Among the responses produced by this child were the following two-word utterances:

| | | |
|---|---|---|
| see bug | my Mommy | all-gone shoe |
| see sock | my Daddy | all-gone vitamins |
| see hot | my milk | all-gone egg |
| do it | bye-bye plane | all-gone lettuce |
| push it | bye-bye man | all-gone watch |
| close it | bye-bye _____ | |
| move it | | |
| buzz it | | |

These utterances seem to show that the young child uses two distinct word classes, with one small class composed of words such as *see*, *it*, *my*, *bye-bye* and *all-gone*, and with one larger class composed of words which occur much less frequently and usually in combination with one of the words contained in the smaller set. Braine has called the smaller set of words a *pivot class*, and the larger set of words, an *open class*. The characteristics of the pivot class seem to be: (1) that they embody an idea such as possession (*my*) or perception (*see*) or disappearance (*all-gone*); (2) that they occur frequently; and (3) that in combination with open-class words they form the pivotal part of many different utterances. Braine feels that the division of words into pivot and open classes forms the basis of adult grammatical form class and represents an early form of grammatical learning. Although not all work on children's language has demonstrated the generality or import- ance of the pivot–open class distinction (see Bloom, 1970), let us postpone a discussion of this newer work until Chapter 16, in which transformational linguists will have their chance to describe how children learn to form sentences.

If we look again at each of the utterances described above, another aspect of pivot words seems obvious; namely, that they always occur in the same position in an utterance. With the exception of *it*, all pivot words occurred in the first position of a two-word utterance, whereas *it* occurred only in the second position. On this basis it is possible to suggest that a child may learn position as a clue to usage and that initially form classes are defined on the basis of positional similarity.

Other observations of child speech by Ruth Weir (1962) indicate some- thing of the same phenomena. Anthony, Mrs. Weir's $2\frac{1}{2}$-year-old son, had the rather helpful habit of engaging in a nighttime monolog just before he dropped off to sleep. In these monologs, there was usually no adult present and Anthony was free to talk about whatever he wanted, in whatever way he wanted. Consequently, his topics of conversation characteristically concerned significant items in his bedtime environment (*blankets, Bobo* (his doll), *milk, lights, Daddy, Mommy*, and *vacuum cleaner*—really the micro- phone used to record his speech). More surprising, however, is the fact that much of his speech involved what could best be called grammatical exercises:

> *What color—what color blanket—what color mop—what color glass. . . . Careful, broke the—Broke the finger—Broke the Bobo—Broke the vacuum cleaner. . . .*

In each of these cases, the child seems to be trying out a series of gram- matical constructions and in each of these cases the child maintains the same position for each of the major pivot words: *what color* and *broke the*. In Anthony's case, these pivot words are more than a single item and perhaps it is possible to argue that at a later stage of grammatical development (Anthony, after all, is 30 months old, whereas Braine's child was only 20 months), the concept of a phrase may come to function as a pivot around which to order other words. Similarly, it also seems possible to argue that phrases such as *what color* may be learned as a paired-associate habit and thereby, at least at this stage of the child's verbal life, function as a single unit.

These tentative speculations were formalized by Braine (1963b), who argues that much of English grammar can be accounted for in terms of *contextual* or *positional generalization*. In its simplest form, this hypothesis assumes that certain types of words recur in the same position in sentences (primarily simple, declarative sentences) and that this positional invariance is used as a clue to form class. Thus an answer to the question "What is learned when the child learns grammar?" might well be "The proper location of words in sentences."

Part of the reason for talking about the location of words in sentences rather than talking about word-to-word or form-class-to-form-class connections is that subjects are able to recognize which is the "noun" and which is the "verb" in nonsense sentences. For example, English speakers after hearing the nonsense sentence, *People kivil every day*, are likely to accept *George kivils* as grammatical.

In order to test his hypothesis that position can serve as a cue in a learning task, Braine had a group of 10-year-old children learn an artificial language consisting of six syllables which were divided into two classes, *A* and *P*. During training, only two nonsense syllables in the *A* class and two syllables in the *P* class were used, whereas during the test for positional generalization a third syllable in each class was used. So, for example, during training, a child learned that *KIV* and *JUF* were *A*-words (occurred in the first position in a "sentence") and that *BEW* and *MUB* were *B*-words (occurred in the second position). During the generalization test, children were presented with problems such as *FOJ* _____ and were asked to pick which of the syllables *KIV* or *BEW* would be correct for the second position. Since *FOJ* had not previously occurred in conjunction with either Class *A* or Class *P* syllables, any correct response had to be made on the basis of position as the cue. Results indicated that about 80% of all problems presented were completed correctly. This means that position can and does serve as a cue to filling in items in nonsense language. When subjects were asked why they filled in a particular syllable, only one specifically mentioned position; all others said "It sounded right" or something to that effect.

In a series of further studies involving this miniature language technique, as well as a different reconstructive memory technique, Braine (1965a; 1965b) was able to show that position is also an effective cue for subjects learning phrase-structure grammars. For example, in one of these experiments stimulus materials were again divided into two classes, *A* and *P*, but in this case the *P* class was itself subdivided in a phrase consisting of two parts, *p* and *q*. As in previous experiments, 10-year-old children were used as subjects, and as in previous experiments subjects were able to solve generalization problems at about a 75% rate. This was true across both *A* and *P* classes, as well as within the *P*-class itself.

More directly pertinent in the present context—since this is a discussion of first language learning—is an *A* + *P* experiment by Braine using $4\frac{1}{2}$-year-old children as subjects. In this particular experiment, "words" for both the *A* and *P* classes were animal sounds such as *moo* or *oink* for *A*, and *meow* or *quack* for *P*. As in tasks involving the 10-year-olds, 4-year-old children were able to solve these $A + P$ problems quite easily, and when tested for positional generalization performed at about a 75% rate, a figure comparable to those reported previously.

All these results then give rise to the view that positional generalization is a helpful principle in exploring how the grammatical order of words might be learned. In order to make the analysis work reasonably well, Braine also made the further assumption that most of the child's early grammar is concerned with simple declarative sentences and that much of adult grammar is a generalization of this simple form. This theory also assumes that position is a good cue to such sentences, i.e., nouns come first and verbs second in this type of sentence. Given position as a cue, generalization takes place across sentence types, with such generalization the critical factor in recognizing novel or nonsense sentences as grammatical. Finally, Braine assumed that other clues are available to help in the acquisition of grammar, and that these consist largely of associative bonds between closed-class morphemes such as inflections and open-class morphemes such as nouns and verbs. Although not all psychologists or linguists (see Bever, Fodor, and Weksel, 1965a; 1965b) are satisfied with this analysis, it does represent an attempt to apply ordinary learning principles directly to the problem of how grammar is acquired.

Although these studies by Lane and Braine are interesting in their own right, it is difficult to know what they mean in terms of how language is learned. It is certainly comforting for an associative analysis to discover that both children and adults are able to learn fragments of phonology and grammar under conditions that are well specified; but it is quite another thing to assume that children—initially without language or speech—go about learning the phonology and morphology of their language in precisely this way. Similarly, it is comforting to know that meaning can be built on the basis of pairing procedures, operationally and conceptually similar to classical conditioning—yet in all three cases, the question must remain as to whether this similarity is enough. There are some psychologists and linguists who feel the answer to this question must be "no," and it is to these objections that we will turn in Chapter 16.

## SUMMARY

Every normal baby comes to language with the same basic repertoire of grunts and coos, yet depending on where he lives, each child contrives to speak his own specific language as an adult. No normal baby comes to any social situation equipped with a repertoire of clichéd or predictable phrases, yet as an adult each comes to say "Sorry," or "Please" or some equivalent phrase in roughly the same situation. These and many other rather ordinary observations serve to place learning at the center of any analysis of the use and development of language.

But what is it that must be learned? Linguists propose, and psychologists agree, that the two primary aspects of language are meaning and grammar. If this is so, then what must be learned are meaning and grammar.

The history of associationist theory, as reflected in *S–R* behaviorism, suggests many different ways to treat meaning and only a few to treat grammar. Indeed it was Pavlov himself who called the conditioned response a *psychic secretion*, and from here it is but a short step to view classical conditioning as the procedure by which word meaning is developed. This assumption is quite congenial to contemporary behavior theory if the further assumption is made that the meaning of a word is given not as an overt response but rather as an implicit disposition known as a mediating response ($r_m$).

The assumption that meaning is an implicit response learned on the basis of classical conditioning procedures has further advantages in that it suggests an empirical test almost immediately. This, of course, was the intent of a series of studies undertaken by Staats and Staats and their associates, in which meaning was developed in the laboratory on the basis of pairing originally meaningless stimuli with meaningful words. Their results suggest that after such pairings, meaningless stimuli come to produce the same semantic differential ratings as those produced by the paired meaningful elements.

But how do we know that a word evokes a specific mediational response? The usual assumption made is that mediational responses can be operationalized by the use of oppositional rating scales, such as *hot–cold*, *good–bad*, etc. Since the total number of adjectives in a language represents a reasonably large pool of words, Osgood, Suci, and Tannenbaum set out to discover whether the total pool could be subdivided into meaningful subclusters and thereby reduce the number of rating scales to an absolute minimum. On the basis of factor-analyzing a great many different adjective scales, which were tested under a great many different conditions, in a number of different languages, Osgood and his collaborators came to the conclusion that adjectival scales tend to segregate themselves into three major factors and a number of variable minor ones. These three main semantic factors were named the *Evaluative Factor* (exemplified by the scale good–bad), the *Potency Factor* (hard–soft), and the *Activity Factor* (active–passive).

Given this analysis, Osgood identified the mediational response ($r_m$) as a compound response containing at least three components. Each of these response components was then coordinated with one of the major factors, thereby leading to the description of a stimulus word as a point in a three-dimensional semantic space. By this type of equation, both the implicit response properties ($r_m$'s) and the rating-scale locations were combined into a single theoretical model. Words, considered as stimuli, evoke responses with the intensity and characteristics of these responses assessed by their location on a set of specific semantic differential scales. Meaning is then both a response and a location, and the two are perfectly coordinated.

Running in parallel to the view that meaning can be construed as an implicit response is the view that words can be defined in terms of the pattern of other words that they give rise to as associative responses. So, for example, Deese used factor analysis to partition a set of meaningful words into associatively defined subclusters. He then speculated that each of these subclusters taped a different aspect of the associative meaning of an initial stimulus word. The recovered components made good intuitive sense and seemed useful in predicting how subjects used these words in other verbal tasks.

A description of how speakers create, and listeners understand, sentences is seen to depend on two types of processes: a sequential or left-to-right process (which in principle is no different from any other behavior such as tying a shoelace or learning a serial list of words) and a hierarchical process (similar in concept to a phrase-structure grammar, but also embodying probabilistic left-to-right connections). The description of grammar as a left-to-right process operating at many different levels (say that of the letter or of the word) encourages an analysis of language in terms of its statistical properties. Here a number of descriptive analyses have been done, all of which can be described in information-theory terms. A brief review of information theory indicates that it is the rare event which carries most information, and that under certain conditions, the highly probable event— the letter $u$ following $q$ in an English word—doesn't tell the listener anything new.

Given a statistical analysis of language performance, we find that a number of intriguing facts turn up, all of which indicate that such performance represents highly predictable bits of behavior. Certain letters or words or phrases recur with great frequency and are highly predictable on the basis of their situational and linguistic contexts. All these results support the view that for some purposes, sequences of verbal behavior that can be designated as "grammatical" are composed of items having high inter-letter or interword transition probabilities. This is the theoretical rationale behind an analysis of the role of sequential dependencies in speech and recall. Similar theoretical considerations also lie behind any attempt to analyze the role and effects of statistical approximations to English in a wide variety of verbal tasks.

But no matter how ingenious the statistical approximation to English, it still does not usually produce English—and what it lacks is grammar. Early experiments by Epstein, which simply demonstrated that grammatical markers do have a facilitating effect in nonsense-syllable learning, and later work (by Johnson and by Martin and Roberts) imply that the role of grammar cannot be ignored even in studies of verbal learning. Osgood has carefully reviewed all this work and has come to the conclusion that grammar, to be handled in the context of an associative analysis, must be described in terms of a phrase-structure grammar. His brand of phrase-structure grammar is different, however, from that usually described by linguists in that it presupposes both hierarchical processes (similar to other linguistically motivated grammars) and linear processes (similar to other probabilistic S–R analysis). The point of Osgood's approach is to emphasize that speakers and listeners alike take advantage of both grammatical organization and sequential probabilities in creating and understanding speech. Speech is both determined and *ad lib.*

Since the major thrust of an associative analysis of language attempts to show that language behavior is no different from other learned behaviors, it is not surprising to find that such analyses often focus on speech rather than on language. Skinner, for example, focuses his analysis entirely on how speech is acquired and maintained and scarcely if ever talks about *la Langue*; that is, about language. In so doing, he specifies in detail the specific properties of *situations* that give rise to *mands, tacts, echoic responses,* etc.— responses which constitute the verbal repertoire of an adult speaker. Skinner is not interested in specifying mental processes; he is concerned instead with describing those observable and manipulatable conditions that initiate and maintain verbal behavior.

The way children go about learning the grammar of their language has been studied in both a natural and a laboratory setting by Braine. The general conclusion emerging from much of this work is that, initially, word classes, and later phrase structures, are learned on the basis of position generalization. That is, in English, nouns seem to come first in sentences and verbs second. When the child comes to make use of pivot words, he has accomplished an early form of grammatical learning. Once this occurs, the child is then able to generalize positional occurrences to other related sentences. The early creativity of child grammar depends on positional generalization built on a base of pivot word classes.

A different set of naturalistic observations, by Weir, provides further support for the concept of pivot classes. Her record indicates that children seem to "practice" the use of particular words and word classes in much the manner of grammatical exercises or drills. In addition to these results, Braine has also shown that position can serve as a cue to complex learning, even in children as young as 4 years. Taken in conjunction with Weir's results, such data suggest that positional generalization is an important aspect of how children learn English grammar.

# CHAPTER 16

# LANGUAGE AND RULES: THE INFORMATION-PROCESSING APPROACH

One hundred years ago there were no motion pictures, airplanes or autobuses and not surprisingly there were no names for these then nonexistent entities. Since that time, however, these things have all come into existence and so too have their appropriate names. Everyone—little old ladies included—now talks confidently and easily about going to the *movies*, or taking a *bus* or a *plane* ride, and it all seems quite normal and casual. Yet behind this casual usage is the important linguistic fact that English has been able to provide new words without any changes in its basic vocabulary structure. English, like all other languages, is able to develop new words to cover new objects and situations.

In the same way that ordinary language grows by the addition of new terms, so too do specific vocabularies. Although this growth may be more self-conscious and consequently more awkward—who in their common-sense mind would invent a term such as *fractional antedating goal response*?—technical additions in vocabulary do seem to follow the same principles as more colloquial ones. What is important in both cases is that language is able to develop and expand without any real change in its basic structure. By its very nature, language provides the wherewithal for infinite innovation, at the word level at least.

But language gains not only by adding new terms, but also by using old ones in new ways. For example, consider a word such as *compact*. Originally this word was used as an adjective meaning small or something very much like that. With the widespread use of cosmetics in the 1920's and 1930's, *compact* came to be used as a noun referring to a small case having a mirror and capable of holding cosmetics. By the late 1950's, *compact* acquired still another connotation so that it now has something to do not only with ladies' cosmetics but with automobiles as well.

James Deese (1967) has recorded part of this change in the meaning of *compact* by examining changes in word associations. Figure 16.1 presents the percentage of word associates given in response to the word *compact* that are codable as referring to automobiles. These examples of associations were gathered at about two-year intervals between 1957 and 1966. Clearly, the use of *compact* in conjunction with automobiles was higher in 1966 than in 1957, although its peak usage seems to have been reached in 1961—the year when *compacts* became a significant factor in the automotive industry. Many other such examples could be presented, but a very complete analysis of such lexical changes is contained in the book *Meaning and Change of Meaning* (1965) by Gustave Stern. In this book, a large number of specific examples are considered, and a general set of change categories proposed.

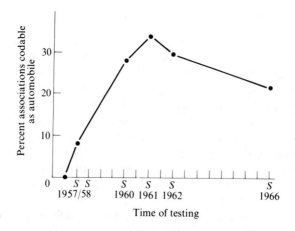

**Fig. 16.1** The percentage of responses in free association to the stimulus "compact," codable as *automobile*, given by male students between 1957 and 1966. (From "Meaning and change in meaning," by James Deese, in *Amer. Psychologist* **22,** 1967)

For example, consider the developmental history of a simple word such as *horn*. Originally *horn* referred specifically to a part of an animal. In the next phase of its development, *horn* referred to an animal's horn used to produce musical sounds, while at a still later stage it referred to a musical instrument made from an animal's *horn*. In its final sense—the one most commonly used today—the word *horn* has lost all connection with its animal origins and refers to a class of musical instruments having at best only a vague and tenuous connection with its original meaning. It is left as an exercise for the reader to develop the further etymological history of *horn* as it occurs in such words and phrases as: *shoehorn; horn in; horn of plenty;* and "He's a *horny* guy."

Returning again to the safer confines of motion pictures, airplanes, and autobuses, it is clear that not only do new words such as these enter the language as they are needed, but that such words are normalized by common usage. In the case of *motion pictures, airplanes,* and *autobuses,* this means the words were shortened as they came into colloquial speech. We go to the *movies* and ride in *planes* and *buses*, rather than view *motion pictures* or travel in *airplanes* and *autobuses*.

Although these words have been regularized by shortening and abbreviation, other changes can also occur.  Roger Brown (1957) has described the evolution of a plural form for the constructed word *schmoo*.  A *schmoo*, as any literate comic-strip reader knows, is a lovable little critter invented by Al Capp, the cartoonist who draws L'il Abner.  Schmoos are so lovable that if you're hungry, they keel over and provide food ; if you need toothpicks, they'll give you their whiskers ; and if you need buttons, the little critters' eyes will do the trick.  Enough of this background material: The important linguistic property of schmoo is its plural—a plural Capp originally specified as Schmoo*n* (perhaps by analogy with *ox → oxen*; *child → children*; or perhaps by his own plain stubbornness).  As Capp saw it, the plural should be formed by the addition of a final *n*.  Such pluralization is contrary to usual English usage and therefore, in accord with the obliging nature of the little critter, the plural of *schmoo* was regularized to schmoo*s*.  The point of this discussion is that novel forms are subject to the same rules of the language system as already existing ones, and that these rules give language much of its productivity.

Creative elaboration is possible not only at the word level but at the level of the phrase or sentence as well.  The stock in trade of many poets is precisely their ability to use old words and phrases to suggest new connotations.  Such productivity does not depend simply on the development of new images or words, but in many cases on the novel use of those that are already familiar.  A young poet talking about the pitfalls of explanation writes: "To explain/is an attempt to give everyone/the same name;/A feat as impossible/ as it is pointless,"* and we understand his meaning immediately.  "To give everyone the same name" is not a very extraordinary phrase and its significance rests not in being esoteric, but rather in being associated with the concept of explanation.  The poet is often defined by his ability to produce novel phrases, or to set usual phrases into unusual contexts, thereby producing unusual effects.

Of perhaps even more importance for the study of language is the response of a listener to these phrases.  Although it is possible to argue that a poet has a very special mentality or gift that enables him to produce novel constructions, we should not miss the important fact that more ordinary and less-gifted speakers are able to understand these novel constructions.  What the poet can produce we can usually understand, even in the absence of knowing the context, mood, or background of either the poet, the poem or both.  This obviously is not completely true, for some poets do attempt to express their meaning by ambiguous constructions.  Many of the symbolist

---

* Peter Cagle, *To explain*; with the author's kind permission.

or surrealist poets achieve their effects by the use of such ambiguity. Even so, most readers do understand each of the sentences, even if not the entire poem, after a few readings.

Here then is an example of creative usage and growth of language. Even if we are not all poets we can usually understand the poet's syntax and often his meaning. It is precisely this point—that language users ranging in ability from little old ladies to creative poets can make productive use of their language—that distinguishes an information-processing analysis of language from more associative analysis of language. As Chomsky (1957) put it:

> "A grammar of a (language) $L$ will thus be a device that generates all of the grammatical sequences of $L$ and none of the ungrammatical ones. [By a language Chomsky means] ... a set (finite or infinite) of sentences, each finite in length and constructed out of a finite set of elements. All natural languages in their spoken or written form are languages in this sense, since each natural language has a finite number of phonemes (or letters in its alphabet) and each sentence is representable as a finite sequence of these phonemes (or letters), though there are infinitely many sentences."*

The phrase "infinitely many sentences" is extremely important, for it is here that the idea of language as an open-ended system is captured. Despite the assertion that language can have infinitely many sentences, the sentences produced by a particular speaker are finite in number, although often quite large. The infinity of sentences is a theoretical concept and relates to the characterization of "language" as a formal system rather than as actual performance. Consider an analogy: Natural numbers go on infinitely, but any particular individual—even one who knows how to count fluently—will be unable to produce the infinity of numbers that potentially can be derived from the number system itself. In terms of both language and numbers, it is necessary to make a distinction between *competence* and *performance*. Any given speaker (as well as any given number user) has the theoretical *competence* to produce infinitely many sentences (or numbers) despite the fact that his performance is limited by his mortality. Although someone knowing the rules of a language *theoretically* could do it, no one *actually* can.

If this is true, how then is it possible to estimate or tap the actual linguistic competence of a given speaker or speakers? Since the number of sentences in a language is infinite, a minimal list of what we might expect in the way of competence would suggest that a fluent speaker is able to provide an interpretation for any sentence of this infinite set. The ability to provide such

---

* From *Syntactic Structures*, by Noam Chomsky, The Hague, Netherlands: Mouton and Company, 1957.

interpretations seems to involve two specific sets of competences, one related to the syntax and the other to the meaning of the sentence. As Garrett and Fodor (1968) have described it, structural or syntactical competence involves the ability:

1. to distinguish structurally well-formed utterances
2. to note when and in what ways an utterance is susceptible to more than one structural interpretation, and
3. to relate sentences to each other by virtue of their structural similarity or difference.

Semantic competence, on the other hand, includes the ability:

1. to detect semantic anomaly,
2. to note when and in what ways an utterance may be semantically ambiguous, and
3. to note paraphrase and synonymy relations among sentences.*

In terms of these criteria, syntactic competence could be tapped by asking subjects to decide whether a given utterance was grammatical or not. For example, in a study by Maclay and Sleator (1960), subjects were asked to judge which of the sentences in a series of sentences were acceptable in terms of their grammar. Results showed that three of 21 college students accepted, as grammatical, deviant collections of words such as *Label break to calm shout and.* One can only assume that since these subjects understood the task instructions—and presumably functioned in a college environment—they must have misunderstood what kinds of judgements were required. For example, they may not even have known what was meant by the term "grammatical." Despite these results, asking subjects for judgments of grammaticalness does seem to be an intuitively reasonable way in which to find out whether they can distinguish grammatical from ungrammatical sentences.

Knowledge of structural bracketing could also be assessed in terms of the pattern of errors subjects make in learning grammatical sentences (for example, as in the studies by Johnson, 1968, and Martin and Roberts, 1967, 1968, reviewed in the last chapter) or in terms of their ability to understand grammatical puns such as: *He likes cleaning ladies* or *Psychologists find conjugating linguists to be difficult* and so on. Similarly, subjects could be asked to explain how two sentences such as: *He is easy to please*; *He is eager to please* differ in terms of what they are trying to say.

---

* From "Psychological theories and linguistic constructs," by M. Garrett and J. A. Fodor, in *Verbal Behavior and General Behavior Theory*, edited by T. R. Dixon and D. L. Horton, Englewood Cliffs, N.J.: Prentice-Hall, 1968, page 452.

Semantic competence could be assessed by a variety of procedures, the easiest of which to use involves asking subjects to paraphrase sentences they hear.  Similarly it should be possible to show that in recall tasks certain types of prompts produce better recall than others.  Blumenthal (1967), for example, has shown that recall of sentences such as (1) *The theorem was proved by John*; and (2) *The theorem was proved by induction* is differentially affected by using the final noun (John or induction) as a prompt for recall of the whole sentence.  This seems reasonable since in sentence (1), *John* is the subject of the entire sentence, whereas *induction* is not the subject of sentence (2).  Using *John* as a prompt should produce better recall than using *induction* largely because *induction* relates to only a small part of the sentence, whereas *John* relates to the whole sentence.  Results of exactly this type were found in Blumenthal's experiment and seem to indicate that different paraphrases were used for storing both sentences, with sentence (1) paraphrased as *John proved the theorem* and sentence (2) paraphrased as *The theorem was proved inductively*.  Neither of these paraphrases would be acceptable for the other.  It is senseless to say: *Induction proved the theorem* or *The theorem was proved Johnly*.

This latter point immediately brings up another distinction important to a transformational analysis: that between *deep* and *surface structure*.  As previous examples indicate, Chomsky's analysis often blurs the usual distinctions between syntax and meaning.  For Chomsky, both are interrelated aspects of the grammar of a language and using paraphrase to determine differences in the intent of a sentence only indicates the close relationship between semantic and syntactic rules in determining meaning.  Deep structure relates to the underlying intention of a sentence, while surface structure represents only one way of "saying the same (deep-structure) thing."

Because this distinction is at once so important and yet so difficult to grasp, perhaps an (admittedly) imprecise analogy will help.  Consider a child who sees a picture of a kitten for the first time after having seen only real-life kittens, and on seeing the picture says "kitty"; or a child who has seen only toy sailboats, and on being shown a picture of an ocean liner says "boat."  In both cases there is clearly little or no physical similarity in the stimuli responded to—rather both stimuli are related to the same concept, that of a kitty or of a boat, whatever the specific properties "kittyness" or "boatness" might be.

This means that the concept of boat, or of kitten, or of whatnot, is the critical competence involved in recognizing any new instance as a "boat" or a "kitty" or a "whatnot."  The physical sailboat and the picture of the liner can be thought to represent two different derivations from the same underlying concept.  In a sense each specific example must also be "generated" from the underlying conceptual competence in much the same way that a mathematical axiom generates many different theorems.  It is really this usage of the term *generate* that is implied in describing a rule approach to language as a *generative theory*. Given an underlying set of competences expressed in the form of rules, each sentence produced or understood may be considered a theorem generated by these rules, a theorem that can be derived by both speakers and listeners.

To return again to the boat–ocean liner example, a further principle also seems involved. In order for the child to label either or both pictures correctly as a boat, he may have to perform a series of *transformations* on one or both stimuli so as to reduce them to their common underlying concept. In the case of language, analogically similar transformations are are involved in paraphrasing to determine whether sentences having similar surface structures also have similar deep structures. For example, *The theorem was proved Johnly* is an unacceptable paraphrase of (1) *The theorem was proved by John*; whereas *The theorem was proved inductively* is a perfectly acceptable transformation of (2) *The theorem was proved by induction*. These simple paraphrases highlight the difference between the sentences: in the case of sentence (1), such paraphrases indicate that *John* is the subject of the sentence, whereas a similar paraphrase indicates that *induction* is clearly not the subject of sentence (2).

## A Word About Rules

One of the more critical concepts in a generative transformational approach to language is that of a rule. In ordinary usage, rules are used in one of two ways: either as a restriction or as a recipe. "Obey the rules—don't smoke" is an example of its use as a restriction, whereas "Take the whites of two eggs, beat in a tablespoon of flour, . . . , etc." represents its use as a guide or recipe. When a linguist talks about rules, he always talks in terms of a procedure (recipe) which, when applied, will produce the desired result ("any and all grammatical sentences and no ungrammatical ones").

Does this mean that the speaker is in any sense aware of grammatical rules when he speaks? The usual answer is "no": Rules are scientific fictions that enable an investigator to characterize a given bit of behavior but need not be introspectively reachable by the subject. But this need not be a troublesome point. Subjects seem perfectly able to perform many complicated and skilled performances in the absence of any ability to describe how they are able to do it. Often, asking the subject to introspect destroys the continuity of action, as when you ask a typist to tell you how she types, or a walker how he walks, and so on.

This is also true in the case of sentence production. Deese (1968) describes the following situation: A group of seventh-grade students were asked to look up the meaning of an unknown word such as *chaste* and then write a sentence including that word. One of the sentences produced was: *The amoeba is a chaste animal.* (Probably the student was using that aspect of the definition having something to do with "simple in design." Presumably he was not commenting on the sex life of the amoeba.) The point here is that even though the boy did not understand the meaning of the word, he was able to use it appropriately in a sentence. This is true despite the fact that he never really considered that from a grammatical point of view, *chaste* is an adjective. We can all use words in perfectly grammatical ways even if we are blissfully unaware of the appropriate range of use for these words.

There is still another reason for making theoretical use of a rule concept in describing language performance, and this has to do with the skilled aspects of speech. Basically the rules used in generative grammar imply a hierarchical structure, and the description of such structure is perfectly congruent with an analysis of skilled performance such as the one presented many years ago by Lashley (1951) and more recently by Lenneberg (1967). Although Chomsky has in fact disclaimed that rules describe how subjects produce sentences: "The hypothesis ... that ... the speaker produces a sentence from top to bottom ... seems to me to have neither any particular plausibility nor any empirical support." (Chomsky, 1964, page 126), many psychologists and linguists have in fact attempted to relate this top-to-bottom characteristic of phrase-structure rules to the skilled aspects of the speech performance itself. For example, Lashley argued that the motor skills involved in playing a piano or typing a letter are much too fast to have been produced by a chain of interconnections (i.e., in typing the letter *h* in the word *the*, *t* couldn't possibly have been the stimulus event to cue the *h* response largely because the inter-response time between *t* and *h* would be too short to allow for feedback). Instead, he argued, the constituent response, *t*, *h*, and *e* form a single unit that is probably produced all at once. The word *the* is a single unit and when one is typing it a total schema must dictate the ordering of individual letters. The manifest sequential stream, namely that *h* follows *t* and that *e* follows *h* is not the same as the underlying process which produces it. The underlying process is hierarchical: Given the intention to produce *the*, the sequence of responses is a foregone conclusion.

Such a hierarchical analysis is obviously required in order to understand Lashley's now famous sentence (for the desired effect the sentence must be read aloud): "Rapid 'riting' with his uninjured hand saved from loss the contents of the capsized canoe." As Lashley noted: "The (factors) which give rise to the meaning of 'riting' (as righting) are not activated for at least three to five seconds after hearing the word." (Lashley, 1951). Only if the sentence is understood as a whole—all at once—is it possible to understand how this particular word is to be interpreted. Anticipation is accounted for in terms of the total structure of the sentence rather than simply in terms of its sequential connections.

## GUIDELINES FOR THE STUDY OF LANGUAGE

All these introductory remarks are necessary to put into perspective the difference between left-to-right and top-to-bottom analyses of language. It does, however, seem reasonable to ask whether these remarks have any direct psychological implications. George Miller (1965), in a presidential address to the American Psychological Association, boiled these implications down to seven admonitions (Miller is quite fond of the number $7 \pm 2$). For purposes of the present chapter, we will reduce these further to the following four specific points:*

1. Not all of the physical properties of speech are significant for vocal communication, and not all of the significant features of speech are represented physically. Let us call this admonition the *Acoustic Postulate for Language*.
2. The syntactic structure of a sentence—both in its surface and deep form—imposes groupings that govern the production and understanding of that sentence. Call this the *Syntactic Structure Postulate*.
3. The meaning of an utterance should not be confused with its reference—meaning depends on the relations of a symbol to other symbols in the language. Call this the *Meaning Postulate*.
4. There is a large biological component that shapes human language acquisition and usage. Call this the *Biological Foundations Postulate*.

These then are Miller's admonitions, preliminaries, postulates, or recommendations for the study of language. In themselves they bring together and pinpoint many of the underlying assumptions guiding contemporary research from a generative–transformational point of view. They stand in strong contrast to the assumptions often made by associationistic psychologists about language. For one thing, learning is not given a major or even a central role in language acquisition; rather strong emphasis is placed on a pretuned organism who develops speech in accordance with his biological destiny. It is not that we can't teach animals to produce poetry; it is simply that they can't learn. Similarly, human infants acquire speech not because they are taught in any ordinary sense of the term, but rather because they are human infants.

Similarly, Miller's Meaning Postulate stresses that Language is to be construed as an abstract system rather than as a series of responses. Words have meaning not only, nor even primarily, because they refer to things in the physical world, but rather because they are involved in a network of

---

* Each of the following statements is a paraphrase of the statements made by Miller. For this reason no quotation marks are used, although in many cases they do use some of Miller's actual wording.

other words and concepts. This network need never be directly observable but may require instead the intuitions of a skillful analyst for its discovery.

Since each of these points represents a major trend in the generative–transformational approach to language, they provide an appropriate organizational scheme for the present discussion. Accordingly the present chapter will concern itself with each of these points in the order presented by Miller. Let us begin then with an analysis of the *acoustic stimulus.*

## The Acoustic Stimulus

Although acoustically the speech signal appears as a fairly continuous stream of changing acoustic energy, the overwhelming psychological effect is that of a regular and segmented signal. For example, consider the sound spectrogram of the words *Santa Claus* as pronounced by an adult male speaker. A sound spectrograph presents the pattern of sound energy produced by a speaker in terms of its intensity at a given frequency over a given time period.

The $X$ axis represents time; the $Y$ axis frequency or cycles per second. The darkness of the line represents the intensity of the sound at a given frequency level. In Fig. 16.2, for example, the /S/ sound has a characteristic frequency range of between 4000 and 7000 cycles per second for a period of slightly more than 0.1 of a second. Note that the vowels /æ/, /a/ and /ɔ/ take more time to produce than the consonants, and that they also tend to produce darker bands.

Despite the fact that this acoustic record gives an impression of continuity (with one bit of acoustic energy merging into the next), the overwhelming psychological impression is one of segmentation—segmentation into words, probably into syllables, and perhaps even into individual sounds. At the receptive level of language—in hearing—segmentation is not in the signal but in the listener.

Given this pattern for listening, it seems reasonable to ask what production processes are like. Here again, the various muscular activities involved in speech are not at all contemporaneous with the production of a given sound, but tend to have a characteristic temporal pattern. Thus the abdomen is active prior to the onset of the actual sound, while the diaphragm is active just before the end of the production of the specific sound. Since Lenneberg (1967) estimates that at least 100 different muscles need be controlled, the production of any given sound must involve a very complicated and precisely timed mosaic of muscular responses. Not only is the sound produced affected by a person's ability to control the appropriate order and timing of the muscles involved, but it is also true that how one sound is produced depends on the preceding and following movements. For the highly skilled act of producing even a single sound, these coordinations need to be carried

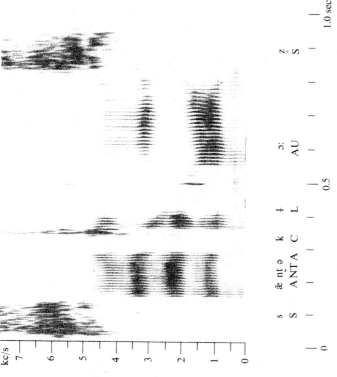

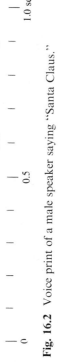

**Fig. 16.2**  Voice print of a male speaker saying "Santa Claus."

out over relatively long time periods, including both anticipatory and sub-sequent movements.

These are some of the problems that arise at the muscular level of sound production. What relevance do they have for speech perception and production? In terms of speech perception, Garrett and Fodor (1968) have noted that two complementary results should be considered by any theory of speech perception: (1) The same acoustic event gives rise to different perceptions, and (2) different acoustic events give rise to the same perception. In general the perception of a single physically defined acoustic event is very strongly dependent on the sound environment in which it occurs. So, for example, in his early review of phonetic analysis, O'Connor (1957) noted that a burst of sound energy at 1440 cycles per second was identified as a /p/ before /i/, as a /k/ before /a/, and again as a /p/ before /u/. Further work with tape cuttings of actual speech also confirmed these conclusions. In these later studies, magnetic tape recordings of /p, t, k/ were combined with /i, a, u/ and results indicated that under these conditions the acoustic representations of the /k/ sounds chosen were identified as /k/ in the context of /ki/, as /t/ in the context of /ka/, and as /p/ in the combination /ku/.

In terms of the second consideration—that different acoustic events can give rise to the same perceived sound—O'Connor reports that although "before all vowels the bursts (of input) between 3000 and 4000 cycles per second were identified by phonetically untrained listeners as /t/ and those at 360 cycles per second as /p/, there was no single burst frequency which was heard as /k/ before all vowels, the optimum frequency decreasing steadily from about 3000 cycles per second before /i/ to 720 cycles per second before /u/." These results complement more ordinary sorts of observations: No fluent speaker of a language has any difficulty in recognizing a given vowel, regardless of whether or not a male or female adult or child produces the sound. Acoustically, the signal differs greatly as a consequence of these seemingly major—but perceptually irrelevant—differences.

How can these facts be reconciled with a theory of speech perception? Although a number of different theories have been proposed, a recent analysis (Neisser, 1967)—summarizing a good deal of prior theory and research—suggests that somehow or other the listener must implicitly be synthesizing along with the speaker; that is, analyzing the incoming speech signal in terms of an expected internal synthesis. This hypothesis is termed an *analysis-by-synthesis model*, and is assumed to depend on two processes. The first of these is essentially a passive nonconstructive one in which the listener tentatively identifies units on the basis of input properties. From such fragmentary information, the subject makes a best guess (his synthesis) as to the specific properties of the input and checks it against subsequent aspects of the input. This of course implies that an organism capable of understanding speech is able to produce it as well. Although Neisser's specific version of the analysis-by-synthesis approach to speech perception (as well as to visual perception) is a good deal more elegant than this brief description suggests, it would be wise to pick it up again after discussing certain other aspects of articulation (speech production) and sentence structure.

The most detailed model of what is required for the production of speech in the way of muscular organization has been presented by Lenneberg (1967, Chapter 3). Lenneberg was extremely impressed by the complex timing required to coordinate the rather large number of different muscular responses involved in even simple speech sounds. He argued that the sequential arrangement of muscular events necessary for the production of a sound, a syllable, a word, and more, must require extensive preplanning and that such preplanning must involve the anticipation of later events. Since timing poses such a crucial problem, Lenneberg speculates that there must be an internal speech clock. In the absence of any complicating factors this speech clock has a duration of about one-sixth of a second, and presumably all temporal aspects of speech are timed against this biological clock. As he puts it:

"The hypothesis is advanced that the temporal patterns on which the neuromuscular automatisms are based have at their roots a physiological rhythm consisting of periodic changes of 'states' at a rate of $6 \pm 1$ cycles per second." (Lenneberg, 1967, page 120)

Most of the discussion up to this point has been at the level of acoustics and physiology. What about language and language users? Experimentally, one way to consider the relationship between articulatory events and language usage is to examine sound preferences for certain grammatical inflections. As we pointed out in Chapter 14, a single inflectional morpheme is often represented by a number of different sounds. So, for example, contentive morphemes such as nouns are usually pluralized by adding the $[Z_1]$ morpheme, which consists of three different phonemic representations /s, iz, or z/, depending on the final sound of the initial morpheme, while past tense, which is indicated by the $[D_1]$ morpheme, also consists of three different allomorphs /t, d, id/.

Given these morphophonemic facts, Anisfeld and Gordon (1968) tried to evaluate the role of generative rules in phonology, as described by Chomsky and Halle (1968). According to Chomsky and Halle, the phonemes of a language can be identified in terms of their distinctive features, while their properties of occurrence can be specified by a series of rules. These rules serve to relate the sounds of the language to the morphology of the language (e.g., the past tense morpheme or the pluralizing morpheme, etc.). If in learning these morphophonemic patterns a speaker learns a set of generative rules, it should be possible to show that such rules will operate on forms that a speaker has never before encountered.

In the Anisfeld and Gordon study, subjects were asked to judge which of two nonsense endings for a nonsense word would make a better plural form. So, for example, the subject was shown a cartoon animal and told that the cartoon was a picture of a *gor*. The subject was then presented with a cartoon containing two *gors* and the subject was asked to judge whether *gort* or *gorsh* would be the better plural. Since there were three different groups of subjects (first-grade students, fourth-grade students, and adults) it was possible to examine the pattern of choices and rejections at all three age levels.

The results indicated that the first-grade and fourth-grade children would accept only /*ch, j, sh*/ as acceptable pluralizations, whereas adult subjects would accept these three, plus the following set of five others: /f, m, n, th, v/. All the sounds preferred by children, and most of the sounds preferred by adults, share two distinctive features; features which also characterize the regular English plural morphemes. In general, these features describe the sound class usually called *fricatives*.

A further experiment by Anisfeld (1969) was concerned with a slightly more complicated problem in generative phonology. Adjectives, such as *extensive*, which are derived from verbs (extend) ending in /d/ require two steps for their transition from verb to adjective (extend → extendzive → extensive), whereas adjectives such as *permissive*, derived from verbs ending in /t/, require only a single step (permit → permissive). If this is true, as Chomsky and Halle suggest, then extenzive would be more readily accepted as the adjective form of *extend* than *permizive* would be accepted for permit. To test this formulation, subjects were asked to select appropriate sound endings for constructed verb forms such as *yermit* (t ending, therefore only one step required) and *dalpond* (d ending, therefore two steps required). Results showed that subjects chose z endings significantly more frequently for artificial d words than for artificial t words.

The important point of both these experiments is that even at the level of phonology, subjects can make novel use of sound features which characterize inflectional morphemes. In one sense these studies are simply generalization studies—but generalization studies with a difference. In these cases the dimensions of generalization can be specified in terms of the pattern of sounds occurring in ordinary English usage as well as in terms of an abstract description of the selection rules used. The results provide some evidence for a view of phonology in which it is possible to describe production processes in terms of rules operating over a set of clearly defined distinctive features. Even at the level of phonology, then, these results lend some support to the view that the phonemic properties of a language are not entirely nor even primarily, memorized. Rather they can be considered to represent a generative rule system no less structured than that involved in sentence production.

## Syntactic Structure—Surface and Deep

The so-called surface structure of a sentence is revealed by its pattern of phrase bracketing. More traditionally oriented studies, such as those done by Johnson (1968) and also by Martin and Roberts (1967) (see Chapter 15) showed that phrase structure does have some demonstrable effects on learning and recall. Since, however, the generative–transformational approach to language is interested in language and language usage rather than in learning and memory *per se*, they have been most interested in examining the role of syntactic structure in sentence perception.

The basic procedure used for this purpose is a simple one: A subject is presented with a tape-recorded sentence and at some point during the presentation of the sentence, a click is introduced and the subject is asked to identify the exact point (word or syllable, etc.) at which the click occurred. The original results (Ladéfoged, 1959, Ladefoged and Broadbent, 1960) showed that subjects almost always misplaced the onset of the click beyond the boundaries of the syllable or sound in which it was located. When subjects were presented with randomly ordered digits, the click was misplaced much less frequently, and when it was misplaced this difference was much less than in the case of sentences.

When the exact location of these displacements was examined, Bever and Fodor (1965) found that clicks tended to move toward the ends of phrases contained in the input sentence. If this was so it might be possible to demonstrate that click displacements move toward the major structural units of the sentence. For example, the sentence *That he was happy was evident from the way he smiled* has a major constituent break between the words *happy* and *was*. If Bever and Fodor's analysis is correct, then subjects should judge the click as occurring between *happy* and *was*, when in fact it may have been located, say, between *he* and *was*. In their actual experiment, clicks (which are indicated by a Δ) were located as follows:

*That he was happy was evident from the way he smiled.*

$$\begin{array}{cccccccc} \uparrow & \uparrow & \uparrow & \uparrow\uparrow & \uparrow & & \uparrow\uparrow \\ 1 & 2 & 3 & 4\ 5 & 6 & & 7\ 8 \end{array}$$

Only click 5 was located at the boundary itself, with clicks 1–4 preceding the break and 6–8 following it. In their particular experiment, Fodor and Bever actually constructed 25 different sentences of this type with clicks scattered at various points throughout the sentence, and subjects were required to write down the sentence and then indicate the location of the click by a slash mark (/).

Over all responses tabulated, results indicated that subjects made about 80% errors in locating clicks. Of all these erroneous responses, 78% were in the direction of the constituent break. That is, for clicks located objectively at Positions 1–3, subjects tended to "move" the click toward the fourth position; whereas for clicks objectively located at Positions 5–8, subjects tended to "move" the click back toward the fourth position. All subjects, therefore, tended to mislocate the click by "moving" it toward the major structural break in the sentence.

The design of this experiment, however, does raise some problems. It is possible to argue that the subjects were not responding to the structure of the sentence in placing the click, but were responding instead to some property of the input signal itself. For example, speakers when reading may tend to pause or to stress words at clause boundaries, and perhaps this is the cue leading the subject to mislocate the click. In order to rule out this possibility, Garrett, Bever, and Fodor (1966) used pairs of sentences such as:

1a. (In *her hope of marrying*) (*Anna was surely impractical*) versus

1b. (Your *hope of marrying Anna*) (*was surely impractical*) or

2a. (As a direct result of their new invention's *influence*) (*the company was given an award*) versus

2b. (The retiring chairman) (whose methods still greatly *influence the company*) (was given an award).

For these particular sentences some part of each pair contains exactly the same wording; the only difference between the two has to do with the structure of the sentence. In preparing these sentences, exactly the same piece of tape containing the identical sound pattern was used for both alternatives. Because of this it would be impossible to argue that click displacement was the result of some difference in the auditory signal, since the signals were identical. In the experiment itself clicks were located at various points in the segments common to both sentences, with the expectation that clicks would be erroneously located in different places in alternative sentences. For example, a click occurring at the same time as the first syllable of *company* in sentence 2a should move back toward *influence*, the point of the major structural break, whereas it should be located in its more or less objective location in sentence 2b. Results, in fact, did agree with this expectation: In sentences like 2a the click was judged as occurring earlier than in sentences like 2b. This is, of course, exactly in accord with the original results derived from the Fodor and Bever experiment.

One critical problem still remains: In both these experiments, subjects had to write down the sentence before inserting the slash mark. Given this procedure, it is possible to argue that the subjects did not "hear" the click as occurring later but only in recalling the sentence did they locate it at the major grammatical break. In order to control for this possibility, Garrett (1965) did not require subjects to reproduce the sentence but asked instead for an immediate judgment. Under these conditions similar results were found indicating that the effect was in perceiving the stimulus rather than in reconstructing it.

All these results fit in nicely with an information-processing analysis of how subjects understand and produce sentences. The basic point is that the information-processing load is higher during the production of a clause and much lower at clause breaks. For this reason, speakers seem to "postpone" the location of clicks from relatively demanding, internal clause positions to the less-demanding conditions which apply at clause boundaries. If this is true, then subjects should be able to react to clicks more rapidly in the immediate vicinity of a major syntactic break than to clicks removed by one or two words from this break. Such a result has, in fact, been reported by Holmes and Forster (1971).

In addition to "clickology," another technique used to assess the surface structure of a sentence has been described by Suci, Ammon, and Gemlin (1967; Ammon, 1968). In this task, subjects were presented with two different sentences and then given a probe word. For example, if a subject were presented with the sentence *The big boy eats red apples* and were then presented with the probe word *boy* he would be expected to respond to this probe with the word *eats*. Obviously the location of the probe can be systematically varied, and for this experiment the probe words were *big*, *boy*, *eats*, and *red*. The purpose of the probe word is obviously to determine whether the location of the probe affects the speed with which the subject produces the next word. The obvious expectation is that latencies will be longer across phrase boundaries.

Figure 16.3 presents two different types of sentences and their associated latency results. These results were obtained from the responses of 16 third-grade children. In general, the results show considerably longer latencies between words occurring in two different phrases. In this same experiment adult subjects were also tested, and although their results conformed to those produced by the third-grade children, they were nowhere near as dramatic.

In order to determine whether the same pattern of results also applies to adult subjects, Ammon (1968) devised a series of much more complicated sentences and presented them, via the same technique, to a series of 20 adult subjects. In just about all cases comparable results were found—the latency to produce the next word was considerably longer across phrase boundaries than within phrase boundaries.

All this work argues that in the perception of speech, the unit of perception is certainly longer than the syllable and probably longer than the word. What may be involved is that subjects first get a general impression of the sentence and on this basis go on to construct a more complete grammatical analysis. This analysis then enables them to anticipate later portions of the sentence. If this is true it should be possible to demonstrate that subjects are able to perceive the same words more accurately when these are embedded in a meaningful sentence than when they are embedded in anomalous or meaningless sentences. In order to provide as stringent a test as possible, one must be sure that subjects know all the words to the same degree of mastery.

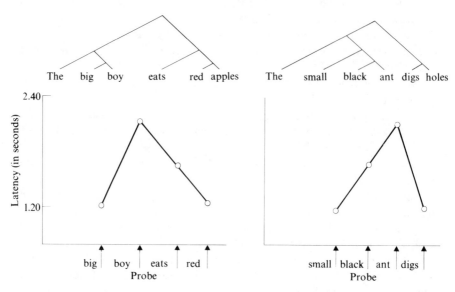

**Fig. 16.3** Response latencies for different probe positions. (Adapted from Suci, Ammon, and Gamlin, 1967)

To run such an experiment takes patience, and George Miller and a set of devoted student subjects spent an entire summer—four afternoons a week—listening to a set of 25 words until both Miller and his subjects, to quote Miller, "became throughly sick of them."

For the major part of the experiment four different conditions were run. For one condition, words were randomly selected from all 25 words (the Random Group); for a second condition words were chosen at random with the provision that they form a sentence (Random Sentence Group); for a third condition, words were selected to form a grammatical and meaningful sentence (Selected Sentence Group); while for the fourth condition all the grammatical sentences of condition three were reversed (Backward Group). The results of this experiment showed that both the Random Sentence and the Selected Sentence groups recognized the input better than either the Random Selection or the Backward Sentence groups. These results were obtained despite the fact that all words were extremely well learned by all subjects.

Another observation was also of some interest: When subjects read the words in each of the lists at a relatively slow rate with pauses introduced between sets of five words, there were no differences among the various conditions. It was only under conditions of time pressure, approximate to actual speech perception, that syntactic structure facilitated perception. Miller interpreted this to mean that... "Sentence context also enables us to organize the flow of sounds into decision units larger than individual words—perhaps into units similar to the linguist's constituents—and so make our perceptual decisions about what we are hearing at a slower and more comfortable rate." (1962, page 208)

As we have said before, *deep structure* is related to surface structure by *transformations*. What this means is that the origin and intent of any given sentence is to be found in its deep-structure form and that the logical form describing the overt sentence is a reflection of this underlying intent (Chomsky, 1967). Since deep structure is not amenable to direct experimental attack, all experiments, by definition, have to take a rather indirect and inferential route.

The earliest studies dealing with grammatical transformations were based on a slightly different view of transformations from that described above. In many of these earlier studies psychologists assumed that in sentence reception and production the speaker or listener began with a simple declarative sentence (the *kernel* sentence) and derived more complicated sentence forms from this kernel. These complications were made possible because speakers were thought to have implicit knowledge of the transformational rules of the language.

If this is true, how do you go about determining the role of transformations in language? One of the simplest ways is to present experimental subjects with a series of Kernel Sentences and ask them to perform various transformations on them. For example, if a subject were presented with the sentence, *Joe liked the small boy*, he might be asked to find a corresponding sentence of the form—*The small boy was liked by Joe* (passive), or *The small boy wasn't liked by Joe* (passive–negative), or *Joe didn't like the small boy* (negative). In a preliminary study (Miller, 1962), and in a more rigorous later one (Miller and McKean, 1964) subjects were presented with two sets of 18 sentences; these sentences were selected to be grammatically similar in certain specifiable ways. In this study, six specific relations were studied—kernel–negative $(K:N)$; passive–passive negative $(P:PN)$; kernel–passive $(K:P)$; passive negative–negative $(PN:N)$; kernel–passive negative $(K:PN)$; and negative–passive $(N:P)$. The subject was presented with two sets of 18 sentences and asked to match one of the sentences in the right-hand column with a sentence in the left-hand column, and so on for all 18 sentences. As the control condition, subjects were simply asked to begin with a sentence in the left-hand column and match it to an identical sentence in the right-hand column.   For the experimental condition, subjects were asked to perform one of the six transformations and then to pick out the appropriate sentence in the right-hand column.

On what basis could predictions be made about the relative difficulty of finding the correct right-hand sentence for each of the six grammatical relationships?   If each sentence type—passive, negative, etc.—represents a separate pattern, then going from one type of sentence to another should be equally time consuming.   If, on the other hand, subjects go through a series of transformations, then relationships between these six sentence pairings should be expressible in terms of two factors: affirmative–negative and active–passive.   Under this view, the $N:P$ and $K:PN$ condition represent two-step transformations, whereas all other pairs $(K:N; P:PN; K:P; PN:P)$ represent only single-step transformations.

The result of this experiment did, indeed, show that relative to the control condition, all single-step transformations were performed more rapidly than all double-step transformations.   In terms of procedure used, this means that subjects produced smaller differences between experimental and control conditions for $K:N$, $P:PN$, $K:P$, and $PN:N$ sentences than for $K:PN$ and $N:P$ sentences.

In a further study, Miller and McKean (1964) used a different procedure, but came up with the same result: Pairs of sentences related by a single transformation take less time to transform than sentences requiring a double transformation.   In this later study, subjects were presented with a sentence tachistoscopically and then asked to perform one of a number of grammatical transformations.   When the subject completed this transformation, he next pressed a switch which turned on a light illuminating another set of 18 sentences.   The subject was then required to select the appropriate trans-formed sentence.   In addition to confirming early results, Miller and McKean discovered that subjects found it easier and faster to perform negative transformations than passive transformations.   As before, however, the *simple active affirmative declarative* sentence (what Miller called the kernel) remained the easiest for all subjects to deal with.

All the experiments considered to this point have used sentences specifically produced for laboratory research.   Frieda Goldman-Eisler and Michele Cohen (1970) took an entirely different tack and tried to determine the relative frequency of occurrence of four different sentence types in spontaneous speech.   Specifically, they wanted to find out how often seven different groups of speakers as varied as members of the English House of Commons and schizophrenic patients used simple active affirmative declarative, passive, negative and passive-negative sentence constructions in spontaneous speech.   Their results are extremely revealing: By far and away declaratives predominate—between 70 and 80% of sentences; negatives come a distant next at between 4 and 10%; passives a poor third at between 0.7 and 11%, and passive-negatives are practically nonexistent. When Goldman-Eisler and Cohen examined the results for all their different speaker groups, they found that Members of Parliament (MP's) used the greatest variety of sentence forms and the schizophrenics the least. Interestingly enough, schizophrenics used more negative constructions (11% to 7%), while MP's used far more passive constructions (11% to 0.7%). In general, planful articulate speech makes use of a greater variety of grammatical construction, whereas schizophrenic speech is primarily characterized by two forms: simple declaratives and negatives.

One conclusion of this study amounts to an admonition as to whether or not $N$, $P$ and $PN$ difficulty is a valid criterion of transformational operation and might well be kept in mind:

> The differences in degree of difficulty between declarative $N$, $P$, $PN$, and so on, as reflected in the indicators used by the various experimenters are not acceptable as quantities on the same yardstick, because they are not based on the same universe of behavior. Differences in difficulty of processing may be assumed to be a by-product of the fact that declarative sentences belong to the class of learned and overlearned behavior, while $N$, $P$, and $PN$ were shown to be relatively infrequent, less practiced, indeed, rare forms of verbal behavior. This fact alone would account for greater facility, fluency, and habit strength in the use of and resort to declarative sentences in preference to $N$, $P$, and $PN$.*

*Grammatical Structure and Sentence Recall.* Contemporaneous with the early experiments on how long it takes to perform and evaluate grammatical transformations was another series of studies concerned with the role of grammatical structure in sentence recall. The first of these was done by Mehler (1963), who attempted to determine how subjects go about learning and recalling eight different types of grammatical sentences. In this experiment subjects were read a series of sentences and asked to write down as many of the sentences as they could. Sentences were presented in random order for each of five trials.

The first result of interest concerns the relative rates at which each of the different sentence types were learned, and here results were clear enough; the easiest type of sentence to learn was the kernel sentence, with all other types considerably more difficult and in roughly the same order of difficulty as found by Miller and McKean. The pattern of memory errors, however, changed significantly from early to late trials: For the first two trials, omission errors were most common—that is, subjects just simply left out some of the

---

* From "Is $N$, $P$, and $PN$ difficulty a valid criterion of transformational operations?" by F. Goldman-Eisler and M. Cohen, *J. Verbal Learning and Verbal Behavior*, **9**, 1970, page 163.

words—while by the third trial the major errors were syntactical in nature—that is, subjects recalled the sentence but changed its syntactic form. The pattern of these syntactical changes was also of interest: In most cases such changes moved in the direction of kernel sentences.

Miller (1962) and later Mehler (1963) have interpreted these results to mean that subjects have to remember or store at least two different things in sentence recall: (1) the meaning of the sentence and (2) its specific grammatical form. The meaning of the sentence is stored in its simplest possible form: as a kernel sentence. This kernel is then supplemented by a grammatical "footnote" that might go something like this: *The car hit the tree; question, active.* Probably what actually gets stored could be simplified even further so that only three items: *car–hit–tree–question, not passive,* would do. The subsequent output of the sentence would then be a reconstruction based on this information. In this case a subject might proceed as follows: "Let's see, the sentence was about a car hitting a tree and it was a question. First let me get it straight—*The car hit the tree.* Now to change it to a question—*Has the car hit the tree?* or *Did the car hit the tree?* Since I'm not sure which one is right, let me try one out on this trial, and see if I can remember if it's *Has* or *Did* on the next one."

Now this is simply a common-sense description of what a subject might do. In terms of contemporary linguistic theory, a to-be-recalled sentence is represented in memory not in terms of its surface structure, but rather in terms of its semantic content plus a set of instructions for deriving surface structure. Meaning is carried in the deep structure, with transformational rules doing the work of producing surface structure. Since what used to be called the kernel sentence represents a sentence type having the minimal number of transformational footnotes, such sentences should be recalled best, and this was exactly the result found. Similarly, those sentences requiring only a single transformation should be better recalled than those requiring multiple transformations, and this expectation was in general also confirmed by the data. Finally, syntactic errors, when these occur, should be in the direction of simplifying the sentence recalled (i.e., moving closer to a kernel sentence). Mehler's results did indeed show that of 648 syntactic errors 400 were in the direction of the simplest sentence form.

An analysis of this sort led to the rather intriguing hypothesis that various grammatical transformations "take up" storage space. That is, if a sentence is stored in its simplest form + grammatical footnotes, then the complexity of the transformation required should effectively reduce recall. For example, in the sentence *The boy hit a ball,* the subject might remember *boy, hit, ball* + kernel, whereas for the sentence: *The ball wasn't hit by the boy was it?* the memory load might be—*boy, hit, ball* + passive, question, negation. Thus the passive–negative–question sentence (*PNQ*) requires more transformations to be stored than the simple declarative sentence.

In order to test one derivation from this hypothesis, Savin and Perchonock (1965) used 11 different sentence types, of which seven presumably required one transformation and four required two transformations. The seven single-transformation sentences involved the same five sentences as those used by Mehler, plus one emphatic sentence (stress or auxiliary) and one *Wh* type (a why, what, where, etc., question). In this experiment, subjects were first presented with a sentence which was then followed by a string of eight unrelated words. Neisser (1966) has termed this method an "overflow" method by analogy to the way in which it is possible to determine "the volume of an irregular object by dropping it into a glass of water and noting how much overflows." For present purposes, the extra words count as the water in the glass and the sentence as the irregular object. By recording how many of the eight words were spilled (that is, not remembered), it is possible to determine the storage requirements of the original sentence. If the original hypothesis is correct there should be poorer recall for double-transformation than for single-transformation sentences.

The actual results of this experiment are presented in Table 16.1. The order of sentence type is determined by the number of unrelated words that were recalled. The obtained ordering is completely congruent with what would be expected on the basis of the original hypothesis: Single-transformation sentences produce less "overflow" than double-transformation sentences and the least "overflowing" of these is the simple declarative sentence. One other aspect of these results that seems noteworthy is that the same transformation, say $Q$, necessitates about the same "overflow" when added to $P$ as when added to declarative sentences. Thus declarative sentences produced a recall value of 5.27, whereas $Q$ produced a value of 4.67, or a difference of 0.60 words. $P$ sentences produced a recall of 4.55 words whereas $PQ$ produced a value of 3.85, or a difference of about 0.70 words. This was true despite the fact that many of the single-transformation sentences were shorter in terms of total words than the comparable double-transformation sentence.

The Savin-Perchonock procedure is a very complicated one, and it is impossible to know precisely how to interpret their results. Foss and Cairns (1970) have suggested that there are really two different parts to this procedure —one concerned with understanding the sentence and one dealing more specifically with sentence rehearsal—and that both must be considered in interpreting Savin and Perchonock's results. In order to separate these two factors experimentally, Foss and Cairns presented their subjects first with a word list of either 0, 2, or 4 unrelated words and then with a single meaningful sentence. The sentences actually used were classified into two different types: Those that were very complex (primarily self-embedded, left-branching sentences) and those that were somewhat less complex (primarily right-branching sentences).

**Table 16.1**  Mean number of words recalled for each sentence type*

| Sentence type | Words recalled | |
|---|---|---|
| Declarative | 5.27 | |
| $Wh$ | 4.78 | |
| $Q$ | 4.67 | |
| $P$ | 4.55 | (Presumably one transformation) |
| $N$ | 4.44 | |
| $Q_{neg}$ | 4.39 | |
| $E$ | 4.30 | |
| $PQ_{neg}$ | 4.02 | |
| $PQ$ | 3.85 | (Presumably two transformations) |
| $EP$ | 3.74 | |
| $NP$ | 3.48 | |

* From Savin and Perchonock, 1965.

Each subject was first asked to recall the unrelated words and if this recall was correct, he was next asked to recall the complete sentence. Not surprisingly, results of this experiment showed poorer sentence recall for longer word lists, and poorer recall for more complex sentences relative to simpler ones. Perhaps the most important condition of this experiment concerns a condition Foss and Cairns called the *Interruption Condition*. In this condition, subjects read a simple sentence. Prior to sentence recall, however, each subject was asked to recall two unrelated words which had just been presented. For the Interruption Condition, the sentence processing was not confounded by having to recall extra words; any effect that might occur would have to occur during the rehearsal part of the experiment, i.e., when the subject would have to interrupt his rehearsal to recall the unrelated words.

Results for this Interruption Condition were exactly the same as for the conditions in which subjects were presented with the two items before the sentence. On this basis, Foss and Cairns concluded that interruption of rehearsal was an important factor in determining sentence recall. This conclusion, however, still left them with having to explain why less-complex sentences were recalled better than more-complex ones. In this case, they assumed that complex sentences take longer to analyze and understand than simple ones, and that less-well-analyzed sentences are forgotten more quickly; for example, a speaker can more accurately recall a sentence that he understands than one he does not. If this is true, then subjects would have analyzed more complex sentences less well than simpler sentences, and therefore, these poorly analyzed complex sentences would be recalled more poorly.

But all these experiments have a smell of the laboratory about them; more often than not, we are interested in recalling what sentences were about rather than their exact form. Although the recall tasks reviewed so far do indicate the psychological reality of grammatical structure, they still do not really tell us very much about what listeners actually remember about sentences when they are not asked for exact reproduction.

In order to investigate this question, Sachs (1967) presented subjects with taped passages. After the subject had listened to a passage under the instruction that the experimenter wanted to "determine how well people can remember what they have just heard," the subject was further told that he would "hear a series of short passages . . . (which) will be interrupted. A bell will sound, and then one sentence from somewhere in the passage will be repeated . . . Sometimes it will be the same sentence (as in the original) . . . and sometimes it will be changed in some small way. Either the meaning of the sentence will be changed, or only the grammatical form."

After these instructions, a number of specific examples were given to show the subject what was meant by a change in meaning and what was meant by a change in grammar. The passages ranged in length from 27 to 180 syllables. Interruptions were made at three different points in the tape: after a delay of 0 syllables, after a delay of 80 syllables (about 27 seconds), and after a delay of 160 syllables (about 46 seconds). The intervening syllables were always a continuation of the passage, so that subjects never knew which sentence would be asked for on the recognition test.

Results were quite clear in showing that at a 0-syllable delay, subjects were equally well able to recognize changes in both semantic or grammatic content. By the 80-syllable delay and continuing on to the 160-syllable delay, subjects were almost never able to detect grammatical changes, but were still able to detect changes in meaning at about an 80% rate. Although subjects were not explicitly told to remember sentence form, it is possible to assume that they might try insofar as they were able to recall the exact wording. In any event, Sachs' results show that in normal memory comprehension, syntactic markers are not retained. Comprehension memory seems to involve paraphrases based on meaning, with sentence structure of importance only insofar as it helps to understand the meaning of the sentence.

There are, however, certain results in the experimental literature which suggest that certain paraphrases are easier or more "natural" than others. For example, Schlesinger (1966) found that passive sentences were more often recalled as actives than vice versa. This was also partially true for Mehler's results described earlier. The results of Sachs' experiment, however, failed to show any differential recall for actives and passives, and so the problem remains as to the exact role of the passive transformation in sentence recall.

To investigate this topic, Slobin (1968) first distinguished between two types of passive sentences: the one in which the subject is known (*They were taken to their seats by a man named Peter*) and the other in which the subject is unknown (*They were taken to their seats*). This second type of passive—the truncated passive—represents the dominant use of passives in ordinary English speech, and in terms of the Miller-Mehler hypothesis of sentence memory raises its own special difficulty. Specifically, according to the meaning + footnote hypothesis, the subject must first transform the sentence to its simple declarative form and include two footnotes, one indicating passive and the other an absence of a specific subject. For truncated passive sentences, the meaning + footnote strategy does seem a bit cumbersome.

Although Slobin tested the recall of full and truncated passives over subjects varying in age from five years to adulthood, for present purposes the data produced by adult subjects is most to the point, and these are presented in Table 16.2.

**Table 16.2**  Characteristics of sentences recalled*

| Sentence type recalled | | | |
|---|---|---|---|
| Sentence type presented | Active | Passive | |
| | | Full | Truncated |
| Full passive | 55% | 23% | 13% |
| Truncated passive | 7% | 4% | 75% |

* Adapted from "Recall of full and truncated passive sentences in connected discourse," by D. I. Slobin, in *J. Verbal Learning and Verbal Behavior*, **7**, 1968, page 878.

Note: Percentages do not add to 100%, as a few S's did produce sentences which could not be categorized as either active or passive.

The most significant result of this experiment concerns the percentage of passive sentences that were recalled as actives: For the full passive, 55% were recalled as active (as against 46% recalled as passive), whereas for the truncated passives only 7% were recalled in the active voice (as against 81% recalled as passives). What this means is that if any transformation is carried out on a passive sentence it occurs primarily for full passives and not for truncated passives. Conversely, and more importantly, these results suggest very good retention of grammatical form for truncated passives. In fact, for this particular type of sentence, the usual result is that a subject will recall both the content and the form, and that the two are not independent of one other.

As Slobin put it: "It would seem, then, that the (Miller-Mehler) coding hypothesis is in need of revision. In the case of truncated passives . . . the syntactic form is not totally irrelevant to the meaning of the sentence, and frequently tends to be retained (or to serve as a ready receptacle for the under-lying semantic content of the sentence) . . . ." The semantic part of the sentence retained in memory therefore need not always be a simple declarative sentence as is implied by the original coding + footnote hypothesis. For truncated passives, recall seems to involve little or no grammatical alteration in the form of the to-be-recalled sentence.

All this research is of course aimed at determining what it is a subject holds onto in memory. The bulk of the evidence seems to suggest that subjects retain meaning and that grammatical information is retained only insofar as it is relevant to the meaning of the to-be-recalled materials. In the case of sentence perception, grammatical information helps to clarify the meaning of the input. Once this clarification is achieved, one of two things may then happen to such grammatical information: If the subject's task is to recall a sentence verbatim, he may hang onto it in the form of a footnote. If the subject is simply expected to understand the sentence (and can indicate this accomplishment by a paraphrase), then specific grammatical footnotes will be lost. During recall the subject probably paraphrases input in the easiest way possible, taking his own feelings about the meaning of the sentence into account. If the grammatical form is relevant to the meaning of the sentence (as in truncated passives), both the meaning and the form of the sentence will be stored. In this case, even if paraphrase is allowed, recall will still follow the same grammatical form as the input not because any additional footnotes have been stored but because the sentence has been stored in its entirety, grammar and all.

There is one other point to be made in connection with studies concerned with the role of syntactic structure in recall—namely, that recall situations have very special properties over and above those imposed by stimulus materials. In a recall or recognition task, subjects make use of any and all strategies in attempting to recall or reconstruct stimulus materials and only one of these concerns the syntactic properties of the input. It is not altogether reasonable to expect a transformational theory set up to explain sentence comprehension and production to account for sentence recall, since this latter situation involves many performance factors irrelevant to language usage in its more usual sense. It is almost as if transformational psycho-linguists have forgotten their own admonition to keep separate linguistic competence and the performance situations in which this competence is assumed to surface.

This extended analysis implies that for sentence reception and sentence recall, meaning is probably more important than syntactic form, and that recall tasks impose special requirements which may be irrelevant for more usual sentence creation and understanding.  In any kind of task in which meaning is either directly involved, subjects seem to be more responsive to the meaning of the input than to its physical form.  If this is the case, it now becomes necessary to ask: What does it mean to say a word has meaning? It is to this question that we now must turn.

## Meaning and the Word Dictionary

Whenever we think of word meaning in common-sense terms, we usually have in mind something like a dictionary or a thesaurus.  As an opening move, it might be instructive to see how these devices work.  The first thing we know about a dictionary is that a prospective user can use it only if he knows the word whose meaning he doesn't know.  That is, a dictionary is organized word by word.  Since there are a great many different words, the elements of the dictionary are themselves further ordered on the basis of a relatively arbitrary principle, that of the alphabet.

How does a dictionary give the meaning of word?  Usually in terms of other words, occasionally by a picture, and often by giving an example of the word's use in a sentence.  Often there are grammatical form class markings— this word is an adjective or a noun, and if the dictionary is a good one there is often a brief history of the word, or at least parts of its historical derivation.

What happens when someone looks up a word?  The process essentially involves a sentence or phrase containing other words that are more frequent in use than the word under consideration.  Sometimes this is not possible so that a definition requires the user to go to another entry.  Often this entry has a different first letter, so that according to the organizational rules of the dictionary, pages have to be turned and time expended before the appropriate next definition can be found.

Given these limitations—that dictionary entries are ordered on the basis of a relatively arbitrary principle, that definitions often contain unknown elements that require further time-consuming searches, and that the final definitions provided may not be immediately usable (see Deese's example of the *chaste amoeba*, described earlier)—a dictionary seems a poor device to provide a speaker or listener with the meaning of a word.  Although it is perfectly usable for reading or other language activities in which time demands are not great, and in which the word is presented in advance of its meaning, it does seem a bit unwieldy for producing words whose meaning we want to express in speech.  For speech production, the essential aspect seems to be "knowing" the meaning first and selecting the word later.

In order to describe this aspect of word usage, consider how a thesaurus works. The primary purpose of a thesaurus is to provide a word when the writer knows what he wants to say but doesn't have the appropriate word immediately available to him. Words are not organized alphabetically, but rather in terms of 990 or so categories which are themselves derived from still more abstract categories. The entire set of more than 20,000 words contained in a thesaurus such as that devised originally by Roget is organized at the highest level into categories such as Abstract Relations, Space, Matter, Intellect, Volition, and Affections. Each of these is further divided into lower-order categories, with some of these lower-order categories having still further subdivisions. For example, under the major heading, *Space*, the first next level heading is *Space in General*, which includes categories such as *Space, Region, Situation, Inhabitant*, etc. Further subdivisions are also provided, so that under *Inhabitant* it is possible to find subheadings such as *dweller, resident, native, settler*, and so on.

Perhaps the best way to characterize the organization of Roget's *Thesaurus* is to say that it goes from very broad categories to very specific ones. If we take this as a model for how words are used in sentence production, it would imply a series of progressively more precise distinctions until the desired word is found. Behind the use of any given word, then, is a highly articulated categorical structure, with the specific location of a word within this structure determining when it will or will not be used.

The dictionary and the thesaurus provide natural models for how subjects using written language understand and choose words, respectively. This division seems natural enough: One compilation of words for giving meaning to a sentence—or more accurately to words in a sentence—and another providing the necessary equipment for presenting ideas in words. Reading and writing involve different word stores, organized along different lines, and that's that. But is that that? Or do other considerations imply that it would be entirely too cumbersome to assume two separate word stores within a fluent language user?

What seems to be required instead is a single word store that can be entered in one of two ways: either in terms of words (like a dictionary) or in terms of meaning (like a thesaurus). It seems unlikely that each of these two tasks—reading and writing or speaking and listening—necessitates the use of a different organizational principle or schema. Indeed there are far too many different things that people can do with words, in addition to understanding and speaking, to require a separate word organization for each. The number of tasks psychologists alone have thought up for subjects to do with words—associate them, recall them, rate them, etc—implies far too many organizations. Indeed it seems reasonable to suppose a single organization of words, and assume that such an organization could serve as a basis for all these tasks. The question then is to determine how such a word store might be organized.

One reasonable and reasonably well-explored topic that might be expected to produce clues is provided by the word-association task. The task is extremely simple to administer and results in large masses of intuitively meaningful data. Somehow it seems reasonable to expect that an examination of the pattern of relations existing among collections of words could provide a convenient starting point by which to discover how a theoretical word store is organized. This, indeed, is the assumption that underlies much of the research initiated by James Deese (1965, 1967) and his coworkers at Johns Hopkins University.

Deese's theoretical and empirical analysis concerns two specific word classes: nouns and adjectives. The basic property relating one noun to another is grouping, whereas the basic property relating one adjective to another is contrast. By *grouping*, Deese simply means the well-documented result that nouns produce similar-meaning nouns as responses in an association task, while by *contrast* he simply means that adjectives usually produce opposite-meaning adjectives as responses. At a first level, then, the problem of the word store becomes one of specifying why nouns produce nouns, and why adjectives produce adjectives.

One important aspect to this particular problem is contained in an observation about word associations made initially by Jenkins (1957) and followed up by Brown and Berko (1960), Ervin-Tripp (1961), and more recently by Entwisle (1966). If a male college student is asked to associate to the word *sour*, he tends to produce responses such as *sweet* and *bitter*. If on the other hand a kindergarten child is asked to associate to this same word, he produces responses such as *kraut* and *lemon*. The young child seems to respond as if he were completing a phrase or sentence while the college student responds as if he were attempting to match the grammatical form class of the target word. The childlike pattern has been termed a *syntagmatic* (or syntactically determined) *associate*, while the adultlike pattern has been termed a *paradigmatic* (or form-class) *associate*.

How frequent are paradigmatic responses at the various age levels? Although there is a general increase over successive age levels, the percentage of paradigmatic increases more dramatically for some form classes than for others. For example, both adjectives and verbs produce only 17% paradigmatics in a population of four-year-olds (kindergarten age), yet both produce more than 65% paradigmatics in a population of college-age respondents. Nouns, on the other hand, show the smallest increase of any grammatical class, but this is largely because young children indiscriminately produce nouns as responses to all kinds of stimulus words. Adverbs, on the other hand, show a very small increase, reaching a maximum value of about only 30% paradigmatics in a college-age population.

The upshot of these results seems to be that the representation of a specific word within a "word dictionary" must contain some marking as to grammatical form class. This obviously agrees with the usual entries found in both a dictionary and a thesaurus. There is one other aspect of these developmental studies that deserves comment, which is that young subjects often produce responses which sound alike, *cocoon–moon*, where no obvious meaningful relationship exists between the two words. This may imply that words also have a phonetic representation that is more significant for child than for adult word usage.

Now that we know both phonetic and grammatical markers are represented in the word store, what other properties might also be involved? Here let us pick up the thread of Deese's argument again (see Chapter 15 for an earlier discussion) and see what it can tell us about the organization of vocabulary. As a beginning, consider the set of overlap coefficients presented in Table 16.3.

First, remember what is meant by an overlap coefficient: Essentially it represents the number of associates two words have in common and is assumed to represent the degree of similarity in meaning between two words. Looking across the first row of the table (the row headed by the word *antelope*), we see that the largest values (greater than .12) occur for *bear*, *deer*, and *moose*. If we lower our cut-off score a bit, a few more words such as *goat*, *muskrat*, *rabbit*, etc., also sneak in, but the point is that all these words seem to belong together in terms of being "animals who live in a forest."

To take another specific example: *cow* and *goat* produce an overlap value of .20. This occurred largely because they share words such as *milk*, *farm*, *meat*, and so on. Note that all these shared words are of the same form-class: They are nouns. Because of the preponderance of paradigmatic responses in adult speakers, very few of the overlapping associates consist of adjectives or other descriptive terms. Yet it is clear whenever a cohesive subgroup does occur, that there are meaningful relations lying beneath the associative surface, relations which could serve to explain the occurrence of a particular word group.

But how should these relations be thought about and described? Basically Deese argues that any word can be considered as a list of attributes: In a simple case, say that of a five-attribute set, the word could be represented as $W_1 = (+, -, +, +, -)$. What this means is that on each of the five attributes relevant to word $W_1$, $W_1$ has a positive rating on the first, third, and fourth attributes and a negative rating on the second and fifth. If we now consider two other words, $W_2$ and $W_3$, and represent their patterns over the same five attributes so that $W_2 = (+ + + + -)$ and $W_3 = (- + + - +)$, it seems obvious that $W_1$ and $W_2$ share attributes 1, 3, 4, and 5, while $W_1$ and $W_3$ share only attribute 3. If this is the case, we might expect that a subject on being presented with $W_1$ would be more likely to produce $W_2$ as an associate than $W_3$.

**Table 16.3**  Intersection coefficients for animal names*

| | Bear | Beaver | Buffalo | Cat | Cow | Deer | Dog | Fox | Goat | Gorilla | Hamster | Horse | Lion | Moose | Mouse | Muskrat | Pig | Pony | Rabbit | Rat | Sheep | Sloth |
|---|---|---|---|---|---|---|---|---|---|---|---|---|---|---|---|---|---|---|---|---|---|---|
| Antelope | 0.14 | 0.07 | 0.09 | 0.01 | 0.04 | 0.26 | 0.02 | 0.08 | 0.11 | 0.03 | 0.12 | 0.03 | 0.06 | 0.15 | 0.04 | 0.12 | 0.06 | 0.03 | 0.12 | 0.03 | 0.06 | 0.12 |
| Bear | | 0.10 | 0.08 | 0.02 | 0.04 | 0.14 | 0.03 | 0.11 | 0.12 | 0.08 | 0.14 | 0.03 | 0.10 | 0.11 | 0.04 | 0.18 | 0.07 | 0.04 | 0.14 | 0.04 | 0.06 | 0.16 |
| Beaver | | | 0.07 | 0.02 | 0.03 | 0.10 | 0.02 | 0.10 | 0.07 | 0.03 | 0.09 | 0.03 | 0.06 | 0.07 | 0.04 | 0.18 | 0.08 | 0.06 | 0.06 | 0.04 | 0.05 | 0.08 |
| Buffalo | | | | 0.01 | 0.04 | 0.07 | 0.02 | 0.05 | 0.09 | 0.06 | 0.07 | 0.03 | 0.07 | 0.09 | 0.04 | 0.08 | 0.08 | 0.04 | 0.06 | 0.08 | 0.08 | 0.06 |
| Cat | | | | | 0.02 | 0.00 | 0.79 | 0.03 | 0.17 | 0.01 | 0.04 | 0.02 | 0.03 | 0.01 | 0.13 | 0.03 | 0.02 | 0.01 | 0.03 | 0.10 | 0.07 | 0.01 |
| Cow | | | | | | 0.04 | 0.02 | 0.04 | 0.20 | 0.02 | 0.04 | 0.16 | 0.04 | 0.08 | 0.03 | 0.04 | 0.03 | 0.08 | 0.04 | 0.02 | 0.01 | 0.04 |
| Deer | | | | | | | 0.03 | 0.12 | 0.09 | 0.03 | 0.08 | 0.04 | 0.06 | 0.16 | 0.04 | 0.11 | 0.07 | 0.04 | 0.12 | 0.03 | 0.06 | 0.10 |
| Dog | | | | | | | | 0.04 | 0.02 | 0.01 | 0.04 | 0.02 | 0.04 | 0.02 | 0.12 | 0.02 | 0.02 | 0.01 | 0.04 | 0.08 | 0.08 | 0.02 |
| Fox | | | | | | | | | 0.05 | 0.04 | 0.07 | 0.05 | 0.05 | 0.10 | 0.05 | 0.13 | 0.06 | 0.05 | 0.13 | 0.06 | 0.07 | 0.06 |
| Goat | | | | | | | | | | 0.03 | 0.10 | 0.06 | 0.04 | 0.10 | 0.04 | 0.10 | 0.10 | 0.05 | 0.10 | 0.03 | 0.21 | 0.10 |
| Gorilla | | | | | | | | | | | 0.03 | 0.03 | 0.09 | 0.05 | 0.03 | 0.03 | 0.03 | 0.03 | 0.03 | 0.03 | 0.03 | 0.05 |
| Hamster | | | | | | | | | | | | 0.04 | 0.04 | 0.07 | 0.20 | 0.17 | 0.09 | 0.04 | 0.10 | 0.21 | 0.05 | 0.15 |
| Horse | | | | | | | | | | | | | 0.04 | 0.06 | 0.04 | 0.04 | 0.05 | 0.38 | 0.05 | 0.05 | 0.05 | 0.03 |
| Lion | | | | | | | | | | | | | | 0.05 | 0.06 | 0.03 | 0.05 | 0.04 | 0.05 | 0.03 | 0.05 | 0.06 |
| Moose | | | | | | | | | | | | | | | 0.03 | 0.09 | 0.07 | 0.04 | 0.07 | 0.02 | 0.05 | 0.07 |
| Mouse | | | | | | | | | | | | | | | | 0.12 | 0.04 | 0.04 | 0.05 | 0.38 | 0.04 | 0.04 |
| Muskrat | | | | | | | | | | | | | | | | | 0.08 | 0.04 | 0.13 | 0.09 | 0.04 | 0.13 |
| Pig | | | | | | | | | | | | | | | | | | 0.05 | 0.08 | 0.03 | 0.08 | 0.12 |
| Pony | | | | | | | | | | | | | | | | | | | 0.04 | 0.04 | 0.04 | 0.04 |
| Rabbit | | | | | | | | | | | | | | | | | | | | 0.04 | 0.06 | 0.09 |
| Rat | | | | | | | | | | | | | | | | | | | | | 0.03 | 0.05 |
| Sheep | | | | | | | | | | | | | | | | | | | | | | 0.05 |

* From J. Deese, *The Structure of Associations in Language and Thought*, 1965.

Since attributes, which are largely represented in language as adjectives, do not readily occur as associates to a target word, one must employ other procedures to recover these latent attributes.  In one attempt to do just this, Deese (1965) asked a group of ten subjects to list as many adjectives as they could to describe the specific animal names presented in Table 16.3. If an adjective were used more than once, it was assumed to represent a significant descriptive attribute for this set.  On the basis of this procedure, a series of 25 adjective pairs was developed and a new group of three subjects asked to choose which of the adjectives best described each of the 21 animal names.  A score was then computed for pairs of words which indexed the degree of agreement in adjectives chosen to describe each of the words in a pair.  This value was then correlated with the overlap coefficients obtained and results produced correlations around .40.  This means that words which produce similar words as associates also tend to select the same adjectives as descriptive attributes.

Given this favorable result, it seems reasonable to represent a word as a list of attributes.  If this is the case, it is also possible to represent a concept as a composite list of attributes.  For example, if we consider $W_1$ and $W_2$ as having the patterns $(+ - + + -)$ and $(+ + + + -)$ respectively, it should then be possible to define a higher-order category $C$ as some combination of the two:  $C = (+ ? + + -)$.  If the category is a usual one, we should expect it to have a name, and this name considered simply as a word should have a good deal of overlap with other relevant words.  In the case of the animal set (in which concept word, $C$, would be *animal*), this implies that the word *animal* should have a higher overlap coefficient than any of the words contained in Table 16.3.  This result has, in fact, been reported by Deese.

Deese's approach to concept description and the organization of vocabulary can be generalized, and one such generalization is presented in Table 16.4.

**Table 16.4**  A hypothetical example of a categorical structure*

| Words | Attributes | | | | | | |
|---|---|---|---|---|---|---|---|
|  | I | II | III | IV | V | V | VI |
| 1 | + | + |   |   |   |   |   |
| 2 | + |   | + |   |   |   |   |
| 3 | + |   |   | + |   |   |   |
| 4 | + |   |   |   | + |   |   |
| 5 | + |   |   |   |   | + |   |
| 6 | + |   |   |   |   |   | + |

* Modified from Deese, 1965, page 155.

The top of this table lists six (VI) different attributes. Six different words are listed down the side. Since this table is meant to represent the structure of a category (such as *animal*), all the words have at least one attribute in common (in this case attribute I). This is obviously the attribute serving to define the category most clearly. For this particular example only a single attribute defines the category. In principle, any number could do the job. Further derivations from this class of model have been presented by Johnson (1970), specifically in regard to a compound word-association task.

One point that should be made about this approach to meaning is that it has a good deal in common with (in fact seems to have been derived from) the distinctive-features analysis of phonemes proposed by Jakobson, Fant, and Halle, 1956 (see Chapter 14 for a fuller discussion of this work). In the case of sounds, Jakobson and his associates assume that a sound is characterized completely by its pattern of +'s and −'s on a series of eight distinctive phonetic–acoustic features. The development of meaning proposed by Deese (and also by Osgood, 1968 and Miller, 1968) strongly resembles the distinctive-features analysis of sound patterns in the language. The only difference so far has to do with the way significant features or attributes are discovered. Obviously, in the case of meaning, these are largely undiscovered as yet and it is doubtful whether any set of features will be universal in the sense implied by Jakobson, Fant, and Halle for sounds.

*The structure of adjectives.* So far we have discussed only nouns; but nouns do not exhaust the properties of associative meaning—there is at least the class of adjectives still to go. Adjectives produce rather special associative patterns, the most important of which is that paradigmatic responses to adjectives tend to be adjectives that are opposite in meaning. This is true despite the fact that most adjectives have both a contrast and noncontrast paradigmatic associate available to them, e.g., *hot* has either *cold* or *warm*; *beautiful*, either *ugly* or *pretty*, and so on. Since the analysis of nouns assumes that one word produces another as an associate because they produce similar attribute lists, the opposite-meaning adjective case obviously requires a special extension of the attribute hypothesis.

The "special extension" required in this case was developed initially by McNeill (1966) and used most extensively by Entwisle (1966). Basically, McNeill proposed that two words that are opposites have an identical attribute pattern with the exception of a single feature or attribute, and that this feature or attribute seems to define the essential nature of the contrast. Thus *hot* and *cold* both have to do with temperature, temperament, etc., and differ only in regard to the degree of temperature (or temperament) they specify.

Now while this is a most attractive hypothesis, it does seem to run into some trouble, both logical and empirical. The logical one first: On the basis of a semantic-attribute hypothesis, there is no reason to assume that synonymous adjectives should have less similar attribute patterns than oppositional adjectives. The list of attributes associated with *cold* could and should be more similar to those associated with *cool* which, in turn, should be more similar than those associated with *hot.*

Empirically, there are also further difficulties. For one thing, the probability with which one member of a contrasting adjective pair produces the other (*hot* → *cold*) should be equal to the reverse probability (*cold* → *hot*). This expectation is not confirmed by data in which the *hot* → *cold* probability is 0.41, and the *cold* → *hot* probability is 0.20. Indeed there is a good deal of asymmetry in most contrastive pairs (see Pollio, 1968), and this asymmetry does not seem to be accountable for by any simple analysis. An even more direct evaluation of McNeill's hypothesis (Pollio, Deitchman, and Richards, 1969) found that even over as limited a set of attributes as the three main semantic differential dimensions, most contrasting adjectives differ significantly on more than a single dimension.

The major problem raised by opposites can be put quite simply: In certain tasks (such as word association), opposites produce each other with great frequency, indicating a good deal of meaningful similarity; in other cases, and by logical definition, they define the most distant points of a meaningful dimension. In terms of both Deese and McNeill's analysis of opposites, they are defined as words which share all attributes but one.

In order to show what effects opposites produce in the context of a learning task, Pollio, Deitchman, and Richards (1969) had subjects learn a series of paired associates in which the stimulus term was a nonsense syllable and the response term was one of five words: *hot, warm, mild, cool,* or *cold.* There were three different nonsense syllables paired with each adjective, yielding a total of 15 pairs. Since this is a rather complex task, subjects made a number of errors on their way to learning the correct pairings. An examination of errors was made with the specific purpose of comparing the relative number of times *hot* was confused with *cold* and *cold* was confused with *cool,* or *hot* with *warm.* This type of comparison pits an opposite pair against a similar pair. Over two sets of experimental results, 62 of 85 subjects showed more confusions of *cold* with *cool* than of *cold* with *hot,* and 55 of 85 subjects showed more confusions of *hot* with *warm* than of *hot* with *cold.* From both ends, then, subjects intruded the "similar" adjective more frequently than the "opposite" one. Similar results have also been found to apply for the word set *beautiful, pretty, fair, homely,* and *ugly. Beautiful* is confused less frequently with *ugly* than *ugly* is confused with *homely,* or than *beautiful* is confused with *pretty* (Pollio, 1966). What this implies is that oppositional adjectives are no more highly similar in terms of their list of attributes than is true for similar adjectives.

How then can this be handled within the context of Deese's analysis of associative meaning? First of all let us assume the essential validity of

Deese's main point; namely that subjects are capable of producing, and actually do produce, associates on the basis of a creative process depending on attribute overlap. In searching through the vocabulary pool for an appropriate word in any task (speaking, understanding, associating, or whatnot), we find that words having similar attribute "profiles" occur together. What this means is that for children, opposites should be less common than for adults. With the growth of syntactic form-class attributes, the occurrence of an opposite (a word of the same form class as the target word) is made more likely, but certainly nowhere near as likely as the similar paradigmatic response.

How then do stable oppositional patterns develop? The motivation for such patterns would seem to depend on the conceptual economy provided by opposites. In most cases it is important to know whether a stove is *hot* or *cold*, not whether it is *tepid* or *warm*. Opposites serve to define a conceptual dimension with great economy. On this basis it would seem that oppositional words are often thought of as the same, and thus may come to have some special learned connection established between them. It is this learned connection, operating as a habit, that probably accounts for Marbe's Law; namely, that oppositional word associations occur with extremely short latency within the context of an association experiment.

Because oppositional adjectives do come to have strong word-to-word connections, there is no reason to assume that they cannot also be described by a specific list of features. Depending on what the subject is asked to do, an adjective can either evoke its paired opposite adjective, or can generate an entire dimension if such is required by a task. Although it may be important to know whether a stove is *hot* or *cold*, it is also important to know whether a baby's bath is *just right* (*lukewarm*).

One word more: The use of an adjective to describe a distinctive feature should not be taken to mean that the underlying feature and the adjective are identical. An attribute may be realized in terms of an adjective, but the use of this adjective is not the same as the concept. For example, in the *hot–cold* case the dimension is *temperature*, whereas in the case of opposites such as *long–short* the dimension is *length*. In the first case, neither adjective defines the dimension; in the second case, one of them has the same name as the dimension. What this means is that attributes or features are probably not directly representable in terms of adjectives. For empirical purposes, however, such words are our best (and only) indicators of the underlying concept involved.

**A marker theory of meaning.** Deese's analysis, however, was not the first to talk about meaning in terms of latent attributes. The first theory to attempt this schematically was proposed by Katz and Fodor in 1963. The easiest way to present this theory is to consider their opening example and see where it leads. Katz and Fodor begin with the word *bachelor* which, according to the Oxford Dictionary, has four different meanings: (1) a young knight serving under the standard of another knight; (2) one who possesses the first or lowest academic degree; (3) a man who has never married; and (4) a young fur seal when without a mate during the breeding time (bet you didn't know that one). Katz and Fodor diagram this entry as shown in Fig. 16.4.

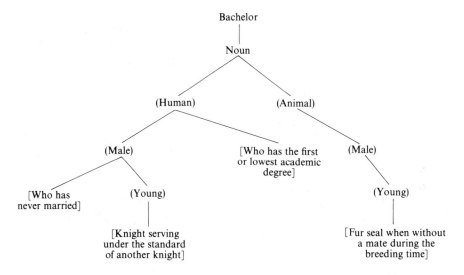

**Fig. 16.4** Hypothetical tree structure for the English word *bachelor*. (From Katz and Fodor, The structure of a semantic theory, *Language*, **39**, 186, 1963)

The first thing to note about this method of diagramming is that it is hierarchical, with the part of speech at the top of the hierarchy. What this means is that when one is interpreting the meaning of a word, the first decision involves grammatical form class. In this sense, grammar is prior to meaning, for a grammatical marking (noun) helps to provide a word with meaning. Going down the hierarchy, it is important to note that some of the words occurring at each node are enclosed in parentheses, while others are enclosed in square brackets. In all cases, those items enclosed in brackets are below those enclosed in parentheses. This is meant to indicate that the "parenthesized" elements are somehow prior to, or more important than, those that have been bracketed. This is in fact meant to be the case: Parenthetical elements are assumed to represent *markers* (that is, classificatory elements having application across a large portion, if not all, of the vocabulary), whereas bracketed elements are thought to distinguish the idiosyncratic components of meaning involved in a given word and are therefore much less general. For obvious reasons, bracketed elements are called *distinguishers.* Each of the specific meanings of a word is characterized by following one path from top to bottom.

There is one question that arises immediately as to how markers are to be ordered. That is, why is the *human–animal* component ahead of the (implied) *male–female* one, and why are both of these prior to the *young–old* marker? This order is presumably set in terms of generality across the entire vocabulary—that is, it seems that the distinction between human and animal is one that organizes a larger portion of the available word pool than the distinction between *male* and *female.* The same is presumably also true of the relative ordering of *male–female* and *young–old.* Whether or not we agree with the order of generality in this particular example, the more general principle of ordering markers on the basis of their breadth of usage does seem a reasonable one.

But does ordering itself pose any problems? Somehow, if we look again at the various entries involved in the *bachelor* example, we note that the two definitions—(1) an unmarried, male, human and (2) a nonbreeding, young, male animal (seal)—are the most different in the set. Technically this means that their terminal positions on the tree are farthest apart. Yet this difference in position is largely due to the fact that the highest-level marker is *human–animal.* If we extracted a different marker as critical, such as *young–old* or *mated–unmated,* and placed the *human–animal* distinction lower down on the tree, definitions (1) and (2) would fill closer positions on the definitional tree.

Now there is a sense in which all these definitions are related, which "transcends" those represented by the superordinate–subordinate marker pattern, and this is in terms of nonliteral or metaphorical usage. There is a common thread running through all the various definitions which can perhaps best be captured in terms of the words *young* and *male.* Although the specific historical development of this word shouldn't trouble us, it seems reasonable to suppose that some of the definitions or meanings aroused by *bachelor* were historically prior to others and that these later usages represented a metaphorical extension of the original use. Some of those extensions emphasized one marker (*young* in the case of knight and baccalaureate), whereas others emphasized a different marker (*mated* in the case of human and seal bachelors). The degree of relationship seems to depend on which marker (attribute) we take as critical.

In any event, the problem or ordering markers is closely related to the more general problem of how such a theory would handle metaphorical usages and extensions (Bolinger, 1965). Presumably, it would involve differential emphasis on one or another marker, with the result a possible temporary reordering of the markers that could then either become permanent or revert back to their initial ordering, depending on custom and usage.

But these objections to the Katz-Fodor model are linguistic or philosophical. What implications does a marker theory have for a psychological
analysis of word usage and interpretation? Certainly, both Deese and Katz
and Fodor are pursuing essentially similar models. Meaning, for both, is
viewed as a multicomponent list of attributes (*features* and *markers*, to use
their terms). The major difference is that for Deese the markers are organized
linearly, whereas for Katz and Fodor they are arranged hierarchically.
Although this latter approach provides generality to the domain potentially
representable by each marker, the problem of metaphorical extension (i.e.,
is a baccalaureate bachelor more similar to an unmarried male or to an
unmated seal?) makes the use of a nonchanging order somewhat difficult to
handle conceptually.

What seems to be implied by these two approaches, and also by Osgood's
most recent (1968) analysis of meaning, is that a word can be represented as
a list of attributes. It seems quite reasonable to take this as a starting point.
From here, it next seems reasonable to propose that for certain purposes this
list is organized linearly, while for other purposes it may be organized
hierarchically. It is even possible to assume that the order of elements
within a hierarchical arrangement is variable, so that for certain tasks—
for example exhibiting meaningful similarity between two words—an
ordering of markers from most general to least general is required. For yet
other tasks—exhibiting the degree of relationship among the various meanings of a single word—an ordering of markers in terms of metaphorically
significant uses is required. In any event, it is evident that semantic attributes, which are primitives in an interpretive theory such as Katz and Fodor's,
must be unordered, and that their usage is situationally determined. The
vocabulary pool need not be static; but must instead change over changing
tasks and situations.

An analysis of meaning, more specifically word meaning, couched in
terms of a shifting array of attributes implies that a thesaurus does not
provide a completely satisfactory model for describing semantic organization. Although it may be true that certain attributes cover a good deal of the
vocabulary pool, it certainly does not seem to be true that all word knowledge
can be organized into a small number of groupings such as Roget's six major
categories. Instead, specific domains and tasks may select specific attributes,
with the specific composition of an attribute matrix determined by the particular segment of vocabulary now under consideration. Words go in families,
and what may be a good way to describe one family may not necessarily
capture the properties of a different family.

This suggests that a componential analysis of meaning does hold some
promise as a theory of vocabulary organization if we grant that there are
few if any all-embracing semantic attributes. We must work instead, as
Wittgenstein suggests and Deese has, with families of words that have a

common thread(s) running through them. The value of a componential view of meaning may ultimately rest on whether or not it is possible to provide a consistent set of attributes for small groups of words which enable a knowledgeable word user to speak, understand, remember, associate, write, and read these words in ways that are mutually complementary. If such turns out to be possible, then componential analysis does provide a clear advance in conceptualizing word meaning and the structure of the vocabulary pool.

## THE DEVELOPMENT OF LANGUAGE

At the age of two, if he can produce any sentences at all, a child will tend to say things such as: "All-gone milk"; "Jono car"; "Bye-bye Mommy" and so on. By the time he is six, he may be able to say such things as: "The stegosaurus has armor like a knight; but that's impossible because he's prehistoric." The difference between these two utterances involves more than just vocabulary; it involves a difference between the crude beginnings of language and the use of language in a delicate and literate form. The set of sentences spontaneously produced by the six-year-old resembles poetry as much as or more than simple prose.

The changes that take a child from vaguely verbal teddy bear to fully productive language user seem to occur in all normal children at about the same time, and more or less at about the same rate. Although most children and perhaps many adults never reach the level attained by our dinosaur-loving six-year-old, most do come to have functional command of their language by the time they are four years of age. In the two-year period between two and four, the child comes to adult language estate.

Lenneberg (1967) has developed a more formal documentation of this conclusion and his results show that the progression of spontaneous verbal output changes systematically from single-word utterances, to two-word phrases, and finally to utterances containing five or more words. By the age of 22 months all children in his sample observed had produced single words; by the age of 36 months all children had produced two-word phrases; while by the 38th month, 80% of the sample produced sentences of five or more words. What is striking about these results is the relatively rapid development of language skills: From start to finish they take no more than two years to emerge. What is also of interest, and will take on greater significance later, is the relatively slower development of two-word phrases in comparison to the rate of development for one- and five-word utterances. The period from 12 to 36 months seems to represent the most critical time for the development of language.

The relatively invariant emergence of these language milestones has led some development psychologists (McNeill, 1966, 1968, Miller and McNeill, 1969; Lenneberg, 1967) to propose that there is a significant biological (innate) component to language acquisition. Basically, this analysis assumes that at certain critical ages (presumably 12–36 months), the child is genetically "tuned" to acquire certain significant aspects of language. These "significant aspects" are assumed to be universal—that is, common to all languages—and during this critical period he is more responsive to these universals than to any other aspects of language, even those that occur more often.

McNeill (1961) provides the following example from his study of a Japanese child, Izanami.*   Unlike English, Japanese is a postpositional language; that is, in Japanese, postpositions often serve the same function as prepositions do in English.   The two postpositions of particular interest in McNeill's analysis are *wa* and *ga.*

*Wa* is used whenever the predicate of a sentence *attributes* something to the surface subject of the sentence . . . often this can be translated into English with the expression *as for*, as in the following example:

*As for* cats, they eat fish.

. . . In the case of *ga*, the predicate of the sentence is not regarded as an inherent part of the subject.   Instead, the two are merely linked together, in a connection usually conceived as momentary and accidental . . . There is no standard translation of *ga* into English, but the Japanese equivalents of the following sentences would all take *ga*:

Izanami-*ga* is making too much noise. . . . The cat-*ga* is eating the fish . . . It-*ga* is on Mt. Everest this morning.

These sentences do not claim that it is an attribute of the cat to eat the fish, or of Izanami to make too much noise.   In fact, they deny attribution and assert instead a momentary connection.   Hence, they receive *ga*.†

These two postpositions therefore have rather different functions in Japanese grammar: *ga* expresses an accidental connection between subject and predicate, while *wa* is used to signal more essential attribution.   In the samples of speech involving Izanami and her mother, Izanami's mother used *wa* about twice as often as *ga*.   Izanami, on the other hand, used *ga* about 12.5 times as often as *wa* (75 to 6).   What this means is that the child's frequency of usage does not mirror the adult's frequency of usage of these postpositions.   Rather, the child seems maximally sensitive both in use and comprehension to the less frequently occurring element because (McNeill

---

* The group of researchers studying language development at Harvard, headed by Roger Brown, inaugurated the tradition of naming their child subjects after biblical characters.   Thus Brown's group often calls male respondents Adam and female respondents Eve.   McNeill, continuing this tradition, calls his subject Izanami after the Japanese goddess who helped create the world.

† From "On theories of language acquisition," by D. McNeill, in *Verbal Behavior and General Behavior Theory*, edited by T. R. Dixon and D. L. Horton, Englewood Cliffs, N.J.: Prentice-Hall, 1968, page 417.

would argue) *ga* captures the needed grammatical relation of "subject of a sentence."

Izanami seemed selectively tuned by her present stage of biological development to learn this particular concept, and not particularly tuned to the more frequently occurring, but not immediately relevant, concept of *attribution*. The use of *wa*, which is so frequent in adult speech, will develop later in order to reflect a distinction significant to Japanese, but not to English.

## Phonological Development

How can the facts concerning a child's language acquisition be characterized? At the outset it is well to realize that behind any overt vocalization, even a simple one-word sentence, is a good deal of phonetic expertise: Muscles have to be coordinated, breathing regulated, tongue positioned, and so on. This expertise, however, is not complete when the child produces his earliest one-word utterance. In fact many of the earliest one-word sentences produced are understood more on the basis of a parent or linguist's intuition than on the basis of the clarity of sound produced. In Ruth Weir's book (1962) dealing with her son's nighttime monologs, she notes that Anthony had trouble with the voiced–voiceless distinction, saying "bik" for "big" and "ret" for "red," and so on.

The interesting aspect of phonological development is that a child begins to produce one-, two-, and even five-word sentences well before phonology is sound-perfect. It is not uncommon for many four-year-olds to say "thith" for "this," confusing the *th* and the *s* sounds. The use and development of language in children in advance of complete phonological mastery is quite different from the pattern used by adults in learning a second language. Here the first step usually consists of acquiring the significant phonological features well in advance of learning the syntactical or lexical aspects of the language. In children it seems as if the child can't wait for his phonology to catch up with his desire to use language creatively.

## The Development of Syntax

But what of the syntactic component? Probably the earliest type of syntax doesn't really involve syntax at all. The first utterances are single words, although careful observation suggests that the intention of a single-word utterance is the same as a complete sentence for an adult. For this reason it seems reasonable to write the first syntactic rule as:

$$S \rightarrow W,$$

meaning that for the very young child the intention to produce a sentence is reflected by the output of a single word.

The second major phase in the development of syntax is represented by what Braine (1963) has called the pivot class. Since the logic of this class has already been discussed previously (see Chapter 15), suffice it to note that words in the pivot class are small in number (such as *bye-bye, all gone, that,* etc.) relative to an open class (of all other words), and that pivot words tend to occur only in conjunction with members of the open class, and then usually in the first position of a two-word utterance. This implies that a next rule of child syntax could be written as:

$$S \rightarrow (P) + O,$$

where $S$ means sentence, as before, $P$ means words in the pivot class and $O$ means words in the open class. The parentheses enclosing $P$ simply mean that using a pivot-class word is optional, but that if it is used, it must be used in the first position. Note that if a member of the pivot class is not used, the rule reduces to one capable of generating one-word sentences, for example, $S \rightarrow O$.

As McNeill (1966) pointed out, words in the pivot class include articles (*a, the*); demonstratives (*that, this*); adjectives; possessives (*my, mine, your*) and a general class of items such as *other, one,* etc., with all these representing successive discriminations of the class of items originally contained in the pivot class. According to data gathered by Brown and Bellugi (1964), there are essentially three phases in the further division of pivot ($P$) words into other grammatical categories. At first,

$$P_1 = \text{(articles)} + \text{(demonstratives)} + \text{(adjectives)} + \text{(possessives)} + \text{(others)}.$$

The first restructuring of $P_1$ occurs about two months after the first systematic use of the $P$ class, and involves the following organization:

$$P_1 = \text{(articles)} + \text{(demonstratives)},$$
$$P_2 = \text{(adjectives)} + \text{(possessives)} + \text{(others)}.$$

The final differentiation occurs about two months later, when $P_2$ is divided into adjectives and possessives with $P_3$ now containing the residual class; for example,

$$P_3 = \text{(other)}; \quad P_2 = \text{(adjectives)} + \text{(possessives)};$$
$$P_1 = \text{(articles)} + \text{(demonstratives)}.$$

Actually, recent work by Lois Bloom (1970) has shown that every combination of pivot and open class occurs except one—$P + P$. That is, Bloom found that children in addition to the $(P) + O$ or $O + (P)$ constructions described by Braine also often made use of an $O + O$ construction. For example, her subjects produced $O + O$ constructions of the following types: (1) cup glass, (2) Kathryn sock, and (3) sweater chair. In talking about these sentences, Slobin (1971) noted that sentence 1 seems to express *conjunction*

(*I see a cup and a glass*); sentence 2, to express possession (*This is Kathryn's sock*); and sentence 3, location (*The sweater is on the chair*). What this means is that although children at this stage produce only two-word sentences, these sentences have many more implicit structures than the relatively simple one captured by the notion of pivot- and open-word class. As Slobin put it: "The child must be aware of the . . . semantic relationships expressed above, but he is apparently limited to sentences of two words in length, and cannot express the full relationship in a single utterance."

All the construction rules considered thus far are essentially linear in nature: Pick one from column *A* and one from column *B*, and so on. The first real development of more general phrase structure emerges somewhat later and involves the early development of a noun phrase as a grammatical constituent. Thus

$$S \to (P) + NP,$$

where $NP \to (P) + N$ or $N + N$. Sentences such as *That Adam coat* are produced by this set of rules. The diagram of this sentence indicates its hierarchical structure.

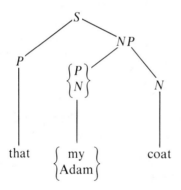

At about the same time that he develops rudimentary noun phrases, the child also comes to develop rudimentary verb or predicate phrases. The rewrite rules governing these sentences can be written as

$$S \to \text{Pred } P,$$

where *Pred P* $\to (V) + NP$, with *NP* defined as before. An example of a sentence produced by this rule would be: *Want that coat*, which can be diagrammed as on following page.

At this stage of syntactic development the child's utterances, even if primitive by adult standards, still reveal a good deal of coherent structure. This structure is different from adult structure, but nonetheless is internally consistent and seems able to account for all utterances produced by a child at this stage.

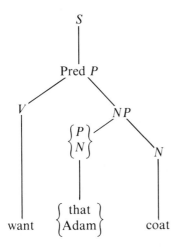

In addition, it is important to note that not all two-word sentences potentially generatable on the basis of these rules occur with equal frequency. Thus the most frequently occurring two-word sentence involves the form $V + N$ (*want coat*) whereas the most frequent three-word pattern is $V + N + N$ (*want Adam coat*). The second most frequently occurring two-word construction has the form $N + N$ (*Adam coat*), and so on. In general, those that are most frequently used seem to have greatest similarity to the adult sentence structure of $S \rightarrow NP + VP$.

But the existence of a phrase-structure grammar does not exhaust all that a child must know in order to become a fluent adult speaker. In particular, he seems to be missing grammatical transformations. Although it is really quite difficult to know for sure whether a child at this stage is, in fact, missing such transformations, the main reasons for denying him the status of "transformation user" would seem to be the child's impoverished output, although this seems a dubious conclusion on at least two counts: (1) The child comprehends more than he produces, and (2) the question of whether or not there are transformations underlying even the very simplest sentences is moot. If, for example, it is assumed that the derivation of single-word sentences includes complex strings, then even the single-word output of the child may have a series of transformations underlying it. The point of this discussion is not to come to any conclusion, but to note that we cannot say, with any degree of confidence, whether or not transformational operations underlie even the earliest outputs of the child.

Despite these theoretical difficulties (or perhaps because of them), many investigators have described the development of selected transformations in the speech of the child. Two transformations which have been studied in some detail have to do with asking a question and with negating a statement. Let us consider the negation transformation first. This is best done by presenting a series of examples drawn from work done by Ursula Bellugi (1966) at Harvard:

Sentence Type 1 :  *no wipe finger*
                     *no sing song*

Sentence Type 2 :  *I don't sit on Cromer coffee*
                     *why not cracker can't talk*

Sentence Type 3 :  *why he didn't know how to pretend*
                     *don't touch the fish*

Sentence Type 4 :  *I can't push it back and forth*
                     *I can't do nothing with no string*

The general impression given by these sentences is that the child is using progressively longer sentences, and that the sentences produced come progressively to resemble those produced by adults. Negative sentences produced during the easiest stage (Type 1) involve adding the word *no* to a standard child sentence. *No wipe finger* is probably best translated into adult speech as *Don't wipe my finger*. What is omitted is use of the verb *do* + negation and the possessive *my*. At this stage, negation is formed simply by prefacing an ordinary sentence with *no*.

Stages 2 and 3 are characterized by an increase in sentence length and complexity, as well as by the use of the *don't* and *why* + negative constructions. In Stage 2 the child uses a double negative (*why not cracker can't talk*) but this drops out during Stage 3. At Stage 2, the double negative is formed by adding the phrase *why not* to the phrase *cracker can't talk*. This may mean that *why not* is not a two-word item, but rather a single term used to express a negative question. The sentence *why not cracker can't talk* seems closer in underlying form to *no wipe finger* than to *why he didn't know how to pretend* (Stage 3).

Stage 4 negations seem to approximate adult language most closely, with the exception of the double negative. The use of the double negative at this stage seems to have a different function from what it did in Stage 2. Here the problem involves the word *nobody*. In negative sentences of this sort the adult may go through the sequence *something* → *anything* → *nothing*, whereas the child is able to express this only in terms of *nothing*. It isn't that the child doesn't understand negation, but rather that he hasn't learned the correct usage of these three terms.

In general there are a number of different factors that bring about the development of the negative transformation. Some of these are semantic and others syntactic. Although it is not altogether clear what motivates the use of *no* in a Stage 1 sentence, informal observation indicates that it depends on attaining the concept of refusal. Only once the child realizes that it is possible to refuse something does there seem to be any desire to express this intention.

The earliest *no*'s represent an attempt to express a refusal, and for this reason the use of *no* preceding a rudimentary affirmative sentence is most appropriate.

With the growth and differentiation of negation, this initial strategy of refusal is too imprecise, and the child becomes more attentive ("tuned") to adult uses of negation. In this way he begins to notice (first as a single lexical entry and later as a more complicated grammatical construction) exactly how it is that adult speakers go about negating statements. These early attempts are clumsy by adult standards and much too particularistic. McNeill estimates that during Stages 2 and 3 the child requires something like 7–8 different sentence types to produce a negation. Under the stress of having to recall many specific sentence types, the child, like the linguist, attempts to reduce this horde by developing transformational rules. From here on in, the rules need only be sharpened, but not changed in any dramatic way.

The question transformation also seems to develop in about the same way. Many parent–child verbal exchanges during the early periods of language seem to involve questions such as: *What does Jono want?*; *Does Jono know what that is called?* *Is this a train?* and so on. Informal observation indicates that the infant first treats questions as no different from other verbalizations; it is not uncommon for a child to go to his room and bring back a picture of a train or a toy train in response to a question such as: "Did Jono see the train yesterday?" The observation and others like it seem to imply that at first the child does not have the concept of a question: The world is assertive and declarative and that's all there is to it!

Once the concept of a question or questioning develops, the general pattern seems to be that the child signals a question by rising intonation rather than by changing word order or by adding auxiliaries and the like. Just as the first negatives involve the simple addition of the word *no* prior to the standard $(P) + O$ sentence, the first questions involve the simple addition of intonation to a standard sentence. The clearest analysis of how the question transformation develops has been undertaken by Brown (1968) in terms of an analysis of *Wh* questions (questions involving *who, whom, what, where,* and *how*). According to Brown's analysis, the earliest uses of *Wh* questions indicate a more or less rote usage on the part of the child. Thus the earliest form of *Wh* question for children is *Wat dat?*, as indeed it was for their mothers. The major difference between the mother's *Wat dat* (in addition to their saying *What is that?*) and the child's *Wat dat?* is that mothers also used other *Wh* variations such as *What's this? What are those? What do you think it is?* etc., whereas none of the children did.

The further development of *Wh* questions seem to involve an intermediary stage in which children produce *Wh* utterances having a form intermediate between the childlike form and the acceptable adult forms. For example, the *Wh* forms: *John will read what?* and *What will John read?* are both acceptable adult forms (assume *what* is stressed in the first sentence). A child past the simple rote stage is likely to produce the pattern *What John will read*? which indicates his ability to prepose a *Wh* form, and his inability to do the appropriate transposing operation required to get *will* into the correct location. Further use of the *Wh* transformation involves learning to use both the transposing and preposing transformations.

As in the case of negation, the development of *Wh* questions proceeds through a series of reasonably well-differentiated stages. These stages begin with the seemingly rote use of a few lexical items, *What dat* for questions and *no* for negations, then pass through a series of one or more intermediary stages until adult usage is achieved. In both cases it seems to suggest that the child develops a particular linguistic transformation in order to express a newly developed concept—that of refusal for negation and that of questioning for questions. Trying out these forms in speech leads to further refinement of the underlying concept, which in turn leads to the necessity for further development of the transformation. In the case of negation, for example, the earliest form represents a relatively simple concept of refusal. With greater linguistic experience, the concept comes to include a more full-fledged understanding of negation in perhaps even its logical sense.

The development of all transformations, then, must involve a constant interplay between an underlying concept and its specific linguistic expression. When the concept is simple, the surface form remains simple. When, however, the concept becomes complex, the corresponding surface form must also increase in complexity. This increases in surface complexity comes to require a large number of highly special rules. As the number of these rules increases, they come to exceed the child's ability to remember them. Given this pressure for cognitive economy, the child pays particular attention to the way in which adult speakers express a particular transformation, and this selective emphasis helps him to induce the underlying structure of the appropriate adult transformational rule(s).

**The Role of the Parent in the Child's Language Development**

Although McNeill (1966) takes a rather strong biological position on language acquisition, Roger Brown (1965; 1968) and others in his group have attempted to describe the growth of language in terms of the dynamics of parent–child verbal interchanges. As he has put it: "The changes produced in sentences as they move between persons in discourse may be the richest data for the discovery of grammar." (Brown, 1968, page 288.)

As an example of how this might occur, consider the four possible forms of interaction involved in developing one of the more significant forms of question transformations. Table 16.5 presents a list of these.

**Table 16.5**  Forms of interaction involving the occasional question*

| | | |
|---|---|---|
| I. | Say again | |
| | (1) Other or Child: "I want milk." | Mother: "What?" | Other or Child: "I want milk." |
| | (2) Other or Child: "Put milk in glass." | Mother: "What?" | Other or Child: "Put milk in glass." |
| II. | Say constituent again | |
| | (1) Other or Child: "I want milk." | Mother: "You want what?" | Other or Child: "Milk." |
| | (2) Other or Child: "Put milk in glass." | Mother: "Put milk where?" | Other or Child: "In glass." |
| III. | Constituent prompt | |
| | (1) Mother: "What do you want?" | Other or Child: ———. | Mother: "You want what?" |
| | (2) Mother: "Where will I put it?" | Other or Child: ———. | Mother: "Put it where?" |
| IV. | Supply antecedent | |
| | (1) Other or Child: "I want it." | Mother: "You want what?" | Other or Child: "Milk." |
| | (2) Other or Child: "Put milk there." | Mother: "Put the milk where?" | Other or Child: "In cup." |

* From "The development of *Wh* questions in child speech," by Roger Brown, in *J. Verbal Learning and Verbal Behavior*, **7**, 2, 1968.

In this table, the interaction role labeled "other or child" is first played by others (older siblings) whom the child overhears. The first pattern is a "say-again pattern" in which the child simply repeats the original sentence. This is probably the most primitive form of a question, although it does provide a simple model for asking a simple kind of question. The second through fourth patterns are pretty well specified by the examples presented. In all cases they have the function of providing the child with a model for asking a question, in which the question serves to remind the child to repeat a particular constituent again (Types II and III) or to supply the antecedent (Type IV).

This specific example implies that the most fundamental or base form of a question is something on the order of *John will read what*? Such questions are called occasional questions by Brown, and have a form somewhat different from more normal questions such as *What will John read*? If occasional questions provide the base form, then rules are needed to show how they change into the more normal question form. Essentially two rules are involved, that of *preposition* and that of *transposition*. The preposing rule changes *John will read what*? to *What John will read*?, whereas the transposition rule changes the position of the verb, producing the more normal form *What will John read*? If this analysis is correct, then the first thing a child must learn about questions is the form of an occasional question. It is for this reason that Brown has described how parent–child interchanges serve to bring about the occasional question rather than the normal question.

In the course of parent–child verbal interchanges, Brown and his coworkers (notably Fraser and Bellugi) have noticed a very specific type of parent–child interchange which they call *expansion*. Consider the following sets of verbal interchange between Adam and his mother.

| Child | Mother |
|---|---|
| Baby highchair | Baby is in the highchair |
| Mommy eggnog | Mommy had her eggnog |
| Eve lunch | Eve is having lunch |
| Mommy sandwich | Mommy'll have a sandwich |
| Sat wall | He sat on the wall |
| Throw Daddy | Throw it to Daddy |
| Pick glove | Pick the glove up |

(Brown, 1965)

The first thing of note about these interchanges concerns Adam's speech: In almost all cases it represents a reduction of the adult pattern. Brown and Fraser (1963) have termed this general aspect of child speech *telegraphic speech*, and note that children often omit items of low information yield that are essentially unstressed in terms of overt production.

A second thing about these interchanges is that adults expand tele-graphic speech in accord both with the dictates of reasonable syntax and in terms of the child's probable meaning.  Thus *Baby highchair* could have been expanded to the perfectly grammatical *The Baby fell out of the highchair*, but this was probably contrary to the fact that *The Baby is in the highchair*. Of particular interest is the fact that Adam's mother tends to preserve the same word order as Adam produced in the first place.  Her expansions consist most often of inserting "missing" words into the word order estab-lished initially by the child.  In general the words that are added are function words, for it is precisely these words that the child omits in the first place.

The interaction between parent and child then provides part of the "instructional" procedure by which the child becomes aware of grammati-cally well-formed utterances.  It is not so much that the parent explicitly attempts to instruct the child (although this may be the case some of the time), but rather that the parent tries to verify his (the adult's) intuition of the intended meaning of the utterance.  Adults seem to expand telegraphic speech a rather large proportion of the time (as much as 30% in Brown's data) and this seems to be their way of checking on whether or not they have understood the child.  In fact, most of the time parents pay little attention to the specific syntax used by their children, preferring to concentrate instead on the truth or falsity of the communication.  As Brown, Cazden, and Bellugi (1967) put it:

> "It seems, then, to be truth value rather than syntactic well-formedness that chiefly governs explicit verbal reinforcement by parents.  Which renders mildly paradoxical the fact that the usual product of such a training schedule is an adult whose speech is highly grammatical but not notably truthful."

## The Development of Meaning

Understanding implies meanings, and so it seems well to ask how children come to learn the meanings of the words and phrases they use.  The associa-tionistic analysis assumes a variety of conditioning explanations, but for the generative approach to language this just won't do.  For one thing, children do not pick up the most frequently occurring words or morphemes in the language (see McNeill's example of *ga* and *wa* in Japanese).  A second important dissatisfaction with a conditioning analysis has been summarized in Miller's fourth postulate: Meaning is not to be confused with or equated with reference.  Meaning depends on a semantic system and not on condi-tioned responses, implicit or otherwise.

But what is the structure of this system?  Linguists are quite fond of illustrating semantic structure in terms of a few well-selected subsets of the speaker's total vocabulary. One of these semantically well-structured sets is represented by the color names, while another is represented by kinship terms. A portion of a kinship system is presented in Table 16.6(a).

**Table 16.6(a)**   The meanings of eight kin terms expressed in the form of a cube.

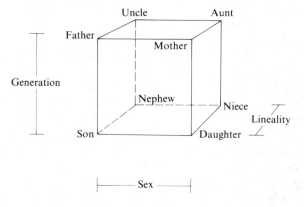

In this table the eight words *father, mother, uncle, aunt, nephew, niece, daughter,* and *son* are arranged according to their properties on three dimensions. A different reorganization of these relationships is presented in Table 16.6(b).

**Table 16.6(b)**   Attribute analysis of the eight kinship terms: distinctive-features analysis

| Word | Sex | | Generation | | Descent | |
|---|---|---|---|---|---|---|
| | M | F | Earlier | Later | Direct | Indirect |
| Father | + | − | + | − | + | − |
| Mother | − | + | + | − | + | − |
| Uncle | + | − | + | − | − | + |
| Aunt | − | + | + | − | − | + |
| Son | + | − | − | + | + | − |
| Daughter | − | + | − | + | + | − |
| Nephew | + | − | − | + | − | + |
| Niece | − | + | − | + | − | + |

This latter type of reorganization is consistent with Katz and Fodor's model, except that all cells in the table are completely filled in. The value of filling in all cells rests in the fact that specifying the meaning of the word as (+ Male + Earlier and + Direct) leads immediately to the word *Father.* Starting at the word end, *Father* is immediately given its meaning in this specific semantic system by the pattern (+, +, +).

An analysis such as this provides for an unambiguous specification of each word in terms of its pattern on a set of significant features. With a table of elements such as this, the language user can start either with the word or with its meaning and expect an unambiguous choice. The use of a componential analysis such as this also exhibits a good deal of cognitive economy; three dimensions with two positions per dimension specify eight words completely. Extrapolating this logic implies that if we allow two positions per dimension, only 17 dimensions are required to allow for unambiguous specification of about 100,000 words, that is, $2^{17}$. (In general, the number of words that can be unambiguously specified by a two-choice dimension is equal to $2^d$, where $d$ represents the number of dimensions.)

This number (of dimensions) would be reassuringly small—within the competence of all language users—if the meaning of all words in the vocabulary could be described in terms of the same set of dimensions. Unfortunately, the number of tightly knit word families such as the color names or kinship terms is quite small, and it therefore seems unlikely that universal semantic dimensions exist. Instead, sadly, we have to realize that only selected portions of the total vocabulary pool can be treated componentially, and that there probably are only a small number of perfectly general dimensions, if indeed there are any at all.

What does all this imply about the development of meaning in children? First it means that studies dealing with the development of componential meaning are quite rare; indeed there are few if any that are even relevant to a componential analysis. This in turn means that all that can be said about the development of meaning in terms of a generative approach must be theoretical, for there are few if any facts.

Given this factual vacuum, let us propose a developmental hypothesis and hope that subsequent attention will be directed toward supplying the empirical data. Let us suppose, by analogy to both phonemic and grammatical development, that meaning develops in terms of a process of differentiation. Just as early phonetic and early grammatical categories or features are much less precise than their adult counterparts, so too are initial semantic distinctions. Perhaps one of these early distinctions has to do with a concept such as approaching and avoiding, a distinction an adult might encode as *good–bad*.

Once the child achieves this type of preliminary categorization, he tends to organize his experience, both linguistic and nonlinguistic, in accordance with this initially simple principle of categorization. In terms of other specific vocabulary items, it is reasonable to propose that the growing child becomes selectively tuned to words relating to a featural distinction, and he in fact seeks out labels to name these newly developed concepts. Lexical items are learned only where categorizations already exist or are in the process of being formed.

What this means is that sheer repetition of a grammatical or even a lexical form (see McNeill's *ga* and *wa*) will not be acquired unless there is some pre-existing category or feature. Once a category is established, an appropriate lexical or grammatical form—even if only occurring infrequently—will be learned almost at once. The child learns words in accordance with his categories, and the form of these categories changes with cognitive and linguistic development. The essential process seems to be one of finer and finer differentiation of various conceptual categories.

But doesn't this analysis run counter to the usual observation that children acquire frequent and so-called concrete words before they acquire less frequent abstract terms? This question was posed a number of years ago by Roger Brown (1958) in an intriguing paper entitled "How shall a thing be called?" He first attacked the question of frequency: The usual observation here is that adults tend to call a thing by the name it is most commonly called, and that what the thing is most commonly called is a frequent word. But, notes Brown, a pineapple (thing) is called a *pineapple* (relatively infrequent word) rather than a *fruit* (relatively more frequent word).

On this basis it seems that things are first named so as "to categorize them in a maximally useful way." It is most often functionally important for the child to know that this thing is a *spoon* (to distinguish its *use* from knives, forks, etc.) rather than that it is a piece of *silverware* (where it is not distinguished from knives, forks, etc.). Similarly it is not important to note that it is Rogers' sterling silverware of such-and-such a date—all that is required is that the child learn a name consonant with his understanding of what the object is to be used for. Frequency then seems to be an accidental by-product of how adults name things for children.

But isn't there another problem? Since we are arguing that the child develops gross undifferentiated categories before more precise, differentiated ones, shouldn't he first learn a word something like *a thing to eat with* before he learns the specific word *spoon*? This raises the more general problem of whether vocabulary items are learned from general to specific or vice versa. In general, some sets of vocabulary items seem to progress from specific to general (*spoon → silverware*), whereas others are learned from general to specific (*fish → bass*). In the specific-to-general case, the child seems to be responding to some least disturbing fit between his gross category system and adult naming preferences. It is as if he is tuned for a general term, but only experiences a specific one. A similar argument seems to apply in the general-to-specific case; the child is always dependent on adult naming preferences. As Brown has concluded:

"Psychologists who believe that mental development is ... from a lack of differentiation to increased differentiation, have been embarrassed by the fact that vocabulary often builds in the opposite direction. This fact need not trouble them, since the sequence in which words are acquired is not determined by the cognitive preferences of children so much as by the naming practices of adults." (Brown, 1958, page 21.)

Given then that vocabulary acquisition is directed by the development of appropriate conceptual categories, it is also reasonable to assume that knowing a specific word must serve in some way to direct the further development of conceptual categories or features.  This interchange between a diffuse category and a specific label should serve, by its interaction, to bring about further differentiation, resulting ultimately in the production of still another new category, which, in its turn, should serve to bring about the "need" for new labels, and so on.  The growth of vocabulary depends on having conceptual features available, with the acquisition of new vocabulary resulting in the differentiation of still further features.

With the growth of further differentiation, features would lose their generality across the now rapidly growing vocabulary pool.  On this basis, features become so differentiated that for the adult, vocabulary is organized across only a few specific subsets of words.  Perhaps, for the adult, there are no perfectly general features; instead, there are features appropriate only to limited samples of words related in quite specific ways, e.g., kinship terms, pronouns, etc.  In this context, an abstract concept may mean one that ties together a number of these subfamilies, or indicates in what ways they are different.  The approach taken by Katz and Fodor represents an attempt in which the most abstract features (animate or inanimate, human or animal, etc.) occur earliest in the tree interpreting a given word.  Since the advantages and problems of such an approach have already been described, it is unnecessary to review them now.

Is there any evidence indicating that vocabulary growth depends on the availability of an underlying cognitive feature which directs the acquisition of specific classes of vocabulary items?  In what is certainly one of the few relevant studies, Richard Cromer (1968) working with Roger Brown's research group at Harvard, studied the development of "temporal reference" in young children.  By "temporal reference" Cromer meant more than simply the use of time words; indeed he meant to analyze how and when the concept of 12 different types of time emerged in the speech of children.

For this analysis, Cromer reexamined the protocols produced by Adam and Sarah.  Each of their recorded utterances from ages two through six were gone over and a series of 12 selected periods chosen for detailed study.  Each utterance in the selected protocol was dealt with in one of three ways: First in terms of tense; that is, all uses of the usual inflected forms of the past, present, future, etc., were recorded, along with all pertinent data as to what the child and his mother were doing when the inflected form was used.  A second way in which the data were examined was in terms of "intended time reference," regardless of the use of tense. For example, if the child says, "Lamp fall, Mommy," it is unclear whether the lamp has already fallen, is about to, or might fall if somebody pushed it. In order to determine the *intended* as opposed to the *grammatical* time reference, Cromer made an intensive analysis of the mother's response to this utterance and of notes made by the observer at the time the utterance was produced. If Mommy said: "Yes, it's fallen," the intended time reference of *Lamp fall, Mommy* was in the past, etc. The third type of data recorded was the actual use of time words such as *before, sometimes, time, never,* etc.

Although Cromer examined each of the tenses in great detail, for present purposes it is enough to note that all three indices showed regular increases as a function of age, with the most dramatic increase occurring around the fourth year (from 4:0 to 4:6). It is at this time that both Adam and Sarah began to use multiple time references in the same utterance: "I will show you what I got for Christmas." (Sarah age 4:6.) Even more significant perhaps are what Cromer calls time reversals: utterances (such as Sarah's quoted above) in which the time references are not kept in the order in which they occurred in experience. Thus Sarah first mentions what she is going to do (future) before mentioning something that happened (past) a long time ago.

All in all, the child's sense of time seems to take a qualitative leap at around the fourth year. Although tense is not perfectly under control at this time, the child's intended and actual time references vary across past, present and future, even to the point of combining tenses in a single utterance. But what about time words? Although coding words into categories does produce some difficulties for the analyst, Table 16.7 presents a schematic analysis of the emergence of time words sorted according to five different categories.

Although each category is not completely unambiguous, the examples provided do give some hint as to what words occurred for the first time at each age. In this case, results are pretty clear in showing that many categories make their first appearance at 4:2, or just about at the same time the child is making intelligent reference to a great many different aspects of time.

After sifting through all the data, Cromer summarized his findings on the relationship of cognitive development to word and tense acquisition as follows:

> "The development of a new cognitive ability leads the child to an active search for new forms to express the relationship he is attempting to formulate. . . . He will be actively directing his linguistic attention into a search for or heightened awareness of particular forms or structures used by adult speakers to express those newly understood relationships." (Cromer, page 169)

**Table 16.7** Emergence of time words in a young child (Sarah)*

| Time category | 2:3 | 2:7 | 2:11 | 3:2 | 3:6 | 3:10 | 4:2 | 4:6 | 4:10 | 5:2 |
|---|---|---|---|---|---|---|---|---|---|---|
| Continuation–repetition versus completion | | | Repetition–continuation begins with "Again" and "One more" | | | | Completion: "all day" "already" | | | |
| Ordering | | | Begins use of "Now" | | Time point naming: "The other day" | Increased time point naming: "Yesterday" <br> Primitive use of "Before" | Much ordering: "Then," "And then," "When," "First" | | | |
| Relevance | | | | | | | | "Remember" "Yet" "Just" | | "Ready to" "Starting to" |
| Timeless | | | | | | | "Sometimes" "Never" | | "Always" | |
| Duration | | | | "Wait a minute" (1 use) | "A long time" (1 use) | "Few minutes" (1 use) | "So long" (1 use) | "A thousand days" (1 use) | "A little while" | "A while" "A ____ minute" Reg. use of duration |

* From "The development of temporal reference during the acquisition of language," by R. F. Cromer, unpublished doctoral dissertation, Harvard, 1968.

In short, cognitive development seems to guide the acquisition of vocabulary items.

One more point needs to be made about these results, and this concerns the role of the mother (the adult speaker) in providing the child with an appropriate model. Although there are a number of interesting points to consider, perhaps the most important one is that there is little systematic change in the mother's use of time words and concepts over the four-year period studied. That is, both Adam's and Sarah's mothers made about the same number of time references at all ages studied. Indeed in one case, Adam's Mommy showed an increase in one category (commands toward the future—*Pick up your coat*) from year to year, while Adam actually showed a decrease. This observation that the child's development is not tied to parental usage in any simple one-to-one way has come up before in connection with McNeill's *wa* and *ga* examples, and Cromer's data provide further confirmation. Children acquire forms, both lexical and grammatical, in accordance with their own cognitive needs, and do not simply copy the input provided. Language acquisition is selective, with this selectivity governed by the prior and contemporary cognitive growth of the child.

## SUMMARY

The hallmarks of a generative–transformational approach to language are two in number: *creative construction* and *cognitive economy*. One concept that seems to provide the potential for both is that of a *rule*. As it is used in linguistics, a rule is a relatively unambiguous concept: It specifies what must be done in order to achieve a desired linguistic result. Neisser has likened the linguist's rule to the cook's recipe or guide, and the analogy is apt. As the linguist uses the term, however, he means to imply that rules provide for an abstract characterization of sentence derivation in the language and not in the speaker. The latter problem—how speakers produce and understand utterances—is the psychological aspect of language usage.

George Miller in his 1966 presidential address to the American Psychological Association noted a number of different implications of linguistic analysis for the psychological study of language. These have been summarized under four major headings, headings which have defined the major sections of the present chapter. The first of these deals with *speech in its overt acoustic and articulatory form*, and stresses that not all the physical properties of the speech signal are significant for vocal communication. The complement of this postulate is also significant: Not all the significant features of speech are represented physically.

Miller's second major point of emphasis has to do with the *syntactical structure of sentences*. Essentially he notes that how the speaker or listener structures a particular utterance affects both the production and understanding of that utterance. Such structure can be described in terms of either the surface bracketing of elements or in terms of their more fundamental orderings. The former type of structure is called *surface structure,* while the latter is called *deep structure.* This distinction is of great importance for the generative analysis of language.

The third major point raised by Miller has to do with *meaning.* The primary point here is that meaning is not to be confused with reference. The meaning of a sentence or word does not depend solely on what it refers to (for often there is no direct reference), but rather on its relationship to other symbols in the language.

The most controversial of Miller's four suggestions concerns the *contribution of an organism's biological endowment to its linguistic ability.* Essentially, the relative speed with which a normal child acquires the ability to use his own language seems to suggest that at certain periods during its early life the child is selectively "tuned" by his genetic inheritence toward language acquisition.

The problems involved in the production and understanding of the physical speech signal all have to do with the difference between the signal as physical pattern and our psychological response to this pattern. Psychologically, the acoustic stream is perceived as a well-segmented and highly regular input, whereas physically it is a fairly continuous stream of changing acoustic energy. In order to bring about effective and useful segmentation of the acoustic stimulus, the listener (and before him, the speaker) must have internalized the implicit phonological rules defining acceptable and unacceptable phonemic sequences. Indeed, recent experiments do indicate the psychological reality of some morphophonemic rules.

Most models of speech production and recognition assume similar processes in the speaker and listener. When formalized in terms of speech recognition, such an approach is called an *analysis-by-synthesis* model. Analysis-by-synthesis models assume that speech recognition begins with a gross preliminary scanning of the input. On the basis of this preliminary scan, the listener constructs or synthesizes an approximation of the incoming material and then checks this approximation against further samples of the input. Only if the listener himself imposes structure on the rather chaotic input does it seem possible to explain how segmentation and regularization occur. Without such analysis-by-synthesis, it seems impossible to explain how the same physical stimulus can give rise to the perception of different sounds, or how different physical stimuli can give rise to the perception of the same sound. Only by assuming that the sound patterns of the language are structured (rule-governed in some abstract sense) and that the listener is able to make use of this structure is it possible to explain the observed properties of speech perception.

But structure is involved not only at the phonological level, but also at *syntactic* and *semantic* levels. It is well to remember that psychologists first became interested in the generative–transformational view of language because of ambiguities in the surface structure of a seemingly small number of tricky sentences. If linguists hadn't produced sentences such as *The shooting of the hunters was terrible*, etc., and had not been able to demonstrate their relevance for the psychological analysis of the sentence, much of the current interest in formal linguistic structure would not have arisen. But they did, and psychology was, and still continues to be, interested.

Although surface structure has been fruitfully explored in terms of learning and recall studies, the *generative–transformation* group has been more interested in the role of surface structure in the perception of connected discourse. Here the basic procedure has been to present a click at various points during an incoming sentence and then determine whether the sound "migrates" toward a major grammatical node of the sentence. Empirically the results of a number of studies—some better controlled than others—indicate that subjects do tend to place the click nearer a major constituent break than it actually is. Such constituent breaks were determined on the basis of a *phrase-structure analysis* of the sentence.

Surface structure, however, does not exhaust the structured properties of language. Generally speaking, overt or surface structure is related to a more basic level of language known as *deep structure*. Since surface structure is related to deep structure by *transformations*, it is therefore not surprising to find that the analysis of deep structure has taken place in terms of an analysis of transformations. Although the earliest studies were concerned with determining how long it took to perform various transformations (see the early work by Miller, 1962), more recent experiments have been concerned with the role of transformations in sentence recall. The basic observation here is that certain types of sentences are more difficult to learn and remember than others.

In order to account for these results, Mehler and Miller both assumed that in remembering a sentence a subject has to remember two different things: (1) the meaning of the sentence and (2) its specific grammatical form. Since the simplest type of a sentence is a kernel sentence, it is reasonable to assume that subjects recall a nonkernel sentence as a simple active declarative sentence with footnotes specifying the appropriate transformations. A number of different experiments have been performed under this assumption, with results generally supporting the hypothesis.

There are, however, two things wrong with this analysis as a general model of sentence recognition. For one thing, exact sentence repetition is a highly artificial task—most subjects would paraphrase the sentence if asked to do so under more natural conditions—while for a second, many transformations significantly affect the meaning of the sentence so that it is unlikely that transformations involve only questions of form.

Since meaning is such an important aspect of sentence comprehension and production, it is necessary to describe the ways in which it is handled by a generative approach. Here the classic paper is by Katz and Fodor, who attempted to analyze the meaning of a word in terms of its *distinctive attributes* or *markers*. The meaning of a word is assumed to be represented by a tree diagram in which the topmost levels of the tree represent the most universal (i.e., the broadest) aspects of meaning, and in which the bottommost arborizations represent an aspect of meaning that is most essential to one or another of the various meanings of the word.

The Katz–Fodor model is meant as a general description of how the lexicon is organized. Although it has provided a stimulus for many different analyses of meaning, it has not gone unchallenged. The topic of semantic universals (i.e., attributes that are general across the vocabulary of all languages) has not been uncritically received, nor has the assumption of semantic markers itself been unchallenged. Bolinger in his careful review of the Katz–Fodor model is quite explicit in demonstrating that in order to handle the distinctions inherent in the various dictionary meanings of the same word, markers would have to be atomized to such an extent that cognitive and conceptual economy would be completely lost.

No normal child begins with a complete command of his language, yet by about age three all are capable of a good deal of creative language use. The development of sound, grammar, and meaning form an important aspect of the generative–transformational analysis of language usage. There are two basic postulates here: (1) that language has a strong biological component, and (2) that language growth is largely a matter of progressive differentiation.

The first postulate has both a weak and a strong form. The strong form asserts an invariant unfolding of capacities which direct language acquisition from sound to meaning. The weak form simply assumes that at certain critical time periods the child is maximally "tuned" to learn certain aspects of his language, even if these aspects occur only rarely in his experience with the language.

The hypothesis that language acquisition represents a progressive differentiation of initially diffuse abilities seems to rest on safer empirical grounds than the assumption of an invariant timetable. There does seem to be some evidence that the phonemes of a particular language become differentiated from one another, rather than being formed along separate lines at more or less the same time. Although some significant features become significant earlier than others—using the lips, as opposed to noticing the distinction between voiced and voiceless—the general rule that later features arise as a differentiation of earlier ones seems reasonably well established.

In terms of syntactic development, results again indicate progressive differentiation. Single word expressions used by infants seem to have the same status as sentences used by adults. Sentencing does not seem to grow by adding new words to core words, but rather by recognizing different classes of words. Once this recognition is made, the child progresses rapidly from sentences formed by the combination of pivot and open classes, to sentences generated by the combination of noun phrases and verb phrases. From here, it is but a short step for the child to use more complicated transformations characteristic of adult language usage.

Vocabulary also develops by a process of differentiation. Increases in the number of words understood and used by a child seem to depend on the progressive enrichment of his cognitive world. Words and forms are acquired as a consequence of newly developed conceptual categories. In the case of time reference, Cromer was able to document this hypothesis with some degree of success: Specific time words are acquired and used only after the child has mastered temporal reference without the use of these words. The child talks (grammatically) about times past well before he uses the words *before*, or *yesterday*, or *Christmas*, etc.

Finally, there is the question of the adult's role in the child's language acquisition. On the basis of both McNeill's and Cromer's data, it seems reasonable to argue that adults provide models for language growth, but that such growth is not contingent on adult tutelage in any direct way. Unless the child "senses the need" for a particular word or grammatical construction, adult repetition has little effect. The child seems to learn what *he* is attuned to learn, with specific training producing only slight effects. The child has a mind of his own about what he should learn and when he should learn it.

# BIBLIOGRAPHY

Adams, J. A., Multiple versus single problem training in human problem solving. *J. Exp. Psychol.* **48,** 15–19 (1954)

Adams, J. A., *Human Memory.* New York: McGraw-Hill, 1968

Adams, S., *Temporal Changes in the Strength of Competing Verbal Associates.* Unpublished doctoral dissertation. University of California, Berkeley, 1962

Adamson, R. E., Functional fixedness as related to problem solving: a repetition of three experiments. *J. Exp. Psychol.* **44,** 288–291 (1952)

Adamson, R. E., and Taylor, D. W., Functional fixedness as related to elapsed time and to set. *J. Exp. Psychol.* **47,** 122–126 (1954)

Alston, W. P., *Philosophy of Language.* Englewood Cliffs, N.J.: Prentice-Hall, 1964

Ammon, P. R., The perception of grammatical relations in sentences: a methodological exploration. *J. Verb. Learn. Verb. Behav.* **7,** 869–875 (1968)

Anisfeld, M., Psychological evidence for an intermediate stage in a morphological derivation. *J. Verb. Learn. Verb. Behav.* **2,** 191–195 (1969)

Anisfeld, M., and Gordon, M., On the psychophonological structure of English inflectional rules. *J. Verb. Learn. Verb. Behav.* **7,** 973–979 (1968)

Asch, S. E., Forming impressions of personality. *J. Abnorm. Soc. Psychol.* **41,** 258–290 (1946)

Asch, S. E., On the use of metaphor in the description of persons. From *On Expressive Language*, edited by H. Werner. Worcester, 1955, pages 29–38

Auden, W. H., An interview with W. H. Auden. *Life Magazine*, June 1970

Averbach, E., and Coriell, A. S., Short-term memory in vision. *Bell Syst. Tech. J.* **40,** 309–328 (1961)


Baddeley, A. D., Short-term memory for word sequences as a function of acoustic, semantic, and formal similarity. *Quart. J. Exp. Psychol.* **18,** 362–365 (1966)

Baddeley, A. D., and Dale, H. C. A., The effects of semantic similarity on retroactive interference in long- and short-term memory. *J. Verb. Learn. Verb. Behav.* **5,** 417–420 (1966)

Barnes, J. M., and Underwood, B. J., "Fate" of first-list associations in transfer theory. *J. Exp. Psychol.* **58,** 97–105 (1959)

Bartlett, F. C., *Remembering.* Cambridge: Cambridge University Press, 1932

Bartlett, F. C., *Thinking.* New York: Basic Books, 1958

Baum, M., Simple concept learning as a function of intra-list generalization. *J. Exp. Psychol.* **47,** 89–94 (1954)

Beckett, R., and Hurt, J., *Numerical Calculations and Algorithms.* New York: McGraw-Hill, 1967

Beilin, H., and Horn, R., Transition probability effects in anagram problem solving. *J. Exp. Psychol.* **63**, 514–518 (1962)

Bellugi, U., Development of negative and interrogative structures in the speech of children. From *Studies in Psycholinguistics*, edited by T. Bever and W. Weksel. New York: Holt, Rinehart and Winston, 1970

Berko, J., The child's learning of English morphology. *Word* **14**, 150–177 (1958)

Berlyne, D. E., *Structure and Direction in Thinking*. New York: Wiley, 1965

Bertalanffy, L. von, On the definition of the symbol. From *Psychology and the Symbol*, edited by J. R. Royce. New York: Random House, 1965, pages 26–69

Beth, E. W., and Piaget, J., *Mathematical Epistomology and Psychology*. Holland: D. Reidel, 1966

Bever, T. G., Associations to stimulus-response theories of language. From *Verbal Behavior and General Behavior Theory*, edited by T. R. Dixon and D. L. Horton. Englewood Cliffs, N. J.: Prentice-Hall, 1968, pages 478–494

Bever, T. G., Fodor, J. A., and Garrett, M., A formal limitation of associationism. From *Verbal Behavior and General Behavior Theory*, edited by T. R. Dixon and D. L. Horton. Englewood Cliffs, N. J.: Prentice-Hall, 1966, pages 421–450

Bever, T. G., Fodor, J. A., and Weksel, W., On the acquisition of syntax: A critique of "contextual generalization." *Psychol. Rev.* **72**, 467–482 (1965a)

Bever, T. G., Fodor, J. A., and Weksel, W., Is linguistics empirical? *Psychol. Rev.* **72**, 493–500 (1965b)

Birch, H. G., The relation of previous experience to insightful problem-solving. *J. Comp. Psychol.* **38**, 367–383 (1945)

Birch, H. G., and Rabinowitz, H. S., The negative effect of previous experience on productive thinking. *J. Exp. Psychol.* **41**, 121–125 (1951)

Bloom, L. M., *Language Development: Form and Function in Emerging Grammars*. Cambridge, Mass.: M.I.T. Press, 1970

Bloomfield, L., *Language*. New York: Holt, Rinehart and Winston, 1933

Blumenthal, A. L., Promoted recall of sentences. *J. Verb. Learn. Verb. Behav.* **6**, 203–206 (1967)

Bolinger, D., The atomization of meaning. From *Readings in the Psychology of Language*, edited by L. A. Jakobovits and M. S. Miron. Englewood Cliffs, N. J.: Prentice-Hall, 1967, pages 432–448

Borko, H., *Computer Applications in the Behavioral Sciences*. Englewood Cliffs, N. J.: Prentice-Hall, 1962

Bourne, L. E., Jr., Concept attainment. From *Verbal Behavior and General Behavior Theory*, edited by T. R. Dixon and D. L. Horton. Englewood Cliffs, N. J.: Prentice-Hall, 1968a

Bourne, L. E., Jr., Development of conceptual rules. Invited address. *American Psychological Association Convention*, San Francisco, September 1968b

Bourne, L. E., Jr., Effects of delay of information feedback and task complexity on the identification of concepts. *J. Exp. Psychol.* **54**, 201–207 (1957)

Bourne, L. E., Jr., *Human Conceptual Behavior*. Boston: Allyn and Bacon, 1966

Bourne, L. E., Jr., Learning and utilization of conceptual rules. From *Concepts and the Structure of Memory*, edited by B. Kleinmuntz. New York: Wiley, 1967, pages 1–32

Bourne, L. E., Jr., and Bunderson, C. V., Effects of delay of informative feedback and length of postfeedback interval on concept identification. *J. Exp. Psychol.* **65**, 1–5 (1963)

Bourne, L. E., Ekstrand, B. R., and Dominowski, R. L., *The Psychology of Thinking*. Englewood Cliffs, N. J.: Prentice-Hall, 1971

Bourne, L. E., Jr., and Jennings, P. C., The relationship between contiguity and classification learning. *J. Gen. Psychol.* **69**, 335–338 (1963)

Bourne, L. E., Jr., and Pendleton, R. B., Concept identification as a function of completeness and probability of information feedback. *J. Exp. Psychol.* **56**, 413–420 (1958)

Bousfield, W. A., The occurrence of clustering in the recall of randomly arranged associates. *J. Gen. Psychol.* **49**, 229–240 (1953)

Bousfield, W. A., and Cohen, B. H., Clustering in recall as a function of the number of word categories in stimulus-word lists. *J. Gen. Psychol.* **54**, 95–106 (1956)

Bousfield, W. A., Cohen, B. H., and Whitmarsh, G. A., Associative clustering in the recall of words of different taxonomic frequencies of occurrence. *Psychol. Report* **4**, 39–44 (1958)

Bousfield, W. A., and Sedgewick, C. H. W., An analysis of sequences of restricted associative responses. *J. Gen. Psychol.* **30**, 149–165 (1944)

Bower, G. H., A multicomponent theory of the memory trace. From *The Psychology of Learning and Motivation: Advances in Research and Theory*, edited by K. W. Spence and J. T. Spence, Volume I. New York: Academic Press, 1957, pages 299–325

Bower, G. H., and Clark, M. C., Narrative stories as mediators for serial learning. *Psychon. Sci.* **14**, 181–182 (1969)

Brace, A., and Nelson, L. D., Preschool child's concept of number. *Arith. Teacher* **12**, 126–133 (1965)

Braine, M. D. S., On learning the grammatical order of words. *Psychol. Rev.* **70**, 323–348 (1963)

Braine, M. D. S., The ontogeny of English phrase structure: The first phase. *Language* **39**, 1–13 (1963b)

Braine, M. D. S., On the basis of phrase structure: A reply to Bever, Fodor, and Weksel. *Psychol. Rev.* **72**, 483–492 (1965)

Broadbent, D. E., *Perception and Communication*. New York: Pergamon Press, 1958

Bronowski, J., Human and animal languages. From *To Honor Roman Jakobson*. The Hague: Mouton, 1967

Bronowski, J., and Bellugi, U., Language, name and concept. *Science*, 669–673 (May 8, 1970)

Brown, R., *Social Psychology*, New York, The Free Press, 1965

Brown, R. W., Language and categories. From *A Study of Thinking*, edited by J. S. Bruner, J. J. Goodnow, and G. A. Austin. New York: Wiley, 1956

Brown, R. W., Linguistic determinism and the part of speech. *J. Abnorm. Soc. Psychol.* **55**, 1–5 (1957)

Brown, R. W., *Words and Things*. New York: Free Press, 1958

Brown, R. W., The development of Wh questions in child speech. *J. Verb. Learn. Verb. Behav.* **7**, 279–290 (1968)

Brown, R. W., How shall a thing be called? *Psychol. Rev.* **65**, 14–21 (1958)

Brown, R. W., The first sentences of child and chimpanzee. From *Psycholinguistics: Selected Papers*. New York: Free Press, 1970

Brown, R. W., and Bellugi, U., Three processes in the child's acquisition of syntax. *Harvard Educ. Rev.* **34**, 133–151 (1964)

Brown, R. W., and Berko, J., Word association and the acquisition of grammar. *Child Develop.* **31**, 1–14 (1960)

Brown, R. W., Cazden, C. B., and Bellugi, U., *The child's grammar from I to III.* Paper read at 1967 Minnesota Symposium on Child Psychology. Minneapolis, 1967

Brown, R. W., and Fraser, C., The acquisition of syntax. From *Verbal Behavior and Learning,* edited by C. N. Cofer and B. S. Musgrave. New York: McGraw-Hill, 1963

Brown, R. W., Leiter, R. A., and Hildum, D. C., Metaphors from music criticism. *J. Abnorm. Soc. Psychol.* **54,** 347–352 (1957)

Brown, R. W., and Lenneberg, E. H., A study in cognition. *J. Abnorm. Soc. Psychol.* **49,** 454–462 (1954)

Brown, R. W., and McNeill, D., The "tip of the tongue" phenomenon. *J. Verb. Learn. Verb. Behav.* **5,** 325–337 (1966)

Bruce, D., and Cofer, C. N., An examination of recognition and free recall as measures of acquisition and long-term retention. *J. Exp. Psychol.* **75,** 283–289 (1967)

Bruner, J. S., The course of cognitive growth. *Amer. Psychologist* **19,** 1–15 (1964)

Bruner, J. S., Goodnow, J. J., and Austin, G. A., *A Study of Thinking.* New York: Wiley, 1956

Bruner, J. S., Olver, R. R., and Greenfield, P. M., *Studies in Cognitive Growth.* New York: Wiley, 1966

Bruner, J. S., Wallach, M. A., and Galanter, E. H., The identification of recurrent regularity. *Amer. J. Psychol.* **72,** 200–209 (1959)

Bulgarella, R., and Archer, E. J., Concept identification of auditory stimuli as a function of amount of relevant and irrelevant information. *J. Exp. Psychol.* **63,** 254–257 (1962)


Cahill, H. E., and Hovland, C. I., The role of memory in the acquisition of concepts. *J. Exp. Psychol.* **59,** 137–144 (1960)

Carroll, J. B., *Language and Thought.* Englewood Cliffs, N. J.: Prentice-Hall, 1964

Carroll, J. B., *The Study of Language.* Cambridge, Mass.: Harvard Univ. Press, 1953

Chapanis, A., The reconstruction of abbreviated printed messages. *J. Exp. Psychol.* **48,** 496–510 (1954)

Chase, S., *The Tyranny of Words.* New York: Harcourt Brace, 1938.

Chomsky, N., Appendix A., The formal nature of language. From *Biological Foundations of Language,* by E. H. Lenneberg. New York: Wiley, 1967

Chomsky, N., *Aspects of the Theory of Syntax.* Cambridge, Mass.: M.I.T. Press, 1965

Chomsky, N., *Current Issues in Linguistic Theory.* The Hague: Mouton, 1964

Chomsky, N., Formal properties of grammar. From *Handbook of Mathematical Psychology,* edited by R. D. Luce, R. R. Bush, and E. Galanter, Volume II. New York: Wiley, 1963

Chomsky, N., *Language and Mind.* New York: Harcourt Brace Jovanovich, 1968

Chomsky, N., On the notion "Rule of grammar." From *Structure of Language and its Mathematical Aspects, Proceedings of the 12th Symposium in Applied Mathematics,* edited by R. Jakobson. Providence, Rhode Island: American Mathematical Society, 1961, pages 6–24

Chomsky, N., A Review of *Verbal Behavior* by B. F. Skinner. *Language* **35,** 26–58 (1959)

Chomsky, N., *Syntactic Structures.* The Hague: Mouton, 1957

Chomsky, N., and Halle, M., *The Sound Pattern of English.* New York: Harper and Row, 1968

Cofer, C. N., Reasoning as an associative process: III. The role of verbal responses in problem-solving. *J. Gen. Psychol.* **57,** 55–68 (1957)

Cofer, C. N., On some factors in the organizational characteristics of free recall. *Amer. Psychologist* **20,** 261–272 (1965)

Cofer, C. N., Bruce, D. R., and Reicher, G. M., Clustering in free recall as a function of certain methodological variations. *J. Exp. Psychol.* **71,** 858–866 (1966)

Cohen, B. H., An investigation of recoding in free recall. *J. Exp. Psychol.* **65,** 368–376 (1963a)

Cohen, B. H., Recall of categorized word lists. *J. Exp. Psychol.* **66,** 227–234 (1963b)

Cohen, B. H., Some-or-none characteristics of coding behavior. *J. Verb. Learn. Verb. Behav.* **5,** 182–187 (1966)

Coleman, E. B., Approximations to English. *Amer. J. Psychol.* **76,** 239–247 (1963)

Coleman, E. B., Sequential interferences demonstrated by serial reproduction. *J. Exp. Psychol.* **64,** 978–982 (1962)

Coleman, E. B., Verbal concept learning as a function of instructions and dominance level. *J. Exp. Psychol.* **68,** 213–214 (1964)

Conrad, R., Acoustic confusion in immediate memory. *Brit. J. Psychol.* **55,** 75–84 (1964)

Conrad, R., An association between memory errors and errors due to acoustic masking of speech. *Nature* **196,** 1314–1315 (1962)

Conrad, R., and Hille, B. A., The decay theory of immediate memory and paced recall. *Canad. J. Psychol.* **12,** 1–6 (1958)

Conrad, R., and Hull, A. J., Information, acoustic confusion, and memory span. *Brit. J. Psychol.* **55,** 429–437 (1964)

Cromer, R. F., *The Development of Temporal Reference during the Acquisition of Language.* Doctoral dissertation. Harvard University, 1968

Cross, D. V., and Lane, H. L., On the discriminative control of concurrent responses: the relations among response frequency, latency, and typography in acoustic generalization. *J. Exp. Analys. Behav.* **5,** 487–496 (1962)

Crowder, N. A., The rationale of intrinsic programming. From *Human Learning in the School,* edited by J. P. DeCecco. New York: Holt, Rinehart and Winston, 1963, pages 183–189


Dallenbach, K. M., Synaesthesis: "Pressury" cold. *Amer. J. Psychol.* **37,** 571–577 (1926)

Dashiell, J. F., *Fundamentals of General Psychology,* third edition. Boston: Houghton Mifflin, 1949

Dattman, P. E., and Israel, H. E., The order of dominance among conceptual capacities: an experimental test of Heidbreder's hypothesis. *J. Psychol.* **31,** 147–160 (1951)

DeCecco, J. P., *The Psychology of Learning and Instruction: Educational Psychology.* Englewood Cliffs, N. J.: Prentice-Hall, 1968, pages 493–494

Deese, J., The associative structure of some common English adjectives. *J. Verb. Learn. Verb. Behav.* **3,** 347–357 (1964)

Deese, J., From the isolated verbal unit to connected discourse. From *Verbal Learning and Verbal Behavior,* edited by C. N. Cofer. New York: McGraw-Hill, 1961, pages 11–31

Deese, J., On the prediction of occurrence of particular verbal intrusions in immediate recall. *J. Exp. Psychol.* **58,** 17–22 (1959)

Deese, J., *Psycholinguistics.* Boston: Allyn and Bacon, 1970

Deese, J., *The Structure of Associations in Language and Thought.* Baltimore: Johns Hopkins Press, 1965

Deese, J., On the structure of associative meaning. *Psychol. Rev.* **69,** 161–175 (1972)

Deese, J., Form class and the determinants of association. *J. Verb. Learn. Verb. Behav.* **1,** 79–84 (1962)

Deese, J., Meaning and change in meaning. *Amer. Psychologist* **22,** 641–652 (1967)

Dixon, T. R., and Horton, D. L., editors, *Verbal Behavior and General Behavior Theory.* Englewood Cliffs, N. J.: Prentice-Hall, 1968

Dodwell, P. C., Children's understanding of number and related concepts. *Canad. J. Psychol.* **14,** 191–205 (1960)

Dodwell, P. C., Relations between the understanding of the logic of classes and of cardinal number in children. *Canad. J. Psychol.* **16** (2), 152–160 (1962)

Dollard, J., and Miller, N. E., *Personality and Psychotherapy.* New York: McGraw-Hill, 1950

Dominowski, R. L., and Duncan, C. P., Anagram solving as a function of bigram frequency. *J. Verb. Learn. Verb. Behav.* **3,** 321–325 (1964)

Dulany, D. E., and O'Connell, D. C., Does partial reinforcement dissociate verbal rules and the behavior they might be presumed to control? *J. Verb. Learn. Verb. Behav.* **2,** 361-372 (1963)

Duncan, C. P., Response hierarchies in problem solving. From *Thinking, Current Experimental Studies,* edited by C. P. Duncan. Philadelphia: Lippincott, 1966

Duncan, C. P., Problem-solving within a verbal response hierarchy. *Psychon. Sci.* **4,** 147–148 (1966)

Duncan, C. P., Effect of word frequency on thinking of a word. *J. Verb. Learn. Verb. Behav.* **5,** 434–440(b) (1966)

Duncker, K., On problem-solving, translated by L. S. Lees from the 1935 original. *Psychol. Monogr.* **58,** No. 270 (1945)


Ebbinghaus, H., *Über das Gedächtnis.* Leipzig: Duncker, 1885, translated by H. Ruger and C. E. Bussenius, *Memory,* Teachers College, Columbia University, New York, 1913

Ebenholtz, S. M., Position mediated transfer between serial learning and a spatial discrimination task. *J. Exp. Psychol.* **65,** 603–608 (1963)

Ebenholtz, S. M., Serial learning: Position learning and sequential association. *J. Exp. Psychol.* **66,** 353–362 (1963)

Ekstrand, B. R., and Dominowski, R. L., Solving words as anagrams. *Psychon. Sci.* **2,** 239–240 (1964)

Ekstrand, B. R., and Dominowski, R. L., Solving words as anagrams: II. A clarification. *J. Exp. Psychol.* **77,** 552–558 (1968)

Entwisle, D. R., *Word Associations of Young Children.* Baltimore: Johns Hopkins, 1966

Epstein, W., The influence of syntactic structure on learning. *Amer. J. Psychol.* **74,** 80–85 (1961)

Epstein, W., A further study of the effect of syntactic structure on learning. *Amer. J. Psychol.* **75,** 121–126 (1962)

Epstein, W., The effect of stimulus and response meaningfulness when response availability is equated. *J. Verb. Learn. Verb. Behav.* **2,** 242–249 (1963)

Ervin-Tripp, S., Changes with age in the verbal determinants of word association. *Amer. J. Psychol.* **74,** 361–372 (1961)

Evans, D. C., Computer logic and memory, *Information*, 1966, pages 20 and 25

Evans, J. J., Glaser, R., and Homme, L., The ruleg system for the construction of programmed verbal learning sequences. *J. Educ. Research* **55,** 513–518 (1966)


Feigenbaum, E. A., The simulation of verbal learning behavior. From *Computers and Thought*, edited by E. A. Feigenbaum and J. Feldman. New York: McGraw-Hill, 1963, pages 297–309

Feigenbaum, E. A., and Feldman, J., *Computers and Thought*. New York: McGraw-Hill, 1963

Feldman, J., Computer simulation of cognitive processes. From *Computer Applications in the Behavioral Sciences*, ed. H. Borko. Englewood Cliffs, N. J.: Prentice-Hall, 1962

Feldman, J., Simulation of behavior in the binary choice experiment. *Proc. West. Joint Computer Conf.* **19,** 133–144 (1961)

Fields, P. E., Studies in concept formation: I. The development of the concept of triangularity by the white rat. *Comp. Psychol., Monogr.* **9,** No. 2, 667 (1932)

Flavell, J. H., *The Developmental Psychology of Jean Piaget*. Princeton, N. J.: Van Nostrand, 1963

Fodor, J. A., and Bever, T. G., The psychological reality of linguistic segments. *J. Verb. Learn. Verb. Behav.* **4,** 414–420 (1965)

Fodor, J. A., *Psychological Explanation*. New York: Random House, 1968

Fodor, J. A., and Katz, J. J., *The Structure of Language: Readings in the Philosophy of Language*. Englewood Cliffs, N. J.: Prentice-Hall, 1964

Forster, K. I., The effect of syntactic structure on nonordered recall. *J. Verb. Learn. Verb. Behav.* **5,** 292–297 (1966)

Foss, D. J., and Cairns, H. S., Some effects of memory limitation upon sentence comprehension and recall. *J. Verb. Learn. Verb. Behav.* **9,** 541–547 (1970)

Freedman, J. L., and Mednick, S. A., Ease of attainment of concepts as a function of response dominance variance. *J. Exp. Psychol.* **55,** 463–466 (1958)

Freibergs, V., and Tulving, E., The effect of practice on utilization of information from positive and negative instances in concept identification. *Canad. J. Psychol.* **15,** 101–106 (1961)

French, N. R., Carter, C. W., and Koenig, W., The words and sounds of telephone conversation. *Bell Syst. Tech. J.* **9,** 290–324 (1930)

Fries, C. C., *The Structure of English*. New York: Harcourt, Brace and World, 1952

Frisch, K. von, *The Dancing Bees*. London: Methuen, 1954

Frisch, K. von, Dialects in the language of the bees. *Sci. Amer.* **207,** 78–87 (1962)


Gagné, R., *The Conditions of Learning*. New York: Holt, Rinehart and Winston, 1965

Gagné, R. M., Problem solving. From *Categories of Human Learning*, edited by A. W. Melton. New York: Academic Press, 1964a

Gardner, R. A., and Gardner, B. T., Teaching sign language to a chimpanzee. *Science* **165** (3894), 664–672 (1969)

Gardner, R. A., and Runquist, W. N., Acquisition and extinction of problem-solving set. *J. Exp. Psychol.* **55**, 274–277 (1958)

Garner, W. R., *Uncertainty and Structure as Psychological Concepts.* New York: Wiley, 1962

Garrett, M., *Syntactic Structures and Judgements of Auditory Events.* Unpublished doctoral dissertation. University of Illinois, 1965

Garrett, M., Bever, T., and Fodor, J. A., The active use of grammar in speech perception. *Perception Psychophys.* **1**, 30–32 (1966)

Garrett, M., and Fodor, J. A., Psychological theories and linguistic constructs. From *Verbal Behavior and General Behavior Theory*, edited by T. R. Dixon and D. L. Horton. New York: Prentice-Hall, 1968, pages 451–477

Gerow, J. R., *The Semantic Differential and Concept Discrimination.* Knoxville: Unpublished dissertation. The University of Tennessee, 1968

Gerow, J. G., and Pollio, H. R., Word association, frequency of occurrence, and semantic differential norms for 360 stimulus words. *Technical Report*, No. 1, University of Tennessee, Grant MH08903, 1965

Ginsburg, H., and Opper, S., *Piaget's Theory of Intellectual Development.* Englewood Cliffs, N. J.: Prentice-Hall, 1969

Glanzer, M., Grammatical category: A rote learning and word association analysis. *J. Verb. Learn. Verb. Behav.* **1**, 31–41 (1962)

Glanzer, M., and Clark, W. H., Accuracy of perceptual recall: an analysis of organization. *J. Verb. Learn. Verb. Behav.* **1**, 289–299 (1963)

Glanzer, M., and Clark, W. H., The verbal loop hypothesis: binary numbers. *J. Verb. Learn. Verb. Behav.* **2**, 301–309 (1963b)

Glaze, J. A., The association value of nonsense syllables. *J. Genet. Psychol.* **35**, 255–269 (1928)

Gleason, H. A., *An Introduction to Descriptive Linguistics.* Revised edition. New York: Holt, Rinehart and Winston, 1961

Gleason, H. A., *Linguistics and English Grammar.* New York: Holt, Rinehart and Winston, 1965

Glucksberg, S., Functional fixedness: problem solution as a function of observing responses. *Psychonom. Sci.* **1**, 117–118 (1964)

Glucksberg, S., and Weisberg, R., Verbal behavior and problem solving: some effects of labeling in a functional fixedness problem. *J. Exp. Psychol.* **71**, 659–664 (1966)

Goggin, J., Influence of the written recall measure on first-list associations. *J. Exp. Psychol.* **65**, 619–620 (1963)

Goldiamond, I., and Hawkins, W. F., Vexierversuch: The log relationship between word-frequency and recognition obtained in the absence of stimulus words. *J. Exp. Psychol.* **56**, 457–463 (1958)

Goldiamond, I., and Dyrud, J. E., Some applications and implications of behavioral analysis for psychotherapy. From *Research in Psychotherapy*, Volume III, edited by J. M. Shlien. Washington, D. C.: American Psychological Association, 1968

Goldman-Eisler, F., Language and the science of man (Discussion and further comments). From *New Directions in the Study of Language*, edited by E. H. Lenneberg. Cambridge, Mass.: M.I.T. Press, 1964, pages 8–22

Goldman-Eisler, F., *Psycholinguistics: Experiments in Spontaneous Speech.* New York: Academic Press, 1968

Goldman-Eisler, F., Speech-breathing activity and context in psychiatric interviews. *Brit. J. Psychol., Med. Sec.* **29,** 35–48 (1956a)

Goldman-Eisler, F., A contribution to the objective measurement of the cathartic process. *J. Ment. Sci.* **102,** 78–95 (1956b)

Goldman-Eisler, F., The determinants of the rate of speech and their mutual relations, *J. Psychosom. Res.* **2,** 137–143 (1956c)

Goldman-Eisler, F., Speech analysis and mental processes. *Language and Speech* **1,** 59–75 (1958a)

Goldman-Eisler, F., Speech production and the predictability of words in context. *Quart. J. Exp. Psychol.* **10,** 96–106 (1958b)

Goldman-Eisler, F., The predictability of words in context and the length of pauses in speech. *Language and Speech* **1,** Part 3, 226–231 (1958c)

Goldman-Eisler, F., and Cohen, M., Is *N*, *P*, and *PN* difficulty a valid criterion of transformational operations? *J. Verb. Learn. Verb. Behav.* **9,** 161–166 (1970)

Goldstein, K., and Scheerer, M., Abstract and concrete behavior; an experimental study with special tests. *Psychol. Monogr.* **53,** No. 2 (1941)

Gordon, W. J. J., *Synectics.* New York: Harper and Row, 1961

Gordon, W. J. J., The metaphorical way of knowing. From *Education of Vision,* edited by G. Kepes. New York: George Braziller, 1965, pages 96–103

Greeno, J. G., and Scandura, J. M., All-or-none transfer based on verbally mediated concepts. *J. Math. Psychol.* **3,** 388–411 (1966)

Grover, D. E., Horton, D. L., and Cunningham, M., Mediated facilitation and interference in a four-stage paradigm. *J. Verb. Learn. Verb. Behav.* **6,** 42–46 (1967)

Gruen, G. E., Experience affecting the development of number conservation in children. *Child Dev.* **36**(4), 963–979 (1965)

Hall, R. A., *Introductory Linguistics.* Philadelphia: Chelton Books, 1964

Harlow, H. F., Learning set and error factor theory. From *Psychology, A Study of a Science,* Volume I, edited by S. Koch. New York: McGraw-Hill, 1959

Harlow, H. F., The formation of learning sets. *Psychol. Rev.* **56,** 51–65 (1949)

Harrower, M. R., Organization in higher mental processes. *Psychol. Forsch.* **17,** 56–120 (1932)

Hartmann, H., Kris, E., and Lowenstein, R. M., Comments on the formation of psychic structure. From *The Psychoanalytic Study of the Child,* Volume II, edited by A. Freud. New York: International Universities Press, 1947, pages 11–38

Haun, K. W., Measures of association and verbal learning. *Psychological Reports* **7,** 451–460, 1960

Hayakawa, S. I., *Language in Thought and Action.* New York: Harcourt Brace, 1949

Hayakawa, S. I., Semantics. *Etc: A Review of General Semantics,* 1952, pages 243–257

Haygood, R. C., and Bourne, L. E., Jr., Forms of relevant stimulus redundancy in concept identification. *J. Exp. Psychol.* **67,** 392–397 (1964)

Haygood, R. C., and Bourne, L. E., Jr., Attribute and rule learning aspects of conceptual behavior. *Psychol. Rev.* **72,** 175–195 (1965)

Hebb, D. O., *The Organization of Behavior.* New York: Wiley, 1949

Hebb, D. O., *A Textbook of Psychology.* Second edition. Philadelphia: Saunders, 1966

Heidbreder, E., The attainment of concepts: I. Terminology and methodology. *J. Gen. Psychol.* **35,** 173–189 (1946)

Heidbreder, E., The attainment of concepts: II. The problem. *J. Gen. Psychol.* **35,** 191–223 (1946)

Heidbreder, E., The attainment of concepts: III. The process. *J. Psychol.* **24,** 93–118 (1947)

Heidbreder, E., The attainment of concepts: VIII. The conceptualization of verbally indicated instances. *J. Psychol.* **27,** 263–309 (1947)

Heidbreder, E., Toward a dynamic psychology of cognition. *Psychol. Rev.* **52,** 1–22 (1945)

Hellyer, S., Frequency of stimulus presentation and short-term decrement in recall. *J. Exp. Psychol.* **64,** 650 (1963)

Helson, H., *Adaptation-Level Theory.* New York: Harper and Row, 1964

Hemingway, E., *The Old Man and the Sea.* New York: Scribner, 1952

Henderson, A., Goldman-Eisler, F., and Skarbek, A., Temporal patterns of cognitive activity and breath control in speech. *Language and Speech* **8,** Part 4, 236–242 (1966a)

Henderson, A., Goldman-Eisler, F., and Skarbek, A., Sequential temporal patterns in spontaneous speech. *Language and Speech* **9,** 207–216 (1966b)

Henle, M., On the relation between logic and thinking. *Psychol. Rev.* **69,** 366–378 (1962)

Herrnstein, R. J., and Loveland, D. H., Complex visual concepts in the pigeon. *Science* **146,** 549–551 (1964)

Hobbes, T., *Human Nature.* London: John Bohn, 1839

Hockett, C. F., Animal "languages" and human language. From *The Evolution of Man's Capacity for Culture*, arranged by J. N. Spuhler. Detroit, 1959, pages 32–39

Hockett, C. F., Logical considerations in the study of animal communication. From *Animal Sounds and Communication*, edited by W. E. Lanyon and W. N. Tovolga. Washington, 1960, pages 392–430

Hockett, C. F., The problem of universals in language. From *Universals of Language*, edited by J. H. Greenberg. Cambridge, Mass., 1963, pages 1–29

Holland, J. G., Design and use of a teaching-machine program. Paper read at the American Psychological Association Convention, Chicago, 1960

Holland, J. G., Research on programming variables. From *Teaching Machines and Programmed Learning II: Data and Directions*, edited by R. Glaser. Washington, D. C.: National Education Association, 1965a, pages 66–117

Holland, J. G., Response contingencies in teaching-machine programs. *J. Program. Instr.* **8,** 1–8 (1965b)

Holmes, E. E., What do pre-first grade children know about number. *Elem. School J.* **63,** 397–403 (1963)

Holmes, V. M., and Forster, K. I., Detection of extraneous signals during sentence recognition. *Perception and Psychophysics* **7,** 297–301 (1970)

Horton, D. L., and Kjeldergaard, P. M., An experimental analysis of associative factors in mediated generalization. *Psychol. Monogr.* **75,** No. 11 (whole No. 515), 279–281, 289 (1961)

Hovland, C. I., A "communication analysis" of concept learning. *Psychol. Rev.* **59,** 461–472 (1952)

Hovland, C. I., Computer simulation of thinking. *Amer. Psychol.* **15,** 687–693 (1960)

Hovland, C. I., and Hunt, E. B., Computer simulation of concept attainment. *Behav. Sci.* **5,** 265–267 (1960)

Hovland, C. I., and Weiss, W., Transmission of information concerning concepts through positive and negative instances. *J. Exp. Psychol.* **45,** 165–182 (1953)

Howes, D., and Osgood, C. E., On the combination of associative probabilities in linguistic contexts. *Amer. J. Psychol.* **67,** 241–258 (1954)

Howes, D. H., and Solomon, R. L., Visual duration threshold as a function of word-probability. *J. Exp. Psychol.* **41,** 401–410 (1951)

Hull, C. L., The mechanism of the assembly of behavior segments in novel combinations suitable for problem solution. *Psychol. Rev.* **42,** 219–245 (1935)

Hull, C. L., *Principles of Behavior. An Introduction to Behavior Theory.* New York: Appleton-Century-Crofts, 1943

Hull, C. L., Quantitative aspects of the evolution of concepts. *Psychol. Monogr.* **28,** No. 1 (whole No. 123) (1920)

Hunt, E. B., *Concept Learning: An Information Processing Problem.* New York: Wiley, 1962

Hunt, E. B., Memory effects in concept learning. *J. Exp. Psychol.* **62,** 598–604 (1961)

Hunt, E. B., and Hovland, C. I., Order of consideration of different types of concepts. *J. Exp. Psychol.* **59,** 220–225 (1960)

Hunt, E. B., Marin, J., and Stone, P. J., *Experiments in Induction.* New York: Academic Press, 1966

Hunt, J. McV., *Intelligence and Experience.* New York: Ronald, 1961

Hunter, I. M. L., Kopfrechnen und Kopfrechner. *Bild der Wissenschaft*, April 1966, pages 296–303. Also from *Thinking and Reasoning*, edited by P. Wason and P. Johnson-Laird. Baltimore: Penguin Books, 1968

Huttenlocher, J., Effects of manipulation of attributes on efficiency of concept formation. *Psychol. Rep.* **10,** 503–509 (1962)


Jacobson, E., Electrophysiology of mental activities. *Amer. J. Psychol.* **44,** 677–694 (1932)

Jacobson, E., *Progressive relaxation.* Chicago: University of Chicago Press, 1929

Jakobson, R., Fant, C. G. M., and Halle, M., *Preliminaries to Speech Analysis.* Cambridge, Mass.: M.I.T. Press, 1952

Jakobson, R., and Halle, M., *Fundamentals of Language.* The Hague: Mouton, 1956

James, C. T., and Hakes, D. T., Mediated transfer in a four-stage, stimulus-equivalence paradigm. *J. Verb. Learn. Verb. Behav.* **4,** 89–93 (1965)

James, W., *The Principles of Psychology.* New York: Dover, 1890 (reprinted 1950)

Jenkins, J. J., Discussion from *Psycholinguistics Supplement*, edited by C. E. Osgood and T. A. Sebeok. *J. Abnorm. Soc. Psychol.* **52,** 114–116 (1954)

Jenkins, J. J., Mediated associations: paradigms and situations. From *Verbal Behavior and Learning*, edited by C. N. Cofer and B. S. Musgrave. New York: McGraw-Hill, 1963, pages 210–245

Jenkins, J. J., Mink, W. D., and Russell, W. A., Associative clustering as a function of verbal association strength. *Psychol. Rep.* **4,** 127–136 (1958)

Jenkins, J. J., and Russell, W. A., Associative clustering during recall. *J. Abnorm. Soc. Psychol.* **47,** 818–821 (1952)

Johnson, D. M., *The Psychology of Thought and Judgment.* New York: Harper and Row, 1955

Johnson, M. G., *The Distributional Aspects of Meaning Interaction in Agrammatical Verbal Contexts.* Doctoral dissertation. Johns Hopkins Univ., Baltimore, Md., 1968

Johnson, M. G., A cognitive-feature model of compound free associations. *Psychol. Rev.* **77**, 282–293 (1970)

Johnson, N. F., The psychological reality of phrase-structure rules. *J. Verb. Learn. Verb. Behav.* **4**, 469–475a (1965a)

Johnson, N. F., Linguistic models and functional units of language. From *Directions in Psycholinguistics*, edited by S. Rosenberg. New York: Macmillan, 1965, pages 29–65

Johnson, N. F., Sequential verbal behavior. From *Verbal Behavior and General Behavior Theory*, edited by T. R. Dixon and D. L. Horton. New York: Prentice-Hall, 1968, pages 421–450

Judson, A. J., Cofer, C. N., and Gelfand, S., Reasoning as an associative process: II. "Direction" in problem solving as a function of prior reinforcement of relevant responses. *Psychol. Rep.* **2**, 501–507 (1956)

Karwoski, T. F., and Odbert, H. S., Color music. *Psycholog. Monogr.* **2**, 60–75 (1933)

Katz, J. J., *Semantic Theory*, New York: Harper and Row, 1972

Katz, J. J., and Fodor, J. A., The structure of a semantic theory. *Language* **39**, 170–210 (1963)

Kemeny, J. A., Man viewed as a machine, *Scient. American* **192**, April, 58–67 (1955)

Kendler, H. H., The concept of the concept. From *Categories of Human Learning*, edited by A. W. Melton. New York: Academic Press, 1964

Kendler, H. H., and D'Amato, M. F., A comparison of reversal shifts and nonreversal shifts in human concept formation behavior. *J. Exp. Psychol.* **49**, 165–174 (1955)

Kendler, H. H., and Kendler, T. S., Vertical and horizontal processes in problem solving. *Psychol. Rev.* **69**, 1–16 (1962)

Kendler, T. S., Concept Formation. *Annu. Rev. Psychol.* **13**, 447–472 (1961)

Kendler, T. S., Verbalization and optional reversal shifts among kindergarten children. *J. Verb. Learn. Verb. Behav.* **3**, 428–433 (1964)

Kendler, T. S., and Kendler, H. H., Reversal and nonreversal shifts in kindergarten children. *J. Exp. Psychol.* **58**, 56–60 (1959)

Kendler, T. S., Kendler, H. H., and Learnard, B., Mediated responses to size and brightness as a function of age. *Amer. J. Psychol.* **75**, 571–586 (1962b)

Keppel, G., Retroactive and proactive inhibition. From *Verbal Behavior and General Behavior Theory*, edited by T. R. Dixon and D. L. Horton. Englewood Cliffs, N. J.: Prentice-Hall, 1968, pages 172–208

Kepros, P. G., Identification of conjunctive concepts as a function of stimulus and response complexity. Unpublished doctoral thesis. University of Utah, 1965

King, H. V., *Guide and Workbook in the Structure of English*, Englewood Cliffs, N. J., Prentice-Hall, 1967

Kintsch, W., *Learning, Memory, and Conceptual Processes.* New York: Wiley, 1970

Kiss, G. R., Words, associations, and networks. *J. Verb. Learn. Verb. Behav.* **7**, 707–713 (1968)

Knight, J., *The Story of my Psychoanalysis.* New York: McGraw-Hill, 1950

Koen, F., An intra-verbal explication of the nature of metaphor. *J. Verb. Learn. Verb. Behav.* **4**, 129–133, April (1965)

Koestler, A., *The Act of Creation.* New York: Macmillan, 1964

Koffka, K. *Principles of Gestalt Psychology*. New York: Harcourt Brace, 1935

Kofsky, E., A scalogram study of classificatory development. *Child Dev*. **37**(1), 191–204 (1966)

Kohler, W., *The Mentality of Apes*. New York: Harcourt Brace, 1925

Kohler, W., *Gestalt Psychology*. New York: Liveright, 1929

Koppenaal, R. J., Time changes in the strength of *A–B, A–C* lists; spontaneous recovery? *J. Verb. Learn. Verb. Behav*. **2**, 310–319 (1963)

Krasner, L., and Ullmann, L. P., *Research in Behavior Modification. New Developments and Implications*. New York: Holt, Rinehart and Winston, 1965

Krumboltz, J. D., and Kiesler, C. A., The partial reinforcement paradigm and programmed instruction. *J. Educ. Psychol*. **3**, 9–14 (1965)

Kuenne, M. R., Experimental investigation of the relation of language to transposition behavior in young children. *J. Exp. Psychol*. **36**, 471–490 (1946)

Kurtz, K. H., and Hovland, C. I., Concept learning with different sequences of instances. *J. Exp. Psychol*. **51**, 239–243 (1956)


Ladefoged, P., The perception of speech. From *The Mechanization of Thought Processes*. London: H. M. Stationery Office, 1959

Ladefoged, P., and Broadbent, D. E., Perception of sequence in auditory events. *Quart. J. Exp. Psychol*. **12**, 162–170 (1960)

Lambert, W. E., and Paivio, A., The influence of noun-adjective order on learning. *Canad. J. Psychol*. **10**, 9–12 (1956)

Lane, H., Programmed learning of a second language. *Int. Rev. Appl. Ling. Lang. Teaching* **II-4**, 249–301 (1964)

Lane, H., Research on second language learning. From *Developments in Applied Psycholinguistics*, edited by S. Rosenberg, and J. Koplin. New York: MacMillan, 1965, pages 66–117

Langer, S. K., *Philosophy in a New Key: A Study in the Symbolism of Reason, Rite, and Art*. New York: The New American Library, 1951

Langfeld, H. S., Note on a case of chromaesthesia. *Psychol. Bull*. **2**, 113–114 (1914)

Lantz, D., *Color naming and color recognition: a study in the psychology of language*. Unpublished doctoral dissertation. Harvard University, 1963

Lashley, K. I., The problem of serial order in behavior. From *Cerebral Mechanisms in Behavior*, edited by L. A. Jeffres. New York: Wiley, 1951, pages 112–135

Lenneberg, E. H., *The Biological Foundations of Language*. New York: Wiley, 1967

Levine, M., Cue neutralization: The effects of random reinforcements upon discrimination learning. *J. Exp. Psychol*. **63**, 438–443 (1962)

Levine, M., Hypothesis behavior by humans during discrimination learning. *J. Exp. Psychol*. **71**, 331–338 (1966)

Levine, M., Mediating processes in humans at the outset of discrimination learning. *Psychol. Rev*. **70**, 254–276 (1963)

Levine, M., A model of hypothesis behavior in discrimination learning set. *Psychol. Rev*. **66**, 353–366 (1959)

Liberman, A. M., Some results of research on speech perception. *J. Acoust. Soc. Amer*. **29**, 117–123 (1957)

Liberman, A. M., Cooper, F. S., Shankweiler, D. P., and Studdert-Kennedy, M., Perception of the speech code. *Psychol. Rev*. **74**, 431–461 (1967)

Liberman, A. M., Harris, K. S., Hoffman, H. S., and Griffith, B. C., The discrimination of speech sounds within and across phoneme boundaries. *J. Exp. Psychol.* **54,** 358–368 (1957)

Lindgren, N., Machine recognition of human language. Part II: Theoretical models of speech perception and language, *I.E.E.E. Spectrum* **2,** 45–49, April 1965

Luchins, A. S., Mechanization in problem-solving. *Psychol. Monog.* **54** (6), 248 (1942)

Luchins, A. S., and Luchins, E. H., New experimental attempts at preventing mechanization in problem solving. *J. Gen. Psychol.* **42,** 279–297 (1950)

Lumsdaine, A. A., Conditioned eyelid responses as mediating generalized finger reactions. *Psychol. Bull.* **36,** 650 (1939)

Luria, A. R., The role of language in the formation of temporary connections. From *Psychology in the Soviet Union,* edited by B. Simon. Stanford: Stanford University Press, 1957, pages 115–129

Luria, A. R., The development of the regulatory role of speech. From *The Cognitive Processes,* edited by R. Harper, C. Anderson, C. Christensen, and S. Hunka. Englewood Cliffs, N. J.: Prentice-Hall, 1964, pages 601–621

Lyons, J., *Introduction to Theoretical Linguistics.* London: Cambridge Univ. Press, 1968

Lysaught, J. P., and Williams, C. M., *A Guide to Programmed Instruction.* New York: Wiley, 1963


McCarthy, D., Language development in children. From *Manual of Child Psychology,* edited by L. Carmichael. New York: Wiley, 1946

McGeoch, J. A., and Irion, A. L., *The Psychology of Human Learning.* New York: Longmans, 1952

McGovern, J. B., Extinction of associations in four transfer paradigms. *Psychol. Monog.* **78** (whole No. 593) (1964)

McLaughlin, K. L., Number ability of preschool children. *Childhood Educ.* **11,** 348–353 (1935)

McLuhan, H. M., *Understanding Media: The Extensions of Man.* New York: Signet Books, 1964

McNeill, D., Developmental psycholinguistics. From *The Genesis of Language,* edited by G. A. Miller and F. Smith. Cambridge, Mass.: M.I.T. Press, 1966, pages 15–84

McNeill, D., On theories of language acquisition. From *Verbal Behavior and General Behavior Theory,* edited by T. R. Dixon and D. L. Horton. Englewood Cliffs, N. J.: Prentice-Hall, 1968

McNeill, D., The origin of associations within the same grammatical class. *J. Verb. Learn. Verb. Behav.* **2,** 250–262 (1963)

Maccoby, N., and Sheffield, F. D., Combining practice with demonstration in teaching complex sequences: summary and interpretation. From *Student Response in Programmed Instruction,* edited by A. R. Lumsdaine. Washington, D.C.: National Academy of Sciences National Research Council, 1961, pages 77–85

Maclay, H., and Sleator, M. D., Responses to language: judgements of grammaticalness. *Int. J. Amer. Linguist.* **26,** 275–282 (1960)

Maier, N. R. F., A Gestalt theory of humour. *Brit. J. Psychol.* **23,** 69–74 (1932)

Maltzman, I., Thinking: from a behavioristic point of view. *Psychol. Rev.* **66,** 275–286 (1955)

Maltzman, I., and Morrisett, L., Different strengths of set in the solution of anagrams. *J. Exp. Psychol.* **44**, 242–246 (1952)

Mandler, G., Association and organization: facts, fancies and theories. From *Verbal Behavior Theory and S-R Behavior Theory*, edited by T. R. Dixon and D. L. Horton. Englewood Cliffs, N. J.: Prentice-Hall, 1968, pages 109–118

Mandler, G., From association to structure. *Psychol. Rev.* **69**, 415–427 (1962)

Mandler, G., Organization and memory. From *The Psychology of Learning and Motivation*, edited by K. W. Spence and J. T. Spence. New York: Academic Press, 1967

Mandler, G., and Pearlstone, Z., Free and constrained concept learning and subsequent recall. *J. Verb. Learn. Verb. Behav.* **5**, 126–131 (1966)

Marks, L. E., and Miller, G. A., The role of semantic and syntactic constraints in the memorization of English sentences. *J. Verb. Learn. Verb. Behav.* **3**, 1–5 (1964)

Marshall, G. R., and Cofer, C. N., Associative indices as measures of word relatedness: A summary and comparison of ten methods. *J. Verb. Learn. Verb. Behav.* **1**, 408–421 (1963)

Martin, E., and Roberts, K. H., Grammatical factors in sentence retention. *J. Verb. Learn. Verb. Behav.* **5**, 211–218 (1966)

Martin, E., and Roberts, K. H., Sentence length and sentence retention in the free learning situation. *Psychon. Sci.* **8**, 535 (1967)

Martin, E., Roberts, K. H., and Collins, A. M., Short-term memory for sentences. *J. Verb. Learn. Verb. Behav.* **7**, 560–566 (1968)

Marton, F., *Structural Dynamics of Learning*. Stockholm: Almqvist and Wiksell, 1970

Mawardi, B. H., Creative use of the metaphor in a cognitive impasse. Unpublished paper. Western Reserve University, 1961

Mawardi, B. H., *Industrial Invention: A Study in Group Problem Solving*. Unpublished doctoral thesis. Harvard University, 1959

Max, L. W., An experimental study of the motor theory of consciousness: III. Action-current responses in deaf mutes during sleep, sensory stimulation, and dreams. *J. Comp. Psychol.* **19**, 469–486 (1935)

Max, L. W., An experimental study of the motor theory of consciousness: IV. Action-current responses in the deaf during awakening, kinaesthetic imagery, and abstract thinking. *J. Comp. Psychol.* **24**, 301–344 (1937)

Mayzner, M. S., and Tresselt, M. E., Anagram solution times a function of letter order and word frequency. *J. Exp. Psychol.* **56**, 376–379 (1958)

Mayzner, M. S., and Tresselt, M. E., Anagram solution times: a function of multiple-solution anagrams. *J. Exp. Psychol.* **71**, 66–73 (1966)

Mednick, S. A., The associative basis of the creative process. *Psychol. Rev.* **69**, 220–232 (1962)

Mednick, S. A., and Halpern, S., Ease of concept attainment as a function of associative rank. *J. Exp. Psychol.* **64**, 628–630 (1962)

Mehler, J., Some effects of grammatical transformations on the recall of English sentences. *J. Verb. Learn. Verb. Behav.* **2**, 346–351 (1963)

Mehler, J., and Carey, P., Role of surface and base structure in the perception of sentences. *J. Verb. Learn. Verb. Behav.* **6**, 335–338 (1967)

Mehler, J., and Miller, G. A., Retroactive interference in the recall of simple sentences. *Brit. J. Psychol.* **55**, 295–301 (1964)

Melton, A. W., Comments on Professor Postman's paper. From *Verbal Learning and Verbal Behavior*, edited by C. N. Cofer. New York: McGraw-Hill, 1961, pages 179–193

Melton, A. W., Implications of short-term memory for a general theory of memory. *J. Verb. Learn. Verb. Behav.* **2**, 1–21 (1963)

Melton, A. W., Learning. From *Encyclopedia of Educational Research*, edited by W. S. Monroe. Revised edition. New York: MacMillan, 1950, pages 668–690

Melton, A. W., and Irwin, J. M., The influence of degree of interpolated learning on retroactive inhibition and the overt transfer of specific responses. *Amer. J. Psychol.* **53**, 173–203 (1940)

Miller, G. A., and McNeill, D., Psycholinguistics. From *The Handbook of Social Psychology*, Volume III, edited by G. Lindzey and E. Aronson. Reading, Mass.: Addison-Wesley, 1969, pages 666–794

Miller, G. A., and Smith, F., editors, *The Genesis of Language*. Cambridge, Mass.: M.I.T. Press, 1966

Miller, G. A., Some preliminaries to psycholinguistics. *Am. Psychol.* **20**, 15–20 (1965)

Miller, G. A., and McKean, K., A chronometric study of some relations between sentences. *Quart. J. Exp. Psychol.* **16**, 297–308 (1964)

Miller, G. A., and Isard, S., Some perceptual consequences of linguistic rules. *J. Verb. Learn. Verb. Behav.* **2**, 217–228 (1963)

Miller, G. A., Decision units in the perception of speech. *Institute of Radio Engineers Transactions on Information Theory*, **IT-8**, 81–83 (1962a)

Miller, G. A., Some psychological studies of grammar. *Am. Psychol.* **17**, 748–762 (1962b)

Miller, G. A., Galanter, E., and Pribram, K. H., *Plans and the Structure of Behavior*. New York: Holt, Rinehart and Winston, 1960

Miller, G. A., Newman, E. B., and Friedman, E. A., Length-frequency statistics of written English. *Inform. and Control* **1**, 370–389 (1958)

Miller, G. A., Free recall of redundant strings of letters. *J. Exp. Psychol.* **56**, 485–491 (1958)

Miller, G. A., and Friedman, E. A., The reconstruction of mutilated English texts. *Information and Control* **1**, 38–55 (1957)

Miller, G. A., The magical number seven, plus or minus two: Some limits on our capacity for processing information. *Psychol. Rev.* **63**, 81–97 (1956a)

Miller, G. A., Human memory and the storage of information. *Institute of Radio Engineers Transactions on Information Theory* **IT-2**, 129–137 (1956b)

Miller, G. A., Information and memory. *Sci. American* **195**, 42–46 (1956c)

Miller, G. A., and Nicely, P. E., An analysis of perceptual confusions among some English consonants. *J. Acoust. Soc. Amer.* **27**, 338–352 (1955)

Miller, G. A., What is information measurement? *Amer. Psychologist* **8**, 3–11 (1953)

Miller, G. A., *Language and Communication*. New York: McGraw-Hill, 1951

Miller, G. A., Heise, G. A., and Lichten, W., The intelligibility of speech as a function of the context of the test materials. *J. Exp. Psychol.* **41**, 329–335 (1951)

Miller, G. A., and Selfridge, J. A., Verbal context and the recall of meaningful material. *Amer. J. Psychol.* **63**, 176–185 (1950)

Miller, N. E., *The influence of past experience upon the transfer of subsequent training*. Unpublished doctoral dissertation. Yale University, 1935

Miller, N. E., and Dollard, J., *Social Learning and Imitation*. New Haven, Conn.: Yale University Press, 1941

Montague, W. E., Adams, J. A., and Kiess, H. O., Forgetting and natural language mediation. *J. Exp. Psychol.* **72,** 829–833 (1966)

Moon, L. E., and Harlow, H. F., Analysis of oddity learning by rhesus monkeys. *J. Comp. Physiol. Psychol.* **48,** 188–194 (1955)

Morris, C. W., *Signs, Language and Behavior.* New York: Prentice-Hall, 1946

Morrisett, L., Jr., and Hovland, C. I., A comparison of three varieties of training in human problem solving. *J. Exp. Psychol.* **58,** 52–55 (1959)

Morrison, H. M., and Black, J. W., Prediction of missing words in sentences. *J. Speech. Dis.* **22,** 236–240 (1957)

Mott, S. M., Number concepts of small children. *Math. Teacher* **38,** 291–301 (1945)

Mowrer, O. H., *Learning Theory and Behavior.* New York: Wiley, 1960a

Mowrer, O. H., *Learning Theory and the Symbolic Processes.* New York: Wiley, 1960b

Mowrer, O. H., The psychologist looks at language. *Am. Psychol.* **9,** 660–694 (1954)

Murdock, B. B., Recent developments in short-term memory. *Brit. J. Psychol.* **58,** 421–433 (1968)

Neisser, U., The multiplicity of thought. *Brit. J. Psychol.* **54,** 1–14 (1963a)

Neisser, U., The imitation of man by machine. *Science* **139,** 193–197 (1963b)

Neisser, U., *Cognitive Psychology.* New York: Appleton-Century-Crofts, 1966

Newell, A., Shaw, J. C., and Simon, H. A., Elements of a theory of human problem solving. *Psychol. Rev.* **65,** 151–166 (1958a)

Newell, A., Shaw, J. C., and Simon, H. A., Chess-playing programs and the problem of complexity. *IBM J. Res. Dev.* **2,** 320–335 (1958b)

Newell, A., and Simon, H. A., Computer simulation of human thinking. *Science* **134,** 2011–2017 (1962)

Newell, A., and Simon, H. A., GPS, a program that simulates human thought. From *Computers and Thought,* edited by E. A. Feigenbaum and J. Feldman. New York: McGraw-Hill, 1963, pages 279–293

Newell, A., Simon, H. A., and Shaw, J. C., Report on a general problem-solving problem, *Proc. Int. Conf. on Information Processing.* Paris: UNESCO, 1960, pages 256–264

*Newsweek,* New peak for newspeak, May 6, 1968, pages 104 and 107

Noble, C. E., An analysis of meaning. *Psychol. Rev.* **59,** 421–430 (1952)

Noble, C. E., Meaningfulness and familiarity. From *Verbal Behavior and Learning: Problems and Processes,* edited by C. N. Cofer and B. S. Musgrave. New York: McGraw-Hill, 1963, pages 76–119

O'Connor, F. D., Recent work in English phonetics. From *Psycholinguistics. A Book of Readings,* edited by S. Saporta and J. R. Bastian. New York: Holt, Rinehart and Winston, 1961, pages 97–111

Oldfield, R. C., and Wingfield, A., Response latencies in naming objects. *Quart. J. Exp. Psychol.* **17,** 273–281 (1965)

Osgood, C. E., The nature and measurement of meaning. *Psychol. Bull.* **49,** 197–237 (1952)

Osgood, C. E., *Method and Theory in Experimental Psychology.* New York: Oxford, 1953

Osgood, C. E., Studies on the generality of affective meaning systems. *Amer. Psychologist* **17,** 10–28 (1962)

Osgood, C. E., On understanding and creating sentences. *Amer. Psychologist* **18**, 735–751 (1963)

Osgood, C. E., Psycholinguistics. From *Psychology: A Study of a Science*, Volume VI, edited by S. Koch. New York: McGraw-Hill, 1963, pages 244–316

Osgood, C. E., Toward a wedding of insufficiencies. From *Verbal Behavior and General Behavior Theory*, edited by T. R. Dixon and D. L. Horton. Englewood Cliffs, N. J.: Prentice-Hall, 1968

Osgood, C. E., Suci, G., and Tannenbaum, P., *The Measurement of Meaning*. Urbana: University of Illinois Press, 1957

Oskamp, S., *Partial reinforcement in concept formation: "Hypotheses" in human learning*. Unpublished master's thesis. Stanford University, 1956


Paivio, A., Abstractness, imagery, and meaningfulness in paired-associate learning. *J. Verb. Learn. Verb. Behav.* **4**, 32–38 (1965)

Paivio, A., A factor-analytic study of word attributes and verbal learning. *J. Verb. Learn. Verb. Behav.* **7**, 41–49 (1968)

Paivio, A., Mental imagery in associative learning and memory. *Psychol. Rev.* **76**, 241–263 (1969)

Paivio, A., and Madigan, S. A., Imagery and association value in paired-associate learning. *J. Exp. Psychol.* **76**, 35–39 (1968)

Paivio, A., Yuille, J. C., and Smythe, P. C., Stimulus and response abstractness, imagery, and meaningfulness, and reported mediators in paired-associate learning. *Canad. J. Psychol.* **20**, 362–377 (1966)

Palermo, D. S., and Jenkins, J. J., *Word Association Norms: Grade School through College*. Minneapolis: University of Minnesota Press, 1964

Pavlov, I. P., *Conditioned Reflexes*, translated by G. V. Anrep. London: Oxford University Press, 1927

Perfetti, C. A., Sentence retention and the depth hypothesis. *J. Verb. Learn. Verb. Behav.* **8**, 101–104 (1969a)

Perfetti, C. A., Lexical density and phrase structure depth as variables in sentence retention. *J. Verb. Learn. Verb. Behav.* **8**, 719–724 (1969b)

Piaget, J., *Judgement and Reasoning in the Child*. New York: Harcourt Brace, 1928

Piaget, J., *The Child's Conception of Physical Causality*. New York: Harcourt Brace, 1930

Piaget, J., *The Moral Judgement of the Child*, translated by M. Warden. New York: Harcourt Brace, 1932

Piaget, J., *The Psychology of Intelligence*. New York: Harcourt Brace, 1950

Piaget, J., *The Child's Conception of Number*. New York: Humanities Press, 1952

Piaget, J., *The Construction of Reality in the Child*. New York: Basic Books, 1954

Piaget, J., *The Language and Thought of the Child*. New York: Meridian Books, 1955

Piaget, J., The stages of the intellectual development of the child. *Bull. of the Menninger Clinic* **26**, 120–128 (1962)

Pollio, H. R., The composition of associative clusters. *J. Exp. Psychol.* **67**, 199–208 (1964)

Pollio, H. R., Some semantic relations among word associates. *Amer. J. Psychol.* **77**, 249–256 (1964)

Pollio, H. R., *The Structural Basis of Word Association*. The Hague: Mouton, 1966

Pollio, H. R., Associative structure and verbal behavior. From *Verbal Behavior and General Behavior Theory*, edited by T. R. Dixon and D. L. Horton. Englewood Cliffs, N. J.: Prentice-Hall, 1968

Pollio, H. R., Deitchman, R., and Richards, S., Law of contrast and oppositional word associates. *J. Exp. Psychol.* **79**(2), 203–212 (1969)

Pollio, H. R., and Foote, R. F., Memory as a reconstructive process. *Brit. J. Psychol.* **61**, 1–5 (1970)

Pollio, H. R., and Gerow, J. R., The role of rules in recall. *Amer. J. Psychol.* **81**, 303–313 (1968)

Pollio, H. R., Kasschau, R. K., and DeNise, H., Associative structures and the temporal characteristics of free recall. *J. Exp. Psychol.* **76**, 190–197 (1968)

Pollio, H. R., and Reinhart, D., Rules and counting behavior. *Cognitive Psychology* **1**, 388–402 (1970)

Pollio, H. R., Richards, S., and Lucas, R., Temporal properties of category recall. *J. Verb. Learn. Verb. Behav.* **8**, 95–102 (1969)

Pollio, H. R., and Whitacre, J. D., Some observations on the use of natural numbers by preschool children. *Perceptual and Motor Skills* **30**, 167–174 (1970)

Pollio, H. R., Wilcox, R., and Sundland, D. M., The effect of context on the production of hostile associates to ambiguous verbal stimuli. *Language and Speech* **9**, 103–113 (1966)

Postman, L. J., Does interference theory predict too much forgetting? *J. Verb. Learn. Verb. Behav.* **2**, 40–48 (1963)

Postman, L. J., The effects of language habits on the acquisition and retention of verbal associations. *J. Exp. Psychol.* **64**, 7–19 (1962)

Postman, L. J., The present status of interference theory. From *Verbal Learning and Verbal Behavior*, edited by C. N. Cofer. New York: McGraw-Hill, 1961, pages 152–178

Postman, L. J., Short-term memory and incidental learning. From *Categories of Human Learning*, edited by A. W. Melton. New York: Academic Press, 1964

Postman, L., and Stark, K., The role of response availability in transfer and interference. *J. Exp. Psychol.* **79**, 168–177 (1969)

Postman, L., Stark, K., and Fraser, J., Temporal changes in interference. *J. Verb. Learn. Verb. Behav.* **7**, 672–694 (1968)

Proust, M., *Swann's Way*, Volume I, *Remembrance of Things Past*, translated by C. K. Scott Moncrieff. New York: Random House, 1934


Reed, H. B., Factors influencing the learning and retention of concepts, I–IV. *J. Exp. Psychol.* **35**, 71–87; 166–179; 252–261 (1946)

Reitman, W. R., *Cognition and Thought: An Information Processing Approach*. New York: Wiley, 1965

Reitman, W. R., Grove, R. B., and Sharp, R. G., Argus: an information-processing model of thinking. *Behav. Sci.* **9**, 270–281 (1964)

Restorff, H. von, Über die Wirkung von Bereichsbildungen im Spurenfeld. *Psychol. Forsch.* **18**, 299–342 (1933)

Richardson, J., and Bergum, B. O., Distributed practice and rote learning in concept formation. *J. Exp. Psychol.* **47**, 442–446 (1954)

Richardson, P., and Voss, J., Replication report: Verbal context and the recall of meaningful material. *J. Exp. Psychol.* **60**, 417–418 (1960)

Rilling, M., *Acquisition and partial reinforcement of a concept under different verbal reinforcement conditions.* Unpublished master's thesis. University of Maryland, 1962
Roberts, W. A., and Smith, I., The effects of categorization and categorical repetition on successive recalls of word lists. *Psychon. Sci.* **5,** 225–226 (1966)
Rosenberg, S., *Directions in Psycholinguistics.* New York: MacMillan, 1965
Rothkopf, E. Z., The Instructional Process. Paper presented at a symposium entitled Research Approaches to the Learning of School Subjects. Berkeley, Calif., 1966
Rothkopf, E. Z., and Coke, E. U., The prediction of free recall from word association measures. *J. Exp. Psychol.* **62,** 433–438 (1961)
Russell, B., *Analysis of Mind.* London: George Allen and Unwin, 1921
Russell, W. A., and Storms, L. H., Implicit verbal chaining in paired-associate learning. *J. Exp. Psychol.* **49,** 287–293 (1955)
Ryan, J. J., Comparison of verbal response transfer mediated by meaningfully similar and associated stimuli. *J. Exp. Psychol.* **60,** 408–415 (1960)

Sachs, J. D. S., Recognition memory for syntactic and semantic aspects of connected discourse. *Perception and Psychophys.* **2,** 437–442 (1967)
Samuel, A. L., Some studies in machine learning using the game of checkers. *IBM J. Res. Dev.* **3,** 210–229 (1961)
Saporta, S., Blumenthal, A. L., and Rieff, D. G., Grammatical models and language learning. *Monogr. Series on Lang. and Linguist.* **16,** 133–142 (1963)
Saporta, S., Blumenthal, A. L., Lackowski, P., and Reiff, D. G., Grammatical models and language learning. From *Directions in Psycholinguistics*, edited by S. Rosenberg. New York: MacMillan, 1965, pages 15–28
Saugstad, P., and Raaheim, K., Problem-solving, past experience and availability of functions. *Brit. J. Psychol.* **51,** Part 2, 97–104 (1960)
Savin, H. B., and Perchonock, E., Grammatical structure and the immediate recall of English sentences. *J. Verb. Learn. Verb. Behav.* **4,** 348–353 (1965)
Schlesinger, I. M., *Sentence Structure and the Reading Process.* The Hague: Mouton, 1966
Schulz, R. W., Problem solving behavior and transfer. *Harvard Educ. Rev.* **30,** 61–77 (1960)
Schulz, R. W., Miller, R. L., and Radtke, R. C., The role of instance contiguity and dominance in concept attainment. *J. Verb. Learn. Verb. Behav.* **1,** 432–435 (1963)
Sells, S. B., The atmosphere effect: An experimental study of reasoning. *Archs. Psycholog.*, 1936, No. 200
Sewell, E., *The Human Metaphor.* South Bend, Indiana: University of Notre Dame Press, 1964
Shannon, C. E., A mathematical theory of communication. *Bell Syst. Tech. J.* **27,** 379–432 (1948)
Shapiro, S. I., Facilitation and interference effects as a function of the free associative strength of mediators. *J. Exp. Psychol.* **84**(1), 69–73 (1970)
Sharp, H. C., Effect of contextual constraint upon recall of verbal passages. *Amer. J. Psychol.* **71,** 568–572 (1958)
Shepard, R. N., Recognition memory for word, sentences, and pictures. *J. Verb. Learn. Verb. Behav.* **6,** 156–163 (1967)

Shepard, R. N., Hovland, C. I., and Jenkins, H. M., Learning and memorization of classifications. *Psychol. Monogr.* **75,** whole No. 517 (1961)

Shepard, R. N., and Tegtsoonian, M., Retention of information under conditions approaching a steady stage. *J. Exp. Psychol.* **62,** 55–59 (1961)

Shepard, R. N., Production of constrained associates and the informational uncertainty of the constraint. *Amer. J. Psychol.* **76,** 218–228 (1963)

Shipley, W. C., An apparent transfer of conditioning. *Psychol. Bull.* **30,** 541 (1933)

Shipstone, E. I., Some variables affecting pattern conception. *Psychol. Monogr.* **74,** whole No. 504 (1960)

Skinner, B. F., *Verbal Behavior.* New York: Appleton-Century-Crofts, 1957

Skinner, B. F., Teaching machines. *Science* **128,** 969–977 (1958)

Slobin, D. I., Recall of full and truncated passive sentences in connected discourse. *J. Verb. Learn. Verb. Behav.* **7,** 876–881 (1968)

Slobin, D. I., *Psycholinguistics.* Glenview, Ill.: Scott, Foresman, 1971

Smedslund, J., The acquisition of conservation of substance and weight in children, Part I. *Scand. J. Psychol.* **2,** 11–20 (1961)

Smedslund, J., The acquisition of conservation of substance and weight in children, Part II. *Scand. J. Psychol.* **2,** 71–84 (1961a)

Smedslund, J., The acquisition of conservation of substance and weight in children, Part III. *Scand. J. Psychol.* **2,** 85–87 (1961b)

Smedslund, J., The acquisition of conservation of substance and weight in children, Part IV. *Scand. J. Psychol.* **2,** 153–155 (1961c)

Smedslund, J., The acquisition of conservation of substance and weight in children, Part V. *Scand. J. Psychol.* **2,** 156–160 (1961d)

Smedslund, J., The acquisition of conservation of substance and weight in children, Part VI. *Scand. J. Psychol.* **2,** 203–210 (1961e)

Smedslund, J., The acquisition of conservation of substance and weight in children, Part VII. *Scand. J. Psychol.* **31,** 69–77 (1961f)

Smith, M. E., An investigation of the development of the sentence and the extent of vocabulary in young children. *University of Iowa Studies in Child Welfare*, No. 5 (1926)

Smoke, K. L., An objective study of concept formation. *Psychol. Monogr.* **42,** No. 191 (1932)

Solarz, A. K., Latency of instrument responses as a function of compatibility with the meaning of eliciting verbal signs. *J. Exp. Psychol.* **59,** 239–245 (1960)

Solomon, R. L., and Howes, D. H., Word frequency, personal values, and visual duration thresholds. *Psychol. Rev.* **58,** 256–270 (1951)

Sperling, G. A., The information available in brief visual presentation. *Psychol. Monogr.* **74,** whole No. 498 (1960)

Sperling, G. A., Successive approximations to a model for short-term memory. From *Attention and Performance*, edited by A. F. Sanders. Amsterdam: North-Holland, 1967

Staats, A. W., Verbal habit-families, concepts, and the operant conditioning of word classes. *Psychol. Rev.* **68,** 190–204 (1961)

Staats, A. W., *Human Learning, Studies Extending Conditioning Principles to Complex Behavior.* New York: Holt, Rinehart and Winston, 1964

Staats, A. W., *Learning, Language, and Cognition.* New York: Holt, Rinehart, and Winston, 1968

Staats, A. W., and Staats, C. K., *Complex Human Behavior*. New York: Holt, Rinehart and Winston, 1963

Staats, A. W., and Staats, C. K., Effect of number of trials on the language conditioning of meaning. *J. Gen. Psychol.* **61**, 211–223 (1959a)

Staats, A. W., and Staats, C. K., Meaning and *m*: Correlated but separate. *Psychol. Rev.* **66**, 136–144 (1959b)

Staats, A. W., and Staats, C. K., Attitudes established by classical conditioning. *J. Abnorm. Soc. Psychol.* **57**, 37–40 (1958)

Staats, A. W., Staats, C. K., and Crawford, H. L., First-order conditioning of meaning and the paralleled conditioning of a GSR. *J. Gen. Psychol.* **67**, 159–167 (1962)

Statts, A. W., Statts, C. K., and Heard, W. G., Denotative meaning established by classical conditioning. *J. Exp. Psychol.* **61**, 300–303 (1961)

Statts, C. K., and Statts, A. W., Meaning established by classical conditioning. *J. Exp. Psychol.* **54**, 74–80 (1957)

Stern, G., *Meaning and Change of Meaning*. First published 1931. Republished Bloomington, Indiana: Indiana University Press, 1954

Strachey, C., Systems analysis and programming. *Information*, A Scientific American Book, London: W. H. Freeman, 1966, pages 56–75

Suci, G. J., Ammon, P. R., and Gamlin, P., The validity of the probe latency technique for assessing structure in language. *Language and Speech* **10**, 69–80 (1967)


Thorndike, E. L., and Lorge, I., *The Teacher's Word Book of 30,000 Words*. New York: Columbia University Press, 1944

Thorson, A. M., The relation of tongue movements to internal speech. *J. Exp. Psychol.* **8**, 1–32 (1925)

Thumb, A., and Marbe, K., *Experimentelle Untersuchungen über die psychologischen Grundlagen der sprächlichen Analogiebildung*. Leipzig: W. Engelmann, 1901

Tighe, T. J., Reversal and nonreversal shifts in monkeys. *J. Comp. Physiol. Psychol.* **58**, 324–326 (1964)

Tinbergen, N., *The Study of Instinct*. London: Oxford University Press, 1951

Trakhtenbrot, B. A., *Algorithms and Automatic Computing Machines*, translated by J. Kristian, J. D. McCawley, and S. A. Schmitt. Lexington, Mass.: D. C. Heath, 1963

Tresselt, M. E., and Leeds, D. S., The effect of concretizing the mental set experiment. *J. Gen. Psychol.* **48**, 51–55 (1953)

Tresselt, M. E., and Leeds, D. S., The Einstellung effect in immediate and delayed problem-solving. *J. Gen. Psychol.* **49**, 87–95 (1953)

Tulving, E., and Pearlstone, Z., Availability versus accessibility of information in memory for words. *J. Verb. Learn. Verb. Behav.* **5**, 381–391 (1966)

Tulving, E., Intratrial and intertrial retention: Notes toward a theory of free-recall verbal learning. *Psychol. Rev.* **71**, 219–237 (1964)

Tulving, E., Subjective organization in free recall of unrelated words. *Psychol. Rev.* **69**, 344–354 (1962)

Tulving, E., Theoretical issues in free recall. From *Verbal Behavior and General Behavior Theory*, edited by T. R. Dixon and D. L. Horton. Englewood Cliffs, N. J.: Prentice-Hall, 1968, pages 2–36

Tulving, E., and Patkau, J. E., Concurrent effects of contextual constraint and word frequency on immediate recall and learning of verbal material. *Canad. J. Psychol.* **16,** 83–95 (1962)

Turing, A. M., On computable numbers, with an application to the Entscheidungs-problem. *Proceedings of the London Mathematics Society* (ser. 2) **42,** 230–265 (1936)

Turing, A. M., Computing machinery and intelligence. *Mind* **59,** 433–460 (1950)


Underwood, B. J., An orientation for research on thinking. *Psychol. Rev.* **59,** 209–220 (1952)

Underwood, B. J., Interference and forgetting. *Psychol. Rev.* **64,** 49–60 (1957)

Underwood, B. J., "Spontaneous recovery" of verbal associations. *J. Exp. Psychol.* **38,** 429–439 (1948)

Underwood, B. J., and Keppel, G., Retention as a function of degree of learning and letter-sequence interference. *Psychol. Monogr.* **77,** No. 4 (1963)

Underwood, B. J., and Postman, L., Extraexperimental sources of interference in forgetting. *Psychol. Rev.* **67,** 73–95 (1960)

Underwood, B. J., and Richardson, J., Some verbal materials for the study of concept formation. *Psychol. Bull.* **53,** 84–95 (1956a)

Underwood, B. J., and Richardson, J., Verbal concept learning as a function of instructions and dominance level. *J. Exp. Psychol.* **51,** 229–238 (1956b)

Underwood, B. J., and Schultz, R. W., *Meaningfulness and Verbal Learning.* Philadelphia: Lippincott, 1960


Verplanck, W. S., The control of the content of conversation: Reinforcement of statements of opinion. *J. Abnorm. Soc. Psychol.* **51,** 668–676 (1955)

Verplanck, W. S., Unaware of where's awareness. From *Behavior and Awareness*, edited by C. E. Eriksen. Durham: Duke University Press, 1962

Vinacke, W. E., *The Psychology of Thinking.* New York: McGraw-Hill, 1952


Walker, C. M., and Bourne, L. E., Jr., Concept identification as a function of amounts of relevant and irrelevant information. *Amer. J. Psychol.* **74,** 410–417 (1961)

Washburn, M., *Movement and Mental Imagery.* Boston: Houghton Mifflin, 1916

Wason, P. C., On the failure to eliminate hypothesis in a conceptual task. *Quart. J. Exp. Psychol.* **12,** 129–140 (1960)

Wason, P. C., The processing of positive and negative information. *Quart. J. Exp. Psychol.* **11,** 92–107 (1961)

Wason, P. C., Response to affirmative and negative binary statements. *Brit. J. Psychol.* **52,** 133–142 (1961)

Wason, P. C., The contexts of plausible denial. *J. Verb. Learn. Verb. Behav.* **4,** 7–11 (1965)

Wason, P. C., On the failure to eliminate hypotheses . . . a second look. From *Thinking and Reasoning*, edited by P. C. Wason and P. N. Johnson-Laird. Baltimore: Penguin, 1968, pages 165–174

Wason, P. C., and Johnson-Laird, P. N., *Thinking and Reasoning.* Baltimore: Penguin, 1968

Watson, J. B., *Behavior: An Introduction to Comparative Psychology.* New York: Holt, Rinehart and Winston, 1914

Watson, J. B., *Psychology from the Standpoint of a Behaviorist.* Philadelphia: Lippincott, 1924

Waugh, N. C., and Norman, D. A., The measure of interference in primary memory. *J. Verb. Learn. Verb. Behav.* **7,** 617–626 (1968)

Waugh, N. C., and Norman, D. A., Primary memory. *Psychol. Rev.* **72,** 89–104 (1965)

Weingartner, H., The free recall of sets of associatively related words. *J. Verb. Learn. Verb. Behav.* **3,** 6–10 (1964)

Weir, R., *Language in the Crib.* The Hague: Mouton, 1962

Wells, R., Meaning and use. *Word* **10,** 235–250 (1954)

Wertheimer, M., *Productive Thinking.* New York: Harper, 1945

Whitfield, J. W., An experiment in problem solving. *Quart. J. Exp. Psychol.* **3,** 184–197 (1951)

Whitman, W., Song of Myself, Section 32. From *Leaves of Grass.* New York: Mentor Books, 1954

Whorf, B. L., *Language, Thought and Reality.* New York: Wiley, 1957

Whorf, B. L., Linguistic relativity and the relation of linguistic processes to perception and cognition. From *Psycholinguistics; A Book of Readings,* edited by S. Saporta and J. R. Bastian. New York: Holt, Rinehart and Winston, 1961, pages 460–468

Wickelgren, W. A., Distinctive features and errors in short-term memory for English vowels. *J. Acoust. Soc. Amer.* **38,** 583–588 (1965)

Wickelgren, W. A., Short-term memory for phonemically similar lists. *Amer. J. Psychol.* **78,** 567–574 (1965a)

Wickelgren, W. A., Acoustic similarity and intrusion errors in short-term memory. *J. Exp. Psychol.* **70,** 102–108 (1965b)

Wickelgren, W. A., Short-term recognition memory for normal and whispered letters. *Nature* **206,** 851–852 (1965c)

Wickelgren, W. A., Short-term memory for repeated and nonrepeated items. *Quart. J. Exp. Psychol.* **17,** 14–25 (1965d)

Wickelgren, W. A., Phonemic similarity and interference in short-term memory for single letters, *J. Exp. Psychol.* **71,** 396–404 (1966a)

Wickelgren, W. A., Distinctive features and errors in short-term memory for English consonants. *J. Acoust. Soc. Amer.* **39,** 388–398 (1966b)

Wickelgren, W. A., Short-term recognition memory for single letters and phonemic similarity of retroactive interference. *Quart. J. Exp. Psychol.* **18,** 55–62 (1966c)

Wicklund, D., Palermo, D., and Jenkins, J. J., Associative clustering in the recall of children as a function of verbal association strength. *J. Exp. Child Psychol.* **2,** 58–66 (1965)

Wittgenstein, L., *Philosophical Investigations.* Oxford: Basil Blackwell, 1963

Wohlwill, J. F., A study of the development of the number concept by scalogram analysis. *J. Genet. Psychol.* **97,** 345–377 (1960)

Wohlwill, J. and Lowe, R. C., Experimental analysis of the development of the conservation of number. *Child Dev.* **33,** 153–167 (1962)

Woodworth, R. S., and Schlosberg, H., *Experimental Psychology.* New York: Holt, Rinehart and Winston, 1954

Woodworth, R. S., and Sells, S. B., An atmosphere effect in formal syllogistic reasoning. *J. Exp. Psychol.* **18,** 451–460 (1935)

Yngve, V. H., Computer programs for translation. *Scient. American* **206,** 68–87, June (1962)

Yngve, V. H., A model and a hypothesis for language structure. *Proceedings of the American Philosophical Society* **104,** 444–466 (1960)

Youtz, R. P., The relation between number of confirmations of one hypothesis and the speed of accepting a new and incompatible hypothesis. *Amer. Psychologist* **3,** 248–249 (1948)

Zipf, G. K., *The Psychobiology of Language.* Boston: Houghton Mifflin, 1935

# AUTHOR INDEX

*As Von Bertalanffy

490

*As Von Frisch, K.

# SUBJECT INDEX

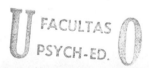